DESIGN FOR WAR

DESIGN FOR WAR

A Study of Secret Power Politics

1937   1941

BY FREDERIC R. SANBORN

Copyright © 2023 Ultimatum Editions.
All rights reserved.

Sanborn, Frederic Rockwell. Design for War: A Study of Secret Power Politics. 1937-1941. First published in 1951 (New York: Devin-Adair Company).

This book or any portion thereof may not be reproduced or used in any manner whatsoever without the express written permission of the publisher except for the use of brief quotations in a book review. The content of this book shall not constitute or be construed or deemed to reflect the opinion or expression of the publisher or editor.

ISBN 978-2-925369-01-1
Printed in the USA.

www.ultimatumeditions.com

CONTENTS

ABOUT THE AUTHOR xi

I. A POLITICAL PROBLEM IS PRESENTED 3
II. COMPLETE ISOLATION FROM WAR 7
III. THE NEW DEAL COLLAPSES 21
IV. OUR FRONTIER IS ON THE RHINE 55
V. A TANGLED WEB IS WOVEN 87
VI. "AGAIN AND AGAIN AND AGAIN" 155
VII. FROM "SEA LION" INTO "BARBAROSSA" 175
VIII. THE SYNTHETIC CRISIS AT THE BIRTH OF LEND-LEASE 205
IX. POWER POLITICS AT CROSS PURPOSES 259
X. JOURNEYS END IN LEADERS' MEETINGS 313
XI. AN UTTERLY FUTILE WAR? 351
XII. TWILIGHT LETS HER CURTAIN DOWN 385
XIII. WAR, WAR IS STILL THE CRY 435
XIV. CHINESE INTRIGUE TRIUMPHS 469
XV. A MORAL PROBLEM IS SOLVED 525

BIBLIOGRAPHY 559
NOTES 562
INDEX 612

To

JANET

ABOUT THE AUTHOR

Frederic R. Sanborn early displayed an interest in international affairs and an aptitude for history, receiving his A.B. degree, with high honors in history, from Columbia at the age of twenty. An A.M. degree in international law and diplomacy, and an L.L.B. degree followed. In 1921 he sailed for England and spent the next three years at Oxford University, working under the great legal historian, the late Sir William Holdsworth, for his doctor's degree. While at Oxford he was named a Carnegie Fellow in International Law for further study and research at the Sorbonne. This honor he subsequently declined, however, in order to return to the United States and to establish himself in the profession of the law.

For over twenty-five years Mr. Sanborn has continuously engaged in the active practice of the law in New York City, where he is a partner in one of the city's oldest firms. He has combined the practical experience of a varied and wide business nature with his avocations of teaching, lecturing, and writing. Mr. Sanborn for many years taught International Law in the postgraduate departments of local law schools and he also taught Administrative Law and Constitutional

Law. He has lectured before the Practicing Law Institute, the Federal Bar Association, the Bar Associations of Philadelphia, Washington and Richmond, and the Institute of Comparative Law of the Association of American Law Schools. He is the author of a highly regarded book on legal history, *Origins of the Early English Maritime and Commercial Law* (1930), which was sponsored by the American Historical Association; of various leading articles in the Encyclopedia of the Social Sciences; and of articles in a number of law reviews. He has also written featured newspaper articles of a nonlegal nature.

During these years Mr. Sanborn's activities have included wide travel in the United States and Europe as well as active participation in local community affairs. He has served as an officer or Board member of numerous charitable organizations and clubs. Not only as a married man and father of two children but also because his ancestral roots in America are very deep, he has a keen sense of obligation to help maintain the nation's heritage of freedom for future generations.

Of little folks it oft has been the fate
To suffer for the follies of the great.

> *La Fontaine's Fables, Book II, Fable IV*
> Wright's translation.

DESIGN
FOR WAR

I | A POLITICAL PROBLEM IS PRESENTED

A GRAVE DANGER TO AMERICA has become apparent in recent years. That danger is, that nowadays there are few, if any, checks and balances upon the conduct of foreign affairs by the President, so that the Nation may unwittingly or unwillingly become involved in a great and terrible war. In modern American practice the President may and sometimes does conduct our foreign affairs personally and single-handed. He takes only such counsel as he may wish to take from such counsellors as he may incline to consult.

It was not always thus. In England it was apparent, centuries ago, that the personal and single-handed conduct of public affairs by the King might become, and sometimes was, arbitrary, erratic, and dangerous. In consequence the Council was developed to check this peril, and the King was prevented from taking any kind of important action except by, through, and with the knowledge and consent of his Council.

The original American constitutional theory and practice was consonant with this principle. President Washington, for example, not only truly consulted the opinions of his cabinet but in important matters involving foreign affairs he invariably took the *advice* of the Senate, as the Constitution intended and still requires in certain ways.

With the passage of one hundred and fifty years there has been a somersault. As this book will show, Mr. Roosevelt almost never consulted the opinions of his cabinet on foreign affairs. Instead of seeking the advice of the Senate, he was more prone to by-pass it or to ignore it. Indeed his conduct of foreign affairs became so secretive that at times the Secretary of State was compelled to ask him for information. Under such circumstances the people of the United States did not know and could not know what was happening. Even the extra-constitutional method of checking official action by the strength of opposing public opinion could not operate under such conditions.

This practice of making one-man decisions in matters of grave importance did not die with Mr. Roosevelt. In the last week of June 1950, Mr. Truman decided to involve the United States and its armed forces in a war in South Korea by a decision which was entirely personal. Such practices are perilous as a matter of principle, however right the ultimate decision may finally prove to be.

Moreover, and quite apart from the problem of the danger and error inherent in the uncounselled opinion of a single man, such action is the antithesis of all that we have in mind when we speak either of the democratic process or of the representative process. It is tyrannical and despotic, as our official survey of World War II states so succinctly: [1]

> * The manner in which Germany and Japan went to war was possible only in governments in which such fundamental decisions were in the hands of a very few individuals who, controlling a propaganda machine, could cloak their decisions in plausibility and could impress their will upon an impotent public.

This book narrates the history of what was largely the personal and single-handed direction of foreign affairs by Mr. Roosevelt from 1937 until the day when the war officially began. It traces what Mr. Roosevelt earlier called the "small decisions of each day [which] lead towards war." Because domestic and foreign politics were so intertwined during those years, this book necessarily has to tell about the domestic policies of the time so far as they appear to have had some influence or bearing upon the course of our foreign policies.

This history is neither pro-Roosevelt nor anti-Roosevelt—it is factual. When history goes beyond an honest attempt to discover what the facts were, and to narrate them, it ceases to be history. It may become apologetics; it may become an attempt at justification of self or policy or party; it may become propaganda, either friendly or hostile, either retrospective or prospective (as some recent books have been)—but obviously it is not history. This is a factual history.

Its author has abstained from passing moral judgments; that function is for each reader to perform for himself after he has familiarized himself with these facts. Indeed—and because nowadays it is so difficult for an objective book on this subject to obtain a fair hearing, and to receive unslanted and unbiased reviews—almost no "anti" Roosevelt sources have been consulted or employed. The citations to such sources can be counted on the fingers of one hand. All the printed sources which have been used have been either official government publications, "neutral" sources such as the New York *Times*, or books written by "pro" Roosevelt authors.

Furthermore this history is neither "isolationist" nor "interventionist." The author has studiously refrained from any attempt to pass any judgment upon the great question of whether it was wise or mistaken for Mr. Roosevelt to involve the Nation in what he once called the "international quarrels and squabbles [and] the wars of the rest of the world." Let each reader form his own opinion for himself upon that problem, giving such weight, if any, as he thinks fit to give to the criterion of the former Under Secretary of State, Mr. Sumner Welles: [2]

> The wisdom of any foreign policy can generally be determined only by its results.*

The scope of this history is more limited than that. It merely tells how Mr. Roosevelt's secret actions from day to day helped to take this Nation into a world war, unwittingly and contrary to the will of a majority of the people. It may be the ultimate verdict of history that Mr. Roosevelt was wiser than the people of the United States, and that he knew better than they did where the best interests of the Nation lay. Or the ultimate verdict of history may be otherwise. That question is neither asked nor answered in this book.

But without regard to whatever ultimate answer history may give to that question, there will still remain the question which this history raises, the question of ways and means and methods and devices and secrecy. Ought one American to be permitted—no matter how wise he may be, no matter how sincere or conscientious or altruistic—to conduct our foreign affairs sometimes personally and single-handed, often with little or no counsel or advice, and frequently in deep secrecy?

Is such a practice consonant with our democratic and representative system?

Is it expedient or safe in an atomic age?

II | COMPLETE ISOLATION FROM WAR

When Mr. Roosevelt was inaugurated President for the first time, on March 4, 1933, no one would have dreamed of predicting that any questions involving foreign power politics would arise while he was in office. Mr. Roosevelt's previous interests as Governor of New York State had seemed to be quite local, and his campaign speeches had been devoted to domestic matters.

The earliest events of his first term, during the so-called one hundred days, emphasized the accuracy of that impression. To mention the various elements of that legislation would fall outside the scope of this book; let it suffice to say that Mr. Roosevelt's program at its inception was exclusively concerned with the internal affairs of the country. When the hundred days were over there was no change in the course or in the direction of public events. As the months and the years went by it was clear that Mr. Roosevelt's interest was concentrated upon domestic matters.

It seemed to be beyond dispute that if there was to be a second World War, America proposed to stand aside and have no part of it. Indeed, having been accused of being an "isolationist," Mr. Roosevelt in substance admitted it as late as August 14, 1936, when he said at Chautauqua: [1]

> We shun political commitments which might entangle us in foreign wars; we avoid connection with the political activities of the League of Nations * . *
>
> We are not isolationists except in so far as we seek to isolate ourselves completely from war. *

A detailed analysis of Mr. Roosevelt's speeches and acts during his first term immeasurably strengthens the conclusion that during those four years, and until the latter part of 1937, his tendencies were genuinely and strongly towards "isolation." Looking backward in 1937, when he wrote the introduction to his volume of 1933 speeches, Mr. Roosevelt stated that the objectives of the New Deal "were, have always been, and still are: * Security against war."[2]

The contemporary 1933 record is not long. The first inaugural address contained only a single sentence referring to world affairs, a dedication to the policy of the Good Neighbor.[3] On March 29, Mr. Roosevelt refused to say, even off the record, whether or not he wanted the Senate to take action on American adherence to the World Court.[4]

On May 16, 1933, he addressed the nations of the world, asking them to agree "to eliminate from possession and use the weapons * of offense * war planes, heavy mobile artillery, land battleships called tanks, and poison gas,"[5] while retaining all defensive weapons. Nothing came of this casual proposal.

In July he abruptly ended the World Economic Conference because it was considering "mere" currency stabilization,[6] which would have interfered with his attempts to affect domestic prices by manipulating the content of the theoretical gold dollar.

On October 13, 1933, in a radio address, Mr. Roosevelt said: [7]

> * As a Nation, we are overwhelmingly against engaging in war. * the United States is opposed to war.

On November 16, 1933, normal diplomatic relations were reestablished with Soviet Russia, so that the two nations thenceforth might cooperate "for the preservation of the peace of the world." [8] Russia agreed, among other things, [9]

> * to refrain from interfering in any manner in the internal affairs of the United States, its territories or possessions.
>
> To refrain, and to restrain * all organizations of the [Russian] Government or under its direct or indirect control * from any act overt or covert liable in any way whatsoever to injure the tranquility, prosperity, order, or security of the whole or any part of the United States * or any agitation or propaganda *.

The entire agreement is most interesting and puzzling to read. Why was it forgotten, or, if not forgotten, why was it not enforced?

At the end of the year, on December 28, 1933, Mr. Roosevelt, stating that he was supplementing an earlier policy of President Wilson, announced that the time had come to make a further declaration: "that the definite policy of the United States from now on is one opposed to armed intervention." [10] Later on in the same address he faintly praised the League of Nations, but immediately added these thoroughly "isolationist" statements [11] (which also serve to illuminate his refusal on March 29, nine months earlier, to approve World Court membership):

> We are not members and we do not contemplate membership. We are giving cooperation to the League in every matter which is not primarily political *.

> I believe that I express the views of my countrymen when I state that the old policies, the old alliances, the old combinations and balances of power have proved themselves inadequate for the preservation of world peace. *

A few days later, on January 3, 1934, Mr. Roosevelt repeated the same theme in his annual message to the Congress: [12]

> * I have made it clear that the United States cannot take part in political arrangements in Europe *.

When the Vinson Navy Bill was signed on March 27, 1934, Mr. Roosevelt took the trouble to prepare and issue a special statement [13] to the country emphasizing that the bill only "authorized" the construction of vessels, that it did not appropriate any money for such construction, and that such construction in the future was very doubtful. At a press conference several days earlier [14] he had also emphasized the same distinction between "authorization" and actual construction of the vessels. And then Mr. Roosevelt concluded his statement with a significant declaration of his policy at that time:

> It has been and will be the policy of the Administration to favor continued limitation of Naval armaments. It is my personal hope that the Naval Conference to be held in 1935 will extend all existing limitations and agree to further reductions.

In a note [15] to the March 27, 1934, statement (which note was written late in 1937), Mr. Roosevelt summarized the entire naval construction of his first term. It shows a progressively steady decline: viz., in 1933, 37 vessels; in 1934 and 1935, 24 each year, and in 1936 only 20 vessels. Of this four-year total construction of 105 vessels, half, or 52, were 1500-ton destroyers and thus almost the exact numerical equivalent of the 50 destroyers which were later transferred to Great Britain at one stroke of his pen on a single day—September 3, 1940. For the rest of 1934, Mr. Roosevelt seems to have been preoccupied exclusively with domestic affairs.

In his annual message to the Congress on January 4, 1935, Mr. Roosevelt, while viewing with gentle alarm the international situation outside of the United States, concluded his brief review with this generality: [16]

> There is no ground for apprehension that our relations with any Nation will be otherwise than peaceful. *

Nine days later the Saar voted for reunion with Germany. On March 16, 1935, Germany reestablished universal military service in violation of the Treaty of Versailles.

Towards the middle of the year, Mr. Roosevelt addressed this "isolationist" observation to the graduating class at West Point:

> * As a Nation, we have been very fortunate in a geographic isolation which in itself has partially protected our boundless resources. *

Somewhat over two months later, on August 31, 1935, the Neutrality Act of 1935 was signed by Mr. Roosevelt. In addition, he issued a general statement of approval, in the course of which he said: [18]

> * the objective is wholly good. It is the policy of this Government to avoid being drawn into wars between other Nations * . * The policy of the Government is definitely committed to the maintenance of peace and the avoidance of any entanglements which would lead us into conflict. *

At the San Diego Exposition, on October 2, 1935, he said: [19]

> The second cloud—"foreign war"—is more real—a more potent danger at this moment to the future of civilization. It is not surprising that many of our citizens feel a deep sense of apprehension lest some of the Nations of the world repeat the folly of twenty years ago and drag civilization to a level from which world-wide recovery may be all but impossible.

In the face of this apprehension the American people can have but one concern—the American people can speak but one sentiment: despite what happens in continents overseas, the United States of America shall and must remain, as long ago the Father of our Country prayed that it might remain—unentangled and free.

Mr. Roosevelt also referred in the same speech to "Our national determination to keep free of foreign wars and foreign entanglements *," which statement he reiterated [20] on November 13, 1935, in answer to an enquiry about another aspect of American foreign policy.

On October 3, the day following the San Diego speech, Mussolini invaded Ethiopia.

On October 5, 1935, Mr. Roosevelt issued a series of neutrality proclamations for the Italo-Ethiopian war, and with them a statement to the public. Annotating these documents in 1937, he pointed out that his neutrality efforts had exceeded what the Act required him to do. [21]

Some days later, on October 17, 1935, Mr. Roosevelt said in a public address read for him in his absence: [22]

* I have pledged myself to do my part in keeping America free of those entanglements that move us along the road to war. *

On October 23, 1935, in the famous "we-are-planning-it-that-way" speech, Mr. Roosevelt again referred to his earlier statements of policy made at the San Diego Exposition, and added: [23]

* I tried to make it clear then, as I continue to make it clear today, that it shall be my earnest effort to keep this country free and unentangled from any possible war that may occur across the seas.

On October 30, 1935, he issued a further statement to the public about the Italo-Ethiopian war, which reemphasized the determination of the Government not to become involved in the controversy, and which also moralized as follows: [24]

> However, in the course of war, tempting trade opportunities may be offered to our people to supply material which would prolong the war. I do not believe that the American people will wish for abnormally increased profits that temporarily might be secured by greatly extending our trade in such materials; nor would they wish the struggles on the battlefield to be prolonged because of profits accruing to a comparatively small number of American citizens.

At the Armistice Day ceremonies in 1935, Mr. Roosevelt delivered an address [25] in which he summarized and strongly reaffirmed these previous declarations. He said:

> The primary purpose of the United States of America is to avoid being drawn into war. We seek also in every practicable way to promote peace and to discourage war. Except for those few who have placed or who place temporary, selfish gain ahead of national and world peace, the overwhelming mass of American citizens are in hearty accord with these basic policies of our Government *.
>
> * We are acting to simplify definitions and facts by calling war "War" when armed invasion and a resulting killing of human beings take place.

Then, referring to a younger generation which had not had any direct knowledge of what war was like, he added:

> * They are not immune to the glamour of war, to the opportunities to escape from the drabness and worry of hard times at home in the glory and heroism of the arms factory and the battlefield. Fortunately, there is evidence on every hand that the youth of America, as a whole, is not trapped by that delusion. They know that elation and prosperity which may come from a new war must lead—for those who survive it—to economic and social collapse more sweeping than any we have experienced in the past. *

At about this time Mr. Roosevelt received from the Bishop of Albany a letter which is not printed in his Public Papers. From Mr. Roosevelt's reply it seems a reasonable inference that this letter from the servant of the Prince of Peace had urged Mr. Roosevelt to intervene in the Italo-Ethiopian war. Mr. Roosevelt's reply to Bishop Oldham, dated November 14, 1935, [26] referred to

> * the unquestioned mandate of our people, expressed in recent legislation and in numerous other ways, through the press, through public gatherings and through petitions and letters, that, above all, the United States should not be drawn into the conflict. *

On October 19, 1935, the League of Nations agreed to apply economic sanctions to Italy, and on November 18 the application of these sanctions by fifty-one nations commenced. The United States did not participate with them.

On December 9, 1935, Mr. Roosevelt wrote [27] to Mr. Norman Davis, Chairman of the American delegation to the London Naval Conference, and urged "a substantial proportional reduction in the present naval levels" of twenty per cent. He specifically referred to Great Britain, Japan, and the United States, and emphasized their existing friendly relations in a sentence which the events of the next six years were to contradict:

> * We three Nations, the principal naval powers, have nothing to fear from one another. *

On the same day Mr. Roosevelt spoke at Chicago, and moralized further as follows: [28]

> You and I know that we have no intention of getting mixed up in the wars of the rest of the world. About the only thing that is left for us to do is to set an example for them, with the hope that * they will stop their local and their international quarrels and squabbles, and take a leaf out of the notebook of the United States.

Mr. Roosevelt delivered his annual message to the Congress on January 3, 1936. Its first half was devoted to a pessimistic synopsis of recent world affairs, after which he asserted that peace was jeopardized, and that a series of wars was in prospect. He concluded this portion of his annual message with a declaration of policy in which he strongly reiterated the American purpose to remain neutral, saying: [29]

> We hope that we are not again at the threshold of such an era. But if face it we must, then the United States and the rest of the Americas can play but one role: through a well-ordered neutrality to do naught to encourage the contest, through adequate defense to save ourselves from embroilment and attack, and through example and all legitimate encouragement and assistance to persuade other Nations to return to the ways of peace and good-will.

On March 7, 1936, German troops marched into and reoccupied the Rhineland. On May 2 the capital of Ethiopia fell, and Haile Selassie fled into exile. Towards the end of that month the first sit-down strikes took place: they were in France, and the date was May 26, 1936.

At a luncheon at Dallas on June 12, 1936, Mr. Roosevelt repeated his then established theme in these words: [30]

> As I have said, we seem to understand very well what the problems of the world are. We have, perhaps, a kind of sympathy for their problems. We want to help them all we can; but they have understood very well in these latter years that that help is going to be confined to moral help, and that we are not going to get tangled up with their troubles in the days to come.

On June 20, 1936, the neutrality proclamations of the Italo-Ethiopian war were revoked, due to the termination of the war by the Italian conquest. [31] On July 18, 1936, the Spanish Civil War commenced. The Neutrality Act had been drafted so casually that it contained no provisions envisaging such an event. [32] However, the State Department requested businessmen not to make sales of goods which would endanger, to quote Mr. Roosevelt, [33]

> * even if only to a slight degree, our desire to be neutral in this unfortunate happening in Spain.

Businessmen cooperated until the end of December, when a manufacturer of planes prepared to send some of them to Spain. [34] Within a week Mr. Roosevelt asked the Congress to amend the Neutrality Act [35] so that he could enforce by law his voluntary neutral policy with regard to the Spanish Civil War.

About four weeks after the outbreak of the Spanish Civil War, Mr. Roosevelt delivered a speech at Chautauqua, on "the subject of peace," [36] which contains his strongest declarations against war until the 1940 political campaign. Some of the crescendo portions of it are as follows: [37]

> We shun political commitments which might entangle us in foreign wars; we avoid connection with the political activities of the League of Nations * . *

> We are not isolationists except in so far as we seek to isolate ourselves completely from war.*

> I have seen war. I have seen war on land and on sea. I have seen blood running from the wounded. I have seen men coughing out their gassed lungs. I have seen the dead in the mud. I have seen cities destroyed. I have seen two hundred limping, exhausted men come out of line—the survivors of a regiment of one thousand that went forward forty-eight hours before. I have seen children starving. I have seen the agony of mothers and wives. I hate war.

> I have passed unnumbered hours, I shall pass unnumbered hours, thinking and planning how war may be kept from this Nation.

I wish I could keep war from all Nations; but that is beyond my power. I can at least make certain that no act of the United States helps to produce or to promote war. I can at least make clear that the conscience of America revolts against war and that any Nation which provokes war forfeits the sympathy of the people of the United States.

* * * * *

The Congress of the United States has given me certain authority to provide safeguards of American neutrality in case of war.

The President of the United States, who, under our Constitution, is vested with primary authority to conduct our international relations, thus has been given new weapons with which to maintain our neutrality.

Nevertheless—and I speak from a long experience—the effective maintenance of American neutrality depends today, as in the past, on the wisdom and determination of whoever at the moment occupy the offices of President and Secretary of State.

It is clear that our present policy and the measures passed by the Congress would, in the event of a war on some other continent, reduce war profits which would otherwise accrue to American citizens. Industrial and agricultural production for a war market may give immense fortunes to a few men; for the nation as a whole it produces disaster. *

* * * * *

Nevertheless, if war should break out again in another continent, let us not blink the fact that we would find in this country thousands of Americans who, seeking immediate riches—fools' gold—would attempt to break down or evade our neutrality.

They would tell you—and unfortunately, their views would get wide publicity—that if they could produce and ship this and that and the other articles to belligerent Nations, the unemployed of America would all find work. *

It would be hard to resist that clamor; it would be hard for many Americans, I fear, to look beyond—to realize the inevitable penalties, the inevitable day of reckoning, that come from a false prosperity. To resist the clamor of that greed, if war should come, would require the unswerving support of all Americans who love peace.

If we face the choice of profits or peace, the nation will answer—must answer—"We choose peace." It is the duty of all of us to encourage such a body of public opinion in this country that the answer will be clear and for all practical purposes unanimous.

* I have thought and worked long and hard on the problem of keeping the United States at peace. But all the wisdom of America is not to be found in the White House *.

No matter how well we are supported by neutrality legislation, we must remember that no laws can be provided to cover every contingency * . * international relations involve of necessity a vast uncharted area. In that area safe sailing will depend on the knowledge and the experience and the wisdom of those who direct our foreign policy. Peace will depend on their day-to-day decisions.

At this late date * we find it possible to trace the tragic series of small decisions which led Europe into the Great War in 1914 and eventually engulfed us and many other Nations.

We can keep out of war if those who watch and decide have a sufficiently detailed understanding of international affairs to make certain that the small decisions of each day do not lead toward war and if, at the same time, they possess the courage to say "no" to those who selfishly or unwisely would let us go to war.

It is to be hoped that the foregoing quotation has been read and reread by the reader with great and attentive care. Many passages in it might well have been italicized, for the sake of emphasis, but such emphasis would perhaps have diverted the reader's attention from other equally significant passages. It will also be observed that the Chautauqua speech rather elaborates upon what the President, Mr. Roosevelt, ought to do in his future conduct of foreign policy. Yet in the future decisions which involved war and peace, Mr. Roosevelt subsequently seems to have done exactly the opposite of what he said he would not do, or ought not to do.

The comment which the Chautauqua speech received was of course favorable, as its author had calculated, because the overwhelming majority of Americans entertained sentiments identical with those declared by Mr. Roosevelt to be his own. [38]

For that very reason the speech was not a sensation and did not receive the studious attention which in the light of subsequent history it deserved to have.

In mid-October Mr. Roosevelt was stumping the country, seeking election for a second term. Asked at Hayfield, Minn., "Are we going to fight?" he replied: [39]

> I hope we will never fight again as long as you and I are alive. * I believe that our foreign policy is really making for peace throughout the world.

At St. Paul he referred to lending "our money to foreign Nations to enable them to buy our own farm and industrial products," and disapprovingly characterized such an act as "frenzied finance." [40]

More or less general remarks praising our search for security from war or our setting an example for peace were made in speeches [41] at Cheyenne, Wyo., Wichita, Kans., St. Louis, Mo., Flint, Mich., and at Madison Square Garden. In the last-mentioned speech Mr. Roosevelt said: [42]

* The Nation knows that I hate war, and I know that the Nation hates war.

I submit to you a record of peace; and on that record a well-founded expectation for future peace * with the world.

Soon after the election Mr. Roosevelt made a four weeks' trip to South America in the course of which his various speeches at Rio de Janeiro and at Buenos Aires dwelt largely, if in generalities, upon the blessings of peace and the prevention of war.

The annual message to the Congress, of January 6, 1937, differed considerably from that of the previous year. It dealt almost entirely with domestic affairs, and gave only about a page and a half to "world problems," which (apart from a couple of uncomplimentary references to oligarchies) consisted in praise of the efforts of the recent Buenos Aires conference to assure peace and improve peace machinery. [44]

On January 8, 1937, Mr. Roosevelt directed the Navy Department to proceed with the construction of two battleships as partial replacements for the *Arkansas*, the *Texas*, and the *New York*, which were then well over twenty years old. [45]

These battleships were the *North Carolina* and the *Washington*, but even these two battleships were not completed and placed in service during Mr. Roosevelt's second term of office prior to Pearl Harbor. [46]

 # THE NEW DEAL COLLAPSES

THE YEAR 1937 was full of frustration and ill omen to Mr. Roosevelt as well as to the United States. In that year he initiated and after a long and bitter struggle failed in his court-packing plans. He also initiated a scheme to reorganize the executive departments, dependent largely on his personal discretion, which failed of Congressional approval, largely due to distrust of his judgment and of his motives. The criticism of the appointment of Senator Black to the United States Supreme Court on August 12, 1937, had flamed up into a national forest fire after the revelations made in September 1937 that Mr. Black was, or had been, a member of the Ku Klux Klan.

Worst of all, the recovery for which Mr. Roosevelt had claimed full credit, as the consequence of New Deal planning, was in full retreat. In September 1937 a new depression had commenced and it developed with almost unprecedented speed. On October 19, 1937, the stock market collapsed, as seven million shares were traded. Seen in the light of retrospect, Mr. Morgenthau rightly thought [1] that this date

* was a date of particular significance in the history of President Roosevelt's administrations. *

Unemployment increased at an astounding rate; [2] stock prices fell abysmally; bankruptcies multiplied; the only sign of expansion was in the number of unemployed people added to the relief rolls which, in the industrial cities of the Middle West, increased 347 per cent between October 1937 and May 1938. [3]

It was thus becoming evident to the electorate that the domestic economic policies of the New Deal had resulted in failure; in consequence, economic planning as practiced by the New Deal was in popular disgrace. [4]

Failure in Congress was thus followed by economic failure, compounded by national wrath at the smart-alecky [5] appointment of Senator Black to the Supreme Court. The wheel of fortune had turned swiftly and far since it had carried Mr. Roosevelt so high at the 1936 election. The New Deal seemed to be headed imminently for the fate of the wonderful one-hoss shay. Something was needed to divert the public attention from contemplation of this dismal situation; some new distraction had to be devised in order to disguise the further economic controls over production and prices which were planned by the New Dealers, but which could no longer be sold to the nation by open daylight.

What to do? Younger New Dealers had privately said that the New Deal could never afford to be caught without a white rabbit in reserve to be pulled out of the magician's hat, but the New Dealers were just about at the end of their supply of domestic rabbits, as the record of domestic legislation shows. By a simple process of elimination all that remained to be produced was a foreign white rabbit.

The state of foreign affairs through the first three-quarters of 1937 reveals how forced this selection was. It seemed to be a time of

THE NEW DEAL COLLAPSES | 23

relative tranquillity in Europe. No new territories were occupied or threatened with occupation by the foreign tyrants, nor were any treaties denounced or violated. It is true that the Spanish Civil War continued, but this was no new development, and during the latter half of 1936 it had given Mr. Roosevelt scant concern. Even Chancellor Hitler's speeches during the first nine months of 1937 were relatively conciliatory and free from threats or predictions of war.

Indeed, so strong was this halcyon feeling in the Government that early in 1937 Mr. Morgenthau had felt serious concern because the European nations were spending an average of twenty per cent of their Government revenues on rearmament, which meant to him that they were gradually going bankrupt, and never could be helped under such circumstances. Mr. Morgenthau took up this problem with Mr. Roosevelt, who agreed that a serious attempt should be made at world disarmament.

> * With the President's backing [6] [wrote Mr. Morgenthau] I sent messages to Neville Chamberlain, then Chancellor of the Exchequer in Britain, urging the exchange of suggestions over how to arrest the arms race.
>
> One message produced no results. The President suggested another. "Let's put a burr under Chamberlain's tail," he said. But Chamberlain replied that the peaceable people of Europe wanted England to arm more, not less. This was a sensible reply * . *

Mr. Roosevelt's earlier pronouncements in 1937 had been few and peaceable. On April 10 he had by letter greeted *The Christian Science Monitor* and had praised its efforts for the preservation of peace. [7] A similar kind of letter had been sent to be read at the opening of the Institute of Public Affairs of the University of Virginia on June 29. [8]

On May 1, 1937, Mr. Roosevelt approved the Neutrality Act, amended so as to apply to civil wars, and the same day by proclamation he prohibited the export of arms and munitions to Spain.[9] As the first legislative act of its session the new Congress had passed a stop-gap resolution on January 8, 1937, so that for the first time, as Mr. Roosevelt later admitted,[10] there was legal authority for his policy of discouraging munitions shipments to Spain.

Violently in contrast was his policy towards China, because he was strongly pro-Chinese.[11] Perhaps the important turning point in Mr. Roosevelt's foreign policy is to be located here. The international event which provided the excuse for his Chicago quarantine speech may be confidently said to have been the increased activity of the Sino-Japanese war after the Marco Polo bridge fighting on July 7, 1937. In contrast to the way in which Mr. Roosevelt had done more than the neutrality laws required with respect to the Italo-Ethiopian war and the Spanish Civil War, he now declined to apply the laws to the war in China on the ground that to do so would be a greater detriment to China than to Japan.

A lawyer who went to Washington at that time to secure the export permits for the Bellanca airplanes to be shipped to China found that the State Department officials were unusually cooperative. When it later transpired that the planes had been shipped from the west coast on a Government-owned vessel, the *Wichita*, public clamor of "sensational proportions" compelled Mr. Roosevelt to order that the planes be unloaded. On September 14 he issued a ruling that thenceforth munitions must not be transported to China or Japan in American Government-owned merchant vessels.[12] The Maritime Commission misinterpreted Mr. Roosevelt's intent and refused all passage to the planes when they arrived back at the east coast to be shipped to England and there transshipped to Hong Kong. Mr. Roosevelt had the Commission "revise" this interpretation, and later in the year privately owned American vessels began to traffic with Hong Kong in arms destined for China.[13]

If Mr. Roosevelt had formed what George Washington called a "passionate attachment" for China, Mr. Hull sheltered an "inveterate antipathy" against Japan. Since August 1937, Mr. Hull said, he had conducted our foreign policy upon the theory that [14]

> Japan definitely contemplates securing domination over as many hundreds of millions of people as possible in eastern Asia and gradually extending her control through the Pacific islands to the Dutch East Indies and elsewhere, thereby dominating in practical effect that one-half of the world.

The American people at this time, as Mr. Roosevelt later admitted, [15] felt an "overwhelming sentiment * of complete isolation *." There was of course no change in their feelings during the summer of 1937 or for years to come.

Some of Mr. Roosevelt's domestic political difficulties of the moment have already been described. The revealing articles concerning Mr. Black were in full swing in mid-September 1937, and Mr. Roosevelt was vehemently refusing any comment upon the topic until Mr. Black returned from Europe. [16] In late September Mr. Roosevelt fled to the Far West and missed (he claimed) the broadcast on October 1, 1937, in which Mr. Black admitted he had been a Klansman. [17] Mr. Roosevelt steadily refused any comment about Mr. Black, [18] but the topic continued to occupy the front pages of the newspapers, and it was politically expedient that something be done to drive it into the inside pages.

Such were the settings of the domestic and of the foreign political stages as Mr. Roosevelt's special train headed eastward in early October. At Chicago on Tuesday, October 5, 1937, he was to make a dedicatory address: he chose this occasion to announce publicly a reversal of his established and professed attitude towards foreign affairs. [19]

After contrasting American peace with the "very different scenes being enacted in other parts of the world," Mr. Roosevelt, the apostle of freedom from fear, painted a terrifying and fearsome picture of the prospects of the world and of the United States. He spoke of "a haunting fear of calamity. * The present reign of terror *.* the very foundations of civilization are seriously threatened," and continued:

> Without a declaration of war and without warning or justification of any kind, civilians, including vast numbers of women and children, are being ruthlessly murdered with bombs from the air. In times of so-called peace, ships are being attacked and sunk by submarines without cause or notice. *
>
> To paraphrase a recent author "perhaps we foresee a time when men, exultant in the technique of homicide, will rage so hotly over the world that every precious thing will be in danger * all will be lost or wrecked or utterly destroyed."
>
> If those things come to pass in other parts of the world, let no one imagine that America will escape, that America may expect mercy, that this Western Hemisphere will not be attacked *.
>
> If those days come "there will be no safety by arms, no help from authority, no answer in science. The storm will rage till every flower of culture is trampled and all human beings are leveled in a vast chaos."
>
> If those days are not to come to pass * the peace-loving nations must make a concerted effort to uphold laws and principles on which alone peace can rest secure.
>
> The peace-loving nations must make a concerted effort in opposition to those violations of treaties and those ignorings of humane instincts which today are creating a state of international anarchy and instability from which there is no escape through mere isolation or neutrality.

After some general pronouncements in favor of morality, Mr. Roosevelt then said (and how mockingly it sounds in retrospect!):

In those nations of the world which seem to be piling armament on armament for purposes of aggression, and those other nations which fear acts of aggression against them and their security, a very high proportion of their national income is being spent directly for armaments. It runs from thirty to as high as fifty per cent. We are fortunate. The proportion that we in the United States spend is far less—eleven or twelve per cent.

How happy we are that the circumstances of the moment permit us to put our money into bridges and boulevards, dams and reforestation, the conservation of our soil and many other kinds of useful works rather than into huge standing armies and vast supplies of implements of war.

Mr. Roosevelt continued:

It seems to be unfortunately true that the epidemic of world lawlessness is spreading.

When an epidemic of physical disease starts to spread, the community approves and joins in a quarantine of the patients in order to protect the health of the community against the spread of the disease.

Having gone thus far, Mr. Roosevelt proceeded no further in that direction, but returned to his leitmotifs of love of peace and of horror of war, although a deviation from that theme is now noticeable for the first time. He concluded his speech with these declarations and promises:

It is my determination to pursue a policy of peace. It is my determination to adopt every practicable measure to avoid involvement in war. *

* We are determined to keep out of war, yet we cannot insure ourselves against the disastrous effects of war and the dangers of involvement. We are adopting such measures as will minimize our risk of involvement, but we cannot have complete protection in a world of disorder in which confidence and security have broken down.

* There must be positive endeavors to preserve peace.

America hates war. America hopes for peace. Therefore, America actively engages in the search for peace.

The exact nature of the action which Mr. Roosevelt proposed to take was designedly left obscure in his speech. At his press conference held on the following day [20] he declined to elaborate on what he intended to do, although he excluded a number of possibilities, but he threw off one extremely significant hint, as the following excerpts show.

Q. Do you care to amplify your remarks at Chicago, especially where you referred to a possible quarantine?

THE PRESIDENT: No.

* * * * * *

Q. But you also said that the peace-loving nations can and must find a way to make their wills prevail?

THE PRESIDENT: Yes?

* * * * * *

Q. Doesn't that mean economic sanctions anyway?

THE PRESIDENT: No, not necessarily. Look, "sanctions" is a terrible word to use. They are out of the window.

* * * * * *

Q. Is there a likelihood that there will be a conference of the peace-loving nations?

THE PRESIDENT: No; conferences are out of the window. You never get anywhere with a conference.

* * * * * *

Q. Wouldn't it be almost inevitable, if any program is reached, that our present Neutrality Act will have to be overhauled?

THE PRESIDENT: Not necessarily. That is the interesting thing.

Q. You say there isn't any conflict between what you outline and the Neutrality Act. They seem to be on opposite poles to me and your assertion does not enlighten me.

THE PRESIDENT: Put your thinking cap on, Ernest [Lindley].

Q. * How can you be neutral if you are going to align yourself with one group of nations?

THE PRESIDENT: What do you mean "aligning"? You mean a treaty?

Q. Not necessarily. I meant action on the part of peace-loving nations.

THE PRESIDENT: There are a lot of methods in the world that have never been tried yet.

Q. But, at any rate, that is not an indication of neutral attitude—"quarantine the aggressors" and "other nations of the world."

THE PRESIDENT: I can't give you any clue to it. You will have to invent one. *I have got one.*

* * * * * *

Q. This is no longer neutrality.

THE PRESIDENT: On the contrary, it might be a stronger neutrality.

* * * * * *

Q. Do you agree or disagree with * the conclusion of the British, that sanctions mean war?

THE PRESIDENT: No. Don't talk about sanctions. *

Q. I meant that in general terms; going further than moral denunciation.

The President: That is not a definition of "sanctions."

Q. Is a "quarantine" a sanction?

The President: No.

Q. Are you excluding any coercive action? Sanctions is coercive.

The President: That is exactly the difference.

Q. *Better, then, to keep it in a moral sphere?*

The President: *No, it can be a very practical sphere.*

(Emphasis supplied.)

The clue as to the nature of Mr. Roosevelt's intentions is to be sought for in the idea of a "quarantine." When a house is quarantined, no body and no thing, speaking generally, is allowed to go in or to come out. By analogy we may therefore presume that Mr. Roosevelt intended to attempt some form of a naval or economic blockade, or both, against an "aggressor" nation. But history has shown that naval blockades have little hope of success when directed against continental nations, such as Germany or Italy. Japan, however, was an island empire, and Japan was the most recent aggressor, and so it seems probable [21] that Mr. Roosevelt contemplated some action against Japan. We have been informed that on October 11, 1937, Mr. Roosevelt consulted some of the American admirals as to an economic blockade of Japan in cooperation with certain European powers, [22] but that England was unwilling to participate in it, due no doubt to a feeling that it was probable war would ensue. In this proposal Mr. Roosevelt seems to have outrun English caution, because there is some evidence to suggest that his speech was at least indirectly prompted by Mr. Churchill and by Mr. Eden. [23]

The American public was of course ignorant, at the time, of the hazardous action which Mr. Roosevelt contemplated as the aftermath of his Chicago speech. All that was then known was contained within the speech itself. To say that the Republic was amazed by the speech would be an understatement. It was not only amazed; it was frightened. The speech was badly received [24] and was the subject of protest. Those who had distrusted Mr. Roosevelt's judgment commenced to distrust his motives and to suspect his purposes. It seem to them (in retrospect, rightly?) that this reversal portended the choice of a path which descended only to war. These intuitive promptings led to the introduction in the Congress of the Ludlow resolution to amend the Constitution. By this amendment a public referendum would have had to be taken before war could be declared. Temporarily frustrated by this new and hostile development, Mr. Roosevelt disappeared behind the screen of silence.

To this day the precise details of this significant reversal remain concealed in the archives of this and other nations. [25] When revealed they will be of great interest. But even when revealed they cannot alter the fact that this fateful reversal of established American foreign policy was commenced not only without the prior knowledge or approval of the people, but indeed contrary to their overwhelming opinion and desire. The reversal probably does not much antedate the date of delivery of the speech, because a year later Mr. Roosevelt was asked at his press conference of October 14, 1938, [26]

> Q. Can you throw any light on the reason which led to this decision to reorganize the whole national defense picture?
>
> THE PRESIDENT: I should say, offhand, that it started about a year ago because of information that was coming in at that time. It has been in progress for about a year * . *

It seems likely that when Great Britain refused to participate in the economic blockade of Japan, she suggested a softer alternative in which Mr. Roosevelt concurred. This was to call a conference of the signatories to the Nine-Power Washington Treaty of February 6, 1922 (in which it was agreed to respect the political and administrative integrity of China), in order to put pressure [27] on Japan to get out of China. In Tokyo, Ambassador Grew felt forebodings that the proposed conference could accomplish nothing. [28] In early October "the Belgian Government, by request of the British Government and with the approval of our government, issued invitations to the signatories of the Nine-Power Washington Treaty to convene in Brussels * in an attempt to provide a formula for peace in the Far East." [29] Russia and Germany, neither of which was party to the treaty, were also invited to attend. Russia accepted, while Germany declined, and "repeated attempts to persuade Japan to send a representative" were unsuccessful. The Japanese accused America of initiating an anti-Japanese front at the conference. Mr. Hull heatedly denied that America took the initiative in calling the conference, and Ambassador Grew, who reported this denial to the Japanese Minister for Foreign Affairs, Mr. Hirota, had previously reported to him earlier denials of our State Department to the same effect. [30] Mr. Grew made a glancing allusion to a speech made by Mr. Eden in the House of Commons, as if to point the finger in the direction of Great Britain. If these denials may be accepted as the truth, it would seem to be the consequence that Mr. Roosevelt was acting in coordination with the British foreign policy of the moment. In any event the conference of November 3–24 was admitted by Mr. Roosevelt to be a failure, but he asserted that he would keep on trying. [31]

The *Panay* incident of December 12, 1937, appeared to offer another opportunity to try to put pressure on Japan. [32] Mr. Roosevelt clearly took the initiative: forthwith he took the matter out of Mr. Hull's hands and wrote the memorandum for Mr. Hull to deliver to the Japanese Ambassador on December 13, 1937. [33] But before it arrived at Tokyo the Japanese Foreign Minister came in person to the American Embassy and apologized. Full indemnity was promised (and subsequently paid), and the Japanese personnel involved in the incident were punished. [34] Thus this quick action by Japan prevented any political capital from being made of the incident. [35]

The last contemporaneously known act of Mr. Roosevelt in 1937 was to write to the chairman of the House Appropriations Committee on December 28, [36] stating that it was "possible" that he might ask for the construction of additional warships during the coming year in view of the fact that other nations were enlarging their armament programs. However, Mr. Roosevelt, in expressing concern, explicitly excluded "any specific nation or * any specific threat against the United States."

Before turning to the events of 1938 it may be well to mention that, while the Sino-Japanese war of 1937 provided the immediate excuse for the reversal of Mr. Roosevelt's previous foreign policy, Mr. Roosevelt's concern with the Pacific and with Asiatic affairs later became at best only secondary, [37] as General MacArthur and many other Americans in service discovered subsequently.

The primary concern of Mr. Roosevelt was with Europe and, more particularly, Britain. As is apparent from the aftermath of the quarantine speech, Mr. Roosevelt's actions were modified by official British opinion, and in this instance were supported or superseded by British use of the Belgian initiative as a catspaw.

Years ago Mr. Moley told us that by January 1938 a policy of active, though unacknowledged, cooperation with Britain was under way. [38] His cryptic reference was to matters which did not come to light for years thereafter. On January 11, 1938, Mr. Roosevelt took the initiative in another move intended to help Great Britain.

He prepared a secret message [39] to the Prime Minister, Mr. Neville Chamberlain, in which he appears to have proposed that he should call a conference at Washington of Great Britain, France, Germany, and Italy to discuss the possibility of reaching a general settlement of their differences. But apparently Mr. Roosevelt also stipulated that his proposal must be kept entirely secret from the other governments, and that he would not invite them at all unless Great Britain was enthusiastically in favor of his action. Sir Ronald Lindsay, the British Ambassador, who transmitted this secret proposal from Washington, commented upon the recent progress which had been made in cooperation between the United States and Great Britain, and recommended that it should be accepted. He viewed it, no doubt, as did other British statesmen, as a commitment of the United States, however tentative, to the support of British policy in Europe.

Mr. Chamberlain seems to have had mental reservations as to Mr. Roosevelt's proposal, and in his reply he expressed doubts as to whether the matter ought not to be postponed, in the light of the current efforts which Great Britain was making to reach agreement with Italy and Germany. Indeed, he wrote, Great Britain was prepared to recognize *de jure* the conquest of Abyssinia, in order to conciliate Italy.

The reply sent the correspondence off upon a different slant. The disappointed Mr. Roosevelt agreed to postpone any thought of a general conference, but he expressed his disapproval of the contemplated recognition of the Italian conquest because he thought it would encourage Japanese policy in respect to China. Mr. Hull amplified this thought, and felt that such a deal in Europe would be at the expense of American interests in Asia.

There was some further exchange of correspondence on the matter and then it appears to have been dropped. But by April 1938 Mr. Emil Ludwig, whose biography of Mr. Roosevelt was almost official, knew enough of Mr. Roosevelt's plans to be able to state [40] that, if there was a war in Europe, America

> * would probably supply the European democracies with everything except troops.

We know now that in December 1937 Admiral Ingersoll, then director of the Navy's War Plans Division, was called to the White House and was directed by Mr. Roosevelt to go to London to enquire what help England could give us in the eventuality of war with Japan, and to declare what the United States intended to do. [41] Admiral Ingersoll was in England during the early part of 1938 and reached some kind of an agreement with the British which seems to have contemplated common action, if not an alliance, in the event of a Japanese war: [42] most of the details are not as yet known. Admiral Richardson said that it provided that the United States was to have Singapore as a base for our fleet, and that [43]

> this understanding * was all based on the assumption that we would be drawn into the war as an associate of Great Britain, and she would be occupied and we would have the rest of the bag to hold. * we would be protecting North America, South America, and Australia.

An earnest of this understanding was demonstrated to the world by a visit of American warships to Australia and then to Singapore in 1938. Already, Mr. Ludwig asserts, [44] Mr. Roosevelt looked "upon Japan as a possible enemy."

Perhaps in consequence of this agreement, Mr. Roosevelt on March 5, 1938, asserted an American claim to Canton and Enderbury Islands, southwest from Hawaii and about two thirds of the distance to Australia. [45] Great Britain had taken possession of the islands about a year previously: therefore, on August 11, 1938, the islands were agreed to be under an Anglo-American condominium, [46] which, on April 6, 1939, was extended for fifty years. [47]

In order to implement his new policy, however, Mr. Roosevelt was compelled to face a number of new problems. First of all it was necessary to "educate" the American public away from historic continentalism, and by means of fear, propaganda, and other publicity methods to persuade them, in the name of national "defense," to participate in what Mr. Roosevelt had earlier characterized as the "international quarrels and squabbles * of the rest of the world." Second, it was necessary to avoid the hampering effect of any war referendum, such as was proposed by Congressman Louis Ludlow. Third, it was necessary to get the Neutrality Act repealed, if possible, or at least modified. Fourth, it was necessary to commence the manufacture of arms for the benefit of Britain primarily and, secondarily, of France. Lastly, it was necessary to make preparations for American entry into the war.

Ten years were to elapse before it was revealed [48] to the American people that the detailed Industrial Mobilization Plan which in 1939 was still so secret that some of the commanding generals of the technical services were unaware of its existence, had actually been commenced some two years earlier, that is, in 1937. It contemplated that no less than twenty thousand factories should be ear-marked for the production of war materials.

Mr. Roosevelt's policy at this time, even the admiring Mr. Ludwig had to confess, [49] was "uneven" and "not easily comprehensible": it could not be a "straight" path, and it lay "between threat and bluff."

Such was the actual shape and the ensuing pattern of the subsequent large and "small decisions of each day [which] lead toward war," and from them the existence of prior plans may be inferred legitimately.

Perhaps the excitement and the high intrigue of power politics furnished to Mr. Roosevelt a welcome escape from his insoluble domestic problems. During the early part of 1938 all of the business indices continued to fall. The census of the unemployed had shown, as of November 1937, about eleven million totally unemployed and five and one-half million partly unemployed. [50] Reversing his "we-are-planning-it-that-way" boast of October 23, 1935, Mr. Roosevelt commenced a publicity campaign to shift the blame for the new depression to business. [51] With his acquiescence this campaign was carried on by a number of subordinates, [52] but not with success.

In the sphere of new domestic legislation, the Fair Labor Standards Act of 1938 stood alone that year, and was the last domestic legislative milestone. And 1938 was also the year of Mr. Roosevelt's ill-fated attempts to purge the Congressional opponents of his court-packing plans. His failure in those plans towards the end of the year not only diminished his prestige but led to serious Republican gains and brought down his political reputation to a new low. It also embittered and emboldened his opponents and strengthened the bi-partisan coalition against him.

It is small wonder that 1938 saw Mr. Roosevelt going more deeply into foreign power politics, [53] and preparing to solve the five new problems in this field which have been enumerated previously.

On January 6, 1938, Mr. Roosevelt wrote the Speaker of the House of Representatives opposing the proposed Ludlow referendum vote as a prerequisite for a declaration of war. He asserted that it was "incompatible with our * form of government" and said that he was convinced that it would not be helpful in keeping the United States out of war, [54] but "would have the opposite effect." In spite of Mr. Roosevelt's opposition, support for the resolution grew, and it was soon thought necessary for Mr. Farley to lend his very considerable influence to block the proposal, in which he was successful. On January 10 the House of Representatives rejected the proposal by the close vote of 209 to 188. [55] "It was a ticklish proposition," wrote Mr. Farley. [56]

At his press conference on January 8, 1938, Mr. Roosevelt said: [57]

> I believe also the time has come for the Congress to enact legislation aimed at * the equalization of the burdens of possible war. * so that the whole nation will engage in war if we unfortunately have one...

But at that time the Congress refused to enact war profits taxes.

On the same day Mr. Roosevelt sent Congress a message requesting increased armaments "for defense." [59] The amounts asked for were not large in themselves—$8,800,000 for anti-aircraft material; $450,000 for the better establishment of an enlisted reserve for the Army; $6,000,000 to manufacture gauges and dies to be used to manufacture army materials; $2,000,000 for ammunition for the Army; an increase of 20 per cent in the authorized Navy program plus the actual commencement of two additional battleships and two additional cruisers, together with $15,000,000 for the experimental construction "of a number of new types of small vessels." In that message Mr. Roosevelt also enunciated his new theory as to what constituted "defense," asserting:

> Adequate defense means that for the protection not only of our coasts but also of our communities far removed from the coast, we must keep any potential enemy many hundred miles away from our continental limits.

Public sentiment remained strongly against Mr. Roosevelt's drive. [60] For the rest of the winter Mr. Roosevelt appeared to be immersed in his domestic problems: nothing whatever appears in his published papers concerning foreign affairs. (Indeed the introduction which he wrote in June 1941 for the 1938 volume does not make so much as a passing reference to foreign affairs.) Nowhere is there mention of the German invasion of Austria on March 12, 1938, or of its annexation on March 13. However, the campaign to "educate" the American people was then resumed with a speech on March 17, 1938, by Secretary Hull [61] in which he advocated "collaboration" along "parallel lines" to prevent the spread of "the contagious scourge of treaty breaking and armed violence." These propaganda efforts were continued through the spring and summer by other subordinates of Mr. Roosevelt, as well as by himself. On April 20, 1938, he met representatives of the Protestant church press. The major part of the interview [62] turned on foreign affairs. It began with neutrality, and there the only omission in the text appears. Conjecturally, Mr. Roosevelt referred to China and Japan, because he next spoke of the case of Spain, and asserted that his policy there was truly neutral. Indeed at that point he gave an excellent definition of "neutrality in the highest sense," which deserves to be better known and remembered—"not to help one fellow more than the other." The conversation then turned to our naval program, and the area which we might attempt to "defend." Mr. Roosevelt suggested the possibility of a German conquest of Mexico; Spain was "three days from Germany, and Mexico is only seven days from Germany," but he was met with skepticism. He then told how the brother of a Chinese friend of his had been killed by bombing in the Chinese interior, "in the Iowa of China," and how Germany, in 1918, was building a Zeppelin to fly "over Iceland, Greenland, and down to New York, to drop a cargo of bombs on New York City." Further skepticism was expressed by his auditors as to how we could "defend" so vast an area. In Mr. Roosevelt's reply lurks the inference that at that early date he was already contemplating simultaneous wars with Germany and with Japan, for he answered:

> Well, of course if you have one enemy, we are all right. But suppose you have two enemies in two different places, then you have to be a bit shifty on your feet. You have to lick one of them first and then bring them around and then lick the other. *

On the following day, in the course of a rather peppery meeting with the American Society of Newspaper Editors, Mr. Roosevelt again elaborated on his neutrality policy and specifically referred to China and Japan, as well as to the Spanish Civil War, [63] repeating his previously stated arguments, but there was no other mention of Europe.

Meanwhile Mr. Roosevelt had been puzzled by the problem of his depression. At first he turned "on the old record" and claimed that he intended to balance the budget. In mid-April he finally came out with a "new" spending program [64] of over three billion dollars. At the end of April he endeavored to divert the public's attention from his depression by the old device of asking for a congressional investigation of monopolies. [65]

There was a lull in May and June while the new spending program was started. The graduation address which Mr. Roosevelt made at Annapolis in early June was wholly peaceable, [66] and a letter to the editor of the *Army and Navy Journal* a fortnight later was also irenic. [67] When the cornerstone of the Federal Building at the New York World's Fair was laid on June 30, 1938, Mr. Roosevelt first revealed [68] that the Navy, which had long been concentrated in the Pacific, would be brought to the Atlantic the following winter. If this betokened an increasing concern with European developments it also seemed to indicate a lessening of the tension in the Pacific.

Shortly thereafter Mr. Roosevelt took a long vacation trip to the west coast, a cruise in the Pacific and back to Florida, ending up at Warm Springs. An address delivered at Treasure Island, San Francisco, [69] spoke of defense, but professed high hopes for peace in 1939.

Before departing on this trip on June 28, 1938, Mr. Roosevelt, perplexed and still undecided what to do with his domestic problems, appears to have announced his conversion to one of Hitler's theories. He said: [70]

* no country has devised a permanent way, a permanent solution, of giving work to people in the depression periods *. The only method devised so far that seemed to give 100 per cent of relief, or nearly so, is the method of going in for armaments *.

Perhaps this statement marked a further significant turning point of Mr. Roosevelt's thinking. The War Department, continuing with the industrial mobilization program, [71] now began to give educational and experimental orders.

On July 1, 1938, the State Department put into effect a "moral embargo" against Japan, notifying aircraft manufacturers and exporters that the United States Government was strongly opposed to the sales of airplanes and aeronautical equipment. [72] As Japanese purchases in the United States of material other than aircraft and aeronautical equipment were relatively unimportant, this embargo operated ultimately to stop the export of arms to Japan.

Before two months had passed, secret negotiations had been commenced with British representatives. Rumors again arose that there was an agreement with Britain envisaging aid from America in the event of war. As signed on November 17, 1938, the agreements officially purported to be trade agreements with Great Britain and Canada. [73] On the other hand the newspapers of the day were full of portentous hints. Thus the headline of one article ran: [74]

Political Effect Interests Britain

and its text stated,

* Britons * are certain that the significance of the conclusion of the agreement at this time will not be lost upon the dictatorships. Authoritative British opinion deprecates discussion of the agreement for its possible political effects. *

Another article rather fulsomely said that this was [75]

* the outstanding diplomatic achievement of the Roosevelt Administration. *

The arrangements were designed to emphasize the importance of treaties which carry both economic and political significance. *

* * * * * *

* It was obvious that the treaty * definitely increases the parallel economic interests of both countries, with the inevitable result that their political interests will become more homogeneous. From this point of view the undertakings are of particular significance. *

* * * * * *

Britain's decision in the first place, while never emphasized in London, was political, because she desired to cement relations with the United States. *

Most curiously, Mr. Roosevelt makes no reference to these treaties or mention of them, in his published papers. Shortly thereafter Washington officials began to talk of M Day, mobilization day.

In late August 1938 Mr. Roosevelt spoke "informally" to his neighbors of Dutchess County and mentioned his travels. He referred to the recently improved defenses of the Panama Canal, saying, [76]

* We are getting airplanes, and submarines, and anti-aircraft guns, and various other things, to try to make reasonably certain that in case of war—which we are all trying to avoid in every possible way—we shall still be able to maintain the link of the Panama Canal. *

At Morgantown, Md., on September 4, 1938, Mr. Roosevelt spoke in the same vein, with an educatory touch: [77]

I suppose there is no nation in the world whose people are more peace-loving than the people of the United States. I suppose there is no nation in the world that is more sincerely desirous of keeping out of war. At the same time, you and I know what world conditions are; and we do have to think sometimes of national defense against some emergency that may come through no fault of our own in the days to come.

On September 6, 1938, Mr. Roosevelt summarized reports which, on March 18, 1938, he had requested to be made, and he asserted concern over "a shortage of [electric] power to meet the needs of the nation's industry in the event of war." [78] He then appointed a committee to study what such war-time needs would be: a year later it was still at work. [79] It was at this time that Mr. Hopkins undertook a secret survey for Mr. Roosevelt as to the national capacity to build military airplanes, because Mr. Roosevelt was convinced at that time that America would get into war. [80] Shortly thereafter General Marshall began to receive, from the relief funds, monies to be secretly used for military expansion. [81]

In the autumn, fear-provoking stories which were intended to further the campaign began to spread mysteriously out of Washington. Some of them were as follows: [82]

1. The Japanese would seize the Dutch possessions in the East Indies;
2. The Germans would conquer England, seize the English Navy, sail it over to our shores, and attack us;
3. The Germans would * secure air bases in Greenland, Iceland and the Faeroes Islands;
4. They would also * establish German bases in the Azores and Cape Verde Islands;
5. They would also * establish colonies on the west coast of Africa and in the Far East, and * [threaten] * the Western Hemisphere;
6. They would also join with the Italians in militarizing the South American states against us;

7. They would also, as the result of some sort of deal with the British * build a base at Newfoundland or Labrador.

Further retaliatory steps were quietly taken against Japan. The private extension of credit was informally discouraged. [83] However, the operation of the most-favored-nation clause in the 1911 commercial treaty barred the adoption of various other retaliatory measures, and so, in order to be free to put them into effect, the United States, on July 26, 1939, notified Japan of the termination of the treaty at the end of the six-month prescribed period. [84]

In 1938 Mr. Chamberlain flew to Berchtesgaden on September 15, and again to Godesberg on September 22, to confer with Hitler. The Munich agreement was signed on September 30, and the Germans occupied the Sudetenland areas on October 1–3.

Meanwhile, on September 9, 1938, Mr. Roosevelt had found it necessary to deny that the United States was allied with European powers in a stop-Hitler movement: this denial is omitted from his published papers. Whatever the truth of this alliance may be, there was some thought in England of attempting to persuade Mr. Roosevelt to join in the resistance to Hitler's manoeuvres. [85] Perhaps these attempts were successful, because on September 26, three days before the Munich meeting, Mr. Roosevelt sent messages to the President of Czechoslovakia, the Prime Minister of Great Britain, the Premier of France, and to Chancellor Hitler, asking that negotiations might continue. [86] On September 27 Chancellor Hitler replied in a noncommittal way on this point, but he rehearsed at length the alleged wrongs done to the Sudeten Germans. Mr. Roosevelt replied on the same day, [87] urging that negotiations continue, and saying:

> * The world asks of us who at this moment are heads of nations the supreme capacity to achieve the destinies of nations without forcing upon them, as a price, the mutilation and death of millions of citizens.

Resort to force in the Great War failed to bring tranquillity. Victory and defeat were alike sterile. That lesson the world should have learned. *

* * * * * *

Allow me to state my unqualified conviction that history, and the souls of every man, woman and child whose lives will be lost in the threatened war, will hold us and all of us accountable should we omit any appeal for its prevention.

The Government of the United States has no political involvements in Europe, and will assume no obligations in the conduct of the present negotiations. *

The conscience and the impelling desire of the people of my country demand that the voice of their government be raised again and yet again to avert and to avoid war.

At this time Mr. Churchill was leading the Opposition in Parliament. He had already drawn, and was to draw, the fire of Hitler's attack for saying in substance that the German regime should be destroyed, while some months earlier he had asserted that Britain was clever enough to bring the whole world into arms against Germany.[88] Mr. Eden had resigned, on February 20, 1938, as Foreign Secretary from Mr. Chamberlain's cabinet because of fundamental differences concerning foreign policy: now, on October 1, the First Lord of the Admiralty, Mr. Alfred Duff-Cooper, resigned in protest against Munich. Presently the French demobilized, but not Mr. Roosevelt. Preparedness for war as the means of enforcing peace became the current new idea in Washington. As early as October 12, 1938, in a Navy Day message, Mr. Roosevelt made a statement [89] which rings slightly hollow in the subsequent light of Pearl Harbor:

> * within the past year unsettled world conditions have made it imperative that we take stock of our national defense and face the

facts. * I believe it entirely consistent with our continuing readiness to limit armaments by agreement, that we maintain an efficient Navy adequate in men and material to insure positive protection against any aggressor. The Fleet must be ready.

* * * * * *

War will be avoided by all honorable means, but should it come, I feel assured that the efficiency * of the Navy will more than justify the confidence of our citizens in their first line of defense.

At his press conference on October 14, 1938, [90] Mr. Roosevelt mentioned that he had sat up late the previous night discussing the European situation with the American Ambassador to France, Mr. Bullitt. He refused to comment on Mr. Baruch's statement, made the previous day, that there was definitely not a first-class organization in the Army because of lack of modern arms, and turned the question by saying that a good many people were very carefully checking up on defense, and were considering the problems of mass production and standardization of weapons and airplanes. These plans, he said, would be presented to the Congress in early January 1939. All this had started, Mr. Roosevelt continued, "about a year ago [right after the Chicago "quarantine" speech], and had been forced to a head by events, developments and information received within the past month." Five days later, on October 26, 1938, Mr. Roosevelt addressed the *Herald Tribune* Forum by radio and asserted [91]

> * that peace by fear has no higher or more enduring quality than peace by the sword.

He called for "discussions, leading to actual disarmament," and saw war as "a disaster * fatal to civilized living." He concluded by asking for unity at home,

* so that we may, if the test ever comes, have that unity of will with which alone a democracy can successfully meet its enemies.

On November 1, 1938, Mr. van Zeeland, the former Belgian Prime Minister, attended the press conference, and Mr. Roosevelt declined to discuss their conclusions reached in prior discussions. [92] Ten days later a great wave of persecution broke out against the German Jews. Mr. Roosevelt dictated a public statement of protest and, at his November 15 press conference, announced that he had sent for Mr. Wilson, the American Ambassador to Germany, to come home; it was not a "recall." [93] Shortly thereafter, on November 18, 1938, Germany called home its Ambassador to Washington. [94]

Washington officials had been overwhelmingly anti-Nazi; it was now observed that feeling was rising portentously against Germany, as it had in 1916–1917, so that the city was war-minded.

Those who had seen their plans to fasten government control over all private industry thwarted by the trend towards conservative practices, which was the consequence of the Roosevelt depression, now began to think that even war itself was not too bad, because it would further their original plans. It was predicted by an astute observer that Mr. Roosevelt, not a person to overlook political capital in world affairs, while conscious that good politics required the gestures of peace, would take further steps towards war, believing that his domestic antagonists would follow his leadership in foreign affairs. It was prophesied that in the name of preparedness old proposed reforms would be presented as measures to aid national defense. New government controls, particularly price controls, were being planned.

After the almost complete failure of Mr. Roosevelt's purges at the polls on November 7, 1938, it became even more requisite to distract the attention of the public from his domestic failures and from his rebuke at that election. Emphasis was therefore to be laid on foreign affairs and on the need of national unity for national

48 | DESIGN FOR WAR

defense: defense, indeed, was to serve as a cloak for the stealthy reentry of the lost reforms and the discredited economic planning.

Consultations held late in 1938 with Ambassadors Bullitt, [95] Kennedy, Phillips, and Wilson appear to have led to agreement that the time had come to stop Germany, Italy, and Japan, and to assist Britain and France. [96] Primary emphasis was to be laid thenceforth on our armament program in preparation for possible war. Next, the Neutrality Act was to be amended so that Britain and France could buy arms in the United States. This in the belief (as later set forth on automobile stickers) that we would "Keep War Out Of America By Aiding The Allies." It must be repeated that none of this program was publicly professed or commonly known at that time.

The first fruits of this new program were soon visible across the Pacific. In December 1938 a loan of twenty-five million dollars was made to China, to be used for the purchase of trucks, tires, gasoline, and machinery in the United States. And by what may have been parallel action in the one case, and coincidence in the other, at about the same time Britain and Russia entered into agreements to furnish credit and supplies to the Chinese. [97]

On December 5, 1938, Mr. Roosevelt made an address at the University of North Carolina. He was in high spirits over receiving another honorary degree, and made what his auditors then thought was a merry jest: [98]

> You undergraduates * have heard for six years that I was about to plunge the Nation into war; that you and your little brothers would sent to the bloody fields of battle in Europe *. *(Laughter)*

One wonders how gaily the echo of that jests rings today in the memories of those undergraduates—and of their little brothers—and of their fathers and mothers.

The next day, on December 6, 1938, at a press conference, Mr. Roosevelt played down the fact that he was about to confer with

THE NEW DEAL COLLAPSES | 49

Mr. Eden, who was no longer a member of the British Cabinet. Further references to Mr. Eden or to the conference do not appear. Asked about extra taxation to pay for the "defense" program "as we go along," Mr. Roosevelt doubted it would be necessary; and he denied that we were far behind technically in airplane production. [99]

The final document in Mr. Roosevelt's 1938 volume pays lip service to peace on a high moral plane. Extending to the whole world the promise which he had so often made to Americans, Mr. Roosevelt said at the conclusion of his address before the community Christmas tree at Washington on Christmas Eve, 1938: [100]

> And so the pledge I have so often given to my own countrymen I renew before all the world * that I shall do whatever lies within my own power to hasten the day foretold by Isaiah, when men "shall beat their swords into ploughshares and their spears into pruning hooks; nation shall not lift up sword against nation, neither shall they learn war any more."

It was the lull before the oratorical tempest broke, to disclose from its dark clouds the terrifying visages of nameless foreign devils.

The real foreign devils were as yet not quite abreast of their supposed villainy. We know now that it was not until the commencement of 1939 that Mussolini considered a clash with the western democracies inevitable and decided to attempt to transform the anti-Comintern agreement into an alliance. [101] The "American lack of political sense" [102] in international affairs may well have helped to influence that fateful decision. Even at a later date the Japanese Foreign Minister was rather indifferent to such an alliance [103] and it was not signed by Japan for many months thereafter. [104] In fact Japan was more interested in a treaty with Russia. [105]

Mr. Roosevelt opened the year 1939 fully cognizant of the "educational" problem which lay before him in his attempt to reverse American opinion. Annotating his volume in the middle of 1941, he wrote this important admission: [106]

There can be no question that the people of the United States in 1939 were determined to remain neutral in fact and in deed *.

The opening gun of 1939 was fired in Mr. Roosevelt's annual message to the Congress on January 4, 1939. [107] Unlike previous annual messages, this message commenced and ended with foreign affairs. Domestic affairs were sandwiched in between, prefaced by the new-born opportunist argument:

> Our nation's program of social and economic reform is therefore a part of defense, as basic as armaments themselves.

In outline the message began with general talk of impending wars, of threats to religion, democracy, and international good faith, which must be defended and saved, together with homes, churches, and civilization itself, all in "the same fight." Mr. Roosevelt then called for weapons of defense, rather vaguely, and for the use of "methods short of war" to let the aggressors know how we felt. He attacked the operation of the Neutrality Act, which had become an obstacle to his plans, and he digressed in order to review briefly, and to praise, all of his own deeds since 1933. Next, the message denied that the nation was overburdened with debt.

Mr. Roosevelt then advanced a new argument in which he claimed that government spending was "government investing * for prosperity." He told the Congress that if there was to be any reduction of government spending it must not only accept the responsibility but also it would "have to determine which activities are to be reduced." He spoke disdainfully of saving "a few million dollars * here or there," and then expressed the hope that if the existing level of government spending was continued, the national income might reach eighty billion dollars a year, at which point he was confident that the budget would be balanced by the additional revenue from the existing levels of taxation. Asserting that the continuance of such spending "is the price of preserving our liberty," Mr. Roosevelt repetitively proclaimed "that this generation of Americans [has] a rendezvous with destiny."

Later, in referring to this "methods short of war" speech, Mr. Roosevelt revealed what his real but undisclosed purposes had then been: [108]

> * One of the methods I had in mind, of course, was to be able to sell implements of war to those nations who [sic] needed them to resist aggression—but who could not get them under this "neutrality" legislation.

It seems to be laboring the obvious to point out that what Mr. Roosevelt secretly had in mind, violated not only the Neutrality Act but also the rules of international law concerning neutrality. Such acts would constitute intervention and would be legally equivalent to making war.

The annual message had said that a special defense message would follow "in the course of a few days." Naturally the special defense message needed to be built up by ballyhoo in order to attract the public attention. Ambassador Bullitt, who had been "having a holiday" at Hyde Park as far back as October 21, 1938, had now for some weeks been having a holiday in Florida, as was Ambassador Kennedy. It was suddenly discovered that they were in the possession of sensational information which must be laid before Congress instantly. There ensued a fully publicized wild dash to Washington where the Military Affairs Committees of the Senate and of the House were convened in secret session to hear the momentous tidings, which have remained a secret to this day. With such alarums and excursions as a prelude, the special message on defense [109] was presented to the Congress on January 12, 1939. The special message symmetrically cautioned against "hysteria" in the second paragraphs from the beginning and before the end.

The third paragraph from the opening not only destroys any claim that Mr. Roosevelt foresaw what the Second World War would be like, but it supports the opinion of contemporary apologists that at that time Mr. Roosevelt honestly believed that American military participation (as distinguished from financial, economic, and naval participation) in the next war would not be needed. In that third paragraph Mr. Roosevelt repudiated as "sensational and untrue" any claims

> * that we must at once spend billions of additional money for building up our land, sea and air forces *.

Asserting that great changes had taken place in conflicts since the First World War, American participation in which he briefly reviewed, Mr. Roosevelt quickly and soothingly said:

> Calling attention to these facts does not remotely intimate that the Congress or the President have any thought of taking part in another war on European soil *. *

Returning to his principal theme of fear, Mr. Roosevelt warned of "sudden attack" and "the possibilities of present offense against us." He then asked the Congress to appropriate "with as great speed as possible" approximately $525,000,000. Yet in contradiction of the need for this speed he said that of this total only $210,000,000 would be spent during the next eighteen months, "before * June 30, 1940."

Of this grand total, Mr. Roosevelt recommended that $300,000,000 be spent for 3,000 army airplanes, observing that it was not advocated to build
* our air forces up to the total either of planes on hand or of productive capacity equal to the forces of certain other nations. *

One hundred and ten million dollars was to be spent for anti-aircraft artillery, semi-automatic rifles, anti-tank guns, tanks, light and heavy artillery, ammunition, and gas masks.

Thirty-two million dollars was to be spent by the army in educational orders "to enable industry to prepare for quantity production in an emergency of * military items. *"

Eight million dollars was to be spent in "improving and straightening the seacoast defenses of Panama, Hawaii and the continental United States *." Guam was not even mentioned.

Forty-four million dollars was to go to the Navy for "bases in both oceans" and twenty-one million dollars for Navy aircraft.

The balance of ten million dollars was to give primary training to twenty thousand civilian air pilots.

Again Mr. Roosevelt reverted to America's peaceful intentions. Again he asserted that "we have no thought of aggression." But he thereafter cast out an ominous hint of the draft which seems to have been quite overlooked at the time:

> The young men of this Nation should not be *compelled* to take the field with antiquated weapons. * (Emphasis supplied.)

The Congress substantially enacted this proposal into law. It was the first of the big appropriations for the new "defense" program.

IV OUR FRONTIER IS ON THE RHINE

MR. ROOSEVELT'S FOREIGN POLICY, quite unknown to the country, had been taking shape since Munich. As a minimum it was to strengthen and encourage Britain, France, and other nations which might get into war with Germany, Italy, and Japan, and to oppose, weaken, and undercut the latter. As a minimum it was also held that the British Empire was our outer ring of security; that the preservation of the sea power of Britain was essential to American security and to our national future, so that we must give active support to Britain [1] and to France in advance of any overt act or demonstrable threat against our own safety.

The maximum was probably greater, but many details are still concealed. Part of the mystery involves the exchange of secret messages between Mr. Roosevelt and various high British political personalities, a story yet to be fully told. At present, and in the light of the known circumstances, it seems fair to infer that at times Mr. Roosevelt may have been encouraging or even influencing Britain and France, and possibly others, either directly or through the promise of some American support. Yet, as late as January 12, 1939, after conversations at Rome with Prime Minister Chamberlain and with Lord Halifax, Count Ciano believed, no doubt reflecting the official British point of view, in contradistinction to that of Mr. Churchill, that the British did not want to fight. [2]

Part of the maximum of our secret power politics at this time included clandestine negotiations with France. In December 1938 a French air mission came to the United States, and on Mr. Roosevelt's instructions, Mr. Bullitt brought them to see Mr. Morgenthau. [3] The deal was not to be a private one, but "direct from one government to the other." The matter was discussed at a cabinet meeting on December 21, 1938, and the Secretary of War, Mr. Woodring, backed by General Arnold, disapproved of it. Subsequently they were reluctant to let the French see our newest and most superior bombers. Mr. Morgenthau took the matter to Mr. Roosevelt at the end of December and backed Mr. Woodring down, but only temporarily. The opposition of Mr. Woodring and of General Arnold continued, and there was a further conference with Mr. Roosevelt on the morning of January 16, 1939, at the White House.

Mr. Roosevelt commenced by saying that he wished every effort made to give the French a view of all available planes. Mr. Woodring still opposed the idea. The Assistant Secretary of War, Mr. Louis A. Johnson, who was hostile to Mr. Woodring, asked Mr. Roosevelt, "Do you wish the Douglas light bomber released to the French?" "I mean exactly that," Mr. Roosevelt replied.

French representatives were accordingly allowed to see the new Douglas attack bomber, and while they were on an inspection flight on January 23, 1939, a bomber crashed and an injured member of the French mission was pulled from the flaming wreck. The sensational news that there was an official French—and also an official British—mission in this country, dealing secretly with various of our executive departments for the purchase of munitions of war was now suddenly revealed to the American people.

There was a great furore, and in consequence, on February 1, 1939, Mr. Roosevelt summoned the Military Affairs Committee of the Senate to the White House, swore them all to secrecy, and addressed them at some length. Subsequently it leaked out that Mr. Roosevelt had said that our frontier in the battle of the democracies versus fascism was on the Rhine, or, according to another version, in France.

Naturally enough, the public's concern was great at this unexpected revelation that Mr. Roosevelt was contemplating playing power politics in Europe. Mr. Roosevelt's reaction to this unwelcome disclosure was vehement. At his next press conference, of February 3, 1939,[4] he angrily said, and repeated, that

> * a great many people, some members of the House, some members of the Senate and quite a number of newspaper owners, are deliberately putting before the American people a deliberate misrepresentation of facts—deliberate.

He then asserted that "The foreign policy has not changed and it is not going to change," and that its "number 1" principle was:

We are against any entangling alliances, obviously.

He then said that what had been printed in the papers had

> * been pure bunk—b-u-n-k, bunk; that these agitators are appealing to the ignorance, the prejudice and the fears of Americans and are acting in an un-American way.

Asked as to what he had said to the Senators, he dodged at first, and then said vaguely that it was information which was believed to be true, but "it may not be true."

He was further asked about our frontier being on the Rhine, or in France, and replied that it was a "Deliberate lie." As to the airplanes for Great Britain and France, Mr. Roosevelt said that they would be paid for in cash, without help from the Reconstruction Finance Corporation. The reporters' questioning returned both to Mr. Roosevelt's asserted "deliberate misrepresentation of facts" by the newspapers, and the "deliberate lie" of the Senators, and they backed down Mr. Roosevelt to the point where he reduced his first statement to an alleged press rumor, and as to the second, "Some 'boob' got that off *."

Eighteen months later Mr. Roosevelt claimed that what he had said was this: [5]

> * I said the existence of certain nations—and I mentioned Finland, Sweden, Norway, and Denmark, and the Baltic States, with Holland and Belgium and France—their continued existence * was a part of our defense *.

But Mr. Morgenthau states that on December 21, 1938, he quoted back to Mr. Roosevelt a prior statement of policy, made by Mr. Roosevelt to him earlier and as follows: [6]

> * it's your theory that England and France are our first line of defense * . *

It seems likely, therefore, that Mr. Roosevelt was not misquoted in spirit, and perhaps not in the letter of what he had said. He had made a propaganda blunder, and was attempting to bluster his way out of it.

As a further maximum Mr. Roosevelt seems to have first commenced the formation of a Pan-American block or alliance at the Lima, Peru, conference [7] in late December 1938, where the "Declaration of Lima," which proclaimed the continental solidarity of America, was adopted. Afterwards special arrangements were made with particular countries, commencing with Brazil, [8] which subsequently sent troops to fight in Europe.

Meanwhile the suspicion was growing in the Congress in both parties that Mr. Roosevelt would welcome a war crisis for third-term reasons. His prestige in the Congress and before the electorate was further lowered by the refusal of the Senate in early February 1939 to confirm the nomination of Mr. Floyd Roberts as a district judge, [9] and by his being compelled in mid-April to withdraw the nomination of Mr. Thomas R. Amlie to the Interstate Commerce Commission. [10] In consequence of these suspicions and conditions the Ludlow war referendum proposal was reintroduced into the Congress in the early part of 1939, and was again opposed by Mr. Roosevelt on "constitutional" and other grounds. [11]

In a press conference held on March 7, 1939, Mr. Roosevelt pressed forward to attack the impediment offered to his plans by the existing neutrality legislation, and said: [12]

> THE PRESIDENT: [interposing] * If you will confine it to the original question, "Has the neutrality legislation of the last three years contributed to the cause of peace?" * I would say, "No, it has not."
>
> Q. The next question was, "Would we be even stronger if we did not have it?"
>
> THE PRESIDENT: We might have been stronger if we had not had it.

This, Mr. Roosevelt admitted, [13] was a complete reversal of his established prior position, because

> * I approved this legislation when it was passed originally and when it was extended from time to time *. *

Mr. Roosevelt thereafter laid a trap for his opponents in his endeavors to abolish the restraints which the Neutrality Act laid on him. Senator Pittman introduced a so-called Peace Act, drafted by the Administration and sent to him by Secretary Hull on May 27, 1939, to replace the Neutrality Act. It was designed to attract the support of those who believed in our historic continentalism, because it would have removed two matters from the scope of the President's discretion. First, a state of war, whether declared or undeclared, would have to be recognized as such; thus the unneutral American attitude towards the Sino-Japanese war would be terminated, and comparable situations would be prevented in the future. Second, goods shipped to belligerents could not be sold on credit, but would have to be paid for in cash, and could not be shipped in American vessels, thus preventing the inception of two of the causes which, it was generally believed, had helped to involve us in the First World War. These two pieces of bait concealed the hook, a provision repealing the existing prohibition against the shipment of arms to belligerents. As soon as the "Peace Act" was passed, Mr. Roosevelt would be free to ship arms to Britain and France.

The quarry were wise enough not to walk into the trap; the fish refused to bite. The Senate declined to act before its adjournment, [14] in spite of pressure from Mr. Roosevelt and an approved statement from Secretary Hull, [15] written after differences on the point between the two men. Mr. Roosevelt publicly denied that there was a "split," [16] but well-informed reporters said that the denial was false.

Meanwhile Europe had boiled up and cooled off again. On March 14, 1939, Hitler had called in the Czech President and Foreign Minister, and had compelled them to accept a German protectorate, which was immediately followed by German occupation. This action was taken without the knowledge of Mussolini, and left him feeling flat-footed and ridiculous: [17] in consequence he determined to seize Albania, and the occupation commenced on April 7, 1939.

On March 17, 1939, Mr. Welles, the acting Secretary of State, issued a brief statement "edited and approved by" Mr. Roosevelt, [18] scolding Germany. The American Ambassador to Italy expressed his indignation against Germany to Count Ciano on the same day, and did not ascertain what the true situation was between Hitler and Mussolini. [19]

It is not only he who would become a great lawyer who must first become a great drudge: he who would become a great statesman, particularly if he be an American, must not be averse from great drudgery. But Mr. Roosevelt was ill-equipped to become a great statesman. There were few men more averse from mental drudgery, and few who were more contemptuous of "mere details." Mr. Roosevelt much preferred five-minute decisions to those which took five weeks. [20] His temperament was impulsive, he loved excitement, he craved action, his native egotism welcomed the concept of playing a bigger part in the world. *Reculer pour mieux sauter* was hardly an operating maxim to Mr. Roosevelt. [21] Save for one almost honeymoon trip, and for two trips during the abnormal conditions of the First World War, Mr. Roosevelt had not travelled in Europe after his childhood days were over. [22] He was thus devoid of relatively recent personal knowledge of Europe's primary interests. Of the secondary interests, and of the cross currents, he seems to have had little cognizance. These deficiencies were not remedied by extensive reading or by laborious collation of the State Department's reports and dispatches. Long ago Mr. Moley noted that it had never occurred to Mr. Roosevelt to look below the surface of events in order to ponder why so many treaties were being broken throughout the world. [23] Mr. Roosevelt tended to look to the surface symptoms rather than to search for the basic causes.

Moreover, Mr. Roosevelt's power diplomacy lacked subtlety and tact. President Wilson, by his skillful and subtle diplomacy, had been able to drive a wedge between the European leaders of our enemies and their peoples, a wedge so profound that those nations fell apart politically before any final military conquest on the field of battle. Mr. Wilson's skill saved thousands of American lives; it shortened the days of war and hastened the days of peace.

On the other hand Mr. Roosevelt's "unconditional surrender" demand of January 1943 prevented the quick collapse of Italy, [24] and strengthened the flagging morale of the German army and people; [25] so also did the Morgenthau plan, which, after sponsoring it, Mr. Roosevelt was compelled to soft-pedal and Mr. Truman to abandon. The German underground movements, which so nearly succeeded in killing Hitler, and which were intended to overthrow the Nazi regime, were not merely not aided in any manner by Mr. Roosevelt; they were "discouraged." [26]

It was not only Japan, as has already been mentioned, which was dubious about joining the military alliance which Hitler proposed in early 1939. Most of the highest political personalities in Italy had even graver doubts. In early 1939, and subsequently, both King Victor Emmanuel III and the Prince of Piedmont were anti-German. [27] Count Ciano, Mussolini, some of the original Quadrumviri, and other leading Italians were opposed to the alliance. [28] The Italian people were violently anti-German. [29]

Mr. Roosevelt seems to have had little idea that within the Axis there existed these tensions, jealousies, disagreements, and cross-purposes, which could have been exploited by a more skillful diplomacy. Instead Mr. Roosevelt scolded and tactlessly lectured these nations in the belief that words could never lead to blows. At about this time he told a story which is in point: [30]

> * Two Chinese coolies were arguing heatedly in the midst of a crowd. A stranger expressed surprise that no blows were being struck. His Chinese friend replied: "The man who strikes first admits that his ideas have given out."

A more solidly grounded diplomatic policy might have capitalized on such divergencies to serve our ends, but instead, Mr. Roosevelt continued with his irritating denunciations. The consequences, at least in part, were visible at Salerno, Anzio, the Rapido River, and Monte Cassino. What this lack of skillful exploitation cost, in terms of lives lost, and through the prolongation of the war, must remain a matter of melancholy conjecture. [31]

In the light of this ignorance of the underlying and basic causes of trouble in Europe, and of this ineptitude, and of a lack of penetrating information from some American diplomats, it is not astonishing, although it is saddening, to read in Count Ciano's diary, under date of March 21, 1939: [32]

> The Western Powers have today lost much ground, which was won by the Germans. News about the attempts to constitute a "democratic bloc" has hardened the Duce in favor of the Germans. The title itself identifies our destinies with those of Germany and makes skeptics of those countries such as Rumania, Yugoslavia, Poland, France and Greece, who, while still concerned about the German progress, must preserve their internal regime built on authoritarian lines *.

On March 31 Mr. Chamberlain stated to the House of Commons that Great Britain and France would fight if Hitler invaded Poland. Mr. Roosevelt, who had been telephoning to Europe—he would not state to whom—interpreted that declaration the same day to his press conference [33] in "words of one syllable * the world is being put on notice as to where the responsibility will lie if there is war."

On April 1 General Franco was recognized: Mr. Roosevelt omits this act from his published papers.

On April 8, 1939, after the invasion of Albania, another "statement" was issued, [34] and Mr. Roosevelt urged the reporters to send out stories which would purport to come from "sources close to the White House," viewing the Albanian invasion as "necessarily bringing us * closer to the time when we shall be faced with a loss of our trade and our shipping *." Then, in general words which would equally well apply to the present Russian occupation of Estonia, Latvia, Lithuania, Poland, Rumania, Bulgaria, Hungary,

Czechoslovakia, and Albania, he said, with reference to Albania at that time:

> * the continued political, economic and social independence of every small Nation in the world does have an effect on our national safety and prosperity. Each one that disappears weakens our national safety and prosperity. *

The next day, April 9, concluding his Warm Springs holiday, Mr. Roosevelt gave the country an "educational" scare by saying, [36]

> * I'll be back in the fall if we do not have a war.

April 14, 1939, was a busy day. Mr. Roosevelt addressed the governing board of the Pan American Union. [37] He criticized Mussolini's speech of March 26 at Rome and Hitler's speech of April 1 at Wilhelmshaven, [38] referred to "the Huns and the Vandals," and spoke belligerently of "matching force to force." After such a prelude, at nine o'clock that night he sent identical messages to Hitler and to Mussolini, [39] asking pledges that for "ten years at the least—a quarter of a century, if we dare look that far ahead," they would not "attack or invade the territory or possessions of" thirty-one named countries in Europe and the Near East.

Mr. Roosevelt ought to have been aware of the fact that such phraseology, impulsively sent under such circumstances, without previous diplomatic preparation, [40] had scant hope of being accepted.

Rather he must have intended it partly as "education" of American voters, perhaps as an alibi. The latter hypothesis is supported by the title which Mr. Roosevelt gave the "message" in his published papers—"The President Again Seeks a Way to Peace." The former hypothesis is supported by the very unusual conduct of Mr. Roosevelt the following day. Much in the manner in which he used to narrate "straw man interviews" in which he was invariably victorious and his verbal opponent was defeated, [41]

Mr. Roosevelt called in the reporters, read them every word of his "message" triumphantly, and, with many asides and interpolations, demonstrated how its apt phraseology would leave the dictators quite discomfited, wholly speechless, [42] and altogether unable to reply to him.

Mr. Roosevelt's running commentary also gave a valuable revelation of his own subconscious ideas. In commenting on that portion of his "message" which had mentioned "self-evident home defense" he said,

> I used the words "home defense" because nobody can get around that. That means "home defense" and does not mean defense *thousands* and *thousands* of miles away. (Emphasis supplied.)

The reader will not fail to observe the fact that Poland, Denmark, the Netherlands, Belgium, France were on the actual frontiers of Germany, and could not be said to be even tens of miles away. Great Britain, Norway, and Russia were not many hundreds of miles distant from the German frontiers. But Germany, Italy, and Japan were "*thousands* and *thousands* of miles away" from America.

Mr. Roosevelt noted with curtness, and omitting either their titles of office, or "Mister," "Herr," or "Signor," [43] that

> No direct answer to the foregoing appeal was received by me from either Hitler or Mussolini.

Actually, however, those two dictators were neither discomfited nor speechless. Il Duce at first refused to trouble to read Mr. Roosevelt's message but finally did so, and then with rudeness characterized it to Count Ciano as "A result of progressive paralysis." [44] And on April 20, 1939, he made a fiery public answer at Rome. [45]

Chancellor Hitler was likewise anything but a straw man. Six weeks prior to sending his message Mr. Roosevelt had said, with the appearance of approving the use of such political stratagems, [46]

* Many other nations envy us the enthusiasm, the attacks, the wild over-statements, the falsehood gaily intermingled with the truth that mark our general elections. *

In the employment of such gay devices Chancellor Hitler was hardly in the beginners' class, and his reply to Mr. Roosevelt, made at Berlin in a speech to the Reichstag on April 28, 1939, [47] was mocking in its comment on, and sarcastic dissection of, the "message." Among other matters he asserted that he had been in touch with twenty-five of the named states in order to enquire "whether they feel themselves threatened," and also whether Mr. Roosevelt's action had been taken "at their suggestion, or * with their consent. * The reply was in all cases negative, in some instances strongly so." Nevertheless, assurances, such as Mr. Roosevelt referred to, would be given to any state asking for them on the basis of reciprocity. There were some states, Chancellor Hitler said, of which he could not make inquiry—Syria, for instance—because they were militarily occupied by the democratic states and so not in possession of their freedom. But the Chancellor's speech was not merely a battle of words. It announced further steps forward—that the German-Polish treaty would be considered as no longer in existence, and that the Anglo-German naval treaty was to be terminated. It cannot be said certainly whether Mr. Roosevelt's lecturing was the cause, or merely the excuse, for these resulting treaty terminations, but in either view his "message" was, to put it mildly, infelicitous. And in the ultimate event it was not the dictators but Mr. Roosevelt who was left discomfited and at least temporarily speechless. For nearly three months thereafter no press conferences are printed among Mr. Roosevelt's papers.

On April 18, 1939, Britain and France had offered guarantees to Greece and to Rumania similar to that offered to Poland. Not long afterwards Britain and France commenced negotiations with

Russia, looking towards a military alliance. On April 28 Ciano [48] erroneously thought it was a concrete and accomplished fact.

As of this time Mr. Roosevelt and some of the American diplomats were taking secret action to support the power politics of Britain and of France. In late March 1939 Mr. Kennedy, our Ambassador to Great Britain, was approached by Lord Halifax, the British Foreign Secretary. Britain, he said, had promised the Commonwealth of Australia to send a fleet to Singapore, but now the British commitments in Europe were so substantial that no warships could be spared to go there: would America oblige? Mr. Kennedy passed this request on to Mr. Hull on March 22, and the request was supported from France by Ambassador Bullitt on April 11. Mr. Bullitt stated that France would decline to go along with Britain in taking joint action to resist Hitler if the British Mediterranean fleet was sent to Singapore, and he urged that prompt action be taken by the United States to transfer the American fleet from the Atlantic into the Pacific. [49] Mr. Bullitt's cable was intended for Mr. Roosevelt, and the latter took the requested prompt action: on April 15, 1939, the American fleet was ordered into the Pacific.

In the endeavor to build up public good will and interest in the United States, King George VI and Queen Elizabeth sailed from England in May to visit Canada, and came to the United States in early June.

On May 17, 1939, in the subsiding ground swell of these speeches and manoeuvres, the American Ambassador to Italy, if correctly quoted by Count Ciano, delivered a warning: [50]

> * He stressed one point, namely, that the American people * intend unanimously to concern themselves in European affairs, and it would be folly to think that they would remain aloof in the event of a conflict. *

Ambassador Davies is supposed to have made a somewhat comparable assertion to Stalin. [51]

And now there came a kind of lull, both in Europe and in America. In Europe, Mussolini had told Ciano on April 20 [52] that "Italy and Germany desire some years of peace and are doing all they can to preserve it." On May 21, 1939, when Ciano conferred in Berlin with von Ribbentrop, he particularly noted that nothing had changed for the worse, and that von Ribbentrop repeated to him [53]

* Germany's interest in and intention to insure for itself a long period of peace at least three years. *

This desire to avoid war for a long time was falsely reaffirmed by von Ribbentrop to Ciano over two months later, on July 27, 1939. [54] Falsely reaffirmed, because at some earlier time there had been a sudden change in the German policy, which Bernardo Attolico, the extremely intuitive Italian Ambassador to Germany, had apparently been the first to sense, a little prior to July 10, [55] and for which he reaped Cassandra's reward for some time. [56] It may be conjectured with considerable confidence that this sudden reversal of Germany policy was due to the feeling that Germany, and not Britain and France, all of whom were then soliciting a Russian alliance, would be successful in the approach.

Considerably prior to this date, it had been well known to high Russian officials that one of Stalin's primary policies had been to come to terms with Germany. [57] Previous Russian approaches had been rebuffed by Germany, but a further guarded approach was made on April 17, 1939, by the Russian Ambassador to Germany, Alexei Merekalov. [58] When Maxim Litvinov, the Soviet Commissar for Foreign Affairs, was suddenly dismissed on May 3, while he was in the midst of negotiations with the British mission, and was replaced by Vyacheslav M. Molotov, the change was viewed in diplomatic circles as being due to Stalin's deep distrust of the democratic nations, which, he feared, intended to draw Soviet Russia into war.⁵⁹ Britain, on the other hand, was supposed to be afraid of driving Japan into the arms of Germany if she guaranteed the defense of all the Russian frontiers, and in consequence she hesitated to accept the Russian proposals.⁶⁰

Meanwhile a guarded flirtation was commenced between Russia and Germany. By early July consideration was being given to the possibility of negotiating a commercial treaty, and by late July the Germans and the Russians were cautiously extending the scope of the negotiations into the sphere of high politics.⁶¹ Simultaneously Molotov was negotiating with the British and the French in a slow and dilatory way, but it was the impression of the German Ambassador that Russia would sign a treaty with them if they would give in to all of the Russian wishes.⁶² The Anglo-French political negotiations were continuing in early August, after which the military negotiations were planned to commence.⁶³

It was at this time that the Germans began to refer to the possibility of trouble developing with Poland.⁶⁴ In a dispatch which was received at Moscow on August 15, 1939, von Ribbentrop asked to make a short visit in order to continue the political conversations,⁶⁵ and every effort was made on the German side to hasten the appointment.⁶⁶ This was because the decision for war with Poland had already been made. Russia insisted, however, that the economic treaty must first be concluded, and this took place on August 19, 1939. Germany immediately began to press for a further political accord, and urged the conclusion of a nonaggression treaty.⁶⁷ Russia presented the draft of a counter-proposal, and insisted on a guarantee of the small eastern Baltic states, and that Germany should bring pressure to bear on Japan in order to improve Russo-Japanese relations.⁶⁸ All of these proposals were agreed to in principle by Germany, whereupon Stalin agreed to receive von Ribbentrop on August 23.⁶⁹

Meanwhile the Japanese Ambassador to Germany had obtained some idea of what was in preparation: he called at the German Foreign Office and showed concern and some uneasiness over relieving Russia of anxiety in Europe, which would permit her to strengthen herself in East Asia and to put new life into the Chinese war. [70]

At Moscow there was a three-hour conference between Stalin, Molotov, and von Ribbentrop, followed by a long night conference. [71] From it there emerged the public nonaggression treaty of August 23, 1939, [72] together with a secret additional protocol. [73] By the latter agreement the northern boundary of Lithuania was fixed as the boundary of the spheres of interest of Russia and Germany; Poland was partitioned along an agreed boundary line, and Germany gave Russia a free hand in the Rumanian province of Bessarabia.

The original German program had apparently been less ambitious than the final result. There is a strong suggestion that at the end of June 1939 the German program as known to Count Ciano did not include any attack on Poland. [74] When the decision was finally made is uncertain, but it was probably in early August, because it was first revealed to Ciano at a conference with von Ribbentrop and then with Hitler at Obersalzburg on August 11–13, [75] although the gravity of the situation was not fully appreciated, even in diplomatic circles, for some days. Count Ciano attempted to dissuade Hitler from making the attack by advancing various arguments, one of which was that [76]

> * Roosevelt's position in America would be seriously weakened after a period of calm in the field of foreign politics, so that he could not be elected president for a third time, which would certainly be the case if a conflict should break out soon.

The springtime lull which existed in Europe found its counterpart in America. Only partly was it due to the rebuff which Mr. Roosevelt had received from Hitler; it was also rooted in American domestic politics, as Count Ciano had observed. Congressional suspicion of Mr. Roosevelt, and opposition to him, were on the increase, as has been mentioned, and his domestic popularity was slipping. Disinterested political observers were predicting that he would not be renominated in 1940 unless there was a war crisis. Recovery from the depression was still around the corner. As early as February 7, 1939, Mr. Roosevelt had had to ask for additional appropriations for W. P. A., [77] because the expected improvement in business, which would have permitted some reduction in the relief rolls, had not materialized. Congress took no action. On March 14, 1939, Mr. Roosevelt again asked for more money and was compelled to admit that not only had there "been no substantial change in the conditions of unemployment. * Since * January and February," but also that "the number of persons now certified as being in need * is actually higher than it was a month ago." [78] On May 22, 1939, in an address to the American Retail Federation, [79] the best claim that Mr. Roosevelt could present for the national income was that it was "running at the rate of better than sixty-five billions," which was the exact mathematical average of the national income, according to his own figures, for the two Roosevelt depression years of 1937 and 1938. Professor Moley, completing his book in August 1939, had already observed despairingly that, due "to our active and tireless participation in the game * of power politics * whether we meant to, or not, we have neglected our unsolved problems at home." [80] A study of Mr. Roosevelt's published papers for that year amply confirms the observation. Mr. Roosevelt, other observers thought, was using world affairs as an excuse for the neglect of home affairs, in the manner of a stage magician, in order to manipulate home affairs while the public's attention was directed by him elsewhere, towards foreign affairs. Dictators solve their internal difficulties by war. [81]

It was asserted that Mr. Roosevelt did not see how this country could remain neutral, and that he was taking chances on American involvement in war. Perhaps in indirect answer to this, on May 22, 1939, he claimed [82] that the New Dealers were the true conservatives,

> * because we simply cannot bring ourselves to take radical chances with other people's property and other people's lives.

By this date it had also been suggested to the railroads that they should build more locomotives and freight cars in order to prepare for the needs of war.

So came the outwardly seeming political lull of late May and June 1939, while undercover political third-term manoeuvering commenced. Writing as early as 1938, Mr. Ludwig had observed that only if war should break out before 1940 would Mr. Roosevelt be elected for a third term. It was also in 1938 that Mr. Farley had said, [84] "Roosevelt has his eye on 1940 as well as the next man," and then he went on to speak of the danger of Mr. Roosevelt's showing his hand too soon. Perhaps that was the case here, for the movement now commenced by Messrs. Hopkins, Ickes, and Corcoran to "draft Roosevelt" attracted far less support than had been hoped for, and was laid aside to ripen further. This third-term movement was particularly promoted by the New Dealers, [85] who were well aware of the political fact that they would lose their positions unless Mr. Roosevelt continued to hold his office.

But while there was this springtime lull in Europe and America, below the surface all was not well. To sapient observers as far distant as Asia, signs of an impending world war were visible and were a source of most serious concern. The Japanese, it is now revealed, were making earnest endeavors to preserve world peace and to avoid being forced into a totalitarian alliance. As we have seen, Great Britain was seeking an alliance with Soviet Russia against Germany during the summer of 1939 and the Japanese were much troubled by the political implications of such an alliance. On the one hand it is clear that by the middle of April 1939 the Japanese had decided to abstain from an alliance with Germany and Italy: indeed Ambassador Grew noted shortly afterwards that Japan was steering away from the Axis. [86] But on the other hand, if there should be an Anglo-Russian alliance, he believed that the Japanese Government would either be forced into an alliance with Germany and Italy, or else that it would fall. Meanwhile he endeavored to persuade the Japanese Government that if there was a general war in Europe the United States would enter it on the side of Britain and France, and if Japan was then on the side of Germany and Italy, war with the United States would be almost inevitable. And, he wrote, [87]

* A Japanese-American war would be the height of stupidity from every point of view. *

These arguments, Ambassador Grew believed, were widely disseminated and ultimately reached the Emperor. Just before the Ambassador was about to leave Japan on a five-month furlough, all of these considerations, coupled with the fact that Japan was sick of the hostilities in China, began to bear a peaceful fruit and caused Japan to attempt to improve her relations with the United States.

The first known conciliatory approach of Japan to America was made on May 16, 1939, at a luncheon at Tokyo to Ambassador Grew. As reported to our State Department by Counselor Dooman of the American Embassy, [88] the tentative proposal was "substantially" this:

Although the Japanese Government has decided not to conclude a military alliance with Germany and Italy, there was being exerted on the Government, not only by Germany and Italy but by reactionary groups in Japan, strong pressure towards entering into some arrangement with the latter countries which would reaffirm the solidarity among the nations whose policies were opposed by the democratic nations. The groups to which he belonged had succeeded in defeating the proposal to conclude the alliance and are now doing their best to defeat the "strengthening of the Anti-Comintern Pact," or at least to prevent it from becoming a political link with Germany and Italy; but it was difficult to meet the argument of those who had advocated the alliance and are now favoring close association with Germany and Italy, that Japan cannot afford to be isolated. Germany and Italy are urging Japan "to come over to their side," while the democratic nations are turning to Japan a very cold shoulder. If, therefore, the democratic nations, especially the United States, could indicate to Japan that restoration of good relations with Japan is desired and that the way is open for Japan to align herself with the democratic nations, but not against the totalitarian states, those Japanese who are working for precisely those objectives would have their hand greatly strengthened.

Mr. Grew expressed interest in these views, but said that, as "a condition precedent to the restoration of good relations between Japan and the United States," Japan must offer China peace terms acceptable to China and approved by the United States. At this early date we thus have this evidence that American foreign policy was already being made the tail to another nation's kite; in this instance, China.

The initial approach was followed up by the Japanese on the next day, May 17, 1939, at a luncheon given by the Japanese Minister for Foreign Affairs, Mr. Hachiro Arita, in honor of Mr. Grew. Mr. Arita expressed a somewhat different angle of approach, a great concern over the subterranean activities of the Soviet Government, and over the pending negotiations in Europe to form an Anglo-French-Russian alliance. He said, [89]

* that there had been a suggestion that he give Mr. Grew an assurance that Japan would withhold any action to "strengthen the Anti-Comintern Pact" until Mr. Grew returned to Washington and had an opportunity to discuss with his Government the possibility of making to Japan some "gesture of welcome." * that there was no important opinion in [Japan] unfavorable to the measure which had been proposed to combat communistic activities, and that, if the time became ripe for the conclusion of the agreement under discussion with Germany and Italy, the Japanese Government intended to proceed with it. He could, however, assure Mr. Grew that the agreement would contain no military, political or economic clauses; but with this proviso—if it were found that these activities were being instigated by the Soviet Government, the countermeasures proposed would have to be directed against that Government.

* that Japan is very anxious to avoid involvement in the affairs of Europe, but that Japan could not ignore the fact that Russia straddled Europe and Asia, and that, whether Japan liked it or not, [Russia's] policies and actions form a bridge by which events in the Far East and in Europe act and react on each other. * that any arrangement which formed the basis for the close collaboration contemplated by Great Britain, France and the Soviet Union in respect of their common interests in Europe would be bound to bring about similar collaboration among them in the conduct of their policies in the Far East. * that decision over Japan's attitude vis-à-vis the situation developing in Europe would have to be withheld until results of the Anglo-Soviet negotiations were known.

The approach, which had begun with an influential Japanese and had moved up to the Foreign Minister, now moved up to a still higher level. On May 18, 1939, a secret proposal to attempt the maintenance of peace in Europe was made by the Japanese Prime Minister, Baron Kiichiro Hiranuma, and was handed to Ambassador Grew for transmission to Mr. Hull, with the specifically expressed hope that it might also be brought to the attention of Mr. Roosevelt. [90]

The Far Eastern Division of the State Department analyzed the proposal, and expressed the opinion that Baron Hiranuma's proposal [91]

> * is evidently inspired by his concern lest in the event of a European war the United States might align itself with the so-called "democratic powers" with the result that the United States and Japan would confront each other from opposite camps. It is because of this concern that Japan would especially regard the eventuality of a European war to be detrimental to Japanese interests.

At a secret conference at Tokyo on May 23, 1939, between Baron Hiranuma and the Counselor of the American Embassy, Mr. Dooman, [92] the Japanese Prime Minister suggested that he might sound out Germany and Italy, if Mr. Roosevelt was prepared at the same time to sound out Great Britain and France, with regard to the holding of a conference to seek a solution of the troubles of Europe. Following Mr. Grew's lead, Mr. Dooman was cool on moral grounds towards the suggestion because of the iniquity of what Japan was doing in China.

As reported by Mr. Dooman to Washington on May 26, 1939, the Japanese Foreign Minister, Mr. Hachiro Arita, had been much worried and "excited over the Anglo-Soviet negotiations" for an alliance. On the other hand he reported Baron Hiranuma as saying to him [93]

* that Japan did not want to tie up with Germany and Italy as there are in those countries undersurface currents which gravely prejudice confidence in any political arrangement which Japan might make with them. * if war broke out in Europe there would be little security for Japan in seeking to maintain neutrality * Japan would greatly prefer to be associated on terms of close friendship with the democratic states than with Germany and Italy through an alliance. *

This telegram was amplified by Mr. Dooman in a long letter to Mr. Hull, dated June 7, 1939. [94] Mr. Hull viewed the letter as "amazing" and directed the attention of Mr. Roosevelt to it in a memorandum dated July 1, 1939. [95] It was, Mr. Hull wrote, "a private *démarche* of the Prime Minister to us. On its face it suggests Japanese-American cooperation in endeavoring to work out a peace agreement between Germany and Italy (through Japan) and France and Great Britain (through us)." Mr. Dooman's letter amplified his cabled version of his interview with Baron Hiranuma on May 23. The Japanese Prime Minister had said,

* the possibility of a war arising in Europe was one which he contemplated with horror. It would inevitably result in the total destruction of civilization, as no nation, however remote from the seat of war, could hope to escape the eventual consequences even though it might be fortunate to avoid direct involvement. He had publicly stated on several occasions that Japan could never be a democracy or a totalitarian state, and that Japan could make its greatest contribution by bringing together in harmonious and peaceful relations the two groups of nations. There were * elements in Japan which considered that Japan could not afford to maintain a condition of isolation and that her security demanded that she enter into "special relations" with Germany and Italy. He was insisting, however, that Japan follow what he termed "moral diplomacy."

A nation's existence was not to be measured by decades, and it was essential, therefore, that statesmen charged with the destinies of nations fix their attention on long term objectives rather than on gaining favorable tactical positions, which were after all, ephemeral. The most important of these objectives was a stabilized peace to replace interludes of preparation for the next war. Japan, like the United States, was not directly involved in the troubles of Europe; and it was his thought that these two nations, which were the only Great Powers situated outside of Europe, were in a position to exercise a moderating influence on Europe. To exercise that influence was a duty which they owed their own peoples, for the downfall of Europe would inevitably bring with it the downfall of the rest of the world. In his opinion, the first step which had to be taken was to check the tendency toward the division of Europe into two politically hostile camps. *

Mr. Dooman felt that Japan's policies and actions in China constituted an obstacle to cooperation with Japan, and he reported that he had rehearsed America's grievances against Japan.

Baron Hiranuma granted that this might be so, and he explained the situation from the Japanese point of view. He dwelt upon the way in which Great Britain had treated Japan with neglect and even hostility after the First World War, amd the way in which Great Britain and the United States were now supporting China against Japan. He continued, rather penetratingly:

The Japanese people * have considerable sympathy for Germany and Italy, as they conceive these countries to be in many important respects in the same position as Japan. It was not to be expected that Germany would have permitted herself to remain under the restrictions of the Versailles Treaty, nor that Italy would have been content to be dependent on other nations for supplies of raw materials. At the same time, the consequences of efforts on their part to redress their grievances by force, or of the stubborn refusal of the democratic nations to offer to correct these grievances could not possibly be confined to the protagonists in the European quarrel but would have to be shared by other nations. He referred to [Mr. Dooman's] observation that the settlement of the China conflict would probably have to be a condition precedent to joint American-Japanese efforts to moderate the situation in Europe. If that were to be the view of the American Government, any hope of proceeding along the course which he had in mind would have to be abandoned. The objectives which Japan has had in China are essential for her security in a world of sanctions, embargoes, closing of markets to foreign competition, and lack of free access to raw materials, and so long as such conditions exist any moderation of her objectives in China and, therefore, of her peace terms could not be considered. Nevertheless if conditions could be brought about which would assure to all nations markets for the world's goods on the basis of quality and price and supplies of the materials which they needed, the importance to Japan of securing a market and sources of raw materials in China would greatly diminish; and by the same token there would not be the urge that there now is on Germany and Italy to expand at the expense of weaker and smaller nations. * the conditions which brought about the situations in the Far East and Europe are not local but universal in character, and * neither situation could be settled in a manner calculated to bring about a stabilized peace unless the conditions which brought them about were corrected.

* the belief was widely held abroad that Japan was considering a military alliance with Germany and Italy. He had endeavored to explain frankly the basis of Japanese sympathy for Germany and Italy, and he could say quite definitely that the basis of what

appeared to be a concerting of Japanese policy with that of Germany and Italy lay in the fact that all three countries are in the same economic [and] strategic position. He personally was of the opinion that Japan, whose government would for all time to come rest on the sanctity of the Imperial Family, could not tie itself by special relations to any foreign government whose stability depended on the continued existence and political prestige of one individual. There were both in Germany and Italy political currents flowing beneath the surface which * would gravely prejudice confidence in any political arrangement, such as an alliance, which Japan might make with those countries. Hidden dissident elements would be certain to make themselves felt in time of war and thus are to be reckoned as a threat to the success of German and Italian arms.

* * * * * *

The United States and Japan were the only powers which could help to prevent the crystallization of the trend toward the division of Europe into armed camps. There can, however, be no confident hope that a permanent peace can be established until the worldwide economic and political conditions which bring about unrest in Europe and in the Far East can be corrected; and if an international conference can be called to solve the problems which create unrest, Japan would be prepared to agree to the inclusion of the Far Eastern situation among the problems to be discussed. Before any call for such a conference could be issued, Great Britain and France and Germany and Italy would have to be sounded out. If the President were prepared to make a confidential approach to the European democracies, he would be glad to approach Germany and Italy; and, if there were returned favorable replies by these nations, he would be glad to have the President call the conference under such conditions as might be agreed upon after discussion through normal diplomatic channels.

Mr. Dooman then offered to our State Department some observations of his own, which deserve serious consideration. He noted that the Japanese were

* groping for security against the gathering storm in Europe. *

Japan had not failed to take note of Mr. Roosevelt's increasing preoccupation with power politics; Mr. Roosevelt's message of April 14, 1939, to Chancellor Hitler had had a tremendous effect in

* persuading the Japanese Government to realize that there may be grave danger of involvement with the United States "not directly across the Pacific but by way of Europe," as one Japanese put it *. *

There are * but two courses for Japan to follow—either to go over unreservedly to the totalitarian side, or to restore good relations with [the democratic] nations *. I am inclined * to doubt whether there are many Japanese who confidently believe that neutrality would afford security. The arguments of those who believe in the superior power of Germany and Italy are obvious and simple: Japan has only to associate herself with those countries and wait for the European war to pick China like a ripe plum. But, for those Japanese who have other views concerning the power of Germany and Italy, there is but one way by which Japan's security can be safeguarded, and that is to bring the conflict with China to an end on some reasonable terms. *

On July 8, 1939, with Mr. Roosevelt's approval, [96] the State Department cabled Mr. Dooman [97] that a reply was coming, not by cable, but by diplomatic pouch. If Mr. Dooman felt that the reply should be made sooner, the Department would consider telegraphing the text. On July 10 Mr. Dooman replied [98] that he was "being asked every few days" for a reply. If the American reply was not definite, which he rather inferred, time was not urgent. But he would welcome some word as to just what the Department's attitude was.

At Washington on July 10, 1939, the Japanese Ambassador, Mr. Kensuke Horinouchi, called on Mr. Hull,[99] obviously to see why there had been a delay of so many weeks. The Japanese Ambassador asked Mr. Hull to comment on the Japanese proposal. Mr. Hull referred censoriously to "peaceful countries" and contrasted them with "countries which are threatening military conquest." Since Japan appeared to be "engaged in military operations for purposes of conquest," Japan could, by ending this situation, exercise her fullest influence along with the United States to discourage aggression. Responding to this idea of the "aggressor" nations, the Japanese Ambassador stated that Japan would not enter into any "military pact with Germany and Italy." He also asked Mr. Hull to express his views on the Chinese situation, and Mr. Hull did so at length and with vehemence.

Mr. Hull asserted that the United States had

> * not the slightest alliance, or secret or other understandings with any nation on earth, and do not propose to have any *.

The Japanese Ambassador had stated that Japan was primarily interested in working against Bolshevism. In response, Mr. Hull made these extremely interesting general statements as to an appropriate foreign policy:

> * of course, this was primarily the business of his country; that my country, of course, strongly opposes the doctrines of Bolshevism *; that it also, as I had indicated, abstains from any entanglements or involvements with European countries; that, of course, if Japan desires to tie herself up with the horribly complicated European controversies, so as to make herself immediately involved in any European war, that still was her business primarily; and I might again reiterate that my Government is keeping itself in a detached position *.

On July 13, 1939, Mr. Hull cabled Mr. Dooman [100] the substance of the Department's reply to Japan, but suggested that he take no action until the full text arrived. The full text of Mr. Hull's reply to Baron Hiranuma did not arrive in Japan until about July 31, 1939. It was tart and barbed. Japan was advised to use its

> * influence toward discouraging among European governments, especially those governments with which your Government may have special relations, the taking of any action, or the pursuance of any policy, that might endanger the general peace. I am confident that any such contribution as this would constitute a high service to those great sections of humanity which live in fear of the devastation of war.

The establishment of "a true world peace * is made the more remote by the existence and the continuance of armed conflict and consequent political disturbances in the Far East today." Those conflicts, wrote Mr. Hull, contributed to the unrest in Europe. It seemed to be "impractical or inexpedient" at present to try to settle Europe's problems, but it was urgently necessary to try to end "armed conflict * in other geographical areas." But the American Government was "sincerely interested" in Baron Hiranuma's suggestion and would be pleased to hear from him further.

Luckily Mr. Dooman had been given some discretion as to the time of delivery of this message. [102] He cabled a strictly confidential message to Mr. Hull on July 31, 1939, and mildly expressed some doubts. [103] Translated into plain English, Mr. Dooman believed that the American reply would lead Japan to think that America had now taken sides, but, as phrased in diplomatic talk, Mr. Dooman stated that the reply

> * would heavily emphasize the impression in official circles as elsewhere in Japan that the United States has now initiated a definitely positive attitude toward Far Eastern problems. *

And Mr. Dooman was not clear as to whether the United States intended to accept or to reject Baron Hiranuma's suggestion that Mr. Roosevelt should call an international conference.

Mr. Hull replied on August 1, 1939. [104] He did not think that the American reply would lead Japan to suppose that America had taken sides, but he was open to further persuasion. With respect to the conference, it was curtly said, "the reply needs no repeat no explanatory comment."

Mr. Dooman cabled back on August 3, 1939. [105] The recent notice which the United States had given on July 26 of its intention to terminate the 1911 Treaty of Commerce with Japan was obviously not motivated by economic reasons but by political reasons. Japan could not as yet comprehend just what the United States was trying to do. All this no doubt fell "within the realm of high policy." Yet Mr. Dooman was compelled to observe that if the reply were delivered it would be interpreted:

> * (a) by the Japanese Government as an indication that the attitude now taken by the American Government requires the termination of the conflict with China as a condition precedent to the betterment by Japan of her relations with the United States; and
>
> (b) by the Prime Minister as a closing of the door to insure peace in the Far East.

This warning jolted the State Department. On August 4, 1939, the Department sent Mr. Dooman a defensively long explanation [106] and gave Mr. Dooman discretion to withhold delivering the reply "for a short time."

Mr. Dooman replied on August 5 [107] and advised withholding action "for the present." Nearly three months had elapsed since Japan had made its conciliatory proposal, and much valuable time had been lost by the dilatory inaction and suspicious reaction of the Department of State. Events had been moving more swiftly in Europe, and Mr. Dooman, also on August 5, 1939, cabled a reliable report [108]

> * that the army supported by a joint recommendation by the Japanese Ambassadors at Berlin and Rome are again vigorously pressing the government for an alliance with Germany and Italy. * the government is resolutely opposing the proposal and has staked its existence on the issue *. *

On August 8, 1939, Mr. Dooman cabled the State Department that, being pressed by the Prime Minister's personal adviser, Mr. Fujii, he had delivered the American reply to the Japanese Foreign Office. [109]

Fortunately the consequences of this error were neutralized by German errors. It was part of the Russian power politics to support China against Japan, and Mr. Molotov had demanded on August 14 that Germany should cease to support Japanese "aggression." [110] Japan had been kept in ignorance of the pending Russo-German negotiations [111] until the very last moment, as has been mentioned, and was troubled and concerned by their probable effects, and discontented by the German neglect. Germany had been annoyed and reproachful at the prior Japanese temporizing. [112] Now, when the event was known, Mussolini feared that there might even be a break with Japan which would result in her return to a position close to the democratic powers, [113] and he therefore attempted to conciliate the Japanese. At Washington on August 26, 1939, the Japanese Ambassador told Mr. Hull that Japan had decided to abandon any further negotiations with Germany and Italy relative to closer relations. [114] Instead of attempting to pick up the pieces, Mr. Hull delivered a cool lecture critical of Japan. [115] And there, so far as is now known, ends the record of a great but wasted opportunity. In this respect history lamentably repeated itself about two years later.

V A TANGLED WEB IS WOVEN

In early August 1939 the Congress adjourned, leaving Mr. Roosevelt's hands still tied by the existing Neutrality Act. Mr. Roosevelt sputtered about it to his press conference and "off the record" tried to convey to the country through the reporters several propaganda arguments. First, that the Senate had put him in the position where there was nothing further that he could do to avert war (nobody knew of the rebuffed Japanese approaches); second, that there was "widespread [and] general approval * regardless of party, for having something done to make the United States neutral and to help to avert war," and last, but most importantly, that the existing prohibition against selling arms was "going to slow up the finest little economic boom that ever happened."[1] On August 8, when Mr. Roosevelt was at Hyde Park, starting a vacation, he asserted that he no longer had the "power * to try to avert [a war crisis] the way I did in September of 1938 and April of 1939 *."[2] It has been claimed that at that time Mr. Roosevelt had in mind nothing specific and that he was quite unaware of the sudden and unfavorable turns which were being taken by European events.³ This claim seems difficult to credit because, if it is true, it contradicts his earlier statements to the reporters.

It is the fact that the preparations for war were proceeding silently and secretly. As early as June 23, 1939, an agreement had been made with Great Britain by which America bartered 600,000 bales of cotton in exchange for rubber from Malaya; ⁴ Mr. Roosevelt accidentally mentioned it much later, on November 10, 1939, when it had not as yet been revealed. ⁵ He also said that "a good deal of money" was being spent

> * to buy various war materials to store up in case of future need. *

On August 9, 1939, Mr. Roosevelt wrote Admiral Land, ⁶ the chairman of the United States Maritime Commission, noting with satisfaction that nineteen new merchant ships had been launched, that by the end of the year contracts would be let for approximately one hundred more, and expressing his thankfulness that the United States would now have auxiliary vessels capable

> * should the unfortunate necessity arise, of serving as the necessary supply force for naval vessels. *

And on August 10, so quietly that all mention of the terms of its creation are omitted from Mr. Roosevelt's published papers, a War Resources Board was created to advise with the Army and the Navy Munitions Board, and to review and complete the Industrial Mobilization Plan which had been prepared for use "in the event of a major war."⁷ It convened and on November 24, 1939, submitted a "comprehensive report" ⁸ which Mr. Roosevelt suppressed. The Board was disbanded shortly thereafter.

When the signing of the Russo-German treaty was announced, it naturally caused confusion and consternation in the public mind as well as in diplomatic circles. While the British and the French were negotiating with Hitler they were simultaneously asserting that they would continue to back Poland. Hitler was unyielding. On August 23 King Leopold III of Belgium and the Scandinavian monarchs issued a general appeal for peace.

On August 24 Mr. Roosevelt chimed in with peace "messages" [9] to Chancellor Hitler, King Victor Emmanuel (thus snubbing Mussolini), and President Moscicki of Poland.

At his press conference in Newfoundland waters on the following morning, August 25, Mr. Roosevelt rather startlingly disclaimed having any special knowledge about the European situation, and he told the reporters, [10]

* quite frankly, you all know just as much about the situation as I do.

Later in the day the affirmative reply of the Polish President was received by Mr. Roosevelt and was forwarded by him within the hour [11] to Chancellor Hitler with a request to agree to the pacific means of settlement accepted by Poland. These two cables were noncommittally acknowledged on August 31. [12] It was on the evening of August 25 that Mr. Roosevelt was first sure of Hitler's purpose to go to war, and he cut short his fishing trip. [13]

Yet by a momentous and tragic quirk of history the situation, as of that moment, was exactly the contrary. It was on August 25 that Hitler cancelled the mobilization orders [14] and through Sir Nevile Henderson, the British Ambassador to Germany, offered Britain an alliance, or something like it, comparable to the new Russian treaty. [15] Hitler had not expected that his Russian alliance would be so unpopular in Europe, or that it would meet with so hostile a Japanese response. He had not anticipated that Britain, France, and Poland would all stand fast and refuse to yield. The final bombshell was the refusal of Italy to join in the proposed war, which led Hitler to perform a political back somersault and call the whole business off.

90 | DESIGN FOR WAR

Feverish negotiations followed, and ultimately failed. In the midst of them German mobilization was resumed and on September 1, 1939, Germany invaded Poland and the Second World War had begun.

That same morning of September 1, Mr. Roosevelt held a press conference at Washington and in substance repeated what he had said in Newfoundland on the previous August 25:

> I do not think there is anything else I can tell you about that you do not know already. *

Quite probably this was correct, because on the same day he sent an "appeal" to Great Britain, France, Italy, Germany, and Poland to refrain from bombing civilians from the air. [16] If Mr. Roosevelt had been better informed he might have known that on August 26 Italy had not only made known to Germany its decision to remain neutral but had also proposed a peaceful political settlement, [17] and that on August 29 Mussolini had advised Hitler to pursue negotiations. [18] Indeed on August 31 Mussolini had suggested that a conference be called for September 5 to review the disturbing clauses of the Treaty of Versailles. Both the British and French Ambassadors welcomed it, and Count Ciano then telephoned it to Lord Halifax, who received the proposal favorably. [19] On September 2 it was transmitted to Hitler, who did not reject it, but when it was coupled with the British condition that Germany must first evacuate Poland [20] it failed, and Britain declared war against Germany on the morning of September 3, France reluctantly following in the late afternoon. There is no evidence as to whether or not any of this was contemporaneously known to Mr. Roosevelt.

At the same press conference of September 1, 1939, Mr. Roosevelt was asked an important question, and authorized direct quotation of his answer, which was a repetition of his numerous earlier professions of peace. The transcript reads as follows: [21]

Q. * I think probably what is uppermost in the minds of all the American people today is, "Can we stay out?" Would you like to make any comment at this time on that situation?

THE PRESIDENT: Only this, that I not only sincerely hope so, but I believe we can; and that every effort will be made by the Administration so to do.

Two days later, on September 3, Mr. Roosevelt made a fireside chat to the nation, [22] and in it his protestations, principally of peace, continued to be strong and profuse. He said,

> You are, I believe, the most enlightened and the best informed people in all the world at this moment. You are subjected to no censorship of news, and I want to add that your Government has no information which it withholds or which it has any thought of withholding from you.

* * * * * *

> Let no man or woman thoughtlessly or falsely talk of America sending its armies to European fields. At this moment there is being prepared a proclamation of American neutrality. This would have been done even if there had been no neutrality statute on the books, for this proclamation is in accordance with international law and in accordance with American policy.

> * I trust that in the days to come our neutrality can be made a true neutrality.

* * * * * *

> * I think it is honest for me to be honest with the people of the United States.

* * * * * *

* The overwhelming masses of our people seek peace—peace at home, and the kind of peace in other lands which will not jeopardize our peace at home.

* * * * * *

I have said not once, but many times, that I have seen war and that I hate war. I say that again and again.

I hope the United States will keep out of this war. I believe that it will. And I give you assurance and reassurance that every effort of your Government will be directed toward that end.

As long as it remains within my power to prevent, there will be no black-out of peace in the United States.

Mr. Roosevelt's assertion that no information was being or would be withheld from the people of the United States was less than accurate. Former Ambassador Winant stated that "at the beginning of hostilities" Mr. Chamberlain had arranged to keep Mr. Roosevelt "informed on the war situation," and that Mr. Chamberlain had "delegated this task to Mr. Churchill" [22] Mr. Churchill, on the contrary, has stated that he was first approached by Mr. Roosevelt on September 11, 1939, and that Mr. Roosevelt asked to have sealed communications sent personally to him through the diplomatic pouches. [24] Mr. Churchill has estimated at one place that there were about two thousand of these interchanges [25] and at another place that there were about seventeen hundred of them. [26] Whatever their final number may prove to be, the great majority of the communications remain secret to this day, except for a few messages revealed during the course of the Pearl Harbor investigations, and more recently by Mr. Churchill. One cannot help but speculate why it has been thought expedient to keep them secret for so long a time, and particularly so because the most important business between Britain and America was ultimately transacted through this personal and secret correspondence. [27]

On September 5, 1939, the customary form of neutrality proclamation under international law was issued, [28] together with an embargo on arms and munitions [29] under the Neutrality Act.

On September 8 at his press conference [30] Mr. Roosevelt referred to his Proclamation of Limited Emergency, which he was about to sign, and did sign and issue that same day. His comment on it was extremely soothing. He wanted no "scarehead stores * written," no "scare headlines." He said,

> What I want to do, and what all of you want to do, is to make it clear that there is no intention and no need of doing all of these things that could be done. There is need of doing a few * simple and minor things within peacetime authorizations. In other words, there is no thought, in any shape, manner or form, of putting the Nation, either in its defenses or in its internal economy, on a war basis. That is one thing we want to avoid. We are going to keep the nation on a peace basis *.

According to Mr. Roosevelt the Army was to be increased a little, "but not anywhere near the 280,000 that are authorized as peace-time strength." The Navy would be increased "by a comparatively small number; but we shall not go to the 180,000 of authorized peace strength." About one third of the 116 laid-up destroyers would be put back into active service. There would be "a small additional number" of Marines, increases in the National Guard, $500,000 to repatriate Americans abroad, and an addition to the Federal Bureau of Investigation, which had been placed in charge of espionage investigation, [31] and similar agencies.

In summing up this activity, Mr. Roosevelt repeated his assurances:

> * we see no other major needs for the future. There may be some minor things * but nothing that can be, in any way, construed as putting this country on a war basis. *

There then ensued these significant questions and answers:

Q. Mr. President, will any of these recommissioned destroyers be used as convoys?

THE PRESIDENT: Not that I know of.

Q. They will be assigned to patrol work, Mr. President?

THE PRESIDENT: Yes.

At this same press conference there was further discussion of a special session of the Congress to be called only to repeal the arms embargo, a matter which Mr. Roosevelt had already mentioned at his press conference the previous week.[32] Mr. Roosevelt was quick to pursue an apparent political advantage, and evidently thought that with the outbreak of the Second World War the chances of repealing the arms embargo had become more favorable—this, in spite of the fact that whereas war abroad was now flagrant, his previous standing argument for the repeal of the embargo had always been that its repeal would help him to maintain peace abroad and to avert war abroad.

Likewise at this September 8 press conference Mr. Roosevelt casually referred to the proposed conference at Panama of the American republics, and in an annotation [33] he mentions various agreements which were made there. The fourth was the Declaration of Panama, providing for a "neutrality patrol along the coastal waters of the entire hemisphere." And Mr. Roosevelt's annotation then states:

* This patrol was of the type which the United States * had *already* undertaken independently. (Emphasis supplied.)

Mr. Roosevelt, perhaps not inadvertently, omitted to state the date or the particulars, but the final act of the Panama Conference was adopted on October 2, 1939, so that the "neutrality patrol" of the United States antedates October 2. It was certainly operating by September 22. [34] Moreover, wholly contrary to the established rules of international law, the so-called "neutral zone" was extended out to sea anywhere from 1000 to 300 miles. On December 19, 1939, it is stated that the U.S.S. *Tuscaloosa* directed and escorted the British destroyer *Hyperion* to the German merchant vessel *Columbus* within this "neutral zone." [35]

Admiral King, as late as 1944, was careful to avoid stating the date when this unneutral "patrol" began "in this extensive area," but he does state that the destroyers already mentioned "were recommissioned for the purpose of making it effective." [36] Later, on October 18, 1939, [37] the submarines of all the belligerents (except Russia) were forbidden to enter American ports or American territorial waters, except in case of *force majeure*. This measure, like that of the Panama conference, was obviously directed against Germany in order to benefit Britain. Indeed, Mr. Churchill got in touch with Mr. Roosevelt in order to welcome the creation of the advantageous "neutral zone." [38]

Returning to the September 8 press conference, Mr. Roosevelt asserted, with reference to the possibility of food shortages:

Of course the real fact is that there is an actual surplus of food of every variety in this country. There is no conceivable shortage; and, as Secretary Wallace said yesterday, all of this fear of shortage of sugar [39] * or a shortage of this, that or the other thing, is ridiculous. * There is not any shortage; and we have plenty of everything in the way of foodstuffs.

On the same day national planning made its reappearance through the creation of the National Resources Planning Board, one of "the most aggressive of Federal agencies": [40] it was to be a division of the executive office of the President. [41]

While the façade of talk thus openly presented to the public bore all of the outward appearances of peace and of staying out of the war, the reality which lay behind it was different. Observers at Washington noted not only that we were committed to aiding Britain and France, but that Mr. Roosevelt wished to participate in the war in some way, considering it improved his chances for a third term, and that he even contemplated the possibility of our being in the war in six months. After the war was over we were told officially: [42]

> As early as the fall of 1939, the President began to think about the administrative arrangements which might be necessary if we were forced to go to war. It was deemed inadvisable to seek from Congress positive legislation for industrial mobilization since, in a campaign year, such a request might set off a partisan debate and if anything resulted it might be restrictive legislation. *

That is, translated out of officialese language, Mr. Roosevelt was unwilling to put the matter of his obtaining additional powers to prepare for entry into the war to the decision of the representatives of the people of the United States.

Other secret preparations for American entry into the war were being made at this time. For example, plans for the draft were being worked on in late September, and by early October they had assumed the essential shape in which they were subsequently enacted: war-time taxation was being studied, as was the increase of the Army and the Navy, and some form of government war-risk insurance was being planned.

On September 13, 1939, [43] Mr. Roosevelt called the Congress to convene in extra session on September 21. Between those two dates, on September 17, and as the result of urgent German representations, [44] Russia entered the war and the Polish army quickly collapsed. The fighting ended in Europe for some months, and the stage which was called the "phony" war began, during which there were many and obscure attempts to make peace. There is some evidence that on or about September 15 the late Mr. William R. Davis conferred with Mr. Roosevelt and informed him that Marshal Goering wanted to make peace. Mr. Roosevelt's attitude was one of indifference: he "pointed out that until some proposal reached him through some Government he could not take any position." [45] This would seem to confirm the report that Mr. Roosevelt was at all times strongly opposed to any negotiated peace. [46]

In such an atmosphere the Congress assembled on September 21, 1939, in extraordinary session. Mr. Roosevelt addressed it at the opening, and asked for the repeal of the embargo provisions of the Neutrality Act on the new and shifted ground [47]

> * that it impairs the peaceful relations of the United States with foreign nations.

In the name of abhorrence of war Mr. Roosevelt next endeavored to cloak his secret purposes [48] from public impugnment. He declared:

> At the outset I proceed on the assumption that every member of the Senate and of the House of Representatives, and every member of the Executive Branch of the Government, including the President and his associates, personally and officially, are equally and without reservation in favor of such measures as will protect the neutrality, the safety and the integrity of our country and at the same time keep us out of war.

Because I am wholly willing to ascribe an honorable desire for peace to those who hold different views from my own as to what those measures should be, I trust that these gentlemen will be sufficiently generous to ascribe equally lofty purposes to those with whom they disagree. * Let no group assume the exclusive label of the "peace bloc." We all belong to it.

Mr. Roosevelt then reviewed recent trends in American foreign policy, according to his own ideas about them, in the course of which he said:

* if and when war [among nations] unhappily comes, the Government and the nation must exert every possible effort to avoid being drawn into the war. * this Government must lose no time or effort to keep our nation from being drawn into the war.

In my candid judgment we shall succeed in those efforts.

Mr. Roosevelt next entered into an argument against the embargo provisions of the Neutrality Act, in the name of "a return to international law." He spoke also of four subsidiary objectives:

1. "* American merchant vessels should, as far as * possible, be restricted from entering war zones. *" But the Executive should be given unfettered discretion to say where and what the limits of such zones were.
2. American citizens should be prevented from travelling on belligerent vessels or in danger areas.
3. Belligerents must take title to goods in this country, and
4. War credits to belligerents should be prevented.

In concluding, Mr. Roosevelt again paid lip service to peace, saying,

To those who say that this program would involve a step toward war on our part, I reply that it offers far greater safeguards than we now possess or have ever possessed, to protect American lives and property from danger. It is a positive program for giving safety. This means less likelihood of incidents and controversies which tend to draw us into conflict, as they did in the last World War. There lies the road to peace!

* * * * * *

* Our acts must be guided by one single hard-headed thought—keeping America out of this war. *

By the next day the Congress was receiving a large and increasing volume of telegrams and messages against Mr. Roosevelt's proposal, and he was aware of this.[49] He himself received "many hundreds of telegrams" asking that a Day of Prayer for peace be proclaimed. Mr. Roosevelt issued a statement giving no reasons for his refusal but saying that he did not want to do so. He suggested, however, a week later, on September 29, that "people throughout the country" might on the coming Sunday "join with him and his family in such a prayer."

This popular sentiment against war found an unexpected ally in the new and startling vicissitudes of the power politics of Europe. Foreign diplomats thought peace quite possible.[51] On October 6, 1939, Hitler addressed the Reichstag [52] and made so clear an expression of his desire for peace that, after reading it, Mussolini thought "the war is now ended."[53] But in Britain only two voices were heard in favor of the conference which Hitler had proposed, those of Messrs. Bernard Shaw and David Lloyd George; and that, as Count Ciano noted in his diary [54] with mordant sapience,

> * proves conclusively that the English consider Hitler's proposals absolutely unacceptable.

M. Daladier first rejected these peace overtures, and after him, Mr. Chamberlain.

Having found by American resistance that war talk was bad politics, and being somewhat checked by the absence of shooting in Europe, Mr. Roosevelt decided to accept the advice of Mr. Hull and veered away from foreign to domestic politics. Indeed word came out of Washington that it would not now be politically feasible to go to war as an active belligerent until after the November 1940 election was won. This quieting down appears in the substantially diminished content of Mr. Roosevelt's published papers for the last quarter of 1939, [55] and in Mr. Churchill's comment as to the unusual American coolness in January 1940. [56]

This lull, and the apparently genuine trend of Mr. Roosevelt in peaceable directions, favored the prospects of the passage of the legislation which he sought from the Congress. In order to ensure its passage Mr. Roosevelt made a radio address on October 26, 1939, the day before the Senate was to vote on his proposals to amend the Neutrality Act. He indulged in vehement and sweeping assertions of his peaceful intentions, saying, [57]

> In and out of Congress we have heard orators and commentators and others beating their breasts and proclaiming against sending the boys of American mothers to fight on the battlefields of Europe.
>
> That I do not hesitate to label as one of the worst fakes in current history. It is a deliberate setting up of an imaginary bogey man. The simple truth is that no person in any responsible place in the national administration in Washington * has ever suggested in any shape, manner or form the remotest possibility of sending the boys of American mothers to fight on the battlefields of Europe. That is why I label that argument a shameless and dishonest fake.

* * * * * *

> The fact of the international situation—the simple fact, without any bogey in it, without any appeals to prejudice—is that the United States of America, as I have said before, is neutral and does not intend to get involved in war. *

In the same speech, and only a few lines below the quoted material, Mr. Roosevelt then made this curious observation which concluded his speech:

* Repetition does not transform a lie into a truth.

On October 27, 1939, the next day, the proposed bill passed the Senate and was sent to the House.

The amended Neutrality Act of 1939 with new cash-and-carry provisions was finally enacted on November 3, 1939, [58] on which day the special session adjourned. [59] Mr. Roosevelt signed the joint resolution the following day, November 4, [60] and, likewise on November 4, he issued a new proclamation of neutrality and a new definition of combat areas permitting the shipment of arms, ammunition, and implements of war to the various belligerents, but not in American merchant vessels. [61]

The ink was hardly dry on the new neutrality proclamation before American vessels were being transferred to foreign registries, principally to that of Panama, in order not to be restricted from this trade. It was slick although legal to do so, and Mr. Roosevelt, who had on other occasions inveighed against violations of the "spirit" of other laws, approved [62] of this obvious violation of the purpose of the amended Neutrality Act.

British and French purchasing commissions were already in this country, awaiting the repeal, and they opened up at once, leading to the hope of a boom or near boom for some months. This hope may have had some influence upon Mr. Morgenthau's opinion that Great Britain and France were not arming speedily enough. [63] As will be seen from the events of 1940 they were arming far beyond their ultimate capacity to pay.

Meanwhile there were ominous developments along the Baltic. As soon as the Polish war had ended, Germany and Russia made further treaties, secret and public, on September 28, 1939, which redefined the new boundaries between the two nations. [64] Russia moved into the little Eastern Baltic states swiftly, and Germany removed thousands of its nationals from these states in a few hours. Under duress Estonia agreed to accept Russian garrisons on September 28: Latvia yielded naval bases on the Baltic to Russia on October 5, and on October 16 Russia obtained additional naval bases from Lithuania. At the same time Russian troops were massed along the Finnish frontier and representatives of the Finnish Government went anxiously to Moscow.

Perhaps as a kind of sop to Hitler the Russians offered the Germans a bay not far from Murmansk as a naval base: by October 10, 1939, a German auxiliary cruiser was being equipped there, and a German repair ship was also to be stationed there. [65]

On October 11, 1939, Mr. Roosevelt voiced the general alarm by a "personal" cable [66] to President Kalinin of Russia, expressing the hope that no demands would be made on Finland inconsistent with peaceful relations and with Finnish independence. On October 13 President Kalinin replied with diplomatically suave but false assurances. [67]

On November 29, 1939, when the news arrived that Russian troops had invaded Finland and that Helsinki had been bombed, there was a wave of indignation which swept America, and which led to further notes from Mr. Roosevelt, [68] together with a request that those who were now free to sell munitions under the amended Neutrality Act should not sell airplanes to countries which bombed civilians. [69] This anger was not unique in America. All Italy was indignant, and there were demonstrations in favor of Finland and against Russia. [70] Italy sent Finland arms, artillerymen, pilots, and planes, and set up a special office at the Ministry for Foreign Affairs: indeed Germany herself supplied arms to Finland. [71] Britain not only encouraged the Italian efforts, but shipped supplies. [72] Russia was expelled from the League of Nations, and for a time it almost seemed as if the Second World War would be redirected into a crusade against

Russia. The American Army was giving technical advice to the Finnish Army which went far beyond the public accounts. But at his press conference on December 5, 1939, Mr. Roosevelt cast off a hint which he declined to make more explicit, saying, [73]

* there are efforts being made at the present time, some of them you do not even know about, for the beginning of negotiations looking toward peace or toward the end of hostilities. *

Perhaps it was in aid of these still-secret negotiations that on December 23, 1939, Mr. Roosevelt sent to Pope Pius XII a guarded and generalized letter suggesting that he would like to send to the Pope [74]

* my personal representative in order that our parallel endeavors for peace * may be assisted.

And on the same day Mr. Myron C. Taylor was named as the "personal representative" of Mr. Roosevelt. [75] Thenceforth all was silence and mystery, except that, some months later, on March 14, 1940, Mr. Roosevelt explained that Mr. Taylor's mission was not to inaugurate "formal diplomatic relations with the Vatican." [76]

Also in December 1939 the Export-Import Bank lent ten million dollars to Finland indirectly, [77] and a liaison committee was formed, composed of Messrs. Stimson, Knox, and Morgenthau, to coordinate foreign military purchases with the program of the United States. [78]

As 1939 drew to an end, Mr. Roosevelt continued to refuse to declare publicly whether or not he was a candidate for a third term. [79] Yet clues or straws might have been found. Many years before, Mr. Roosevelt had said, [80]

No one ever willingly gives up public life—no one who has tasted it.

Indeed it had been noted of Mr. Roosevelt, as of the end of 1911, [81] that

> One year in Albany had * developed within him a consciousness of power to lead men, and given him a taste for public life which has never left him.

By March 1940 the insiders already knew that Mr. Roosevelt wanted a third term "if it could be handled properly." [82]

When 1940 opened, the lull of the "phony" war continued and was to continue for several months. Writing in mid-July, 1941, and evidently not foreseeing the disaster of Pearl Harbor, Mr. Roosevelt made this observation as part of the introduction to his 1940 volume of papers:

> * increased appropriations for our Navy, had, by 1940, brought it back to a high state of efficiency, equipment and striking power *. * [83]

In his annual message to the Congress on January 3, 1940, Mr. Roosevelt referred to the war only generally, and he specifically renewed his earlier pledges of peace in a defensive way, saying, [84]

> I can understand the feelings of those who warn the nation that they will never again consent to the sending of American youth to fight on the soil of Europe. But, as I remember, nobody has asked them to consent—for nobody expects such an undertaking.
>
> The overwhelming majority of our fellow citizens do not abandon in the slightest their hope and their expectation that the United States will not become involved in military participation in these wars.

* * * * * *

* The time is long past when any political party or any particular group can curry or capture public favor by labeling itself the "peace party" or the "peace bloc." That label belongs to the whole United States and to every right thinking man, woman and child within it.

Toward the end of the speech Mr. Roosevelt called again for "national unity," and he warned the nation against [85]

> Doctrines that set group against group * class against class, fanning the fires of hatred in men too despondent * to think for themselves * used as rabble-rousing slogans on which dictators could rise to power.

With unconscious humor he denounced

> Overstatement, bitterness, vituperation * [which] have contributed mightily to ill-feeling * between nations. [and which] are also harmful in the domestic scene. *

On January 16, 1940, using the payment by Finland of the installment of her debt to the United States as a springboard, Mr. Roosevelt asked the Congress to double the amount of one hundred million dollars which the Export-Import Bank could lend, saying, [86]

> There is without doubt in the United States a great desire for some action to assist Finland to finance the purchase of agricultural surpluses and manufactured products, not including implements of war. There is at the same time undoubted opposition to the creation of precedents which might lead to large credits to nations in Europe, either belligerents or neutrals. No one desires a return to such a status.

* * * * * *

> An extension of credit at this time does not in any way constitute or threaten any so-called "involvement" in European wars. That much can be taken for granted.

A skeptical Congress took no immediate action on this request. At this date we have a glimpse of the extent to which Mr. Roosevelt had already secretly gone in power politics. Admiral

James O. Richardson became Commander-in-Chief of the United States Navy early in 1940, in which year on January 26 he wrote warnings to Admiral Stark, the Chief of Naval Operations: [87]

> The remarks in your letter of 18 Jan. about the situation in the Far East, the possibility of something breaking without warning and my need to be mentally prepared are some what disquieting.
>
> When the China incident started and on every opportunity until after I left the job as Asst. C[hief of] N[aval] O[perations] [88] I used to say to Bill Leahy "Be sure to impress on the boss [Mr. Roosevelt] that we do not want to [be] drawn into this unless we have others so bound to us that they can not leave us in the lurch."
>
> There is a possibility that this constant repetition had something to do with the trip of Ingersoll.
>
> When this understanding [with England] was reached it had some value but under present conditions it has little value as it affords us the use of a base [Singapore] [89] in exchange for an obligation to protect about 2 ½ continents.
>
> I strongly feel that you should *repeatedly impress on the boss* that an Orange [90] [Japanese] war would probably last some years and cost much money, my guess is 5 to 10 years 35 to 70 Billion dollars.
>
> * *I do not know* * what you are telling the boss, what is the meaning of our diplomatic moves * or our neutrality patrol. But you are the *principal and only Naval advisor* to the boss and he should know that our Fleet can not just sail away lick Orange and be back at home in a year or so. Also the probable cost of any war should be compared [to] the probable value of winning the war.
>
> * * * * * *
>
> All of this letter may be needless but I know that if you do not tell the boss what you really know and feel about the probable cost and duration of an Orange war NOBODY WILL. (Emphasis in original.)

The next development was on February 9, 1940, when Mr. Roosevelt announced at his press conference [91] that the Under Secretary of State, Mr. Sumner Welles, was going to

> * Italy, France, Germany and Great Britain. * solely for the purpose of advising the President and the Secretary of State as to present conditions in Europe.
>
> Mr. Welles will, of course, be authorized to make no proposals or commitments in the name of the Government of the United States.
>
> Furthermore, statements made to him by officials of Governments will be kept in the strictest confidence and will be communicated by him solely to the President and the Secretary of State.

Mr. Roosevelt declined to elaborate on this in any substantial way, although he did say that he had not advised any congressional leaders of Mr. Welles's journey. [92] When Mr. Welles had returned, Mr. Roosevelt issued a statement on March 29, 1940, [93] which was likewise vague and noncommittal. Mr. Welles was charged with three and perhaps four cognate tasks: [94]

1. To ascertain the strength of the Anglo-French determination to continue the war;
2. To ascertain the nature and extent of the pending peace negotiations, but
3. To oppose any proposed peace terms which would leave Germany strongly armed, or in an advantageous position, and
4. (In the opinion of some European political observers) to ascertain what further military moves Germany was planning.

At this same press conference of February 9 Mr. Roosevelt spoke guardedly of selling "surplus" arms to Norway and to other neutral countries. [95] It seems legitimate to infer that the rumors of further German attacks, which will shortly be mentioned, had been reported to him.

At almost the same moment Mr. Taylor left for Rome. On February 16 he had an interview with Mr. Roosevelt in which four possible bases for establishing peace in Europe were discussed. Mr. Taylor was to explore the possibilities for an "early ending of the war * in all quarters with which I would come in touch." [96] At this interview one can also trace some germs of the four freedoms: freedom of religion, freedom of communication of news and knowledge, reduction of armament, and freedom of trade between nations. Mr. Taylor formally presented himself to the Pope on February 27, 1940, but by March 16, [97]

> * conversations with His Holiness and with various foreign officials at the Vatican had confirmed the view that there was no hope of reestablishing peace. Any effort of mediation by neutral states would be untimely and would surely be rebuffed by the Axis Governments. * Under-Secretary of State Sumner Welles was arriving at the same conclusions from the direct conversations he was then having with heads of governments in Europe. *

The Pope had in fact been having conversations through an intermediary with the German underground, and through the British Minister to the Vatican had passed this information on to Lord Halifax. [98] Likewise there had been direct conversations between a representative of Lord Halifax and von Hassell. [99] And during early March there had been many mysterious visits of the Papal Nuncio at Berlin to the German Foreign Office. [100] Goering had been negotiating with London, [101] and the King of the Belgians thought that there were definite opportunities for peace. [102]

Mr. Welles came and went through the European capitals, and on March 16 he told Count Ciano that [108]

> * in London and in Paris there does not exist any of the uncompromising attitude which their speeches and the papers indicate. If they had certain guarantees of security they would be ready to give in more or less and to recognize the *fait accompli*. *

On that or the next day Mr. Welles telephoned Mr. Roosevelt and asked for his "permission to undertake a certain vague initiative for peace." Mr. Roosevelt refused, [104] apparently being opposed to any negotiated peace, although at that time the territorial dismemberment of Germany was not an American aim. [105] However, on March 19 Mr. Welles was suggesting the possibility of a meeting between Mr. Roosevelt and Mussolini at the Azores. [106] But before leaving Rome for good Mr. Welles is reported to have made a declaration of American foreign policy: [107]

> * The United States is there with all the weight of her power to guarantee this victory [of the French and English]. *

This commitment to the British and to the French would have been news if it had been known to Americans, and yet at that very instant some of the people to whom we were committed, the British, were secretly tattling to the Italians the most confidential remarks which Mr. Welles had made in England. [108]

It is only fair to add that this declaration by Mr. Welles was coupled with the assertion that

> * Even without undertaking any offensive, Germany will be exhausted within a year. * the war already [has been] won by the French and the English. *

Prior to the arrival of Mr. Welles in Rome on February 25, 1940, there had been a considerable leakage of the German plans for new offensives in the hope of imposing peace. In early October 1939 Hitler was planning to break through the Maginot line and to drive through Belgium and the Netherlands. [109] This was originally planned for January 17, 1940, but was postponed because a German airplane, bearing the plans with all details, landed in Belgium by mistake about a week earlier. [110] Count Ciano had heard of these plans in November and again in December 1939 and had passed the information on to the Belgian Ambassador and to the former Premier of the Netherlands in early January 1940.[111] In late February 1940 an observant American had heard the essentials of the planned attack on the Scandinavian countries; had noted daily troop trains passing through Berlin, west bound, and knew of heavy troop concentrations against the Netherlands.[112] These matters seem to have been common knowledge among many Germans by the middle of March 1940 and were known to Swedish diplomats at least a week in advance of the attack on Norway.[113]

Mr. Welles must have been familiar with all this news, and perhaps Count Ciano confirmed it. Likewise it seems proper to assume that Mr. Welles passed this information back to Mr. Roosevelt, and that this was the reason why Mr. Roosevelt belatedly put pressure on the Congress so that on March 2, 1940, he was able to approve the bill which doubled the capital of the Export-Import Bank. Fifty-six millions was lent at once to Finland, Norway, Sweden, Denmark, and Iceland. Finland made peace with Russia in ten days after the loan was made, much to the consternation of Britain and France. Indeed, Mr. Churchill had for some time been planning landings in Norway, partly to help the Finns, and partly to cramp the Germans.[114]

As for the other countries to which we made these loans Mr. Roosevelt wrote that [115]

> * the course of events in Europe * prevented the actual use of the major part of these credits.

Before mid-April, loans to Britain and to France were being discussed. Mr. Churchill believed that, as of this time, the opinion in Washington was confident that Britain and France would win the war.[116]

By March 19, 1940, Mr. Roosevelt was confessedly allowing our advanced types of airplanes to be sold to Britain and France, except for "three or four devices" on them, [117] while the American Army and Navy then and for many months thereafter were compelled to wait for them.

On March 29 the German Foreign Office released a White Book containing sixteen documents said to have been found in the Polish archives, being secret reports from various Polish ambassadors abroad.

On April 9, 1940, the Germans invaded Denmark and Norway, and the next day Mr. Roosevelt "froze" all their credits and assets within the United States, [118]

> * primarily to prevent the aggressor nations from using [them] for their own purposes * . * to carry on their program of world conquest and destruction of democratic nations and democratic principles. * and used against our own national interest. *

When the war was over, Admiral Doenitz's attorney attempted to prove that the German invasion of Norway took place with at least the tacit approval of Russia, but quick Russian objections to this attempt were sustained, and prevented the development of any evidence on the matter. [119] On April 13 Mr. Roosevelt issued a two-paragraph statement of disapproval of the invasions; [120] by comparison with earlier statements it was noticeably restrained.

Two days later, on April 15, 1940, Mr. Roosevelt addressed the Pan American Governing Board over the radio. [121] His theme, four times repeated, was, "Peace reigns among us today." "The value of love," he said, would "always be stronger than the value of hate * . * The value of a belief in humanity and justice is always stronger * than the value of belief in force * . * The value of truth and sincerity is always stronger than the value of lies and cynicism. *" The speech was altogether gentle; it could not have aroused suspicion in anyone's mind.

By April 20 the pre-convention political campaigns were in full swing. That day Mr. Roosevelt by radio addressed the Young

Democratic Clubs of America assembled in meetings throughout the United States. [122] Most astutely he played down foreign affairs, repeating and reaffirming his many prior pledges of peace. He put the entire emphasis of his speech on domestic affairs, saying,

It is the domestic scene which I stress tonight. *

Mr. Roosevelt's only references to power politics were these:

> I am not speaking tonight of world affairs. Your Government is keeping a cool head and a steady hand. We are keeping out of the wars that are going on in Europe and in Asia * . *

He particularly denied either warlike design or diplomatic ineptitude, stating,

First, our opponents are seeking to frighten the country—by telling people that the present Administration is deliberately trying to put this nation into war or that it is inevitably drifting into war. You know better than that.

On April 22, 1940, Count Ciano had assured Ambassador Phillips that there was no prospect of any immediate entry of Italy into the war. [123] Before another week was up it was known in diplomatic circles that Italy was considering the matter. [124] On April 28 the Pope wrote Mussolini a letter praying for peace, [125] and by prior arrangement with the Pope, who was not consulted as to its substance, [126] Mr. Roosevelt presented a message to Mussolini on May 1. It has been omitted from Mr. Roosevelt's published papers and from the United States and Italy Documentary Record, so that it is necessary to rely on Count Ciano's summary of it. [127] It was a "covertly threatening" warning to stay out of the war, coupled with the implied threat that if Italy entered the war, the United States, which had intended to remain neutral, would be obliged to revise its position at once. To the Pope's letter Mussolini's reaction was skeptical, but Mr. Roosevelt's threats impelled him to feel that he must enter the war in spite of powerful Italian opposition, [128] and quickly obtain a victory because of the "hidden threats of American intervention." In consequence his reply to Mr. Roosevelt was hostile. [129] On May 14, 1940, Mr. Roosevelt wrote Mussolini another letter, much of which is still secret. [130] The tone of the correspondence had now changed; the letter was discouraged and conciliatory, [131] and Mussolini's reply on May 18 [132] was brief and dry.

Yet, when Mr. Roosevelt was asked at his press conference on May 14 if there was any special reason behind Mr. Hull's warning to all Americans to leave Italy, he disingenuously answered, [133]

Not that I know of.

Mr. Churchill now took a try, and on May 16 wrote a message to Mussolini which contained the covert threat that Britain would be aided in increasing measure by the United States. [134] He too was repulsed, [135] whereupon Mr. Churchill and M. Reynaud asked Mr. Roosevelt to intervene. They authorized him to say that they would consider any reasonable Italian territorial claims in the Mediterranean, and that Mr. Roosevelt could guarantee the performance of any agreement which might be reached. [136] This was on May 25. Mr. Roosevelt acted promptly in the interests of Britain and France; on May 27 Ambassador Phillips brought to Count Ciano Mr. Roosevelt's message, which was dated May 26. Most of the significant portions of this dispatch remain secret, [137] but Count Ciano wrote that in this amazing proposal [138]
* Roosevelt offers to become the mediator between us and the Allies, becoming personally responsible for the execution, after the war, of any eventual agreements. *

This approach was likewise unsuccessful. [139] A portion of the conversation between Ambassador Phillips and Count Ciano has been omitted from the published report. [140] Belgium capitulated, and Mr. Roosevelt reverted to his original policy of covert threats. On May 31 Ambassador Phillips brought to Count Ciano another dispatch from Mr. Roosevelt [141] in which Mr. Roosevelt emphasized the possibility that Italian entry into the war "might well bring with it the involvement of countries at present remote from the scene of the hostilities." [142] Mr. Roosevelt likewise emphasized "the historic and traditional interests of the United States in the Mediterranean" which had "been upheld over a period of almost one hundred and fifty years." And in conclusion, if Italy entered the war, Mr. Roosevelt threatened that the result would "at once" be

> * an increase in the rearmament program of the United States itself and * a redoubling of the efforts of the Government of the United States to facilitate in every practical way the securing within the United States by the Allied Powers of all the supplies and matériel which they may require.

Mussolini's reply, delivered on June 1, was negative. [143] The American note proved to him that America had already "chosen the Allied side." And "any further pressure," he observed, "would only stiffen his attitude."

It seems almost superfluous to repeat that the American people were then uninformed and generally still remain ignorant of these manoeuvres in power politics, and of these secret pledges and secret threats. In fact on June 4, 1940, the White House authorized the statement that

> * not a single true and accurate report on the President's correspondence with Mussolini has yet come from Rome. *

This was for the reason that, as noted at that time by Washington observers, the reaction of public opinion was feared by Mr. Roosevelt if the extent of his financial and economic back-door support to the Allies became known. It was stated that if the election was not impending this help would be much greater, and yet it seems probable that the Washington observers of those days did not know (and could not know) how great it really was.

Elsewhere in Europe, events had been moving with incredible speed. Although Mr. Churchill had taken over general control of the British fighting forces by April 4, the British troops landed in Norway were being steadily forced back and their evacuation was commencing. On May 7 and 8 Mr. Chamberlain was bitterly attacked in the House of Commons. At dawn on May 10, 1940, the Germans invaded the Netherlands, Belgium, and Luxembourg: later in the day Mr. Chamberlain resigned. Mr. Churchill formed a coalition cabinet and became Prime Minister. The British had been informed of this exact date of the German attack "weeks ahead" by Dr. Joseph Müller, one of the plotters against Hitler. [144]

In America on May 10, 1940, Mr. Roosevelt had addressed the Eighth Pan American Scientific Congress. [145] He commenced with a reference to the invasion of Belgium, the Netherlands, and Luxembourg that day, and said he was "glad" that it had "angered" all Americans. It presented, he continued, "a definite challenge to the continuance of * civilization * . *" After contrasting the freedom of the search for truth in the Americas with its suppression "in other parts of the world," he asserted that the "fear" that the destruction on "other Continents" would require "the Americans * to become the guardian of Western culture, the protector of Christian civilization" had "become a fact." Mr. Roosevelt then attacked

> * a false teaching of geography—the thought that a distance of several thousand miles from a war-torn Europe to a peaceful America gave to us some form of mystic immunity that could never be violated.

The distance from Europe to Chile or to San Francisco was now relatively less, he claimed, than the distances which ancient conquerors, such as Alexander or Julius Caesar, had traversed. The modern conquerors, asserted Mr. Roosevelt,

> * seek to dominate * every human being and every mile of the earth's surface.

Guardedly Mr. Roosevelt called for intervention in Europe. Rhetorically he questioned whether the way of life in the New World is

> * permanent or safe if it is * just for us alone? * Can we continue our peaceful construction if all the other Continents embrace by preference or by compulsion a wholly different principle of life? No, I think not.

Having gone thus far in one direction he faced about and paid a tribute to peace, asserting,

> I am a pacifist. You, my fellow citizens of twenty-one American Republics, are pacifists too.

After this, and in his closing paragraph, he returned to his theme song of defense, saying,

> But I believe that by overwhelming majorities in all the Americas you and I, in the long run if it be necessary, will act together to protect and defend by every means at our command our science, our culture, our American freedom and our civilization.

Europe was hoping for something more tangible than words from Mr. Roosevelt. King Leopold III in Belgium's hour of need cabled Mr. Roosevelt for help. The text of his cable for help is not printed, but Mr. Roosevelt's answering cable of May 11, 1940, is given. [146] Mr. Roosevelt repeated a phrase out of the previous day's Pan American speech, hoped that Belgium might preserve its integrity and freedom, and, by way of tangible help, sent the king his "warm personal regards."

At his press conference on May 14, [147] Mr. Roosevelt referred to the message on national defense which he was about to send to the Congress in a day or two. He was about to ask for an additional $896,000,000 [148] but had given no thought as to how the money was to be raised, whether by increased taxation or by loans. That, he said firmly, was "a completely minor detail." The transcript shows the following questions and answers:

> Q. Mr. President, you said that expenditures [for defense] would have to be met by taxes or by borrowing. Would you make any definite recommendation on increasing the statutory debt limit?
>
> THE PRESIDENT: No.
>
> * * * * * *
>
> Q. Do you think it is necessary at this session to do that, Mr. President?
>
> THE PRESIDENT: I think it is a completely minor detail. * I think it is a minor detail, because the Government has got to spend the money anyway.

At this same press conference on May 14 Mr. Roosevelt was asked whether we needed a two-ocean navy. In a reply in which there appears to be some omission from the transcript he repelled the notion, saying,

> * it is an entirely outmoded conception of naval defense * . * it is not sensible to talk of naval defense in those terms *

Yet it was not seven months later, on December 5, 1940, that Mr. Roosevelt [149] spoke contradictorily of a two-ocean navy as having been part of

> * a program covering many years * . *

118 | DESIGN FOR WAR

During the period of the "phony" war it had become the fashion to belittle the German war power by minimizing the strength and skill of Polish resistance, although Poland, attacked from two sides by vastly more powerful nations, had held out against them for nearly three weeks. Now, on May 14, after only four days of Nazi blitzkrieg, the armies of the Netherlands ceased to resist.

Britain was swiftly losing her new-found allies, and the hopes of Mr. Churchill, in office only a few days, turned to the west. On May 15 he cabled Mr. Roosevelt with a long list of requests for help. [150] He asked for everything short of armed forces, including an abandonment of American neutrality, and listed some of the more specific items:

1. For forty or fifty of the older American destroyers;
2. For several hundred of the latest types of airplanes;
3. For anti-airplane guns and ammunition;
4. For steel and other materials, for which Britain would pay dollars while she could, but Mr. Churchill asked for an assurance that when Britain could no longer pay for them she might have them as gifts;
5. That vessels of the United States Navy might go to Irish ports and make a prolonged stay there; and
6. That the United States would hold the Japanese in check in the Pacific, using Singapore if we wished.

Mr. Churchill also expressed a gloomy estimate as to the immediate developments of the war.

On May 16, 1940, Mr. Roosevelt sent to the Congress a message asking additional appropriations "for National Defense," [151] the first in a 1940 series. The appropriations for which he asked were moderate enough; $896,000,000, together with the authority to contract ahead to the extent of an additional $286,000,000. This money was to be used principally for the production of airplanes, anti-aircraft guns, and the training of troops to use these weapons, [152] but the body of the message seems to have reflected Mr. Churchill's gloom. It spoke of

> * ominous days * . * The brutal force of modern offensive war * horror. * New powers of destruction, incredibly swift and deadly * those who wield them are ruthless and daring. * the dangers which confront us * . * Motorized armies [which] sweep through enemy territories at the rate of two hundred miles a day. * Lightning attacks, capable of destroying airplane factories and munition works hundreds of miles behind the lines *. 153

Mr. Roosevelt recalled that an "opponent" (Great Britain, destined soon to be one of the two greatest beneficiaries of American bounty) in a former war had once captured and then burned our national Capitol. Next, in a series of imaginary conquests he portrayed unnamed enemies arriving in the heart of the Mississippi Valley in five easy jumps. From the Cape Verde Islands these enemies could be over Brazil in seven hours. The second jump brought them to Venezuela in four hours; the third to the Canal Zone in two and one-half hours, and the fourth to Tampico, Mexico, in two and one-quarter hours. The final jump brought them to Kansas City, Omaha, and St. Louis in two and one-quarter hours. [154] Thus the heart of America was distant only eighteen hours from the peril of invasion. It will be plain to the reader that Mr. Roosevelt was not sound either as to strategy or as to logistics. Was he attempting to create fear or hysteria in the American people?

Even after its surrender it took the able General MacArthur more than eighteen hours to make an unopposed landing in Japan, while the problems and difficulties of Hitler in attempting to cross the narrow width of the English Channel are undisputed. [155] Similarly the equally able General Eisenhower thought of crossing the Channel, not in terms of hours of preparation, nor weeks, but months. [156] All this lay in the future at that time, it is true, but there was also a valid present consideration—what of the

American Army, Navy, and Air Corps? Mr. Roosevelt had then been President for well over seven years, and upwards of six billion dollars had admittedly been spent on national defense during his administrations. Had it all been spent to no avail? That very question had been raised in the Senate earlier that week. [157] Gloom must not be overdone, because it might lead to unfavorable inferences. Consequently Mr. Roosevelt attempted to anticipate and to avert such criticism by attacking the "Loose talking and loose thinking" of some people, which gave

> * the false impression that our own American Army and Navy are not first-rate, or that money has been wasted on them.
>
> Nothing could be further from the truth.

High words of praise were also spoken for the Navy, the Army, the National Guard, and the Air Corps. For the last named, Mr. Roosevelt asked the production of at least 50,000 planes a year, without hampering or delaying the delivery of the other American airplanes which foreign nations had ordered or might order here. Finally, towards the conclusion of his message Mr. Roosevelt paid his customary tribute to peace, saying,

> I, too, pray for peace * . *
>
> Our ideal, yours and mine, the ideal of every man, woman and child in the country—our objective is still peace—peace at home and peace abroad. *

It has already been mentioned that in early September 1939, about 40 of the 116 laid-up destroyers were to be put into active service. At some unknown later time another 40 destroyers were activated, because on May 17, 1940, [158] Mr. Roosevelt said that it was planned

> * to commission * thirty-five of the old World War destroyers, which are still out of commission; all the rest of them have been put into commission. *

It may be assumed that this was the first step towards giving them to Britain, because when Mr. Roosevelt replied the next day to Mr. Churchill's request he did not refuse it except for the moment, on the ground that the time was not opportune. [159] As to Mr. Churchill's second, third, and fourth items, Mr. Roosevelt promised the utmost help. He was politely noncommittal as to the touchy Irish situation, while as to Japan he referred to the fact that the American fleet was being concentrated at Hawaii.

We now know that it was the original plan for the United States Fleet, after holding its annual manoeuvres near Hawaii, to depart from that area for the West Coast on May 9, 1940. [160] Instead, on May 7 it was ordered to remain in Hawaiian waters "for a couple of weeks." [161] Admiral Richardson objected on May 13 that to maintain the security of the Western Hemisphere was vital; that a move towards Asia meant hostilities and would be a grave mistake because it would reduce American ability to defend the Western Hemisphere. [162] On May 22 Admiral Stark replied to Admiral Richardson, [163] stating that on May 7

> * it looked as if Italy were coming in almost immediately and that a serious situation might develop in the East Indies, and that there was a possibility of our being involved. *

* * * * * *

> I wish you would keep constantly in mind the possibility of a complete collapse of the Allies, including the loss of their fleets. *

Mr. Roosevelt's cable to Mr. Churchill of May 18 very likely crossed one of Mr. Churchill to him on the same day, in which the latter begged for American assistance soon. [164] Then on May 20 Mr. Churchill cabled again. [165] It appears that Mr. Roosevelt had been conferring with Lord Lothian, the British Ambassador, about the gift of the destroyers, and the inference is clear that

Mr. Roosevelt had enquired whether Britain would surrender and what would become of the British fleet. Mr. Churchill tied strings to his assurances. First, he asked that fighter planes be taken away from the American Army and delivered to Britain in the largest possible numbers at the earliest possible time. Then, if Britain could get the help for which she had asked she would fight on to the end, but if Mr. Churchill's cabinet fell and another cabinet was formed, and if the United States had left Great Britain to its fate, the British Fleet might be surrendered to Germany. For some months to come Mr. Churchill dangled this bogey man before Mr. Roosevelt, as will be told in the following pages. As comment upon it here, we may quote what Mr. Churchill said when the Russians were importunate to Britain in 1941:

> The Soviet Government had the impression that they were conferring a great favour on us by fighting in their own country for their own lives. The more they fought, the heavier our debt became. This was not a balanced view. * 166

In his reply 167 Mr. Roosevelt pointed out that the British navy could always withdraw to Canada, and he promised Mr. Churchill that the United States would never permit Germany to occupy Canada or any other part of the British Empire in the Americas. Mr. Roosevelt asserted that Britain could put no trust in any peace terms proffered by Hitler, so that if such a time should come Mr. Roosevelt urged Mr. Churchill to see that all ships building in Britain were destroyed and that all merchant ships should depart to other ports in the Empire. But, he thought, Germany could not conquer Britain so long as the British and French navies were in being. Meanwhile the United States was doing all that it could to speed up the delivery of munitions. Finally—and this was fateful—

---

* He promised to give every possible consideration to specific requests Churchill might send him.

On May 24 the House of Representatives passed a statute to permit unlimited expansion of the Air Corps, and Mr. Roosevelt on the same day announced that fifty thousand volunteer pilots would be trained during the year commencing on July 1, 1940. [168]

It was probably at about this time (for the exact date is not given) that Secretary Ickes wrote to Mr. Roosevelt [169]

> * and stated that while a big pipe line from Texas to the east coast might not be economically feasible, it might become an absolute necessity in the event war should come to America.

At Washington administrative confusion and inefficiency prevailed. [170] Secretary of War Woodring was alleged to be incompetent for the job ahead, but the real basis for his disqualification in Mr. Roosevelt's eyes was that he was rather less pro-war than Mr. Roosevelt. [171] Yet care had to be taken to handle him gently; situated as he was, Mr. Woodring could have made embarrassing revelations in an election year. At a much later date Mr. Louis A. Johnson, the Assistant Secretary of War, who was hostile to Mr. Woodring, claimed that the Secretary of War "was a sincere pacifist." [172] Certainly it is clear from Mr. Johnson's testimony that there was dissension within the Cabinet itself over Mr. Roosevelt's war policies. The Secretary of Labor, Miss Perkins, was "violently opposed" to Mr. Johnson's scheme to use the Civilian Conservation Corps's camps as a training ground for military training. And Mr. Johnson also testified that as early as 1938 it was Mr. Roosevelt's opinion that war was inevitable and that America could not stay out of it.

Returning to 1940, at this time there was a feeling which was on the increase that Mr. Roosevelt intended to take the nation into the war after he had won the election. [173] There was the opinion that a large part of the monies previously spent on defense had been wasted; there was doubt whether the American way of life could be maintained in the face of the defense appropriations made, requested, and foreseeable.

In order to still some of these doubts Mr. Roosevelt made a long fireside chat on May 26, 1940. [174] This was the "on hand or on order" speech. It began on a note of sadness and sympathy for the refugees of Belgium and France, and thence, by a deft transition, it continued as an "educational" attack on historic American continentalism, based on generalized, fear-breeding assertions. (Only nine days previously Mr. Roosevelt had made the narrowly careful distinction between such generalizations and "a definite, concrete, immediate threat of attack on us * . *"[175]) Then, as in his message to Congress ten days previously, Mr. Roosevelt quickly tacked away from the lee shore of criticism by entering upon a long narrative exposition of the asserted splendid current condition of national defense. This new topic began on a defensive note as follows:

> In the past two or three weeks all kinds of stories have been handed out to the American public about our lack of preparedness. It has even been charged that the money we have spent on our military and naval forces during the last few years has gone down the rat-hole. I think it is a matter of fairness to the nation that you hear the facts.
>
> We have spent large sums of money on the national defense. This money has been used to make our Army and Navy today the largest, the best-equipped, and the best-trained peace-time military establishment in the whole history of this country.

* * * * * *

> But between 1933 and this year, 1940—seven fiscal years—your Government will have spent one billion four hundred eighty-seven million dollars more than it spent on the Navy during the seven years that preceded 1933.
>
> What did we get for this money?

A TANGLED WEB IS WOVEN | 125

* * * * * *

During this period 215 ships for the fighting fleet have been laid down or commissioned, practically seven times the number in the preceding seven-year period.

As talk, such statements sound most impressive, but when "the facts" are verified a totally different picture appears. Plate II of the official report of Admiral King, dated March 27, 1944, shows the "status of combatant vessels, U. S. Navy" as of January 1 in each year from 1923 to 1944. Adopting the Rooseveltian phrase used in the present speech, it shows the total tonnage of vessels "on hand," and from that plate it appears:

1. That there was no substantial increase in the total of such tonnage from January 1, 1940, to January 1, 1942, both inclusive.

2. The total tonnage on January 1, 1923, 1924, and 1929, was substantially the same as on January 1, 1940.

3. The tonnage was at its lowest from January 1, 1932, to January 1, 1937, both inclusive. Five of these six years were Rooseveltian years.

4. While there was some increase in tonnage after January 1, 1942, the substantial increase appears after January 1, 1943.

5. Between January 1, 1940, and January 1, 1941 (and thus during the year when this speech was made), there was an actual decrease of tonnage "on hand"!

As is well known, the Navy was Mr. Roosevelt's pet and, as much as his stamp collection, his hobby: he relished referring to himself as "Commander in Chief."[176] It cannot be assumed that he was ignorant of these facts, so that the conclusion seems warranted that Mr. Roosevelt was using the figures mentioned in his speech in order to create a false impression in the minds of the American people.

The conclusion that Mr. Roosevelt was attempting to create false impressions is strengthened by the transition in this fireside chat to the "on hand or on order" passages. Exactly ten days previously Mr. Roosevelt had inveighed against weapons which existed only on paper. He had told the Congress on May 16 that it was [177]

> * essential that we have the physical, the ready ability to meet * attacks *.
>
> This means military implements—not on paper—which are ready and available * . *

But in this fireside chat of May 26, 1940, Mr. Roosevelt lumped together actual arms and "paper" arms, saying,

> * And, speaking of airplanes that work with the Navy, in 1933 we had 1,127 useful aircraft and today we have 2,892 on hand and on order. *
>
> * * * * * *
>
> In 1933 we had only 355 anti-aircraft guns. We now have more than 1,700 modern anti-aircraft guns of all types on hand or on order. *
>
> In 1933 there were only 24 modern infantry mortars in the entire Army. We now have on hand and on order more than 1,600.
>
> In 1933 we had only 48 modern tanks and armored cars; today we have on hand and on order 1,700. *

But was this planned production to be made directly by the political appointees of the Administration? No, indeed; when asked the question at an earlier press conference Mr. Roosevelt interrupted the questioner and hastily interposed: [178]

No Government operated plants.

The fireside chat of May 26, 1940, therefore made it clear that the New Deal would not attempt, itself, to perform such staggering feats of production as to build fifty thousand planes a year. In order to accomplish that, said Mr. Roosevelt,

> * We intend to harness the efficient machinery of these manufacturers *.

The same was to be true in all other fields:

> We are calling upon the resources, the efficiency and the ingenuity of the American manufacturers of war material of all kinds *. The Government of the United States itself manufactures few of the implements of war. Private industry will continue to be the source of most of this matériel * . *

* * * * * *

> We are calling on men now engaged in private industry to help us in carrying out this program * . *

> * Private industry will have the responsibility of providing the best, speediest and most efficient mass production of which it is capable. *

None of this, however, was to impair in the slightest

> * any of the great social gains we have made in these past years. *

The forty-hour week (concerning which Mr. Roosevelt had vacillated on May 17 [179]) would be maintained in order to give employment on armaments to

> * tens of thousands of people, who are now unemployed *.

As for old-age pensions and unemployment insurance, they should now be

> * extended to other groups who do not now enjoy them.

There must be "no new group of war [sic] millionaires," and the general cost of living must be maintained at a reasonable level. Nor must discord be disseminated: there must be unity. Every man and woman should make some contribution to the security of the nation.

Finally, employing what by now appears to have become his standard formula, Mr. Roosevelt paid a tribute of lip service to peace, concluding the chat thus:

> Day and night I pray for the restoration of peace in this mad world of ours. It is not necessary that I, the President, ask the American people to pray in behalf of such a cause—for I know you are praying with me.
>
> I am certain that out of the heart of every man, woman and child in this land, in every waking minute, a supplication goes up to Almighty God; that all of us beg that * peace may return to the world. *

At this point it is useful to verify a few more of "the facts" mentioned in Mr. Roosevelt's speech. Not "tens of thousands" but millions of people were put to work to produce munitions of war. There were still nine million unemployed people in June 1940, but by December 1941 their number had diminished to about four million. [180] Notwithstanding this increase, the progress in the production of war material from this time to the end of the year 1940 was not impressive in terms of articles actually manufactured. [181] By the end of 1940 only a trickle of arms was coming off the production line. [182] And at even a later date Mr. Roosevelt diverted from the American forces large quantities of these limited products and sent them abroad, [183] which explains the shortages suffered here and at Hawaii and in the Philippines up to the time of Pearl Harbor.

On May 27, 1940, Admiral Stark wrote Admiral Richardson as to the grand, if nebulous, strategy of the Pacific: [186]

> Why are you in the Hawaiian Area?
>
> Answer: You are there because of the deterrent effect which it is thought your presence may have on the Japs going into the East Indies. In previous letters I have hooked this up with the Italians going into the war. The connection is that with Italy in, it is thought the Japs might feel just that much freer to take independent action. We believe both the Germans and the Italians have told the Japs that so far as they are concerned she, Japan, has a free hand in the Dutch East Indies.
>
> Your natural question may follow—well, how about Italy and the war? * we have had Italy going into the war on 24 hours' notice on several different occasions *. Others have stated that it would occur within the next ten days. * It is anybody's guess. *.
>
> The above in itself shows you how indefinite the situation is.
>
> Along the same line as the first question presented you would naturally ask—suppose the Japs do go into the East Indies? What are we going to do about it? My answer is, * I don't know and I think there is nobody on God's green earth who can tell you.*
>
> * even if the decision here were for the U. S. to take no decisive action if the Japs should decide to go into the Dutch East Indies, we must not breathe it to a soul, as by so doing we would completely nullify the reason for your presence in the Hawaiian area. Just remember that the Japs don't know what we are going to do and so long as they don't know they may hesitate or be deterred. These thoughts I have kept very secret here.

The above I think will answer the question "why you are there." It does not answer the question as to how long you will probably stay. Rest assured that the minute I get this information I will communicate it to you. Nobody can answer it just now. Like you, I have asked the question, and also—like you—I have been unable to get the answer.

Next day, at the press conference of May 28, 1940, [185] Mr. Roosevelt elaborated on the theme

> * that we are not going to upset, any more than we have to, a great many of the normal processes of life. * we are * going to have * new automobiles next year, new models, * a lot of other things that could be put into the luxury class * cosmetics, lipsticks, ice-cream sodas *.

And in answer to the thought that troops were going to be conscripted Mr. Roosevelt referred to the 1917 army of four million men and gave what appeared to be a flat denial, the guarded provisos in it having escaped the general attention. He said:

> * This is not like April, 1917 * when we were attempting to organize an army of 4,000,000 men. We have not, certainly at this time, that in mind.

* * * * * *

> * We are not talking at the present time about a draft system, either to draft men or women or money or all three. *

Mr. Roosevelt then turned to another topic which illustrates the casualness of his administrative methods, and how commission was imposed on commission. Mr. Roosevelt announced that, acting under "an old 1916 statute which had not been repealed," [186] he was appointing a seven-member advisory commission to the

Council of National Defense, which he was re-creating. The advisory commission was rather vaguely to

> * act as a clearing house * . * act as the coordinating agency for Government orders * . *

And now there ensued between the reporters and the author of the "we-are-planning-it-that-way" speech this revealing dialogue: [187]

Q. Did you say this Commission had no chairman? Did you say there is no chairman of this Commission?

THE PRESIDENT: May [Miss Craig], I do not know. Why bring up the subject? I don't know.

Q. It is hard to function without a chairman.

THE PRESIDENT: * I do not know what the procedure will be. *

Q. Will you have to have a special appropriation to finance this Commission, or have you the funds out of which to pay?

THE PRESIDENT: I do not know. *

Q. Have you decided where this Commission is going to be housed?

THE PRESIDENT: * Oh, Gosh! I do not know.

It was on this same day, May 28, 1940, that King Leopold III surrendered the Belgian armies after eighteen days of warfare. The stage was set for the British evacuation through Dunkirk, which commenced on May 29.

On May 29 Secretary Hull modified the restrictions of the Neutrality Act and permitted American pilots to deliver American war planes by flying them into Canada.

On May 31, 1940, Belgium having surrendered, and the evacuation of Dunkirk being in full course, Mr. Roosevelt sent to the Congress a second request [188] for additional appropriations for defense. It was hastily drawn, so hastily that the amounts requested are not mentioned in the message. They were to be found in "plans and proposals" which the War and Navy Departments were later to send to Congress. Pursuant to this request Congress appropriated over $1,763,500,000 additional. Mr. Roosevelt also inched forward with the general observation that

> * There is definite danger in waiting to order the complete equipping and training of armies after a war begins.

Consequently he asked the Congress to authorize him to call the National Guard into active service, and also to recall the Army's reserves to active service. The Congress refused to grant him such authority for almost three months.

Mr. Churchill's appeals for help bore fairly quick fruit. The latest of them resulted in an order from Mr. Roosevelt to the Army and the Navy on June 1, 1940, to investigate the quantity of arms which could be transferred, and on June 3 a list was approved by General Marshall, following hasty conferences between the British, the French, the Army, the Navy, the State Department, and the Treasury.[189] It may seem odd that the Treasury Department should appear in this otherwise military group, but Mr. Morgenthau had been ceaselessly working for Britain, which had already been urged to be financially bold and had been assured that when its money ran out some way of financing it would be found.[190]

There is as yet no direct information as to the political terms of this deal, which involved half a million rifles, nine hundred 75 mm. field guns, 80,000 machine guns, much ammunition, an assortment of bombs, TNT, and smokeless powder, but by inference the terms are clear. General Marshall justified his approval of the transaction on the ground that "the military issue immediately at stake was the security of the British fleet to dominate the Atlantic," which seems to involve the idea of a promise to be made by Mr. Churchill to that effect, in exchange for the weapons. If this inference is correct Mr. Churchill for the moment kept his part of the bargain promptly. He spoke in the House of Commons on the following day, June 4, and acknowledged that a colossal military disaster had been suffered by the evacuation from Dunkirk. His concluding paragraph was, he declares, aimed at the United States. [191] In it he not only repeated a part of the substance of his cable of May 20 to Mr. Roosevelt, but he answered Mr. Roosevelt's two questions by making two promises and coupling them with the expectation of further American help:

> * we shall never surrender, and even if, which I do not for a moment believe, this island or a large part of it were subjugated * then our Empire beyond the seas, armed and guarded by the British Fleet, would carry on the struggle, until, in God's good time, the New World, with all its power and might, steps forth to the rescue and the liberation of the Old.

Mr. Roosevelt, writing some thirteen months later, made a guarded statement which supports the inference that there was a *quid pro quo* in these transactions. He said, [192]

> * So long as the friendly British Navy is in existence, we need not fear that the freedom of the seas will be endangered. [193] But if Great Britain were to fall, particularly if its Navy were to be surrendered or immobilized, the seas of the world might fall under Nazi domination.

* * * * * *

In June of 1940, as France was falling * [it] appeared to be perfectly clear. * that the chief hope upon which America could rely for the necessary time required to carry on this rearmament program was the continuance of the British resistance to the Nazis. * To gain that time it was necessary for Great Britain to maintain its defense, for if Britain were to fall it was clear that we would have to face the Nazis alone *.

Therefore the two great objectives—our own rearmament and our aid to Britain * —were tied together hand in hand.

Until we have the full details of all the exchanges between Mr. Roosevelt and Mr. Churchill, we can only conjecture whether Mr. Roosevelt sought from Mr. Churchill the original pledge about the continued existence of the British Navy in exchange for assistance from America, or whether it was Mr. Churchill who first asked for such further assistance [194] and, in exchange for it, offered in return the pledge about the British Navy. What is certain is that on the very next day, on June 5, Mr. Roosevelt's Attorney General, Mr. Robert H. Jackson, rendered an opinion that at least 600,000 army rifles and 2500 field guns, with ammunition, might be sold to England as "surplus."

This transaction, if such it was, was viewed by Mr. Churchill as merely a beginning. On June 5 Mr. Churchill cabled to the Canadian Prime Minister, Mr. Mackenzie King, and urged him to put pressure on Mr. Roosevelt—"our best friend"—for the desired destroyers, for airplanes, and to send some of the American Navy to Irish ports.[195] If America were in the war, Mr. Churchill emphasized, his promises just given would hold good, but if America remained neutral and England fell—out popped the bogey man—there would then be a pro-German cabinet and nobody could tell what would happen. The British Ambassador, Lord Lothian, was having further conversations with Mr. Roosevelt, no doubt in order to support Mr. Churchill's ungranted requests, and on June 9 Mr. Churchill cabled to him in the same sense as to Mr. King,[196] making the dread more specific. Not only would a pro-German cabinet surrender the British fleet; it would also surrender islands and naval bases which would threaten the United States, and this should be made very clear to Mr. Roosevelt.

Also, on June 5, the Germans having attacked the French along the Somme on a 125-mile front, Premier Reynaud telephoned Mr. Roosevelt and asked for help, particularly for more American airplanes. [197] What Mr. Roosevelt said, we do not know as yet, but on June 6, the next day, fifty Curtiss-Wright dive bombers, which had just been delivered to the Navy, and ninety-three light attack bombers, which had just been delivered to the Army, were ordered returned to their manufacturers in order to be sold to France and to Britain. [198]

On June 8 a spokesman in the United States for the Allied Purchasing Commission said that 2000 planes had thus far been delivered to the Allies, and that 6000 more were on order.

On June 9 Mr. Roosevelt wrote the chairman of the Federal Power Commission in order to ensure an "Adequate Supply of Electric Power in the Event of War Emergency," as the caption runs. [199] The letter itself referred to an "expansion of distribution systems to meet war industry requirements *." These two references to "war" were no doubt accidental and inadvertent slips, because the program of the moment was supposed to be referred to officially always as for "national defense."

On June 10 the Allied Purchasing Commission stated that, as the result of this ruling, there would be an immediate increase in the export of all kinds of munitions to the Allies. Mr. Roosevelt states that the material sent in the month of June to Great Britain alone had originally cost us $300,000,000 to manufacture, and that it presumably had a great effect upon the success of Great Britain's resistance in the summer and fall of 1940. [200] These weapons were in truth so "surplus" that our own Army at a later date, in August 1940, had to use dummy guns at its manoeuvres. General Marshall and Assistant Secretary of War Patterson began to feel that they had stretched the law to a breaking point in declaring American military material to be "surplus." [201]

On June 10, 1940, the day Italy declared war against France, Mr. Roosevelt was to deliver the commencement speech at the University of Virginia. [202] It may be assumed that he had had sufficient advance word of Mussolini's plans to be able to prepare his formal speech. It may likewise be assumed that it was anger and irritation over Mussolini's brusque treatment of his prior proposals, briefly and inadequately summarized in the speech, which led Mr. Roosevelt into making his attack on Italy—

> On this tenth day of June, 1940, the hand that held the dagger has struck it into the back of its neighbor.

The ensuing furore caused most people to overlook the far more important, if guarded, statement by Mr. Roosevelt of a further advance in his publicly professed policy:

> * we will extend to the opponents of force the material resources of this nation *.

But not all of the public clamor came from this side of the Atlantic. Premier Reynaud, who had again telephoned Mr. Roosevelt that day, [203] cabled him, [204] thanking him
* for the generous aid that you have decided to give us in aviation and armament.
Then, grandiloquently echoing Mr. Churchill, Premier Reynaud asserted, boastfully and erroneously,

> We shall fight in front of Paris; we shall fight behind Paris; we shall close ourselves in one of our provinces to fight and if we should be driven out of it we shall establish ourselves in North Africa to continue the fight and if necessary in our American possessions.

But, the Premier continued,

> * it is my duty to ask you for new and even larger assistance.

* I beseech you to declare publicly that the United States will give the Allies aid and material support by all means short of an expeditionary force. I beseech you to do this before it is too late. *

In justification of this expectation of aid, M. Reynaud quoted two paragraphs from Mr. Roosevelt's Chicago "quarantine" speech of October 5, 1937, and said in conclusion that "The hour has now come" to make "these" declarations good.

Next day, on June 11, Mr. Churchill cabled Mr. Roosevelt, asking him to say or to do something which would help France, and once again asking for American naval vessels to be sent to Irish ports. [205] Presumably in response to this appeal, eighty additional attack bombers were released by the Army on June 12 for use by the Allies.

This was, however, almost a supplementary message. Earlier in the day on June 11 Mr. Churchill had sent to Mr. Roosevelt a much longer cable in which, while he asked that hope be held out to France, he begged for the thirty or forty old destroyers which had been put into commission. [206] This was in the name of the "Common Cause," to which he welcomed Mr. Roosevelt as a new adherent. On June 12 Mr. Churchill cabled Mr. Roosevelt from France, saying that the situation was very serious, but that the French fleet was to be sent to Canada and that there was a prospect of resistance being continued from the French colonies. [207] Mr. Roosevelt was also asked to do his utmost to strengthen M. Reynaud.

Russia was busy capitalizing on these troubled times and gobbling up weak neighbors. In Europe, demands were made on Lithuania on June 12, 1940, and on Estonia and Latvia on June 16, which led to the swallowing up of these countries by the Soviet. On June 27, Rumania ceded Bessarabia and other territory to Russia. From Tokyo, Ambassador Grew had reported on June 3, 1940, [208] with reference to a rumored Russo-Japanese partition of China:

* It is reported that Russia made some such proposal to Japan last autumn and that Japan turned it down. Informants have told us that Russia has recently renewed the proposal, desiring a free hand to cope with eventualities in Europe, including the Balkans and the possibility of eventually having to fight the Germans for control of the Baku oil fields * . *

On June 10, 1940, Russia and Japan had signed a treaty delimiting the frontier between Manchukuo and Outer Mongolia: some observers inferred that Russia and Japan had settled their differences and were about to negotiate a neutrality treaty which would free Japan for adventures in any direction. [209]

On June 13 the French position was believed to be desperate, and the French Cabinet contemplated asking for an armistice. Mr. Churchill, Lord Halifax, and Lord Beaverbrook flew to Tours and conferred there with Premier Reynaud, who asked that France might be released from her agreement not to conclude a separate peace. Mr. Churchill argued rather desperately, trying to make the most he could of the possibility of help from America, or even of a declaration of war. [210] It was finally agreed that M. Reynaud would again appeal to Mr. Roosevelt and that Mr. Churchill would support the new appeal.

Late in the evening of June 13 Mr. Roosevelt's reply to the June 10 appeal was received. He declared that the United States was doing everything in its power to make available to the allied governments the material which they so urgently required, and that American efforts to do still more were being redoubled. He praised the resistance of the Anglo-French armies, suggested that that resistance should continue, whether from North Africa, the colonies, or the Atlantic, and drew attention to the combined strength and importance of the Anglo-French naval power. [211] Mr. Churchill felt that Mr. Roosevelt had now gone a long way and that the United States was deeply committed to enter the war if France should continue to participate in it.[212] To M. Reynaud he telegraphed that this message had committed America beyond recall.[213] But in order to make such a secret commitment binding, it needed to be publicly known. Accordingly Mr. Churchill at once replied to Mr. Roosevelt, stating that the French situation was critical, asking for support for M. Reynaud's June 13 appeal, praising Mr. Roosevelt's message fulsomely, and asking permission to publish it at once.[214]

On the evening of June 13 M. Reynaud broadcast that he had sent to Mr. Roosevelt "a new and final appeal," which Mr. Roosevelt omitted from his published papers. M. Reynaud set forth that France had to choose whether to continue resistance or seek an armistice.[215] If France was not saved Britain would probably be defeated, and the only way to avert this was to throw into the balance "this very day the weight of American power" and to send the American Navy across the Atlantic. M. Reynaud called for "clouds of war planes" to speed across the Atlantic "to crush the evil force that dominates Europe"; and he stated that each time he had asked Mr. Roosevelt to increase the American aid it had been done, which, he claimed, met with the approval of the American people. France, he said,

* has the right to turn to other democracies and to say: "We have claims on you."

He enquired whether the American people would

* hesitate still to declare themselves against Nazi Germany.

Finally he said that if Mr. Roosevelt could not give to France very quickly the certain assurance that the United States would enter the war within a very short time, "the fate of the world will change."

Paris fell on the next day, June 14, when Mr. Roosevelt replied.[216] He repeated that the United States had made it possible for the allied armies to obtain airplanes, artillery, and munitions during the weeks that had just passed, and promised that America would redouble its efforts so long as the allied governments continued to fight. He believed that he could say that every passing week would see additional munitions on their way to the allies, and as long as the French people continued to defend their liberty, so long could they rest assured that they would receive war supplies in ever-increasing quantities and kinds. And in accordance with established American policy we would not recognize any conquests of French territory or any attempts to infringe the independence of France. But, Mr. Roosevelt concluded, only the Congress could make any military commitments. On the same day Mr. Roosevelt sent in substance the same answer to Mr. Churchill,[217] and refused permission to publish his message to M. Reynaud.

Mr. Churchill was disappointed but persistent. He has written that he appreciated the great risks which Mr. Roosevelt ran; first, of being charged with violating the Constitution, and second, of losing the election "on which [the] fate [of Britain] depended."[218] But, notwithstanding these considerations, Mr. Churchill continued his pressure on Mr. Roosevelt in a cable sent on the night of June 14–15.[219] The original bogey man became twins: Hitler would likely compel the French government to surrender the French Navy. Mr. Churchill then embellished the circumstances under which Britain would also be compelled to surrender the British Navy, leaving the American Navy alone against the combined navies of Britain, Germany, Japan, France, and Italy. All this peril could be avoided by a declaration that the United States would enter the war if necessary. But in any event Britain should be given thirty-five American destroyers.

The nature of Mr. Roosevelt's reply, if any was made, is not known.

At noon on June 15 Mr. Roosevelt conferred with the British and French ambassadors for an hour. The discussion appears to have included: [220]

1. Whether French resistance would continue in North Africa, and elsewhere abroad, as M. Reynaud had boasted; and
2. What steps would be taken to prevent the French Navy from falling into German hands.

On June 16, 1940, Mr. Churchill sent a kind of circular message to the Prime Ministers of the four Dominions, [221] containing his estimate of the posture of the war at that moment, and expressing his hopes for the future. Absent from it was the threat of the contingent surrender of the British Navy, but very much present was the continuing hope that somehow the United States would be drawn into the war at some future time, perhaps because of the bloodshed and turmoil that would ensue from a German invasion of England.

Late in the day on June 16 the British proposed to the French an "Act of Union" between the two countries, in the hope of keeping the French in the war by a dramatic proposal. [222] As was becoming customary at that time, the proposed Franco-British Union intended to appeal to the United States

> * to fortify the economic resources of the Allies, and to bring her powerful material aid to the common cause.

These last two words were copied by Mr. Churchill from his June 11 cable to Mr. Roosevelt, which has been mentioned previously.

Meanwhile the French Cabinet was studying Mr. Roosevelt's cable of June 14, which had been received on June 15. [223] It was used as a strong argument by those who were in favor of asking Germany for terms. [224] They ultimately prevailed; the Cabinet resigned in consequence, and Marshal Pétain formed a new Cabinet for the purpose of obtaining an armistice from Germany, the terms of which it asked for on June 17. [225] On June 17 Mr. Roosevelt sent a message to the new Cabinet concerning the disposition of the French Navy. He said that if France should fail to get its Navy out of the way of its enemy before it concluded an armistice it would not only fatally impair the preservation of the French Empire and the eventual restoration of French independence, but also

> * the French Government will permanently lose the friendship and good-will of the United States. [226]

On the same day Mr. Roosevelt sent to M. Reynaud an unpublished message which expressed his personal regret over the fall of the Cabinet and the cessation of French resistance. [227]

Also on June 17, 1940, the War Department sent word to General Herron at Hawaii to alert his entire organization immediately "to deal with possible trans-Pacific raid." [228] Two days later the alert was eased up. [229]

The extent of American political and military confusion at this time is revealed by the minutes of a conference of certain Generals in General Marshall's office on the morning of June 17, 1940. [230]

> [General Marshall] remarked that in going over the various possibilities it seems that we may suddenly find Japan and Russia appear as a team operating to hold our ships in the Pacific. If the French navy goes to Germany and Italy, we will have a very serious situation in the South Atlantic. Germany may rush the South American situation to a head in a few weeks.
>
> Are we not forced into a question of reframing our naval policy, that is, purely defensive action in the Pacific with a main effort on the Atlantic side. There is the possibility of raids with resultant public reaction. The main effort may be south of Trinidad, with any action north thereof purely on the basis of a diversion to prevent our sending material to South America. This seems to indicate that we are reaching a point where we should mobilize the National Guard.

General Strong stated that the Navy reports that they have a definite information that the French Fleet has already been turned over to and incorporated in the British fleet. (NOTE: Later information from the Navy Department indicates that this is questionable.) If this is so, and if the next move of the Germans, possibly through Ireland, results in the capitulation of Great Britain proper, the combined Atlantic fleets may move to the western hemisphere. In this case, they must operate from our ports as there are no others adequate. *

[General Marshall] commented that if the British and French fleets come here the Navy point of view is OK; if not, it is all wrong. We have to be prepared to meet the worst situation that may develop, that is, if we do not have the Allied fleet in the Atlantic.

* * * * * *

Both General Andrews and General Strong recommend ordering the National Guard into Federal service. General Strong anticipates a desperate need within 60 days for troops in South America (Brazil and Uruguay). [General Marshall] thought that although we cannot at once send expeditions, we might be able to guarantee to some of the South American governments the occupation and holding of certain key ports.

With respect to further equipment for the Allies as per the President's statement, we have scraped the bottom so far as the Army is concerned.

On June 18 M. Paul Baudouin, then the French Minister for Foreign Affairs, gave the desired assurance to Ambassador Biddle

* in the name of the French Government in the most solemn manner that the French fleet would never be surrendered to the enemy. [231]

On June 18 and 19 von Ribbentrop, who wanted peace, told Count Ciano of [232]

vague contacts between London and Berlin by means of Sweden.

On June 19 identical notes were delivered to the German and Italian Governments by the American representatives in their capitals. After mentioning the French request for an armistice the note referred to the Monroe Doctrine and stated that the United States would neither recognize nor acquiesce in any transfer of territory in the Western Hemisphere from one non-American power to another. [233]

On June 20 Mr. Roosevelt urged Congress to enact a pending bill to provide government marine war-risk insurance, [234] much of which was written in London, for American vessels, cargoes, and crews, on the ground that such private insurance might "suddenly" become unavailable. Also on June 20, although Mr. Roosevelt omits all mention of it in his papers, he formed a "coalition" cabinet by nominating two Republicans to it. The first was the elderly Mr. Stimson as Secretary of War, in place of Mr. Woodring, who complained that he had been ousted because he refused to strip the nation of its defenses in order to aid the Allies. The second appointment was that of Mr. Knox as Secretary of the Navy, in place of Mr. Edison. This manoeuvre was of course largely political and was designed to create confusion in the Republican national convention which was to convene at Philadelphia on Monday, June 24. But it was not wholly party politics. Both of the new nominees were ardent interventionists. In May 1940 Colonel Knox, with the approval of Mr. Roosevelt, had announced a plan to train ten thousand civilians as airplane pilots. Mr. Stimson had for long advocated peace-time conscription, and Mr. Roosevelt was now about to thrust it on the nation.

On June 20 a bill was introduced in the Senate to compel peace-time conscription: it was essentially the same bill which had been drafted in September and October 1939 and since then had been held in abeyance to await a favorable time for introduction. From Mr. Roosevelt's point of view such a law was necessary because, if enlistments in the Army are any criterion of the state of public opinion, the country was still overwhelmingly against Mr. Roosevelt's policies. The Army's recruiting drive had ended in dismal failure: only nine thousand men had enlisted in six weeks, including 364 of New York's seven million people. [235] In North Carolina there was only one enlistment for every ten thousand males of enlistment age: in Montana it was .0014 per ten thousand, and in Michigan it was .00008, the lowest in the country. [236]

Mr. Roosevelt opened this new campaign cautiously, and began by reverting to the ideas of government service which he had already proposed during his original militarist era, that of the First World War. He did this at a press conference on June 18, 1940, [237] but has omitted the transcript from his published papers. There had been an editorial in the New York *Times* of Sunday, June 16, [238] which had advocated compulsory military training under the title "The Need To Be Ready," and Mr. Roosevelt had remarked that he liked the idea. Now, cautiously, he said that he supposed he should not have spoken so fast, and should not have said "military." He didn't mean that everybody should be trained as an infantryman, a machine gunner, or a flier, because there must be others behind the lines helping with the supplies. Perhaps he had meant military training, but not combat training. Non-uniformed young people should necessarily be trained to work in clothing factories, in airplane factories, in conservation, and so forth. We are undoubtedly coming to some form of government service for everyone in each class, said Mr. Roosevelt. Even service for eighteen to twenty-year-old girls was being studied. It will be noted how the military aspect of such conscription was minimized and kept in the background by Mr. Roosevelt, although it was his primary objective—an excellent illustration of the Rooseveltian technique.

It was at this time that the veil of secrecy parted on the destroyer deal with Britain. Senator Walsh broke the story on June 21, 1940, and stated [239] that it had been discovered "only by the merest accident." About the middle of June 1940 the Senate Naval Affairs Committee had heard rumors that American destroyers were to be transferred to a foreign power, but the Navy flatly denied it. Then, according to Senator Walsh, he received a telephone call from the Assistant Secretary of the Navy, Mr. Lewis Compton, who said that, on his own authority, he had disposed of eleven motor torpedo boats and twelve submarine chasers. The negotiations for transferring these smaller vessels had been pending only for about three weeks, but the negotiations for transferring the destroyers had been commenced about the middle of March [*sic!*] 1940. Mr. Compton denied that he had consulted Mr. Roosevelt in any way. Thereupon Mr. Early said that Mr. Roosevelt had personally approved of the sale, but on June 24, 1940, Mr. Roosevelt called off the deal. In consequence Section 14 was added to the Naval Appropriations Act of June 28, 1940, to prevent such transfers of naval vessels.

Meanwhile another deal was in the making, a transfer of twenty of our newest and fastest light torpedo boats to Britain, but the Attorney General, Mr. Jackson, could not as yet discover any plausible authority for doing this. It was abandoned, but another and more extensive scheme was shortly to be improvised. In addition to this proposed deal there was already some evidence, as has been mentioned, that our Navy was secretly cooperating with the British Navy.

On June 21 Mr. Roosevelt issued a statement [240] suggesting the creation of an "inter-American organization, an export corporation with a capital of one or two billion dollars, in order to protect

* our economy and the economies of the other American Republics from the repercussions of the disturbed international situation.

This proposal Mr. Roosevelt wrapped in the cloak of

* a part of a program of economic defense designed to supplement our military defense program. *

Nothing came of this impulsive scheme to create an all-American cartel. It quietly faded into oblivion.

On June 22, 1940, the French signed an armistice with Germany in the forest of Compiégne at the same place where, and in the same railroad car in which, the armistice ending the First World War had been signed.

This foreseen development had been causing disquieting thoughts in the minds of responsible Americans in the Navy. Suppose that the worst should happen? Ought not preparations to be made now in order to maintain the British Navy if, in accordance with Mr. Churchill's promise, it was withdrawn to the western Atlantic? Ought not ammunition to fit the calibres of the British guns and appropriate spare parts for repairs to be stockpiled here? These or similar questions were raised with the British Ambassador, and by him transmitted to Mr. Churchill, whose answer, on June 22, 1940, was a curt refusal. [241] When, coupled with this refusal to take any preliminary steps to implement his promise, one is informed that even as of seven months later there was not even the vestige of any plan for transferring the British Government overseas, [242] one may well ask oneself searching questions as to the worth of the promises which Mr. Churchill had given. In some extenuation it should be pointed out that the British Prime Minister believed himself to be in a desperate situation, and that he was doing whatever he could to obtain assistance for his own country. Even as of this time the bogey continued to appear. To Mr. King, the Canadian Prime Minister, Mr. Churchill cabled on June 24, denying that any bargain could be made about the British Navy with the United States. [243] Instead, Mr. King was urged to impress on Mr. Roosevelt the danger that if Mr. Churchill's government fell, after being deserted by the United States, the successor government would make peace with Germany on German terms. It is perhaps not unjust to Mr. Churchill to suggest that he did not intend to sell his promise as to the British Navy once and for all; rather he intended to sell it day by day and over and over again. This same leitmotif was impressed by Mr. Churchill on Lord Lothian under date of June 28. [244] The British Ambassador was instructed never to cease to impress on Mr. Roosevelt—even though "We know President is our best friend *"—that if Britain was successfully invaded and largely occupied some new cabinet would make peace by surrendering the British Navy, and Britain would become a German protectorate. Then, although the weapons already mentioned were now on the high seas, [245] Mr. Churchill complained that

> * We have really not had any help worth speaking of from the United States so far. *

Meanwhile steps were being taken in the United States to move forward the production of war materials. On June 27, 1940, the National Defense Research Committee was created to "correlate and support scientific research on the mechanisms and devices of warfare," and the development of the atom bomb and of bacteriological warfare commenced. [246] On June 28 the Rubber Reserve Company and the Metals Reserve Company were created as subsidiaries of the Reconstruction Finance Corporation. Later the Defense Plant Corporation was created, on August 22, and the Defense Supplies Corporation on August 29.

Also on June 28 Mr. Hull had a conversation with Lord Lothian and with the Australian Minister in which policy against Japan was discussed.[247] Mr. Hull stated that the United States had been exerting economic pressure against Japan for a year; that the United States had stationed its fleet in the Pacific, and that everything possible was being done to contain Japan "short of a serious risk of actual military hostilities." This course, he added, was the best evidence of the intentions of the United States in the future. As of this time Mr. T. V. Soong had been at Washington for several weeks pleading for the gift of war planes to China.[248]

In order to limit the danger of fifth-column activities, an unprecedented Alien Registration Act was passed, and on June 29 it was approved by Mr. Roosevelt.[249]

So ended June. It had been a bewildering and sobering month for Mr. Roosevelt. He had been "astounded" by the collapse of France[250] and, we may safely assume, by the ensuing frenzy. This is reflected in his *Public Papers*, which, as printed, number 644 pages for the calendar year, but less than 23 for June: no mention is made in them of most of the important events of that month.

The downfall of France was followed by peace manoeuvres. Some came to England from the Pope through Switzerland before June 28, and were brusquely repulsed.[251] Notwithstanding this, there was confusion in Europe and in Washington. Whether the outcome would be peace or a German victory seemed to depend on what Hitler might decide, and if he should decide for peace, on what terms he might offer.[252] No one could be sure until he spoke.

Hand in hand with the possibility of peace went the rations for war. It was probably at this time[253] that General Marshall and Admiral Stark sent a military and naval mission to Britain, composed of Generals George V. Strong (Assistant Chief of the United States Army Staff and Assistant Chief of the United States War Plans Division) and Delos C. Emmons (of the Air Corps), together with Admiral Robert L. Ghormley. Nominally it was an exploratory mission, but out of it the secret joint Anglo-American staff plans of January 1941 ensued. After Lend-Lease had been enacted our military and naval personnel was "ostensibly" [254] connected with it, but Admiral Ghormley, for example, was working with the British Admiralty on what the American Navy was secretly doing in the Atlantic. We are indeed told by an official publication that after the fall of France the first American objective "was to keep Britain and her fleet in being as fighting entities." [255] Concern with the French Navy was also serious as July 1940 began.

Thus on July 1 Ambassador Bullitt received assurances from President Le Brun that "France would under no conditions deliver the fleet to Germany"; from Marshal Pétain that orders had been issued to every captain in the French Navy to sink his ship rather than to permit it to fall into German hands, and from Admiral Darlan that he had "given absolute orders to the officers of his fleet to sink immediately any ship that the Germans should attempt to seize." [256] Yet on the other hand one of the terms of the German-French Armistice required that the French ships should be collected in specified ports and there disarmed under German-Italian control. Which would prevail? The French ships were widely dispersed. Some were in English ports, some were at Alexandria, some at Oran, some at Algiers, some at and near Martinique; one capital ship lay at Casablanca and another at Dakar. Britain decided to take immediate action, probably with Mr. Roosevelt's previous knowledge. [257] The ships in England were seized, and those at Alexandria were immobilized. Those at Martinique were observed and for all practical purposes blockaded by American ships; they were later immobilized by agreement. At Oran a note was presented to the French Admiral in command offering him several choices, one of which was to entrust the French ships to the United States until the end of the war. [258] He refused, and the

British attacked the French on July 3, 1940. Most of the French ships were sunk or destroyed, but one escaped to Toulon, as did the ships at Algiers. The great battleship at Dakar was injured but neither sunk nor captured. Both Foreign Minister Baudouin and Premier Pétain protested vehemently to Mr. Roosevelt, apparently believing that he had some connection with, or influence on, British action. [259] On July 5 France broke off diplomatic relations with Great Britain as the consequence of this attack.

Next, and on July 1, Mr. Roosevelt approached one facet of paying for the cost of armaments, and he recommended [260]

> * the enactment of a steeply graduated excess profits tax *.

On July 2 Mr. Roosevelt by proclamation prohibited the export of arms, ammunition, war implements, basic materials, chemicals, various products, and machine tools except under license. [261] Annotating this document a year later, he said that it had been used to promote "the policy of helping Great Britain," [262] and by clear implication that it had prevented any exports to Germany and Italy. On the same day Mr. Knox and Mr. Stimson appeared respectively before the Senate's Naval Affairs and Military Affairs Committees. They gave guardedly cautious statements as to their opinions concerning intervention, and were confirmed. In about three weeks Mr. Johnson, the Assistant Secretary of War, who had been at odds with Mr. Woodring, also resigned.

On July 3, 1940, Count Ciano asked Ambassador Phillips whether the United States was ready to enter the war. He replied [263]

> * For the moment we don't intend to enter the conflict. We are arming on a very large scale, and are helping the British in every way. However, some new fact might decide our intervention, such as a bombardment of London with many victims among the civilian population. *

Mr. Roosevelt's press conference of July 5 saw the first public revelation of the "five freedoms," four suggested by him, and the fifth, which he immediately adopted, by a reporter. It is not without significance that when Mr. Roosevelt edited these "freedoms" six months later, he edited out his own "terribly important" first freedom, freedom of information. [264] A reporter had asked Mr. Roosevelt what his own peace desiderata were, and after a long and rather wistful disquisition upon the "extremely efficient * corporate state" and the necessary inefficiency of a representative government, Mr. Roosevelt said: [265]

> * you might say there are certain freedoms. The first I would call "freedom of information," which is terribly important. It is a much better phrase than "freedom of the press" * . * you will never have a completely stable world without freedom of knowledge, freedom of information.
>
> The second, of course, is freedom of religion * . *
>
> Then, a third freedom is the freedom to express one's self as long as you don't advocate the overthrow of Government. *
>
> Fourth, freedom from fear, so that people won't be afraid of being bombed from the air or attacked * . * disarmament. *
>
> * * * * * *
>
> Does that cover it pretty well?'
>
> Q. [Mr. Harkness] Well, I had a fifth in mind which you might describe as "freedom from want"—free trade, opening up trade?
>
> The President: Yes, that is true. I had that in mind but forgot it. * That is the fifth, very definitely.

By this time Mr. Roosevelt was contemplating asking for additional appropriations for "defense" for the third time in eight weeks. The amount of over four billion, eight hundred million dollars which Mr. Roosevelt on July 10, 1940, asked Congress to appropriate [266] was almost double the two prior additional appropriations combined. As in his previous request Mr. Roosevelt did not attempt to itemize or even lump these figures. In his message, after refusing to attempt to define the word "defense," Mr. Roosevelt rehearsed some of his remarks during the prior eighteen months. In a reprise of the theme of his September 21, 1939, speech, Mr. Roosevelt said:

> * I said that this Government must lose no time or effort to keep this nation from being drawn into the war, and I asserted my belief that we would succeed in these efforts. We have succeeded. I believe we shall continue to succeed.

And as he came to the middle of his speech, he proclaimed,

> That we are opposed to war is known not only to every American, but to every government in the world. We will not use our arms in a war of aggression; we will not send our men to take part in European wars.

Mr. Roosevelt then gave a "broad outline [of] our immediate objectives":

1. * to build up the Navy to meet any possible combination of hostile naval forces."
2. To equip an army of 1,200,000 men, "though of course this total of men would not be in the Army in time of peace."
3. To procure reserve stocks of equipment for a further 800,000 men "if a mobilization of such a force should become necessary."
4. To provide manufacturing facilities for this equipment, and to produce the ordnance required for the aircraft program.
5. To procure 15,000 additional Army planes and 4000 additional Navy planes.

This being a public address, Mr. Roosevelt then skated swiftly over the thin ice of the pending draft act, saying, with the appearance of casualness:

> * The Congress is now considering the enactment of a system of selective training for developing the necessary man power to operate this matériel, and man power to fill army non-combat needs. In this way we can make certain that when this modern matériel becomes available, it will be placed in the hands of troops trained, seasoned, and ready, and that replacement matériel can be guaranteed.

Mr. Roosevelt then praised the efficiency of his own administration, and concluded his speech by calling on the country for sacrifice, hard work, and unity.

VI. "AGAIN AND AGAIN AND AGAIN"

1. THE VOICE FROM THE SEWERS

THE SCOPE OF THIS CHAPTER is such that it will only be noted here that it was not until after the Democratic National Convention had met at Chicago that Senator Barkley, on July 16, 1940, by authority of Mr. Roosevelt, announced that "He Does Not Seek to Be a Candidate for a Third Term." [1] The hollowness of this pretense was universally recognized. Mr. Roosevelt, having been nominated on the first ballot, spoke to the convention over the radio at 12:25 A.M. on July 19 [2] and carried forward the sham. As Commander-in-Chief of the Army and Navy he had lain awake many nights asking himself if he could decline to serve his country, but his conscience would not let him turn his back on a call to service if the people should draft him. This speech did not refer to the Democratic platform's qualified anti-war plank, unanimously passed, but Mr. Roosevelt in his later campaign speeches at Washington on

September 11 and at Philadelphia on October 23 adopted it and quoted it: ³

> We will not participate in foreign wars, and we will not send our Army, naval or air forces to fight in foreign lands outside of the Americas, except in case of attack.

The Republican Party's plank on this topic was altogether unqualified. It read: ⁴

> The Republican Party is firmly opposed to involving this nation in foreign war.

It is a revealing fact that Mr. Roosevelt, who had asked Mr. Byrnes to represent him at the convention, was particularly interested in the phraseology of the anti-war plank. As introduced, that plank lacked the final weasel clause, "except in case of attack," which Mr. Byrnes had originated and suggested. Mr. Byrnes had telephoned Mr. Roosevelt three times on this topic ⁵ and, over Mr. Hull's reluctance, secured Mr. Roosevelt's consent to accept the qualified and weakened anti-war plank because

> * it was the best we could hope for. The alternative would be a bitter fight in the convention that would disclose a serious split in the President's party and impair his prestige abroad.*

In some respects the Democratic convention at Chicago had marked the nadir of American political life. Publicly Mr. Roosevelt was sitting aloof in Washington, playing the gaunt Lincolnian part of a President toiling under the burden of affairs of state too great to be borne by one harassed man, too great to leave him any time to participate in the petty intrigues of party politics. Privately Mr. Roosevelt had arranged for a direct wire ⁶ to the Chicago room of his house guest since May, Mr. Harry Hopkins (then Secretary of Commerce), and kept himself minutely informed of the manoeuverings and intrigues of the city machine bosses, Kelly, Nash, Flynn, and Hague, [7] who had combined with the high-minded idealists and reformers of his official family, such as Secretaries Wallace, Ickes, Perkins, Hopkins, and Attorney-General Jackson, to engineer his "draft." It was an example of Mr. Roosevelt's deviousness. When Mr. Morgenthau had complained to Mr. Roosevelt that "sometimes it seems to me that your right hand doesn't know what your left hand is doing," Mr. Roosevelt had replied, "I always make it a practice to keep one hand on top of the desk and one hand under it." [8]

"America Needs Roosevelt," screamed the signs with which Boss Kelly had plastered the Chicago walls and store windows. "We Want Roosevelt—The Whole World Needs Roosevelt!" boomed the secret stooge voice of the Chicago Superintendent of Sewers, the henchman of Kelly and Nash, over his clandestinely connected microphone. The shabbiness of it suggested Fascist tactics,

> * the welcome that is given him by "the applauding squad," which was very well mobilized by the police commissioner. [9]

The same pretense was perpetuated by Mr. Roosevelt in his acceptance speech, [10] which referred to a

> * deep personal desire for retirement * . * one world crisis after another * . * no call of Party alone would prevail upon me to accept reelection to the Presidency. * my conscience will not let me turn my back upon a call to service. * Only the people themselves can draft a President. *

> * it has become my duty to remain either in the White House itself or at some near-by point where I can reach Washington and even Europe and Asia by direct telephone—where, if need be, I can be back at my desk in the space of a very few hours. *

* I shall not have the time or the inclination to engage in purely political debate. But I shall never be loath to call the attention of the nation to deliberate or unwitting falsifications of fact, which are sometimes made by political candidates.

In 1916 a man of great personal integrity, President Wilson, had felt moral scruples against conducting a political campaign from the White House, [11] because, in the American spirit of fair play, he felt that it gave one candidate an immense and an unfair advantage over the other candidate. Prompted by these decent and scrupulous motives, Mr. Wilson therefore removed himself and his family in the summer of 1916 from the White House to a rented home at Spring Lake, N. J., from which he conducted his political campaign. With Mr. Roosevelt the the situation was not the same. He was not only "remote alike from religion and philosophy"; [12] he was remote alike from fair play and scruples, when it came to politics. [13] Mr. Roosevelt proposed to campaign and did campaign with the prestige which the presidency and the aura of the White House could confer upon him. But between the concentrated excitement of the national convention and the hullabaloo of the campaign there lay an outwardly seeming lull of eight weeks.

2. "PEACE DURING THE NEXT FOUR YEARS"

Domestic American political matters were beginning to come to the fore by the time Mr. Roosevelt had signed the peace-time draft act on September 16. Mr. Willkie had commenced to assert that while Mr. Roosevelt intended to get the nation into war, he, Mr. Willkie, would do no such thing. Mr. Willkie said at Rushville, on September 7, 1940, forthrightly, that

> If I am President I shall never lead this country into war.

and at Chicago on September 13,

If you elect me President I will never send an American boy to fight in any European war.

Mr. Willkie had admittedly got off to a poor and a fumbling start in his campaign, but he was now coming up fast from behind: tens of thousands of independent voters were rallying to him with an enthusiastic fervor not seen in politics in eight years. His warnings were not only being heeded; they were making converts. It was time for Mr. Roosevelt to bestir himself, abandon all the pretense of being "drafted," and actively seek election.

In the endeavor to portray himself to the Republic as the zealous Commander-in-Chief, Mr. Roosevelt prepared a selection of well-publicized junkets to "inspect" plants, shipyards, and factories. The first trip was made at the end of July, [14] ten days after he had accepted the third-term nomination; there were two in August (six cities in five states), three in September (five places in three states), six in October (eleven cities in eight states), and one on Saturday, November 2, [15] three days before election. Then they abruptly ceased, in much the same manner as in previous years the padding of relief payrolls had ceased soon after election day.

They were occasions such as Mr. Roosevelt's political address on September 11 [16] to the convention of the A. F. of L. Teamsters Union, where, with a straight face, he said,

I do not know whether this is a political speech or not. I do not know *.

And he then appealed for the political support of the Teamsters on the ground that he was the champion of the laboring man against the employer, narrating at considerable length the things which he claimed to have done for the benefit of "organized labor," and promising labor "certain definite" benefits "in the near future." The second principal topic of the Teamsters speech was "defense," and in answer to Mr. Willkie, whom he did not name, Mr. Roosevelt denied his charges and repeated his own older themes, giving the nation new and additional pledges of peace in these words:

> In all these plans for national defense, only those who seek to play upon the fears of the American people, discover an attempt to lead us into war. The American people will reject that kind of propaganda of fear *. *
>
> I hate war, now more than ever. I have one supreme determination—to do all that I can to keep war away from these shores for all time. I stand, with my party, and outside my party as President of all the people, on the platform, the wording that was adopted in Chicago less than two months ago.

When, on the occasion of receiving an honorary degree from the University of Pennsylvania on September 20, 1940, Mr. Roosevelt addressed the convocation, [17] his speech was almost demagoguery, as he belittled the value of the opinions of educated men and quoted what he said the President of Harvard University had told him a quarter of a century previously:

> * if the ballot were to be confined to the holders of college degrees, the Nation would go on the rocks in a very few years—

while he extolled the value of the opinions of uneducated people. It seems clear that Mr. Roosevelt was aware of the fact shown by various surveys that the percentage of those who voted for him was greatest in the least educated group, and that the percentage of his support progressively decreased in the more educated groups and reached its lowest point amongst those with the best educations.

At the dedication of the Washington airport on September 28, 1940, Mr. Roosevelt referred to the planes which had flown overhead, and observed, [18]

They are here upon a peaceful mission. We all hope that their missions will always be in the ways of peace. We shall strive with all our energies and skills to see to it that they are never called upon for missions of war. But the more of them we have, the less likely we are to have to use them—the less likely are we to be attacked from abroad.

The improvement in Mr. Willkie's chances, implying the possibility of Mr. Roosevelt's defeat at the polls, revealed the bad sportsmanship of some New Dealers, both high and low, which was evidenced by abuse, vilification, and even personal assaults. Critics of Mr. Roosevelt were called appeasers, fifth columnists and even traitors. The curmudgeonly Puritan, Mr. Ickes, sneered that Mr. Willkie was

> The rich man's Roosevelt. *The simple barefoot Wall Street lawyer.

The Christ-like Mr. Wallace (as the principal proponent of a peacetime draft,[19] Senator Pepper, once characterized him)[20] intemperately vilified Mr. Willkie as a pro-Hitlerite and said in substance that Mr. Willkie was Hitler's candidate. Government employees[21] and other supporters of Mr. Roosevelt threw fruit, eggs, and even a metal basket at the opposition's candidate.

On October 12, in the course of one of his "inspections," Mr. Roosevelt spoke over the radio on "hemisphere defense,"[22] and once again he interjected political matters into his speech in order to defend himself again against Mr. Willkie's charges; once again he spoke in defense of his peaceable purposes. Mr. Roosevelt declaimed,

> There are some in every single one of the twenty-one American Republics who suggest that the course the Americas are following is slowly drawing one or all of us into war with some nation, or nations, beyond the seas.

> The clear facts have been stated over and over again. This country wants no war with any nation. This hemisphere wants no war with any nation. *
>
> For many long years every ounce of energy I have had has been devoted to keeping this nation and the other Republics at peace with the rest of the world. That is what continues uppermost in my mind today—the objective for which I hope and work and pray.
>
> We arm to defend ourselves. The strongest reason for that is that it is the strongest guarantee for peace.

Without naming Mr. Willkie, Mr. Roosevelt then called him an appeaser:

> It can no longer be disputed that forces of evil which are bent on conquest of the world will destroy whomever and whenever they can destroy. * We know now that if we seek to appease them by withholding aid from those who stand in their way, we only hasten the day of their attack upon us.
>
> The people of the United States * reject the doctrine of appeasement. They recognize it for what it is—a major weapon of the aggressor nations.
>
> I speak bluntly. *
>
> That is why we arm. Because, I repeat, this nation wants to keep war away from these two continents. Because we, all of us, are determined to do everything possible to maintain peace *. Because great strength of arms is the practical way of fulfilling our hopes for peace and for staying out of this war or any other war. *

But Mr. Willkie continued to gain, to gain so fast that almost all pretense of a reluctant man submitting to a "draft" had to be abandoned. Mr. Roosevelt found himself forced to campaign personally or else not be "drafted." He therefore called in the reporters [23] on October 18 and issued a "White House Release" stating [24] that he would personally campaign. The "White House Release" attempted to preserve a few shreds of the political fiction that Mr. Roosevelt would not campaign, but anger appears to be the dominant note. It ran:

> In the speech of acceptance to the Democratic Convention on July 19, 1940, the President said:
>
> "I shall not have the time or the inclination to engage in any purely political debate. But I shall never be loath to call the attention of the nation to deliberate or unwitting falsifications of fact."
>
> There has been in this campaign, however, a systematic program of falsification of fact by the opposition. The President does not believe that it has been an unwitting falsification of fact. He believes it is a deliberate falsification of fact.
>
> He has, therefore, decided to tell the American people what these misrepresentations have been and in what respect they are false. With that purpose in mind, the President will make five speeches between now and election day.

The reader will not fail to notice how, unlike President Wilson, Mr. Roosevelt attempted to envelope his own candidacy to be "drafted" with the aura of the White House and with the prestige of the presidential office.

In fact Mr. Roosevelt made a great many more than five speeches. Some of the additional speeches are printed in his papers; [25] others are merely referred to. [26] Those which are printed, such as the "remarks" at Wilmington, [27] are usually campaign speeches: they seldom purport to correct any pretended misrepresentations of fact.

The first of Mr. Roosevelt's longer campaign speeches was made at Philadelphia on Wednesday, October 23, 1940. [28] It covered a great deal more ground than pretended misrepresentations. The opening gambit was a statement of the responsibilities of the president, day and night, in crises and in possibilities of crises in world affairs. Then followed a brief résumé of the "White House Release," after which there were some moral generalities. Next came some straw-man denials, with a reprise of the leitmotif that "the only thing we have to fear is fear itself." At the end of this portion there were some denials, which ran as follows:

> My friends, the Presidency is not a prize to be won by mere glittering promises. It is not a commodity to be sold by high-pressure salesmanship and national advertising. The Presidency is a most sacred trust and it ought not to be dealt with on any level other than an appeal to reason and humanity.
>
> The worst bombshell of fear which the Republican leaders have let loose on this people is the accusation that this Government of ours, a Government of Republicans and Democrats alike, without the knowledge of the Congress or of the people, has secretly entered into agreements with foreign nations. They even intimate that such commitments * have pledged in some way the participation of the United States in some foreign war. It seems almost unnecessary to deny such a charge. But so long as the fantastic misstatement has been made, I must brand it for what it is.
>
> I give to you and to the people of this country this most solemn assurance: There is no secret treaty, no secret obligation, no secret commitment, no secret understanding in any shape or form, direct or indirect, with any other Government, or any other nation in any part of the world, to involve this nation in any war or for any other purpose.

* * * * * *

Tonight there is one more false charge—one outrageously false charge—that has been made to strike terror into the hearts of our citizens. It is a charge that offends every political and religious conviction that I hold dear. It is the charge that this Administration wishes to lead this country into war.

That charge is contrary to every fact, every purpose of the past eight years. Throughout these years my every act and thought have been directed to the end of preserving the peace of the world, and more particularly, the peace of the United States—the peace of the Western Hemisphere.

* * * * * *

To Republicans and Democrats, to every man, woman and child in the nation I say this: Your President and your Secretary of State are following the road to peace.

We are arming ourselves not for any foreign war. [Here Mr. Roosevelt repeated his stand on, and quoted again the peace plank of the Democratic platform.]

It is for peace that I have labored; and it is for peace that I shall labor all the days of my life.

So ended the speech. The reader may form his own opinion as to which candidate was making "deliberate falsifications of fact."

There were other passages in the Philadelphia speech, which had been almost verbally lifted from Mr. Roosevelt's campaign speeches of eight years previously. But there were two paragraphs which, in the light of the war shortages so soon to come, deserve perverse commemoration because every item (save one) specifically mentioned by Mr. Roosevelt later became difficult or impossible to obtain:

> * the American people this year are building more homes, are buying more pairs of shoes, more washing machines, more electric refrigerators * more textile products than in the boom year of 1929.
>
> This year there is being placed on the tables of America more butter, more cheese, more meat, more canned goods—more food in general than in that luxurious year of 1929.

On Monday, October 28, Mr. Roosevelt made at Madison Square Garden the second of his five longer speeches,[29] one of the most equivocal of his career.[30] In it he largely referred to what he had said and done prior to 1937, and on the basis of that obsolete record he claimed to be a consistent lover of peace: indeed his final paragraph, according to his current formula, was a promise of future peace. He said:

Today our Navy is at a peak of efficiency and fighting strength. *

* * * * * *

For eight years our main concern, as you know and as the nation knows, has been to look for peace and the preservation of peace.

Back in 1935, in the face of growing dangers throughout the world, your Government undertook to eliminate certain hazards which in the past had led us into war.

By the Neutrality Act of 1935, and by other steps:

We made it possible to prohibit American citizens from travelling on vessels belonging to countries at war. Was that right?

We made it clear that American investors, who put their money into enterprises in foreign nations, could not call on American warships or American soldiers to bail out their investments. Was that right?

We made it clear that ships flying the American flag could not carry munitions to a belligerent; and that they must stay out of war zones. Was that right?

In all these ways we made it clear to every American, and to every foreign nation that we would avoid becoming entangled through some episode beyond our borders.

Those were measures to keep us at peace. And through all the years since 1935, there has been no entanglement and there will be no entanglement.

* * * * * *

I am asking the American people to support a continuance of this type of affirmative, realistic fight for peace. *

And here Mr. Roosevelt referred cuttingly to

* those who * are willing recklessly to imply that our boys are already on their way to the transports.

He was, he claimed, engaged in an

* affirmative search for peace * . * [mobilizing] every active force for peace in all the world. [including] * the greatest force of all—religious faith, devotion to God.

Therefore, Mr. Roosevelt promised, in concluding,

We go forward with firm faith, And we shall continue to go forward in peace.

At Boston Mr. Roosevelt made his third long speech on Wednesday, October 30. [31] It was a mélange of claimed efficiency in increasing the Navy, a kind mention of the Boston Navy Yard, a claim of speed and efficiency in providing equipment for the Army, a pledge which will be quoted below, a boast about airplane engine output, an announcement of increased British purchases of armaments, a pat on the back for "that Boston boy," Ambassador Kennedy, further reprises from the theme songs of the 1932 campaign speeches, some slurs at Representative Martin of Massachusetts, and a confused ending in which freedom and peace and love and laughter faced the future with confidence and courage, waving the American flag—a good example of what Mr. Roosevelt delighted to call "glittering generalities," or, cynically, "turning on the old record" again.

The pledge, which to this day evokes memories in many an American home, came a little before the middle of the speech. The draft numbers of young American civilians had been drawn only the day before, and already there were reports of lagging and poor construction of the barracks in the Army camps to be. This, said Mr. Roosevelt, was a

> * brazen charge * . * the most inexcusable, most unpatriotic misstatement of fact about our Army—a misstatement calculated to worry the mothers of the Nation * . *

Mr. Roosevelt "very simply and very honestly" assured the mothers and fathers of America,

> * that each and every one of their boys in training will be well housed and well fed.
>
> Throughout that year of training, there will be constant promotion of their health and their well-being.

And then, carried on by his own political necessities, Mr. Roosevelt proclaimed another pledge:

> And while I am talking to you mothers and fathers, I give you one more assurance.
>
> I have said this before, but I shall say it again and again and again:
>
> Your boys are not going to be sent into any foreign wars.

Mr. Sherwood thought that this speech was even "equivocal" than the second one, and he was ashamed of it. [22] Mr. Roosevelt's more ardent defenders have been apologetic about it. Perhaps by now there can be general agreement that there was

> * a need for restoring honor in the written and spoken word. * [33]

Two days elapsed before the delivery of the fourth long speech at the Academy of Music at Brooklyn on Friday, November 1. [34] That speech made no pretense of correcting any alleged misstatements of fact: it was just a campaign speech. Since it was almost entirely domestic in its contents, it hardly falls within the scope of this book, except that immediately before its conclusion Mr. Roosevelt repeated his standing pledge of lip service to peace:

> I am fighting to keep this Nation prosperous and at peace. I am fighting to keep our people out of foreign wars * . *

At Rochester the next day, November 2, 1940, Mr. Roosevelt made a shorter speech. ³⁵ Part of it was devoted to self-congratulation that the Army and the National Guard had never been called out during Mr. Roosevelt's terms of office "except in a cause of humanity." From this rehearsal of his acts Mr. Roosevelt glanced by a clear implication at the conduct of foreign affairs which the electorate might expect from him, and he specifically asked them to believe that he had

* his feet on the ground, rather than his finger on the trigger.

Mr. Roosevelt then directly approached foreign policy, and said this:

> Your national Government down in Washington, in all of its component parts, is equally a Government of peace—a Government that intends to retain peace for the American people.
>
> As your great Secretary of State said last night: "Outstanding is the wholly unwarranted and utterly vicious charge that the President is leading us into war." *

Later in the same day Mr. Roosevelt made another shorter speech at Buffalo. ³⁶ It, too, was devoted to foreign affairs. Referring to our long-extended peace with Canada, Mr. Roosevelt expanded that idea into the statement:

> * we have and we seek the kind of unarmed peace that we are looking for, some day, throughout the world.

He then gave these pledges:

> Our eyes are on the goal of peace; and this Administration will strive to continue an eight year record of peace in the next four years.

* * * * * *

I hope and I believe that this Administration will be able to keep this country at *peace during the next four years* * . * (Emphasis supplied.)

Mr. Roosevelt then referred to an unnamed Republican (but not Mr. Willkie) who, said Mr. Roosevelt—himself adept at that art—had

* peddled out to the press of this country surreptitiously by the "don't quote me process"—

a statement that after election day the American fleet would be moved further into the Pacific in the course of taking more aggressive action against Japan. That was a "falsehood," said Mr. Roosevelt, with indignation. Moreover,

* that kind of action is more dangerous to our peaceful international relations, than anything that has ever been done in Washington by this Government.

There were other such rumors, continued the candidate,

* all of them untrue, but every one of them tending to make people believe that this country is going to war.

Then, without any of the "weasel words"[37] of qualification which Theodore had thought so despicable, Mr. Roosevelt made another promise bolstered by the prestige of his high office:

Your President says this country is not going to war.

In conclusion, Mr. Roosevelt asked the "good people" of Buffalo and of the nation to vote for him in order to show their resentment of "these unfounded charges" made by the opposition that his policies were leading the country to war.

"AGAIN AND AGAINAND AGAIN" | 171

The fifth and last long speech was delivered at Cleveland, Ohio, on Saturday night, November 2. [38] Once again it did not purport to correct pretended misstatements of fact. Once again its content was principally "glittering generalities" in which Mr. Roosevelt dangled before the electorate a portrait of a quadrennium full of "the good things of life created [not by politicians but] by the genius of science and technology * not for the enjoyment of the few, but for the welfare of all."

In this speech Mr. Roosevelt abandoned the pretense of a "draft." He asked for a "vote of confidence" so that he could "continue for four more years" a "march" into

* a future which holds the fulfillment of our hopes for real freedom, real prosperity, real peace.

"The true reason" why he was a candidate, said Mr. Roosevelt, is

* that I would like to stick by these people of ours until we reach the clear, sure footing ahead.

He would not run again, for a fourth term, Mr. Roosevelt promised. If he were given a third term, [39]

When that term is over there will be another President *.

As for foreign policy, said the candidate,

There is nothing secret about our foreign policy. It is not a secret from the American people * . * Let me restate it like this:

The first purpose of our foreign policy is to keep our country out of war.

* * * * * *

The second purpose of this policy is to keep war as far away as possible from the shores of the entire Western Hemisphere. *

Towards the conclusion of his speech Mr. Roosevelt sought the sympathy of the voters by telling them of his

* hard task. * from which there is no escape day or night.

But through all his tasks two thoughts had ever been uppermost in Mr. Roosevelt's mind; the second, to make democracy work; but the more important and first of these was

* to preserve peace in our land *.

The final paragraph of Mr. Roosevelt's Cleveland speech invoked the strength of all America, the spirit and the faith of God, and

The spirit of the common man [which] is the spirit of peace and good will. *

But even with all this long sequence of promises of peace Mr. Roosevelt feared that some of the voters might yet have their doubts. He therefore sought the last word, and "in this last hour before midnight," on Monday, November 4, on the eve of the election, Mr. Roosevelt took to the air with a hybrid speech [40] which was partly religious exhortation and prayer, and partly a political appeal to the ward workers of the city machines to get out all the voters tomorrow to vote for him. And in that speech Mr. Roosevelt made no fewer than nine references to peace, saying,

* millions of families * have eaten their supper in peace, they will be able to sleep in their homes tonight in peace. Tomorrow they will be free to go out to live their ordinary lives in peace * . *

* * * * * *

* I think I speak the minds of all of you when I say that we thank God that we live in the sunlight and in the starlight of peace, that we are not in war and that we propose and expect to continue to live our lives in peace—under the peaceful light of Heaven.

"AGAIN AND AGAINAND AGAIN" | 173

* * * * * *

* there can be no arguments about * our desire to remain at peace *.

* * * * * *

On this election eve, we all have in our hearts and minds a prayer for * the peace of our beloved country.

And the concluding prayer included an invocation to Almighty God to

* Endue with the spirit of wisdom those to whom in Thy Name we entrust the authority of government, that there may be * peace at home * . *

The results of the election showed that Mr. Roosevelt's popularity had declined both absolutely and relatively since 1936. [41] Absolutely he secured 233,000 fewer votes and carried eight fewer states, while the votes cast for the Republican party increased by almost six millions: it was, indeed, estimated that if 250,000 voters in pivotal states had switched their votes, Mr. Roosevelt would have lost the election. Relatively Mr. Roosevelt secured not quite 55% of the popular vote in 1940, whereas he had had almost 65% in 1936. His forced decision to campaign politically had been made just in the nick of time.

As has already been shown, Mr. Roosevelt was opposed to, and had succeeded in heading off, a national referendum on war. But not even the most ardent of Mr. Roosevelt's New Dealers could truly claim that the 1940 election was a "mandate" to go to war. [42] Mr. Willkie's declarations were universally and consistently against war: therefore no one who had voted for Mr. Willkie did so for the purpose of abandoning our historic American continentalism. Every vote for Mr. Willkie was a "peace" vote.

Mr. Willkie had also charged that Mr. Roosevelt, either deliberately or by mistaken conduct of our foreign relations, was getting

America into the war. If Mr. Roosevelt had been content to let such charges lie unanswered, it could perhaps be argued fairly if weakly that those who wanted to go to war had voted for Mr. Roosevelt. But, as has been shown, the actual fact was to the contrary. When faced with such charges Mr. Roosevelt and his henchmen sprang to their oratorical arms. Such assertions of warlike intent, they claimed, were "deliberate misstatements of fact"—and many another fancy epithet, which need not be repeated here. Nor did Mr. Roosevelt content himself with the negative policy of denials: he affirmatively portrayed himself as a peaceable man, his foreign policy as that of peace; and his representations were coupled with innumerable pledges of future peace. It is therefore clear that everyone who voted for Mr. Roosevelt was explicitly invited to do so in reliance upon his solemn and repeated promises to preserve American peace, and must be assumed to have done so on that basis. There was no war candidate, there were no war votes in 1940, and so there was still no "war" referendum.

Rather there was an overwhelmingly unanimous "peace" referendum. And as Mr. Roosevelt had pointed out in his election eve radio speech, the candidates selected at the election become

> * only the instruments to carry out the will of all the people. [43]

Notwithstanding all this, inside of two months from the date of the election (on January 3, 1941) Mr. Roosevelt was asserting to the Congress that [44] he had received

> * the mandate of the people * [to embark] on a program for the total defense of our democracy. *

The promises of peace had been discarded almost as swiftly as the campaign buttons. Yet it was no war crisis which had persuaded the people to confer a third term upon Mr. Roosevelt: they were persuaded by his promises to keep the country at peace during the next four years.

 FROM "SEA LION" INTO "BARBAROSSA"

1. THE CONTINENT IS ISOLATED

By the middle of 1940, English history seemed to have repeated itself. Almost exactly one hundred and thirty years earlier, western Europe, except for relatively trifling areas, was under the control of a single tyrant. Britain stood alone. Coalition after coalition of nations had been defeated, and Britain, not being a continental power, could not hope to prevail until she could find new and powerful allies on the continent. In principle, the situation was identical at the end of June 1940. General Fuller's terse analysis [1] deserves quotation:

> * Britain was now left his [Hitler's] sole enemy. She had lost not only her footing on the Continent but also the requisite fighting manpower—that of France—to wage a continental war. Further, she had lost the assistance of the French fleet, and, with Italy now in the war, she had lost the command of the Mediterranean and with it the direct sea route to Egypt. *

Single-handed, Britain could not possibly win the war however long it might last. Henceforth, and until she could recruit another ally, her problem was a purely defensive one. *

* without American economic support she could not * have continued the struggle.

* * * * * *

* In spite of her first coalition having been smashed, she was undefeated yet impotent until she could establish another. The first step taken toward this end was a gratuitous one on the part of Germany: the German invasion of Russia gave her a new continental ally.

* All that was now wanting in order to establish a powerful second coalition against Germany was a military alliance between Britain and America, and, on December 7, 1941, the Japanese surprise attack on Pearl Harbor cemented it.

The extreme military weakness of Britain in mid-1940 is not generally appreciated. When Mr. Churchill was broadcasting his famous "we will fight on the beaches" speech on June 4, 1940, he put his hand over the microphone and said in an aside, [2]

> And we will hit them over the heads with beer bottles, which is all we have really got.

Almost all of the British artillery and other equipment had been sent abroad to the continent with the British expeditionary force and had been lost at Dunkirk. All of this material had to be replenished, if British resistance was to continue, as Mr. Roosevelt specifically noted. [3] It was promptly and secretly replenished from American army arsenals in response to urgent appeals from Mr. Churchill, as has been mentioned. In addition, American private stocks were swept clean—not only Springfield rifles but the older Krags and even shotguns to outfit the Home Guard poured into Britain. Fifty per cent, sixty per cent, and sometimes more, of the new arms production of American factories was being currently sent to Britain. [4] Over eighty per cent of the new military planes were delivered to Britain, and the American Army and Navy were so stripped that, after giving effect to the addition of the new planes from the manufacturers, they had lost combat planes on balance. [5] As will soon be told, the British Navy was bolstered by the addition of fifty American destroyers, and by the American Navy's "patrol" of the Western Atlantic.

The final great deficiency of Britain, that of man power, could not—as yet—be supplied by Mr. Roosevelt. Just before the outbreak of the Second World War it was stated that [6]

> * The wisest diplomat I know has reminded me again and again that "England has just one more big war left in her."

It is not necessary to attempt to judge where the right lay in the disputes between the French government and Mr. Churchill as to whether or not twenty-six British divisions had been promised and only ten sent to France, or as to whether or not there had been at that time an insufficient mobilization of British man power, [7] because we do know that at a vastly more critical time, just before the invasion of France, in late April 1944, one of the great British ships, H. M. S. *Malaya,* had to be left in port as the consequence of the shortage of British man power. [8] Neither is it necessary to endorse the hard saying of Mr. Mencken [9] concerning Mr. Roosevelt's error in

> * pulling ashore the corpse of the British Empire

in order to recognize the kernel of meaty truth within the hard nut. In consequence there were two great questions to be answered during the second half of 1940—first, would the weakness of Britain combined with the necessities of Germany result in peace, and, second, if peace was not made, when and where and how would the war be extended?

Mr. Churchill's estimate of the situation was penetrating, but his conclusion seems unsatisfying and perhaps incomplete. [10] As he viewed the immediate future,

> * Hitler's need to finish the war in the West was obvious. He was in a position to offer the most tempting terms. * it did not seem impossible that he would consent to leave Britain and her Empire and Fleet intact and make a peace which would have secured him that free hand in the East * which was his heart's main desire. 11 * No one was under any obligation to Soviet Russia. Why should not Britain join the spectators who * might watch with detached interest, or even relish, a mutually destructive struggle between the Nazi and Communist Empires? *

In the light of subsequent history it would have been interesting if Mr. Churchill had set forth his reasons against peace as of that time. Instead, he offers as a conclusion of this topic:

> * Future generations will find it hard to believe that the issues I have summarized here were never * even mentioned in our most private conclaves. *

Not "hard to believe" but rather, "incredible," one might suggest. Mr. Churchill recognized that probably his Cabinet would fall and be replaced by another if peace was made or to be made. Consequently it is difficult to escape the opinion that domestic political necessities influenced his conduct of foreign affairs, as they did Mr. Roosevelt. [12] And Mr. Roosevelt, as has been mentioned, opposed a negotiated peace for his own complicated reasons. Yet one's fancy cannot help speculating about another "if."

On July 19, 1940, Hitler addressed the Reichstag at Berlin, and as "the victor speaking in the name of reason" appealed to Great Britain to make peace.[13] His offer was serious,[14] and there were seasoned observers who believed that Britain would have been tempted to accept it, instead of rejecting it, had it not been for Mr. Roosevelt.[15] Even so, there appears to have been some feeble possibility of peace at that time. To an extent, the details of which are unknown, Germany and Britain were negotiating through the King of Sweden[16] until late August, while Lord Halifax's speech on August 22 did not exclude the possibility of peace.[17] Other approaches were made through the Pope and through a German diplomat at Washington.[18]

We know that the Tyrannies, as it will be convenient to call them, had not prepared any detailed or specific plans, either collectively or singly, for world conquest: the fact is that they had no long-range plans at all. They improvised as they went along, as we are now officially told:[19]

> It is now perfectly clear that the Axis countries had not planned adequately beyond their initial aggressive thrusts. Their objectives in beginning wars on either side of the world were limited * . * the planners of war assumed that short, quick military campaigns would accomplish their objectives. They moved in a series of separate thrusts at nations even less prepared than they. No prolonged war against superior resources effectively mobilized was contemplated.

* * * * * *

The failure of England to capitulate after the fall of France forced Hitler to consider invasion. *

It is therefore not surprising to know that it was not until July 16, 1940, that Hitler ordered the commencement of plan making for the invasion of England. The code name for this operation was "Sea Lion." The opening sentence of this "Top Secret" General Order No. 16 suggests the existence of earlier negotiations and a hope that they might be resumed: [20]

> Since England, despite her militarily hopeless situation still shows no sign of willingness to come to terms, I have decided to prepare a landing operation against England, and if necessary to carry it out.

And Hitler ordered that the plans should be completed by the middle of August. Of necessity it took considerable time to prepare the first tentative plans for so vast an enterprise, and it was not long before a serious conflict arose between the German Navy and the German Army as to the nature of the plans and as to what each of the two services could and could not do to carry them out in conjunction with the activities of the other. Weeks were lost in the conduct of this acrimonious debate, and the time was very shortly approaching when weather conditions would make both the crossing and the operation of supporting aircraft impossible. Meanwhile, on July 29, 1940, the first of the mass air raids began. They were intended partly to intimidate the British into asking for peace and partly to prepare the way for the subsequent invasion. At the end of September they were abandoned, along with the invasion plans, [21] for the reason that Russo-German relations had deteriorated to the point where war preparations against Russia had already been verbally authorized by Hitler. [22]

Hitler's intention to invade Russia appears to have become ultimately almost an open secret in Germany. [23] The first inklings of it were observed as early as December 23, 1939, [24] and the same acute observer noted on June 24, 1940: [25]

* Molotov has told Schulenburg [German Ambassador to Russia] Russia is preparing to attack Rumania. * it is clear that Russian policy is increasingly anti-German. The capital in which there is the greatest amount of conspiracy against German victory is Moscow. * in August and September [1939] the Bolsheviks * didn't believe in a German triumph. They wanted to push Germany into a conflict and Europe into a crisis because they were thinking of a long and exhausting struggle between the democracies and Hitler. Things have moved fast, and now Moscow is trying to trouble the waters.

In June 1940 there were some observers in Berlin who were convinced that Hitler sincerely wanted peace with Britain in order to be able to attack Soviet Russia,[26] while in mid-July a correspondent of the New York *Herald Tribune* was expelled from Germany for sending a dispatch stating that Russo-German relations were not so friendly then as previously.[27] Prior to July 29, 1940, Hitler had already made known to Generals Keitel and Jodl his purpose to attack Russia in the spring of 1941.[28]

By early August 1940 Hitler's purpose had been disclosed to various other generals, and to the German military attachés in foreign capitals. The necessary plans for the attack were being prepared under the first operational code name of "Auf-bau Ost."[29]

On September 19, 1940, von Ribbentrop, when discussing with Count Ciano the Tripartite Treaty to be signed eight days later at Berlin, pointed out that it was also directed against Russia.[30] As early as September 26, 1940,[31] Hitler was discussing with Admiral Raeder the plans of the attack on Russia and the abandonment of any invasion of England. On October 4, at the Brenner Pass conference, Count Ciano noted that Hitler was "again extremely anti-Bolshevist."[32] In Moscow, Stalin had been showing a "strong reserve" in public towards the German Ambassador.[33] Notwithstanding this situation, von Ribbentrop, on October 13, 1940, invited Molotov to come to Berlin in order to discuss the future relations between the two countries. [34] Von Ribbentrop appears to have had three matters in mind: the situation on the Finnish frontier in the Arctic Circle, the general situation in the Balkans, and an improvement of Russo-Japanese relations. A month's delay ensued until Molotov arrived at Berlin for conversations held on November 12 and 13 with Hitler and with von Ribbentrop. At the first of these conferences, which was with von Ribbentrop, the latter suggested that in Europe, in Asia, and to Central Africa, the spheres of interest of Russia, of Japan, of Italy, and of Germany should be defined by agreement, in order to avoid the possibility of any future conflicts among these four powers. [35] Von Ribbentrop then dangled possibilities in the Bosporus and in the Straits before Molotov's eyes, but disclaimed any intent to make concrete proposals. Next he turned to the Sino-Japanese situation, and mentioned that he had recently heard that Japan as well as China desired to seek a compromise. Molotov agreed with him as to the advantages of such an accord, but was suspicious as to the meaning of the Greater East Asian Sphere as well as of the New Order in Europe. As for the general spheres of influence he limited himself to the Russo-German situation, wherein "particular vigilance was needed." He felt that "only a partial solution" had been reached, with the possible exception of Finland, where there was none.

The second conference was also held on November 12 and Hitler was present, doing most of the talking. [36] His generalities were large and sweeping, and little was said that was tangible. The conversation was terminated by the approach of an air raid on Berlin.

The third conference began on November 13, 1940, [37] and soon came around to Finland. Hitler disclaimed any political interest in Finland, but asserted that it had a very substantial economic importance for Germany during the war. This was equally true of Rumania. Molotov was stubborn as to Finland, and objected to the presence of German troops there at any time or at any place. He hinted that there might be war with Finland, and Hitler strenuously objected to the idea. Molotov remained stubborn, after which von Ribbentrop and Hitler tried to smooth the matter over. Hitler then turned to the British Empire, which he asserted was "bankrupt," and he began to discuss how it should be partitioned. Molotov seemed to show little interest in this topic and brought up the matter of a Russian guarantee to Bulgaria, and of coming to some arrangement with Turkey which would give Russia a special position in the Straits. On these topics Hitler was evasive and sought to terminate the discussion. Molotov said that a number of new and important questions had been raised. In concluding the meeting he glanced towards the Orient and spoke in defense of the Chinese interests. The air raid which Mr. Churchill had thoughtfully provided [38] terminated the third conference.

The fourth one was held in von Ribbentrop's air-raid shelter until midnight that same evening. [39] The German returned to the topic of spheres of influence and proposed to the Russian a new ten-year treaty, amplifying the Tripartite Pact of September 27, 1940, by Russia's adherence. The four powers would respect each other's spheres of influence (which would be defined in a secret agreement), and would assist each other in every way in economic matters. Von Ribbentrop also said that Japan was anxious to conclude a nonaggression treaty with Russia, after which Japan would recognize the Russian spheres of influence in Outer Mongolia and in Sinkiang, provided an understanding with China was reached. Molotov was vague as to the Japanese situation and did not refer to the proposed treaty at all. He turned the conversation to the Straits, to Bulgaria, to Rumania, and to Hungary, all of which were material and of interest to Russia. He also referred to an exit from the Baltic Sea, and mentioned Yugoslavia, Greece, and Poland. Von Ribbentrop was evasive, and objected that he had been questioned too closely by Molotov: to him the one great question was whether Russia would cooperate with Germany in the liquidation of the British Empire. Molotov expressed doubt that Germany had won the war. He approved of collaboration, but first they had to come to a thorough understanding about it. However these were issues of tomorrow; the issues of today and the fulfillment of existing agreements must first be settled. All of these questions could now be dealt with through their respective ambassadors. On this note the conference and the visit terminated.

The parties had reached no agreement, and never did. On November 26, 1940, Russia offered to adhere to the proposed Quadripartite Pact on four conditions: [40]

1. All German troops to be withdrawn from Finland at once.
2. A mutual assistance treaty with Bulgaria, and military and naval bases there within range of the Bosporus and the Dardanelles.
3. The area from Batum-Baku south to the Persian Gulf to be recognized as the center of Russian aspirations.
4. Japan to renounce her concessions in Northern Sakhalin.

No answer was received from Germany, and on January 17, 1941, Molotov inquired why. [41] Germany's reply on January 21, 1941, was evasive in part, and in part negative: [42] it hardly seems worth while to develop the sterile diplomatic exchanges further.

Hitler did not allow these conversations to delay the preparation of his military plans. On November 12, 1940, the day the conferences began, part of his "top secret" order read as follows: [43]

5. *Russia.* Political discussions have been initiated with the aim of clarifying Russia's attitude for the time being. Irrespective of the results of these discussions, all preparations for the East which have already been verbally ordered will be continued.

Instructions of this will follow, as soon as the general outline of the army's operational plans have been submitted to, and approved by, me.

The German plan to attack Russia became known later in Germany by the cynically humorous code name of "Barbarossa"— Red Beard. On December 18, 1940, Hitler, by his Secret Directive No. 21, ordered that all preparations must be complete by May 15, 1941. [44] At that time the campaigns in the Balkans against Greece and against Yugoslavia had not been foreseen: they compelled a postponement of the opening of the Russian campaign to June 22, 1941.

As an epilogue to the loyalty of tyrants it should be mentioned that Russia was planning to attack Germany in the Autumn of 1941. [45]

But in the summer of 1940, as Mr. Roosevelt began to collaborate more closely with Mr. Churchill, the prospect of an actual war between Russia and Germany seemed remote. There were more immediate matters which required attention.

2. FINDING A WAY TO CIRCUMVENT CONGRESS

Lord Lothian had continued to work behind the scenes on the destroyer gift, but the problem was complex. On the one hand Washington was beginning to take Mr. Churchill's scares seriously, and to insist on buying once and forever a firm assurance about the British warships. Moreover Mr. Churchill's additional suggestion had sunk in, that the Germans would insist upon receiving bases in the British possessions. On the other hand Mr. Roosevelt was angry at the Congress's deep distrust of him, and he was determined to find a way to circumvent the Congress and the restrictive provision which had been inserted in the Naval Appropriation Act of June 28, [46] Mr. Ickes arguing that it should be done "by hook or by crook." However it was an election year and there was always public opinion to consider.

Early in July Lord Lothian cabled Mr. Churchill that perhaps public opinion could be brought around to favor the deal if it was tied in to a promise about the British ships. [47] Just how the publicity was arranged is uncertain, but publicity was already on the way. In an issue of *Life* [48] which appeared on the newsstands on July 12, 1940 (and which naturally had gone to press some days earlier), a trial balloon was sent up. The brief propaganda article read:

> * Britain has been asking the U. S. for the right to buy 35 [of the older] U. S. destroyers. *
>
> The question now before the American people is how best to use their ships to guarantee their ultimate safety against Adolf Hitler. * the U. S. is open to certain and swift destruction if the British Navy falls into the hands of Adolf Hitler. In this perilous dilemma, we are asked to sell England 35 destroyers. *
>
> One destroyer released to Britain now is worth a hundred airplanes, of which the U. S. has supplied 2,000.
>
> Deserted by the U. S., the English might in bitter defeat surrender their fleet to Hitler. Aid now might save the British Navy for the U. S.
>
> The American *and* British Navies could defend the Western Hemisphere in perpetuity.

In this article the essence of Mr. Churchill's argument is repeated, and it even seems possible to conclude that Mr Churchill's cable of June 14–15, 1940, was shown to the writer of the article. This is for the reason that the article and that particular cable mention the number of thirty-five destroyers, whereas the May 15 cable asked for 40 to 50, and the June 11 cable asked for 30 to 40.

While this was pending, Mr. Roosevelt, through Mr. Hull, moved to strengthen America's position in the Western Hemisphere. On July 21 the foreign ministers of the twenty-one American republics met at Havana. [49] There they considered three topics. The first was the possible transfer of the French or Netherlands possessions in the Caribbean; as to this they adopted a resolution which not only affirmed Mr. Hull's note of June 19, 1940, but which declared that any attempt on the part of a non-American state against the integrity or inviolability of the territory, the sovereignty, or the political independence of any one American state would be considered an act of aggression against all of the other states. The second topic related to subversive activities, and each state agreed to take domestic measures against them and to exchange information about them with the others. The third was pure sugar, to provide for the surpluses of the other countries. While the Havana conference was in session, Mr. Roosevelt asked the Congress to increase the lending power of the Export-Import Bank by $500,000,000 in order to provide the necessary funds for such purchases, and this was subsequently done. [50]

On July 31, 1940, Mr. Churchill resumed his requests to Mr. Roosevelt. He asked for fifty to sixty destroyers, for motor boats, and for seaplanes, but offered no promises of any sort as to future British action. [51] On August 3 he cabled Lord Lothian to let Mr. Knox know that the "second" alternative, to lease bases but not sell them, would be acceptable provided Britain received the destroyers and the seaplanes immediately. [52] What the first alternative was, is not stated, but it seems safe to assume that it was the formal pledge as to the British ships. Mr. Churchill wrote a memorandum to Mr. Eden on August 7 [53] which strongly supports this inference, as does his cable of the same date to Lord Lothian, [54] in which he insisted that the bugaboo was not for sale at all—"We have no intention of relieving the United States from any well-grounded anxieties on this point"—except at the price of a declaration of war:

> * You foresaw this yourself in your first conversation with the President, when you said you were quite sure that we should never send any part of our Fleet across the Atlantic except in the case of an actual war alliance.

The negotiations therefore dragged along. It was known that something was going on about the destroyers, for Mr. Roosevelt was asked about it at his press conference on August 2 [55] but refused to make any public comment. On August 16 he was asked again. [56] He refused to tell about the destroyers, but said that we were negotiating with Britain on the matter of naval and air bases for the defense of the Western Hemisphere and particularly the Panama Canal.

Meanwhile Mr. Roosevelt had been in touch with Mr. Churchill, who replied to him on August 15, 1940, asking not only for the destroyers and the seaplanes, but also for motor torpedo boats and for as many more rifles as possible, preferably a million. [57]

On August 20, with Mr. Roosevelt's consent, Mr. Churchill addressed the House of Commons and mentioned the matter of the leasing of the bases for 99 years. In connection with this he predicted that Britain and America would for the future have to conduct some of their affairs jointly.

There was still no agreement on the method of handling the deal, as Mr. Churchill refused to put it on any basis which resembled a contract, [58] while Mr. Roosevelt was explicitly unwilling to put it in the proper form of a treaty, which would have required approval by the Senate. [59] Mr. Churchill cabled his objections on August 25; [60] Mr. Roosevelt telephoned him and discussed them on August 26 and then apparently discussed the problems further with Lord Lothian, who cabled his views to Mr. Churchill. The matter seems by now to have become more definite and to have begun to take documentary form, as appears from Mr. Churchill's cable to Mr. Roosevelt of August 27. [61] On that same day a formal offer was cabled to the United States [62] of the eight bases. In addition Mr. Churchill consented to be asked formally whether his statement made to the House of Commons on June 4, 1940, as to the disposition of the British ships represented the settled policy of the British Government, and to reply that it did. [63] The principals were now agreed, but public announcement [64] of the consummation [65] of the deal, which took place after the Labor Day week end, on September 3, 1940, had to wait for a week while the Attorney General, Mr. Robert H. Jackson, wrote a long and criticized [66] opinion asserting that Mr. Roosevelt could circumvent the provisions of the Naval Appropriations Act, and that the deal did not need to be ratified by the Senate. [67] Neither the American people, nor their elected representatives in the Congress were consulted by Mr. Roosevelt; indeed they had no way of knowing that any such deal was contemplated. Thoughtful citizens were justifiably alarmed at this further revelation that Mr. Roosevelt was not only personally conducting a secret and clandestine one-man foreign policy, but also that he did not hesitate to confront the country with a *fait accompli*. By committing this quite unneutral act [68] Mr. Roosevelt had deliberately deprived the American people of any opportunity to choose whether or not they wished to take this further step towards war. Mr. Willkie said that [69]

> It is regrettable * that the President did not deem it necessary * to secure the approval of Congress or permit public discussion prior to adoption.

and that the deal for the fifty destroyers had been [70]

> * the most arbitrary and dictatorial action ever taken by any President in the history of the United States.

Mr. Roosevelt, exhibiting small restraint, claimed that the deal

* is probably the most important thing that has come for American defense since the Louisiana Purchase. *

Some extracts from this press conference, [71] which was held on the train returning to Washington after he had dedicated the Great Smoky Mountains National Park, are of interest:

Q. No connection between those bases and the destroyers?

* * * * * *

THE PRESIDENT: * there is no exchange in relation to them.

Q. No *quid pro quo?*

THE PRESIDENT: No *quid pro quo* on those at all. You see the point? [Matter omitted from the transcript as printed.]

* * * * * *

Q. Mr. President, when will the destroyers be sent to Great Britain?

THE PRESIDENT: Oh, some of them are [72] —I don't know; reasonably soon.

Q. Where are the destroyers now?

THE PRESIDENT: I don't know.

Q. Mr. President, does this require Senate ratification?

* * * * * *

THE PRESIDENT: It is all over; it is all done.

But that was not all. There were obviously further agreements, even though Mr. Roosevelt claimed that one of them was "fortuitous":

THE PRESIDENT: * I have not finished the story. There is also to be given out in Washington, simultaneously—you will have to leave this off the record as coming from me; make it just pure information—a restatement by Prime Minister Winston Churchill on what he said on the fourth of June to Parliament * to the effect that the British Fleet, in case it is made too hot for them in home waters, is not going to be given to Germany or sunk.

* * * * * *

Q. Is that part of the deal?

THE PRESIDENT: No, it happens to come along at the same time.

Q. Fortuitously?

THE PRESIDENT: Fortuitously, that is the word.

* * * * * *

Q. Does this understanding postulate the establishment of an agreement?

THE PRESIDENT: No, there is nothing said here.

Q. In other words, would it postulate that—

THE PRESIDENT: [interposing] * don't say this is the forerunner of this, that, or the other thing. You might hit, but the chances are ten to one that you would miss." [Matter omitted from the transcript as printed.]

The agreement to defend Canada formed a part of the larger arrangements. While these negotiations had been going on, Mr. Roosevelt telephoned Mr. Churchill on August 16, and, having reached agreement on defending Canada, Mr. Roosevelt by telegraph arranged a conference with Mr. Mackenzie King, the Canadian Prime Minister, for August 17. Immediately afterwards, on August 18, Mr. Roosevelt announced [73] the creation of a Permanent Joint Board on Defense to

> * consider in the broad sense the defense of the north half of the Western Hemisphere.

It was to

> * consist of four or five members from each country, most of them from the services. *

Here was another instance of Mr. Roosevelt's personally conducted foreign policy, without benefit of the advice and consent either of the Senate or of the American people. No one knew what it meant specifically in the way of plans: as to them Mr. Roosevelt wrote almost a year later: [73]

> * Obviously, these [plans] cannot be made public because of existing military considerations.

However, a magazine [74] which seemed at the moment to have excellent sources of information stated that the Joint Defense Board

> * agreement will mean as much as Roosevelt thinks he can get away with in the face of isolationist opinion.

And that it would specifically include

> U. S. destroyers to patrol Canadian waters, thus releasing Canadian destroyers for Britain.

In Germany it was believed that these arrangements were steps preliminary to the American or British occupation of the Azores and the Canary Islands; perhaps of the French colonies in West Africa and, especially, of Dakar. Consequently Germany began to consider plans to forestall such occupations. [75]

Nor were these secret commitments all. A closer association and collaboration with the British Empire was already being prepared in secret. On July 3, 1940, Mr. Hull, having been authorized by Mr. Roosevelt to do so, requested the Canadian Prime Minister to send the appropriate Canadian military and naval personnel to Washington to initiate staff conversations. [76] Several weeks earlier Mr. Churchill and Lord Lothian had suggested that British and American officers should hold comparable conferences, [77] and this was arranged at a later date.

Mr. Roosevelt's penchant for secrecy and for personal conduct of foreign policy was at times extreme. In 1940 Ambassador Bullitt had a code private to himself and to Mr. Roosevelt, and often telephoned directly to him, so that there were times when Mr. Hull was in the dark and could find out what was going on only by asking Mr. Roosevelt. [78] In 1941 our Ambassador to France, Admiral Leahy, wrote frequent personal letters to Mr. Roosevelt: he never corresponded with Secretary Hull, although at times he was in touch with Under Secretary Welles. [79] This secrecy was the subject of serious concern and it naturally resulted in an increasing measure of distrust. It bewildered and confused the Congress and made it restive, as did reports that plans were being prepared to put the United States upon a full war status as soon as it was politically feasible to do so.

Mention has already been made of Mr. Roosevelt's request that the Congress grant him authority, when it was not in session, to order the National Guard into active service, should an "emergency" require such action. On July 29, not having received such authority, Mr. Roosevelt attempted to reach the result by a different route. He wrote to the Congress [80] asserting in general terms that it was necessary to bring the National Guard "to the highest possible state of training efficiency *." He then requested authority to order the National Guard into active service, but only for training purposes, and he promised that such service would be in rotation, each increment being released after training. Somewhat dubiously Congress granted this plea by a statute approved August 27, 1940. [81] On August 31 Mr. Roosevelt began to call out the first units of the National Guard. [82] There was considerable surprise when it was discovered that the orders did not mention training, and that the men were ordered to serve for twelve months. In fact many of them—those who were not killed or wounded—served for about five years.

During this period the Congress was also debating the proposed draft law. It was felt by some that a period of voluntary recruiting might first be tried. Mr. Roosevelt did not wish to wait, and on August 2 he authorized a quotation that he was in favor of "selective training," as the peacetime draft was sugarcoatedly called, and that he considered it essential to adequate national defense. [83] Asked if women should be trained, Mr. Roosevelt backed away from his previous position with the reply, [84]

Not in legislation at the present time. *

But he suggested

* that when we get to what we call home defense, and possibly without legislation, we shall follow * Europe, where the women * [help] to the best of their ability.

Later in the day he touched on the topic again, speaking informally to various women's groups, [85] and he referred to the ways in which English women had "fitted into the national defense picture *. We have not reached that point *" said Mr. Roosevelt. He then spoke of "what we might call community defense" and said that later

* we * shall give everybody a job to do in practically every community in the United States.

On August 6, 1940, Mr. Hull issued a statement [86] which glanced at both the Havana Conference and the draft debate. With reference to the former he said that it was believed by the conferees that "the military and other sinister activities on the part of some nations in other parts of the world" endangered the American republics; that a threat to one was a threat to all, and that preparations for defense could not be taken too soon. "The one and only sure way" for the United States to avoid being drawn into actual war was for Americans

> * to make up their minds that we must continue to arm, and to arm to such an extent that the forces of conquest and ruin will not dare make an attack on us or on any part of this hemisphere.

Each American must be ready and willing for real sacrifice, both of time and of his substance, and for hard personal service. In the face of such terrific problems "we cannot pursue complacently the course of our customary normal life."

At his press conference on August 23, 1940, [87] Mr. Roosevelt spoke even more earnestly against a proposal of the Senate to postpone conscription until January 1, 1941. He referred to the pending orders for new equipment, and said that while

> * manpower without equipment was no use, we are getting to the point now of saying that equipment without manpower is no use.

Mr. Roosevelt then quoted Mr. Stimson to the effect that to fill up the Army, the National Guard, and the Reserves to full strength would require nearly 400,000 men:

> * and that, even at the present high rate of voluntary recruiting * will require a year. *

But, said Mr. Roosevelt, another 400,000 men would be necessary as "supporting troops" and to recruit them would take yet another year.

> * Now, we cannot afford a year. In other words, time is of the essence. *

Passage of the bill was necessary "in the next couple of weeks" to get "our team together." Just why the haste was so extreme and why the need for men was so great, Mr. Roosevelt did not explain, and no one asked "Why?"

So, Mr. Roosevelt continued on August 23, still quoting Mr. Stimson:

> * all of this new training * is thorough and novel, and * the Army cannot practice efficiently as a team until it is filled up to full strength and until the men are physically hardened.

Congress, he said, after two months was

> * still talking about it. * I am asking for action now.

Then the question was asked,

> * does this contemplate an army of 1,200,000 a year from this fall?
>
> THE PRESIDENT: I don't know. I haven't got the tables down here, but I should say so, offhand—about. Of course you have about 400,000 now and need two more increments. It would be about a million and a quarter men. [Matter omitted from the transcript as printed.]

Yet on August 27, when the slowness of the administration in giving orders for "defense" material was under attack by Democratic Senator Byrd and others, Mr. Roosevelt reversed his argument and directly contradicted [88] what he had said on August 23:

> Q. * Will you explain why the Draft Bill is holding up any speed or anything? I cannot quite say I understand it.
>
> THE PRESIDENT: Because if and when the Draft Bill goes through we shall need a lot of other things, undoubtedly, and we cannot—there are all kinds of preparations we cannot make until the thing goes through.

Across the Atlantic Mr. Churchill's needs continued to be large. Perhaps he had not read Mr. Hull's statement of August 6, or perhaps he did not put too much credence in it; in any event in late August he asked General Strong that at least two sixteen-inch guns and their carriages be removed from the American coast defenses and sent to Britain, and General Strong, without committing the United States, believed that this could be arranged.[89] A trifle more than three weeks later, on September 22, 1940, he was cabling, and through Lord Lothian asking, for more supplies, including a quarter of a million army rifles [90] which were promptly given.[91]

At the dedication of the Great Smoky Mountains National Park on September 2, 1940,[92] Mr. Roosevelt assumed the cloak of his cousin Theodore and asserted that Americans had "grown soft in many ways." We could not survive, he said, if we were soft in a world in which Americans were threatened by dangers far more deadly and more close than those which threatened the frontiersmen—the airplane, the bomb, the tank, and the machine gun.

> Therefore, to meet the threat—to ward off these dangers—the Congress * and the Chief Executive * are establishing by law the obligation * to serve our forces for defense through training in many capacities.
>
> * the greatest attack that has ever been launched against freedom of the individual is nearer the Americas than ever before. To meet that attack we must prepare beforehand— * preparing later may and probably would be too late.

* * * * * *

It is not a change from the American way of life to advocate or legislate a greater and a speedier preparedness. It is a positive protection to the American way of life. You and I know that in the process of preparing against danger we shall not have to abandon and we will not abandon the great social improvements that have come to the American people in these later years. We need not swap the gain of better living for the gain of better defense. I propose that we retain the one and gain the other.

It was on September 11 that Mr. Hull declared to the French Ambassador, M. Henri-Haye, what the "fixed" and unsubtle policy of the United States had been for several years, and now was. [93] All American action and utterances had been based on the "assumption" that

> * Hitler was out to become the ruthless and utterly destructive conqueror of Europe, and that the Japanese military clique was bent on the same course in the Pacific area from Hawaii to Siam.

On September 30, in a conversation with Lord Lothian, Mr. Hull expanded his views and declared [94] that it was certain that Japan would assume that the special relations between the United States and Great Britain were such that they could overnight easily establish cooperative relations for the mutual use of naval and air bases in the Pacific, including Singapore, whether or not the two countries had "definite" agreements on the point. And Mr. Hull "emphasized" to Lord Lothian that it was "the special desire" of the United States to see Great Britain succeed in the war, and that American acts and utterances with respect to the Pacific area would be affected by the question as to what course would most effectively aid Great Britain in winning the war. In addition, Mr. Hull also asserted that Mr. Roosevelt and he himself and the heads of the Army and the Navy recognized that it was unadvisable to risk involvement in war by resort to drastic economic measures against Japan, as the United States was not adequately prepared to defend itself "in both oceans." [95] In this last statement there lurks the tacit assumption that a war with Japan would necessarily involve war with Germany.

All of this was of course kept secret from the people who in person and over the radio listened to Mr. Roosevelt's speech at the

Great Smoky Mountains National Park. Nor did they know that there were people who were secretly motivated in their desire for war by the opinion that a war would hasten the advent of socialism. All this lay far below the surface. Neither did the good people who assembled at the park realize that, instead of retaining the promised "gain of better living," they would for five years swap their butter for guns; do without new houses, new refrigerators, new automobiles, new radios, and other electrical equipment; have little meat, sugar, or gasoline, and few and poorer clothes, shoes, and tires, while income taxes would commence at twenty per cent on the income of everyone and rise steeply to harsh and unprecedented levels. Without the gift of prophecy they could not translate into such specific items and tangible events Mr. Roosevelt's echo of Mr. Hull's statement, which they probably took for an oratorical generality:

* It will require sacrifices from us all.

On September 16, 1940, Mr. Roosevelt signed the peacetime draft bill [96] which Congress had enacted. Augmented distrust of Mr. Roosevelt's motives and policies had caused the Senate to insert in the bill a provision that the draftees might not be sent outside of the Western Hemisphere, except to American territories. Furthermore it was provided that this "training" of the draftees should be for only one year. Mr. Roosevelt set the registration day for October 16, [97] asked the state Governors to appoint draft boards, [98] set the drawing of numbers for October 29, [99] and then, in contradiction of his earlier argument that a draft was needed so that men particularly well equipped with industrial skill would not be lost to production through volunteering, [101] opened the doors to one-year volunteers. [101]

With a careful eye to the political effect on the pending election Mr. Roosevelt insisted that this was merely registration: [102] no one was actually to be drafted until later. Moreover, in these draft documents Mr. Roosevelt was studious to minimize the number of men to be drafted—[103]

> * eight hundred thousand * this coming year and somewhat less than one million men each year thereafter. *

> * * * * * *

> * a little less than 5 per cent of the total registration.

—and to emphasize that their service would be only for one year; [104] that the draftees would derive many benefits from it, [105] and that, as he had so often previously claimed, his policy was one of peace. He reasserted: [106]

> Universal service will bring * a wider * understanding to enjoy the blessings of peace.

> * * * * * *

> We prepare to keep the peace * . * It is a program obviously of defensive preparation and of defensive preparation only.

> * * * * * *

> * Such a nation must be devoted to the cause of peace. And it is for that cause that America arms itself.

> It is to that cause—the cause of peace—that we Americans today devote our national will *.

> * * * * * *

> Your Government will devote its every thought; its every energy, to the cause that is common to all of us—the maintenance of * the peace of our country.

We are all with you in the task * of keeping the peace in this New World of ours.

Effective aid to help Britain win the war, as promised by Mr. Hull to Lord Lothian, was by no means limited to the secret power politics of the Pacific area. [107] When Mr. Churchill was about to launch his unsuccessful attack against Dakar, he cabled Mr. Roosevelt first and asked him to impress upon the French Government that if they should declare war against Great Britain in consequence of the attack, the United States would make it "very bad indeed" for France. [108] This was on September 23, 1940, and at the same time Mr. Churchill asked that American warships should be sent to visit Liberia and the British colony of Sierra Leone, where they would be close to Dakar in the French colony of Senegal. Presumably the requested warning was sent, because when Mr. Roosevelt verbally gave Admiral Leahy his instructions as Ambassador to France a little more than two months later, one of the warnings which he was to renew whenever he thought it necessary was that France was to undertake no hostile operations against the British. [109] On October 20, 1940, Mr. Churchill again asked for American pressure to be exercised against France, this time on account of a rumor that the French were about to join the Germans against the British, and to turn over to them the ships at Toulon. [110] Mr. Roosevelt immediately sent a very severe personal message of warning to Marshal Pétain, in the course of which he threatened France with the possible loss of her colonies after the war was over. [111] Mr. Roosevelt reported his action promptly to Mr. Churchill, and was not only thanked for it under date of October 26, but was asked to go back to the French and to add to his threats the warning that no naval bases might be made available to Germany. [112] Mr. Churchill ended his cable with a general appeal for more supplies, saying, "* all contributions will be thankfully received."

It was at this time that Mr. Hull spoke again. On October 26, 1940, he delivered a further message of impending doom, saying that all peaceful nations were gravely menaced. [113] These wars were not local or regional wars; they represented an organized and determined movement for steadily expanding conquest. The first need for all nations was to create for themselves impregnable means of defense; and the United States, in order to strengthen its own defense, was affording all feasible facilities to obtain supplies to nations which were checking the spread of violence and thus reducing our danger. America intended to continue this policy to the greatest possible extent because of our "inalienable right of self-defense." If the would-be conquerors should gain control of other continents, they might strike at the life of this hemisphere and ultimately we might find ourselves compelled to fight on our very own soil in defense of our independence and of our lives.

In the early part of October 1940, well-informed Washington observers predicted that our future steps into war would consist of sending bombers to England, of somehow lifting the statutory prohibition against the extension of credits to belligerents, and of sending American merchant ships into the war zones.

Between July and October 1940 there had been a noticeable change in the political climate at Washington. This was observed by Admiral Richardson, who had been absent at Hawaii during this period. And the "entirely different impression" which he had formed was, as he wrote Admiral Stark on October 22, [114] "* that the United States had more closely identified itself with Great Britain*."

By late October 1940 it was supposed that some kind of an agreement had been reached between Mr. Roosevelt and Mr. Churchill, because British sources were leaking the future American plans; it was noted that the British government knew more than the American public about what America would do.

Additionally, and while it was not publicly known for years, [115]

> * it was in 1940, the fall of 1940, that [Admiral Stark] communicated with Admiral Sir Dudley Pound of the British Navy, requesting that he send his naval experts to the United States to discuss collaboration between the two navies * in case of war.

The secret collaboration continued between Mr. Roosevelt and Mr. Churchill, and the aid increased. Three days after the election had been won Mr. Roosevelt announced a "rule of thumb" for the division of American munitions as they were produced. [116] Half were to go to Britain and Canada, and the American forces might have the remaining half. On that same day the Supply Priorities and Allocations Board approved a British request to order another twelve thousand airplanes.

On November 10, 1940, Mr. Churchill requested more diplomatic aid. [117] He had heard rumors that the two largest French warships were to be brought back to France to be completed: would Mr. Roosevelt please issue another warning? Mr. Roosevelt not only did so; he went further and attempted to buy the two ships from France, as he reported to Mr. Churchill. Finally Mr. Roosevelt obtained an assurance from Marshal Pétain that he would keep the two battleships where they were, and that he would give Mr. Roosevelt previous notice if they were to be moved. This too was promptly reported back to Mr. Churchill. [118]

About a fortnight later, on November 23, 1940, Mr. Churchill wanted yet more diplomatic help. He had heard that Spain was near starvation, and he believed that if Mr. Roosevelt would offer Spain some food on a monthly basis so long as she kept out of the war, the manoeuvre might be successful. [119] It turned out, however, that Spain's intentions were not warlike, and that no such action was needed.

Yet all of this aid was as nothing when compared to the aid for which Mr. Churchill was about to ask. In dollars, at least, Britain was about to be bankrupt. [120] It was now Mr. Churchill's task to persuade Mr. Roosevelt and through him the United States to purchase a large percentage of Britain's interest in the war. Such an appeal took thought and time. It was commenced prior to November 16, but it was not ready to send until December 8, 1940. [121]

This was the seed out of which lend-lease grew.

VIII THE SYNTHETIC CRISIS AT THE BIRTH OF LEND-LEASE

ADMIRAL STARK wrote to Admiral Hart on November 12, 1940, on the strength of a report from Vice-Admiral Ghormley, already present in England as a "naval observer," [1] that

> * the British expected us to be in the war a few days after the re-election of the President *.

However that might be, a study of "possible naval war operations" was now in Mr. Roosevelt's hands. In the same letter of November 12, 1940, Admiral Stark wrote Admiral Hart as to British proposals for a new understanding:

> *They have been talking, in a large way, about the defense of the Malay Barrier, with an alliance between themselves, us, and the Dutch, without much thought as to what the effect would be in Europe.

But we have no idea as to whether they would at once begin to fight were the Dutch alone, or were we alone, to be attacked by the Japanese. Then again, the copy of the British Far Eastern War Plan * obtained at Singapore, shows much evidence of their usual wishful thinking. Furthermore, though I believe the Dutch colonial authorities will resist an attempt to capture their islands, I question whether they would fight if only the Philippines, or only Singapore, were attacked.

With reference to current political conditions Admiral Stark expressed the opinion that

I do not believe Japan will attack us if she can avoid doing so. In fact, I believe she will go far to avoid hostilities with the United States. It is even doubtful if she wishes at this time to fight the British or the Dutch. * Should we refrain from imposing additional economic sanctions, present conditions * might be stabilized over a considerable period of the future. *

Possibly, however, a war might "develop between Japan and an alliance of British, Dutch and Americans." The War Plan, Rainbow III, "for this possible war is about completed," having been under way for at least three weeks. Meanwhile he hoped to send naval attachés to Singapore, Batavia, Soerabaja, Balikpapan, and Ceylon.

As soon as the British Ambassador, Lord Lothian, had returned to Washington from London he sought out Mr. Hull: this was on November 25, 1940. [2] Lord Lothian urged that there should be conferences between the British and American naval officers "with respect to what each [government] would or might do in case of military outbreaks on the part of Japan." He also advocated basing the American Navy "largely" at Singapore.

Doubtless our then Ambassador to Great Britain, Mr. Kennedy, who was about to retire, knew much of what was going on, and

THE SYNTHETIC CRISIS AT THE BIRTH OF LEND-LEASE | 207

was troubled by the conflict between his duty to his country and his loyalty to Mr. Roosevelt. He had returned to the United States, leaving it obscure as to when and whether he would return to England, [3] and at last, after the election was over, he spoke out bluntly on January 18, 1941, and urged America to stay out of the war. On January 20, 1941, Mr. Roosevelt hastened his retirement and promptly replaced him by Mr. Winant.

November 1940 brought grapevine rumors of peace negotiations, [4] which informed German sources do not mention. Was this, one wonders, a method of putting more pressure on Mr. Roosevelt, now that the election was over? Mrs. Clapper, who was in a position to be well informed, wrote this estimate of the situation as of the turn of the year: [5]

> Churchill needed our direct intervention. * He felt after Roosevelt's re-election that since Roosevelt was in the White House for four years * he should be willing to lead the country into direct intervention. *
>
> * Churchill feared that if the British people ever got the idea that the United States was not coming in to help them, they would not stick. * Churchill tried desperately to keep up the appearance that we were coming in. *

On December 8, 1940, Mr. Churchill's letter was ready. It was cabled to Washington [6] and on December 9 a plane delivered it alongside the *Tuscaloosa*, on which Mr. Roosevelt was cruising in the Caribbean with Mr. Hopkins. [7] As printed, [8] the letter is almost ten pages long. It reviewed past events and appraised the possibilities of future developments in the light of British needs. In summary the essence of the letter was as follows:

1. Previous American commitments:

> To equip in 1941 the entire British army as "already planned" (its size not being stated), and to equip another ten British divisions in time for the 1942 campaign.

2. Future requirements:

A. *Military*. At the moment the danger of invasion has diminished very much. However Britain cannot meet the German army at any place where its full strength can be exerted. Britain can fight only in places where Germany cannot deploy more than comparatively small forces. In the Far East Britain has no forces which could resist Japan. Yet— "* Even if the United States were our ally instead of our friend and indispensable partner, we should not ask for a *large* American expeditionary army. *" (Emphasis added.)

B. *Naval.* The United States Navy should control the Pacific and the British Navy should control the Atlantic. But Britain needs vastly more naval and merchant vessels.

Many more American warships, particularly destroyers, should be given or lent to Great Britain.

Many more merchant vessels should be built. American merchant ships should be sent everywhere, and they should be convoyed by American warships.

The United States Navy should extend its control of the western side of the Atlantic further out.

The United States should obtain bases in Eire, and it should put the greatest pressure on Eire in order to obtain bases there for Britain. [9]

3. *Production of War Munitions.*

Britain needs many more fighting airplanes. They should be produced at the rate of 2,000 per month, with special emphasis on heavy bombers.

The American production of arms, artillery, and tanks should be expanded to the utmost limits, because it will later become necessary for the United States to arm other European countries.

THE SYNTHETIC CRISIS AT THE BIRTH OF LEND-LEASE | 209

4. *Lack of Cash.*

Britain will shortly be unable to pay cash even for the supplies which she herself has previously ordered. She leaves it to the United States to discover how to overcome this difficulty. But if Britain were financially "stripped to the bone," then, when the war was over, she would be unable to buy goods from the United States in consequence of which there would be a severe depression and great unemployment.

This was no small order, and it is understandable that Mr. Roosevelt should sit silent and pondering in his deck chair on the *Tuscaloosa* for several days. Perhaps the spark of something which Mr. Churchill had written him earlier [10] glowed in his memory, "that we are two friends in danger helping each other as far as we can." Whether or not this conjecture is correct, Mr. Roosevelt evolved the concept of lend-lease (which he first named "lend-spend," and which was next called "lease-lend" before the name took its final form) before the cruise was over, and before his return to Washington on December 16, 1940.

But in addition to these top-level problems, work was being carried on in the echelons just below. By December 12, 1940, staff conversations with the British had been secretly undertaken in Manila, [11] in London, and in Washington. They concerned "an Allied operating plan and command arrangements" and were based on the assumption "that war would be fought with the United States, the British, and the Dutch Colonial Authorities as Allies." [12]

On December 17, 1940, Mr. Roosevelt met with his press conference [13] and adumbrated further help to England, and a further step towards war in the form of lend-lease. For the last three or four weeks, said Mr. Roosevelt,

> * I have been * exploring other methods of continuing the building up of our productive facilities and continuing automatically the flow of munitions to Great Britain. *

* * * * * *

* we should do everything to help the British Empire to defend itself."

* * * * * *

* it may still prove true that the best defense of Great Britain is the best defense of the United States, and therefore that these materials would be more useful to the defense of the United States if they were used in Great Britain *.

We could make a gift to Great Britain, observed Mr. Roosevelt, but that was a "somewhat banal" method, and besides,

* I am not at all sure that Great Britain would care to have a gift from the taxpayers of the United States. I doubt it very much.

As has been shown, the actuality at this time was very different. Indeed, writing in July 1941, Mr. Roosevelt himself pointed out that [14]

As 1940 drew to a close, Britain's financial assets reached a dangerously low point. * her gold reserve and dollar exchange assets left small leeway for additional purchases in this country. Action became imperative to bolster her position *.

But on December 17, 1940, Mr. Roosevelt glossed this over, both generally and specifically. The generality was:

* in all history, no major war has ever been won or lost through lack of money.

He then mocked,

* the best economic opinion in the world that the continuance of war was absolutely dependent on money in the bank. *

THE SYNTHETIC CRISIS AT THE BIRTH OF LEND-LEASE | 211

Britain was fast approaching just such a desperate situation, but Mr. Roosevelt attempted to create the opposite impression, stating:

> Q. You referred to future orders * the orders the British have given * would be paid for?
>
> THE PRESIDENT: Yes, I think so. They have plenty of exchange, you know. There doesn't seem to be very much of a problem about payment for existing orders, but there might be a problem about paying for additions to those orders *.

"Now what I am trying to do," said he, grandiloquently, "is to eliminate the dollar sign. That is something brand new in the thoughts of practically everybody in this room, I think—get rid of the silly, foolish old dollar sign." Really, explained Mr. Roosevelt, with oversimplification, it was just like being a good neighbor; if your neighbor's house caught fire, you would lend him, not sell him, your garden hose, and he would either return it later or replace it if damaged. We would have with the British

> * the understanding that when the show was over, we would get repaid sometime in kind, thereby leaving out the dollar mark in the form of a dollar debt and substituting for it a gentleman's obligation to repay in kind. *

Where would the title to all this property be? asked a reporter. "I haven't the faintest idea," replied Mr. Roosevelt; "I don't know, and I don't care."

How would the goods be delivered; by us? Mr. Roosevelt skated over this thin ice airily:

> Oh, I suppose it would depend on what flag was flying at the stern of the ship. * It might be even a Bolivian flag. That question is a detail.

But wouldn't this take us "more into the war"? Mr. Roosevelt was soothing in his reply:

> No, not a bit. * we are furnishing everything we possibly can at the present moment. This will make easier a continuation of that program. That's all there is to it.

The matter probably would not come before the Congress before January 3, 1941, said Mr. Roosevelt,

> * because the thing has not only to be worked out here, but in London too.

On January 3, 1941, [15] Mr. Roosevelt announced that Mr. Hopkins was going over to London very soon

> * as my personal representative * just to maintain—I suppose that is the best word for it—personal contact between me and the British Government. He will only be over there a couple of weeks, and then come back here.
>
> Q. Does Mr. Hopkins have any special mission *?
>
> THE PRESIDENT: No, no, no! * he will have no powers. * He's just going over to say "How do you do?" to a lot of my friends!

Mr. Roosevelt's answer was so preposterous that the reporter noted (*"Laughter"*). Actually Mr. Hopkins was sent over to size up Mr. Churchill; to arrange a meeting between Mr. Churchill and Mr. Roosevelt, tentatively set for April 1941; to avert any British contretemps which might endanger the passage of the Lend-Lease bill; to ascertain the strength of any peace sentiment in Britain; to find out if Britain would continue in the war if given further American aid; to estimate how great that aid should be, and to discuss the next moves on the chessboard of power politics. [16]

The remainder of the December 17 press conference was devoted to the muddled progress of production, which Mr. Knudsen had recently said was lagging. It continued to lag, and on December 20, after a meeting of the National Defense Advisory Commission, Mr. Roosevelt called a special press conference [17] to announce the superimposition of a headless Office of Production Management upon the Commission. At the close of that conference Mr. Roosevelt stated his existing policy:

> * Today we give everything to England that we can possibly spare in the judgment of the military experts.

Mr. Roosevelt ended the year of 1940 with another one of his educational fireside chats, intended to sidle America a little more into participation in the war. It was delivered over the radio on Sunday night, December 29, 1940, [18] and is generally referred to as "the arsenal of democracy" speech. Mr. Roosevelt began on a reassuring and soothing note:

> This is not a fireside chat on war. It is a talk on national security; because the nub of the whole purpose of your President is to keep you now, and your children later, and your grandchildren much later, out of a last-ditch war * . *

Mr. Roosevelt then ominously referred to "a world crisis," a "new crisis," and he declared that

> Never before since Jamestown and Plymouth Rock has our American civilization been in such danger as now.

That new danger, that world crisis, it appeared, was the slightly stale Tripartite Treaty of September 27, 1940, between Germany, Italy, and Japan, the importance of which Mr. Hull had casually dismissed more than three months previously. [19] The Nazi masters of Germany, Mr. Roosevelt proclaimed, "intend * to enslave the whole of Europe, and then to use the resources of Europe to dominate the rest of the world." They are being blocked on the other side of the Atlantic by the British and the Greeks, and in Asia by the Chinese, but particularly by the British Navy.

They must not be allowed to gain control of the oceans which lead to this hemisphere. "If Great Britain goes down, the Axis powers will control the continents of Europe, Asia, Africa, Australasia [sic] and the high seas." Then "all of us * would be living at the point of a gun * loaded with explosive bullets *."

We should enter upon a new and terrible era *.

There is no longer any safety in the broad oceans, he asserted, and fearsomely he said, "Frankly and definitely there is danger ahead." If the Nazis were to win they would attack us, and the attacks of the Nazis and their misdeeds were paraded at considerable length. We must support Great Britain because "Our own future security is greatly dependent on the outcome of that fight." There is far less risk of our getting into war if we do so, he argued, and he continued:

> The people of Europe who are defending themselves do not ask us to do their fighting. They ask us for the implements of war, the planes, the tanks, the guns, the freighters which will enable them to fight for their liberty and for our security. *

* * * * * *

There is no demand for sending an American Expeditionary Force outside our own borders. There is no intention by any member of your Government to send such a force. You can, therefore, nail any talk about sending armies to Europe as deliberate untruth.

Our national policy is not directed toward war. Its sole purpose is to keep war away from our country and our people.

THE SYNTHETIC CRISIS AT THE BIRTH OF LEND-LEASE | 215

Mr. Roosevelt called for greater production of war munitions, and he paid this tribute to private industry:

> American industrial genius, unmatched throughout the world in the solution of production problems, has been called upon to bring its resources and its talents into action. *

But even so,

> We must have * more of everything.

> The notion of business as usual must be discarded. To the needs of "defense" the production of consumer or luxury goods must yield.

Then came the catch-line of the speech:

> We must be the great arsenal of democracy. *

> We have furnished the British great material support and we will furnish far more in the future.

Then, at the speech's conclusion, came the customary lip service:

> * We have every good reason for hope—hope for peace *.

So, in consequence, we must make a great national effort to increase the production of all kinds of war munitions.

On December 30, 1940, Mr. Arthur Purvis, the head of the British purchasing mission, sponsored by Mr. Morgenthau, called with him at the White House, and asked for fifteen billion dollars. [20] Mr. Roosevelt "took this figure in his stride" and told Mr. Morgenthau that the Treasury Department should prepare the proposed lease-lend bill.

Mr. Churchill cabled Mr. Roosevelt on December 31, [21] nominally to thank him for the "arsenal of democracy" speech, but actually to enlarge the scope of the desired assistance, and to ask for haste in providing it. Britain, he said, would be unable to make any further payments in the United States in a few weeks. If the debate in the Congress concerning Mr. Roosevelt's proposal should be long, what would Britain do meanwhile? And in addition to the needs of Britain there were the needs of the Dominions, of Greece, and of all the "refugee allies." Then there were other British commitments around the globe for which Mr. Churchill would not ask direct American aid: Britain would take care of them in the first instance and then she would look to America for reimbursement in gold or in dollars: Sir Frederick Phillips, representing the British Treasury, would explain all this to Mr. Morgenthau.

As the old year was ending, the first step was taken towards censorship of the news. On December 31, 1940, Secretary of the Navy Knox called in the newspapermen and imposed on them a "voluntary" censorship [22] by which they were required to refrain from mentioning

1. Actual or intended movements of vessels, aircraft or personnel;
2. "Secret" U. S. weapons, or technical developments;
3. New U. S. Navy ships or aircraft;
4. U. S. Navy construction projects ashore; and
5. After the arrival of H.M.S. *Malaya* in broad daylight at New York in 1941, the arrival in U. S. ports of damaged British ships for repairs under Lend-Lease.

On January 3, 1941, Mr. Roosevelt announced [23] that

> * because it is perfectly obvious that so much tonnage in the way of ships has been going to the bottom for a year and a half * we have begun taking the first steps toward a program of building about 200 merchant ships—a program which will cost * between $300,000,000 and $350,000,000 * . *

The ships were to be about 7500 tons each.

Also on January 3, 1941, Mr. Roosevelt sent to the Congress his annual budget message. [24] Sixty-two per cent of the seventeen and a half billion dollars which it called for was for "national defense," but Mr. Roosevelt, following his usual method of asking for appropriations piecemeal, declined to "predict the ultimate cost of [the] program," which did not include lend-lease.

On January 6, 1941, Mr. Roosevelt addressed the Congress. [25] Contrary to the pattern of his earlier annual message, this one was devoted to foreign affairs exclusively except for less than one page which called for the extension and improvement of social and economic benefits. In this speech Mr. Roosevelt asked for "lend-lease" aid and also proclaimed the so-called "four freedoms." The more significant passages were:

> In the recent national election there was no substantial difference between the two great parties in respect to [our] national policy. No issue was fought out on this line before the American electorate. *
>
> * * * * * *
>
> I also ask this Congress for authority and for funds sufficient to manufacture additional munitions and war supplies of many kinds, to be turned over to those nations which are now in actual war with aggressor nations.
>
> Our most useful and immediate role is to act as an arsenal for them as well as ourselves. They do not need man power, but they do need billions of dollars worth of the weapons of defense.
>
> The time is near when they will not be able to pay for them all in ready cash. *
>
> I do not recommend that we make them a loan of dollars with which to pay for these weapons—a loan to be repaid in dollars.
>
> I recommend that we make it possible for these nations to continue to obtain war materials in the United States * . *
>
> * * * * * *
>
> For what we send abroad, we shall be repaid within a reasonable time following the close of hostilities, in similar materials, or, at our option, in other goods of many kinds, which they can produce and which we need.

* * * * * *

In fulfillment of this purpose we will not be intimidated by the threats of dictators that they will regard as a breach of international law or as an act of war our aid to the democracies. Such aid is not an act of war, even if a dictator should unilaterally proclaim it so to be.

Mr. Roosevelt then referred to his new position, although briefly, when he said that

We must all prepare to make * sacrifices * . *

Towards the end of the speech he named the four freedoms, and then, in a significant departure from his previous pattern of ending, he ceased to pay any tributes to peace: he called, instead, for "victory."

The next day, on January 7, 1941, Mr. Roosevelt by sarcastic implication denied a report that American troops had landed on Greenland.[26] Mrs. Roosevelt, at her press conference that day, criticized the members of Congress who had failed to applaud her husband's speech.[27] Representative Mason of Iowa retorted, "We do not usually applaud * during funerals."[28]

And now a further but not publicly known step towards war was taken. There had been some conflict between Mr. Roosevelt and the top admirals as to the expediency of his secret policies and, particularly, as to whether or not the Japanese Navy could be defeated quickly by the American Navy. Involved with this main problem were two subsidiary problems; one, how safe was it to weaken the Pacific fleet by withdrawing warships from the Pacific in order to send them into the Atlantic so as to aid the hard-pressed English? And, two, if it be assumed that the safety of the United States was imperilled, ought the United States to give away such tremendous quantities of munitions? This conflict within the Navy was known to informed Washington observers by the middle of October in 1940. Admiral Stark was said to be complaisant towards Mr. Roosevelt's views. Admiral Richardson, commanding the Pacific fleet, had prudent misgivings: it was noted that if Admiral Richardson was shifted it would be a war sign.

On January 8, 1941, this conflict was resolved. [29] Admiral Richardson was relieved from his command and sent to Washington, to languish thenceforth: Admiral King's report makes no mention of Admiral Richardson or, indeed, of this shift in the high command. Admiral Richardson was replaced in command of the Pacific Fleet by Rear-Admiral Husband E. Kimmel, who was given forthwith a double promotion to the rank of full Admiral: furthermore Admiral Kimmel was simultaneously put in command of the entire United States fleets, wheresoever afloat, and this arrangement was still in effect at the time when Pearl Harbor was attacked. [30]

Mr. Roosevelt was personally hand picking the Admirals. As Admiral Stark wrote on January 13, 1941, to Admiral Kimmel, when congratulating him on his promotion: [31]

* incidentally, and very incidentally, and *in all cases, the White House finally decides. This*, of course, *is White House* prerogative and *responsibility*, and believe me, it is used these days. (Emphasis supplied.)

Such evidence would appear to justify the conclusion that in Mr. Roosevelt's opinion Admiral Kimmel was the ablest commander among all the American Admirals.

At the same time the Navy was broken up into three fleets, the Pacific Fleet already mentioned, the Atlantic Fleet, and a pitifully "small Asiatic Fleet" which could not "muster sufficient strength to put up any real resistance" * against Japan after Pearl Harbor. For instance, the Asiatic Fleet had but "13 over-age destroyers," [33] of the same general type as the fifty over-age destroyers which had earlier been given away to Britain. These arrangements indicate that Mr. Roosevelt had now abandoned his first concept of one great overall navy, his second concept of a two-ocean navy, and had adopted the concept of a three-ocean navy.

All the signs and portents betokened greater support to be given to England by the United States. Mr. Hopkins had on January 6, 1941, [34] left this country for London to advise Mr. Churchill, it was publicly stated, what Mr. Roosevelt thought the content should be of the Prime Minister's promised statement of British war aims, and to ascertain the post-war social and economic objectives of Britain. [35] In exchange, Lord Halifax, leaving the cabinet, was about to depart for the United States in H.M.S. *George V* as ambassador *vice* Lord Lothian, deceased on December 12, 1940. Mr. Churchill, in a speech [36] to the Pilgrims in London on the occasion of Lord Halifax's departure, after praising Mr. Roosevelt at fulsome length, and after uttering fervent congratulations upon the breaking of the third-term tradition, had emphasized the importance of the new ambassador's mission by saying that it

> * is as momentous as any that the monarchy has entrusted to an Englishman in the lifetime of the oldest of us here.

The momentousness of Lord Halifax's mission was echoed on this side of the Atlantic by Mr. Roosevelt. Breaking all diplomatic precedents, an American president, for the first time in our history, left the White House and went out into Chesapeake Bay in order to greet and to meet a foreign ambassador. [37] The momentous mission, insofar as it was that day publicly revealed, was to ask for quick and generous help to Britain, [38] glancing towards, without directly referring to, the then pending Lend-Lease bill.

This line of approach may well have been inspired by Mr. Hopkins, who had already arrived in England on January 9, 1941, the day of the Pilgrims' dinner. Mr. Hopkins had had luncheon and a long talk on January 10, with at least Mr. Churchill, and had [39]

> * managed to convey the impression that his visit here was connected somehow *with a crisis* confronting the United States and Britain of greater urgency than a discussion of Britain's war aims. (Emphasis supplied.)

Because of the circumstance that the American newspapers were to be filled with scare stories of a "crisis" during the opening of the Lend-Lease debate immediately thereafter, it may be of help to turn aside for a moment, in order to review the political situation in Europe in January 1941.

— 2 —

With the aid of Russian treachery, Hitler had won a quick and cheap victory in Poland, as he had expected. But on August 22, 1939, in a secret talk to his top generals at Obersalzburg he had quite frankly admitted that [40]

* we cannot conduct a long war. *

Hitler therefore sought to make peace immediately after the conclusion of his Polish campaign, and much to his regret found himself unable to do so. This check to his plans was unexpected and immediately led to a most careful secret review of Germany's prospects in international affairs. That analysis, dated October 9, 1939, [41] at the end of topic after topic concludes in substance just as the estimate of German-American prospects concludes:

* Here, too, time is to be viewed as working against Germany.

In the hope, therefore, of forcing a quick peace an attack on the West was improvised. It was of necessity first proposed for mid-November 1939 [42] but various considerations led to a series of postponements until May 10, 1940. Prior to January 30, 1940, we have it on the contemporaneous authority of Goering that [43]

> The Fuehrer is firmly convinced that he will succeed in reaching a decision of the war in the year 1940 by a big attack in the west. He reckons that Belgium, Holland and Northern France will get into our possession * . *

From the technical military point of view the attacks in the West were successful beyond any reasonable expectation. Once again Hitler had won a series of cheap and quick victories which laid five more nations of the Continent prostrate at his feet.

That England would refuse attractive, because generous, peace offers seems to have been quite outside of any possibility which Hitler contemplated up to mid-July 1940. In consequence there were no previously prepared plans on hand for the invasion of England. Indeed, as has been shown, the first order for the formulation of such plans was not issued until July 16, 1940, and in eight or ten weeks, by the end of September 1940, operation Sea Lion was abandoned.

Dazzling military victories had not brought political peace to Hitler: he was now face to face with the unwelcome prospect of a vastly longer war than he had originally intended to bargain for. The German resources of raw materials were anything but unlimited and many of them flowed into Germany from, or through, Russia. In a long secret memorandum by Schnurre, dated September 28, 1940, the economic relationships between Russia and Germany were anxiously but exhaustively analyzed. [44] The large totals of imports from Russia were itemized, and it was pointed out that Germany had received from Russia, among other raw materials, nearly one million tons of grain. The dependence of Germany upon Russia was noted frankly:

> To date the Russian deliveries have been a very substantial support of the German war economy. * Our only economic connection with Iran, Afghanistan, Manchukuo, China, Japan, and beyond that to South America is the way through Russia, which is being exploited to an increasing degree for German raw material imports (soya from Manchukuo).

From the viewpoint of power politics it was plain that in order to support a much longer war than had been anticipated, Germany would have to be provided with an assured and German-controlled source of raw materials; particularly, of food. This sole consideration would seem to have made the German attack upon Russia politically inevitable in the light of the constraining circumstances of the moment. Probably a minor consideration was Hitler's deep-seated hatred of Bolshevism.

Another and major factor was the chimerical belief that this victory, like all of the preceding victories, would be quick and cheap, and thereafter peace would be made or compelled. That belief is exemplified in Hitler's Secret Directive No. 21, dated December 18, 1940, which reads, in part: [45]

> The German Armed Forces must be prepared to crush Soviet Russia in a quick campaign before the end of the war against England.

In its inception the Russian attack appears to have been an improvisation, born of the necessity of the political situation of the moment. Hitler, we may safely conjecture, was badly rattled. He felt that he had to have peace, and he could not see any clear way to get it. He was so badly rattled, indeed, that such military pipe dreams as attempts to take the Canary Islands, or the Cape Verde Islands, or Madeira, or the Azores—which attempts, even if they had succeeded, would merely have wasted, dissipated, and dispersed German power, and would not have tended remotely towards a decisive conclusion of the war—were dignified by preliminary discussions on November 12, 1940, [46] and then were promptly abandoned for what should have been the obvious reasons originally. One embryo brain-storm child of this rattled Directive No. 18 had a brief and abortive existence—a tentative plan to bring Spain into the war and take Gibraltar, which was wrecked by the intelligent resistance of Serrano Suñer. [47] That General Franco and Señor Suñer had by that time formed a poor opinion of Germany's ultimate prospects and that they did not choose to invest in the future of a rattled and failing concern would appear to be clear,

Apart from the possibility of this side-show attack on Gibraltar, the whole German might was being aimed at Russia in January 1941, and for several prior months had been thus aimed. Rumors of the projected German attack had become widespread. It seems probable that the British, who had excellent sources of information on the Continent, had had express word of it at a fairly early date. Presumably they also had had direct word that the invasion of Britain had been abandoned, which was well known in Berlin. [48] But whether or not the latter information was explicitly known to the British would appear to be unimportant. Knowledge that Russia was soon to be invaded was sufficient to indicate clearly that of necessity the whole German power would have to be turned towards the East, and that it could not be thrown across the Channel.

It is incredible that Mr. Churchill would have dared to gamble in sending out of England and to Egypt the armed and equipped divisions whose presence made possible the attack on Libya which had its inception in the offensive of December 9, 1940. Rather, Mr. Churchill must have been aware of the German plans towards the end of 1940, and he must have been convinced in the light of such knowledge that, the English invasion having been abandoned, Egypt could safely be reinforced without hazard.

Indeed, so well were the Axis plans to attack Russia known to American and to British officials that in mid-January 1941 the American State Department at Mr. Roosevelt's specific instructions [49] warned the Russian Ambassador, Constantine Oumansky, of the impending German attack. This warning was repeated by Mr. Sumner Welles on March 20, 1941, [50] and was additionally reinforced by British officials. [51] Other evidence permits the fixing of the latest date of the first warning with some exactitude. The "moral" embargo against the sale of airplanes to Russia was lifted on January 21, 1941; [52] obviously as the consequence of this information. The only inkling given to the public was a brief and unfeatured news item stating that there were reports from Russia that

that country expected that it would have to fight Germany, but that it would need at least another year and a half to be ready for such a war.[53] In actual fact Russia seems to have made no preparations to meet the planned attack.[54] Perhaps this was because, as Anne O'Hare McCormick pointed out in a thoughtful article on Russo-German relations, Stalin hoped to bring about a stalemate in the war between Germany and England.[55] An earnest of the carrying out of the German plan to attack Russia was quickly given by the movement of German troops to the Russian border, which movement had commenced by early February 1941.[56] Bearing in mind the possession of this useful knowledge by the highest officials both in America and in England, one is now in a position to examine the synthetic crisis which accompanied the Lend-Lease campaign.

— 3 —

When Mr. Morgenthau's assistants commenced drafting the lease-lend bill, it transpired that Mr. Stimson had already prepared a draft.[57] The two drafts were blended, and Mr. Roosevelt then sought the approval of various cabinet officers. Vice-President Garner, at the Cabinet meeting of January 9, 1941, argued for an hour that the British Empire was rich and could pay: Mr. Morgenthau got so excited and mad that it took Mr. Roosevelt to quiet him.

Mr. Hull thought that there should be a limitation of five billion dollars on the American loan: he also asserted that the British should put up their holdings of foreign securities as collateral. There previously had been some discussion as to this point. Mr. Roosevelt told Mr. Morgenthau that he did not want the British fleet as collateral "because by the time we get it, it would be too antiquated." As for the British West Indies, he believed that they would not have any value as collateral.

Mr. Stimson consequently observed that Mr. Hull's position on collateral was "preposterous." He did not want the United States to become the pawnbroker of the British Empire, he said indignantly. And Mr. Stimson said that Great Britain had always subsidized her allies and had not lent to them: this was the normal relationship between a neutral country and a nation fighting for its life when they had a common cause.

It was on January 10, 1941, that H.R.1776, the Lease-Lend bill, as it was originally styled, was introduced in Congress.[58] The Washington reporters noted at once that it gave "blank check" authority to Mr. Roosevelt to employ not "short of war," but—a new slogan, now that the election had been won—"all out" methods against the Axis.

At his press conference held the same day, Mr. Roosevelt was the pattern of a diffident and reluctant executive. He said that someone had to have authority to act quickly in this world *crisis:* he did not want the power granted by the bill, but someone had to have it, so that quick action could be taken.[59] Thus, it will be noted, Mr. Roosevelt made the novel and unspecified *crisis* serve as his excuse for the demanded grant of unprecedented power. In retrospect we know that there was no impending crisis and particularly that no impending crisis threatened England. Knowing the German plans, knowing them well enough to warn Russia, Mr. Roosevelt knew this too, but the Congress did not know it, and the country did not know it, and they were misinformed by Mr. Roosevelt, by his cabinet, and by others.

To reread the papers of this time gives one a curious feeling of living in an unreal world. The progress of the Libyan campaign is day-to-day history, but other events seem to be taking place not in America but in Alice's topsy-turvy Wonderland.

Mayor LaGuardia was planning to create a New York City Defense Unit and referred terrifyingly to London's experiences in being bombed and burned from the air:[60] Governor Lehman's annual message to the New York State Legislature dealt solely with defense problems in New York State.[61]

THE SYNTHETIC CRISIS AT THE BIRTH OF LEND-LEASE | 227

But on January 12, 1941, Senator Wheeler had warned the country [62] that the lease-lend bill represented another

> * New Deal triple A foreign policy—plow under every fourth American boy.

* * * * * *

> * nothing could be more unpatriotic than to try to fan the passions of the American people to the point where they will accept a program that will eventually send American boys to be killed upon foreign battlefields.

Mr. Willkie, on the other hand, promptly declared himself to be in favor of lease-lend, but with reservations, and sensing an opportunity to continue to keep himself in the public eye, he announced that he would go to Britain in order to see for himself what conditions there were really like. [63] Maladroitly this played directly into Mr. Roosevelt's hands, because the imaginary crisis in Britain was to be the new oratorical flood upon which the lease-lend bill was to be floated to passage: Mr. Roosevelt gladly authorized Mr. Willkie's passport, perhaps as a reward.

Lease-lend was contrary to the elementary rules of international law: it was of course contrary also to the platform promises of both the Democratic and Republican parties in 1940.

Mr. Landon noted this clearly when he said, [64]

> There is no essential difference between Mr. Willkie's position and Mr. Roosevelt's position, which is to go to war if necessary to help England win. If Mr. Willkie had revealed it before the Republican National Convention he would not have been nominated, and if Mr. Roosevelt had revealed it before election he would not have been reelected.

And Mr. Krock endorsed the accuracy of Mr. Landon's statement. [65] Indeed readers of the New York *Times* were warned in a played-down article that the ambit of Mr. Roosevelt's purposes extended far beyond the war, that in the back of his mind he intended to create "a New Deal for the world" after the end of the war. [66]

The hearings before the House Foreign Affairs Committee on the lease-lend bill commenced with swiftness, and with a parade of cabinet members on Wednesday, January 15, 1941. The Secretary of State, Mr. Hull, [67] led off with a statement said to have been edited by Mr. Roosevelt. [68] In substance he urged that all "technical" considerations be brushed aside because the United States was faced with the grim necessity of subordinating its ideal of neutrality and the finer points of international law to the urgency of sheer self-defense against the tidal wave of totalitarian conquest pointed unmistakably towards the Western Hemisphere. He warned America to beware lest we meet the fate of Norway, Holland, Belgium, and other defenseless countries. Mr. Hull, of course, as Secretary of State, could not have been ignorant of the fact that the tidal wave of totalitarian conquest was pointed unmistakably towards Russia and not towards the Western Hemisphere. All of the first part of Mr. Hull's statement [69] was a long rehearsal of grievances against Japan, which by no conceivable stretch of anybody's imagination was going to attempt the conquest of the Western Hemisphere. Mr. Hull's statement next dealt rather briefly with Italy, which was not only quite incapable of conquering the Western Hemisphere, but which was meeting with disaster in Libya, and which had caught a tiger by the tail in its attempted conquest of Greece. [70] Finally Mr. Hull's statement dealt at more length with Germany, but there was not the slightest mention of Russia. In the light of all these circumstances a curiously significant episode deserves attention. Mr. Hull was being questioned, [71] after testifying, by Representative Tinkham, one of the ablest, most widely informed Congressmen, who may well have had an inkling of what was in the wind. Mr. Tinkham asked Mr. Hull:

> "If Russia is attacked, will we help her?"
>
> "That's so theoretical that it hardly deserves an answer," Mr. Hull snapped.

In other words, the United States Department of State would tell and retell information to the Russian Ambassador, Constantine Oumansky, but the Secretary of State of the United States would indignantly refuse to tell the same information to a duly elected Representative of the people of the United States.

The second "witness," who testified the same day, was the Secretary of the Treasury, Mr. Morgenthau.[72] The substance of what he said was that Britain was practically out of gold; that British dollar exchange was fast running out, and that it would by no means be sufficient to pay for what Britain needed. These figures, he testified, had come to him from officials of Great Britain. Mr. Morgenthau's statement flatly contradicted what Mr. Roosevelt had said at his "silly, foolish old dollar sign" press conference slightly less than a month previously.

And on that same day, by an ironic coincidence of history, the first publicly mentioned American soldiers sailed away from our shores for foreign duty: they were going to garrison Newfoundland.[73]

Next day, on January 16, 1941, the Secretary of War, Mr. Stimson, was the third "witness" on behalf of the lease-lend bill.[74] His advent was the signal for sending up a barrage of terror propaganda. In substance Mr. Stimson said, on the first day of his appearance, that he saw a real and great danger of invasion of England by air if the British Navy should surrender or be destroyed. Being questioned as to whether what was believed then to be the greatest of American military inventions, the secret Norden bomb sight, had been given away to foreign nations, he refused to answer.[75] The inference to be drawn was clear, but the unanswered question still remains open.

Mr. Stimson's appearance ran over into the following day, January 17, and he was followed by the Secretary of the Navy, Mr. Knox, who also spoke in favor of the lease-lend bill.[76] The two gentlemen combined to exhibit to the nation an hypothetical chamber of horrors.

Both said in substance that Great Britain faced the possibility of the greatest "crisis" in the island kingdom's history within the next sixty to ninety days. The only way to keep the control of the seas from passing to Germany, they asserted, was to keep the British fleet supplied and fighting. To do that would also involve keeping Great Britain alive, because the British fleet would go down in the last desperate struggle should Britain finally be defeated.

For the benefit of those whose memories had retained for seven months the promise of Mr. Churchill's "we shall never surrender" speech, the secretaries cast doubts on the keeping of that promise. They questioned the value of Mr. Churchill's assurances given to Mr. Roosevelt the previous August concerning the British Navy on two grounds, which echoed the secret cables sent to Mr. Roosevelt by the Prime Minister. First (they claimed) the assurances only bound the Churchill cabinet; second, all sorts of circumstances might arise to make it impossible to carry out the assurances.

While Mr. Knox was ultimately generous enough to conjecture that probably the British Navy would go down fighting, he seized the occasion to add another waxwork to the chamber of horrors. If, he confidently speculated, Great Britain should fall, Germany would inevitably seize bases and territory in South America.

Upon questioning at the close of their statements both of the secretaries said, several times, that there was no intention of using the American Navy to convoy merchant ships, whether British or American. In spite of these assertions each secretary sturdily insisted that the proposed bill should not be amended so as to prohibit convoying. The President, they said, needed the greatest latitude to provide for unforeseen circumstances.

Each secretary carefully dodged the politically dangerous topic of using American soldiers to fight England's wars. In answer to such a question by Representative Tinkham, Mr. Stimson said that the material aid which it was proposed to give England should suffice "so that we do not have to send man power."

Secretary Knox, being asked how he thought Germany could be defeated, expressed the Churchillian opinion that it would be accomplished by bombing German cities and by the resulting collapse of the German people.

The lack of candor of Mr. Stimson and of Mr. Knox is highlighted by a confidential memorandum which Mr. Stimson sent to Mr. Roosevelt on January 22, 1941. It had been read and approved by Mr. Knox in draft form. [77] Mr. Stimson was estimating the "situation relative to Bill 1776," and with respect to the effectiveness of the aid which it might give England in the "crisis," he expressed these opinions: [78]

> 1. The above described immediate dangers to the United States arising from a defeat of Great Britain and a loss of the British fleet during the coming spring or summer cannot be entirely eliminated by anything which it is possible for us to do in respect to selling munitions to Britain between now and next September.
>
> 2. Whatever benefit Britain would derive during that period from the passage of Bill 1776 would be mainly in the increased morale which such passage would undoubtedly give to the British people. The enactment of the Bill would undoubtedly somewhat expedite the furnishing to her of American munitions owing to the centralization of purchasing and the flexibility of operations which it permits. But the immediate material advantages would, in my opinion, be far from sufficient to greatly increase her defensive power. For example, our production of the items of planes, guns (including aircraft guns, tank and anti-tank guns), and ammunition, will not be greatly increased until 1942.

Mr. Stimson concluded as follows:

> The prompt passage of Bill 1776 offers probably the last possible opportunity of, to any extent, contributing more fully to the defense of this country by aid to Britain which is short of military action. That extent is mainly limited to the increase of British morale which would be effected. In materiel the assistance rendered by this Bill during the coming six months would be insignificant. And when a people are suffering from such strain and shortage of supplies, including food, as will soon be the case with the British people, preservation of morale is difficult. I therefore think that the President should consider whether the American government has not reached the time when it must realize that the policy it has thus far followed of limiting its aid to measures which are short of military action will not probably secure a British victory. It is my belief that consideration should be given to measures which will at the same time secure the life line of British supplies across the Atlantic and relieve of their convoy duty units of her fleet which are sorely needed elsewhere.

The conflict between some of the statements made in the public testimony of Mr. Stimson and of Mr. Knox, and their opinions as revealed by this contemporary letter, cannot be reconciled.

Towards the close of the January 17 hearing a letter was read from the greatest American authority on international law, Mr. John Bassett Moore, which spotlighted the vice of the pending bill. Its most important paragraph read:

> There can be no doubt that, under the guise of certain phraseology, the pending bill assumes to transfer the war making power from the Congress, in which the Constitution lodges it, to the Executive. This is evident upon its face.

Also on the same day, January 17, Mr. Roosevelt held a press conference [79] at which he laughed off all attempts to limit the sweeping powers which the proposed bill would give him. He made it clear that he believed that the numerous suggestions publicly advanced for limiting the powers given him by the lease-lend bill verged on the absurd. Mr. Roosevelt also took this occasion either to repudiate a portion of the testimony which had been given by his cabinet members, or else to deny the existence of the "crisis." Mr. Roosevelt was asked if he had had word from the British that they were urgently in need of aid, and answered the question with an emphatic "no." Finally Mr. Roosevelt dodged confirming the report that Mr. Winant was about to be appointed Ambassador to Great Britain in the place of Mr. Kennedy.

Other propaganda came out of England on that same day, January 17. Mr. Churchill visited Glasgow to make a speech which was in reality beamed to the United States. He was accompanied by Mr. Hopkins and, the reporter noted, [80] "ostentatiously" called "attention to the presence of Mr. Roosevelt's representative on the platform."

Mr. Churchill said that, as to war aims, he asked to be excused from making peace aims his theme. If there was any dreadful and imminent "crisis," Mr. Churchill's auditors did not learn of it from him that day. The speech was gentle and almost soothing. Since the speech was meant for the American audience, and because it was timed to precede anything which Mr. Kennedy, the retiring ambassador, might say in his expected radio speech, Mr. Churchill was disarming, even if limitedly so. He said:

> We do not require in 1941 large armies from overseas. What we do require is weapons, ships and airplanes. All that we can pay for we will pay for, but we require far more than we will be able to pay for * . *

One can only wonder whether Mr. Hopkins, who had so swiftly sensed the existence of a great "crisis" the moment he arrived in England, had directly, or on instructions, [81] inspired the further news of the reporter. The reporter stated that the crucial weeks, or even days, of the war lay immediately ahead. The outcome of the Battle for Britain depended pretty much upon the speed and the extent of the aid which the United States gave England. It was generally believed there that Hitler would strike soon and hard. Hitler's logical strategy was to try to invade England as soon as the weather permitted. The fear in England was that American help, which could save the day if given in time, might come too late. And, the reporter concluded,

> * it is a fundamental precept here that the war will be won or lost *
> by the political manoeuverings now going on in Washington.

Next day, on January 18, 1941, a voice was heard in partial opposition when Mr. Kennedy spoke over the radio and urged the passage of a less drastic lease-lend bill. [82] We ought to stay out of the war and we can stay out of the war, he asserted. He justifiably complained of the increasing growth of intolerance, and of having been "smeared" because of his views. Rather movingly he argued that the problem before the country should be viewed only in the light of what was best for the United States. Glancing towards the testimony of Messrs. Stimson and Knox, he said that he was "aware of and [had] reported on the serious obstacles to British victory." Negating some of the terror propaganda, he suggested that in view of the fact that Hitler had been unable to cross the channel [83] one might well be skeptical of his ability to cross the Atlantic. As if gifted with prophecy he interpreted Mr. Churchill's speech of the previous day to mean, "Our boys are expected over there in 1942." What, he asked, are our war aims? What are the war aims of Great Britain? No statement of war aims, he noted, had ever been made. Are we being asked to sign a blank check?

With greater powers of prophecy he foresaw that Russia might well be the strongest nation at the end of the war. "Are our children's and our grandchildren's lives to be spent standing guard in

THE SYNTHETIC CRISIS AT THE BIRTH OF LEND-LEASE | 235

Europe?" England, he said, is fighting to preserve its own existence; England is not fighting our battle. This is not our war. We should stay at peace.

Mr. Kennedy could not have known how right he was about the difficulty of invading England. By an odd coincidence of history, Hitler was meeting with Mussolini at Salzburg on that very same day. Hitler had quite abandoned any idea of landing in England.

> Hitler said that the undertaking would be extremely difficult and that if it failed the first time it could not be attempted again. [83a]

On January 20 Mr. Roosevelt delivered his third inaugural address. [84] The transition continued which was noticeable in his annual message of two weeks previously. After saying some kind words about democracy in general and, in particular, during his own prior terms of office, he spoke of the spirit of America and then of American destiny. He next spoke of

> * sacrifice * in the cause of national defense. * great perils never before encountered. * We do not retreat. * we go forward in the service of our country.

There was no longer any talk about "short of war." There was no longer even lip service to the cause of peace: indeed the word "peace" does not appear even once in the course of the entire speech.

At his press conference on the following day, Tuesday, January 21, 1941, Mr. Roosevelt made statements which were intended to prevent the Congress from placing any limitations upon the powers to be conferred on him by the lease-lend bill. He laughed at any suggestion of convoying ships to Iceland, and said that he had never considered using American naval vessels to convoy ships bearing supplies to Great Britain. [85] Then, employing a form of obtaining publicity for a statement without assuming responsibility for it, Mr. Roosevelt, as reported, said obliquely:

Sources close to the White House said it was obvious that if the United States Navy convoyed ships * shooting was pretty sure to result and shooting came "awfully close to war."

Those responsible for foreign policy wanted to avoid that and the last thing they wanted was to compel shooting to start.

And Mr. Roosevelt, who was always extremely sensitive about the Constitution when it was a question of his own powers, said that to adopt the suggestion of a Supreme Defense Council to administer lease-lend would be unconstitutional because it would be a limitation on the power of the Executive.

Mr. Roosevelt's plans, so far as he had let them be known and insofar as they were then understood by Washington observers, were explained by Mr. Krock: [86]

* to wage war without declaring it, if possible to escape participating in it, and to manage the risks implicit in such a program. *

Anne O'Hare McCormick said that Mr. Roosevelt was engaging in an experiment in national policy. He was trying to wage and win a world war without actually fighting it. And she commented that it was a dangerous game, full of the most appalling risks. [87]

More terror stories began to appear in the papers. On the day when Lord Halifax arrived with a fanfaronade of publicity, one such story's headlines screamed, "British Expect Nazis To Hurl All Into Invasion To Win War By May—Set To Repel It By Suffering Huge Losses in Men, Planes And Ships," and the text of the article elaborated upon how the British [88]

* expect the mightiest onslaught in history * to be launched * within three months.

But a delay of three months was inconsistent with the earlier propaganda. Congressmen were quick to point out the discrepancy between this and the prior thirty-to-sixty-day stories. "Washington officials" quickly hastened the advent of Armageddon. The headlines on the front pages now screamed, "All-Out Attack by Axis Forecast." It was said that "Washington officials" are convinced [89]

> * that the world is only a few weeks away from perhaps the most critical period, in which Germany will attempt a knockout blow against Britain with no weapons barred.

On the following day a similar article also gained front-page publicity. [90]

Mr. Bullitt, our Ambassador to France, now joined Mr. Kennedy in principle, and urged that we should stay out of the war. [91] He weakened the force of his argument by adding that in order to gain time for our rearmament we should help Great Britain. No matter what aid we furnished Britain, he said, the dictators would hesitate to declare war against us until they had first conquered Great Britain. Congress suspected that perhaps all of the underlying facts were not fully known, but the Administration continued to suppress them, while the State Department refused to make public the diplomatic reports which it had received from Mr. Bullitt and from Mr. Kennedy. [92]

The House of Representatives ended the testimony on lease-lend. [93] Its Foreign Affairs Committee recommended four restrictions on the powers sought by Mr. Roosevelt: [94]

1. No defense article to be given away except after consultation with Army or Navy officers;
2. Lease-lend to terminate on June 30, 1943;
3. No convoying, and
4. The President to report to Congress every ninety days concerning his acts.

The minority of the Foreign Affairs Committee skeptically foresaw, if lease-lend became law, [95]

> * the probable result that [we] will soon go to war.
>
> This bill will not provide any additional war supplies for aid to Britain within the sixty or ninety days of her alleged crisis * . *

What was not known either to the Congress or to the American people was acknowledged in a secret memorandum dated January 27, 1941, prepared by General Marshall and Admiral Stark for the use of the British Staff representatives at the secret conferences just commencing, that the United States had already adopted [96]

> * the policy of affording * diplomatic assistance to the British Commonwealth in that nation's war against Germany.

The Senate hearings began before the Foreign Relations Committee on January 28, 1941. Secretary Morgenthau stuck to his story. He said [93] that Great Britain, Greece, and China could not continue to fight unless Congress passed the pending lease-lend bill: "they haven't any dollars left." Secretary Knox repeated himself: Great Britain's crisis may come within sixty to ninety days. [97]

The pendency of the great debate on lease-lend, which, as can be seen in retrospect, was an ambiguous, obscure, and concealed debate as to whether this nation should once again participate in a great world war, caused to pass almost unnoticed the genesis of Mr. Roosevelt's first and perhaps principal war aim, the extension of the New Deal to the rest of the world, and the consequent destruction of the colonial empires and other established institutions of our future allies. The New Dealish Mr. Winant was, on January 21, 1941, publicly named [98] the successor as Ambassador to Great Britain of the more conservative Mr. Kennedy. Mr. Winant's nomination was confirmed on February 10, 1941, and it was also announced that the more New Dealish Mr. Benjamin V. Cohen would accompany him to London to act as counselor to the embassy. [99] Mr. Krock alone

THE SYNTHETIC CRISIS AT THE BIRTH OF LEND-LEASE | 239

seems to have caught the full import of those appointments: in two extraordinarily inspired articles, [100] he suggested Mr. Roosevelt's desire for a transatlantic New Deal, and he predicted that there would be American manoeuverings in Britain designed to aid Mr. Bevin to bring a Socialist government to power there at the end of the war. The accuracy of Mr. Krock's foresight is confirmed by later information concerning Mr. Roosevelt's subsequent proposals of a New Deal for the British colonies, [101] for the French Empire, [102] for Morocco, [103] for the Dutch colonies, [104] and for Arabia. [105] To develop the details of those matters would, however, fall outside of the scope of this book.

— 4 —

Meanwhile the representatives of our War and Navy Departments were initiating a further series of secret staff conversations with military and naval experts (disguised in civilian clothes) [106] from Great Britain, Canada, and the Netherlands. [107]

In the earliest 1941 meetings it seems to have been agreed [108]

> * that the major offensive effort of the United States is to be exerted in the Atlantic, rather than in the Pacific, and * that a "waiting attitude" will be taken in the Pacific, pending a determination of Japan's intentions. *

The first of these further meetings was held in Washington from January 29 to March 27, 1941; the second at Singapore, commencing February 22, 1941, [109] and out of them American-British-Dutch war plans developed for combined operations against Germany and against Japan. The first plan, for operations against Germany, was, for short, known as "ABC-1," [110] and the later plan, for operations against Japan, was known as "ADB." [111] Mr. Roosevelt approved [112] these plans "except officially," [113] as

Admiral Stark put it. Yet, curiously enough, Admiral King's official report of 1944 does not make the remotest reference to those plans and conversations unless he intended to cover the topic with the utmost generality by his opening confession [114] that

> * we have been closely and deeply involved with our Allies in all the political * and military problems and undertakings which constitute modern war.

The "ADB" plan provided that the military and naval staffs of the various countries "should * advise [their] respective Governments to authorize [military] action" against Japan not only in the eventuality of a direct act of war by Japan, but also if Japanese troops or "a large number" of warships moved into certain defined areas of the high seas, or if Japan moved into certain French or Portuguese Colonies, or into Siam. [115] The technicality that Mr. Roosevelt had approved of this secret plan, but not "officially," hardly seems to be important, because he acted thenceforth in concert with the British and the Dutch as much as if the agreement was "officially" binding. [116] Indeed there appears to be some evidence that there was an ABCD (American, British, China, and the Dutch) bloc constituted at about this time, and that there was also a Joint Action Agreement between the United States, Great Britain, and the Netherlands, [117] but the secrecy of the details has thus far been successfully preserved.

A gleaning of contemporary clues tends to establish the fact that such a bloc had been constituted. Thus on April 2, 1941, it was reported from Manila that Air Chief Marshal Sir Robert Brooke-Popham (who subsequently held the chief command in Malaya) was there for what was guardedly characterized as "defense talks." [118] Next day it was mentioned that staff talks were being held at Washington concerning a joint convoy system with the British: it was reported that the American share of responsibility for these convoys would extend as far as to Iceland. [119] On April 8, 1941, there was a brief reference to Sir Robert Brooke-Popham's recent visit to Batavia, and a cryptic mention of "the British-Netherland-United States defense conferences in Manila." [120]

In the outcome it is perhaps not too important to attempt to establish one way or the other the relatively trifling difference between a secret alliance constituted by a formally executed treaty and a secret alliance established by a gentleman's agreement which had in fact been approved and established, "except officially."

What is more important is that the Japanese acted upon the justifiable belief that the United States, Great Britain, China, and the Netherlands had formed a secret bloc to oppose Japan. [121]

— 5 —

The conclusion that some secret commitment had been made by the United States to England at about this time finds further support in the conduct of the English top officials, who began to seek increased American aid in their manoeuvres in the sphere of power politics, particularly in Asia. Thus on February 7, 1941, Mr. W. M. Butler, Counselor of the British Embassy at Washington, acting under the instructions of the British Foreign Office, approached Mr. Maxwell M. Hamilton, Chief of the Division of Far Eastern Affairs in our State Department. The British Foreign Office had received a number of rumors (all of which subsequently proved to be inaccurate) that there was some new Japanese "scheme of cooperation with Germany"; that this plan was "linked up with the Soviet Government and Chinese Communists," and that perhaps war was planned, or at least a push to the southward, directed against British territories and the Netherlands East Indies. [122]

On February 11, 1941, the British Foreign Office cabled the British Embassy at Washington, amplifying these rumors, and begging for American diplomatic aid. War with Japan, it was asserted," [123]

> * would weaken their whole war effort against Germany. Indeed, if the threat to Singapore became imminent, the British authorities might be forced temporarily to transfer the British fleet from the Mediterranean in order to free naval forces for action in the Indian Ocean.
>
> It will be appreciated what a profound set-back this last step would constitute. Thus war with Japan would inevitably lengthen the war with Germany and would, indeed, make ultimate British success improbable *without the full participation of the United States.*
>
> Hence, while the direct danger to American interests in the Far East constituted by a further Japanese movement is clear, the indirect danger to the United States is even more serious. Indeed, it seems evident that Japanese aggression against British interests in the Far East represents a serious threat to the safety of the United States on account of its effect on the British war effort as a whole. It is essential, therefore, in the interests not only of the British Empire but of the United States, to take steps which will prevent the Japanese from taking the plunge. (Emphasis supplied.)

The reader will be repaid if he rereads the foregoing welter of words critically and determines for himself just how much the British Foreign Office was concerned with American interests in the Far East (and, indeed, how substantial American concern should have been with the political fate of some of the British possessions, which, like India, were afterwards to be abandoned).

The British Foreign Office note of February 11, 1941, was brought by Lord Halifax to the attention of Mr. Hull the same day, a copy being sent to the White House. Lord Halifax annexed a copy of the telegram already mentioned and also a copy of a second cable from the Foreign Office, which attempted both to

THE SYNTHETIC CRISIS AT THE BIRTH OF LEND-LEASE | 243

lay down the line of American foreign policy and to influence the movements of the American Navy. The second telegram read, in part, [124]

> * The only thing likely to avert war is to make it clear to Japan that further aggression will meet with the opposition both of the United States and of ourselves.
>
> A joint declaration to the Japanese by the United States and the British Empire that any attack on the Netherlands East Indies or on the British possessions in the Far East would involve Japan in war immediately and irreparably with both the United States and the British Empire is obviously the course most likely to achieve this end. *
>
> * Speaking to the Japanese Ambassador on February 7th, Mr. Eden said that while His Majesty's Government had no aggressive intentions they did not intend to sacrifice the British possessions in the Far East at the dictation of any Power. Nor were His Majesty's Government prepared to agree that Japan alone was entitled to control the destinies of the peoples of the Far East. Great Britain intended to discharge her obligations to those people in that part of the world for whom she was responsible and if British territories were attacked, the British people would undoubtedly defend them with the utmost vigour.
>
> It would be most useful if the President, when seeing the new Japanese Ambassador [Admiral Nomura] on his arrival, could speak to him in somewhat similar terms and make plain beyond the possibility of misunderstanding the interest of the United States in Far Eastern affairs. If a joint declaration on the lines indicated above is impracticable then it is clearly of the greatest importance that the United States Government should independently go as far as they can to make plain their attitude to the Japanese Government.
>
> With this object in view you should seek an interview with the President * . *

You should furthermore point out that in the view of the British authorities the situation would be greatly improved if in addition to any statement or warning that the United States Government may see fit to make to Japan, the American naval forces in the Far East were to be increased, either by sending reinforcements to Manila or despatching a detachment to Singapore. At this stage of events the most effective check upon further Japanese adventures would appear to be some definite move on the part of the American Fleet.

At this time Lord Halifax apparently did not see Mr. Roosevelt, for the reason expressed in his letter of February 11, 1941, to Mr. Hull, [125]

> * because I know that you are already giving the whole question your earnest consideration and also because in my recent conversations with the President and yourself I had already to a large extent anticipated the Foreign Office instructions.
>
> * I need not emphasize how greatly my Government hope that the United States Government will feel able to take some effective action in the very near future to deter the Japanese.

What the clue was to this frenzied pressure by the British may best be set forth in the contemporary language of General Sherman Miles, the head of our Military Intelligence Division (G-2), in a shrewd and skeptical report to General Marshall, dated February 11, 1941; [126]

> The British staff conferees *. At their meeting yesterday * presented strong arguments for the dispatch of an American [naval] force * to Singapore.
>
> Within the past four days similar pressure has apparently been exerted by the British, or through British influence * . *

THE SYNTHETIC CRISIS AT THE BIRTH OF LEND-LEASE | 245

* * * * * *

It is difficult to believe that all of this pressure, coming almost simultaneously * is coincidental, or indeed that the various reports are founded on any definite indications of the imminence of a Japanese attack on Singapore *. *It all looks very like concerted British pressure on us to commit ourselves in the Far East—a pressure that has been applied rather consistently during the past three months.* (Emphasis supplied.)

On February 15 Mr. Churchill cabled Mr. Roosevelt in order to put additional pressure behind the move which England desired: [127]

There are indications, from many drifting straws, that the Japanese mean to make war on us, or to do something which would compel us to make war on them, during the next few weeks or months. * should the weight of the Japanese Navy be thrown against us, situations beyond the capacity of our own naval strength would confront us.

* * * * * *

Should there be a threat of a major attack of [sic:—on?] New Zealand and Australia we would be compelled, of course, to remove our navy from the eastern Mediterranean. Such an action would result in disastrous military possibilities in that area, a certainty that some accommodation would have to be made by Turkey, and the reopening of German oil supplies and German trade from the Black Sea. Thus, Mr. President, you will see what an awful weakening of our war effort would come about, merely should Japan send her battle cruisers and her 12 cruisers carrying 8-inch guns into the eastern oceans, and still more should there be any serious invasion threat against New Zealand and Australia.

There are some who consider that in Japan's present mood she would have no hesitation to entertain an attempt to make war against both your country and mine. Although it is my personal belief that the odds are definitely against such an event, one cannot tell. Whatever you are able to do to instill in Japan anxiety as to a double war may succeed in averting this danger. Nevertheless should we alone be attacked, it would be difficult to overstate the grave character of the consequences.

When Mr. Roosevelt first saw Ambassador Nomura on February 14, 1941, it seems likely that he made threats of the sort requested by Mr. Churchill, because some of the material contained in the report of that meeting has been omitted from the printed official version.[128] Later, on February 22, 1941, Mr. Churchill cabled Mr. Roosevelt,[129]

Have received better news concerning Japan. It seems Jap Foreign Minister [Matsuoka] is shortly going to Moscow, Berlin and Rome for the purpose of covering the failure of action against us. The fear of the U. S. appears to have postponed attack which seemed imminent. While completely understanding your situation pending enactment of Bill on which our hopes depend ["Lend-Lease"], the more these fears can be aroused the better.

— 6 —

It was shortly after the inception of the secret conferences with the disguised British military and naval officials that the newspaper reporters at Washington were fingerprinted in a further move to censor naval news.[130]

On February 7, 1941, General Marshall was considering "the possible occupation of the Azores."[131]

On February 8, 1941, Mr. Roosevelt addressed the Boy Scouts.[132] Their peaceful motto of "be prepared" he turned into another context, as he referred to the needs of defense in "* these grave hours * these critical hours." As previously, the word "peace" is conspicuous by its absence from the speech.

On Sunday, February 9, Mr. Churchill broadcast from London, answering in part Mr. Kennedy's assertion that "our boys are expected over there in 1942." Just as Mr. Roosevelt had given America promises during the 1940 campaign that American troops would not be sent to Europe, so Mr. Churchill now set out to demonstrate to America that England would not need nor ask for American troops, but that she could achieve victory without them, and therefore the passage of the lease-lend bill would not involve the American nation in war. Mr. Churchill said: [133]

> It seems now to be certain that the government and people of the United States intend to supply us with all that is necessary for victory. In the last war the United States sent two million men across the Atlantic, but this is not a war of vast armies, hurling immense masses of shell at one another. We do not need the gallant armies, which are forming throughout the American Union. We do not need them this year, nor the next year, nor any year that I can foresee.
>
> But we do need most urgently an immense and continuous supply of war materials and technical apparatus of all kinds. We need them here and we need to bring them here. We will need a great mass of shipping in 1942, far more than we can build ourselves if we are to maintain and augment our war effort in the west and in the east.

Mr. Churchill then purported to address Mr. Roosevelt across the Atlantic and said, in concluding his broadcast,

> Put your confidence in us. Give us your faith and your blessing, and under Providence all will be well. * Give us the tools and we will finish the job.

Mr. Hopkins was with Mr. Churchill while this speech was being prepared, and the two men consulted at length over it. [134] It was intended to influence American opinion and especially the American Senate, which now had the bill, the House having passed it on February 8. [135]

Mr. Churchill's references to Mr. Hopkins's visit are brief. He quotes only the "Give us the tools" sentence from his entire broadcast. But in this connection his comment is significant: [136]

> * This could only be an *interim* pronouncement. *Far more* was needed *. (Emphasis supplied.)

Vessels, aircraft, arms, money, cooperation in power politics—what more could be needed—*far more* needed—unless it were American soldiers and a declaration of war against Germany? So Mr. Hopkins's visit ended. He was supposed to know all the English secrets, it was said as he left London, and an air of complete mystery continued to cloak him: [137]

> Only a few government officials know what Mr. Hopkins was here for, and perhaps not even they are sure.* The effect may not be known until the full history of this war comes to be written.

Meanwhile Mr. Willkie returned home, telling his interviewers [138] the same story as Mr. Churchill's recent broadcast. "What the British desire from us is not men, but materials and equipment," he asserted. To give aid to Britain would be likely to enable the United States to stay out of the war, Mr. Willkie argued: to withhold aid from Britain would probably involve us in war.

Mr. Churchill and Mr. Willkie had brought "short of war" back into the debate. [139]

The lease-lend debate was now shifting to the Senate. Senator Taft proposed amendments to the bill [140] which would:

1. Forbid the entry of American ships into the combat zones;
2. Forbid the use of American warships to convoy merchant ships to Great Britain and to other countries at war;
3. Forbid the use of American ports as bases for English warships;
4. Forbid giving away American warships or American military and naval equipment, and
5. Require specific Congressional approval of any funds for foreign aid.

On February 11, 1941, Mr. Willkie testified before the Senate on behalf of lease-lend. [141] It was his opinion that all-out aid to England did not finally involve the entry of America into the war. [142] While in England, he declared,

> * I never heard one person suggest that America should become an active ally and belligerent in this war.

Mr. Willkie was cross-examined by various senators, and in the course of his cross-examination passages from his 1940 campaign speeches were quoted to him. In one of these passages Mr. Willkie set forth his own standard of sincerity:

SENATOR NYE: One more assertion of yours, that of October 30 [1940]:

"On the basis of his"—that is, Roosevelt's—"past performance with pledges to the people you may expect we will be at war by April, 1941, if he is elected."

Do you still agree that that might be the case?

MR. WILLKIE: It might be. It was a bit of campaign oratory (laughter).

On February 13 the Senate's committee, 15 to 8, [143] recommended the adoption of the lease-lend bill. Three days later Mr. Hopkins arrived back in the United States: Great Britain, he said, needs our help "desperately," and needs it "now." [144] Thereafter the adoption of lease-lend was urged in the Senate, even at the risk of war. [145]

A war note now began to appear in duly reported slips of the tongue by high administration officials, perhaps not inadvertently. Mr. Jesse Jones, speaking before the House Currency and Banking Committee, said,

> We're in the war; at least we're nearly in the war; we're preparing for it.

And then he asked to have the remark stricken from the record. [146] Mr. Ickes declared himself to be in favor of the adoption of daylight saving time, [147]

> * now that we are at war; I mean to say, now that we are preparing our country for national defense.

Mr. Roosevelt, it was reported, was already preparing to create administrative machinery to function as soon as the lease-lend bill was passed. [148]

Mr. Hopkins was promptly named a member of the new Production Planning Board; it was observed that his appointment to this key post in the defense administration was particularly significant in connection with the planned economic collaboration between England and the United States to deprive Japan of vital supplies. [149]

The only intimation received by the public of the then current staff conversations appeared in a guarded and unfeatured report that plans for Anglo-American naval cooperation had been discussed among some military experts and New Deal political strategists in Washington. [150] This report casts doubt upon Admiral Stark's claim that he initiated purely military conversations [151] upon his own sole responsibility.

More alarming to the public was a front-page report on February 21, 1941, that General Marshall, the Chief of Staff, had told the Senate Military Affairs Committee that war planes were being speeded to Pacific areas; that the administration believed that Germany was urging Japan to enter the war and to come to grips with the United States in the Far East in order to divert American attention away from our program to aid Great Britain. [152]

Years later it transpired that these were combat planes for the Chinese, sent perhaps as early as January 1941; that General Marshall had "personally initiated the procedure" and had done the "maneuvering to get the planes." [153]

In an effort which seems to have had a dual motive, partly to advance the increasing censorship of news, and subsidiarily to control the flow of propaganda, Mr. Roosevelt delivered to the reporters a severe lecture at his press conference on February 21. [154] He put defense secrecy up to the press and the radio. He questioned the ethics, morals, and patriotism of the press and of the radio in giving the public the information about General Marshall's testimony concerning the increase of American air strength in the Pacific. To give such information to the nation, Mr. Roosevelt said,

> * would lead the American people to think in a way which was not accurate and thus hurt defense.

Mr. Roosevelt then went off to Hyde Park for a long week end to discuss further with Mr. Hopkins, his "personal envoy, the situation in Great Britain." [155] The creation of what was to become the Truman Committee was recommended. [156]

At the beginning of the next week Mr. Roosevelt asked Congress for $3,812,311,197 in order to purchase airplanes for England and for the American Army. [157] In London, Sir Walter Citrine observed that the people of the United States are "definitely opposed to entering the war." [158] Sir Walter also noted that decisive American aid from war-material production could not be expected before September 1941. The incident likeliest to plunge the United States into the war would, he predicted, come from Japan.

On Tuesday, February 25, Mr. Roosevelt returned to the White House and had his usual press conference.[159] He expressed the opinion that there need be no concern about the possibility of a rubber shortage, for the United States was in no danger of running short of rubber. There was a good-sized supply on hand, he said, and if necessary enough rubber could be obtained from old tires and similar used rubber to keep us going until synthetic rubber plants could be put up.

Mr. Roosevelt was cool towards the recent Japanese proposals for peace in Europe, which will be mentioned subsequently. Peace in Europe, he stated, must await a British victory. The first thing to do was to win the war. After victory had come, it would be time enough to outline the basis of peace.

As to lease-lend, Mr. Roosevelt emphasized that he was opposed to any amendments which would hamper him in extending all possible aid to Great Britain. He referred specifically to the proposed Ellender amendment which would restrict the use of American armed forces to the Western Hemisphere. No definition of the Western Hemisphere was necessary, Mr. Roosevelt opined, because the administration had already adopted a common-sense definition. *The Western Hemisphere did not include the Azores nor Iceland.*

Next day Mr. Roosevelt took steps to be ready to transfer to Great Britain about $500,000,000 worth of arms from American arsenals and Navy yards as soon as Congress acted.[160] Mr. Krock noted that, whatever it might be saying, the administration was squarely contemplating the prospect of war.[161]

All this time the lease-lend debate continued, and quite the opposite opinion was expressed therein by the proponents of the measure. This was typical of the confused state of the nation, due to its trust in Mr. Roosevelt's promises and assertions. The confused trust in what Mr. Roosevelt had promised is well illustrated by what Senator Brown of Michigan said, in carrying forward the debate on the lease-lend bill. [162] He said that the people of the United States had approved of Mr. Roosevelt's course the previous November but "including his promise not to participate in foreign wars. I base my vote on the bill upon that promise," he concluded. "I base my support of his leadership upon that promise. I trust him in this crisis. My countrymen told me to trust him." In Senator Brown's words there seems to lurk an uneasy echo of Job's mournful phrase, "Though he slay me, yet will I trust in him."

The result was by now so probable that the War Department did not hesitate to let it be known that legislation would be sought to extend the term of service of the National Guard by six to twelve months. [163] But to ensure against any last-minute narrowing of Mr. Roosevelt's desired power, Secretary Hull stated his opposition to the Ellender amendment: it might, he feared, encourage Japan to become more aggressive. [164] Meanwhile Mr. Roosevelt made it clear at his March 4, 1941, press conference that when the lend-lease bill was enacted he would run the defense program personally. [165]

Party hacks, New Deal zealots, the trust-papa group, and beyond doubt some sincere men combined in the Senate to pass the lend-lease bill on March 8. It became a law on March 11, 1941. On the same day Mr. Roosevelt proclaimed that the defense of Britain and Greece was "vital to the defense of the United States," and on March 15 China was included.

It was a fateful decision. The American people had lost control. Congress had surrendered to Mr. Roosevelt another of its constitutional powers, and had enabled him to make war, declared or undeclared, anywhere in the world. Seen in retrospect it becomes quite clear that thereafter American entry into the Second World War would be inevitable. The only remaining uncertainties about our belligerency were those of when and where and how; "completely minor details," to employ Rooseveltian phraseology.

That the die had been cast for ultimate war was clearly apparent to the military and naval men still meeting secretly at Washington. "ABC-1," their final plan, dated March 27, 1941, did not say *if* the United States becomes involved in war; it bluntly said "*when* the United States becomes involved in war*." [166]

A secret letter of Admiral Stark, dated April 3, 1941, and referring to these plans, is of great importance: [167]

> Staff conversations with the British have been completed and a joint United States-British war plan drawn up. * This report has been approved by [General Marshall] and by myself, and, at an appropriate time, is expected to receive the approval of the President. *
>
> * * * * * *
>
> The question as to our entry into the war now seems to be *when* and not *whether*. Public opinion * may or may not be accelerated. My own personal view is that we may be in the war (possibly undeclared) against Germany and Italy within about two months *.
>
> * * * * * *
>
> * The time has arrived, I believe, to perfect the technique and the methods that will be required by the special operations which you envisage immediately after the entry of the United States into war. (Emphasis in the original.)

For all practical purposes an Anglo-American alliance had now been constituted, "except officially." Indeed a post-war government publication says, [168]

> With the passage of the Lend-Lease Act on March 11, 1941, the United States openly allied its welfare with that of the United Kingdom and other countries fighting the Axis. *

THE SYNTHETIC CRISIS AT THE BIRTH OF LEND-LEASE | 255

As of March 1941 the word "openly" is erroneous. Mr. Sherwood was nearer to accuracy when he wrote [169] of the alliance that

> * if the isolationists had known the full extent of it their demands for the impeachment of President Roosevelt would have been a great deal louder. *

But Mr. Sherwood likewise was not entirely accurate. The existence of this alliance was not concealed solely from "isolationists"—it could not have been concealed from them alone. It was concealed from all of the people of the United States without regard to the nature of their political views.

The first fruit of this new alliance was a visit by American officers to Britain in March 1941. The purpose of this visit was to select naval bases and air fields, and as soon as they had been selected the work of construction began. [170] Some time late in January or early in February 1941 another quarter of a million rifles, with half a billion rounds of ammunition, had been given to Britain. It was so relatively insignificant, by now, that Mr. Churchill's brief cable of thanks to Mr. Hopkins for the gift referred to it as a "packet." [171] In April two million tons of merchant shipping was obtained and sent through the Red Sea to aid the British campaigns in the Mediterranean area. [172]

In order to perfect the technique of cooperation within the secret Anglo-American alliance, Mr. Roosevelt, it seems, instructed Admiral Stark in late April 1941 that the units of the American Navy should not be moved about without notifying the British Chief of the Naval Staff, and inviting his advice concerning such movements. [173] Accordingly in late April and early May 1941 there was considerable correspondence with the British over transferring a part of the American fleet from the Pacific into the Atlantic. The matter went to the Defense Committee of the British Cabinet, from them to Australia and

New Zealand, and back to Mr. Knox and to Mr. Roosevelt. [174] This transfer of American warships was the prelude to the proposed expedition to capture the Azores.

Only one restraint could now operate to deter Mr. Roosevelt from an immediate entry into the war, and that was the state of American public opinion, which was still overwhelmingly opposed to going to war. Some incident had to be found so as to reverse the general public opinion; to overcome the passive resistance of the American people to war, and to unite the nation in martial efforts.

Ardent and frankly acknowledged interventionists, like Mr. Sevareid, felt compunction over the deceit which accompanied the enactment of the Lend-Lease Act. He wrote: [175]

> Churchill had said: "Give us the tools and we will finish the job," and the President argued that the grant of the tools would be the cheapest way to buy our own salvation. Neither one, it was certain even then, believed in his heart that either proposition was the truth. Their opponents knew this and taunted them, daring them to tell the people the truth of their conviction that America must enter the war. This bothered me; I wondered whether there was not something fundamentally undemocratic and dishonest in this gradual procedure of moving from one objective to the next—from lend-lease to the taking of bases in the Atlantic, to the arming of merchant ships, and so on. *

Moreover, continued Mr. Sevareid: [176]

> * It was harder to contest the far more modern objections of men like Robert Hutchins of Chicago, who broadcast his cogent warning that the American people were "intellectually unprepared" for war, that they would enter it, if they did, not knowing precisely why they fought and unlikely therefore to make fruitful the victory they would win. * His premise was correct *. * I was to see at first hand as victory approached in other lands how right his premise had been, how badly we misused our triumph *.

Mr. Herbert Agar, who was also an interventionist, likewise made this subsequent confession of the deceit that was practiced, when agitating for the enactment of the Lend-Lease Act: [177]

> Our side kept saying in the press and in the Senate that it was a bill to keep America out of war. That is bunk. And I think this failure to say exactly what a thing means is an illustration of why our democratic world is being threatened now.

It is an old problem. Can a corrupt tree bring forth good fruit? Does the end justify the means?

Lease-lend being an accomplished fact, Mr. Roosevelt went off with Mr. Hopkins on another cruise on March 19, 1941. There he stated the extent of his purposes, according to his relative, Mr. Alsop, [178] as follows:

> * As long as two months ago he acknowledged to the intimates whom he invited to join him on his yachting holiday after passage of the lend-lease bill that the war could not be won without American intervention. At the same time he said that he could not intervene without an incident * . *

While thus absent on the *Potomac*, Mr. Roosevelt by radio from Fort Lauderdale, Florida, addressed the Democratic Party diners at the Jackson Day dinners on March 29, 1941. [179] He apologized for his second vacation in about three months but claimed that at Washington he usually worked fifteen hours a day. The times, he said, called "for courage and more courage—for action and more action." If Germany should win the war then the Gestapo would organize and rule the world. How long, asked Mr. Roosevelt, edging towards the war, how long could we maintain our ancient liberties under such terrible conditions? Mr. Roosevelt then attacked and attempted to "smear" his recent adversaries, saying,

Propagandists, defeatists and dupes, protected as they are by our fundamental civil liberties, have been preaching and are still preaching the ungodly gospel of fear. * They have tried to shatter the confidence of Americans in their government. *

* * * * * *

* They have attempted to exploit the natural love of our people for peace. They have represented themselves as pacifists, when actually they are serving the most brutal warmongers of all time. They have preached "peace—peace!" In the same way the devil can speciously quote the Scriptures.

Before we leave the fateful events of lend-lease a postscript should be added. In the 1942 campaign another attempt was made at a purge, this time of all those who had formerly opposed America's entry into the war. But the Democrats received only 47.4% of the total vote in 1942, and about four-fifths of the Representatives who had voted against lend-lease were re-elected; indeed, a larger proportion of them were reelected than of the Representatives who had voted in favor of that bill. [180]

— 7 —

In Europe thirty days passed, sixty days passed, ninety days passed, but the synthetic greatest crisis in the island kingdom's history utterly failed to develop.

Everything pointed towards an extension of the war on the Eastern front of Germany, but Anglo-American power politics succeeded in delaying the attack on Russia.

IX POWER POLITICS AT CROSS PURPOSES

L. IN EUROPE

ON FEBRUARY 10–12, 1941, General Franco conferred at Bordighera with Mussolini, [1] and on February 12 he met Marshal Pétain there. [2] It had been suspected that Italy was manoeuvering towards peace, [3] but we know now that that report was incorrect. In fact it was intended to persuade Spain to join the Axis, [4] so that Gibraltar could be captured, [5] but General Franco and Señor Suñer resisted these attempts; [6] Spain remained neutral, and Hitler was involuntarily preserved from a further and useless dispersal of his military power.

Concurrently the Axis had trouble in the Balkans and in North Africa. Bardia fell, Tobruk fell, [7] Bengazi fell, Italian East Africa fell, while the Greeks took the offensive and pushed the Italians back into Albania. [8] Rumania was in turmoil. [9] Hitler had to prop up his tottering Italian partner, send armored divisions to North Africa, and postpone for five weeks his planned attack upon Russia [10] while he made secure what was to become his right flank in the Balkans. On March 1, 1941, German troops entered Sofia, and Bulgaria joined the Axis, [11] being promptly reproved for doing so by Russia. [12] This may have represented a setback for Col. William J. Donovan, who, it was reported, had in recent weeks flown to many of the Balkan countries and had delivered personal messages from Mr. Roosevelt to the heads of these respective states. [13] This policy was directly guided by Mr. Roosevelt, and even the State Department was not consulted. [14]

In Yugoslavia, American intrigues had begun in January 1941, and in Greece they had begun in February. [15] After the Bulgarian submission German troops were massed along the Yugoslav frontiers, and on March 25, 1941, Yugoslavia joined the Axis by a treaty signed at Vienna. On March 27 an American-engineered revolution, [16] coupled with pledges of American support if the Yugoslav army would revolt, [17] led to the overthrow of Prince Paul and to the arrest of various ministers. It was a great American diplomatic triumph while it lasted. On April 6 Germany declared war on Yugoslavia. Belgrade was blotted out by aerial bombing: the Yugoslav armies were crushed in three days, and most of the remnants surrendered within two weeks. Anglo-American power politicians had forced a showdown with Germany, and Yugoslavia got it.

In Greece the melancholy story was not different in principle. [18] While the Germans were attempting to negotiate a peaceful end to the Italo-Greek war, Mr. Eden, the Foreign Secretary, and Sir John Dill, the British Chief of Staff, went to Athens in February 1941 to aid continued resistance. [19] The Germans then issued an ultimatum, which caused the Greeks to hesitate. American representations were made, and it is said that Greece was promised that she would share generously in the spoils of victory when Germany was eventually defeated. In late March 1941 it was reported that American lend-lease help was being given to Greece: President Roosevelt in fact disclosed that guns were being sent "as a showdown impends in the Balkans."[20] Even earlier a British expeditionary force had been landed in Greece, together with its necessary appurtenances, and thereafter it had been reinforced [21] from time to time. Greece decided that with English and American help it could resist Germany successfully as it had resisted Italy. Accordingly, on Sunday, April 6, 1941, Germany also attacked Greece. On April 9 the Germans were in Salonika, and on April 27 they captured Athens. King George II and the Greek government fled to Crete, together with the remnants of the British expeditionary force. [22] Adding insult to injury, the Germans made an air-borne surprise attack on Crete on May 20, [23] and from May 28 to May 31 the remainder of the British troops were evacuated from that island, having admittedly suffered "severe" losses. [24] The naval action of the British Mediterranean Fleet around Crete, Admiral Stark wrote, led to such a wounding defeat that no important British naval strength could for some months thereafter be brought to bear to defend either India or Malaya against a Japanese attack. [25] Meanwhile, due to the weakening of the North African army by withdrawing the forces sent to Greece, [26] the Germans had driven the English out of Libya and back into Egypt. Mr. Demaree Bess, reflecting contemporaneously upon these unfortunate and unsuccessful political events, wrote gloomily: [27]

> As far as * Americans were concerned, the happenings in Jugoslavia were of first-class importance. * Commitments made for us there swept far beyond "measures short of war." *
>
> * Last March our representatives pledged us to rescue Jugoslavia and Greece. There is little evidence in Europe that such a rescue will be possible without American soldiers.

These commitments, like a bird of ill omen, returned to roost at long last. In March of 1947 the original Anglo-American commitment to Greece was thrust back solely upon American shoulders. It caused a temporary political crisis in America, the more particularly so because the original background of the aged political deal was so generally unknown in the United States.

Returning to April 1941, Mr. Roosevelt's frame of mind may be gathered from an Easter message which he sent to the Pope. [28] The word "peace" does not once appear therein. Mr. Roosevelt listed and elaborated upon the four freedoms, which were stated as freedom of worship, freedom of information, freedom from fear, and freedom from want. These freedoms, he said in concluding his message, were once more attainable, but only by

> * the resolute action of men who answer bravely the clear call to their ancient fidelity to the Lord and to their fellowmen.

The response of His Holiness [29] deplored the horrors of war, and elaborated with considerable emphasis upon the blessings of peace.

American cooperation with Britain continued in the various spheres of power politics and was intensified after the passage of lend-lease. In early April, at Mr. Churchill's request, further pressure was put on France in respect to certain proposed movements of part of the French Navy, and France submitted to Mr. Roosevelt. [30] Similar action was taken in early May. [31]

In early April the United States secretly set up a large supply base at Basra [32] and in June and July more supplies were being sent to Egypt. [33]

At the beginning of April 1941 arrangements were made to repair the damaged British warships in American navy yards, [34] while in early May one third of the American training capacity for pilots was turned over to the British in order to prepare the candidates for the R. A. F. [35]

American power politics were extended to the Eastern Mediterranean in order to aid Britain. In May 1941 lease-lend supplies were "secretly and indirectly" shipped to neutral Turkey through nominally British destinations.[36] These shipments were sent to Turkey at this and subsequent times in order to induce Turkey to support the British political manoeuvres in the Near East.

Even beyond the eastern part of the Mediterranean there was political manoeuvering. There was a *coup d'état* in Iraq, and a government was formed hostile to Britain. A few days later the revolt was more or less terminated by British troops, but German and Italian planes were flown out to that area, based on the French-mandated territory in Syria. Marshal Pétain and Admiral Darlan seemed now to be attracted into a strong anti-English position, which was intensified when English and Free French forces invaded Syria on June 8. On May 16, 1941, Mr. Roosevelt warned France against any collaboration with Germany, which, he said, would constitute a menace to the Western Hemisphere. On June 5, 1941, Mr. Hull in a strongly worded note to Vichy asserted that, by collaborating with Germany and Italy, France was practically aligning herself with the aggressors.[37] A second and somewhat similar denunciation was sent on June 14.

2. IN AMERICA

In the United States, following the enactment of the lend-lease law, Mr. Roosevelt's covert preparations for war continued. His son Elliott tells us an unknown fact, that by March 1941 he was in Newfoundland with an Army aviation group, doing patrol work over the North Atlantic against German submarines.[38]

On April 4, 1941, Admiral Stark wrote Admiral Kimmel. He enclosed a memorandum on convoying which had already been prepared for Mr. Roosevelt.[39] The letter stated,

Our officers who have been studying the positions for bases in the British Isles have returned, and we have decided on immediate construction of one destroyer base and one seaplane base in Northern Ireland. We are also studying Scotland [and] Iceland bases for further support of the protective force for shipping in the northward approaches to Britain. [40]

Prior to April 9, 1941, the Coast Guard cutter *Cayuga* had landed American personnel in Greenland to conduct various surveys there: [41] on April 9, 1941, the United States entered into an agreement with a Danish official for the defense of that island, and simultaneously American Marines were landed there.

At some later date, which cannot yet be fixed with accuracy, Pacific bases were being built in the British and French colonies: Admiral Kimmel wrote, [42]

> * Our Army is now engaged in building air fields at Christmas, Canton, Fiji, and New Caledonia, and consideration is being given to other installations in the New Hebrides and Solomon Islands. In addition, discussion has been made from time to time over the establishment of American bases in the Gilberts, Bismarck Archipelago and other places.

It was during 1941 that "almost the entire administrative structure essential for war" was being created. [43] On March 27 Mr. Roosevelt had appointed Mr. Hopkins "to advise and assist" him in carrying out lend-lease; Congress the same day had appropriated seven billion dollars for that purpose. [44] Another element was added to the machinery for bureaucratic economic control through the creation of the Office of Price Administration and Civilian Supply by Executive Order on April 11, 1941: [45] in a little more than three months, on July 30, Mr. Roosevelt asked for price-control legislation. [46]

As of March 22, 1941, the Office of Production Management, by Order M-1, created preferences which aluminum producers were bound to observe in filling orders: copper, iron, steel, cork, certain chemicals, nickel, rayon, rubber, silk, and other materials were brought under similar priorities control in the following months. [47] By May 1941 the Director-General of the O.P.M., Mr. Knudsen, had persuaded the automobile industry to agree that automobile production would be cut 20% for the year beginning in August 1941. [48]

On Friday, May 16, at his usual press conference, Mr. Roosevelt announced his conversion to one of the repugnant concepts of the Tyrannies, the idea of an undeclared war. [49] Mr. Roosevelt began by a recital of earlier American history. He said that already there had been two undeclared wars; one against the Barbary pirates in the Mediterranean in 1803–1804, and the second in the West Indies a few years later.

When a reporter asked Mr. Roosevelt what his remarks meant, Mr. Roosevelt said "he should use his head." [50] Mr. Roosevelt evaded making a forthright statement, but in the light of subsequent events his inferential statement is of assistance in understanding his purposes.

On May 20 the Office of Civilian Defense was created, replacing the Division of State and Local Cooperation, [51] which had been established in late July 1940. [52] On June 4 the wartime censorship plan, which had been prepared earlier by the Joint Army and Navy Board, was approved by Mr. Roosevelt. [53]

On May 27 in a broadcast speech made to the governing board of the Pan American Union, not in a message to the Congress, Mr. Roosevelt proclaimed the existence of a state of "unlimited emergency" [54] (whatever that may mean).

Mr. Roosevelt opened his broadcast by setting forth the agreements which had been reached with all the other American republics. His theme was still that of "defense" at the beginning of this speech, and in the name of defense he summarily itemized the quantities of "aid for the democracies" which America had furnished. This included mention of the fact that America had "rushed arms [to Britain in June 1940] to meet her desperate needs." Mr. Roosevelt then painted a lurid picture of an imaginary Nazi conquest of the world. Latin America would first be conquered, then America and Canada. The American laboring man would be enslaved and forced to work for low wages. Farmers would be grievously harmed, because they would have to sell their products at prices which would be fixed by the government—by a Nazi Government, that is. The interests of business would be injured. Mr. Roosevelt continued, in this somber vein,

> Yes, even our right of worship would be threatened. * the Nazis are as ruthless as the Communists in the denial of God. *

Hitler, he said, was planning to dominate Europe, and that domination was a step preliminary to his accomplishment of a vaster plan to dominate the world. Therefore, for the safety of the whole Western hemisphere, Hitler must be stopped.

Indeed, Mr. Roosevelt continued, the Germans might take Portugal and Spain: they were threatening various points vital to American defense, such as the Azores, the Cape Verde Islands, Dakar, and Iceland. America must be ready to forestall such occupations.

> The war is approaching the brink of the Western Hemisphere itself. It is coming very close to home.

Consequently aid to Britain and to *any* country which would resist Hitlerism must be assured. (This was likely the first preparation to persuade the American people to aid Russia when it should be attacked.)

A short lecture on sea power followed, in the course of which Mr. Roosevelt revealed, with British permission, that Nazi sinkings of merchant ships were at a rate three times greater than the capacity of British shipyards to replace them, which rate was also twice the combined British and American capacity for production.

A deft transition then appeared in the speech. Mr. Roosevelt reasserted that American purposes were only for defense and to repel attack, after which, "attack" was defined in a new sense. In consequence of this redefinition the defensive "patrols" by our warships would be extended both in the North and South Atlantic oceans.

Our new policy, Mr. Roosevelt said, would be, first, actively to resist every attempt by Hitler to "threaten" the Western Hemisphere, and second, to give every possible assistance to Great Britain. Sneering at the "timid ones among us," Mr. Roosevelt admitted that there was "a small group of sincere, patriotic men and women" who had a "real passion for peace," but he smeared them subtly, saying that they were being supported by

* the enemies of democracy in our midst, the Bundists, the Fascists and the Communists. *

So, concluded Mr. Roosevelt,

We in the Americas will decide for ourselves whether and when and where our American interests are attacked or our security threatened.

We are placing our armed forces in strategic military positions.

We will not hesitate to use our armed forces to repel attack.

"Peace" had long since vanished from Mr. Roosevelt's vocabulary, to be replaced by "defense" and then by "acts short of war." Now "defense" died somewhere about the middle of this speech and was replaced by "attack," a glance towards the pledge of the anti-war plank of 1940.

The Congress was not consulted about this new declaration of American foreign policy. It had been by-passed. Count Ciano, who was in a position to form an opinion on the topic, now noted "that Roosevelt is a real dictator." [55]

What lay behind this speech of Mr. Roosevelt's was quite unknown to the Republic at the time. Our knowledge is now sufficient to state that Mr. Roosevelt was making a zig-zag step towards war from which he later withdrew. We know now that on the afternoon of May 22, 1941, Mr Roosevelt had called in Admiral Stark and given him: [56]

> * an over all limit of 30 days to prepare and have ready an expedition of 25,000 men to sail for, and to take the Azores. * The Army, of course, will be in on this but the Navy and the Marines will bear the brunt.

Three battleships, one aircraft carrier, four cruisers, and eighteen destroyers were detached "with the utmost possible secrecy" [57] from the Pacific fleet to the Atlantic in order to engage in this expedition. [58] This transfer is not mentioned by Admiral King in his official report. It resulted in a further deterioration of our relative position to the Japanese Navy, according to Admiral Inglis. [59]

If Mr. Roosevelt's plans resulted from a genuine fear, he had been badly misinformed by his intelligence service, because this improvised sideshow had been abandoned by the Germans at least by February 3, 1941, [60] over three and one-half months earlier.

It is also possible that Mr. Roosevelt ordered this attack in order to carry into effect, anticipatorily, a portion of the new Basic War Plan, WPL-46, also known as Rainbow No. 5, which was promulgated secretly but officially on May 26, 1941. [61] War Plan-46 superseded earlier plans with lower numbers, and it incorporated both ABC-1 and the Joint Canada-United States Plan (ABC-22). [62] It specifically provided that when agreements were "reached with Associated Powers other than those with the British Commonwealth, including Canada" the plan would be amended. [63] Meanwhile, [64]

Agreements have been reached between the United States and the United Kingdom relating to war operations.

Among the details of WPL-46 were:
Prepare to capture the AZORES, CAPE VERDE * ISLANDS. [65]

* * * * * *

* the movement of Army troops to ENGLAND, SCOTLAND and NORTH IRELAND. [66]

* * * * * *

Relieve, as soon as practicable, the British garrison in Iceland * [67]

* * * * * *

Provide a token force for the defense of the British Isles. [68]

* * * * * *

The early elimination of Italy as an active partner in the Axis. [69]

We cannot yet fix the date of temporary abandonment of this projected attack against the territory of a truly neutral nation, bound loyally to England by a succession of treaties for the better part of six hundred years. [70] However the fleet units, after the attack was abandoned, were not returned to the Pacific "but were employed further to augment the Atlantic Fleet, particularly in the vicinity of Iceland." [71] Officially American troops are not supposed to have been landed in Iceland until July 7, 1941, "where," Admiral King writes, "we *originally* established a base for forces engaged in escorting Lend-Lease convoys."[72] (Emphasis supplied.) This fleet transfer was, it is further said, [73] "in line with the basic *war* plans * . * an inextricable part of the over-all military policies *." (Emphasis supplied.)

There is some contemporary evidence as to the nature of Mr. Roosevelt's plans and purposes at this time. [74] He had adopted Mr. Churchill's views that to "conquer" Germany no large American expeditionary force would be needed. These were among Mr. Roosevelt's plans:

> * active American aid * will take the form of supplementing Britain's strength with American air and naval power * to sweep from the seas and the air above the seas all the German warcraft. This is, in fact, the next step.
>
> * The system * called for a mixture of convoying and policing sea lanes * . *

* * * * * *

> * At the same time, or a little later, the President may also order preventive occupation of * the Atlantic Islands and Dakar. Plans to do this are also in readiness *.

But what pretext could be found by Mr. Roosevelt to put these plans into effect? He had for long had in mind the possibility of some incident which would bring America into the war, even though that incident happened "by mistake." [75] Perhaps Hitler would now be obliging. There is contemporary evidence that Mr. Roosevelt was hoping for a German incident. [76] He was stated in an article to

> * wish to force the Germans to give him a pretext for action. *

It was explained that Mr. Roosevelt found it politically impossible to take the country into the Second World War by any direct route because of

> * the various commitments * he has made in the last year against convoying, against taking the country into war. *

A momentary digression into the state of public opinion at this time may be helpful. Admiral Kimmel wrote bluntly in late May 1941: [77]

> As preparation for war, the current mental and moral preparation of our people * is utterly wrong. To back into a war, unsupported or only half-heartedly supported by the public opinion, is to court losing it. A left-handed * approach to a very serious decision is totally destructive of that determination and firmness of national character without which we cannot succeed. The situation demands that our people be fully informed of the issues involved *. When we go in, we must go with ships, planes, guns, men and material, to the full extent of our resources. To tell our people anything else is to perpetrate a base deception *.

But a direct method of going to war presented no insuperable obstacle, the article continued. Mr. Roosevelt could accomplish it successfully with the aid of one kind of pretext or another, and no doubt would, because of

> * the President's penchant for doing a job the smart way. * If the Germans can only be persuaded to shoot first, they will have the major responsibility for what follows. * That is what appears to be in the President's mind.
>
> * As long as two months ago he acknowledged to the intimates whom he invited to join him on his yachting holiday after passage of the lend-lease bill that the war could not be won without American intervention. At the same time he said that he could not intervene without an incident. *
>
> * he has not acted, because he hopes to drive the Germans into shooting first.

* * * * * *

The problem was mentioned in this space in a recent discussion of the Atlantic patrol, in which it was pointed out that the President and the men around him privately hope the patrol will produce an incident. The patrol is by no means the only expedient, moreover, which the President has at his disposal. *

* no one can doubt the German high command will do everything possible to avoid shooting first.

This final conjecture of the columnists was exceedingly shrewd, and, as will be shown below, the Germans took careful steps to avoid any "incident" which might serve as a pretext for Mr. Roosevelt's purposes. Indeed we are now officially told that [78]

> * it is true that Hitler and his colleagues originally did not consider that a war with the United States would be beneficial to their interest * . *

Consequently there were no immediate German "incidents" to serve Mr. Roosevelt as a pretext for entry into the European war. Temporarily Mr. Roosevelt was stymied.

In fact the Atlantic patrol had been secretly commenced on April 24, 1941, the order stating, [79]

> The execution of this plan shall give the appearance of routine exercises where the departure of units from port are being made.

By May 1, 1941, confidential Navy tabulations were bracketing our total Naval strength against the "Axis" and with the British as "Allied."[80] There was a secret intercommunication system between the American and the British ships.[81]

However the Atlantic patrol was by no means the only expedient which Mr. Roosevelt had at his disposal. There are back doors as well as front doors. There was always the uneasy state of political affairs in the Far East.

3. IN THE FAR EAST

A peaceful solution of the Japanese question would have released much American power for use in Europe. On the other hand if certain diplomatic officials were correct in believing that Japan could be quickly defeated, perhaps a Japanese "incident" would serve Mr. Roosevelt's purposes without involving too much delay in his will to "conquer" Germany. Maybe the longest way round was the shortest way home.

It was complicated. Either way there were pros and cons. It is quite possible that in his own mind Mr. Roosevelt did not fully commit himself to the latter choice until late in November 1941. Without elucidating the cryptic remark, Miss Perkins tells us that Mr. Roosevelt was then attempting to solve a "terrible moral problem." [82] Moreover, [83]

> Franklin Roosevelt was not a simple man. That quality of simplicity which we delight to think marks the great and noble was not his. He was the most complicated human being I ever knew *.

* * * * * *

> He was many things—not clear, not simple, with drives and compulsions in a dozen different directions *. There was undoubted conflict within him. *

And Miss Perkins also refers to [84] "the complexity and variety of his * intentions." His "plans were never thoroughly thought out." [85]

It may therefore be true that there was a complex ambivalence, not thoroughly thought out for a long time, in Mr. Roosevelt's attitude toward the possibilities of peace or war between America and Japan. By his express declarations, hereafter mentioned, we know that there was deliberate temporizing, and temporizing is sometimes merely a way of postponing the making of a decision. But sometimes temporizing may also be simply a way of awaiting a favorable opportunity to put into effect a decision already made. It is therefore difficult to attempt to fix the time when Mr. Roosevelt first became willing to let war ensue between Japan and America.

Consequently some attention must now be given to the development of political affairs in the Far East.

We must turn back to 1940 in order to survey the further development of the diplomatic relations between Japan and the United States. As has already been pointed out, and as will become increasingly clear, the relationships between Germany, Russia (until June 22, 1941), Italy, and Japan—let us call them the Tyrannies, for convenience of reference—were anything but unified, harmonious and loyal.

The Tyrannies were jealous [86] of each other, contemptuous, [87] resentful, [88] and spiteful. [89] The Tyrannies trusted each other so little [90] that, by spying or other methods, they obtained each other's secret codes. [91] Each Tyranny at times kept one or more of the other Tyrannies quite in the dark concerning the next manoeuvre planned, [92] or even obstructed it as it was developing. [93] Their suspicions of each other seem hardly ever to have been at rest, [94] because each Tyranny was conducting its own affairs for its own sole benefit in a coldly selfish way [95] and therefore took it for certain that the other Tyrannies were equally free from any encumbering altruism.

Any concept, therefore, of the Tyrannies as a coordinated and well-integrated group, as an harmonious team playing a wicked and far-seeing game in loyal concord, is not merely inexpressibly naïve; it is utterly wrong. [96]

The spirit of unity was not only lacking from Tyranny to Tyranny in external politics, it was lacking within the national frontiers. The same conditions prevailed in Japan, within which there was a pronounced division of opinion as to policy, a division at times so extreme and so bitter that it had led to the murder of more than one political leader by the adherents of another political group. [97] Japan was by no means one coherent group, one cohesive mixture: [98] it was, to use a pharmacist's term, an emulsion, a rather unstable emulsion at that. After all, substantially less than one century had passed since Commodore Perry had cracked the shell of the Hermit Kingdom in 1854; only eighty years had elapsed since the first delegation of Japanese notables had visited President Buchanan in 1860. The old and the new had not yet been firmly engrafted together in Japan.

Just as Don Quixote was blindly bemused by the obsolete mediaeval traditions and romances of chivalry, so there were in Japan many military men, and others, who were equally blindly bemused by the obsolete traditions and romances of the samurai and by tales of the mediaeval power of the Japanese Empire. The "Japanese schoolboys," on the other hand, who had been a not-inconspicuous feature of the American scene prior to the First World War, had been educated abroad, had finished their Occidental travels, and were now middle-aged men at home, well aware of the power and the wealth of the western world. So were the Japanese merchants, whose commerce with that younger world yearly increased. So were the Japanese seamen, whose growing marine plied constantly the further seas, and so, on the whole, was the Japanese Navy. To some extent, so were the stay-at-home industrialists, building modern machinery in modern factories. And so, to varying degrees, was many a convert to Christianity. In late 1939 the Japanese people were overwhelmingly and intensely anti-German. [99]

As was the case in America, not everyone in Japan knew what the men who were operating the machinery of his national government intended to do. Nor, as in America, did everyone, who thought he knew, approve. [100]

As is now well known and generally recognized, two very different principal groups were contending for the governance of

Japan, the liberals and the military. By 1939, as has already been shown, neither group was enthusiastic about Hitlerian Germany. Both groups were even more suspicious of the trends which might be involved in the Russo-German rapprochement. Reciprocally, as early as 1935 the Russians were spying on Japanese diplomatic activities. [101] There was traditional bad blood between Japan and Russia, dating back to the Russo-Japanese war of 1904, augmented by the Japanese occupation of Siberia towards the end of the First World War and afterwards, and enhanced by the short undeclared wars along the Mongolian frontiers in the summers of 1937 and 1938. [102]

Assuming, therefore, that an American felt bound to engage in power politics, as Mr. Roosevelt was doing, the line to be adopted in the Far East was fairly obvious. By exploiting Russo-Japanese hostility, and German-Japanese suspicions and doubts, it should have been possible to drive a wedge between the Russo-German group and the Japanese. The facts of geography were such that Japan could never have given much direct aid to Germany in Europe, and Japan was plainly not disposed to be helpful to Russia. If friendly relations with Japan had been cultivated and maintained by America, the size of the American Army, Navy and Merchant Marine, together with our production of munitions and armaments, would, so to speak, have been doubled, because all of it could have been directed against Hitler, instead of our having to use a large portion of it in the Pacific. It is, furthermore, an elementary principle of strategy that one ought not to be compelled to fight two simultaneous wars on widely distant and separated fronts.

Even if truly friendly relations with Japan had proved difficult to achieve, a wisely Machiavellian foreign policy would have striven to create a false appearance of that kind, so that our will could have been later imposed on Japan, if necessary, by turning against her singly the full power of all the victors at the end of the

European war, but so that meanwhile Japan would have remained quiet and reasonably friendly. If it be objected that this would have involved duplicity and the disregard of moral considerations, the plain answer is that those who choose to engage in power politics must also be prepared to engage in such faithless conduct—as almost invariably they are.

For these reasons it would seem that American power politics towards Japan should have:

1. Done everything possible to aid, encourage, foster and strengthen the liberal political elements in Japan;
2. Done everything possible to undercut the military political elements in Japan, but surreptitiously, and without forcing an outward break;
3. Striven to prevent the creation of incidents which would have permitted the military to unify the dissident elements with them by invoking the "national honor," or comparable emotional shibboleths;
4. Emphasized the Japanese suspicions of Germany, and the bad blood towards Russia;
5. Offered additional peaceful trade and business opportunities with America in exchange for a diminution, on a progressive basis, of the war with China, and
6. Abstained from lecturing and hectoring.

But Mr. Roosevelt's policy towards Japan was none of these things. Clearly it was not friendly, but for equally clear political reasons it was not completely hostile in 1940.

American foreign policy during 1940 in the Far East was thus officially summarized by Mr. Hull: [103]

> Throughout this period the United States *increasingly* followed a policy of extending all feasible assistance and encouragement to China. * (Emphasis supplied.)

Japan's counter-policy was stated by Premier Konoye as follows: [104]

*Japan is now engaged in diplomatic maneuvers to induce Russia, Britain and the United States to suspend their operations in assisting the Chiang regime.

When 1940 opened, the war in China was two and a half years old, and gave no signs of coming to any decision. Japan had a million or more troops in service, and the burden of maintaining them had become a severe financial strain. Inflation was developing, and social unrest was increasing.[105] American pressure was augmenting the Japanese troubles. On January 26, 1940, the necessary notice having previously been given, the almost thirty-year-old treaty of commerce with Japan was ended.[106] Further aid, although not of a decisive nature, was extended to China.[107] Twenty-five million dollars had been "lent" to China towards the end of 1938, but Mr. Roosevelt records no official aid in 1939. In 1940 a total of two hundred and eighty-five million dollars was "lent" in progressively larger amounts; twenty millions on March 7, fifty-five millions on September 25, and the balance of two hundred and ten million dollars on November 30.

When the Japanese set up a Chinese central regime at Nanking under Wang Ching-wei in March 1940, the United States refused to recognize it and Mr. Hull issued an official statement denouncing it.[108]

In early April Ambassador Grew thought [109]

*that the futility of the China campaign * is steadily coming home to the great majority of thinking Japanese.

There now occurred an excellent example of power politics at cross purposes. Just before the German invasion of the Netherlands, Mr. Arita, the Japanese Foreign Minister, heard a report that the United States contemplated taking the Netherlands East Indies under its protection in such an event. [110] On April 15, 1940, he therefore issued a statement that Japan could not view with equanimity any alteration in the *status quo* of the islands. Mr. Hull suspected, erroneously, that Japan intended to move into the East Indies, and on April 17 he issued a counter-declaration in favor of their *status quo*. [111]

The German victories in Europe during May and June strengthened the political position of the Japanese militarists. They were emboldened to demand the cutting off of the war supplies which were arriving in China via Indo-China, Burma, and Hong Kong, and pressure was put on Britain to close the Burma Road. [112] Hearing such reports, Mr. Hull stated to the reporters on July 16, 1940, that the United States Government had a "legitimate interest in the keeping open of arteries of commerce in every part of the world" and that if the road were closed it "would constitute unwarranted interpositions of obstacles to world trade." [113] In spite of this statement the Burma Road was closed for three months on July 18. The United States promptly took single-handed action against Japan. On July 31 we cut off the export of aviation gasoline and most types of machine tools: [114] on August 1 the licensing system was applied to certain types of iron and steel scrap, and on September 26, 1940, it was announced that the export of scrap iron to Japan would be prohibited, effective October 16. Later in 1940, and in 1941, limitations were placed upon the export of arms, ammunition, war implements, iron and steel manufactures, petroleum products, lead, aluminum, copper, brass, bronze, zinc, potash, and other materials. [115] When, therefore, Hitler secretly [116] approached Japan in August 1940, after the new Government under Prince Konoye had come to power, [117] it proved possible ultimately to persuade the Japanese to sign the Tripartite Treaty of September 27, 1940, by which, if Germany, Italy, or Japan were attacked "by a power at present not involved in the * war," the others agreed to aid. The Tripartite Treaty was intended and understood to be a diplomatic counter-manoeuvre to the destroyer deal with Britain. [118] Mr. Roosevelt contemporaneously attached so little importance to it that he did not even refer to it in his 1940 volume, while the Secretary of State said, [119]

> * That such an agreement has been in progress of conclusion has been well known for some time, and that fact has been fully taken into account by the Government of the United States in the determining of this country's policies.

In addition to cutting off the supply of munitions of war to China through Burma, the Japanese wished to cut off their entry through French Indo-China. This pressure continued through the summer of 1940, and on September 22 a military agreement was concluded between the French and the Japanese authorities. [120] Before it was made Mr. Hull tried to block it on September 4 by issuing a declaration as to the *status quo* of Indo-China, [121] and after it had been made he issued a statement of disapproval on September 23. [122] As a result of this agreement Japanese forces moved into northern Indo-China.

As far back as September 1939 Mr. Roosevelt had decided to base a detachment of the American fleet at Pearl Harbor. [123] On May 7, 1940, Admiral James O. Richardson was directed to hold the entire fleet at Hawaii temporarily. [124] As the delay lengthened and continued, he first inquired and then protested, on the ground that the fleet was quite unprepared for war. [125] Admiral Richardson continued to protest over the hazards involved, and finally came to Washington on October 8, 1940, when he lunched with Mr. Roosevelt at the White House. [126] Mr. Roosevelt justified keeping the fleet at Hawaii on the grounds that it exercised a restraining influence on the actions of Japan.

Admiral Richardson said the Japanese knew the fleet was undermanned, that it was unprepared for war, and that it had no train of auxiliary ships, without which the fleet could not undertake active war operations. Therefore it could not exercise a restraining influence on Japan. [127] To accomplish that purpose, the Admiral said, we should withdraw the fleet to the Pacific coast, assemble a train of auxiliary ships, strip for war operations, and return.

Mr. Roosevelt replied that he *knew* that the fleet had had, and was then having, a restraining influence on the actions of Japan. Admiral Richardson retorted that he did not believe it. He knew that the fleet was disadvantageously disposed either for preparing for or initiating war operations. And he bluntly asked Mr. Roosevelt, are we going to enter the war?

Mr. Roosevelt answered

> * that if the Japanese attacked Thailand, or the Kra Peninsula, or the Dutch East Indies we would not enter the war, that if they even attacked the Philippines he doubted whether we would enter the war, but that they [the Japanese] could not always avoid making mistakes and that as the war continued and the area of operations expanded sooner or later they would make a mistake *and we would enter the war*. (Emphasis supplied.)

On October 10, 1940, Mr. Knox told Admiral Richardson, to the latter's amazement, that Mr. Roosevelt had also said that he was considering the creation of two long sea patrol lanes, or lines, of light ships to blockade Japanese commerce if the Japanese should take drastic countermeasures against Great Britain, which was planning to reopen the Burma Road on October 17. [128] This was a kind of rewarming of Mr. Roosevelt's similar plan of three years earlier, after his Chicago "quarantine" speech.

This plan of October 10, 1940, was to establish one long and unsupported line of light American warships from the Philippines to Hawaii, and a second line from the Netherlands East Indies to Samoa, in order to shut off all Japanese trade with North and South America. On this occasion, in addition to expressing his amazement, Admiral Richardson warned Mr. Knox that the Fleet was not prepared to put such a plan into effect, nor for the war which would certainly result from such a course of action.

Admiral Richardson's prudent warnings cost him his post before three months had elapsed. When, in late March 1941, he asked Mr. Knox why he had been so summarily shifted, the Secretary of the Navy replied, referring to the luncheon, "The last time you were here you hurt the President's feelings." [129]

In early October 1940 it was known to high officials that it was our policy to put more economic pressure on Japan and, in alliance with Great Britain, to be ready for war against Japan, hoping that it would not be necessary. [130]

British weakness had compelled Mr. Churchill to yield to Japan in July 1940 when the Burma Road was closed. But as the expiration approached of the three months' period, not only was Britain stronger but a better appraisal could be made of Japanese intentions. About mid-August Mr. Churchill believed that Japan would not attack the British Empire until Hitler had successfully invaded Britain. By October 4, 1940, the situation was clarified enough for the cabinet to decide to reopen the Burma Road on October 17. Mr. Churchill took this opportunity to ask again that American warships should be sent to Singapore—"the bigger the [squadron] the better"—at which time military and naval problems could be discussed with the British and the Dutch. [132] It seems safe to assume that this British action was taken in reliance upon the assurances, mentioned above, which Mr. Hull had given to Lord Lothian on September 30.

It was also in October 1940 that Mr. Roosevelt caused a secret approach to be made to the Australian Minister and that he urged that the Australians should ship arms into French Indo-China (from which country they could easily be sent to China) to be used against the Japanese; he promised that these arms would later be replaced from America. [133]

By mid-October 1940 there were some Congressmen who foresaw a war in Europe, started by a backdoor war with Japan, and there were some rash State Department officials who speculated that a war with Japan would end quickly in her defeat "in a few weeks." [134]

Another matter which seems to have had its inception near this time passed almost unnoticed at the moment, and was thereafter kept a secret for many years. In a dispatch from Wellington, N. Z., dated January 14, 1941, but delayed by censorship for nearly three weeks, [135] it was stated, from a highly authoritative source, that Australia and New Zealand had "an understanding" with the United States concerning future events in the South Pacific area, and that it was intended to block Japanese expansion. Washington was very reticent about this news item, and would neither confirm it nor deny it.

The passage of time had enabled the moderates in Japan to gain ground from the military extremists. The Tripartite Pact was unwelcome to them, as it was to the Emperor, and the general Japanese attitude was one of dismay. [136] Germany had not made any attempt to invade Britain, and as Mr. Hull had told Lord Lothian, the Japanese were assuming the existence of some secret and special relationship between Britain and America. In November 1940 Japan made a secret peace offer to Chiang Kai-shek and hoped for United States mediation to secure peace. [137] Late in 1940 Japan was approaching a political crisis. No longer could anyone, even in the military group, claim seriously that the occupation of Chinese territory had turned out to be a success. Except officially and publicly the "China Incident" was an acknowledged failure, [138] but the problem still to be solved was how to liquidate a losing venture without likewise losing face. General Tomoyuki Yamashita, who had been the Japanese military attaché to Austria, had been sent on a six-month inspection tour of Europe in 1940 by General Tojo. [139] As a result of this, when General Yamashita returned to Japan in 1941, he recommended that the China Incident be brought to an immediate close, and that the relations with Great Britain and America be maintained on a peaceful basis at all costs. [140]

If, therefore, American statesmen truly wanted peace, theirs was not a difficult task, particularly so because they were at all times fully acquainted with Japanese hopes and plans through the breaking of the Japanese code. [141] On the other hand, if American statesmen either wanted war or at least welcomed it as a backdoor means of entrance into the European war, their task was equally easy. Perhaps for the only known occasion in diplomatic history the Americans had everything at their finger tips. It was a complete set-up for them. And it eventuated in war.

By the middle of January 1941 anyone who could read the front page of a good newspaper [142] was made aware of the increasingly moderate foreign policy of Japan. This had found an earlier and tangible expression in the appointment of Admiral Kichisaburo Nomura on November 8, 1940, as the new Japanese Ambassador to the United States. The Germans viewed this as an unfavorable development, because, said von Ribbentrop: [143]

> * at heart Nomura inclined rather toward the Anglo-Saxons.

Admiral Nomura had been Foreign Minister only a few months previously, and Ambassador Grew judged that he was "fundamentally friendly to the United States." [144]

This favorable turn of Japanese policy received a greater impetus in December 1940, when Bishop James E. Walsh, the Superior General of the Roman Catholic institution at Maryknoll, N. Y., being in Japan with Father Drought, engaged in secret conversations for the readjustment of Japanese-American relations with Colonel Iwakuro of the Military Affairs Bureau of the Army Ministry and with Mr. Tadao Ikawa. [145] On January 27, 1941, Bishop Walsh wrote the Postmaster General, Mr. Frank C. Walker, that a plan had been worked out, and he suggested that a representative be sent from the United States to Japan. [146] Mr. Walker brought the letter to Mr. Roosevelt's attention, and the latter, on February 3, 1941, sent it to Mr. Hull. [147] Mr. Hull was skeptical and preferred to await the arrival of Ambassador Nomura. [148] It would appear that Bishop Walsh had seen Mr. Roosevelt in person in order to urge his plan, and that he had left a copy of it with Mr. Roosevelt. [149] In that plan it was stated that in October 1940 Chiang Kai-shek had secretly offered truce terms to Japan, and that Japan was now ready to accept them. [150]

Admiral Nomura had left Japan for Washington on January 23, 1941, and the news article which noted his departure [151] stated that his mission was to try to improve Japanese-American relations. The foregoing facts therefore elucidate the somewhat cryptic statement of the official version: [152]

> During the latter part of January 1941, through private Japanese and American citizens, the suggestion had reached President Roosevelt and Secretary Hull that the Japanese Government would welcome an opportunity to alter its political alignments and modify its attitude toward the "China Incident." *

In diplomatic language, "to alter its political alignments" means that Japan was thinking of drawing away from its loose and nebulous ties with the Axis.

Mr. Hull, therefore, knew of this potentially great opportunity, but he did not reveal it to the Congress at a later date, when he set forth the considerations which he claimed that he had in mind at so momentous a time. First, he says, he was utterly and completely pessimistic about maintaining peace: [153]

> * I estimated from the outset that there was not * even one [chance] in 100 of reaching a peaceful settlement. *

Second, Mr. Roosevelt's primary purpose was not to seek peace, but rather to play for time while American armaments increased: [153]

* Moreover, the President and I constantly had very much in mind the advice of our highest military authorities who kept emphasizing to us the imperative need of having time to build up preparations for defense vital not only to the United States but to many other countries resisting aggression. *Our decision to enter into the conversations with the Japanese was*, therefore, *in line with our need to rearm* for self-defense. (Emphasis supplied.)

Japan, then, wanted at this time to pull away from the Axis; to make peace with China; to be at peace with the United States. It is difficult to imagine any reasons why an accomplishment of these objectives would have injured any of the interests of the United States, or of Britain, the protection of whose interests was certainly in the forefront of Mr. Roosevelt's and Mr. Hull's thoughts at that time. Under date of January 21, 1941, Mr. Roosevelt wrote to Ambassador Grew in Japan: [154]

> The British need assistance * at many points, assistance which in the case of the Far East is certainly well within the realm of "possibility" so far as the capacity of the United States is concerned. *
>
> * The conflict may well be long and we must bear in mind that when England is victorious she may not have left the strength that would be needed to bring about a rearrangement of such territorial changes in the western and southern Pacific as might occur during the course of the conflict if Japan is not kept within bounds. *

Certainly in Germany the Japanese tendencies towards peace were viewed with considerable alarm as injuring the interests of Germany. German attempts were made in Tokyo to prevent Admiral Nomura from being sent to Washington, and Ambassador Grew [155] was well aware of the basic German policy, which was

> * to bring about a partial or complete break in diplomatic relations with the United States, and * to intensify their efforts to embroil the two countries * . *

In Europe, von Ribbentrop met the Japanese Ambassador, General Hiroshi Oshima, at Fuschl on February 13, 1941, and attempted to persuade him that Japan should attack the British possessions in the Far East. This manoeuvre had been contemplated by Hitler as early as December 27, 1940. [156] Mr. Roosevelt, said von Ribbentrop, was the most bitter enemy of Germany and of Japan: Mr. Roosevelt [157]

> * would like to enter the war. However we have an interest in keeping America out of the war. * it should be possible to keep America out of the war by skillfully coordinated politics of the allied powers.

Most of von Ribbentrop's argument is not of particular interest [158] except to someone who requires additional evidence of the way in which one of the Tyrannies attempted to use another as a catspaw: it seems patent on the face of the interview that Germany was trying to influence Japanese foreign policy so as to divert Mr. Roosevelt's attention away from Europe by an Oriental war. Unless von Ribbentrop was wholly unaware of the meetings going on at that very moment in Washington with an eye to American defense of the British colonial empire, he was giving Oshima very bad advice when he urged this Japanese action: [159]

> A surprising intervention by Japan [against England] was bound to keep America out of the war. America, which at present is not armed as yet and would hesitate greatly to expose her Navy to any risks West of Hawaii, could do this even less so in such a case. If Japan would otherwise respect the American interests, there would not even be the possibility for Roosevelt to use the argument of lost prestige to make war plausible to the Americans. *

Mr. Churchill must have been swiftly informed concerning this German manoeuvre because on February 15, 1941, he urged Mr. Roosevelt to "instill in Japan anxiety" that any such Japanese move would mean war with the United States. [160]

Mr. Roosevelt's first idea, as appears in a memorandum from Admiral Stark, dated February 11, 1941, was to send a detachment of warships to the Far East and perhaps to permit a leak as to their destination, so as either to "bluff" Japan or even perhaps to create an "incident" which would lead to war and thus unify American public opinion. Admiral Stark quoted Mr. Roosevelt as stating that while he did "not mind losing one or two cruisers" he "did not want to take a chance on losing five or six." [161] Presumably for this reason the first idea was abandoned.

The second idea of Mr. Roosevelt's seems to have been to employ diplomatic threats. At an interview in Tokyo on February 14, 1941, between the Counselor of the American Embassy, Mr. Dooman, and the Japanese Vice Minister for Foreign Affairs, Mr. Ohashi, [162] the latter asked, "Do you mean to say that if Japan were to attack Singapore there would be a war with the United States?" Mr. Dooman replied, "The logic of the situation would inevitably raise that question." When Ambassador Grew saw Mr. Matsuoka the next morning he stated that Mr. Dooman's remarks "were made with my prior knowledge and have my full approval."

Apparently Mr. Churchill's hopes were realized. The well-informed Mr. Hugh Byas cabled from Japan, [163] noting

> * Matsuoka's anxiety to avoid war with the United States. Virtually all diplomatic observers agree that the avoidance of a clash with the United States is a fixed point in the present Cabinet policy.

When, on February 14, 1941, Ambassador Nomura was received by Mr. Roosevelt at Washington, the official version of their meeting, as given to the press, was to emphasize their anxiety for peace in the Orient. [164] Mr. Hull's version, years later, of his early conferences with the Japanese Ambassador in February 1941 seems intended to convey a different picture of bleak reserve: Mr. Hull [165] had

* expressed the hope that the Ambassador might have something definite in mind that would offer a practical approach to dealing with the present course of his Government.

For the next two months, as will be shown, Britain was trying to push the United States into aggressive action against Japan; Germany was trying to push Japan into aggressive action which would have had repercussions on the United States, and Japan was trying to create peace both in Europe and in Asia.

Hardly had the ink dried on mid-February news articles stating that women and children of the British and American embassies were leaving Tokyo; [166] that the British were mining a zone off Singapore, and that there were various war rumors, [167] when it appeared that Japan had offered to mediate to end the war! [168] Under Secretary of State Sumner Welles rushed into the news as being "Cold To Tokyo Plea For Peace" [169] even before the English Foreign Under Secretary, Mr. Richard Austen Butler, could officially announce the Japanese mediation offer to the House of Commons. [170] Five days later Mr. Churchill rejected the peace offer. [171]

Britain was once again attempting to influence the action of the United States. A London despatch stated that the British were urging a curb on the export of goods to Japan. It was noted that this plan had been outlined to Mr. Hopkins, who had left London only a few days previously. "Mr. Hopkins, it was said, took the list of proposals [172] back to Washington for submission to Mr. Roosevelt." And there was one prophetic note of warning: the British believed that the Japanese might consider an oil embargo provocative. [173] As so often happened, there was an immediate echo from Washington: [174]

> Early economic collaboration between the United States and Britain to deprive the Japanese war machine of vital war supplies is a distinct possibility, unofficial administration sources said tonight.

All Tokyo's hopes were peaceful, cabled Mr. Byas: [175]

> Not to have war with the United States if it can possibly be avoided is one of the fixed points of Foreign Minister Yosuke Matsuoka's foreign policy *. *
>
> Mr. Matsuoka's great ambition is to be the architect of peace.

On March 4, 1941, at London, Mr. Churchill talked with the Japanese Ambassador, Mamoru Shigemitsu. Japan was reported as emphasizing her desire to keep the war from spreading into the Pacific and as expressing friendly intentions. [176]

The existence of these purposes was confirmed by a dispatch from Mr. Byas, who reported from Japan that the Japanese were stressing a peaceful policy; that they did not wish war with Britain.

Meanwhile Germany was trying, with a notable lack of success, to incite the Japanese to warlike action. A Top Secret "Basic Order No. 24," countersigned by General Keitel, was issued from Hitler's headquarters as Hitler's order on March 5, 1941. [178] It provided:

> 1. It must be the *aim* of the collaboration based on the Three Power Pact to induce Japan as soon as possible *to take active measures in the Far East*. Strong British forces will thereby be tied down, and the center of gravity of the interests of the United States of America will be diverted to the Pacific.
>
> * * * * * *
>
> 3. * * *
>
> *a*. The *common aim* of the conduct of war is to be stressed as forcing England to the ground quickly and thereby keeping the United States out of the war. Beyond this Germany has no political, military or economic interests in the Far East which would give occasion for any reservations with regard to Japanese intentions.

* * * * * *

c. The *raw material situation* of the *pact powers* demands that Japan should acquire possession of those territories which it needs for the continuation of the war, especially if the United States intervenes. Rubber shipments must be carried out even after the entry of Japan into the war, since they are of vital importance to Germany.

d. The *seizure of Singapore* as the key British position in the Far East would mean a decisive success for the entire conduct of war of the Three Powers.

In addition, attacks on other systems of bases of British naval power—extending to those of American naval power only if the entry of the United States into the war cannot be prevented—will result in weakening the enemy's system of power in that region and also, just like the attack on sea communications, in tying down substantial forces of all kinds (Australia).

* * * * * *

5. The Japanese must not be given any intimation of the Barbarossa operation. (Emphasis in the original text.)

The reader will not have failed to note how anxious Hitler was to keep the United States out of the war, or at least to divert its energy and attention towards the Pacific. No secret document has to date revealed any plans by Hitler to make a direct attack on the United States.

Even the diversionary manoeuvre just mentioned failed of its purpose. On March 18, 1941, at a meeting of Hitler, Generals Keitel and Jodl, and Admiral Raeder,[179] the last named delivered a temporizing and possibly ironical reply from the Japanese: they would attack Singapore only after the Germans had effectuated a landing in England. Raeder noted, also, that "Japan wishes if possible to avoid war against U. S. A." Raeder could only suggest a renewal of the already unacceptable arguments:

> * the opportunity will never again be as favorable (whole English fleet contained; unpreparedness of U. S. A. for war against Japan; inferiority of U. S. Fleet vis-a-vis the Japanese). * Germany must therefore concentrate all her efforts on spurring Japan to act immediately. *

In the midst of these intrigues and cross-currents the Japanese Foreign Minister, Mr. Matsuoka, decided to see for himself. Leaving Tokyo on March 12, 1941, [180] he went visiting to Moscow, Berlin, Rome, and Vichy. There were meetings at Berlin on March 27, 28, 29, April 4, and April 5, 1941, [181] at which Hitler and von Ribbentrop continued their attempts to push Japan into the war. Matsuoka expressed his sympathetic regrets. On the whole he agreed with the German views, but the influential politicians in Japan would always delay "and act partly from a pro-British or pro-American attitude." He had been strongly in favor of an attack on Singapore, but he had not prevailed. He wanted to have Japan attack Singapore but

> * Unfortunately he did not control Japan, but had to bring those who were in control around to his point of view. * at the present moment he could under these circumstances make no pledge on behalf of the Japanese Empire that it would take action.

* * * * * *

Matsuoka then requested urgently that the representations which he had made be treated as strictly confidential, since, if they became known in Japan, those among his Cabinet colleagues who thought differently from him would probably become alarmed and would seek to get him out of office.

At the second conference Matsuoka enquired from von Ribbentrop what attitude Germany would take towards the United States if Britain was crushed, but the United States had not yet entered the war; would Germany leave the United States in peace? Von Ribbentrop replied

* that Germany did not have the slightest interest in a war against the United States. Matsuoka noted this with satisfaction *. The Reich Foreign Minister replied that each would exercise dominion in its own sphere. Germany, together with Italy, would do this in the European-African sphere; the United States would have to limit itself to the American Continent; and the Far East was reserved for Japan. As far as Russia was concerned, it would be very carefully watched and would in no case be permitted any kind of subversive propaganda. In the future only the three aforesaid spheres of interest would remain as great centers of power. The British Empire would disappear.

Again and again von Ribbentrop kept urging that Japan should attack Singapore and declare war against Britain, and Matsuoka discussed some possible aspects of this situation with him and at a later conference with Hitler. At the later conference some of the interesting passages were as follows:

* Japan would do everything in her power to avoid a war with the United States. In case his country determined on a stroke against Singapore, the Japanese Navy must, of course, also make preparations against the United States, for in such a case America might possibly come out on the side of Great Britain. Personally, he (Matsuoka) believed that the entry of the United States into the war on the side of Great Britain could be avoided. The army and navy must, however, prepare for the worst, i.e., for a war against America. They believed that such a war would last over five years and be fought out as a guerrilla war in the Pacific Ocean and South Seas. *

* * * * * *

The Fuehrer agreed to this and added that Germany also considered a war with the United States to be undesirable *. *

* * * * * *

In the further course of the conversation the Fuehrer declared that if Japan got into a conflict with the United States, Germany on her part would take the necessary steps at once.

* * * * * *

Matsuoka continued that it seemed important to him to give the Fuehrer the true story about the actual situation in Japan. Therefore he must inform him of the regrettable circumstances that he (Matsuoka), as Japanese Foreign Minister, in Japan itself did not dare to say a word about the plans which he had set forth to the Fuehrer and the Reich Foreign Minister. In political and financial circles it would do him much harm. *

* * * * * *

In addition Matsuoka expressly requested that nothing be cabled on the subject of Singapore, since he feared that by use of telegrams something might slip out.

The Fuehrer agreed and assured him that he could rely fully and completely on German discretion.

Matsuoka preserved his liberty of action partly by emphasizing his political difficulties, and partly by asserting that the Germans must not believe what they might hear about Japanese negotiations with Britain and with America. Thus on March 29 Matsuoka had pointed out to von Ribbentrop *that he was doing everything to reassure the English about Singapore. He acted as if Japan had no intention at all regarding this key position of England in the East. Therefore it might be possible that his attitude towards the British would appear to be friendly in words and in acts. However, Germany should not be deceived by that. He assumed this attitude not only in order to reassure the British, but also in order to fool the pro-British and pro-American elements [in Japan]*.

In this connection, Matsuoka stated that his tactics were based on the certain assumption that the sudden attack against Singapore would unite the entire Japanese nation with one blow. *

* * * * * *

* He believed he could stave off any danger which threatened from America for six months. If, however, the capture of Singapore required still more time and if the operations would perhaps even drag out for a year, the situation with America would become extremely critical and he did not know as yet how to meet it.

Matsuoka also reported

* that the United States or rather their ruling politicians had recently still attempted a last maneuver towards Japan, by declaring that America would not fight Japan on account of China or the South Seas provided that Japan gave free passage to * rubber and tin to America. However, America would war against Japan the moment she felt that Japan entered the war with the intention to assist in the destruction of Great Britain. *

Matsuoka was seeking to neutralize Russia's power, but he was likewise seeking to gain something from Germany. Italy had long since recognized the puppet regime in China of Wang Ching-wei: this had been done on March 3, 1940, over German objections.[182] We may assume with confidence that Matsuoka sought to obtain a similar recognition from Germany, but he did not get it at this time. It was delayed for about three months and was not given until June 26, 1941, [183] after the Russian attack had been commenced.

Indeed, while on the topic of anomalous power politics, it should be pointed out that, at that moment, Mr. Roosevelt's policy in China was identical with that of Stalin, [184] to help Chiang Kai-shek against the Japanese and the Wang Ching-wei puppet government.

Matsuoka's primary purpose seems to have been [185] to lighten the Japanese commitments in China, partly by diminishing the threat of Stalin's power when in alliance with Hitler, and not to be tempted into new and extravagant adventures.

Germany, Matsuoka may have finally concluded, wanted for her own purposes to lead Japan into additional expensive and dangerous enterprises. How about a direct approach to Russia? Russia also had been helping Chiang Kai-shek by economic and other methods, and Russia, like Germany, had refused to recognize Wang Ching-wei. But perhaps Russian politics had changed: certainly all the rumors flying about in diplomatic circles seemed to indicate some pending change.

Even though the Japanese had not received any clear word from the Germans of the pending "Barbarossa" plan, von Ribbentrop and Hitler were compelled to hint to Matsuoka that the Russo-German honeymoon was at an end. Von Ribbentrop tried to prevent Matsuoka from resuming the impending talks with Russia: [186]

> * He expressed the opinion that it would probably be best, in view of the whole situation, not to carry the discussions with the Russians too far. He did not know how the situation would develop. One thing, however, was certain, namely, that Germany would strike immediately, should Russia ever attack Japan. He was ready to give Matsuoka this positive assurance, so that Japan could push forward to the South on Singapore, without fear of possible

complications with Russia. The largest part of the German army was anyway on the Eastern frontiers of the Reich, and fully prepared to open the attack at any time. * Should Germany however enter into a conflict with Russia, the U.S.S.R. would be finished off within a few months. *

He could not know, of course, just how things with Russia would develop. It was uncertain whether or not Stalin would intensify his present unfriendly policy against Germany. He [von Ribbentrop] wanted to point out to Matsuoka, in any case, that a conflict with Russia was anyhow within the realm of possibility. In any case, Matsuoka could not report to the Japanese Emperor upon his return, that a conflict between Russia and Germany was impossible. On the contrary, the situation was such, that such a conflict, even if it were not probable, would have to be considered possible.

Quite possibly this was exactly the information that Matsuoka wanted to receive. He returned to Moscow on April 7, 1941.[187] The Russians were at first extremely cool to Matsuoka, and it seemed as if here, too, he would be unable to work out any deal. He had at first planned to leave upon April 10, but he hopefully extended his stay to April 13.[188] He was getting nowhere, and finally on April 12 saw Stalin in order to bid him farewell.[189] Thereafter, overnight, and on the very eve of his departure, there was a typical Muscovite back somersault. The Russians completely reversed themselves, blew hot in a frenzy, and decided to take out some diplomatic insurance against the possibility of a later attack by Japan on Siberia.

At 11 A.M. on April 13 Matsuoka was suddenly and altogether unexpectedly summoned to the Kremlin, where a neutrality treaty, to last for five years, was drawn up and signed at 2:30 P.M. the same day. It was a whirlwind performance which came as a diplomatic bombshell to Axis circles. At 5:55 P.M. Matsuoka and his entourage departed for Japan in happy triumph. Stalin and Molotov, in equal happiness, unprecedentedly and for the first time in Soviet history came down together to the railroad station in order to bid the Japanese mission a fond farewell. [190] The reason immediately assigned for making this treaty, so far as Russia was concerned, was that Russia was "alarmed by recent rumors that Germany might attack Russia by summer." [191]

4. AT WASHINGTON

Meanwhile three dilatory weeks elapsed at Washington from the time of the reception of Ambassador Nomura by Mr. Roosevelt on February 14, 1941, until March 8, when Secretary Hull says he had his "first extended conversation" [192] with Admiral Nomura. Secretary Hull gravely condemned Germany and Japan: Admiral Nomura said that "all of the people in Japan, with very few exceptions * were very much averse to getting into war with the United States *." [193]

On March 14 Mr. Roosevelt and Secretary Hull conferred with Ambassador Nomura. Mr. Roosevelt agreed with Nomura's suggestion

> * that * matters between our two countries could be worked out without a military clash and [Mr. Roosevelt] emphasized that the first step would be removal of suspicion regarding Japan's intentions. *

Mr. Roosevelt and Mr. Hull viewed the projected trip of Matsuoka to Berlin with "serious concern and suspicion." [194]

In consequence a draft of a proposed agreement was prepared in collaboration with Admiral Nomura by Japanese and American citizens and was presented to the State Department on April 9, 1941. [195] Mr. Hull expressed skepticism that the time was opportune for negotiations, when, at his request, on April 14, Mr. Hull again saw Admiral Nomura. [196] Mr. Hull then seems to have modified his prior position, because two days later, on April 16, he asked Ambassador Nomura for a "definite assurance in advance" that Japan would abandon conquest by force and that she would agree to four general statements of principle. [197] Conditioned upon such an agreement, Mr. Hull said that he "had been told" (obviously, by Mr. Roosevelt)

> * that the document on which the Ambassador and the private group of individual Americans and Japanese were collaborating [the proposals of April 9, 1941] contained numerous proposals with which my Government could readily agree; on the other hand, however, there were others that would require modification, expansion, or entire elimination, and, in addition, there would naturally be some new and separate suggestions by this Government for consideration. *

Ambassador Nomura cabled this statement to Tokyo, where it was deemed to be of the highest importance and was brought promptly to the attention of the Prime Minister, Prince Konoye. [198] He immediately summoned a conference of high government and military leaders, who seem to have been enthusiastically in favor of accepting the American proposal, partly because it "would be the speediest way toward disposal of the China Incident." Unfortunately the Japanese also felt bound in a measure to Germany by their treaty. Moreover the Japanese purpose was to promote world peace: if, therefore, Mr. Roosevelt intended that the understanding was "to relieve America of her commitments in the Pacific and thus afford her an opportunity for increasing her support of Britain," the Japanese thought that this would be improper. Nevertheless, after the Japanese conference of April 18, 1941, Mr. Terasaki, Chief of the American Bureau of the Japanese Foreign Office, wished to instruct Admiral Nomura to transmit Japan's "acceptance in principle," but he was overruled on the ground that the Foreign Minister, Matsuoka, who had not yet returned from Moscow, ought to be consulted. Prince Konoye telephoned Matsuoka as soon as he had reached Dairen, and went personally to the airport when Matsuoka reached Japan. But Matsuoka was full of his experiences in Europe and was not willing to think about American topics for several days. "Ill-feeling" towards Matsuoka consequently "increased among Army and Navy leaders" and "some" of them "in their anger demanded that resolute steps be taken, even at the cost of changing the Foreign Minister." Prince Konoye attempted to pacify them, and then both he and Matsuoka fell sick for some days, but even during this period attempts were made to secure Matsuoka's approval "so that Japan's answer might be sent to America as soon as possible."

Finally there was another conference on May 3, 1941, at which Matsuoka managed to prevail in requiring "that the conclusion of a neutrality treaty should be proposed to the United States as a test." Germany and Italy were informed of this, and Admiral Nomura, "growing impatient at the delay," was instructed to make the neutrality treaty proposal to Mr. Hull. This interview took place at Washington on May 7, 1941. When Ambassador Nomura proposed a nonaggression treaty Mr. Hull, in his own words, [199] "did not hesitate but promptly brushed it aside." Mr. Hull then launched a double-barrelled diatribe against Matsuoka and Hitler, at the conclusion of which he urged the commencement of negotiations speedily.

Matsuoka's test plan had now failed, and there appears to have ensued a Japanese political dispute which was carried by both sides straight to the Emperor, who decided in favor of Prince Konoye. Accordingly a revised Japanese proposal was prepared and sent.

On May 12 Admiral Nomura submitted a new or second draft [200] containing, among others, this proposed paragraph: [201]

The Government of the United States maintains that its attitude toward the European War is, and will continue to be, *directed by no such aggressive measures as to assist any one nation against another. The United States maintains that it is pledged to the hate of war, and accordingly, its attitude toward the European War is, and will continue to be,* determined solely and exclusively by considerations of the protective defense *of its own national welfare* and security. (Emphasis supplied.)

Secretary Hull declined to bind this country to such a commitment: the italicized matter in the quoted paragraph above was deliberately *omitted* from the subsequent American redraft. This particular and express omission, when coupled with Mr. Hull's brushing aside of the Japanese proposal for a nonaggression treaty, should make it clear to the reader just what the ultimate end of Mr. Roosevelt's foreign policy then was.

As we now know, it was a golden moment for establishing Japanese-American peace, and this situation must have been equally clear at that time to those who, like Mr. Roosevelt and Mr. Hull, were reading all of the supposedly secret messages between the Japanese diplomats and Japan. Furthermore, German diplomatic ineptitude was defeating its own purposes in Japan.

On May 12, 1941, just too late, Germany and Italy delivered at Tokyo a joint note inviting Japan to adopt an anti-American stand. The gist of the note was, according to Prince Konoye, [202]
* that, since America's underlying motive in planning conciliation with Japan apparently was that she wished to enter the war against Germany, it was desirable that the Japanese Government make it clear to the American Government that:

1. The patrolling and convoying being carried on by America was recognized as an act deliberately provocative of war, and one which would inevitably cause Japan to enter the war, and that;
2. If America refrained from such actions, Japan would be ready to study the American proposal.

Furthermore, the German reply ended with the request that, in view of the effect of the present negotiations upon the Tripartite Pact, Germany be consulted before a final answer [was] sent to America. * Count Ciano noted in his diary [203] skeptical doubt "whether the note will have any great effect," the reason being that "Matsuoka does not conceal his great friendliness and respect for the United States." And he noted, gloomily, that the American Ambassador, "Phillips, with whom I spoke today, no longer excludes the possibility of intervention by his country * . * "

On May 13 there was a conversation between von Ribbentrop, Mussolini and Count Ciano at Rome, [204] in the course of which von Ribbentrop said that it was unfavorable that the discussions with Mr. Roosevelt were being carried on by Admiral Nomura, "for at heart Nomura inclined rather towards the Anglo-Saxons." The fact was also mentioned that in the course of the American negotiations Matsuoka had enquired if the United States would agree not to enter the European war. Mussolini observed suspiciously that, while of course it would be favorable if the United States did not enter the war, perhaps Matsuoka's motives were that Japan herself wanted to keep out of the war. Most of the conversation was concerned with Rudolf Hess's flight to Scotland three days earlier and with von Ribbentrop's attempts to play down Hess's peace proposal. [205]

Next day, on May 14, Ciano wrote that "in Japan, things are not going as they should * . *" [206] On the same day, at Tokyo, Matsuoka had advised Ambassador Grew that he and Prince Konoye were determined that any southward movement by Japan should be carried out only by peaceful means "unless circumstances render this impossible." [207]

On May 16 Mr. Hull submitted to Admiral Nomura what may be called a third draft. [208] Mr. Hull was far from being willing to agree that the United States would not enter the European war. Rather, in his own words, [209] he insisted upon

* the necessity of Japan's making clear its relation to the Axis in case the United States should be involved in * the war in Europe *. *

Translated into simple English, Japan was to abandon her treaty commitments and remain neutral while America entered the war in Europe. This bellicose purpose is clarified by an episode which took place at the May 16 interview: Mr. Hull presented to Admiral Nomura a redrafted statement agreeing that Japan's commitments were not inconsistent with American intervention. [210]

From Berlin the Japanese Ambassador, General Oshima, [211]

* repeatedly sent cables, reporting that German national leaders were harboring extreme antipathy toward the Japanese-American proposal. He also declared his own opposition in strong language.

At Tokyo, on May 19, 1941, the German Ambassador, General Eugene Ott, made what Prince Konoye felt were "highhanded representations" [212]

* concerning the displeasure of his Government with Japan's having replied to America without waiting for the German reply. The German representations, by implication, expressed Germany's objection in principle to the Japanese-American negotiations, and pointed out that any treaty concluded by any one of the signatories of the Tripartite Pact with a third country would weaken the common front of the Tripartite Pact signatories. The reply requested that at least "The American Government's obligation not to interfere with the war between England and the Axis countries" and "Japan's obligations accruing from the Tripartite Pact" be clearly defined. Lastly, the representations stated that "The German Government was obliged to express its desire for total participation by Germany in the Japanese-American negotiations and for an immediate report regarding the American reply. It constituted an infringement upon the articles of the Tripartite Pact for Japan

to listen to American representations and to determine Japan's future policy without entering into a previous understanding with the German Government regarding all the important problems included in the proposal." *

In consequence "the originally vague attitude of" Matsuoka became "more and more vague," and it was "more and more obvious" to Prince Konoye that Matsuoka "was standing alone in his opposition" to a Japanese rapprochement with the United States; so much so that on May 23, Matsuoka naively complained to Prince Konoye

> "* that Army and Navy leaders were trying to have the Japanese-American understanding put through, even at the cost, more or less of disloyalty to Germany and Italy—what could be accomplished by such a weak-kneed attitude?"

And now another momentary glimpse is given of another projected attack by the United States. It was proposed to seize the French island of Martinique by sending there an expeditionary force of Marines, and the Army's 1st Division. It was to be "primarily a Naval mission," but General Marshall thought that the Army Air Corps "should participate, both for the help it could give and the experience it would gain." These plans were discussed at a conference in Mr. Stimson's office on May 19, 1941, [213] and a considerable part of the report [214] has been suppressed. When these plans originated, and why they were abandoned, is not surely known. It seems probable that it was connected with the last voyage of the German battleship *Bismarck,* which, it was believed, intended to make Martinique her destination. Perhaps the seizure of Martinique was an alternative to Mr. Roosevelt's tentative thought that he might order American submarines to torpedo the *Bismarck.* [215]

By the middle of May, Britain and the United States had adopted a common line of policy towards Japan, [216] so much so that Mr. Churchill thought it probable that if Japan should attack Singapore the United States would enter the war at the side of Britain. [217] The new alliance against the Axis was beginning to assume substance and form.

In the opposite camp the question was whether Japan could be split away from the Axis: four months later Stalin thought that it was still possible. [218]

It was perhaps in resistance to Mr. Hull's demand that Japan abandon the Axis that Mr. Matsuoka, in late May, stated that Japan was bound to support Germany if the United States should intervene in Europe. Just how far any Japanese support could have extended in view of the Japanese political situation just mentioned is problematical. Perhaps Matsuoka was not willing to abandon the German ties until he had obtained a firm commitment from the United States; perhaps this statement was only intended to serve as a lever by which better terms could be obtained from the United States in the course of the pending negotiations. Perhaps it was completely irresponsible. Looking at the other side of the coin we do know that a contemporaneous top-secret report from the German Military Attaché at Tokyo, [219] dated May 24, reveals the meagre extent to which Japan was willing to commit herself to Germany at that moment. If the United States entered the war Japan would acknowledge her treaty obligations but "would not open hostilities immediately." She would prepare a later attack on Singapore and on Manila. Also if a "possible war Russia-Germany causes U. S. A. entry into war" Japan would likewise not go to war immediately, but at later dates she would attack Singapore and Manila, and possibly Vladivostock and Blagovestchensk. For German purposes so qualified and indefinite a promise could have had but scant political or military value. Obviously Japanese support of Germany was undependable.

Mr. Hull's reply to Matsuoka's statement was to call in Admiral Nomura on May 28 [220] and to say that there would be "difficulty" in continuing to negotiate unless Japan was willing to concede that America might have a free hand in aiding Britain, even if that meant American involvement in the war in Europe. Nomura suggested that Matsuoka had made his speech for domestic political consumption, and, in effect, asked Mr. Hull to strengthen the Japanese moderates who wanted peace, by observing that as soon as the proposed agreement was signed it "would cause a weakening in the influence of the jingoes." He added, also, this very significant statement,

> * that the Japanese Government would make its own independent decision and would not be dictated to by Germany and Italy in the matter of interpreting Japan's obligations under the Alliance.

How lamentable it was that Mr. Hull did not, or would not, accurately evaluate the true political situation in Japan at that time. How equally lamentable it was if Ambassador Nomura felt unable to say plainly and frankly to Mr. Hull how unrepresentative of Japanese Army, Navy, and official opinion Matsuoka's statements were. Whether Ambassador Nomura did or did not say precisely this to Mr. Hull is in dispute. The Japanese Navy intercepted a cable from Lord Halifax, at Washington, to London, in which Nomura is so quoted. [221] This made Matsuoka very angry and he telegraphed a rebuke to Nomura. Nomura replied that "the accusation was totally unfounded on fact."

On May 27, as has been mentioned, Mr. Roosevelt proclaimed the existence of a state of "unlimited national emergency." On May 31, 1941, Mr. Hull presented what may be called the fourth draft. [222] Its most important change from the previous draft was the insertion of this significant proviso:

* Obviously, the provisions of the pact do not apply to [American] involvement [in the war in Europe] through acts of self-defense.

Mr. Hull was insisting upon one fundamental point, that the American path to war in Europe should be clear of any obstruction. And, as appears in the Pearl Harbor Committee report at page 506,

> The duty of conducting negotiations with foreign governments * was vested in President Franklin D. Roosevelt, under the Constitution, laws, and established practice of the United States, and he could delegate to the Secretary of State, Cordell Hull, such correspondence and communications relating thereto as he deemed fitting and proper. In respect of matters assigned to him it was the duty of Secretary Hull to keep the President informed of all transactions that were critical in nature and especially those involving the possible use of the armed forces of the United States.

On June 2, Ambassador Nomura asked Mr. Hull for some changes in its phraseology, but otherwise he was prepared to accept the May 31 draft in principle. [223] Even this did not satisfy the suspicious Mr. Hull, who doubted whether the Japanese were really trying to reach a settlement. For the next two or three weeks there were a number of indeterminate "informal conversations," [224] in which the two principal topics discussed were whether Japan really would stand aside if the United States entered the European war, and the withdrawal of Japanese troops from China. [225]

While these discussions were ambling along, Mr. Hull, on June 5 and again on June 14, issued notes denouncing Admiral Darlan's new policy of collaboration with Germany. [226]

At his press conference on May 16, 1941, Mr. Roosevelt had announced that some twenty-four cargo ships were ready to depart for the Red Sea in spite of the German proclamation of a war zone in that area. [227] Since the movements of American warships were being kept secret at this time, Mr. Roosevelt's announcement, made in advance of this projected sailing of merchant vessels carrying contraband of war, can be regarded as intended to provoke an "incident." These vessels, of course, sailed between South America and Africa in order to round the Cape of Good Hope, and in that general area an American vessel, the *Robin Moor*, was sunk by a German submarine on May 21, although the news was not released until June 12. On June 20 Mr. Roosevelt sent a denunciatory message to the Congress [228] in which he attempted to capitalize on this "incident," saying that the sinking was "the act of an international outlaw," and, later, that it was an "act of piracy." Professing great respect for the rules of international law, Mr. Roosevelt scolded Germany for her lawless conduct. Mr. Roosevelt would not be intimidated by Germany, he said, and he ended the message:

> We are not yielding and we do not propose to yield.

But Mr. Roosevelt was unlucky in his timing, since the German attack on Russia immediately blanketed the episode.

It was on June 14, 1941, that a proclamation was issued "freezing" all funds, securities and property not only of German and Italian nationals within the United States but of all continental Europeans, including the neutrals. [229] On June 16 Mr. Roosevelt ordered that all German and Italian consulates within the United States be closed [230] by July 10. On June 19 Germany and Italy took comparable retaliatory action. [231] "Which means that we are moving headlong toward an open state of war," wrote Count Ciano. [232]

Hitler's projected invasion of Russia was, as has been mentioned, hardly a diplomatic secret. On April 24, 1941, the German Naval Attaché nervously reported from Moscow the considerable extent of the current rumors about a Russo-German war. [233] He reported that the

> * English Ambassador *predicts* as day of outbreak of war *22 June!* (Emphasis in original.)

The imminent war was the subject of recorded diplomatic concern on various occasions in June, [234] the general substance of which must have been known to Mr. Hull. One is therefore compelled to assume either maladroitness or else Machiavelian subtlety on the part of Mr. Hull, who selected the day before the commencement of the attack, June 21, 1941, to present a fifth draft [235] of American proposals to Admiral Nomura.

Even in the light of the expected attack upon Russia Mr. Roosevelt's purpose to enter the European war was as unswerving as before. There was to be an exchange of notes by which Japan would agree to remain at peace in the Pacific when the United States entered the war in Europe. China and Japan were to negotiate "for a termination of hostilities and resumption of peaceful relations." [236] The Philippines were to be neutralized, and there were various subsidiary matters. At the time when this fifth draft was presented, Mr. Hull again emphasized American concern with European power politics. He said in substance to Admiral Nomura that it was "illusory to expect * substantial results" from any such agreement so long as certain Japanese leaders were committed to supporting Germany. [237]

But by now the hour was late, and the fifth draft languished in Tokyo, where the Japanese ministers debated and redebated what Japanese foreign policy should be in the light of the astounding new development of the war. While the Japanese unquestionably had some hints of what was in the German wind, it has been shown that Operation Barbarossa was to be kept wholly secret from them, so that the German attack on Russia on June 22, 1941, caused "utter consternation" in Japan. [238] It was, indeed, felt "that those who had taken Japan into the Axis alliance had misled the country." [239] The first fruits for Japan of the German attack was the recognition of the Wang Ching-wei government by Berlin on June 26, 1941, [240] no doubt as a part of the German campaign to persuade Japan to attack Russia at once. Intensive consideration was immediately given in Tokyo to this question, and Foreign Minister Matsuoka urged that it be done. [241]

It was not only in Japan that the German attack upon Russia seemed to the local militarists to give them the signal to enter the war. In Washington, Admiral Stark wrote, [242]

> Within forty-eight hours after the Russian situation broke, I went to the President, with the Secretary's [Knox's] approval, and stated that * we should immediately seize the psychological opportunity presented by the Russian-German clash and announce and start escorting immediately, and protecting the Western Atlantic on a large scale; that such a declaration, followed by immediate action on our part, would almost certainly involve us in the war *. I reminded him that * I have been maintaining that only a war psychology could or would speed things up the way they should be speeded up *.

Admiral Stark also proposed to Mr. Roosevelt that Britain and the United States should assume a joint protectorate over the Netherlands East Indies.

While we do not as yet have the German diplomatic correspondence of that particular moment, we do know that von Ribbentrop immediately sent a note to Matsuoka. Its substance may be inferred from the contents of the two Japanese replies of July 2, 1941. [243] The first read:

> Japan is preparing for all possible eventualities regarding Soviet in order [to] join forces with Germany in actively combatting Communist [sic] and destroying Communist system in eastern Siberia. At same time Japan cannot and will not relax efforts in the south to restrain Britain and [the] United States. New Indo-China bases will intensify restraint and be vital contribution to Axis victory.

The second Japanese reply to Berlin read, somewhat reproachfully:

> Oshima delivers above note and tells Ribbentrop in part, "Matsuoka will soon submit a decision. If you Germans had only let us know you were going to fight Russia so soon we might have been ready. We were planning to settle South Seas questions and China incident hence decision cannot be reached immediately, but Japan will not sit on fence while Germany fights Russia."

From the ultimate result it can be soundly inferred that some of the leading Japanese personalities were skeptical of the Japanese power and ability to continue the China Incident, attack Russia, and expand into Indo-China and beyond. They wanted to cut Japan's losses and achieve peace. Moreover, in view of Germany's secretiveness, there were other Japanese who were quite prepared to look with a single eye towards their own concept of Japan's sole interest and, if it seemed expedient, to sit on the fence while Germany fought Russia, in order to see what might ensue. [244] And there was yet another group which was in favor of expansion southward only, without regard to Russia.

X | JOURNEYS END IN LEADERS' MEETINGS

JAPANESE CONFLICT OF OPINION was so great, and the impending decision was thought to be so important that an Imperial Conference was called at Tokyo for July 2, 1941: there had been but five in the previous twenty-seven years.[1] At that conference Japan decided to go on her separate way independently of Germany. Matsuoka's policy was overruled, at least temporarily, and the question of war with Russia was put aside until it was clearer to the Japanese fence sitters how successful the German attack on Russia might prove to be. The secret report read:[2]

> * As regards the Russo-German war, although the spirit of the Three-Power Axis shall be maintained, every preparation shall be made at the present and the situation shall be dealt with in our own way. In the meantime, diplomatic negotiations shall be carried on with extreme care. *

Instead of attacking Russia it was decided that [2]

> * preparations for southward advance shall be reenforced and the policy already decided upon with reference to French Indo-China and Thailand shall be executed. *

And finally,

> * Although every means available shall be resorted to in order to prevent the United States from joining the war, if need be, Japan shall act in accordance with the Three-Power Pact and shall decide when and how force will be employed.

This final decision was interpreted by the Japanese Prime Minister, Prince Konoye, in his Memoirs,[3] as meaning:

> In case all diplomatic means fail to prevent the entrance of America into the European War, we will proceed in harmony with our obligations under the Tri-Partite Pact. However, with reference to the time and method of employing our armed forces we will take independent action.

It was also on July 2 that Japan approached our State Department and stated, on the basis of direct information from sources within the State Department to J. P. Morgan & Co., that the United States had firmly closed these conversations, and that it was understood that the freezing of Japanese funds in the United States could be expected in the near future.[4] The former allegation was not denied by the State Department, and the latter allegation was proved to be correct in twenty-three days. It would therefore appear to be the fact that by this early date Mr. Roosevelt had ceased to be interested in attempting to reach a peaceful solution of the problems in the Pacific area. The statute providing for export controls had been signed on July 2, 1940, and, following its passage, it is officially stated that [5]

* restrictions were imposed * on an ever-increasing list of exports of strategic materials. These measures were intended also as deterrents and expressions of our opposition to Japan's course of aggression.

Mr. Roosevelt's justification for this action was presumably the Japanese movement into southern Indo-China. Far from being something which the Axis powers had planned as part of an integrated policy, it was a separate and selfish Japanese move which, as the intercepted messages prove, was quite unwelcome to the Germans. On June 16, 1941, Tokyo cabled Berlin and Vichy: [6]

> Matsuoka requests Ribbentrop's aid in demand on French for following * bases *. Japan determined acquire above quickly, diplomatically if possible or by force if necessary in order expand and strengthen them. Chief reason given is to prevent British moving in.

Berlin replied to Tokyo on June 21: [7]

> Ribbentrop reluctant to force issue now.

Tokyo immediately answered the next day: [7]

> Matsuoka will negotiate directly with French. Repeats determination get bases soon.

On June 28 Tokyo cabled to Vichy: [7]

> French Indo-China base question this date receives Imperial sanction.

And Tokyo further cabled Vichy on June 30: [7]

> Japan now considers it absolutely essential to force France accede to demands for above bases.

On July 29, 1941, France finally gave in. [8]

If Japan wanted to maintain peace with America at this time, the desire of the American people to stay at peace remained no less great. Writing in guarded terminology, Mr. Welles complained: [9]

> By the summer of 1941 the overwhelming issue was [Mr. Roosevelt's] need to obtain the support of the people of the United States, and of their Congress, for those measures which were indispensable if the United States was to be prepared to defend herself should she be drawn into war. * Isolationist sentiment was still widespread.

In order to obtain such popular support for entering the war Mr. Roosevelt therefore pressed forward by words and by deeds. In words, Secretary Knox spoke to the Governor's Conference at Boston, Mass., on June 30, 1941, and enumerated reasons why Americans should act now. He spoke of matching British blood "with American blood." "Now is the time to strike." He concluded his speech by saying, [10]

> The time to use our Navy to clear the Atlantic of the German menace is at hand.

At a later press conference, on July 2, 1941, Mr. Knox denied that our warships were convoying vessels or that they had been in action against hostile submarines. [11] This was, of course, a quibble. Admiral Pratt noted that [12]

> * we have instituted a sea patrol * which naturally includes aircraft carriers, protecting destroyers and cruisers.

In an undated entry which falls between March 11, 1941, and April 9, 1941, Admiral King wrote, [13]

> * Naturally, we were unwilling to see a large part of the [Lend-Lease] material built with our labor and money lost in transit, and our only recourse was to give the British assistance in escorting the convoys carrying that material within North American waters.

In another entry immediately after August 11, 1941, Admiral King wrote: [14]

For some months * our naval forces had been patrolling waters in the vicinity of the convoy routes, and had been broadcasting information relative to the presence of raiders * . * (Emphasis supplied.)

Writing as of about July 1, 1941, it was reported [15] that the Atlantic patrol was being stepped up in order to ensure the safe delivery of munitions to England, and, further:

The United States has greatly accelerated preparations for large-scale naval shooting in the Atlantic if and when necessary. Already Navy activities are in that zone somewhere between "patrolling" and "convoying."

Mr. Roosevelt, at his press conference on July 1, declined to comment on Secretary Knox's speech. [16] He still hoped the country could avoid fighting, he said, but he could not be very confident about it. As for the polls which showed public opinion to be against the war, he derided them: of course people were against war; that was like being against sin.

American naval cooperation in the Atlantic was constantly on the increase. It would appear that seven Coast Guard cutters were turned over to Britain in early June 1941, [17] and by the end of the month discussions were under way over having American destroyers patrol to the far side of the Atlantic. On July 11 Mr. Roosevelt drew a map of the waters in the Atlantic for which the American Navy would assume responsibility and thus relieve the British. [19]

It is perhaps indicative of this relief that in early July Mr. Churchill was arranging to requisition large quantities of food from the United States. [20]

On July 3, 1941, Senator Wheeler asserted that the administration was planning to send American troops to occupy Iceland. [21] In fact, by a secret understanding with the English Government, the first American expeditionary force was then already on its way to Iceland. [22]

Also on July 3 General Marshall asked to have the law amended so as to keep the draftees in service for more than one year and to remove the prohibition of sending American troops outside the Western Hemisphere. [23]

On July 3 Admiral Stark expressed the opinion to Admiral Kimmel, among others, that Japan was likely to move southwards by late July in order to seize and develop naval, army, and air bases in Indo-China. [24] Japanese merchant vessels in the Atlantic had been ordered to be west of the Panama Canal by dates which supported Admiral Stark's inference.

On July 4, in a brief speech from Hyde Park, [25] Mr. Roosevelt paraphrased the "American blood" speech of Mr. Knox, and called on the Nation to "pledge * if it be necessary, our very lives." He did not say, to what. But it was a "childlike fantasy * simpleminded," to suppose that we could "save freedom * after a dictator combination" had "gained control of the rest of the world."

On the same day Mr. Roosevelt had Mr. Hull by-pass Matsuoka by sending a message which Ambassador Grew delivered directly to Prince Konoye on July 6. It said, [26]

> We have information that Japan is starting military operations against the Soviets. We request assurance that this is contrary to fact.

At Cairo, on July 4, 1941, General Sir Archibald P. Wavell, who was about to retire as the Commander in Chief in the Middle East, said in an interview that "tools" only would not be sufficient for England to win the war; that the outcome of the war in Europe would be decided by man power, and that the war could not be won without American man power. [27] Three days later his successor, General Sir Claude Auchinleck, said that the war would have to be won in Europe by beating the Germans on their own soil, and that it would take American man power to do it. [28]

At this time, at least two American divisions were being trained in the operations expected of expeditionary forces. [29] As early as May 24, 1941, the Navy had secretly been "preparing" a Force "to go to North Ireland and Scotland on the outbreak of war," but at that earlier date Admiral Stark stated [30] "the Army has neither the equipment, the ammunition nor the aircraft to defend *these bases.*" (Emphasis supplied.)

On July 7, 1941, Mr. Roosevelt notified the Congress that American troops had landed in Iceland to take it over from the British. [31] Mr. Churchill had stated (Mr. Roosevelt said) on June 24 that the fifteen thousand British troops there were required elsewhere, and Mr. Churchill had asked the Prime Minister of Iceland to invite the Americans to come in. [32] Our troops will be withdrawn, Mr. Roosevelt promised, "upon the termination of the present international emergency." At the same time Mr. Roosevelt stated that he had ordered the American Navy to clear the Atlantic Ocean between Iceland and the United States. This action was described as [33]

* a seven league stride nearer to war.

Mr. Hanson Baldwin went further, writing that it meant that the administration intended to help England with military means, and that it marked the beginning of American participation in a shooting war. [34]

At Tokyo, on July 8, 1941, the American inquiry of July 4 was answered by delivering a copy of the Japanese communication to Russia, dated July 2. [35] Prince Konoye, who had noted that

> America showed a profound interest in Japan's attitude toward the German-Soviet War,

turned the tables on Mr. Roosevelt by asking a counterquestion, whether

> The American Government really intended to enter the European War.

At his regular press conference on July 8 Mr. Roosevelt was both evasive and defiant.[36] In the first vein he said that the lines of the Western Hemisphere were geographically dim, although previously, on February 25, 1941, he had said that the Western Hemisphere did not include Iceland, and on January 21, 1941, he had laughed at the suggestion that ships might be convoyed as far as to Iceland. In the vein of defiance, Mr. Roosevelt said that anyhow he would act beyond the lines of the Western Hemisphere when and if it was necessary. He declined to comment on General Marshall's request for the repeal of the draft act's restrictions.

Next day, on July 9, 1941, Mr. Churchill differed from Mr. Roosevelt in some particulars.[37] Instead of having the Americans merely taking over from the British in Iceland, he attempted to tie in the two nations a little closer together by saying that the military and naval forces of both countries would "cooperate closely" with "the same object in view."

Also on July 9 Mr. Knox was asked at his press conference if the American Navy would shoot if necessary to keep the North Atlantic clear. He replied that the reporters ought to be able to answer that one for themselves.[38] Next day the Senate Committee on Naval Affairs decided to call in Mr. Knox to ask him whether our Navy had done any such shooting.[39]

The hope that the anticipated "incident" might arise out of the occupation of Iceland was hardly concealed in a letter to Captain Charles M. Cooke, Jr., which Admiral Stark wrote on July 31:[40]

> The Iceland situation may produce an "incident." You are as familiar with that and the President's statements and answers at press conferences as I am. Whether or not we will get an "incident" because of the protection we are giving Iceland and the shipping which we must send in support of Iceland and our troops, I do not know. Only Hitler can answer.

Likewise there was almost a note of disappointment in Mr. Knox's voice when, on August 16, at Raleigh, N. C., he denied that any American ship had fired on an Axis flag in the North Atlantic, because, he explained, [41]

> They're keeping out of our way, apparently, and the sinking of ships in that area has stopped for some reason or other

On July 10 the Congress received from the War Department drafts of two bills which broke faith with the Americans then in service. [42] The first bill extended—involuntarily—for the duration of the "emergency" the terms of service of those who had enlisted. The second bill proposed to authorize Mr. Roosevelt to send the draftees, or any other part of the Army, anywhere,

> * within or beyond the limits of the Western Hemisphere, as he shall deem necessary in the interests of national defense.

We may assume that it was at this time that General Marshall sent to Mr. Roosevelt, who approved it, an undated memorandum in which he endorsed the views of Generals Wavell and Auchinleck, and said, [43]

> * Britain is reaching [the] limit of usable manpower. We must supplement her forces. * Germany cannot be defeated by supply of munitions to friendly powers, and air and naval operations alone. Large ground forces will be required.

This memorandum also mentioned providing American "security forces for air and naval bases in the British Isles and Ireland." It listed a number of "Organized forces for overseas expeditions. * especially trained for landing attacks." Some listed possible uses for those forces were, "Azores, Cape Verdes, Martinique. * Africa * England, Middle East. *." It mentioned the need of "reinforcement of expeditionary forces."

Looking to the future the memorandum continued:

* In the final decisive phase we must come to grips with and annihilate the German military machine. Forces deemed necessary at this time to accomplish role of ground units in supreme effort to defeat Germany comprise five field armies of about 215 divisions *. If the United States remains committed to the policy of defeating Germany, making an all-out effort mandatory, then we must build toward these forces as rapidly as possible. *

It is noteworthy that General Marshall wrote that the Expeditionary Force was "Essential * for carrying out commitments of ABC-1," the Joint War Plan, dated March 27, 1941, the commitments of which he thus deemed to be binding upon the United States, and in force.

By early July the headstrong Japanese decision to move southward into Indo-China was well known to Germany. As has been stated, it was not acceptable, but von Ribbentrop put the best face on it that he could, while he continued to attempt to persuade Japan to attack Russia. On July 10, 1941, he telegraphed the German Ambassador to Japan, General Ott: [44]

> 4. Please take this opportunity to thank the Japanese Ambassador in Moscow for conveying the cable report. It would be convenient if we could keep on receiving news from Russia this way. In summing up, I would like to say: I have now, as in the past, full confidence in the Japanese Policy, and in the Japanese foreign minister, first of all because the present Japanese government would really act inexcusable [sic] toward the future of its nation, if it would not take this unique opportunity to solve the Russian problem, as well as to secure for all times its expansion to the South and settle the Chinese matter. Since Russia, as reported by the Japanese Ambassador in Moscow, is in effect close to collapse, a report which coincides with our own observations as far as we are able to judge at the present war situation, it is simply impossible that Japan does not solve the matter of Vladivostok and the Siberian area as soon as her military preparations are completed.

It is, of course, also in our interest that Japan wants to secure for herself further possessions in the South, Indo-China, etc., just as every measure of Japan direct[ed] toward expansion is principally welcomed by us. I shall give you detailed instructions, within the near future, relative to the consequences which might, and no doubt will, result from the occupation of Iceland by American military forces, and the attitude which we will take toward Japan in this connection. As directive for talks we can advise you already today that the sending of American military forces to the support of England into a territory which has been officially announced by us as combat area, shows not only Roosevelt's aggressive intentions, but the fact of the intrusion of American military forces into the combat area to the support of England is in itself an aggression against Germany and Europe. After all, one cannot enter a theater of war in which two armies are fighting, and join the army of one side without the intention of shooting and without actually doing so. I do not doubt for a moment that in case of the outbreak of hostilities between Germany and America, in which case today already it may be considered as an absolutely established fact that only America will be the aggressor, Japan will fulfill her obligations, as agreed upon in the Three Power Pact. However, I ask you to employ all available means in further insisting upon Japan's entry into the war against Russia at the soonest possible date, as I have mentioned already in my note to Matsuoka. The sooner this entry is effected, the better it is. The natural objective still remains that we and Japan join hands on the Trans Siberian railroad, before winter starts. After the collapse of Russia, however, the position of the Three Power Pact states in the world will be so gigantic, that the question of England's collapse or the total destruction of the English islands, respectively, will only be a matter of time. An America totally isolated from the rest of the world would then be faced with our taking possession of the remaining positions of the British Empire which are important for the

Three Power Pact countries. I have the unshakable conviction that a carrying through of the new order as desired by us will be a matter of course, and there would be no insurmountable difficulties if the countries of the Three Power Pact stand close together and encounter every action of the Americans with the same weapons. I ask you to report in the near future as often as possible and in detail on the political situation there.

RIBBENTROP.

General Ott replied on July 13, 1941: [45]

I am trying with all means to work towards Japan's entry into the war against Russia as soon as possible. Especially using arguments of personal message of Foreign Minister and telegram cited above, to convince Matsuoka personally, as well as the Foreign Office, Military elements, Nationalists and friendly business men. * The greatest obstacles [sic] * is the disunity among Activist groups which, without unified command, follows various aims and only slowly adjusts itself to the changed situation.

OTT.

On July 12, after a Japanese Cabinet meeting, "revolutionary control" over the nation's wealth was announced. By one sweeping decree all private banks and financial institutions were made virtual subsidiaries of the Bank of Japan, and the government took control of all industry, production, and distribution. General mobilization was ordered. [46] On the same day at Moscow, England and Russia by treaty pledged each other all assistance in the war against "Hitlerite Germany" and agreed not to conclude a separate peace. England was now well on the way to reconstituting a second and stronger coalition.

A dispatch sent from Japanese military officials at Canton to Tokyo on July 14 sets forth the extent of the ambition of the Japanese extremists. [47] It was intercepted, and in connection with later developments it may have given the impulse for the later Atlantic Conference meeting between Mr. Roosevelt and Mr. Churchill. The plans of the military extremists were:

> The recent general mobilization order expresses Japan's irrevocable resolution to end Anglo-American assistance in thwarting Japan's natural expansion and her indomitable intention to carry this out with the backing of the Axis if possible but alone if necessary. *
>
> Immediate object will be to attempt peaceful French Indo China occupation but will crush resistance if offered and set up martial law. Secondly our purpose is to launch therefrom a rapid attack when the international situation is suitable. After occupation next on our schedule is sending ultimatum to Netherlands Indies. In the seizing of Singapore the Navy will play the principal part. * With air forces based on Canton, Spratley, Palau, Singora in Thailand, Portuguese Timor and Indo China and with submarine fleet in Mandates, Hainan and Indo China we will crush British American military power and ability to assist in schemes against us. *

By July 15 Admiral Stark had heard that "within [the] next day or two" Japanese demands would be made on Vichy France. [48] On July 16 the American Ambassador to France, Admiral Leahy, reported these demands in such a way as to leave the inference that they were sure to be complied with. [49]

On July 16, 1941, the American answer to Prince Konoye's counterquestion was delivered to him. [50] He thought that the answer was "bitterly ironical": it stated that

> * it was quite proper to exercise the right of self-defense against Germany, [also]
>
> * any country using force to keep America an indifferent bystander would be considered a partisan of the countries conducting armed invasion.

The Japanese Cabinet resigned in a body on July 16 and was reconstituted on July 18. The principal change was the elimination of Foreign Minister Matsuoka, the proponent of close collaboration with Germany, and the substitution of Vice-Admiral Teijiro Toyoda, who was known to be a moderate. [51] Secondarily, Baron Kiichiro Hiranuma became Vice-Premier: he had very recently been heading a drive to suppress clandestine German activities in Japan. [52] Matsuoka's views as to the nature of the reply which should be made to the American proposals of June 21 had been the principal cause of disagreement within the Cabinet, and its resignation was due to that disagreement. [53] Consequently it should have been clear to Mr. Roosevelt that the reconstruction of the Japanese Cabinet indicated an increase in the strength of the moderates and a greater purpose to reach an agreement with the United States. It was certainly a repudiation of the extreme military policies depicted in the intercepted message of July 14. Nor ought a person experienced in the devious ways of power politics to have attached too much importance to the *pro forma* intercepted declaration which Tokyo soothingly sent to Berlin on July 19:

> The Cabinet shake up was necessary to expedite matters in connection with National affairs and has no further significance. Japan's foreign policy will not be changed and she will remain faithful to the principles of the Tripartite Pact. [54]

On the other hand, in the light of the political tensions and forces within Japan, it was less than realistic to suppose that the plans for expansion within Indo-China would be straightway abandoned, and in fact they were not, in spite of Prince Konoye's efforts. [55] The six-point demands [56] which had been sent to France clearly were not, as Admiral Darlan suggested, [57] welcome to Germany, but Germany, in the light of larger objectives, was not willing to support any French opposition to them, and France was compelled to accede on July 21.

Mr. Roosevelt's policy of waging an undeclared naval war [58] against Germany in the western and middle Atlantic Ocean was not challenged by Germany: quite to the contrary, a secret order, dated July 18, 1941, [59] was issued forbidding attacks on United States war ships and merchant vessels in the operational area of the North Atlantic and on the sea route from the United States to Iceland, but authorizing such attacks in the so-called "blockade" zone close to England.

This action was taken, Grand Admiral Karl Doenitz later testified, at Hitler's direct order: [60] he "wanted to avoid conflict with the United States." And Doenitz added, "When American destroyers in the summer of 1941 were ordered to attack German submarines, I was forbidden to fight back." Hitler's conduct created another dilemma for Mr. Roosevelt, whose tactics at about that time were apparently improvised and variable. Thus, in mid-April, Mr. Roosevelt, Admiral Stark writes, was "debating in his own mind" undisclosed plans, while Mr. Hull was "counselling something less aggressive," [61] Later, in July 1941, Admiral Stark wrote sadly, [62]

> To some of my very pointed questions, which all of us would like to have answered, I get a smile or a "Betty, please don't ask me that." Policy seems to be something never fixed, always fluid and changing. There is no use kicking on what you can't get definite answers. God knows I would surrender this job quickly if somebody else wants to take it up and I have offered to, more than once. *

Four months afterwards, in late November 1941, Admiral Stark, immediately after a conference with Mr. Roosevelt and with Mr. Hull, wrote Admiral Kimmel: [63]

> I won't go into the pros or cons of what the United States may do. I will be damned if I know. I wish I did. The only thing I do know is that we may do most anything * or we may do nothing—I think it is more likely to be "anything."

The Germans had "broken" the English Navy's code prior to September 7, 1940. [64] From these messages, sent from Washington to London, the Germans may have had rather more than an inkling of the projected political and diplomatic moves of their opponents. Whether this information was shared with Japan is not now known; it seems to be improbable. But this was not the only Axis source of secret information.

As early as June 1940 Ambassador Bullitt believed that the American diplomatic code was being "broken." [65] The Japanese Foreign Minister, wishing to send a highly confidential message to Washington through Ambassador Grew in August 1941, guardedly hinted that the Germans and Italians had "broken" the code. [66] In this same month Admiral Darlan warned Admiral Leahy that the Germans could read the American diplomatic code. [67] Therefore if the reader should wonder at the quick accuracy with which Hitler riposted to Mr. Roosevelt's schemes, one reason for it has just been explained. By July 20, 1941, at least the American diplomatic code had also been "broken" by the Italians, [68] although we do not know what information, if any, they may have passed on to the Japanese. Secret diplomacy was henceforth a goldfish bowl to a few of the insiders: it was only the people who were kept in ignorance of the diplomatic and political manoeuverings of their leaders. But with such open diplomatic secrecy came certain disadvantages. Thus, Count Ciano feared to talk openly to Ambassador Phillips, whose report to Washington of the conversation would be read by Italian decoding and intelligence officials, who might put the wrong interpretation on Ciano's statements. "This," he noted in discouragement, "paralyzes any possibility of a rapprochement with the Americans."[69]

On July 21, 1941, Mr. Roosevelt endorsed and adopted General Marshall's proposals concerning Army service. Mr. Roosevelt asked the Congress for legislation to compel the continued service of the draftees, the National Guard, the Reserves, and the retired personnel of the Army after their statutory one year of service under the

Draft Act of 1940 had expired. He also asked for the removal of all restrictions on the draftees, both as to the number—900,000— which might be inducted each year, and as to the parts of the world in which they might be compelled to serve. As usual, vague terrors constituted the justification for this action. Mr. Roosevelt said: [70]

> Today it is imperative that I should officially report to the Congress what the Congress undoubtedly knows: That the international situation is not less grave but is far more grave than it was a year ago. It is so grave, in my opinion, and in the opinion of all who are conversant with the facts, that the Army should be maintained in effective strength and without diminution of its effective numbers in a complete state of readiness * . *

And Mr. Roosevelt asked Congress to find, within the meaning of the Draft Act,

> * that the national interest is imperiled.

Two days later, on July 23, 1941, General Marshall testified secretly before the House Military Affairs Committee. When Germany had attacked Russia it had been the general opinion in the highest military circles in Washington that Russia would be defeated in a brief period. [71] Some military authorities believed that the occupation of Russia to the Urals was inevitable. [71] Others, more hysterical and more panicky, expected an immediate German conquest of Siberia to its easternmost tip, opposite Alaska; indeed the Army and Navy immediately rushed preparations for air, submarine, anti-aircraft, and heavy artillery concentrations to Alaska. [72] Either General Marshall sincerely believed in this extreme fear, or else he consciously participated with Mr. Roosevelt in the campaign of terror, because he is reported to have warned the House Committee of a possible Axis conquest of Siberia, and of danger to Alaska. [73] Mr. Stimson also appeared and asked for the power to keep the troops in service indefinitely.

There were those, in and out of Congress, who doubted the sincerity of the request. It was, they said, merely the disguised forerunner of a move to send a mammoth A.E.F. to fight on the continent of Europe. [74] But Mr. Roosevelt's control over the Senate was still sufficiently strong and the amendments were passed there by a vote of 45 to 30. The conscience-troubled Senate threw the soldiers a bone, as it were, by increasing their pay $10 per month. [75] The House reflected public opinion more accurately, and there the outcome appeared to be highly uncertain. Finally, and by the narrowest possible majority, the House, on August 12, passed the amendments by a vote of 203 to 202. [76] One more acknowledged obstacle to American involvement in the Second World War had been removed. The affirmative vote in the House of Representatives was sectional and political. In the Solid South and in the Southwest the affirmative vote was 120 to 10. [77] But from New England, New Jersey, and Pennsylvania across the mid-West and out to the Northwest every single state delegation voted two to one, or more strongly yet, against the extension of the draft, except for Montana, Connecticut, and Rhode Island, which split 50-50. The tired and jaded Congress, which had been in almost continuous session for twenty months, then took a series of three-day recesses to September 15, 1941.

It was written officially nearly five years later, [78]

> * After this crucial decision * the Government was free to make dispositions of troops as the circumstances warranted and to move on various domestic questions which had been crying for attention but which had been postponed until settlement of the paramount question of the maintenance of the forces in being. During the following weeks further steps were taken quickly in the improvement of defense organization; several major agencies acquired, in the essentials, the form and functions which they were to exercise, under other names, during the entire war. *This stage had been reached by a zigzag route* and had necessitated involved judgments concerning the state of public opinion * . * (Emphasis supplied.)

As Mr. Roosevelt and his group conceived of their worldwide strategy at this time, the decisively important theater of war was in the Atlantic and particularly in Europe. The Far East and the Pacific was a side-show. [79] On the chessboard of power politics this relegated Japan to the position of a piece of minor importance, to be pushed about as might seem to be expedient. The State Department was under the impression that Japan could be defeated in military action in a few weeks. [80] The handling, therefore, of Japanese affairs received only secondary attention and was sometimes indifferent, as it was in late July 1941.

By July 15, 1941, Admiral Stark, in a dispatch to Admiral Kimmel, had reached the conclusion, based on the intercepted messages, that Japan did "not intend to move further south" than Indo-China "or interfere with colonial government." [81] Even so, Mr. Roosevelt was planning to take severe action against Japan under the new statute. The imposition of an oil embargo was under consideration, and high Navy officials were, no doubt among others, requested to submit an analysis of its expected effects. While this analysis was in process, Admiral Nomura, who had somehow got wind of it, on July 20 called on the officer in charge of the study, Rear Admiral Richmond K. Turner, the head of the Navy's War Plans Division, and hinted broadly that if the United States would only let up on Japan, Japan would not take action under the Axis treaty if Germany and the United States should become involved in war. [82]

On July 22, 1941, in a well-reasoned analysis in which Admiral Stark generally concurred, Admiral Turner recommended against the contemplated embargo on the ground that its effects would probably compel Japan to attack Malaya and the Netherlands East Indies, and lead to involving the United States in early war in the Pacific, [83] as it ultimately did. [84] This report was sent to Acting Secretary of State Welles.

Mr. Welles saw Admiral Nomura the next day, on July 23, and demanded of him an explanation of the proposed Japanese move into southern Indo-China. Not finding it satisfactory, he inaccurately attributed the agreement with France to German initiative, and he characterized it as assistance to German policies. Mr. Welles further observed that not only would the reaching of an agreement with America be to Japan's economic advantage, but if such an agreement had been concluded (and here is one of the earliest hints of the formation of a bloc), Great Britain, the British Dominions, the Netherlands, and China would have joined in supporting the United States. Then, stating that the United States for self-defense and safety's sake must assume that Japan was about to proceed on "a policy of totalitarian expansion and conquest in the South Seas," Mr. Welles terminated the negotiations at the request of Secretary Hull, with whom he said he had talked a few minutes previously. [85] Next day, on July 24, Mr. Welles issued a public statement [86] largely in the same terms, but containing the additional observations that the actions of Japan endangered the use and the safety of the Pacific and jeopardized the American defense program.

In consternation Ambassador Nomura immediately sought to see Mr. Roosevelt, and did so late in the afternoon of July 24. [87] Acting Secretary Welles was present, and also Admiral Stark. Mr. Roosevelt was by now acting in concert with Mr. Churchill: [88] he was more threatening than Mr. Welles had been: he prophesied a Japanese war with the Dutch, that "the British would immediately come to their assistance," and he then hinted that America would join in. As a last-moment alternative, which he had not even discussed with Mr. Welles, Mr. Roosevelt asked that all Japanese troops be withdrawn from Indo-China, and that it be neutralized by general agreement. Admiral Nomura felt that, considering the problem of saving face, the difficulties were likely insuperable. Nevertheless Mr. Roosevelt seems to have been pleased with the interview, because on July 26 he cabled Mr. Hopkins [89] at London, to tell Mr. Churchill,

> * our concurrent action in regard to Japan is, I think, bearing fruit. I hear their Government [is] much upset and no conclusive future policy has been determined on. *

Mr. Roosevelt then mentioned "in great confidence" his proposal to neutralize Indo-China. The answer, he thought, would "probably be unfavorable but we have at least made one more effort to avoid Japanese expansion to [the] South Pacific."

On July 25, from Hyde Park, Mr. Roosevelt issued an Executive Order, effective July 26, 1941, freezing all Japanese assets in the United States. This order brought under Government control all financial and import and export trade transactions in which Japanese interests were involved. In effect it virtually terminated all trade between the two countries. [90] It was contemporaneously viewed as a declaration of economic war. [91] The British Empire and the Netherlands promptly followed suit with similar measures, as Mr. Churchill did not believe that Japan wanted war. [92]

Incidentally, at this same time the United States embargoed the shipment of petroleum products and of most other goods to Spain. [93]

It is superfluous to say that there was consternation in Tokyo over the joint freezing orders of the Anglo-American-Dutch bloc. Admiral Turner's prophecy was almost copied in the bleak view of the possibility of maintaining peace which Foreign Minister Toyoda set forth in an intercepted dispatch of July 31, 1941, to Ambassador Nomura: [94]

> Commercial and economic relations between Japan and third countries, led by England and the United States, are gradually becoming so horribly strained that we cannot endure it much longer. Consequently our Empire, to save its very life, must take measures to secure the raw materials of the South Seas. *

Toyoda's dispatch, rather naturally under such circumstances, referred to cooperation with Germany, but in a qualified way which reserved to Japan liberty of independent action. And, as printed in the Pearl Harbor Committee Report, this very important passage is omitted: [95]

> 5. I know that the Germans are somewhat dissatisfied over our negotiations with the United States, but *we wished at any cost to prevent the United States from getting into the war, and we wished to settle the Chinese incident.* * (Italics supplied.)

On August 1, 1941, Mr. Roosevelt and Mr. Churchill, supplementing the economic sanctions, decided that the United States and Great Britain should take further parallel action to warn Japan against new moves of aggression. [96]

Japanese concern was indeed so great that finally, on August 4, 1941, the Prime Minister, Prince Konoye, who had been considering the expediency of a personal meeting between Mr. Roosevelt and himself, called in the War and Navy Ministers and asked their opinions about it. [97] Neither one felt able to give an immediate reply, but before the day was over the Navy expressed complete accord and, moreover, it anticipated the success of the conference. The Minister of War, General Tojo (who was to succeed Prince Konoye as Prime Minister in two and a half months), replied in writing. He was of the opinion that failure was the greater likelihood, and felt that the meeting was not a suitable move. If, however, Prince Konoye was prepared to assume leadership of a war against America in the event that the meeting was a failure, the Army, he stated, was not necessarily in disagreement with the plan to hold such a meeting. There is no known evidence to indicate that Prince Konoye agreed to General Tojo's condition.

On August 7, 1941, Prince Konoye was received by Emperor Hirohito and laid this problem before him. The Emperor instructed the Japanese Prime Minister to proceed immediately with arrangements for the meeting, [98] and on the same day Prince Konoye telegraphed Ambassador Nomura: [99]

> We are firm in our conviction that the only means by which the situation can be relieved is to have responsible persons representing each country gather together and hold direct conferences. They shall lay their cards on the table, express their true feelings, and attempt to determine a way out of the present situation.
>
> In the first proposal made by the United States mention was made of just such a step. If, therefore, the United States is still agreeable to this plan, Prime Minister Konoye himself will be willing to meet and converse in a friendly manner with President Roosevelt.
>
> Will you please make clear to them that we propose this step because we sincerely desire maintaining peace on the Pacific. *

On August 8, 1941, Admiral Nomura enquired of Mr. Hull whether such a meeting could be held. [100] Mr. Hull replied coldly that it remained for the Japanese Government to decide whether it could find means of shaping its policies along lines that would make possible an adjustment of views between the two Governments. As of August 8 Mr. Roosevelt had already been gone secretly for five days on his way to hold his first personal meeting with Mr. Churchill.

Mr. Roosevelt was a great believer in personal meetings and held many of them with important political personalities of other countries. It was only a few months later that Mr. Roosevelt said to Ambassador Hayes [101]

> * that he would be willing to meet and talk with General Franco in the Canary Islands or elsewhere outside of Spain if a real crisis threatened, and that, at my discretion, I might communicate this suggestion to the Chief of the Spanish State. He was, he said, a strong believer in the advantages to be derived from personal contacts between chiefs of state. It was quite obvious to me that the President would go to unusual lengths to forestall Spain's cooperating with the Axis.

But to forestall Japan's cooperating with the Axis, Mr. Roosevelt seemed to be unwilling to go to any lengths at all. Without imposing any conditions in advance, Mr. Roosevelt was willing to meet with General Franco at Ambassador Hayes's discretion. Ambassador Grew in Japan was not given broad discretion; indeed he was given no discretion at all. As will appear subsequently, before agreeing to meet Prince Konoye Mr. Roosevelt sought to impose all sorts of advance conditions and was, in addition, so dilatory that Opportunity not only ceased to knock at the door; she died of old age upon the doorstep. The attempts to impose these prior conditions, and the dilatory tactics, all took place after the Atlantic Conference. It may be assumed with confidence that this new and changed policy resulted in part from the agreements arrived at that Conference, to which our attention must soon be turned.

Meanwhile and at London on August 6, 1941, Mr. Eden, then Foreign Secretary, had made the statement in the House of Commons that a threat to the independence of Thailand would constitute a menace to Indo-China and to Singapore, and would not be tolerated by the British Government: the Governments of Australia and of New Zealand promptly took the same position. [102]

Following this up, Lord Halifax called on Mr. Hull on August 9, 1941, to ask what aid the United States would give if Singapore or the Netherlands East Indies should be attacked by Japan. Mr. Hull replied that American resistance or discouragement to such a Japanese move would be affected by the number of American warships which at such a time the British would be requiring in the Atlantic. [103]

Several days later, Mr. Grew and the British Ambassador to Japan, Sir Robert L. Craigie, called on Admiral Toyoda, the Japanese Foreign Minister, and stated that any action which would threaten the independence of Thailand would be a matter of immediate concern to Great Britain and to the United States, both of which countries were prepared to meet any step Japan might take, move for move, [104] a further instance of concurrent action by the two countries.

As has already been noted, the German attack on Russia immediately led to the public and formal creation of the nucleus of Britain's second coalition. The United States was not publicly and formally a part of that coalition. In order to achieve completely this purpose American accession to the second coalition had to be official and public. Furthermore Mr. Roosevelt wished to aid Russia from the American cornucopia of lend-lease. And then there was the subsidiary problem of Japan.

The first known preparatory step was to send Mr. Hopkins secretly to London on July 13, 1941. [105] This, it was contemporaneously said, [106] was done so that he might not be available in the United States to testify in connection with Mr. Roosevelt's request to the Congress to appropriate an additional six billions for lend-lease. It was believed that to give Russia more aid would mean less for England. On July 25 Mr. Hopkins was at London, cabling Mr. Roosevelt for permission to go to Moscow as Mr. Roosevelt's personal representative to confer with Stalin. It was currently reported that he had Mr. Roosevelt's authority to offer material aid against Germany; [107] he did have a message from Mr. Roosevelt to Stalin. In fact Mr. Hopkins had impulsively cabled Mr. Roosevelt from London on July 25, saying, [108]

> * I have a feeling that everything possible should be done to make certain the Russians maintain a permanent front even though they be defeated in this immediate battle. If Stalin could in any way be influenced at a critical time I think it would be worth doing by a direct communication from you through a personal envoy. I think the stakes are so great that it should be done. Stalin would then know in an unmistakable way that we mean business on a long term supply job. * Prime Minister [Mr. Churchill] does not believe Japan wants war. Russian Ambassador told me this morning he did not believe Japan would attack Russia immediately. *

By July 31 it was a settled matter that "We shall give aid to Russia." [109] There was also some inconclusive discussion about "the degree of cooperation that will prevail between that country and ourselves if and when we become active participants in the war *." [110] Mr. Hopkins was duly granted permission to go to Russia. Stalin is said to have given Mr. Hopkins a note for Mr. Roosevelt. [111] Mr. Bullitt states that Mr. Hopkins concluded that the Russians were fighting earnestly, [112]

> * and that it would be in our national interest to give them Lend-Lease aid.
>
> In return for the offer of such aid he asked nothing. *

It is noteworthy that the pattern of Russian intransigence begins at this very beginning. When something was asked for by America—an urgent request from Under Secretary of State Welles that American military observers be permitted to visit the combat zones—it was quietly refused without explanation. [113] On August 2, 1941, Admiral Stark wrote to Admiral Kimmel: [114]

> We nor the British have no one at the front in the Russian-German war though both the Army and Navy have made every effort to this end. From the press, therefore, you have about as much information as we have. *

On August 19 Admiral Stark wrote Admiral Kimmel: [115]

> * On 11 August 1941, the Russian Mission, headed by Ambassador Oumansky * was received by Secretary Knox. The Ambassador stated that his country had pressing need for all manner of military supplies, planes—and anti-aircraft guns in particular. He announced that "quantities" of bombs, ammunition, and machine tools were needed. *

And on August 28 Admiral Stark wrote Admiral Hart: [116]

> * Ambassador Oumansky and some of their military men from Russia are coming in tomorrow, and I know that their demands will be very urgent.

At his press conference on Friday, July 25, 1941, Mr. Roosevelt promised that aid to Russia would *not* be under lend-lease, but that it would be strictly on a cash basis. [117] And Russia was to get more than token aid. [118] It was noted that General De Gaulle had agreed with Generals Wavell and Auchinleck that American man power would eventually be needed to win the war. Mr. Roosevelt refused any comment on that one.

On this same day, July 25, 1941, Admiral Stark wrote Admiral Kimmel [119] that Mr. Roosevelt might order the latter admiral to send a carrier load of airplanes to Russia at one of the Russian ports in Asia. Knowing already of Mr. Roosevelt's willingness to produce an "incident," Admiral Kimmel in his reply did not express moral indignation, astonishment, or surprise. It was simply technical: [120]

> I entertain no doubt that such an operation, if discovered, (as is highly probable), will be tantamount to initiation of a Japanese-American War. If we are going to take the initiative in commencing such a war, I can think of more effective ways for gaining initial advantage.

* * * * * *

> In short, it is my earnest conviction that use of a carrier to deliver aircraft to Asiatic Russian ports in the present period of strained relations is to invite war. If we have decided upon war, it would be far better to take direct offensive action. *If for reasons of political expediency, it has been determined to force Japan to fire the first shot,* let us choose a method that will be more advantageous to ourselves. *
> (Emphasis supplied.)

It may be conjectured that this attempt to create an incident was abandoned for the reasons testified to by Admiral Turner. [121]

> * It was felt in the Navy Department, that there might be a possibility of war with Japan without the involvement of Germany, but at some length and over a considerable period, this matter was discussed and *it was determined that* in such a case *the United States would,* if possible, *initiate efforts to bring Germany into the war against us in order that we would be enabled to give strong support to the United Kingdom in Europe.* * (Emphasis supplied.)

Further demands were being made upon the United States at this time by Mr. Churchill, and plans were being made for a somewhat distant future of full American participation in the war. On July 25, 1941, Mr. Churchill was urging Mr. Roosevelt to build the specialized landing ships for tanks in order to be able to land the "armies of liberation" in Europe at a later date. [122] More tanks were to be built for the military campaigns of 1942 and 1943, and it was suggested that the British troops to man the tanks should be trained in the United States. [123]

The pressure on the United States to participate in the war as an official belligerent was also increased. In a speech made to Parliament on July 29, 1941, Mr. Churchill proclaimed [124] that the United States is "giving us aid on a gigantic scale and is advancing * to the very verge of war." His right-hand man, Lord Beaverbrook, in a propaganda article published in the September issue of the *American Magazine,* listed five reasons why the United States ought to enter the war and why "We Must Fight." [125]

On August 1, 1941, the United States closed down on all silk manufacturing as of August 2. [126]

Beginning on August 3, 1941, Mr. Ickes asked all filling stations along the Atlantic seaboard to close from 7 P.M. to 7 A.M. in order to relieve the shortage of gasoline. [127] This closing, it transpired, was made necessary because fifty American tankers had been transferred to England, and four more to Russia. [128]

It was also on August 3 that Mr. Roosevelt boarded the *Potomac* at New London. [129] On August 5 he transferred from the *Potomac* to the *Augusta*, which anchored off Argentia, Newfoundland, on the morning of August 7. [130] All this was then a great secret, but only to the American public, for on August 7 Admiral Nomura reported to Tokyo that Mr. Roosevelt, accompanied by high Army and Navy officials, was meeting with Mr. Churchill. [131] Mr. Churchill, together with Mr. Hopkins, arrived in the ill-fated *Prince of Wales* on August 9, and the meetings continued on August 10, 11, and 12.

The exact nature of all the commitments which Mr. Churchill sought to obtain from Mr. Roosevelt is not yet entirely clear, but it seems to be true that in any event he sought more than Mr. Roosevelt was prepared to give.

Mr. Elliott Roosevelt says his father told him that the purpose of the meeting was to work out production and delivery schedules for the British under lend-lease. [132] Perhaps a more accurate way of putting it would be to say that the question was one of apportioning the lend-lease production between Britain and Russia. [133] But Mr. Roosevelt expected that Mr. Churchill would ask for more than an increase of American giving.

As a minimum Mr. Churchill wanted a declaration which would indicate a hard and fast Anglo-American alliance, [134] and thus publicly advertise to the peoples of the Axis the growing strength of England's second coalition.

As a maximum Mr. Churchill wanted the United States to declare war on Germany forthwith: it is known that he sought to obtain this at the conference. [135]

In either event Mr. Roosevelt is reported to have declared just before the conference commenced, that Mr. Churchill was coming there because he [136]

* knows that without America, England can't stay in the war.

* * * * * *

* Churchill's greatest concern is how soon will we be in the war * . *
He knows that to mount an offensive, he needs American troops.

It seems unlikely that as yet we have a complete account of what took place in the harbor at Argentia. Certainly there was not an immediate declaration of war by the United States against Germany. But in the light of the more aggressive orders which were given to the Atlantic Fleet soon after Mr. Roosevelt's return to Washington, as will appear below, it may be inferred that Mr. Roosevelt was seeking—and perhaps agreed to attempt—to force the commission of an "incident" which would speed up American entry into the European war. He had repeated to Mr. Churchill his predilection for an undeclared war, saying, [137] "I may never declare war; I may make war. If I were to ask Congress to declare war, they might argue about it for three months."

Neither was there any publicly acknowledged Anglo-American alliance, although it is manifestly impossible to exclude the possible existence of secret verbal agreements. Presumably the Atlantic Charter represented a compromise between Mr. Churchill's hopes and Mr. Roosevelt's sense of what was politically possible at the moment: a joint declaration which did not openly purport to be an alliance, but from which many would infer the existence of a secret alliance, so that the hand could be played either way as might seem to be expedient in the light of the political circumstances of the moment.

While it has been claimed that the Atlantic Charter was originated by Mr. Welles "from the time it was first considered, back in Washington," Mr. Welles, who certainly ought to know, stated that there had been no prior exchange of views between Mr. Roosevelt and Mr. Churchill about a declaration such as the Charter, and that Mr. Churchill took the initiative after his arrival at Argentia on the evening of August 9, 1941. [139] Mr. Churchill's first draft was presented to Mr. Roosevelt on the morning of August 10. The second draft was an alternative which Mr. Welles submitted to Mr. Roosevelt early on the morning of August 11: the third draft, likewise by Mr. Welles, was prepared later that same morning: the fourth draft, by Sir Alexander Cadogan and by Mr. Welles, was made late that afternoon, and the final text was agreed on between Mr. Roosevelt and Mr. Churchill on August 12. [140]

The Atlantic Charter, in providing for Anglo-American cooperation in "the policing of the world" during a transition period following the close of the Second World War, assumed by a tacit but inescapable inference that the United States would presently become involved in the war. [141] This inference is fortified by Mr. Roosevelt's previously quoted statement to his son, from which it is manifest that Mr. Roosevelt appreciated the fact that Britain could not continue to stay in the war without American aid, nor win the war without the power of American troops in an American Expeditionary Force.

This inference is further strengthened by the preponderance of top military and naval staff personnel who attended the conference, such as General Marshall, General Arnold, and Admirals Stark and King for the United States, and comparable personnel from Great Britain such as General Sir John Dill, Admiral Sir Dudley Pound, and Vice Chief Air Freeman. What was on the agenda of the Chiefs of Staff is not fully known as yet, but it is known that there was further discussion of an American Expeditionary Force to seize the Azores, and of similar British or American expeditions to take the

Canaries and Cape Verde Islands.[142] There was also to be an extension of the activity of the American Navy in the North Atlantic.[143]

The situation in the Far East was discussed from the outset. Mr. Churchill asked and Mr. Roosevelt agreed to issue a declaration to Japan that any further move by the latter nation in the southwest Pacific would require the United States to take counter-measures even if such action led to war.[144] Mr. Churchill contemplated, apparently, that after the United States had assumed the onus of such leadership, "parallel declarations" would follow from England and the Netherlands, while Russia would be kept informed, and perhaps also would be protected from attack by the declarations.[145]

There is some reason to believe that the Chiefs of Staff felt that their forces were not as yet ready for war [146] and that they dissuaded Mr. Roosevelt and Mr. Churchill from taking drastic action immediately. Mr. Roosevelt and Mr. Churchill nevertheless agreed that they would take parallel action in warning Japan,[147] and [148]

> The President expressed the belief that by adopting this course any further move of aggression on the part of Japan *which might result in war* could be held off for at least *thirty days.* * (Emphasis supplied.)

According to another version, which seems more probable in the light of subsequent events, Mr. Roosevelt is quoted as saying to Mr. Churchill that he could delay the Japanese for three months.[149]

This "parallel action" was to be initiated by Mr. Roosevelt on his return to Washington. Mr. Roosevelt [150]

> * stated that in that interview he would inform the Japanese Ambassador that provided the Japanese Government would give the commitment contained in the first paragraph of the proposal * of August 6, namely, that the Japanese Government "will not further station its troops in the Southwestern Pacific areas, except French Indochina, and that the Japanese troops now stationed in French Indochina will be withdrawn," specifically and not contingently, the

United States Government, while making it clear that the other conditions set forth by the Japanese Government were in general unacceptable * would, nevertheless, in a friendly spirit seek to explore the possibilities inherent in the various proposals made by Japan for the reaching of a friendly understanding between the two Governments. The President would further state that should Japan refuse to consider this procedure and undertake further steps in the nature of military expansions, the President desired the Japanese Government to know that in such event in his belief various steps would have to be taken by the United States *notwithstanding the President's realization that the taking of such further measures might result in war* between the United States and Japan.

Mr. Churchill immediately declared that the procedure suggested appeared to him to cover the situation very well. * (Emphasis supplied.)

Mr. Roosevelt was in touch with Washington both by messenger and by radio, and must have known of Prince Konoye's recent and pending proposals for a personal meeting already delivered to Mr. Hull on August 8, 1941, but there is no evidence that this topic was discussed at the conference, or indeed that there was any consideration of the possibility of reaching some kind of an agreement with Japan by a peaceable approach.

Eleven months previously it had been Mr. Roosevelt's policy, privately acknowledged, [151] to appease Japan, but only in order to gain time to build up a first-rate Army and a first-rate Navy. No possibility of reaching a *modus vivendi* was expected in September 1940. Now, in August 1941, the same point of view appeared to persist: delay for another three months until the United States and England were further prepared for what seems to have been thought of as an inevitable war. In the light of such an attitude it is not easy to presume that the negotiations which were to be carried on in Washington for the next three months were carried on with any genuine purpose of reaching a happy issue.

In any event, and as soon as the weather had cleared after the conference was over, Mr. Welles was rushed back to Washington ahead of Mr. Roosevelt. There he conferred with Mr. Hull, drafted and redrafted the proposed warning to Japan, and submitted it to Mr. Hull for further revision by him and by his advisors on Far Eastern Affairs. [152]

Meanwhile Mr. Roosevelt in the *Augusta* coasted southwards, and on August 14, 1941, "for the record" and for the "information" of the Congress, he released the eight-point Declaration of the Atlantic, [153] written in noncommittal talk: "they *desire * wish * will endeavor * hope * believe.*" And, since it was hoped that General Stalin would accede to the Declaration, the sixth point of the Declaration mentioned only the third and the fourth items of Mr. Roosevelt's "Four Freedoms," freedom from want and fear. It did not even noncommittally declare a benediction upon the second freedom, freedom of religion, nor upon the first freedom—"Freedom of speech and expression—everywhere in the world." [154]

As printed upon many occasions, [155] the Declaration has annexed to it the names of Mr. Churchill and of Mr. Roosevelt. It has already been shown how carefully it was drafted and redrafted. Later, when even its weak declarations had become politically embarrassing, Mr. Roosevelt attempted to minimize its importance by saying that it had been scribbled on the back of an old envelope and had never actually been signed by Mr. Churchill or by himself. [156] But all this was in the future when, at an inter-allied meeting held at London on September 24, 1941, the Declaration was formally adopted by the Governments of Belgium, Czechoslovakia, Greece, Luxembourg, the Netherlands, Norway, Poland, Russia, Jugoslavia, and the Free French. [157]

Receiving the reporters at Rockland, Me., on August 16, 1941, Mr. Roosevelt told them [158] that Anglo-American understanding was now complete concerning possible developments on every continent of the world. Mr. Churchill and he, Mr. Roosevelt said, had outlined a course of action for any eventuality which might develop anywhere.

Observers did not fail to draw appropriate inferences from the circumstances; they noted that it would not have been necessary to take along so many generals and admirals merely to draw up a new kind of Magna Carta. [159]

Likewise, hopes intended to be construed as pledges had been held out by Britain and by America through the Declaration both to the conquered peoples of Europe and to the Germans themselves. The conquered peoples were reassured that they would not be sold out at the peace table, particularly not to Russia: the German people were assured of the falsehood of Goebbels's assertions that defeat would mean the dismemberment of Germany and enslavement in Russian communism. [160]

The subsequent record is indeed depressing. (1) There was no peace table, but nevertheless many of the conquered peoples were sold out. (2) Before the Morgenthau plan was finally abandoned the German people had been given reason to believe that in the wild ranting of a Goebbels there lay more truth than in the Declaration of a Roosevelt and a Churchill. [161] (3) British collapse in 1947 caused Britain to default upon her single affirmative promise, and thrust upon America the sole burden of policing the world. (4) The promise of the eighth point of the Declaration, to "lighten * the crushing burden of armaments" and to achieve "the disarmament of * nations" has become an illusion. What Mr. Welles said in another connection [162] may be repeated here:

> * In the fundamentals of international relationships there is nothing more fatally dangerous than the common American fallacy that the formulation of an aspiration is equivalent to the hard-won realization of an objective. *

Returning to Washington, in mid-August of 1941 Senator Harry S. Truman's investigating committee commenced its revelation of inefficiency by reporting the extent of the needless waste in the construction of the new Army camps. The original estimate of the cost had been $320 per draftee; the actual cost was $702 per draftee for a total loss of one hundred million dollars. [163] Even at today's inflated prices twelve or fifteen thousand homes for veterans could have been built with the wasted money.

On August 14 Mr. Stimson asked the Senate [164] for much more equipment than had been planned for the then publicly admitted possible future army of three million men. This was likely because of the gifts made and contemplated to Britain [165] and Russia. But in order to lull public opinion Mr. Stimson broadcast to the Army on August 15, [166] and denied that the Government was "seeking any wild adventures in foreign wars," or "planning any expeditionary forces for the benefit of other nations."

On August 15, 1941, Mr. Roosevelt and Mr. Churchill sent a joint message to Premier Stalin, stating that the United States and Great Britain had consulted together as to how they could best help the Soviet Union; that they were cooperating to provide it with the very maximum of supplies most urgently needed; that many shiploads had already left for Russia, and that more would leave in the immediate future. [167]

On August 16 Admiral Nomura called on Mr. Hull in order to press for an early meeting between Mr. Roosevelt and Prince Konoye. Admiral Nomura, according to Mr. Hull, [168]

> * said that his Government was very desirous of working out peaceful relations between our two countries and he elaborated further along this line and against the idea of war. He stated that he would favor concessions in order to avoid war and that from what he heard from his Government, it would make concessions in order to avoid war. *

> The Ambassador repeatedly said that his country was very desirous of peaceful relations with this country in the future as well as now and that he believed his Government would make some concessions in order to resume conversations to this end. *

* * * * * *

The Ambassador then pointedly inquired of me whether conversations such as he and I had been conducting could be resumed between our two Governments. *

Mr. Hull's response was a reprise of the theme song which Mr. Welles had sung for him on July 23, 1941, when the conversations had been discontinued. Mr. Hull said that if Japan were to invade "the South Sea area * it * would be a serious *menace to British success in Europe and hence to the safety of* * the United States,* and that, therefore, this Government could not for a moment remain silent in the face of such a threat *.*" (Emphasis supplied.) Mr. Hull suggested that the situation "was very serious," but "expressed interest" in the possibility that Japan might make some concessions in order to resume the conversations.

Admiral Nomura ended the conversation by saying that he would telegraph Japan

> * for instructions as to what concessions it might be willing to make in connection with a resumption of conversations.

This statement by Mr. Hull, that any serious menace to British success in Europe likewise menaced the safety of the United States and (translating the diplomatic language) would lead to American intervention to stop it, was a new factor in the negotiations. Coupled with what he had already heard, and reading the realities between the lines, Ambassador Nomura cabled his estimate of the political situation to Tokyo that same day: [169]

> * I understand that the British believe that if they could only have a Japanese-American war started at the back door, there would be a good prospect of getting the United States to participate in the European war. *

XI AN UTTERLY FUTILE WAR?

ON SUNDAY AFTERNOON, August 17, 1941, Mr. Roosevelt summoned the Japanese Ambassador to the White House and commenced the stalling process. After some tendentious observations about Japan [1] he noted the existence of a new factor, Ambassador Nomura's request to reopen the conversations, and saying "that the next move is now up to Japan," he enquired of the Ambassador "if he had anything in mind to say in connection with the situation."

Admiral Nomura then read an instruction from the Japanese Government which

> * asserted very earnestly that it desired to see peaceful relations preserved between [the] two countries; that Prince Konoye feels so seriously and so earnestly about preserving such relations that he would be disposed to meet the President midway, geographically speaking, between [the] two countries and sit down together and talk the matter out in a peaceful spirit.

This irenic approach was manifestly quite unexpected by Mr. Roosevelt: he made no responsive answer to the statements of the Japanese Ambassador. Instead, saying "that he regretted the necessity of * offer[ing] certain observations about the position of this Government * but that he had no other recourse," he read the statement of the proposed warning to Japan [2] which Mr. Welles had been specially rushed back from Argentia to prepare [3] with the aid of Mr. Hull and his advisors on Far Eastern affairs, in order to carry into effect [4] the "parallel action" which had been agreed upon between Mr. Roosevelt and Mr. Churchill. The statement warned Japan to respect, not the possessions of the United States, but "neighboring countries," and used diplomatic language which meant that "any further steps" by Japan would result "immediately" in war. [5] In American military and naval circles it was viewed as an ultimatum. [6]

The inference seems clear that Mr. Roosevelt felt obliged by his commitment to Mr. Churchill to deliver this threatening statement or ultimatum, which circumstances had already rendered obsolete, and which ought not to have been delivered at all if the defense only of American interests had been the sole guiding determinant. That inference is buttressed by Mr. Hull's embarrassed, or naïve, mention of the fact [7] that Mr. Roosevelt, after keeping his promise to Mr. Churchill to hurl the thunderbolt, then provided for

> * some little delay in the conversation so as to set apart the first statement which he read to the Ambassador *.

After the brief intermission for meditation Act Two was more friendly. Mr. Roosevelt read a considerably longer statement, [8] much of it a rehash. At one point the second statement proclaimed that "the policy" of the United States was to "extend * assistance to any country threatened" by Japan, but the procrastinating conclusion was peaceful in appearance:

> * The Government of the United States * feels that * it would be helpful * before undertaking a resumption of such conversations or proceeding with plans for a meeting [between Prince Konoye and President Roosevelt], if the Japanese Government would be so good as to furnish a clearer statement than has yet been furnished as to its present attitude and plans *.

At some point in this part of the conference Mr. Roosevelt seized upon an opportunity to baby along the Japanese for at least two months: he said [9]

> * if such meeting was to be held, that it might be arranged for about October fifteenth. *

Mr. Roosevelt thus had created two ways of delaying any rapprochement; first, the requested statement of Japanese plans, and second, an indefinitely distant date for the proposed conference.

Admiral Nomura

> * reiterated from time to time that his Government was very desirous of preserving peaceful relations between the two countries *.

and the conversation ended. The Ambassador immediately reported it to Tokyo, [10] emphasizing the "graveness with which [Mr. Roosevelt] views Japanese-U. S. relations." But he also expressed the hopeful view that the Japanese proposal for a "'leaders' conference' had considerably eased" Mr. Roosevelt's attitude, and that there was "no room for doubt * that the President hopes that matters will take a turn for the better."

Next day, on Monday, August 18, 1941, Mr. Roosevelt sent a report of his meeting with Ambassador Nomura to Mr. Churchill, from which it appears that not until after his return to Washington on Sunday had Mr. Roosevelt learned of Admiral Nomura's démarche to Mr. Hull on Saturday. Mr. Roosevelt advised Mr. Churchill that [11]

> *The statement I made to him [Nomura] was no less vigorous than and was substantially similar to the statement we had discussed.

When it came to taking "parallel action" Mr. Churchill seems to have let Mr. Roosevelt down. Mr. Welles stated that he took it for granted that the British also had taken such parallel action, and that the records of the State Department would probably show it, but Mr. Hull testified, and the State Department reported, [12] that its files contained no record of any such action.

It was also on August 18 that Mr. Hull conferred in Washington with the Minister from Thailand (Siam). Mr. Hull was asked what the attitude of the United States would be if Thailand were attacked by Japan, and in response he promised the same sort of aid as was being given to China. [13]

In Japan almost desperate efforts for peace were made on August 18. First of all the Director of the American Bureau of the Japanese Ministry for Foreign Affairs, Mr. Terasaki, requested Mr. Dooman, the Counselor of the American Embassy, in whose judgment and views Ambassador Grew had "full confidence," [14] to call upon him early in the afternoon. [15] Mr. Terasaki attributed "the greatest importance" to the pending interview between the Japanese Foreign Minister, Admiral Toyoda, and Ambassador Grew, and he expressed the "high hopes [which] were being held in all influential quarters with regard to the outcome of the conversations which would be initiated by today's interview.*" Should they fail, Mr. Terasaki was gloomily accurate in his vaticination:

> * If these conversations should prove unsuccessful, he did not believe that another attempt could be made. If a Cabinet under the leadership of Prince Konoye should prove unable to adjust relations with the United States, it would be inconceivable for any other Japanese statesman to succeed where he had failed.

Later that same afternoon Ambassador Grew met with Admiral Toyoda for two and a half hours to receive a peace offer in what might have been an interview of great historic significance.[16]

Admiral Toyoda first

* pointed out the supreme importance of avoiding any leakage, especially to the Germans or Italians*.

Admiral Toyoda continued with a review of recent Japanese-American relations, and he then solicited American cooperation

* for the settlement of the China affair which is the obstacle to peace in the Far East. * If the United States really desires peace in the Far East *.

The Foreign Minister next pleaded for high statesmanship. The situation was, he thought, "critical," and he referred to "the breakdown of peace." He recognized that

* the present relations between the United States and Japan have become extremely strained as a result of misunderstanding between the two countries and *sinister designs by third powers* *. (Emphasis supplied.)

He then begged for a direct meeting at Honolulu between Mr. Roosevelt and Prince Konoye, pointing out:

Needless to say the Premier's going abroad would have no precedent in Japanese history and the Prime Minister, Prince Konoye, has made up his mind with an extremely strong determination to meet the President notwithstanding the fact that he is fully aware of the objections in certain parts of this country. This determination of Prince Konoye is nothing but the expression of his strongest desire to save the civilization of the world from ruin as well as to maintain peace in the Pacific by making every effort in his power *.

The Japanese Foreign Minister then begged that there be no humiliation of Japan, and he requested some face-saving gesture, saying,

> * it is absolutely necessary to avoid arousing misunderstanding or giving an impression both inside and outside this country that the Japanese Government has entered into negotiation with the American Government as a result of American pressure. Based upon this point of view the Minister deems it desirable that various measures of economic pressure against Japan be immediately stopped or highly moderated and the Japanese Government is of course ready to reciprocate at once in this respect. The Minister wishes to draw the attention of the American Government to this point.

Ambassador Grew replied that in the interests of peace he would give the proposal his own personal support. In transmitting his report of this interview to Washington Mr. Grew added these observations:

> The foregoing is the substance of the highly serious and absolutely secret proposal for which the Minister especially asked me to visit him today. In view of its importance and delicate nature he does not need to ask me to keep this only to myself as it is not difficult to imagine what would occur if it should leak out. *

Ambassador Grew had reached the opinion that if the Roosevelt-Konoye meeting should not be held, or if it should be long delayed, the Konoye Cabinet might fall.[17] He seems to have feared a negative decision from Washington, as appears from the placatory form of his telegraphed plea:[18]

> * naturally he is not aware of the reaction President Roosevelt will have to the proposal *. The Ambassador urges, however, with all the force at his command, *for the sake of avoiding the obviously growing*

possibility of an utterly futile war between Japan and the United States, that this Japanese proposal *not be turned aside* without very prayerful consideration. Not only is the proposal unprecedented in Japanese history, but it is an indication that Japanese intransigence is not crystallized completely owing to the fact that the proposal has the approval of the Emperor and the highest authorities in the land. The good which may flow from a meeting between Prince Konoye and President Roosevelt is incalculable. The opportunity is here presented, the Ambassador ventures to believe, for an act of the highest statesmanship, such as the recent meeting of President Roosevelt with Prime Minister Churchill at sea, with the possible overcoming thereby of apparently insurmountable obstacles to peace hereafter in the Pacific. (Emphasis supplied.)

Whether "the highest statesmanship" was exhibited by Mr. Roosevelt may be left to the subsequent judgment of the reader. What is indisputable is that the Japanese proposal never received a timely and an affirmative response from Mr. Roosevelt. The result was, in Ambassador Grew's own words, "an utterly futile war."

When Ambassador Grew was meeting with Admiral Toyoda on August 18, 1941, the question of utter secrecy was discussed, as has been mentioned. The Japanese Foreign Minister said that [19]

> * he hoped that in my [Grew's] report to Washington no risk would be incurred of my telegram being read by others. I said that the telegram would be sent in a code which I hoped and believed was unbreakable. *

As has also been mentioned, one or more of the American codes had apparently been deciphered by at least the Italians. Perhaps in consequence, on the very next day, August 19, 1941, the German Ambassador, General Ott, called on the Japanese Vice Minister for Foreign Affairs, Mr. Eiji Amau. [20] As the Japanese Vice Minister noted, the German Ambassador was attempting to find out what the Japanese attitude was. Herr Ott renewed the old proposal that Japan should attack Russia from the East: he also attempted to persuade the Japanese to stop the American shipments of oil to Russia at Vladivostok. Mr. Amau's replies were noncommittal.

On August 21 Mr. Roosevelt sent a message to the Congress describing the meeting at Argentia. [21] This message embodied the text of the Atlantic Charter and referred in general terms to other matters discussed at the meeting, but it suppressed all mention of the agreement to take parallel action with England in issuing a warning to Japan, and of the Japanese proposal for a leaders' meeting. What was revealed by this message was not as important as what was left untold.

On Saturday, August 23, 1941, Ambassador Nomura called on Mr. Hull and was first lectured by him at some length. [22] When the lecture was over, Ambassador Nomura mildly explained that while he did not wish to make "a diplomatic incident" of it, the United States had cut off the sale of all oil to Japan and yet was actually shipping oil to Russia at Vladivostok "through Japanese waters"; that this "would naturally give the Japanese real concern at an early date." Mr. Hull responded

> * that we are determined to aid every country—to the fullest extent and as quickly as possible—that is resisting Hitler, and that relates to the present situation. *

Mr. Hull then added a thinly veiled threat to go to war in order to aid the Soviets:

> I said to the Ambassador that, of course, if Japan * should project herself militarily into the Russian-German situation or into other military situations that would directly affect this Government, an entirely different question would be presented. *

There then occurred a curious and perplexing episode, which can only be explained if one assumes that not only was there an agreement for "parallel action" between Britain and America, but also that America did not know what the basic British policy was, and had had no share in determining that policy. Mr. Hull noted that:

> The Ambassador then said that he supposed we had abandoned the sale of any oil at all to Japan under the freezing system which requires licenses and thus far no licenses have been issued for the sale of oil. I replied that I had not checked fully on the details of this matter; that it ramifies through other departments of the Government. I then stopped long enough to enquire *if the Ambassador knew what was taking place between Great Britain and Japan in this respect* and he said he did not. *I replied that I did not either, but that I would soon check this* and our own situation *as it related to his inquiry.* (Emphasis supplied.)
>
> The Ambassador then departed, again emphasizing his hope for better relations between the two countries.

Later that same day Ambassador Nomura received a cable from the Japanese Foreign Minister [23] that "everything in our power" was being done to comply with Mr. Roosevelt's two delaying items, that is, "to rush our reply to the United States and at the same time to bring about the 'leaders' conference' at an earlier date" than October 15, 1941. Therefore, still later on August 23, 1941, Admiral Nomura went to Mr. Hull's apartment [24] in order to ask that the date for the proposed meeting be advanced. Mr. Hull was at first sarcastic in his comments and then concluded the conference upon a note of indifference:

> * I made no promises of any kind in regard to a meeting of responsible heads of the American and Japanese Government or when it would be held, if it should be held at all.

On Sunday, August 24, 1941, Mr. Churchill made a broadcast, purportedly a report to the British people on the Atlantic Conference, but obviously intended in part for American consumption. It contained much more information than Mr. Roosevelt's message to the American Congress three days previously. Mr. Churchill, humoring Mr. Roosevelt's taste for mystification, said, in part, [25]

> Exactly where we met is a secret, but * it was somewhere in the Atlantic. * And there for three days I spent my time in company, and I think I may say in comradeship, with Mr. Roosevelt, while all the time the chiefs of the staff and naval and military commanders, both of the British Empire and the United States, sat together in continual council.
>
> * * * * * *
>
> We had the idea when we met there, the President and I, that without attempting to draw final and formal peace aims, or war aims, it was necessary to give all peoples, and especially the oppressed and conquered peoples, a simple, rough-and-ready wartime statement of the goal toward which the British Commonwealth and the United States mean to make their way * on a road which will certainly be painful and may be long.
>
> The United States and Great Britain do not now assume that there will never be any more war again. On the contrary, we intend to take ample precaution to prevent its renewal in any period we can foresee by effectively disarming the guilty nations while remaining suitably protected ourselves.
>
> * * * * * *
>
> You will, perhaps, have noticed that the President of the United States and the British representative in what is aptly called the Atlantic Charter have jointly pledged their countries to the final destruction of the Nazi tyranny. That is a solemn and grave undertaking. It must be made good. It will be made good. And, of course, many practical arrangements to fulfill that purpose have been and are being organized and set in motion.

AN UTTERLY FUTILE WAR? | 361

The question has been asked, "How near is the United States to war?" There is certainly one man who knows the answer to that question. If Hitler has not yet declared war upon the United States *. It is certainly not because he could not find a pretext. He has murdered half a dozen countries for far less.*

* * * * * *

* if he can succeed in beating the life and strength out of us * then is the moment when he will settle his account, and it is already a long one, with the people of the United States *.

There was criticism of Mr. Churchill's attempt to commit the United States with reference to performing the pledges of the Atlantic Charter:

It must be made good. It will be made good.

In addition, however, Mr. Churchill adumbrated in his broadcast the inception of a new English propaganda line. After he had reviewed the recent history of Japanese advances, and had mentioned other possible Japanese advances, [26] he asserted:

It is certain that this has got to stop. Every effort will be made to secure a peaceful settlement. * But this I must say: That if these hopes should fail we shall, of course, range ourselves unhesitatingly at the side of the United States.

A little over six and a half months previously, on the morning of March 6, 1941, Mr. Roosevelt had expressed his purpose to the new Polish Ambassador: [27]

* we Americans will have to buy this war as such. Let us hope at the price of Lend-Lease only. But who can say what price we may ultimately have to pay *?

By right of purchase, therefore, America now owned the Second World War. And, intimated Mr. Churchill, Britain would comradely help out America in what had now become America's war. This new British theme was later to be repeated and augmented: *crescit eundo*, like Fame in the Æneid.

On August 25, 1941, Mr. Roosevelt gave secret orders to the Atlantic Fleet to destroy "hostile forces which threaten [United States and Iceland flag] shipping": [28] this was War Plan 51.

On August 26 Tokyo cabled Admiral Nomura asking Mr. Hull to reconsider his stand upon oil shipments through Japanese waters to Russia in the light of the prior Japanese request [29] that the United States abstain from humiliating actions. On that same day it was publicly announced that the United States had decided to send to China an American military mission commanded by General John A. Magruder. [30] Several weeks earlier Admiral Stark had frankly written to Captain Cooke, [31]

> We are doing what we can for China and taking unheard of chances on neutrality; or rather unneutrality. This along with sanctions on Japan make her [Japan's] road certainly not less easy.

Apparently Admiral Stark felt that it was a great mistake to let the existence of the Magruder mission be known to the American people: he wrote to Admiral Hart on August 28, 1941: [32]

> I know about the very indiscreet radio and other leaks with regard to those recently sent to China. I have taken it up with those concerned, and here's hoping for at least some semblance of secrecy on the next one. Anyway, we shall try.

At about this time American Army aviators on active service were permitted to enter the Reserves and to join the Chinese armed forces: comparable support in men and in planes was also presently sent from Britain. [33]

At Tokyo on August 27, 1941, Mr. Terasaki delivered to Counselor Dooman a message for Ambassador Grew,[34] imploring that the American tankers going to Vladivostok be recalled, or if that was not possible, that they at least be rerouted so as not to pass through Japanese home waters. Mr. Terasaki's pleadings and warnings were almost frantic. Mr. Grew was further requested

* to urge upon the United States Government the desirability of giving favorable consideration to the holding of [the Roosevelt-Konoye] meeting as soon as possible.

Mr. Terasaki also stated

* that the internal situation in Japan was extremely grave and that should there be any premature disclosure at this time of the recent Japanese proposal [for the meeting] while these tankers were en route to Vladivostok it would probably bring about further attempts on the lives of leading members of the Japanese Government.

That same day, August 27, Ambassador Nomura called on Mr. Hull to support the request.[35] Mr. Hull delivered a preliminary scolding, which Admiral Nomura tried to pass off peaceably before coming to the problem of the tankers. Mr. Hull was cold and delivered a second lecture. He restated the Ambassador's request in the form of a question, and then Mr. Hull writes of his own monologue:

* I proceeded to answer for him by saying that would be preposterous. *

Eleven days having elapsed since the Japanese Ambassador had last seen Mr. Roosevelt, there was a conference at the White House, attended also by Mr. Hull, on the morning of August 28, 1941, in which a message from Prince Konoye was presented, dated the previous day, together with the requested statement of the views of the Japanese Government.[36]

The message from Prince Konoye was immediately read by Mr. Roosevelt. Prince Konoye set forth his hopes for peace and for the improvement of Japanese-American relations. Lack of understanding, mutual suspicions and misapprehensions and "the machinations and maneuvers of Third Powers" had, he wrote, caused a deterioration in those relations. In order to eliminate these causes he wished to meet Mr. Roosevelt "personally for a frank exchange of views." He continued, with grave seriousness,

> I consider it, therefore, of urgent necessity that the two heads of the Governments should meet first to discuss from a broad standpoint all important problems between Japan and America covering the entire Pacific area, and to explore the possibility of saving the situation. Adjustment of minor items may, if necessary, be left to negotiations between competent officials of the two countries, following the meeting.

In conclusion he requested that the meeting "take place as soon as possible."

Mr. Hull writes that Mr. Roosevelt "read it with interest and complimented the tone and spirit of it." But, in order to baby along the situation, Mr. Roosevelt "elaborated on * the difficulty of going [to] Hawaii." (The Roosevelts were notoriously reluctant travellers.) Perhaps Juneau in Alaska would be easier, Mr. Roosevelt suggested.

> * The only point raised by the Ambassador in this connection was that the conversation be held as early as possible.

Mr. Roosevelt then skimmed quickly over the longer statement of Japanese views, making several brief but critical comments. However,

> * he stated each time, study would later, of course, be given to the subject. *

Nevertheless Mr. Roosevelt then authorized Ambassador Nomura to say to the Japanese Government

> * that he considered this note a step forward and that he was very hopeful. He then added that he would be keenly interested in having three or four days with Prince Konoye, and again he mentioned Juneau.

So the conversation ended, and Mr. Roosevelt had been smart enough to avoid naming any date.

Later in the day Admiral Nomura called at Mr. Hull's apartment. [37] He was full of hope and discussed the details of the proposed meeting at length, even to fixing a date, September 21 to 25. Mr. Ballantine's memorandum on this point covers twenty-one lines. Mr. Hull's reply was evasive and curt: he

> * said that he would refer these points to the President for consideration.

Mr. Hull then brought up the Japanese statement of views, which he criticized at considerable length. In the course of this discussion Ambassador Nomura made this extremely important and interesting statement:

> * with regard to Japan's relations with the Axis there should be no difficulties, as the Japanese people regarded their adherence to the Axis as merely nominal and as he could not conceive of his people being prepared to go to war with the United States for the sake of Germany. He said he thought our attitude in regard to self-protection was entirely reasonable. The only difficulty that he saw was that to ask that Japan give a blank check for action that the United States might take against Germany in the name of self-defense was equivalent to asking for a nullification of the Tripartite Pact.

Mr. Hull continued to find obstacles in the Japanese statement of views, and at the conclusion of the interview he had successfully managed to bring the matter right back to the indefinite and dilatory status in which Mr. Roosevelt had left it on August 17. Mr. Hull agreed with the correctness of Ambassador Nomura's recapitulation of his position, that prior to the holding of the meeting there must be an agreement in principle, so that the meeting would merely serve to ratify an agreement already reached. Ambassador Nomura concluded the conference with a blend of despondency and hope. He

> * had misgivings as to how far the Japanese Government could go on account of the internal political difficulties in Japan. He said, however, that Prince Konoye was a man of great courage and was prepared to assume great risks in bringing to a successful conclusion an effort to improve relations.

On this same day, August 28, Mr. Roosevelt secretly extended his Atlantic Ocean shooting order to certain defined areas of the Pacific Ocean. The Navy's order read: [38]

> Certain operations prescribed for the Atlantic by W[ar] Pl[an] 51 are hereby extended to areas of the Pacific Ocean as described herein *. Formal changes in W[ar] Pl[an] 51 will be issued, but meanwhile action addressees will execute immediately the following instructions. * Destroy surface raiders which attack or threaten United States flag shipping. Interpret an approach of surface raiders within the Pacific sector of the Panama naval coastal frontier or the Pacific Southeast sub area as a threat to United States flag shipping. *

Soon after the morning conference on this day, August 28, 1941, it became known to the American press by a brief statement from Mr. Hull that Admiral Nomura had delivered to Mr. Roosevelt a personal message from Premier Konoye.[39] A diplomatic earthquake followed.⁴⁰ Less than four hours after the news was known in Tokyo ⁴¹ the suspicious German Ambassador, General Ott, called on Mr. Amau, the Japanese Vice Minister for Foreign Affairs. ⁴² General Ott was obviously trying to find out the import of the message from Prince Konoye: he demanded to know whether it departed from the policy determined at the Imperial Conference on July 2, 1941 (which had been secretly communicated to the German Government), and whether the Japanese Cabinet was contemplating any change in that policy.

Mr. Amau responded that the message did not mean that there had been

> * a change in Japan's policy, nor that we are contemplating any change in our relations with the Axis.

He said, rather vaguely, that he understood

> * that the reason for sending the message was to clarify the atmosphere in the Pacific.

General Ott then inquired whether the proposed negotiations between Japan and America involved only old matters or entirely new problems. Mr. Amau was again indefinite. General Ott then warned that

> * precautions must be taken against America's scheme to prolong these negotiations, so that this might work to her advantage.

Mr. Amau quickly explained that

> * we have also given the matter careful thought so that the carrying on of negotiations by Japan with America might not have any disadvantageous consequences upon Germany and Italy. *

Mr. Amau then gave a résumé and explanation of the Japanese policy towards the United States, which by adroit implication criticized the then current German policy of doing everything possible to avoid an "incident":

> Moreover, if next I may express my own personal opinions, our aim at the time when Matsuoka was Foreign Minister was to keep America from participating in the war, and for this reason we took a firm attitude toward America. In order to prevent her from joining in the war, we considered it necessary to get her to reflect upon her attitude, and, judging from the situation at the time, it was no mistake at all for us to think that it was quite proper for us to take a firm attitude toward her. Nevertheless the results proved to be just the opposite, and we can not deny that American public opinion has grown stronger and stronger, speeding up American preparations for war. Meanwhile Germany took a very mild attitude toward America. That is, America in all kinds of ways gave aid to England, instituted a system of convoy, and invaded Iceland, on the other hand freezing German funds in America and even closing German Consulates, while Germany took a very gentle attitude. Even at present Japan's policy of preventing America from participating in the war remains unchanged, and our aim is to keep her from joining in the war. Even now there is no change whatever in that objective. However it will be necessary for us to consider a policy that is adequate for the attainment of said objective, depending upon the time and occasion. In the present situation, America being a country of wide expanse and plentiful raw materials, we might possibly think it preferable, just at this time when the hostile feeling of the people toward the situation is on the point of becoming violent, to appease them and bring about a domestic disintegration, rather than to excite and unify them.

General Ott was apparently not satisfied by Mr. Amau's noncommittal replies, and he asked to receive a secret report of the contents of the message to Mr. Roosevelt. Mr. Amau attempted to dodge this, and General Ott finally asked for arrangements to be made so that he might see Foreign Minister Toyoda the following day.

On the following day, August 30, 1941, there was such an interview. It appears to have been inconclusive, and so far as can be ascertained General Ott did not receive a copy of the message. Foreign Minister Toyoda said, equally noncommittally, that the purpose of the Tripartite Pact (*not* of Japan) was "to prevent American participation in the war, and that this view is the same as in the past; nor will it change in the future."

So ended August 1941, the close of one period or stage of the American preparation to enter the war officially, and the beginning of a new period or stage, as the official government historians have noted. [43] Mr. Roosevelt was vacationing at Hyde Park and putting the final flourishes on his Labor Day speech. It was intended, in part, to open a campaign for increased production, but it was also intended to make the country more war conscious. Without saying that this country was all but officially at war, that impression was given, and the speech abounded in some nine references to the "enemy," who was now openly proclaimed to be Hitler. [44]

Mr. Roosevelt said, incitingly,

> There has never been a moment in our history when Americans were not ready to stand up as free men and fight for their rights.

* * * * * *

> I give solemn warning to those who think that Hitler has been blocked and halted, that they are making a very dangerous assumption. When in any war your enemy seems to be making slower progress *, that is the very moment to strike with redoubled force, to throw more energy into the job of defeating him, to end for all time the menace of world conquest and thereby end all talk or thought of any peace founded on a compromise. *

Mr. Roosevelt then called for a greater effort by labor to produce, and he talked in terms appropriate to a country at war, saying,

> The single-mindedness and sacrifice with which we jointly dedicate ourselves to the production of the weapons of freedom will determine * the length of the ordeal through which humanity must pass.

* * * * * *

> Yes, we are engaged on a grim and perilous task. Forces of insane violence have been let loose by Hitler upon this earth. We must do our full part in conquering them. *

> The task of defeating Hitler may be long and arduous. *

> I know that I speak the conscience and determination of the American people when I say that we shall do everything in our power to crush Hitler and his Nazi forces.

September 1, 1941, was the date contemplated by the secret ABC War Plan when America might enter the war.[45] It was on this day that Mr. Churchill, who had been meditating the approach for some little time,[46] asked Mr. Roosevelt for twelve American liners and twenty cargo ships, manned by American crews, to transport two British divisions to the Middle East.[47] Mr. Roosevelt promptly agreed to furnish Mr. Churchill with "our best transport ships."[48] These ships were to be absent from October 1941 to February 1942. At the time of Pearl Harbor they were near the Cape of Good Hope, and some of the British troops in the U.S.S. *Mount Vernon* were diverted to Singapore.[49]

It was also in early September that Mr. Roosevelt put into effect "the agreements" which he had made with Mr. Churchill at the Atlantic Conference "to intervene more directly in the Atlantic,"[50] and "attack any Axis ship found in [the] vast area" to which he was soon to make reference.[51] The American public were not to be informed about the vast area to which the new attacking orders were to be applied.

On the same day, September 1, 1941, Admiral Nomura called on Mr. Hull to express his hope for an early reply to Prince Konoye's unanswered request for a leaders' meeting. [52] There followed some discussion as to possible Chinese reactions to a Japanese-American settlement, and in connection with this obstacle, real or fancied, Mr. Hull returned to his major obstacle and

> * repeated his suggestion that we endeavor to reach an agreement in principle on fundamental questions before the meeting should take place.

There was then some discussion of the publicity concerning the proposed meeting, and Ambassador Nomura was able to make the constructive statement:

> * that nevertheless the press reaction in Japan had been favorable, which indicated that public opinion in Japan would support a *rapprochement* between Japan and the United States.

Mr. Hull objected to what he called "the Japanese press campaign" for certain of the Japanese objectives, and without directly using the word, by very clear implication asked that it be suppressed by the Japanese Government.

At Tokyo, Foreign Minister Toyoda feared the publicity both because of "the exceedingly complex domestic situation" and because of its effect upon "our relations with Germany and Italy." In a cable sent to Admiral Nomura on September 3 [53] he warned him of local political difficulties:

> Since the existence of the Premier's message was inadvertently made known to the public, that gang that has been suspecting that unofficial talks were taking place, has really begun to yell and wave the Tripartite Pact banner.

The same day, at Tokyo, Ambassador Grew was urged to speed a *fait accompli* of peace. He reported to Mr. Hull the troubled concern of the Japanese Foreign Office that [54]

> * the result of this publicity would be to increase the opposition to Japanese Government on the part of rightist elements since it would be alleged that the Government was yielding to American pressure. * while the Japanese Government does not fear those elements, nevertheless in view of Japan's association with the Axis powers in the Tripartite Pact it would be desirable to be in a position as soon as possible to produce, for their effects in uniting the nation, definite results from the Prime Minister's approach, since it is believed that if the pro-Axis elements promptly could be confronted with a *fait accompli* any mobilization of these elements against the Japanese Government could be halted.
>
> * Admiral Toyoda considered it extremely important that an official announcement of the meeting and its approximate date should be issued as soon as possible. * Prince Konoye wished to inquire whether the President would find it possible to meet [him] on or about the twentieth of September or as soon thereafter as possible *.

At Washington, Mr. Roosevelt and Mr. Hull met with Ambassador Nomura on the afternoon of September 3, 1941. Mr. Roosevelt handed two papers to the Ambassador, [55] which in substance required the Japanese to agree on all the unsettled and outstanding matters which were involved, prior to the holding of any personal meeting. At one place Mr. Roosevelt expressed to Prince Konoye his

> * desire to proceed as rapidly as possible toward the consummation of arrangements for a meeting at which you and I can * endeavor to bring about an adjustment in [our countries'] relations *.

but a few paragraphs later he deferred the desired meeting until prior agreement was reached.

In oral conversation with the Ambassador, Mr. Roosevelt imposed a new and startling obstacle: [56] he

> * also emphasized that if and when we had secured sufficient assurances from the Japanese Government * it would be necessary for us to discuss the matter fully with the British, the Chinese and the Dutch, since there is no other way to effect a suitable peaceful settlement for the Pacific area *.

This policy, we are officially told, [57]

> * was deliberate and well considered.*

We have already mentioned that the Atlantic Conference resulted in an "alliance" between Great Britain and the United States. In the light of Mr. Roosevelt's startling new condition only one hypothesis appears to be logically tenable. Was not Mr. Roosevelt also actually creating at this time some sort of formal alliance, or informal understanding, with China, the Netherlands—and Russia, as Mr. Churchill indicates [58] —so that he felt bound to conduct American foreign policy so as to subserve and support the interests of those nations?

Testifying several years later [59] as to this decision, Mr. Hull mentioned four palliatory "considerations" which appear to have had no logical connection with excusing this unfortunate step backward and away from peace.

First, "Japanese leaders were unreliable and treacherous." (But were they, at this time? And why would further delay have made them more reliable and less treacherous?)

Second, and contradictory of the first, he doubted "whether the military element in Japan would permit the civilian element * to revert to peaceful courses." (The diplomatic correspondence indicated just the opposite. But why would further delay have strengthened the peaceful civilian element?)

Third, any such meeting "would have had a critically discouraging effect upon the Chinese." (Did the Chinese believe that American leaders might be unreliable and treacherous? [60] If not, why would sincere American attempts to secure peace in China be "critically discouraging" to the Chinese?)

Fourth, contradictory of the first, and this was perhaps the real nub of the matter, though concealed in equivocal diplomatic circumlocutions:

> * The Japanese had been consistently unwilling in the conversations to pledge their Government to * . * state that Japan would refrain from attacking this country if it became involved through self-defense in the European war. *

That is, and translated into plain-spoken English, Japan would not agree to the repeated American demands for *carte blanche* in European power politics. But, as will presently appear, in another fifteen days Japan was prepared to give even this required "pledge." Yet all the while, Mr. Hull asserts,

> Our government ardently desired peace.*

For American purposes the need for such a Japanese pledge was becoming acute. At long last an "incident" occurred on September 4, 1941, in connection with an American destroyer, the *Greer,* and a German submarine far out in the Atlantic. Presumably acting under the secret and then unknown shooting orders of August 25, the Greer probably first depth-bombed the German submarine [61] which, in retaliation, fired two torpedoes at the *Greer.* [62] The official version, as made public at the moment, was that while conducting herself in a peaceable way upon a lawful occasion the vessel was wantonly attacked. [63] But the Navy Department refused to furnish the log of the *Greer* to the United States Senate. [64]

It was also on September 4, at London, that Mr. Mackenzie King, the Canadian Prime Minister, asked that the United States should guarantee armed assistance to Britain if British soil were threatened.[65] Mr. Churchill endorsed Mr. Mackenzie King's sentiments and, in a glancing bid for an American expeditionary force, stated that Germany could be defeated only by the full cooperation of all nations which as yet lay outside the range of the conqueror's power.

At Tokyo on September 4 Ambassador Grew called on the Japanese Foreign Minister at the latter's request.[66] Admiral Toyoda

> * emphasized to me the intention of Prince Konoye and himself to leave no stone unturned to arrange the suggested meeting at an early date * and to ensure the success of that meeting since, should it fail to achieve its basic aim, he was afraid that further efforts would be useless. *

The Foreign Minister then gave to Mr. Grew a document accepting various of the prior American proposals, and containing the Japanese commitments.[67] In particular Japan was prepared to back away from her obligations under the Tripartite Pact, and decide "independently" on its "interpretation and execution." In transmitting these proposals Ambassador Grew commented on their closer approach to American ideas, and he concluded,

> * I believe that this difference in tone and substance is indicative of the earnest wish of the Japanese Government to achieve a basic settlement with the United States.

At Washington on this same day, September 4, there was an even more encouraging development. Ambassador Nomura called on Mr. Hull[68] and handed him a "statement"[69]. It had seven topics, as did the earlier and last American draft of June 21, 1941.[70] *Six* of these seven topics *were identical* with the American draft of June 21, and the seventh (Item No. III), which referred to the proposed peaceful settlement with China, did not differ from the American draft in any important respects. Indeed the American obligation towards China was, if anything, reduced, while Japan explicitly stated by way of addition that Mr. Roosevelt was entitled to reply upon the policy of the Japanese Government.

It is difficult to suppose that Mr. Hull really comprehended how completely Japan had met the original American demands, since he gave no indication of any satisfaction. Instead, he re-emphasized [71]

* the necessity before entering into any formal negotiations of consulting with the Chinese, the British and the Dutch in order to enlist their support for a broad program of peace in the Pacific area. He pointed out that this was especially necessary with the Chinese who might otherwise be apprehensive lest we betray them. * [72]

And then Mr. Hull asked for more! He

* suggested the desirability of further broadening our proposed commitments affecting trade. *

Ambassador Nomura asked if there might not be some sort "of a public announcement in regard to the proposed meeting *." Mr. Hull flatly refused:

* he felt strongly that any announcement in regard to *negotiations* should be deferred until we had completed our preliminary discussions *and had approached the other interested governments.* (Emphasis supplied.)

The Ambassador may well have wondered whether there was any sincere American desire to reach an agreement, and he may likewise have been stunned by the chilly reception which the Japanese capitulation (for it was tantamount to that) had received. Subsequently, and prior to September 13, it was withdrawn, the face-saving reason assigned [73] being that it represented Admiral Nomura's

* personal and private views and it was consequently an unofficial document. *

At Washington, on September 4, 1941, the Chinese Ambassador saw Mr. Hull [74] to make it

* clear that China did not desire any peace at this time. *

Mr. Hull suggested to him

* the possibility that the governments opposed to Japan, including the United States, might refuse to enter into a peace settlement at the present time. *

In Tokyo the American obstacles and delays were beginning to have an effect. Prince Konoye met the Emperor informally on September 5 in preparation for an Imperial Conference which was held on September 6, 1941. [75] In essence the Japanese plans assumed the existence of an alliance between America and England and the Netherlands. The plans were:

* we will endeavor by every possible diplomatic means to have our demands agreed to by America and England. *

If by the early part of October there is no reasonable hope of having our demands agreed to * we will immediately make up our minds to get ready for war against America (and England and Holland.)

And these war preparations were to

* be completed approximately toward the end of October.

Emperor Hirohito feared that these plans might

* give precedence to war over diplomatic activities. *

He stated that he was striving for an international peace, and on both occasions he insisted upon receiving assurances that diplomacy should have precedence. It is said that, upon his intervening, he was also assured that the Chiefs of the Supreme Command were conscious of the importance of diplomacy and that they

> * advocated a resort to armed force only when there seemed no other way out. *

On September 5 Ambassador Grew cabled from Tokyo with further reference to the official proposals which he had transmitted the previous day.[76] He commented that while these proposals might not be entirely satisfactory,

> * It is clear that the first step * involves the cessation on the part of Japan of its progressive acts of aggression. It would appear that the commitments contained in the latest Japanese proposal, if implemented, would fulfill this requirement. *

He then recommended that, as Japan performed these commitments, the United States should, step by step, relax

> * the military and economic measures * which are now inexorably pressing on Japan. *

The dispatch concluded with this humane and pregnant observation:

> * If an adjustment of relations is to be achieved some risk must be run, but the risk taken in the pursuance on our part of a course which would not only provide inducements to the Japanese to honor their undertakings but would also leave to the United States Government a certain leverage of compulsion would appear to be relatively less serious than the risk of armed conflict entailed in the progressive application of economic sanctions which would result from a refusal to accept these proposals.

Next day, on September 6, 1941, Ambassador Grew went first to see the Foreign Minister, [77] to whom, on direct instructions from our Department of State, he delivered two severe rebuffs: the sailing of the American tankers to Vladivostok would not be delayed, and the freezing orders would not be suspended, pending the Roosevelt-Konoye meeting.

Second, Mr. Grew saw Mr. Terasaki, the Director of the American Bureau of the Japanese Foreign Office. Mr. Terasaki warned Mr. Grew that

> The Germans and Italians are endeavoring in every way through subordinate officials in the Foreign Office and the Vice Minister for Foreign Affairs [Mr. Amau] to obtain knowledge of the character and progress of the conversations between the United States and Japan. Every precaution, however, is being taken to ensure secrecy * . * the German influence is * considerable.

Moreover, Mr. Terasaki had information on the basis of confidential reports that extremist and pro-Axis elements were plotting some form of coup for September 27. Mr. Terasaki therefore expressed the opinion, which Mr. Grew noted that he himself had also expressed, that the *fait accompli* of reaching a peaceful agreement, prior to this date, would not only forestall such plans, but that it would also be favorably received in Japan and "supported by the great majority of the people."

On the evening of September 6, after the Imperial Conference was over, Ambassador Grew secretly met Prince Konoye at a private house. [78] They discussed the situation "with entire frankness," and Prince Konoye asked to have his statements transmitted personally to Mr. Roosevelt. The Japanese Prime Minister gave assurances of his support by "the responsible chiefs of both the Army and the Navy. * and other high ranking officers of the armed forces who are in entire accord with his aims." He promised satisfactory commitments and stated his conclusive and whole-hearted agreement with Mr. Hull's four principles.

> Prince Konoye repeatedly stressed the view that time is of the essence. * since resentment is daily mounting in Japan over the economic pressure being exerted by other countries, he could not guarantee to put into effect any such program of settlement six months or a year from now. He does, however, guarantee that at the present time he can carry with him the Japanese people *.
>
> Prince Konoye * expressed the earnest hope that in view of the present internal situation in Japan the projected meeting with the President could be arranged with the least possible delay. Prince Konoye feels confident that all problems and questions at issue can be disposed of to our mutual satisfaction during the meeting with the President, and he ended our conversation with the statement that he is determined to bring to a successful conclusion the proposed reconstruction of relations with the United States regardless of cost or personal risk.

At Washington, also on Saturday, September 6, 1941, Admiral Nomura called on Mr. Hull [79] and handed him a document [80] which was a copy of the draft proposal which had first been given to Ambassador Grew at Tokyo on September 4. [81] Mr. Hull said that it had been received on September 5. [82] Admiral Nomura related the document's proposals to the previous notes and conversations, and particularly directed Mr. Hull's attention to two of the proposals, the second and the third.

By the second proposal Japan agreed not to extend the military occupation of French Indo-China, nor, without any justifiable reason, to take any military action to the south. That is, Japan agreed not to attack Singapore or the Netherlands East Indies.

By the third proposal Japan said that, in case the United States should participate in the European War, Japan would "independently" decide concerning "the interpretation and execution of the Tripartite Pact." That is, Japan intimated that under such circumstances she would not consider herself bound to act in coordination with the Axis.

These were important advances for the policy which Mr. Roosevelt was following, and Ambassador Nomura stressed his own opinion that in the light of circumstances in Japan these were the maximum concessions which Japan "could offer at this time."

Mr. Hull said that the proposals would be studied over the week end, and claimed that he was "anxious to proceed as rapidly as possible." Admiral Nomura at once took up this opening and again requested haste, both in the discussions and in an announcement. Mr. Hull now withdrew his earlier objections to publicity and said that the Japanese Government might let it "seep out that informal and exploratory conversations were proceeding."

On September 9 Mr. Hull telegraphed Ambassador Grew [83] a long statement [84] to be delivered to the Japanese Minister for Foreign Affairs, Admiral Toyoda. It dealt exclusively with the settlement of Chinese affairs, and in that connection it raised new difficulties about the proposed settlement, concerning which it propounded a series of questions regarding the intentions of the Japanese Government. Once again Mr. Hull asserted

> * that the peace of the Pacific is not a question which can be decided by the United States and Japan alone *.

And once again it was repeated that it was

> * the intention of the United States Government * to confer with the Government of China, Great Britain, The Netherlands, et cetera, before it could agree to embark on any definitive negotiations with the Japanese Government regarding a settlement involving the Pacific area. *

This Chinese settlement was, indeed, the only matter still left open on which there could be the slightest excuse for quibbling, because, as has been pointed out, Japan had already yielded, or had indicated an intention to yield, on all of the other matters. Mr. Hull's statement was delivered by Ambassador Grew to Admiral Toyoda at Tokyo on September 10, 1941.

At Washington Admiral Nomura called on Mr. Hull on the morning of September 10, [85] in order to follow up the September 6 proposals. Mr. Hull then expressed the view that the Japanese proposals were narrower than previously, but he was promptly corrected on this point. Admiral Nomura in polite diplomatic language requested Mr. Hull to terminate the delay which was being prolonged by lengthy conversations about details, and once again the Japanese Ambassador asked to proceed with the settlement negotiations as rapidly as possible. It is to be inferred that he also asked to have Ambassador Grew permitted to do some of the negotiating in Tokyo, but Mr. Hull declined to permit this, saying that the American Government "desired to conduct the conversations here at Washington." Ultimately Mr. Hull agreed to let two of his immediate subordinates, Messrs. Hamilton and Ballantine, confer with the Japanese diplomats that afternoon.

On the afternoon of September 10, 1941, Messrs. Hamilton, Ballantine, and Schmidt conferred with Ambassador Nomura, Mr. Obata, his occasional translator, and Mr. Matsudaira. [86] Admiral Nomura made it clear that Japan was not now narrowing her earlier proposals—"all points previously tentatively agreed upon were 'to stand' and that * the other assurances" sent by Japan more recently were "in addition." The discussion again turned on China, and in this connection the Americans submitted a draft of an enlarged demand for American participation in "international trade and international investment" in the Pacific area. But at the end of the discussion the Americans evaded the Japanese proposal that the

Americans should "prepare a complete draft" of everything they wanted to ask Japan for, and left the matter to be further delayed until an answer could be obtained to the new but rather minor questions raised that afternoon.

Meanwhile Mr. Roosevelt was concerned with carrying into effect one of the decisions of the Atlantic Conference, to give aid to Soviet Russia. This decision affected the consciences of Roman Catholics, because the encyclical *Divini Redemptoris* of Pope Pius XI of March 18, 1937, [87] had broadly condemned atheistic communism and forbade collaboration with it. In the hope of changing the Pope's attitude Mr. Roosevelt sent Mr. Taylor to Rome on his second mission, bearing a letter dated September 3, 1941, [88] which was delivered to His Holiness on September 9. [89]

Mr. Roosevelt stated that

> * the fact is that Russia is governed by a dictatorship, as rigid in its manner of being as is the dictatorship in Germany *.

He then expressed the opinion (which the passage of time has shown to be erroneous),

> * that this Russian dictatorship is less dangerous to the safety of other nations than is the German form of dictatorship. *

Mr. Roosevelt wrote that he had been informed that the Russian churches were open, and he then stated a further erroneous opinion, that as a result of the war Russia might recognize freedom of religion.

We are not told of the full scope of Mr. Taylor's discussions with the Pope, but it is stated that a number of Mr. Roosevelt's views concerning the Atlantic Charter were conveyed. His Holiness, we are informed, continued to condemn atheistic communism and the Soviet's practices regarding individual liberty. On September 20, 1941, he wrote Mr. Roosevelt a friendly, noncommittal, and astute reply. [91] It has already been pointed out how the word "peace" had earlier vanished from Mr. Roosevelt's vocabulary. His Holiness's letter was largely a plea for peace, which was repeatedly mentioned, with some adverse comment upon "the appalling and heart-sickening consequences of modern warfare." Mr. Taylor was also asked to report orally the Pope's "point of view regarding the important matters which were dealt with in [the] conversations." As yet, these remain secret, but in the light of the letter of September 20 they may be inferred to have been a plea to maintain the peace. Whatever they were, they do not seem to have pleased Mr. Roosevelt, because a full year passed before there was another exchange of letters. [92]

XII TWILIGHT LETS HER CURTAIN DOWN

THE INCREASED INTENSITY of war preparation which was so noticeable in Washington after September 1, 1941, [1] was augmented by a grim "fireside chat" by Mr. Roosevelt on September 11, [2] in which he announced that he had ordered American warships to shoot on sight at German or Italian war vessels in North Atlantic waters. This order was of course not new, although the American public thought so; it was merely a public announcement of the substance of the secret War Plan 51 of August 25, 1941. In the course of his radio speech Mr. Roosevelt used the word "attack" an unusual number of times. Mr. Roosevelt opened his speech with the claim that the *Greer* had been "attacked" in full daylight; "the German submarine fired first upon this American destroyer without warning and with deliberate design to sink her." Without mention of the fact that under international law the United States had no right to attempt to control vast stretches of the open ocean, Mr. Roosevelt stated that the *Greer* was sailing in waters which the American Government had declared to be "waters of self-defense":

> This was piracy, piracy legally and morally. It was not the first or the last act of piracy which the Nazi Government has committed against the American flag in this war, for attack has followed attack.

It was of course not "piracy," as Mr. Roosevelt should have known very well, but Mr. Roosevelt was not trying to state the law accurately; he was attempting to arouse American passions by an emotional appeal, and seeking an apparent justification for the public announcement of his previous secret order. Probably, too, he was seeking moral liberation from the 1940 Democratic platform plank's pledge by way of its escape clause—"except in case of attack." Mr. Roosevelt therefore mentioned the *Robin Moor* and other instances of "attack." The Nazis, he proceeded to say, design to abolish the freedom of the seas, and then to dominate the United States, dominate the Western Hemisphere, by force of arms. He mentioned Nazi plots in South America, and then returned to an older argument for the support of Britain:

> I think it must be explained over and over again to people who like to think of the United States Navy as an invincible protection that this can be true only if the British Navy survives. And that, my friends, is simple arithmetic.

Mr. Roosevelt's explanation of the simple arithmetic was, that if the Nazis controlled the rest of the world they would have much greater shipbuilding facilities than the Americas. He therefore developed the theme of the freedom of the seas, for which America had battled from generation to generation. Hitler had begun a campaign to control the seas: "* we Americans are now face to face * with cruel, relentless facts." The attack on the *Greer* was not a mere episode: it "was one determined step toward creating a permanent world system based on force, on terror and on murder." The time has come to say "* you have now attacked our own safety. You shall go no further." The "normal practices of diplomacy * are of no possible use in dealing with international outlaws." Mr. Roosevelt proclaimed,

> No matter what it takes, no matter what it costs, we will keep open the line of legitimate commerce in these defensive waters of ours.
>
> We have sought no shooting war with Hitler. We do not seek it now. But neither do we want peace so much that we are willing to pay for it by permitting him to attack our naval and merchant ships while they are on legitimate business.
>
> * We cannot bring about the downfall of Naziism by the use of long-range invective.
>
> * When you see a rattlesnake poised to strike, you do not wait until he has struck before you crush him.
>
> These Nazi submarines and raiders are the rattlesnakes of the Atlantic. * They are a challenge to our own sovereignty. They hammer at our most precious rights when they attack ships of the American flag—symbols of our independence, our freedom, our very life.

The Americas, said Mr. Roosevelt, must be defended:

> Do not let us be hair splitters. *
> The time for active defense is now.
> Do not let us split hairs *.
> This is the time for prevention of attack *.

The "very presence" of German and Italian submarines "in any waters which America deems vital to its defense constitutes an attack." We will no longer wait for the Axis to strike first:

> * our patrolling vessels and planes will protect all merchant ships—not only American ships but ships of any flag—engaged in commerce in our defensive waters. They will protect them from submarines; they will protect them from surface raiders.

* * * * * *

But let this warning be clear. From now on, if German or Italian vessels of war enter the waters the protection of which is necessary for American defense, they will do so at their own peril.

Mr. Roosevelt then announced, in the phrase which he loved, that as Commander in Chief of the United States Army and Navy he had given orders to carry out this policy "at once." His auditors did not know that for some time it had already been in effect.

Mr. Roosevelt then sought sympathy for himself. He was doing his duty "in this crisis." He was well aware of its "gravity"; indeed, he declared,

> * I have not taken it hurriedly or lightly. It is the result of months and months of constant thought and anxiety and prayer. *

But what if this was a "crisis"? The American people had faced other crises, and they knew that we needed "a bold defense against these attacks." So Mr. Roosevelt ended this long speech by declaring, in a last strophe of flag waving, that the American people would "stand their ground against this latest assault upon their democracy, their sovereignty and their freedom."

From Pearl Harbor, Admiral Kimmel, pricking up his ears, immediately wrote Admiral Stark, the letter being dated September 12, 1941,[3] to ask whether, not only in the Atlantic, but also in the Pacific, he should "change * to direct offensive measures":

> * Should we now bomb contacts, *without waiting to be attacked?* (Emphasis supplied.)

Next day, on September 13, Mr. Roosevelt ordered the Atlantic fleet to escort convoys in which there were no American vessels.[4]

Interpreting this order, Mr. Knox spoke to the American Legion convention on September 15, 1941, and said: [5]

> Beginning tomorrow the American Navy will provide protection as adequate as we can make it for ships of every flag carrying these aid supplies between the American continent and the waters adjacent to Iceland. These ships are ordered to capture and destroy by every means at their disposal Axis controlled submarines or surface raiders encountered in these waters. This is our answer to Hitler's declaration that he will try to sink every ship his vessels encounter on the route leading from the United States to British ports.

Two days later Mr. Knox cryptically added the statement that "the escort of convoys by war vessels is only one of the methods * being used * . *" [6]

Admiral Stark's current interpretation of the shoot-at-sight order was that America was now assisting England "openly." [7] And he correctly predicted:

> * Unless the Axis powers withdraw their men-of-war from this area, contacts are almost certain to occur. *The rest requires little imagination.* (Emphasis supplied.)

Admiral Stark also referred to recent "contacts" of American warships with German submarines, and stated,

> * We should have gotten at least one SS [Submarine], *which was attacked* under favorable circumstances. (Emphasis supplied.)

In Japan on September 13 Ambassador Grew called on the Foreign Minister, at the latter's request, for a lengthy interview [8] at which the replies to the questions were also received. [9] Admiral Toyoda repeated that Japan was not narrowing any points on which prior agreement had been reached but, instead, was extending those agreements. Agreement was likewise expressed with the substance of the new and extended American demand of September 10, relating to trade and investment in the Pacific area. Several times Admiral Toyoda urged the advisability of a prompt meeting between Mr. Roosevelt and Prince Konoye, and of obviating the "long drawn out discussion of details at the present time *."

The Japanese Foreign Minister also indicated the existence of doubt in his mind as to whether Mr. Roosevelt was aware of the details of the current negotiations. Ambassador Grew replied

> * that the Secretary of State was in constant communication with the President in regard to the conversations in progress *.

In conclusion Admiral Toyoda "earnestly and seriously" expressed his hopes for a prompt Roosevelt-Konoye meeting. "In view of the great weight which he attributed to the urgency of speedy action," Ambassador Grew promised again to transmit the Foreign Minister's views to Mr. Hull. It was at Washington, Ambassador Grew said, that "any definitive discussions concerning the reaching of an agreement on principle" would have to be continued.

Such, in substance, was the message which Ambassador Nomura cabled to Foreign Minister Toyoda on September 15. [10] The United States, he added, would not act as intermediary with China for the proposed Japanese peace terms unless they "were fair and just"; such terms, therefore, must be outlined in advance of the "leaders' conference." Moreover the United States would have to explain everything to Great Britain, China, and the Netherlands in advance, so that those countries would not be suspicious.

In addition Admiral Nomura attempted to quiet Foreign Minister Toyoda's doubts, as expressed to Ambassador Grew, as to whether Mr. Roosevelt really was informed about, and approved of, what Mr. Hull was doing. Admiral Nomura's message also stated:

Whatever we tell to Secretary Hull you should understand will surely be passed on to the President if he is in Washington. It seems that the matter of preliminary conversations has been entrusted by the President to Secretary Hull, in fact he told me that if a matter could not be settled by me and Secretary Hull it would not be settled whoever conducted the conversations. *Hull himself told me that during the past eight years he and the President had not differed on foreign policies once, and that they are as "two in one."* (Emphasis supplied.)

Other hopeful hints must also have been dropped to Admiral Nomura, because on September 17 he cabled [11] that "According to information from [my] usual source," [12] at a recent United States Cabinet meeting there were

* considerable signs of anticipation of a Japanese-U. S. conference. *

and that

* There is no mistaking the fact that the President is prepared to attend the meeting if the preliminary arrangements can be made.

At Tokyo on September 17 the Japanese Ambassador to Great Britain, Mr. Shigemitsu, called on Ambassador Grew. [13] He pointed out that the Japanese Government was united in support of its current endeavors to improve Japanese relations with the United States, and that its policy had the support of the responsible chiefs of the armed forces. Mr. Shigemitsu also told Mr. Grew

* in the strictest confidence that the initiative in the direction of an understanding with America and England had come from the Emperor personally and that his own recall from London was related to this general subject. *

So far as Japanese good faith was concerned, Mr. Shigemitsu said * that although it was a physical impossibility to set down ahead of time all details relative to the carrying out by Japan of the undertakings which the Japanese Government might assume, the sincerity and will of the Konoye Government is such that the faithful execution in the course of time of any agreement which may be reached can be counted on with complete confidence.

On the same day Mr. Tomohiko Ushiba, the Private Secretary to the Japanese Foreign Minister, sought and had a long interview with Mr. Dooman, the Counselor of the American Embassy.[14] Three principal points were covered. The first was the method of the communication of the Japanese peace terms with China. The third was the importance of holding the proposed meeting "as soon as possible."

The second was amazing, for Japan was prepared to give to Mr. Roosevelt *carte blanche* to take *any* action he pleased against Germany and, in effect, to desert the Three Power Alliance. What Mr. Roosevelt had been seeking from Japan appears clearly in Mr. Ushiba's preliminary résumé. The Private Secretary

> * said that it was impossible for Japan to give to the United States a prior undertaking that it would interpret as a *defensive* act *any* action on the part of the United States against Germany *which might lead to war* between the United States and Germany. * He added, however, that an understanding had been reached among the various influential elements in Japan which would enable Prince Konoye to give *orally* and *directly to the President an assurance* with regard to the attitude of Japan *which*, he felt sure, *would be entirely satisfactory to the President*. (Empasis supplied.)

One of Mr. Roosevelt's major diplomatic objectives had thus been achieved, but as will presently appear he no longer was satisfied with his original objectives.

On September 22, 1941, at Tokyo, the proposed basic Japanese peace terms with China were delivered by Foreign Minister Toyoda to Ambassador Grew.[15] They had largely been copied from Mr. Hull's draft proposal of June 21, 1941.[16] Thus, Japan agreed verbatim to items

1. Neighborly friendship.
7. No annexation.
8. No indemnities.

Mr. Hull's original item 4, "Mutual respect of sovereignty and territories," was strengthened in its phraseology as 2, "Respect for sovereignty and territorial integrity."

Mr. Hull's original item 2, "Cooperative defense against injurious communistic activities," which had been subject to further discussion, was the new item 8, and while the phraseology was amplified, the scope of legitimate Japanese activity was defined.

The new Japanese item 4 (the old American item 6) called for the "Withdrawal of Japanese armed forces" from China, and was agreed to!

American insistence upon this demand, the American military experts felt, was a serious strategic error. In a secret Military Intelligence Estimate, prepared by G-2 and dated October 2, 1941, these statements appear:[17]

> * as a matter of fact, at this stage in the execution of our national strategic plan, a cessation of hostilities in China followed by the withdrawal of twenty-one Japanese divisions, 20 independent brigades, and 1,000 aircraft therefrom would be highly detrimental to our interests.

* * * * * *

> * it seems imperative, for the present at least, to keep as much of the Japanese Army as possible pinned down in China. In other words we must cease at once our attempts to bring about the withdrawal of Japanese armed forces from China *.

The new Japanese item 5 (the old American item 3) dealt with "Economic cooperation," and accepted Mr. Hull's principle of "non-discrimination."

Fusion of the two Chinese Governments was asked (Japanese item 6) and, in place of negotiations in regard to Manchoukuo, Chinese recognition was asked.

On September 22, 1941, the general Japanese situation was reviewed by Ambassador Grew in an extremely significant personal letter to Mr. Roosevelt.[18] Mr. Grew begged for peace, and spoke highly of Prince Konoye, who, he wrote,

> * in the face of bitter antagonism from extremist and pro-Axis elements in the country is courageously working for an improvement in Japan's relations with the United States. * I am convinced that he now means business and will go as far as is possible, without incurring open rebellion in Japan, to reach a reasonable understanding with us. In spite of all the evidence of Japan's bad faith in times past in failing to live up to her commitments, I believe that there is a better chance of the present Government implementing whatever commitments it may now undertake than has been the case in recent years. It seems to me highly unlikely that this chance will come again or that any Japanese statesman other than Prince Konoye could succeed in controlling the military extremists in carrying through a policy which they * resent and oppose. The alternative to reaching a settlement now would be the greatly increased probability of war *. I therefore most earnestly hope that we can come to terms, even if we must take on trust, at least to some degree, the continued good faith and ability of the present Government fully to implement those terms.

From Batavia the American Consul cabled Mr. Hull on September 22, 1941, reporting that the Rt. Hon. Alfred Duff Cooper had stated:[19]

> An effective liaison exists between the British and the Dutch *.

In response to a question concerning the use of the base of Singapore he said that there is no "agreement on paper but the answer is obvious." Asked if the ABCD front was merely wishful thinking, he said "Emphatically no. It is a fact." *

From Washington on the same day, September 22, 1941, Admiral Nomura sent a long, analytical report to the Foreign Minister [20] which concluded with this optimistic hope:

> Finally, though the United States Government does not wish to compromise with Japan at the expense of China, should Japan give up forceful aggressions, Japanese-American trade relations could be restored, and the United States would even go so far as to render economic assistance to Japan.

On Tuesday, September 23, 1941, Admiral Nomura called on Mr. Hull in order personally to deliver to him another copy of the same proposed basic Japanese peace terms with China which had been delivered to Mr. Grew in Tokyo on Monday, September 22. In the course of the conversation, Admiral Nomura urged [21]

> * that the holding of a meeting such as suggested would be of great value in counteracting the influence of the pro-Axis elements in the Japanese Government and in providing support for those elements desiring peaceful relations with the United States.

Mr. Hull raised the Admiral's hopes by mentioning

> * the great opportunity that was now presented for Japan and the United States to work together along peaceful and progressive lines and he said he could not emphasize too much his view that by following such a course both countries would stand to gain more than through any other course. *

Ambassador Nomura fully agreed, whereupon Mr. Hull tartly ended both Admiral Nomura's hopes and the interview by saying,

> * that as this country had been following courses of peace and was committed to these courses there was very little that we could offer offer Japan in the way of bargaining. *

There is some evidence to show that by this time Mr. Hull had about closed his mind to the possibility of coming to any agreement with Japan. On September 23, 1941, Admiral Stark wrote Admiral Kimmel. [22] Admiral Stark had just talked to Mr. Hull, who had informed him *"that conversations with the Japs have practically reached an impasse."* (Emphasis in original.) In a postscript to this letter, dated September 29, Admiral Stark writes that he had received the impression from Mr. Hull that he might make one more try. This pessimism was the antithesis of the constructive policy which Mr. Grew was urging and was to urge.

In a further attempt to meet Mr. Hull's objections the Japanese Government submitted a set of proposals [23] to Mr. Grew at Tokyo on September 25. They consisted of a long declaration, or preamble, and six numbered topics.

The declaration, or preamble, was essentially the same as Mr. Hull's own draft of June 21, 1941, [24] except for one addition which will be mentioned under "Topic V."

Topic I, "The concepts of Japan and of the United States respecting international relations and the character of nations," was identical with Mr. Hull's earlier draft.

Topic II, "The attitudes of both Governments toward the European War," was far more favorable to Mr. Roosevelt's purposes than Mr. Hull's draft had been. Mr. Hull's phrase, applicable only to the attitude of the United States, that its policy would be determined "by considerations of protection and self-defense," was now likewise adopted by Japan, and was thus a clear diplomatic expression of a Japanese refusal to act aggressively in collaboration with Hitler. Japan likewise promised "in case the United States should participate in the European War" to interpret the Tripartite Pact "entirely independently" of Germany. On this point, it will be recollected, the Japanese had on September 18 stated that Prince Konoye would at the proposed meeting give "an assurance * entirely satisfactory to" Mr. Roosevelt.

Topic III, "Action toward a peaceful settlement between Japan and China," was redrafted, but only two new matters were added to the substance. By the first, while the peace negotiations were pending, the United States would

> * refrain from resorting to any measures and actions which might hamper the measures and efforts of the Government of Japan directed toward the settlement of the China Affair.

By the second, Japan voluntarily offered to agree

> * that the economic cooperation between Japan and China will be carried on by peaceful means and in conformity with the principle of non-discrimination in the international commercial relations * and that the economic activities of third Powers in China will not be excluded so long as they are pursued on an equitable basis.

To this topic was annexed the draft of the basic peace terms already mentioned.

Topic IV, "Commerce between Japan and the United States," was also redrafted, but seems to be in substance about the same as Mr. Hull's proposal, if one assumes that Mr. Hull was acting in good faith. By Mr. Hull's draft "normal trade relations" were to be resumed, and "available" commodities supplied as soon as both governments gave "official approbation to the * understanding." [25] By the Japanese draft "normal trade relations" would be resumed "without delay," the "freezing" orders would be discontinued "immediately," and "available" goods would be supplied.

Topic V, it will be remembered, had already been redrafted by the Americans on September 10. The Japanese draft followed the new American draft verbatim with one exception, which also characterizes the declaration, or preamble. Topic V was originally captioned, "Economic problems in the Pacific Area." It was now redrafted by the Japanese to read, "Economic problems in the *Southwestern* Pacific Area"; as thus rephrased, it unquestionably appeared to be a narrowing—so far as the phraseology went—of the geographical area which the proposal was to cover. But there was involved another important and very material consideration, to be explained below.

Topic VI, "The policies of both nations affecting political stabilization in the Pacific area," as redrafted by the Japanese, explains the apparent, but not real, narrowing of Topic V. Mr. Hull's original draft of Topic VI was merely a generality in favor of peace in the Pacific area. That generality was now amply covered in the first paragraph of Topic II. But the area in which the trouble had been developing which threatened the peace of the Pacific was the Southwest Pacific, where Indo-China, Thailand (Siam), the Philippines, and the Netherlands East Indies were situated. Indeed, when the official American version [26] of our Japanese policy was written, it was stated that, as of this time, it was anticipated, and by plain inference feared, that Japan would [27]

> * take advantage of American preoccupation in the Atlantic area by seizing territories in the *southwest* Pacific region *. (Emphasis supplied.)

There in the southwest the root of the anticipated trouble was to be found, and it was there that the Japanese proposed to give, not general, but precise and specific assurances. The new Japanese draft proposed that "the situation in the Southwestern Pacific area" be stabilized promptly, and that no "measures and actions" be taken which might "jeopardize such stabilization." The American, British, and Dutch military and political officials had for long feared, and rightly continued to fear, a Japanese advance to the southwest. Japan now proposed to agree flatly not to advance out of French Indo-China in any direction whatsoever (excepting China only), and, upon the establishment of peace, to withdraw the Japanese troops from Indo-China, Japan also specifically proposed a new item, to "respect the sovereignty and territorial integrity of Thailand and Netherland [*sic*] East Indies," and with this proposal was was combined an expressed agreement with Mr. Hull's original topic VII, neutralization of the Philippine Islands by treaty when they achieved independence. These specific new Japanese proposals went far beyond anything ever requested by Mr. Hull (so far as the records show). It is therefore very difficult to understand why they should not have been acceptable if Mr. Roosevelt and Mr. Hull were sincerely attempting to find a way to maintain peace.

The indifferent handling and casual rejection of the Japanese proposals of September 25, 1941, is one of the historical mysteries of that era. Volume II of the Foreign Relations, Japan, 1931–1941, contains a sixty-one-page narrative concerning these negotiations in 1941. It is the official version of, the official apology for, what happened subsequently. Many minor matters receive therein paragraphs and even pages of comment. But the substance of these important Japanese peace proposals is curtly dismissed in less than two lines as printed therein: [28]

> * The new redraft did not indicate any modification of the attitude of the Japanese Government on fundamental points.

As will be seen from the previous analysis such a claim is not true.

While the official version expresses dubiety as to the proposed Roosevelt-Konoye meeting, [29]
* unless the Japanese could be brought either before such a meeting *or at such a meeting* to the making of specific and substantially detailed pledges * (emphasis supplied),

the Japanese were now voluntarily offering specific pledges. Moreover, so far as the record shows, Mr. Hull never at any time indicated to the Japanese just what specific pledges were desired from them. His draft of June 21, 1941, already referred to, was neither specific nor detailed. Nevertheless it represented the official American position, so that the Japanese were quite warranted in relying upon it and in copying it so substantially when they made their proposals of September 25, 1941.

It is also justifiable to assume that the Japanese proposals of September 25 received only a cursory consideration at Washington. The American Embassy at Tokyo had to put them into code, they then had to be telegraphed, and at Washington they had to be decoded. But at Washington, on Thursday, September 25, as Mr. Roosevelt was rushing away for one of his week ends at Hyde Park, Mr. Hull gave him this memorandum in pencil: [30]

> My suggestion on Jap situation—for you to read *later*. C. H.
>
> When the Jap Prime Minister requested a meeting with you he indicated a fairly basic program in generalities, but left open such questions as getting troops out of China, Tripartite pact, nondiscrimination in trade in Pacific.
>
> We indicated desire for meeting, but suggested first an agreement in principle on the vital questions left open, so as to insure the success of the conference.
>
> Soon thereafter, the Japs *narrowed* their position on these basic questions, and now continue to urge the meeting at Juneau.
>
> My suggestion is [1] to recite their more liberal attitude when they first sought the meeting with you, [2] with their much narrowed position *now*, and [3] earnestly ask if they cannot go back to their original liberal attitude so [4] we can start discussions *again* on agreement in principle *before* the meeting and [5] reemphasizing your desire for a meeting. (Emphasis in original: numerals supplied.)

Whether or not Mr. Roosevelt ever had the full text of the Japanese proposals before him does not appear.

In Japan on September 27 Foreign Minister Toyoda requested Ambassador Grew to call on him, and for two hours there was a discussion of Japanese-American relations. [31] Admiral Toyoda's

> * main purpose in conversation with me [Mr. Grew] today, however, was to have conveyed to the President, through the Secretary of State and myself, the anxiety of Prince Konoye and the entire Cabinet lest the proposed meeting between the heads of our two Governments might be indefinitely delayed, and orally to present various considerations regarding the position of the Japanese Government in connection with the present informal conversations *.

These considerations included a narration of the Japanese desire to reestablish good relations with the United States, and for peace, but not at the price of abject and face-losing surrender. It was emphasized by Admiral Toyoda that there was no "precedent in Japanese history for a Prime Minister to go abroad to confer with the head of a foreign Government," but that Prince Konoye, in his desire to create good relations with the United States, had determined to break all precedent. All of the Japanese details for the proposed meeting had been completed. Full admirals and generals had been appointed to accompany the Prime Minister, "in order to dissipate doubt as to the collaboration of the Japanese Navy and Army with the Prime Minister's undertaking."

Time was of the essence, Admiral Toyoda urged, because "opposition groups * are moving against the policy of the Cabinet in its endeavors to bring about an improvement in relations with the United States." If the meeting were held, "an epochal improvement in Japanese-American relations would evolve," but "The favorable atmosphere and auspicious opportunity obtaining at present, however, would be subverted and would not soon recur" if America delayed or interposed "obstructions."

Japan was of course not "setting a time limit," but would not "the American Government * be pleased to assign some date between October 10 and 15 for the meeting"?

Finally, "Admiral Toyoda wanted to emphasize the essential necessity for mutual confidence and faith." Mr. Grew promised to report the substance of his statement completely and precisely, and seems to have done so conscientiously, but both at Hyde Park and at Washington it fell on deaf ears.

At Hyde Park on September 28, 1941, Mr. Roosevelt prepared his instructions for Mr. Hull. [32] They were in substance a paraphrase of Mr. Hull's recommendations:

> I wholly agree with your pencilled note—[1] to recite the more liberal original attitude of the Japanese when they first sought the meeting, [2] point out their much narrowed position now, [3] earnestly ask if they cannot go back to their original attitude [4] start discussions again on agreement in principle, and [5] reemphasize my hope for a meeting. (Numerals supplied.)

Being very troubled at the constant American delays and obstructions and the consequences which he foresaw would flow from them, Ambassador Grew sent to Mr. Hull a long advisory cable from Tokyo on September 29, 1941. [33] After reviewing the general situation Mr. Grew noted that the Japanese efforts were

> * increasing steadily and intensified lately, to arrange a meeting between Prince Konoye and President Roosevelt without further delay. *

He noted almost wistfully that he had become reduced to being

> * chiefly * a transmitting agent in these conversations * . *

Mr. Grew stated his firm belief that "a complete readjustment of relations between Japan and the United States" could now be brought about, and that

* the United States is now given the opportunity to halt Japan's program without war, or an immediate risk of war. *

and, further, that

* through failure to use the present opportunity, the United States will * face a greatly increased risk of war. *

Japanese psychology, wrote Mr. Grew, was different from that of the Western nations, and the inference is plain that he felt Mr. Roosevelt and Mr. Hull did not understand the Japanese psychology correctly. Then, in highly prophetic language, he continued,

> Should the United States expect or await agreement by the Japanese Government, in the present preliminary conversations, to clear-cut commitments which will satisfy the United States Government both as to principle and as to concrete detail, almost certainly the conversations will drag along indefinitely until the Konoye Cabinet and its supporting elements desiring *rapprochement* with the United States will come to the conclusion that the outlook for an agreement is hopeless and that the United States Government is only playing for time. * The logical outcome of this will be the downfall of the Konoye Cabinet and the formation of a military dictatorship which will lack either the disposition or the temperament to avoid colliding head-on with the United States. *

The reason why detailed agreement could not be reached through correspondence, Mr. Grew explained, was that the former Foreign Minister, Matsuoka, and many of his supporters who remained in the Japanese Foreign Office were telling everything to the Germans, and that they would not scruple to reveal both to the Germans and to the Japanese extremists any information which might lead to the downfall of Prince Konoye and his Cabinet.

Japan was willing, Mr. Grew thought, to reduce her adherence to the Axis "to a dead letter," and he believed that in direct negotiations with Mr. Roosevelt Prince Konoye would

> * offer him assurances which, because of their far reaching character, will not fail to satisfy [him]. *

Mr. Grew therefore expressed his opinion that American objectives would not be reached by current methods. A reasonable amount of confidence, he believed, should be placed in Prince Konoye. Only by doing so was there any hope either of improving relations or of avoiding "ultimate war * in the Pacific." If there was war the Japanese military machine could be discredited only "through wholesale military defeat *."

In the light of later events Mr. Grew's message appears to be unanswerable, so much so that some of the official administration apologies omit all reference to it, while the embarrassed majority of the Pearl Harbor Committee tried to minimize its effect by quoting its politely deferential final sentence, [34] in the hope of leaving an impression with the reader that perhaps Mr. Roosevelt at Washington knew better than Mr. Grew what the local situation at Tokyo was really like.

At Washington, on September 29, 1941, Ambassador Nomura called on Mr. Hull [35] and left a document [36] containing the gist of what Admiral Toyoda had said to Mr. Grew on September 27. In the course of the conversation, and about as it was concluding, Admiral Nomura expressed as his opinion

> * that if nothing came of the proposal for a meeting * it might be difficult for Prince Konoye to retain his position and that Prince Konoye then would be likely to be succeeded by a less moderate leader. He suggested that this was one reason why the Japanese Government desired to move as speedily as possible. *

As is now evident, history at this point hung in the balance. By making the right choice Mr. Roosevelt would probably have avoided the Pacific war. Why, then, did he make the wrong choice? It is plain that Mr. Roosevelt did not accept Mr. Grew's advice nor heed his warnings, and because of this we must necessarily infer either that Mr. Roosevelt disagreed with Mr. Grew's opinion that it was possible to maintain the peace, or else that Mr. Roosevelt intended war at some later date. Perhaps there is a third possibility, that Mr. Roosevelt believed that war with Japan was ultimately inevitable, but that meanwhile Mr. Roosevelt was playing for time and babying along the Japanese. Whatever Mr. Roosevelt's motives may have been, Mr. Grew's advice and warnings had no perceptible effect in changing the line of conduct of Mr. Roosevelt's foreign policy towards Japan. It is odd that Mr. Grew's advice should have had no effect, because, while Mr. Grew had no knowledge of the secret intercepts, Mr. Roosevelt did, and Mr. Grew's opinion that the Japanese were negotiating in good faith found striking confirmation in an intercepted message of September 30 from the Japanese Ambassador in Rome to the Foreign Office at Tokyo: [37]

> Our recent negotiations with the United States have put a bad taste in the mouths of the people of this country. Our attitude toward the Tripartite Alliance appears to them to be faithless. Recently the newspapers have been growing more critical in tone where we Japanese are concerned. Official comment, too, has been none too complimentary. As for Italy's attitude toward the recent celebration of the first anniversary of the * Alliance, its coolness reflects the attitude of the whole Italian people. *

Further confirmation is to be found in another intercepted message of October 1, 1941, from the Japanese Ambassador in Berlin to Tokyo. [38] He reported that because of the Japanese-American negotiations everyone in the German Foreign Office was "thoroughly disgusted with Japan." Likewise the feeling of the German leaders and people in general was plainly bad towards Japan, and he warned Tokyo that if the negotiations continued, without consulting Germany,

> * there is no telling what steps Germany may take without consulting Japan.

These intercepted secret messages made it abundantly clear that Japan was not acting in collusion with the Axis, but quite independently of it. It is therefore difficult to understand why Mr. Grew's advice was not taken, and why the opportunity to establish good relations in the Pacific, and to avoid a long, bloody, and desperate war, was so casually or so obdurately lost.

Almost simultaneously another opportunity was being lost in another part of the world. Mr. W. Averell Harriman and Lord Beaverbrook, heading the Anglo-American mission, conferred with General Stalin from September 29 to October 1, 1941. [39] General Stalin demanded very large quantities of all kinds of war materials, most of which was granted, but in exchange no commitments were asked for from General Stalin with regard to Europe. [40]

The contemporary opinion in diplomatic circles was [41] that

> * both the United States and Great Britain are fearful lest the Soviet Union enter into an independent peace. The United States and Britain are giving determined aid to the Soviet Union in order to prevent such a peace from materializing * . *

It was, indeed, not until January 1, 1942, that General Stalin adhered to the Atlantic Charter. [42] American publicists and American newspapers had been saying frequently that freedom of religion had been omitted from the Charter as a sop to Stalin and Mr. Roosevelt was very sensitive upon the point. Moreover Congressional hearings were about to commence on the second

Lend-Lease appropriation bill, and there was opposition to giving aid to Russia.[43] It was, additionally, necessary to persuade American public opinion of the expediency of forgiving Russia's promise to pay for such large quantities of war materials—one billion dollars' worth, to begin.[43] When, therefore, Mr. Roosevelt heard from the Polish Ambassador, Mr. Ciechanowski, that Catholic and Jewish chaplains were being assigned to the Polish Army forming in Russia, he sent Colonel Donovan to Mr. Ciechanowski on September 27, 1941, in order to get a fuller report. At his request a letter was written, and then a report to the State Department,[44] which Mr. Roosevelt used in an exaggerated form at his press conference of September 30. Knowing now, as people did not know then, of Mr. Roosevelt's recent unsuccessful attempt to remove His Holiness's objections to aiding Russia, we can conjecture that Mr. Roosevelt intended to create a favorable attitude towards aid to Russia in the minds of the Roman Catholic hierarchy.

On his return to England, Lord Beaverbrook made a radio speech, on October 12, in which he praised Russia. He said that England could best aid the Soviets by supplying war material, and he advocated setting a goal of thirty thousand tanks for Russia.[45] From Washington Mr. Roosevelt immediately echoed the British, and he announced on October 13 that large amounts of war material had already been shipped to the Reds, and that more was on the way.[46]

Meanwhile the German forces were approaching Moscow. An Anglo-American start was just being made in satisfying this first set of Russian demands when the Russian demand was renewed insistently that a second front be opened by British invasion of the Continent.[47] Needless to say, nothing was offered by the Russians in exchange for, or to counterbalance such demands. Contemporaneous accounts describe them as "tough * realistic * good traders,"[48] as "inflexible bargainers" and as "inquisitive, acquisitive and secretive":[49] these characterizations seem to be conservative. Five months later, in early February 1942, the Italians intercepted a telegram to Washington from the American military attaché at Moscow in which Russian threats appear. [50] It

> * complains about failure to deliver arms promised by the United States, and says that if the U.S.S.R. is not aided immediately and properly she will have to consider capitulating. *

Fulfilment of the Russian demands was given a first priority by Mr. Roosevelt over everything else. [51] Thus we are officially told that shipping for Russia was given "a first priority * * * at the expense of the Red Sea operations" [52] to aid the British forces in Egypt, which may have been a contributing cause of the reverses sustained there in the first part of 1942. Likewise it is officially stated that [53]

> * The problem of allocating resources among civilian, military and foreign uses became increasingly difficult with the competition most keen between military and Russian requirements. *

Materials, equipment, and tools were diverted to Russia in late 1941 "over opposition" and "strong protest" from the armed forces, [54] Mr. Roosevelt having packed the Supply Priorities and Allocations Board with Messrs. Wallace, Hopkins, and Henderson [55] in order to ensure this result. It seems indisputable that the shortage of fighter planes and anti-aircraft guns at Hawaii on December 7, 1941, was due to the extremely great diversions of lend-lease. [56]

Certainly the contrast is striking between the inflexibility shown towards Japan at this time and the complaisance shown towards Russia, with America asking for nothing in return.

We now return to the Japanese-American negotiations as they stood at the crossroads of better and worse.

Mr. Roosevelt and Mr. Hull adhered to their predetermined dilatory course. The note which Mr. Hull had prepared [57] and which he delivered [58] to Ambassador Nomura on October 2, 1941, was a masterpiece of negativism. Specific reference was made to the Japanese proposals of September 6, 1941, but the later Japanese proposals of September 25 were referred to, if at all, only under a generalized reference to "subsequent explanatory statements." It was said that these communications "narrow and restrict" the prior conversations and assurances.

No one who had read only the American note of October 2, 1941, would have been informed by it that much of the Japanese proposals of September 25 had been copied *verbatim* or taken in substance from Mr. Hull's own earlier proposals.

One of the defects of the American note of October 2 was that nearly all of it was vaguely negative. Mr. Hull did not point out the acceptability of much of the Japanese proposals of September 25. He did not ask for definite changes in specified unacceptable proposals in order to make them acceptable. Oddly, in the light of the history of the prior conversations, Mr. Hull contradictorily asserted:

> * It has not been the purpose of this Government to enter into a discussion of details *.

More oddly, the American note failed to touch upon the third item mentioned in Mr. Roosevelt's instructions of September 28: nowhere does the note ask the Japanese "if they cannot go back to their original attitude."

Most importantly, nowhere does Mr. Hull specify what the Administration wanted from Japan; what assurances would satisfy it. If it was Mr. Hull's purpose to leave the Japanese mystified and bewildered as to what it was requisite for them to offer in order to reach an agreement with the United States, then his note of October 2 was a success.

The projected Roosevelt-Konoye meeting was viewed in the note with doubt, and its holding was warily postponed into the sweet bye-and-bye, while the parties engaged in "discussion of the fundamental questions."

After Mr. Hull had read this statement he invited Admiral Nomura to comment. Admiral Nomura said that

> * he feared that his Government would be disappointed because of its very earnest desire to hold the meeting. * he wished to assure the Secretary that he was convinced that the Japanese Government was entirely sincere in this matter and had no ulterior purpose. * in view of the difficulties of the internal situation in Japan he did not think his Government could go further at this time. *

It was recognized in Washington that Mr. Hull was making a fateful decision. In a memorandum bearing the same date, October 2, 1941, which was distributed to President Roosevelt, Secretary Hull, Secretary Stimson, General Marshall, and others, the Acting Assistant Chief of Staff, Intelligence Division, expressed his erroneous views of our proper policy towards Japan as follows: [59]

> 10. This Division is of the opinion that neither a conference of leaders nor economic concessions at this point would be of any material advantage to the United States unless a definite commitment to withdraw from the Axis were obtained from Japan prior to the conference. *
>
> 11. Since it is highly improbable that this condition can be met by the Japanese Government at the present time our course lies straight before us. This Division still believes that forceful diplomacy vis-a-vis Japan, including the application of ever increasing military and economic pressure on our part, offers the best chance of gaining time, the best possibility of preventing the spread of hostilities in the Pacific area, and the best hope of the eventual disruption of the Tripartite Pact. The exercise of increasingly strong "power diplomacy" by the United States is still clearly indicated.

And on his copy of this memorandum Mr. Stimson wrote similar views: [60]

> Quite independently I have reached similar conclusions and hold them strongly. I believe however that during the next three months while we are rearming the Philippines great care must be exercised to avoid an explosion by the Japanese Army. Put concretely this means, that while I approve of stringing out negotiations during that period, they should not be allowed to ripen into a personal conference between the President and P.[rime] M.[inister Konoye]. I greatly fear that such a conference if actually held would produce concessions which would be highly dangerous to our vitally important relations with China.

The explosive danger of the diplomatic situation, of which some American military personalities appeared to be oblivious, was not only apparent to Ambassador Grew; it was also observed with alarm by other diplomatic experts in Japan. The British Ambassador to Japan, Sir Robert Craigie, was so troubled by the worsening situation that on October 3, 1941, he cabled Mr. Eden, the Secretary for Foreign Affairs, at London, and Lord Halifax, at Washington, saying [61] in substance,

> 2. Among the difficult points in the materialization of a Japanese-United States conference, is that with Japan speed is required. * By pursuing a policy of stalling, the United States is arguing about every word and every phrase on the grounds that it is an essential preliminary to any kind of an agreement. It seems apparent that the United States does not comprehend the fact that by the nature of the Japanese and also on account of the domestic conditions in Japan, no delays can be countenanced. It would be very regrettable indeed if the best opportunity for the settlement of the Far Eastern problems since I assumed my post here, were to be lost in such a manner.

3. Prince Konoye is sincerely desirous of avoiding the dangers which Japan may face through her connections in the Tripartite Pact and in the Axis for which the Prince, himself, feels responsibility. Opposition within the country to the Prince's reversal of policy is fairly strong. Therefore, unless the Japanese-U. S. conversations are held in the very near future, the opportunity will probably be lost. Moreover, if by some chance, meetings fail to materialize, or if they are unduly delayed, the Konoye cabinet will be placed in a precarious position.

From Washington, Admiral Nomura cabled to Foreign Minister Toyoda on October 3, 1941. Admiral Nomura was obviously reluctant to admit that his mission had been a failure, but even so, he could find but little about which to be cheerful. He said: [62]

> Although there is a feeling that the Japanese-U. S. talks have finally reached a deadlock, we do not believe that it should be considered as an absolutely hopeless situation. We are of the impression that the United States worded their memorandum in such a way as to permit a ray of hope to penetrate through.

The majority of the Pearl Harbor Committee has acknowledged the bewilderment of the Japanese Government by the negations and by the lack of affirmative suggestions in Mr. Hull's note of October 2, 1941: [63]

> During the next two weeks the Japanese Foreign Office made repeated efforts both in Washington and in Tokyo to have the United States Government state what further assurances it desired from the Japanese Government, emphasizing that the position of Premier Konoye was daily growing more difficult. *

It is needless to say that these "repeated efforts" were made in vain by the Japanese and resulted only in frustration.

The receipt of Mr. Hull's note of October 2 caused an avoidable political crisis to develop in Japan, the consequences of which were the downfall of the peace party of moderates, the rise to power of the military extremists, and ultimately the war which began at Pearl Harbor and lasted for the major part of four years. This was diplomatic maladroitness of a high degree.

On October 4, 1941, Prince Konoye had an audience with the Emperor, following which there was a joint conference attended by the chiefs of the Japanese high command. [64]

On the evening of October 5 Prince Konoye conferred with General Tojo, the War Minister (who was so soon to become the new Prime Minister), to whom he expressed his determination to "continue negotiations [with the United States] to the very end." [64]

In consequence Mr. Ushiba, Prince Konoye's Private Secretary, had breakfast at Tokyo on October 7 with Mr. Dooman, the Counselor of the American Embassy. Mr. Ushiba said that [65]

> * the Prime Minister's position had been made difficult by the failure of the preliminary conversations with the United States to make any progress. Prince Konoye was at a loss to know what further he could do, the opposition had now something concrete to use in their attacks on the Cabinet, and the future looked dark. *

> * pessimism in Japanese official quarters had been strengthened by failure on the part of the American Government to lay any of its cards on the table. * it had not precisely specified what it wanted the Japanese Government to undertake. Although several months had elapsed since the conversations began, the apparently great care being taken by the American Government not to give the Japanese any specifications was extremely discouraging. * an increasing number of persons in Japanese Government circles were of the opinion that Japan had fallen into a trap, the argument running somewhat as follows—the United States never had any intention of coming to any agreement with Japan *.

* * * * * *

* the actual memorandum [of October 2] was * "extremely disagreeable." * argumentative and preceptive * quite uncompromising, and it contained no suggestion or indication calculated to be helpful to the Japanese Government toward meeting the desires of the American Government. * Why was there not provided some indication of the kind of undertaking the Japanese Government was expected to give?

Later that same morning Ambassador Grew called on Foreign Minister Toyoda, at the latter's request. [66] Admiral Toyoda asked "whether unofficially and privately" Mr. Grew "felt able to offer an opinion on the position of the United States Government as outlined in the * memorandum of October 2." Mr. Grew felt compelled to respond with generalities.

That evening General Tojo called on Prince Konoye to express a stronger opposition to his peace policies. General Tojo declared that the Army would find it difficult to submit to the proposed withdrawal of its troops from China. [67]

Because of this opposition, Prince Konoye conferred the next day, October 8, with the Navy Minister and with Admiral Toyoda (also the Foreign Minister) concerning "methods of avoiding a crisis." [68] That afternoon Mr. Terasaki, the Chief of the American Bureau of the Japanese Foreign Office, called on Mr. Grew [69] in a further attempt to ascertain "the desires of the United States for action by Japan in order to reach a mutual agreement." Mr. Grew mentioned several generalities, and

> I then pointed out to Mr. Terasaki that I had no authority from my Government to interpret the memorandum of October 2 and as I had said to the Foreign Minister * in connection with his suggestion that the conversations be transferred from Washington to Tokyo, it was Mr. Hull's wish, in view of the active interest of

the President in these conversations, that they continue to be held in Washington *. I therefore suggested that * it might be well for Admiral Nomura to seek an interview with Mr. Hull and to put these questions to him.

Meanwhile various moves towards war were being made by Mr. Roosevelt at Washington. On October 7 he approved of the Moscow Protocol by which it was agreed to furnish war materials to Russia. [70] On October 8 Mr. Roosevelt secretly ordered units of the Atlantic fleet to engage in convoy duty in the Atlantic, and to attack and destroy any German or Italian vessels or planes. [71] As Admiral Stark wrote to Secretary Hull, under date of October 8, 1941, [72] Hitler

> * has every excuse in the world to declare war on us now, if he were of a mind to. *

This was the secret prelude to Mr. Roosevelt's public request to the Congress, on October 9, 1941, to modify the Neutrality Act so that American vessels might be armed and might carry contraband of war to any ports of any belligerent. [73]

On October 11, 1941, Mr. Roosevelt caused to be issued a secret order [74] providing that American, Canadian, and English warships might be brigaded together, American vessels being sometimes under English or Canadian command, and English or Canadian warships being sometimes "under the strategic direction of the United States."

Japan did not abate her efforts to find out specifically what Mr. Roosevelt wanted. On the morning of October 9, 1941, a further approach at Tokyo by Mr. Terasaki to Mr. Dooman [75] led to the American's saying cautiously that he did not see that he was in a position to add anything to what Mr. Grew had said the previous night. In the course of the conversation one interesting and important point developed, that the Japanese reference to "Southwestern" in the preamble and in Topic V of the September 25 proposals

> * was not [intended] to confine the application of the principle of equality of opportunity to the southwestern Pacific—that it was intended as an affirmation of a positive intention with regard to an area in part of which the Japanese Government now exercise *de facto* control * it was not intended by implication to exclude the application of the principle from other areas under which the Japanese exercised control. *

In Washington, Admiral Nomura called on Mr. Hull on the morning of October 9 in order to attempt to obtain an expression of the latter's views,[76] but Mr. Hull managed to avoid saying anything definite, and suggested that his subordinates, Messrs. Hamilton and Ballantine, might see the Ambassador.[77] Admiral Nomura asked if he might speak frankly, and being so permitted said that

> * Japan was now at the crossroads and the Japanese Government was in a very difficult position. * 99 per cent of the Japanese people did not want trouble with the United States but that they were a disciplined people and would fight if commanded to do so. * there were agitators in Japan who were trying to cause trouble * probably * with funds from other countries. * war * whatever might be the final outcome, would be a very serious undertaking *. therefore * everything possible should be done by both sides to avert the possibility of a conflict between the two countries. *

All that Japan wanted, it must be remembered—all that Mr. Hull was being asked to do—was to state specifically what America's terms were. By the frank and moving appeal of Admiral Nomura Mr. Hull apparently remained unmoved: his answer was to thank

> * the Ambassador for having expressed his views freely.

Mr. Hull's subordinates called on Admiral Nomura on the afternoon of October 9, 1941.[78] For "almost two hours" the Japanese, according to the official American version, "numerous times" attempted to find out specifically and concretely

> * wherein the American Government found objection to the Japanese proposals [of September 25] in order that the Japanese Government could consider the question of meeting, if possible, the desires of the American Government.

Mr. Hull's subordinates successfully frustrated these Japanese attempts to reach an understanding with the United States by talking indefinitely about "broad-gauge principles," reporting that

> * We said that we had sought to avoid being placed in a position of possible criticism for having tried to tell the Japanese Government what it must do or must not do.

At the conclusion of this fruitless conference the American subordinates

> * expressed our readiness to meet the Ambassador and his associates at any time and to be helpful in any way that we could.

It was also on October 9, although the dispatch has been omitted from the published volume, that Ambassador Grew sent home another warning. He reported that the frozen credits policy of the United States was driving Japan into national bankruptcy, and that she would be forced to act.[79]

In Tokyo, Foreign Minister Toyoda simply could not bring himself to believe in the accuracy of the apparently vague reports which he had received from Admiral Nomura of these conferences.

On October 10, 1941, he telegraphed Admiral Nomura a scolding and querulous demand for "the complete minutes of what" was said at such conferences, both current and future.[80] Then, in despair, that same afternoon he requested Mr. Grew to call on him, and he asked Mr. Grew to request a plain reply from the American Government to this simple question: [81]

> * Will the American Government now set forth to the Japanese Government for its consideration the undertakings to be assumed by the Japanese Government which would be satisfactory to the Amercan Government?

So far as the official American record shows, this reasonable question was never answered.

Admiral Toyoda also assured Ambassador Grew [82]

> * that the Japanese Government would find it possible to make commitments of a far-reaching character at such a meeting but that under present conditions the full extent of the undertakings which the Japanese Government was willing to assume could not be set forth prior to the meeting. He reiterated his concern lest the Government be unable to control extremist groups in Japan if matters remain in their present undetermined conditions.

At Tokyo on October 12, 1941, there was a meeting, called by Prince Konoye and attended by the Ministers of War, Navy, and Foreign Affairs, together with the President of the Planning Board, at which there was a four-hour discussion of what to do: whether to attempt to bring the apparently hopeless diplomatic "negotiations to fruition, no matter what happens," as the Minister of the Navy urged, which was also Prince Konoye's wish, or else to abandon all hope of a peaceful solution through diplomacy and determine on war. [83] Even the truculent General Tojo, the Minister of War, thought it a mistake to be hasty in deciding on war. He wished to know if anyone was in a position to give an informed estimate as to the diplomatic problem, which, as he stated it, was

> * whether or not there is any possibility of bringing the negotiations to fruition? *

No one was able to say, and the meeting adjourned without having reached any conclusion. Next day, on October 13, Prince Konoye seems to have taken his problem to the Mikado and to the leading elder statesman, Marquis Kido.[84] Inferentially, he was told to work on in the hope of maintaining peace.

At Washington the Minister-Counselor of the Japanese Embassy, Mr. Wakasugi, who had just returned to Washington from a short stay in Japan, called on Mr. Welles, the Under Secretary of State, on the afternoon of October 13. Mr. Wakasugi emphasized [85]

> * that the Imperial family, as well as the present Cabinet, was earnestly desirous of maintaining peace with the United States and of adjusting rapidly the problems which had arisen between Japan and [America].

But, he said,

> * the present Japanese Government * could not indefinitely continue the conversations with the United States. It would have to show some results. * if the present Japanese Government fell * there was no telling what the result might be. * in all probability it would be replaced by a cabinet composed of military representatives *.

And so Mr. Wakasugi returned to the great unanswered questions:

> * what in reality were the desires of the United States and what in reality was the agreement which the United States desired to achieve. * could [Mr. Welles] tell him what the reasons for the delay might be or what the points of clarification were which this Government still desired to obtain from his Government.

Mr. Welles replied in generalities, referred Mr. Wakasugi to the prior statements and correspondence, and said that there was nothing more which he could add.

Nevertheless Mr. Wakasugi persisted. Referring to the apparent limitation of Topic V of the Japanese proposals of September 25, 1941, to the Southwest Pacific, he said that Japan would be quite willing to agree to the American proposals on this topic. But he went further and said that

* the Japanese Government was prepared to make a full commitment to undertake no aggressive activities to the north, south or anywhere else in the Pacific region.

Finally he "said that the Japanese Government was willing to evacuate all of its troops from China."

Mr. Welles was so startled by this very great concession that he noted:

* (Thinking I had misunderstood him I asked him to repeat this statement which he did, in the same terms, twice.)

Finally Mr. Wakasugi said that the American administration

* should be in no doubt that if an agreement could be reached before it was too late the control of the Army and Navy under present conditions was such as to make it sure that the [Japanese] Government would be able to carry out and implement the terms of such agreement.

While the substance of this conversation was ultimately telegraphed to Ambassador Grew in Japan,[86] the record does not show that any eagerness or willingness was expressed at Washington to accept these far-reaching Japanese offers, and in consequence a political crisis now overtook the Japanese peace cabinet.

On October 14, 1941, Prince Konoye met with General Tojo before the Cabinet meeting.[87] There was a discussion about withdrawing the Japanese troops from China, which Prince Konoye advocated, in order to

* save ourselves from the crisis of a Japanese-American war. * the future of which I can not at all foresee.

In the light of American conduct during the negotiations General Tojo opposed the policy of making any further concessions, because, he said,

> If at this time we yield to the United States, she will take steps that are more and more high-handed, and will probably find no place to stop. *

Thus no agreement was reached, and at the ensuing Cabinet meeting General Tojo urged strongly that the negotiations should no longer be continued, but no decision was made by the Cabinet.

Following out his ideas, General Tojo is reported to have sent a message [88] to Prime Minister Konoye that same evening, in which he urged Prince Konoye and the Cabinet to resign, and

> * declare insolvent everything that has happened up to now, and reconsider our plans once more. *

Accordingly on October 15, 1941, Prime Minister Konoye again conferred with the Emperor, and there was a discussion concerning who should be the next Prime Minister. [89] On October 16, 1941, the entire Cabinet resigned.

It was probably on October 15 that the Emperor summoned a conference of leading Japanese personalities, including those of the armed forces, and bluntly asked "if they were prepared to pursue a policy which would guarantee that there would be no war with the United States." [90] An ominous silence was the only response, whereupon the Emperor ordered the armed forces to obey his wishes.

On the afternoon of October 16, 1941, Admiral Nomura sought an interview at Washington with Lord Halifax in the hope of somehow, even if indirectly, reaching an agreement with the United States. [91] Admiral Nomura began the talk by a reference "to the desirability of maintaining peace in the Pacific." He stated that in his talks with Mr. Hull "three principal points of difficulty had emerged." According to Lord Halifax Admiral Nomura said,

The first point concerned the Tri-Partite Pact. The Ambassador did not develop this in detail beyond saying that the United States Government wished for some more precise definition of the Japanese attitude than they had hitherto felt able to give, but he thought that the United States Government understood the Japanese position pretty well.

The second point concerned non-discrimination and equality of treatment in economic matters. These he thought could be adjusted.

The third point, which was the only one on which he anticipated serious difficulty, concerned the admission of a right for Japan, secured by agreement with China, to station troops for an agreed period, in North China and Inner Mongolia to control the communist armies there.

So far no solution had emerged in his conversations with Mr. Hull on this third point.

The resignation of the Japanese Cabinet was due to internal differences between on the one hand the Prime Minister and those who wished to reach agreement with the United States by not insisting on the third point mentioned above, and on the other hand those who thought that not to insist on this point would involve too great a loss of face.

But the Ambassador did not anticipate any sudden change of policy. The Emperor was in favour of peace, and even if a general were made Prime Minister, it was unlikely that the Emperor's wishes would be disregarded.

* * * * * *

Everybody in the Japanese Cabinet wanted understanding with the United States, and the only difference was as to the price that should be paid for it.

Reverting to the Tri-Partite Pact, the Ambassador said that * the Japanese Government * had regarded adherence to it as the only policy * possible for Japan to pursue, having regard to the evidence of * Anglo-Saxon co-operation against Japan.

After some disclaimers of this fact by Lord Halifax, who also expressed some advice to Japan on various topics, Admiral Nomura came to what may have been the essential purpose of his call, and proposed the type of political armistice which in diplomatic language is called a *modus vivendi:*

> Returning to his main point, he asked me whether I thought that it would be possible to find any modus vivendi in the Pacific that might be of value in giving time for the atmosphere to calm, and make easier the solution of the third point to which he had referred * which he thought it would be extremely difficult for any new Government to solve quickly.

> He knew how close the relations of the British Government and the United States Government were, and hoped that I [Lord Halifax] would take an opportunity of speaking with Mr. Hull about it. This I said I would certainly do.

Admiral Nomura then issued a prophetic warning to those who were so ill-advisedly belittling the naval might of Japan: he remarked that

> * some Americans spoke of finishing off the Japanese Navy in a few days. But the Japanese Navy was well trained, and, as I knew never surrendered, and he thought it could be relied upon to give a good account of itself.

Lord Halifax returned a diplomatic answer to this assertion, and asked Admiral Nomura

* whether he had any opinion as to what might be General Chiang Kai Shek's view of his third point as to temporary occupation by Japanese troops of an area in North China by agreement with the Chinese Government.

He said he had not, but he had an impression that though the Chinese army were not now very keen on fighting, Chinese diplomacy was extremely shrewd, and vastly better than that of Japan.

The whole conversation was very friendly, and left on my mind the clear impression that the Japanese Government or certainly that part of it for which Admiral Nomura can be held to speak, felt their position to be one of extreme difficulty.

As events were so swiftly to prove, Chinese diplomacy was not only vastly better than that of Japan; it was better than that of the United States.

Lord Halifax reported this conversation to Mr Hull the next day, on October 17, 1941, [92] and subsequently, as will appear, Admiral Nomura's constructive proposal of a *modus vivendi* would have borne peaceful fruit, had it not been for Chinese diplomacy.

The serious view taken in England of the diplomatic situation is illuminated by Foreign Office communications sent through Ambassador Winant to Washington, commencing on October 18, 1941, in which plans were recommended for exchanging urgent telegraph messages between the British, the Americans, and the Dutch [93] in the event of war with Japan.

That Mr. Roosevelt and his cabinet were aware of the explosive possibilities of the situation which they had helped to bring about is proven by a dispatch which Admiral Ingersoll drafted and Admiral Stark sent to Admiral Kimmel, dated October 16, 1941: [94]

> The resignation of the Japanese Cabinet has created a grave situation. If a new Cabinet is formed it will probably be strongly nationalistic and anti-American. If the Konoye Cabinet remains

the effect will be that it will operate under a new mandate which will not include rapproachment [*sic*] with the U. S. In either case hostilities between Japan and Russia are a strong possibility. Since the U. S. and Britain are held responsible by Japan for her present desperate situation there is also a possibility that Japan may attack these two powers. In view of these possibilities you will take due precautions including * preparatory deployments * . *

Fifty-one days were to separate the new Japanese Prime Minister from war. Admiral Stark's "possibility" was really a probability which, with the passage of time, became a certainty. Why, one wonders, did Mr. Roosevelt risk war with Japan? Was it a "bluff"? [95] Was he maladroit? Was he seeking for some "incident" to bring America into the war?

Simultaneously German pressure on Japan was increasing. Early in October 1941, according to an intercepted message from Japan, [96] the Germans had

> * demanded that the Japanese Government submit to the American Government a message to the effect that the Japanese Government observes that if the Roosevelt Administration continues to attack the Axis Powers increasingly, a belligerent situation would inevitably arise between Germany and Italy on the one hand and the United States on the other, and this * might lead Japan to join immediately the war in opposition to the United States. We have not, as yet, submitted this message * in view of the Japanese-American negotiations *. The German authorities have been repeatedly making the same request and there are reasons which do not permit this matter to be postponed any longer. While Japan on the one hand finds it necessary to do something in the way of carrying out the duties placed upon her by the Three Power Alliance she had concluded with Germany, on the other hand, she is desirous of making a success of the Japanese-American negotiations. *

On October 15, Mr. Amau, the Japanese Vice Minister for Foreign Affairs, told Ambassador Grew that [97]

> * the German Government is insistently pressing for the issuance of a statement by the Japanese Government in confirmation of the interpretation given to the Tripartite Pact by Mr. Matsuoka, to the effect that Japan will declare war on the United States in the event of war occurring between Germany and the United States. As a reply * the Japanese Government is considering a formula of a noncommittal nature *.

The German Ambassador continued to press Admiral Toyoda's successor for action. [98]

On October 17, 1941, General Tojo became the new Prime Minister: he continued as Minister of War. In deference to the Emperor's command the new Cabinet let it be known that the conversations would continue. [99] Admiral Nomura, who wished to resign as Ambassador [100] because he doubted that he would "be able to accomplish much in the future," was asked to stay on at his post. [101] His instructions, however, contained a new note of increased urgency, as appears from an intercept of October 21, 1941; [102]

> The new cabinet differs in no way from the former one in its sincere desire to adjust Japanese-United States relations on a fair basis. Our country has said practically all she can say in the way of expressing of opinions and setting forth our stands. We feel that we have now reached a point where no further positive action can be taken by us except to urge the United States to reconsider her views.
>
> We urge, therefore, that, choosing an opportune moment, either you or Wakasugi let it be known to the United States by indirection that our country is not in a position to spend much more time discussing this matter. Please continue the talks, emphasizing our desire for a formal United States counter proposal to our proposal of 25 September.

The military estimate of the current Japanese-American diplomatic situation as sent by the Adjutant General of the American War Department to General Short at Hawaii on October 20, 1941, was this: [103]

> *Tension between [the] United States and Japan remains strained but no repeat no abrupt change in Japanese foreign policy appears imminent.

In effect this was also Mr. Churchill's view—the stronger our actions the better the chances for peace. [104] Mr. Roosevelt and his cabinet seem to have entertained a different view. It was on October 24, 1941, that the Secretary of the Navy, Mr. Knox, said publicly that war between Japan and the United States was inevitable, and that, consequently, the United States Navy was on a twenty-four-hour basis. [105] Senator Pepper likewise made an inflammatory statement in the Senate on October 28, 1941, [106] asserting that if another American expeditionary force was necessary to defeat Hitler, he would vote for it. Former Ambassador Bullitt asked for a declaration of war at once against Germany: war, he asserted, was inevitable. [107]

It was on the afternoon of October 24, 1941, that Mr. Wakasugi called on Mr. Welles at Washington. [108] In accordance with the instructions from Tokyo to Admiral Nomura of October 21, Mr. Wakasugi stated, first, that the new Cabinet desired to continue the conversations "without delay" in the hope of reaching a satisfactory agreement; second, the new Japanese cabinet was constrained by tense domestic public opinion to such an extent that the conversations should be pressed to a satisfactory conclusion "speedily"; and, third, did the United States have any counterproposals to make to the Japanese proposals? Mr. Welles thereupon scolded Mr. Wakasugi because of recent inflammatory statements publicly made in Japan. Mr. Wakasugi promptly countered with a *tu quoque*—he referred to Secretary Knox's outburst that very day. Mr. Welles abandoned that topic of recrimination: he then claimed that the American point of view had been set forth previously "with complete clarity," and by clear implication he declined to make any counterproposals. He would, however, be willing to "consider any * changes in phraseology" of the Japanese proposals which Mr. Wakasugi might be willing to suggest. Thus the interview terminated in futility.

From Japan Mr. Grew telegraphed Washington on October 25, 1941, [109] mentioning the prominence given in the Japanese press to Mr. Knox's belligerent remarks. Even now, Ambassador Grew wrote, it was not yet too late, because it was still

> *the fact that the present Japanese leaders are willing to give up their expansionist plans through armed forces if a workable understanding can be reached with the United States.

Mr. Grew referred again to some of his observations in his important telegram of September 29, 1941, emphasizing by such reference that the United States could still halt the Japanese expansion without war provided that during the preliminary conversations America did not narrowly insist upon full agreement about details. The alternative was war. The Emperor, Mr. Grew noted, had intervened with "the announced aim of reaching an agreement with the United States"; if the Emperor had not done so, war would probably have developed.

On October 27, 1941, Mr. Roosevelt delivered a Navy Day speech at the Mayflower Hotel in Washington. [110] Eyen the friendly Mr. Lindley was compelled to characterize it as "of the scare-mongering election-eve type," but it indicated, he thought, "that the moment for grave decision is near." [111] One of the excuses for the speech was the "incident" in which a new destroyer, the U.S.S. *Kearny*, had been torpedoed on October 17,

1941. This, Mr. Roosevelt asserted, was an *"attack"*—"America has been attacked"—and in consequence he seized the opportunity to arouse the nation with the declaration that

> * the shooting has started. And history has recorded who fired the first shot.

Then, in a passage the importance of which seems to have been overlooked at that time, when the American people were uninformed of the extent of Mr. Roosevelt's involvement in secret power politics, he guardedly told the Republic that it was already bound by secret agreements, saying significantly,

> Very simply and very bluntly—we are *pledged* to pull our own oar in the destruction of Hitlerism. (Emphasis supplied.)

A portion of the speech was devoted to propaganda. Having attempted, about four weeks earlier, to rehabilitate General Stalin and to portray him, if not as a lover of God, at least as a tolerator of God, Mr. Roosevelt now moved in the opposite direction against Hitler. Relying on a document of dubious authority,[112] Mr. Roosevelt claimed that a plan to abolish all existing religions had been "made in Germany by Hitler's government," which plan they "are ready to impose on a dominated world—if Hitler wins." Also, said Mr. Roosevelt, Hitler's government planned to conquer Latin America and to redistrict it into five vassal states, as proved by a questionable German map which he claimed he had.

In America this Navy Day speech provoked much discussion of its various points, but principally on the question of the truth of Mr. Roosevelt's assertion that America had been "attacked." The memory of political observers went back to the Democratic platform's anti-war plank of 1940, with its escape clause, "except in case of attack." In a thoughtful article Mr. Arthur Krock reviewed this topic and expressed the opinion that Mr. Roosevelt would now claim that he was released from his profuse campaign pledges, and that the promise of the anti-war plank had been automatically cancelled. [113]

There was also contemporary skepticism about the truth of Mr. Roosevelt's assertion that the *Kearny* had suffered an unprovoked attack. It was stated by a careful and reputable magazine that [114]

> Despite official silence on the subject (even after the Greer and Kearny incidents), there is now no doubt the U. S. Navy has had its destroyers aggressively pursuing and depth-bombing German U-boats * . * a number of U. S. destroyer commanders have already reported that they believed they had scored hits.

Admiral Stark's contemporary secret letter of October 17 to Admiral Kimmel states by implication that the *Kearny* began the attack. [115]

The alleged German map was never revealed. At his next press conference Mr. Roosevelt was asked about it. [116] He said that it was somewhere among the papers on his desk, but he declined to show it to any of the reporters on the ground that to do so would reveal to Germany the source of his information. And so the map, if any there was, was never seen by any enquiring or critical eye.

The Navy Day speech produced perhaps a greater effect in Germany than anywhere else. Count Ciano, who happened to be visiting at the German General Headquarters, noted in his diary that the cautious German policy continued: [117]

> * The Germans have firmly decided to do nothing which will accelerate or cause America's entry into the war. *

It has been stated that in early September 1941 Mr. Roosevelt had agreed to transport two British divisions to the Middle East in American Navy transports. To replace their strength in the islands Mr. Churchill, whose eye was ever glancing towards Ireland, asked Mr. Roosevelt on October 20, 1941, to send to Northern Ireland a United States Army Corps, an armored division, and all the air force possible. [118] Almost at the same moment the United States was planning to intervene in French North Africa, in Morocco, with about 150,000 troops [119] but apparently no action could be taken on either project at that time because of the absence of so many of the American Navy transports on the Middle East voyages for Great Britain.

In late October the Japanese Government began to send additional troops to French Indo-China and to nearby regions. Generalissimo Chiang Kai-shek inferred from these movements that an attack on Kunming and the Burma Road was imminent. As was to happen again in about another four weeks a great Chinese clamor arose. Messages were sent by the Generalissimo; by Mr. Gauss, the American Ambassador in Chungking; by General Magruder, the head of the recently arrived American military mission to China; by the American naval attaché, and on October 30, 1941, by Mr. T. V. Soong in Washington, to the champion of China, Secretary Morgenthau, who sent them to Mr. Roosevelt, who relayed them to Mr. Hull. [120] Military support from outside sources, asserted the Generalissimo, was the sole Chinese hope for defeat of this new Japanese threat. He urged that Mr. Roosevelt intercede with London to make available the Singapore air forces to support his defense. Moreover Mr. Roosevelt should be urged to bring diplomatic pressure on Japan and to appeal as well to Britain jointly to warn Japan that an attack upon Kunming would be considered inimical to American interests. American air forces from the Philippines were also appealed for, all "in order [to] save democratic position in Far East," failing which he predicted that Chinese resistance would end.

In Tokyo on October 30, 1941, the new Foreign Minister, Mr. Shigenori Togo, received the diplomatic corps. Speaking to Ambassador Grew, [121] Mr. Togo noted the progressive worsening of

Japanese-American relations to a point which if not remedied, "was fraught with the gravest dangers." And he asked that the Japanese-American conversations be continued "and without delay be successfully brought to a conclusion."

On October 31, 1941, an older destroyer, the *Reuben James*, was torpedoed about 700 miles to the east of Newfoundland, [122] and ninety-five lives were lost. Some of her seamen were convinced she had already sunk a U-boat or two, [123] prior to her own sinking. In connection with this event Admiral Stark wrote Admiral Hart, [124] "whether the country knows it or not, *we are at war*." And to Admiral Kimmel he wrote, [125]

> Things seem to be moving steadily towards a crisis in the Pacific. Just when it will break, no one can tell. * A month may see, literally, most anything. Two irreconcilable policies can not go on forever—particularly if one party can not live with the set up. *
>
> * * * * * *
>
> Believe it or not, the *Reuben James* set recruiting back about 15%. *

Also on October 31 the oil agreement between Japan and the Netherlands East Indies expired: the latter government had promised to deliver to Japan about 11,400,000 barrels of oil, but actually had delivered only half of that amount. [126] The American embargo had shut Japan off from about twenty-three million barrels, and Japan, with an annual consumption of thirty to thirty-five million barrels, now had no certain source of supply except her own production of seven million barrels. There was but little oil for the Japanese fishing boats, and already fish was unobtainable in some sections of Tokyo. By the time the war broke out the Japanese Navy had consumed about 22% of its oil reserves. [127]

October 1941 had been a fateful month. When it began, it was still possible to avoid war in the Pacific: when October ended, war in the Pacific, if not yet absolutely certain, appeared probable. In the Atlantic an undeclared naval war had become a reality and was in full swing.

But this was not enough. Under the American Constitution the war powers could not be exercised until there was a formal and declared war, and of that there was no immediate prospect.

According to Mr. Hopkins, [128]

> Both Stimson and Marshall feel that we can't win without getting into the war but they have no idea how that is going to be accomplished.

Mr. Roosevelt likewise had no idea how to accomplish it. As of the end of October, 1941, [129]

> * He had said everything "short of war" that could be said. He had no more tricks left. The hat from which he had pulled so many rabbits was empty. *

The only thing that he could think of to do was to continue to stall. [130]

 WAR, WAR IS STILL THE CRY

THE BRITISH ADMIRALTY on October 31, 1941, created a new command in the Far East, replacing the Commander in Chief, China, by a new Commander in Chief, Eastern Fleet. Among his secret duties, jurisdiction and instructions were the following:

B. * the preparation of plans and war orders for whole eastern theatre in collaboration with * U. S. and Dutch authorities.

* * * * * *

D. The degree of strategic control exercised by [him] over naval forces of U. S. A. should latter be a belligerent will be governed by such agreement as may be in force at the time between U. S. and Great Britain.

* * * * * *

H. The eastern theatre comprises:—

1. While U. S. are non-belligerent, the existing East Indies, China, Australia and New Zealand naval stations.
2. If U. S. are belligerent, the existing East Indies, China, Austalian, New Zealand naval stations bounded north and south by the following lines:—the parallel 030° N. from the coast of China to meridian of 140° E.; down latter to equator; along equator to 180° meridian, and down latter. The Pacific Ocean to east of this line will be an area of U. S. strategic responsibility.

This secret dispatch was forwarded from Washington to three of the highest American naval officers in the Pacific on November 1, 1941, [1] for their official guidance and to indicate to them the areas in which they would have to assume strategic responsibility.

In the Indian Ocean, England was also forming a new squadron, as our Navy officials had been informed. Mr. Churchill cabled Mr. Roosevelt of this, and that the *Prince of Wales* was being sent out to join it, asserting with ill-starred boastfulness: [2]

* This ought to serve as a deterrent on Japan. There is nothing like having something that can catch and kill anything. * The firmer your attitude and ours, the less chance of their [Japan's] taking the plunge.

On November 1, 1941, Mr. Hull called a conference at the State Department for the purpose of discussing what action should be taken in answer to Generalissimo Chiang Kai-shek's strident messages. The chief of the Army's War Plans Division was present, and also the Navy's liaison Admiral for the State Department. Mr. Hull, glancing towards war, observed that there was no use in issuing "any additional warnings to Japan if we can't back them up," and he enquired if the military authorities were prepared to do so. [3] Apparently no conclusion was reached at this meeting, or at a similar meeting held at the State Department on the following day, Sunday, November 2.

At Tokyo, on November 2, 1941, Prime Minister Togo saw the Emperor, and advised him of the decision as to how far the Cabinet was prepared to go in implementing the Emperor's desires for better relations with the United States. [4] For some days previously the Japanese Prime Minister, who was also War Minister and Home Minister, had been in conference, day and night, with the Minister of the Navy and the Foreign Minister.

Something of the highest importance was brewing in Japan, and Ambassador Grew seems to have had accurate information about it. On November 3, 1941, he again telegraphed a warning to Mr. Hull. [5] After referring to his prior advices, to which he adhered, Mr. Grew cautioned against accepting

> * the view that continuation of trade embargoes and imposition of a blockade (proposed by some) can best avert war in the Far East.

If the Japanese efforts to conciliate the United States should fail, it was "not * possible but * probable" that Japan would make

> * an all-out, do-or-die attempt, actually risking national hara-kiri, to make Japan impervious to economic embargoes abroad rather than to yield to foreign pressure. *

> * the view that war probably would be averted, * by progressively imposing drastic economic measures is an uncertain and dangerous hypothesis *. War would not be averted by such a course * . *

> * The Ambassador's purpose is only to ensure against the United States becoming involved in the war with Japan because of any possible misconception of Japan's capacity to rush headlong into a suicidal struggle with the United States. * it would be shortsighted for American policy to be based upon the belief that Japanese preparations are no more than saber rattling * . *

And with extraordinary perception Mr. Grew concluded his message with this prophetic sentence:

> * Action by Japan which might render unavoidable an armed conflict with the United States may come with dangerous and dramatic suddenness.

Knowing its unreadiness, the Army shared Mr. Grew's prudent caution. On November 3, 1941, at Washington, General Marshall, the Chief of Staff, received a report from General L. T. Gerow, the chief of the War Plans Division. [6] The report mentioned the skepticism of the Military Intelligence Division about the panicky Chinese claim that Japan was about to attack Kunming. It was stated that sending any considerable force of airplanes out of the Philippines would seriously risk the capture of Luzon. The strong opinions of the War Plans Division were stated to be:

> The policies derived in the American-British Staff conversations remain sound, viz:
>
> 1. The primary objective is the defeat of Germany.
> 2. The principal objective in the Far East is to keep Japan out of the war.

* * * * * *

> Strong diplomatic and economic pressure may be exerted from the military viewpoint at the earliest about the middle of December, 1941, when the Philippine Air Force will have become a positive threat to Japanese operations. It would be advantageous, if practicable, to delay severe diplomatic and economic pressure until February or March, 1942, when the Philippine Air Force will have reached its projected strength, and a safe air route, through Samoa, will be in operation.

General Marshall then attended the weekly meeting of the Army-Navy Joint Board, which had been scheduled for November 5, but which, because of the apparent Chinese emergency, had been moved forward to November 3, 1941. The principal topic discussed was aid to Generalissimo Chiang Kai-shek. At this meeting there was read a memorandum by Mr. Hull's political adviser, Dr. Stanley K. Hornbeck, which advocated a firm representation to Japan, even if war should result.[7]

In tactful language the Army and the Navy expressed their horror at this ill-considered and bellicose proposal.[8] General Marshall by implication criticized the blundering American conduct of the entire Japanese negotiations, which had secretly led America almost to the brink of war, saying that

> * Until powerful United States Forces had been built up in the Far East, it would take some very clever diplomacy to save the situation. It appeared that the basis of U. S. policy should be to make certain minor concessions which the Japanese could use in saving face. These concessions might be a relaxation on oil restrictions or on similar trade restrictions.

It seems clear that General Marshall did not agree with the illogical idea expressed in the subsequent official apology:[9]

> * There would be no method by which the American Government could remove economic pressure upon Japan merely step by step as and when Japan took successive steps away from courses of aggression and towards policies of peace.

The reader will of course recollect the fact that the embargoes and other measures which Mr. Roosevelt had put into effect against Japan had come into effect piecemeal and step by step, over several years.

In order to avoid a premature war with Japan, the Army and the Navy therefore concluded at this November 3 Joint Board meeting that they must oppose the diplomatic policies contemplated. They decided that the [10]

> War Plans Division of the War and Navy Departments would prepare a memorandum for the President, as a reply to the State Department's proposed policy in the Far Eastern situation. The memorandum would take the following lines:
>
> Oppose the issuance of an ultimatum to Japan.
>
> Oppose U. S. military action against Japan should she move into Yunnan.
>
> Oppose the movement and employment of U. S. military forces in support of Chiang Kai-shek.
>
> Advocate State Department action to put off hostilities with Japan as long as possible.
>
> Suggest agreements with Japan to tide the situation over for the next several months.
>
> Point out the effect and cost a U. S.-Japanese war in the Far East would have on defense aid to Great Britain and other nations being aided by the U. S.
>
> Emphasize the existing limitations on shipping and the inability of the U. S. to engage in a Far Eastern offensive operation without the transfer of the major portion of shipping facilities from the Atlantic to the Pacific.

On the evening of November 3, 1941, there was received at Washington a telegram [11] from Ambassador Gauss at Chungking, stating that while land invasion was not certain, it was believed to be certain that large Japanese air forces would attack the Burma Road and the "volunteer" air forces. Therefore if Anglo-American air units were sent into Yunnan, they should be in force sufficient to defend themselves against heavy Japanese attack. "Half or token measures would prove disastrous," advised Mr. Gauss.

On the morning of November 4 the Chinese drums were beaten even more loudly. The Generalissimo had sent a personal message to Mr. Roosevelt, [12] which commenced by quoting a strident message which he had sent to Mr. Churchill. In the long telegram to Mr. Churchill, received in England on November 2, [13] the Generalissimo asked for help from the "British air force in Malaya with American cooperation" to prevent the Japanese capture of Kunming. If that city fell,

> * the morale of the Chinese armies and people will be shaken to its foundation. * a real collapse of resistance would be possible.

Addressing himself to Mr. Roosevelt, [12] the Generalissimo urged

> * my conviction that British determination in dealing with Japan waits at present upon the lead and stimulating influence of America; if the United States would draw on its arm in the Philippines to provide either an active unit or a reserve force in the combined operation. * You are, Mr. President, recognized as the leader in the front of democratic nations fighting aggression. *

That same day Mr. Hull held separate conferences with Mr. Knox, and with General Marshall and Admiral Ingersoll. [14] The views of General Marshall and of Admiral Ingersoll were "that United States armed forces should not be sent to China for use against Japan," and Mr. Hull was "in thorough accord with [these] views." [15] Inferentially Mr. Knox's views were not so cautious.

On November 4, 1941, the Japanese Foreign Minister sent to Ambassador Nomura a long telegram, which, as usual, was intercepted, and which emphasized the highly critical state of Japanese-American relations. It read: [16]

1. Well, relations between Japan and the United States have reached the edge, and our people are losing confidence in the possibility of ever adjusting them. In order to lucubrate on a fundamental national policy, the Cabinet has been meeting with the Imperial Headquarters for some days in succession. Conference has followed conference, and now we are at length able to bring forth a counter-proposal for the resumption of Japanese-American negotiations based upon the unanimous opinion of the Government and the military high command. This and other basic policies of our Empire await the sanction of the conference to be held on the morning of the 5th [November].

2. Conditions both within and without our Empire are so tense that no longer is procrastination possible, yet in our sincerity to maintain pacific relationships between the Empire of Japan and the United States of America, we have decided, as a result of these deliberations, to gamble once more on the continuation of the parleys, but this is our last effort. Both in name and spirit this counter-propsal is, indeed, the last. I want you to know that. If through it we do not reach a quick accord, I am sorry to say the talks will certainly be ruptured. Then, indeed, will relations between our nations be on the brink of chaos. I mean that the success or failure of the pending discussions will have an immense effect on the destiny of the Empire of Japan. In fact, we gambled the fate of our land on the throw of this die.

When the Japanese-American meetings began, who would have ever dreamt that they would drag out so long? Hoping that we could fast come to some understanding, we have already gone far out of our way and yielded and yielded. The United States does not appreciate this, but through thick and thin sticks to the selfsame propositions she made to start with. Those of our people and of our officials who suspect the sincerity of the Americans are far from few. Bearing all kinds of humiliating things, our Government has repeatedly stated its sincerity and gone far, yes, too far, in giving in to them. There is just one reason why we do this—to maintain peace in the Pacific. There seem to be some Americans who think we would make a one-sided deal, but our temperance, I can tell you, has not come from weakness, and naturally there is an end to our long-suffering. Nay, when it comes to a question of our existence and our honor, when the time comes, we will defend them without recking the cost. *

The balance of the message consisted principally of instructions to Admiral Nomura as to how to conduct himself during the conversations.

In addition, and conditioned upon their approval by the Imperial Conference the following day, two Japanese proposals were cabled, with explanations. [17]

"Proposal A" was described as

> * our revised ultimatum made as a result of our attempt to meet, insofar as possible, the wishes of the Americans, clarified as a result of negotiations based on our proposals of September 25. *

From the Japanese point of view the proposals were several times described as "toned down." There was yielding on the question of nondiscrimination in trade, on the question of the Japanese understanding and application of the Tripartite Alliance, and on the evacuation of troops from French Indo-China. The army influence in the new Japanese Cabinet was reflected in the question of evacuating Japanese troops from China; here the proposal was more a matter of form than of substance. Mr. Togo advised Admiral Nomura

> * that in all probability the question of evacuation will be the hardest. * In any case, our internal situation also makes it impossible for us to make further compromise in this connection. *

"Proposal B" was to come into effect,

* If there appears to be a remarkable difference between the Japanese and American views, since the situation does not permit of delays *.

This second formula was to be presented, in such an emergency, "with the idea of making a last effort to prevent something happening." In substance, by this proposal, neither country would militarily invade any area in Southeast Asia and the South Seas, except Indo-China; both countries would cooperate to obtain needed materials from the Netherlands East Indies; both countries would reverse their freezing decrees; the United States would engage in no activity which might put an obstacle in the way of Japanese efforts to make peace with China, and, when such peace was made, Japan would evacuate her troops. Additionally, Japan would continue to offer the proposals concerning nondiscrimination in commerce and the Three Power Pact contained in "Proposal A."

All of these intercepted messages were decoded and translated at Washington on November 4, 1941.

Precisely what happened at the Imperial Conference on November 5 is unknown, but the proposals in the form sent to Admiral Nomura were approved. He was notified that [18]

* this is the Imperial Government's final step. Time is becoming exceedingly short and the situation very critical, Absolutely no delays can be permitted. * I wish to stress this point over and over.

But at the same time the Ambassador was cautioned,

We wish to avoid giving them the impression that there is a time limit or that this proposal is to be taken as an ultimatum. *

As early as October 10, 1941, the Japanese Foreign Minister had received the impression that Ambassador Nomura was very fatigued, and he was giving serious consideration to the question of sending to Washington a high-ranking diplomat to assist him.[19] This eventuated in the sending of Mr. Saburo Kurusu, with the rank of Ambassador. He called on Mr. Grew at Tokyo, on the evening of November 4, before leaving for Hong Kong [20] to catch the Clipper on November 7, and telegrams were sent from Tokyo to Ambassador Nomura, stating that he was coming.[21]

Tokyo was so hopeful of reaching an agreement that Ambassador Nomura was instructed [22] as to its form: it was not to be a treaty, but an Executive Agreement, which the President could put into effect forthwith. Also, because Great Britain and the Netherlands were concerned, Admiral Nomura was instructed [23]

> * to impress upon the American officials the importance of this essential measure and have them agree to make Great Britain and the Netherlands both simultaneously sign those terms in which they are concerned. *

Finally there was a grave warning, by separate message,[24] "of utmost secrecy," and to be kept strictly and only to Admiral Nomura himself:

> * it is absolutely necessary that all arrangements for the signing of this agreement be completed by the 25th of this month. *

Admiral Nomura immediately made arrangements through Mr. Hull to meet with Mr. Roosevelt, but could not get an appointment for a definite date:[25] there is no reference to this in the official American version of these happenings.

About midday on November 5, 1941, Mr. Roosevelt received a telegram from Mr. Churchill, stating his views as to Chiang Kai-shek's recent appeal for air assistance.[26] Mr. Churchill said that he would be willing to send pilots and even some planes from Singapore if they could arrive in time. He continued:

> Two. What we need now is a deterrent of the most general and formidable character. *When we talked about this at Placentia *you spoke of gaining time,* and this policy has been brilliantly successful so far. *But our joint embargo is steadily forcing the Japanese to decisions for peace or war.* (Emphasis supplied.)

Mr. Churchill then continued with some observations as to the dangerous consequences of a Japanese attack on Yunnan, and he asked Mr. Roosevelt to warn the Japanese against this, promising "to make a similar communication" if Mr. Roosevelt should do so. Mr. Churchill concluded his message:

> Five. No independent action by ourselves will deter Japan because we are so much tied up elsewhere. But of course we will stand with you and do our utmost to back you in whatever course you choose. I think, myself, that Japan is more likely to drift into war than to plunge in. Please let me know what you think.

But Japan was not drifting into war; she was in fact secretly preparing for the plunge. On November 5, 1941, Order No. 1, the Japanese Navy's "Combined Fleet Top Secret Operation," [27] was promulgated, stating that preparations for war were to "be completed by the first part of December," because it was "feared that war with the United States, Great Britain, and the Netherlands is inevitable*." [28]

At Washington the top American military and naval authorities were now pleading for more time. In consequence of the November 3 conference General Marshall, as Chief of Staff, and Admiral Stark, as Chief of Naval Operations, submitted a secret joint memorandum to Mr. Roosevelt on November 5, 1941, concerning the Far Eastern situation. [29] After reviewing Generalissimo Chiang Kai-shek's dispatch and the other recent messages, and the prospective military operations of the Japanese, they warned

Mr. Roosevelt that "offensive military operations with U. S. forces against Japan * *however well-disguised,* would lead to war." The memorandum then analyzed the difficulties of an American war with Japan at that time, commencing the analysis with the unqualified statement that

> At the present time the United States Fleet in the Pacific is inferior to the Japanese Fleet and cannot undertake an unlimited strategic offensive in the Western Pacific. *

In fact, they wrote, to reinforce the Pacific Fleet "all" or "practically all" American warships would have to be withdrawn from the Atlantic, and the result of such a withdrawal might be that England would "lose the Battle of the Atlantic in the near future." Correcting a reference to "The *only existing* plans for war against Japan" so that it read, "The *current* plans for war against Japan," they pointed out that only "defensive war, in cooperation with the British and Dutch," was planned. The southwest area of the Pacific was weak; by February or March 1942 it would be much stronger. Therefore, they concluded:

(a) The basic military policies and strategy *agreed to* in the United States-British Staff conversations remain sound. The primary objective of the two nations is the defeat of Germany. *

(b) War between the United States and Japan should be avoided while building up defensive forces in the Far East, until such time as Japan attacks or directly threatens territories whose security to the United States is of very great importance. * (Emphasis supplied.)

At the end of their report they specifically recommended

> That the dispatch of United States armed forces for intervention against Japan in China be disapproved.

* * * * * *

> That no ultimatum be delivered to Japan.

This memorandum evidently had a sobering effect on Mr. Roosevelt. On November 6, 1941, Mr. Stimson had an hour's talk at the White House alone with Mr. Roosevelt,[30] who

> * was trying to think of something that would give us further time. He suggested he might propose a truce in which there would be no movement or armament for six months and then if the Japanese and Chinese had not settled their arrangement in that meanwhile, we could go on on the same basis.

Unfortunately Mr. Stimson "did not approve of a truce on such a basis and told him so." Mr. Stimson wished to continue to reinforce the Philippines and, moreover, like Mr. Morgenthau, he set a very high value on the military prowess of the Chinese:

> * it was still very important that we keep the Chinese in the war, and I believed that they would feel that such a truce was a desertion of them, and that this would have a very serious effect on Chinese morale.

We are not told more than this, or whether the discussion continued, and, if so, to what conclusion, but we may infer from an incident which occurred the following day that Mr. Stimson disagreed with the joint report of General Marshall and Admiral Stark. Mr. Stimson's attitude and opinions in this connection may have been affected by the urgings of Dr. Hornbeck, then Mr. Hull's immediate subordinate. Dr. Hornbeck was opposed to the current cautious views of the Army and of the Navy and as of November 5, 1941, was in favor of conciliating and strengthening the Chinese. At a slightly later date he did not hesitate to write Mr. Stimson his critical views,[31] "without quotation or attribution," on a "strictly personal and strictly confidential" basis, of General Marshall's estimate of the Far Eastern situation. It is difficult to resist the suspicion of intradepartmental intrigue.

There was a Cabinet meeting on Friday afternoon, November 7, 1941, at which a momentous decision was made, but unfortunately we know little about it. Mr. Roosevelt opened the Cabinet meeting by turning to Mr. Hull and asking him whether he had anything in mind. Mr. Hull says that [32]

> * I thereupon pointed out for about 15 minutes the dangers in the international situation. I went over fully developments in the conversations with Japan and emphasized that in my opinion relations were extremely critical and that we should be on the lookout for a military attack anywhere by Japan at any time. When I finished, the President went around the Cabinet. All concurred in my estimate of the dangers. *

Mr. Stimson's diary now takes up the story [33] and adds an extraordinarily significant matter which Mr. Hull omits. After over eight and one half years in office Mr. Roosevelt took

> * what he said was the *first* general poll of his Cabinet and it was on the question of the Far East—*whether the people would back us up in case we struck at Japan down there and what the tactics should be.* *
> [The Cabinet] was unanimous in feeling the country would support us. Mr. Roosevelt said that this time the vote is unanimous, he feeling the same way. * The thing would have been much stronger if the Cabinet had known—and they did not know except in the case of Hull and the President—what the Army is doing with the big bombers and *how ready we are to pitch in.* (Emphasis supplied.)

It therefore seems right to infer that Mr. Stimson believed that the Army was ready for war, contrary to General Marshall's considered view. Mr. Stimson's statement that "the thing would have been much stronger," leads on to the further inference that, while the Cabinet may not have had grave doubts as to the political feasibility of striking at Japan, it did doubt the military expediency of such an attack in disregard of the advice of General Marshall. What had become of Mr. Roosevelt's idea of a six-months' truce, we do not know. Indeed, in the light of the extreme secrecy so generally prevalent at this time we cannot even be sure whether the minor members of the Cabinet were aware of the Marshall-Stark memorandum or, if they did know of it, why it was so casually disregarded.

We do not even know in full the decision of the Cabinet on "what the tactics should be" in order to prepare for striking at Japan, but Mr. Hull does tell us [34] that "this critical situation" was to be emphasized "in speeches in order that the country would, if possible, be better prepared for such a development."

So far as Admiral Stark was concerned it appears to be the fact that his opposition to Mr. Roosevelt's policy was only to being at war with Japan as well as with Germany. In his opinion we were already at war with Germany. On November 7 he wrote Admiral Hart: [35]

> The Navy is already in the war of the Atlantic, but the country doesn't seem to realize it. Apathy, to the point of open opposition is evident *. Whether the country knows it or not, *we are at war.* (Emphasis in the original.)

From the viewpoint of history the fateful day was perhaps not December 7, 1941, but November 7, 1941, because it was on that day that Mr. Roosevelt and his cabinet arrived at the decision which made war with Japan inevitable, in the absence of a complete reversal of policy. Consequently the narrative of the events of the next thirty days becomes to some extent an historical epilogue.

Perhaps in consequence of this secret decision, and of its logical aftermath, Mr. Roosevelt extended the benefits of lend-lease to Soviet Russia on November 7, [36] making an initial commitment of one billion dollars, after having officially declared that the defense of Russia was vital to the defense of the United States. [37]

So far as we know at present, Mr. Churchill was at first kept in the dark about this momentous decision. Mr. Roosevelt's reply to Mr. Churchill's message was sent from Washington at 9:00 P.M. on November 7.[38] It was restrained and almost soothing. It counselled against a "new formalized verbal warning or remonstrances" to Japan, because their tendency might be, "in Japan's present mood," to induce a decision for war. Instead, an increase in lend-lease aid to China, building up of the American volunteer air force there, and of the defenses of the Philippines and of Singapore, and comparable measures, were recommended because they would "tend to increase Japan's hesitation." Perhaps the message owed the moderation of its tone to the fact that it had been drafted in the State Department [39] prior to the time of the fateful Cabinet meeting.

Being unable to reach Mr. Roosevelt, Ambassador Nomura had to content himself with an interview with Mr. Hull at the latter's apartment on the evening of November 7.[40] Mr. Hull, "Before the Ambassador had said anything in regard to the purpose of his call," began to scold him, saying that three American missionaries had been arrested at Harbin. When this polemic flurry was over, Admiral Nomura commenced to deliver his message just as it had been telegraphed to him on November 4. He stated that the Japanese proposals represented "the utmost concessions that they could make." And he

* went on to say that in view of the gravity of the situation he was very conscious of his responsibility and in order to minimize the possibility of any blunder on his part he had asked the Japanese Government for the assistance of an experienced diplomatist and that in accordance with his request the Government was sending Mr. Kurusu to assist him.*

Ambassador Nomura then handed Mr. Hull a document containing formulas [41] which were copied from "Proposal A" of November 4, 1941. Mr. Hull "glanced over" it, and after a short discussion came up with what appears to be a diplomatic red herring, suggesting that if "the Chinese were now to say that they desired a real friendship with Japan and would do everything in their power to work together along peaceful ways," this would be "a wonderful opportunity for Japan to launch forth on a real new order" and to adopt "a new policy of conciliation and friendship with China," and "a real opportunity for progressive leadership in which Japan and the United States could cooperate to save the world." Supposing that this was a diplomatic approach tentatively made by China through the United States, Ambassador Nomura rose swiftly to the bait, "appeared to be very much impressed with this suggestion," and said that he would refer it to the Japanese Government. In his report to Tokyo, sent off that night, Ambassador Nomura gives a much fuller account of this part of the conversation than appears in the guarded official American Version: [42]

> Hull went on to say that as he had said on previous occasions, Britain, China, the Netherlands and other countries had to be consulted regarding Japanese—U. S. talks of maintaining peace on the Pacific. He let it leak out in this connection that China was being consulted *.
>
> Hull then said that he had happened to wonder what Japan's attitude would be if there were the following developments: Supposing an influential and reliable representative of China were to join in these talks. Supposing, further, that this representative states that China is desirous of resuming friendly relations with Japan, giving his pledge of true friendship and sincerity. What would Japan's reaction be?

* * * * * *

We got the impression that he may have already discussed this matter with the Chinese and that his plan was a consequence thereof. * Hull requested that this plan be * relayed to the government of Japan and its attitude on it be ascertained. *

When this message was received in Tokyo, it led to a brief period of great hopefulness, as is shown by an intercepted message sent on Sunday, November 9, from Tokyo to Ambassador Nomura. [43] This hopefulness was quickly to be dispelled by various American political speeches.

On November 10, 1941, Mr. Churchill, who had presumably been informed by that time of Mr. Roosevelt's November 7 decision, joined in the speech-making tactics which were to prepare and to condition the American people for a Japanese war. He referred to the darkening prospects for peace in the Pacific, but promised to help the United States if it should become involved in the war:— [44]

> * it is my duty to say * that, should the United States become involved in war with Japan, a British declaration will follow within the hour.

On Armistice Day, November 11, 1941, Mr. Roosevelt, in a brief speech, asserted that the United States once again faced the danger of a World War. [45] Mr. Knox was slightly more explicit, since his speech was deliberately made in pursuance of the decision reached at the November 7 Cabinet meeting. Speaking at Providence, R. I., on November 11, 1941, [46] Mr. Knox Delphically warned a nation ignorant of these secret parleys "that grave questions are about to be decided—that the hour of decision is here." Mr. Knox stated to a Republic from which the facts had been concealed, and which therefore could not appraise the trend of foreign affairs on the basis of his assertions, that America was "not only confronted with the necessity of extreme measures of self-defense in the Atlantic," but also that we were "likewise faced with grim possibilities on the other side of the world—on the far side of the Pacific." The Pacific, no less than the Atlantic, he said, called "for instant readiness for defense."

Mr. Welles also spoke on the same day.[47] Beyond the Atlantic, he said, "a sinister and pitiless conqueror" had reduced more than half of Europe to abject serfdom, while in the Far East the same forces of conquest were menacing the safety of all the nations bordering on the Pacific. "The waves of world conquest are breaking high both in the East and in the West," and were threatening more and more with each passing day "to engulf our own shores." The United States, he claimed, was in "far greater peril" than in 1917: "at any moment war may be forced upon us."

At Tokyo on November 10, 1941, the Japanese Foreign Minister, Mr. Togo, had a long interview with Ambassador Grew at the American Embassy.[48] Mr. Togo expressed the opinion that the "preliminary and exploratory conversations" had gone on long enough and that it was now time "to enter into formal and official negotiations." Moreover, after reviewing the documents concerning the prior conversations, Mr. Togo felt

> * that the knowledge and appreciation of the United States with regard to the realities of the situation in the Far East are unfortunately inadequate.*

For more than six months the Japanese had made proposals, but

> * the United States sticks to her first proposals and will not bend an inch. *
>
> * we in Japan are led to wonder what is the degree of sincerity of the American Government in continuing with the conversations. *

Mr. Togo then spoke against further delay and urged a settlement of the outstanding problems "with one sweep." Stating that these were "the maximum possible concessions" [Mr. Grew's report] or "the maximum compromise *. There is absolutely no possibility of our yielding any further" [Togo to Nomura], he handed Mr. Grew "Proposal A." There was some discussion of the terms contained in this proposal, and then Mr. Togo expressed the hope

> * that the American Government would * realize the possibility that the Japanese people, if exposed to continued economic pressure, might eventually feel obliged resolutely to resort to measures of self-defense.

Indeed, argued Mr. Togo, on the other hand,

> * the American Government is now resorting, under the plea of self-defense, to measures over and beyond those that are generally recognized by international law. *

At Washington, on the morning of Monday, November 10, 1941, Ambassador Nomura had finally managed to secure an audience with Mr. Roosevelt.[49] Mr. Hull and Minister Wakasugi were also present. Admiral Nomura began by presenting "Proposal A." When he came to the Tripartite Pact he explained that Japan could not go "any further to write in black and white" what it intended, but, he said,

> * All I have to ask you is to read between the lines and to accept the formula as satisfactory.*

This statement he subsequently deleted from the minutes of the conversation, no doubt as exceeding the limits of diplomatic propriety. Ambassador Nomura, appearing to be "very much in earnest," then briefly reviewed the course of the negotiations, and made a statement which in substance was about the same as that which Foreign Minister Togo had made to Ambassador Grew at Tokyo.

Mr. Roosevelt spoke of "the extreme need that the world come back to ways of peace," and said that, in the spirit of fair play, the American Government would do its best to establish peace in the Pacific. He also said that we would continue to do our best to expedite the conversations, and he asked the Japanese Government clearly to set forth its intention of following peaceful courses. Ambassador Nomura mentioned the economic pressure on Japan, and Mr. Roosevelt said that it was necessary to find a *modus vivendi,* a method of living, he explained, which Admiral Nomura erroneously thought might mean a provisional agreement. Mr. Roosevelt then said that at the end of the week he was leaving Washington to vacation at Warm Springs for ten days. No date was set for the next conversation.

In consequence, later that same day, at Washington, Minister Wakasugi called on Mr. Ballantine,[50] first, to ask for hastening the conversations, and second, to follow up Mr. Hull's red herring of Chinese peace, and to develop more fully just what Mr. Hull had had in mind in making his suggestions. Mr. Ballantine said that he would consult Mr. Hull, and then he put off Mr. Wakasugi with an indefinite reply.

Earlier that day the legal adviser to the Japanese Embassy had been sent to contact Senator Thomas of the Foreign Relations Committee, and also Mr. Hull. After talking to them he reported to the Japanese Ambassador:[51]

> The United States is not bluffing. *If Japan invades again, the United States will fight with Japan.* * The Navy is prepared and ready for action. (Emphasis supplied.)

Admiral Nomura had already had confidential contacts with one unidentified Cabinet member,[52] who had expressed skepticism to him, on Sunday evening, November 9, 1941, over the outcome of the forthcoming negotiations. This Cabinet member also guardedly hinted at war, telling Nomura that[53]

* *the United States cannot stop now* because if Japan moves *something will have to be done* since it is a question of the United States saving its face. (Emphasis supplied.)

Foreign Minister Togo at Tokyo was so much concerned when he heard of Mr. Roosevelt's indefiniteness that he cabled Admiral Nomura at once, [54] on November 11, 1941, pointing out that the situation in Japan was exceedingly critical. He repeated that November 25 was a "definite deadline * that the situation is nearing a climax, and that time is indeed becoming short." Admiral Nomura was asked to redouble his efforts and secure a "speedy approval to our final proposal." The Admiral replied the same day, November 11, 1941, that he had an appointment with Mr. Hull for November 12. [55]

Also on November 11 Sir Robert Craigie, the British Ambassador to Japan, called on Mr. Togo to follow up the October 26 warning. The Japanese Foreign Minister said: [56]

> * he had a strong impression that, for reasons best known to themselves, the United States Government were deliberately dragging out the negotiations. If this were so it would of course be impossible for the Japanese Government to continue them.

The British Ambassador deprecated the absurd notion that Mr. Roosevelt was babying along the Japanese; he felt that the Japanese assurances and proposals had not been "sufficiently definite"—hence the hitch. Sir Robert urged on Japan

> * the advantage of a supreme effort to reach agreement with the United States, as against the desperate risks to Japan of allowing a situation to develop in which it might no longer be possible to control the issue of peace or war.

He said that the British believed a settlement to be in the best interests of England and of Japan, and that when the matter reached the stage of "actual negotiations" the British Government would be very ready to collaborate.

Mr. Togo said [57] that Japan had "already submitted its final proposal"; that the "maximum concessions" had been made, that the situation was critical, and that it was "absolutely impossible that there be any further delays." Sir Robert "listened * very attentively," and Mr. Togo thought he realized "for the first time how critical the situation was": he said he would report to his own government at once. Sir Robert not only did so, but his report was forwarded to Washington, where Lord Halifax brought it to Mr. Welles on the morning of November 12.

At Tokyo on the morning of November 12, 1941, a representative of the Foreign Office called on Ambassador Grew [58] and repeatedly requested haste, setting forth the urgency of the situation. He also referred to Mr. Hull's mention of a Chinese peace offer, and Mr. Grew said that that should be taken up at Washington.

At Washington on November 12, 1941, Ambassador Nomura and Minister Wakasugi met with Mr. Hull and Mr. Ballantine. [59] Mr. Hull first dealt with the "Chinese peace offer," and handed Admiral Nomura a statement [60] which consisted of generalities and platitudes. With more adroitness Mr. Hull next said that he assumed that the Japanese Government had not changed its position, and that it would be appreciated if the Japanese would confirm the correctness of this assumption. Mr. Hull then handed Admiral Nomura a second statement [61] in which all of the peaceable pledges of Japan towards the peace of the Pacific, towards Indo-China, towards Thailand, towards Soviet Russia, and towards peace generally, were listed for Japanese confirmation. Three qualifications of peace were listed for Japanese disavowal. Ambassador Nomura asked for an agreement to be reached in a week or ten days. There was then a discussion of several of the items of "Proposal A," after which Ambassador Nomura asked just how Mr. Hull's fictitious peace terms between China and Japan would be worked out: would it be left to the two countries alone to arrange for a meeting, or would the United States bring them together? Mr. Hull necessarily answered this vaguely: he suggested that "basic matters" be disposed of now, "and that questions of procedure could thereafter be more satisfactorily settled." Mr. Ballantine, who reported this meeting, notes at this spot that

> * the Japanese appeared to find difficulty in understanding [this], possibly because of a preconception that the Secretary's suggestion contained more than appeared on its face.

The conversation turned for a time to the peace declarations of Japan, and then Ambassador Nomura brought it back to China and the hoped-for peace meeting. Mr. Hull managed to keep the conversation vague. In the course of this discussion Admiral Nomura made a sapient remark, that if the negotiations failed

> * simply over an unwillingness on the part of China to agree * the situation would then be one in which China held the key to future relations between Japan and the United States which might result in war.

Mr. Wakasugi asked for haste, and another meeting was set tentatively for November 14, 1941.

However, Ambassador Nomura was not satisfied and sent Mr. Wakasugi to call on Mr. Ballantine on November 13. [62] Minister Wakasugi insisted on a point of diplomatic procedure, that actual diplomatic negotiations were now being carried on between Japan and the United States, not "exploratory" talks. He asked for a clear reply from Mr. Hull at the next meeting tomorrow, "in black and white," to three questions:—

1. Does the United States accept the Japanese proposals of September 25, including those made on November 7 and 10?

2. If not, will the United States submit a counter proposal, "clearly indicating the revision desired?"
3. If not, is the American proposal of June 21 a final proposal?

Mr. Wakasugi said that many people in Japan thought "that the United States is purposely stalling the procedure." Mr. Ballantine acknowledged that "the United States is * aware of the fact that matters have reached an exceedingly critical stage," but he denied "that the United States [was] pursuing a stalling policy." Mr. Wakasugi asked to have these matters referred to Mr. Hull.

Meanwhile the State Department had been drafting a reply to Chiang Kai-shek's message for Mr. Roosevelt, who received the draft on November 10.⁶³ On November 12 Mr. Roosevelt saw the Chinese Ambassador,⁶⁴ but what assurances, if any, were given him we do not know. After the interview the draft was approved by Mr. Roosevelt; it was sent out on November 14.⁶⁵ In form most of it followed the essence of the Marshall-Stark recommendations, but one of the final paragraphs was perhaps intended to convey more meaning than appeared on its face:⁶⁶

> This Government has on numerous occasions pointed out to the Government of Japan various consequences inherent in pursuit of courses of aggression and conquest. We shall continue to impress this point of view upon Japan on every appropriate occasion.

Also on November 14 Admiral Stark wrote Admiral Kimmel a secret letter⁶⁷ as to British troop movements:

> * The large fast ships which we now have and which *could* be converted for the duty you have in mind are currently engaged in an *important mission* (transporting British troops to the Middle East—*obviously most secret)* and will be so engaged for a number of months. I would give a lot if we had those ships *now* converted to carriers and fully equipped for combat purposes. (Emphasis in original.)

On November 14 Foreign Minister Togo cabled "Proposal B" in formal form to Ambassador Nomura, [68] who was to present it at some subsequent time, when so instructed.

On November 14 Ambassador Nomura made an earnest and judicious appeal to Tokyo. [69] He telegraphed that the policy of the American Government in the Pacific was to stop any further Japanese moves either northward or southward: *"now they are contriving by every possible means to prepare for actual warfare."* He elaborated on the progress of American military and other preparations, and observed, "they would not hesitate * to fight us." Such a war would also involve Britain; perhaps Russia; the nations of Central America, "already the puppets of the United States," and the nations of South America. Chinese relations "might become the stumbling block." Japan seems to be tying up closer with the Axis, but "the apex of German victories has been passed. * the possibility of a separate peace has receded." The Admiral continued:

> It is inevitable that this war will be long, and this little victory or that little victory, or this little defeat or that little defeat do not amount to much, and it is not hard to see that whoever can hold out till the end will be the victor.

While the United States is gradually getting in deeper in the Atlantic, he observed, this was merely a convoy warfare, and at any moment America's main naval strength might be transferred to the Pacific. Great Britain had doubtless moved considerable naval strength into the Indian Ocean.

Moreover, he telegraphed, it is being thought more than ever that American participation in the war will be carried out through war in the Pacific. Consequently Admiral Nomura cautioned "patience for one or two months in order to get a clear view of the world situation."

Tokyo replied to this message from Admiral Nomura on November 16, [70] and said that to wait and see was quite out of the question: "the deadline" had been set for November 25 and there would be no change. Admiral Nomura was instructed to do his best to bring about an immediate solution.

Meanwhile the meeting tentatively set for November 14 was postponed to Saturday, November 15. As before, there were present Messrs. Hull and Ballantine, Ambassador Nomura and Minister Wakasugi. [71] Mr. Hull led off with a proposal of a joint United States-Japanese declaration on economic policy. His "oral statement" [72] was a long statement concerning his prior efforts to establish unconditional most-favored-nation treaties, the principle of which he urged Japan to adopt. The proposed draft of a "joint declaration" [73] was on the whole favorable to Japan, particularly as it proposed the restoration of commercial, financial, and other relationships to a normal basis. This was the bait; the hook was the restoration of "Complete control over its economic, financial and monetary affairs * to China" and the abandonment by Japan of any kind of a preferential position both there and everywhere else in the Pacific area. Mr. Wakasugi enquired whether this proposal was the American answer to the Japanese nondiscrimination proposal, and Mr. Hull answered in the affirmative.

Ambassador Nomura then insisted that the "exploratory conversations" were over; that these were "actual negotiations." Mr. Hull replied that until he could go to Great Britain, to China, and to the Netherlands, and say that the attitudes of Japan and of the United States were such as to afford a basis for negotiation, the meetings would have to continue to be of an "exploratory" nature.

Mr. Wakasugi asked for an answer on the two other outstanding questions. Mr. Hull turned to the large questions of peace, and asked first to have a definite reply from the new Japanese cabinet in answer to his own questions of November 12. At the same time Mr. Hull asked whether, if an agreement was reached with Japan, the Tripartite Alliance "would be automatically abandoned," or "become a mere scrap of paper," or "automatically become a dead letter." Mr. Wakasugi asked if this was the answer of the American Government on the question of Japan's relations with the Tripartite Pact. Mr. Hull backed away, and said that when Japan answered his questions of November 12 we would be better able to reply. In addition to this, when the question of nondiscrimination was cleared up, as suggested in that day's American proposal, together with the question of the Tripartite Pact, Mr. Hull believed they "could sit down like brothers" and solve the question of stationing Japanese troops in China. He asserted that America did not desire any delay. The Japanese said that their Government would no doubt be very disappointed at the results of that day's conversations.

After reporting this conversation to Tokyo, Ambassador Nomura was sufficiently pessimistic to follow it with a long cable [74] enquiring as to the routine to be followed if diplomatic relations between the two countries were broken off immediately.

Tokyo ominously cabled detailed instructions to Admiral Nomura later on November 15, 1941, as to how to destroy the code machines "in the event of an emergency."[75] The Japanese Embassy at Washington was instructed to relay the message to Mexico City, Rio de Janeiro, and Buenos Aires.

Ambassador Kurusu had arrived at Washington on Saturday afternoon, November 15. On Monday morning, November 17, 1941, Ambassador Nomura brought Ambassador Kurusu to see Mr. Hull [76] at 10:30. Mr. Kurusu emphasized General Tojo's "desire to reach a peaceful settlement with the United States." Ambassador Nomura handed Mr. Hull two documents. The first [77] answered Mr. Hull's questions of November 12, and affirmed the new cabinet's adherence to the older peaceful declarations: it also explained and disavowed the three qualifications as applying only to the anomalous position of Soviet Russia: they "were not intended to limit or narrow down in any way the peaceful intentions of the Japanese

Government." The second document [78] eliminated "southwestern" from Topic VI of the September 25 proposals, and specifically stated that the principle of political stabilization which it set forth should be extended "to the entire area of the Pacific *."

Japan had once again yielded to the American position, and energetic and affirmative American action could still perhaps have preserved the peace of the Pacific.

Over the previous week end Ambassador Nomura had heard a rumor that during the past two days something had happened which made Mr. Roosevelt strongly desire the maintenance of peace with Japan. When the Japanese next met with Mr. Roosevelt on Monday morning, November 17, at 11:00 Ambassador Nomura thought that Mr. Roosevelt was outlining in his mind some formula to preserve peace in the Pacific. Also the Ambassador had been making other quiet enquiries in the State Department, and had been told that the solution of the economic problems was a comparatively simple matter. [79] The Japanese adherence to the Tripartite Pact, and the problems of China, were "the stumbling points," but even a solution of these was "apparently quite possible." The basic difficulty was

> * spiritual * the suspicion that the United States harbors of Japan. * that immediately subsequent to * [an agreement] the Japanese Government may be forced by Germany or by the Japanese military to pursue a course entirely different *.

The conference with Mr. Roosevelt that morning [80] was largely concerned with diplomatic formalities and with empty generalities: it did not get down to serious business nor attempt to solve any of the open questions. At its conclusion it was agreed that the Japanese Ambassadors were to meet with Mr. Hull the following morning.

From Japan, on November 17, Ambassador Grew sent an even more pointed warning, [81] emphasizing the need of the American authorities, independently,

> * to guard against sudden Japanese naval or military actions in such areas as are not now involved in the Chinese theatre of operations.
>
> * the probability of the Japanese exploiting every possible tactical advantage such as surprise and initiative. *

He warned that the Embassy staff was so situated, in the light of the conditions then prevailing in Japan, that it was likely that it could not give "prior warning" to Washington of any warlike measures.

At Washington the Congress by joint resolution on November 17, 1941, repealed more of the Neutrality Act. With amendments the repeals had passed the Senate, 50-37, on November 7, and on November 13 the House had passed the amended version, 212-194. [82] Mr. Roosevelt now had the power to arm American merchant vessels and to have them carry cargoes of contraband of war to belligerent ports anywhere.

On the evening of November 17, 1941, the Japanese Ambassadors called on "a certain cabinet member," [83] who advised them: [84]

> The President is very desirous of an understanding between Japan and the United States. In his latest speech he showed that he entertained no ill will towards Japan. I would call that to your attention. Now the great majority of the cabinet members, with two exceptions, 85 in principle approve of a Japanese American understanding. If Japan would now do something real, such as evacuating French Indo-China, showing her peaceful intentions, the way would be open for us to furnish you with oil and it would probably lead to the reestablishment of normal trade relations. The Secretary of State cannot bring public opinion in line so long as you do not take some real and definite steps to reassure the Americans.

On the morning of November 18, 1941, the Japanese Ambassadors conferred with Mr. Hull for about three hours. [86] The greatest emphasis was placed on the existence of the Tripartite Alliance, and in diplomatic language Mr. Hull stated that no agreement could be reached with Japan while she adhered to the Tripartite Pact. This amplified his pessimistic earlier remark that

> * he frankly did not know whether anything could be done in the matter of reaching a satisfactory agreement with Japan; that we can go so far but rather than go beyond a certain point it would be better for us to stand and take the consequences. *

At another point, Ambassador Nomura

> * repeated that the situation in Japan was very pressing and that it was important to arrest a further deterioration of the relations between the two countries. *

Mr. Kurusu took up this theme, and coupled a warning with an entreaty, saying that the American

> * freezing regulations had caused impatience in Japan and a feeling that Japan had to fight while it still could. If we could come to some settlement now * it would promote an atmosphere which would be conducive to discussing fundamentals. *

Mr. Hull did not respond to this, but returned to his own topic and asked if "something could be worked out on the Tripartite Pact."

The conversation then got off on other controversial topics. Mr. Hull insisted that the talks were "exploratory conversations," not "negotiations," and that he had nothing "substantial" to take as an offer from Japan to Great Britain or China. There was then some heated conversation about the Japanese troops in China and, next, about American delay, which Mr. Hull denied. Finally Ambassador Nomura made the offer of a *modus vivendi*, first originated by him, and most recently suggested by the American cabinet member:—

> * the possibility of going back to the status which existed before the date in July when, following the Japanese move into southern French Indo-china, our freezing measures were put into effect. *

No doubt the Japanese were astonished, in the light of receiving such a lead, to find Mr. Hull "not * particularly receptive to this suggestion." Mr. Hull responded that

> * if we should make some modifications in our embargo on the strength of [such] a step by Japan * we do not know whether the troops which have been withdrawn * will be diverted to some equally objectionable movement elsewhere. *

Ambassador Nomura placatingly said that

> * what he had in mind was simply some move toward arresting the dangerous trend in our relations. *

Mr. Hull was skeptical. Ambassador Nomura then said that

> * the Japanese were tired of fighting China and that Japan would go as far as it could along a first step. *

Cautiously and noncommittally Mr. Hull answered that

> * he would consult with the British and the Dutch to see what their attitude would be toward the suggestion * . *

This was substantially the end of the meeting.

On the afternoon of November 18 Mr. Hull transmitted this information, with some amplification, to the British Minister, Sir Ronald Campbell, [87] and on November 19 to the Ministers of the Netherlands [88] and of Australia. [89] On November 19 Mr. Hull also met with the Japanese Ambassadors, [90] but the conversation was devoted almost entirely to diplomatic shop talk. Hs only items of interest were, first, a declaration by Mr. Hull

> * that this country is determined to keep Hitler from getting control of the seas no matter how long it took us. *

And, second, a rather amazing bit of advice from Ambassador Nomura that the United States might impair its strength if it sent military forces to Africa. This remark implies not only that that invasion had already been planned, but also that the Japanese diplomat had somehow obtained news about it! Finally, third, a remark of Mr. Hull's was misconstrued by the Japanese as welcoming a "reasonable" peace bid from Germany, and

> * Mr. Kurusu interrupted at this point and said that he thought that Hitler would be willing to enter into peace negotiations. *

Mr. Hull was frigid to this response; all "he meant was abandonment entirely by Hitler of his program of conquest."

# CHINESE INTRIGUE TRIUMPHS

Various conciliatory plans now suddenly appeared on the diplomatic scene in Washington. Mr. Maxwell M. Hamilton, Chief of the Division of Far Eastern Affairs in the Department of State, sent a "strictly confidential" proposal to Mr. Hull on November 18, 1941, suggesting that Japan might purchase part or all of New Guinea with funds supplied by the United States, in exchange for Japanese "merchant ships or possibly certain categories of naval vessels," and for Japanese withdrawal from China.[1] No action was taken on this proposal.[2]

Meanwhile Mr. Morgenthau had been preparing "An Approach to the Problem of Eliminating Tension with Japan and Insuring Defeat of Germany": it was dated November 17, 1941,[3] and was sent by Mr. Morgenthau to Mr. Roosevelt and to Mr. Hull, accompanied by a brief letter dated November 18, 1941. This proposal was revised [5] and approved by all of the senior officers of the Far Eastern

Division as being "most constructive." The Chief of that Division, Mr. Hamilton, under date of November 19, submitted it to Mr. Hull, writing, [6]

> I urge that most careful consideration be given promptly to the proposal. To that end I suggest that copies * be made available to Admiral Stark and to General Marshall and that you arrange to confer with them in regard to the matter as soon as they have had an opportunity to examine the proposal.

In 1941 the new Thanksgiving Day fell officially on November 20, and it seems probable that the revised Morgenthau proposal was not received by the Navy and War Departments before the morning of November 21. [7]

Both sides recognized that the diplomatic situation was now *in extremis*. On November 19 the State Department cabled the American Embassy at Tokyo, and various other points, [8] instructing them to

> * call to the attention of American citizens in the Japanese Empire, Japanese-occupied areas of China, Hong-Kong [an *English* colony], Macao [a *Portuguese* colony], and French Indochina the advice previously given in regard to withdrawal and in so doing emphasize that the shipping problem in the Pacific is very difficult and that because of urgent demands elsewhere there is no assurance that it will be possible to retain in the Pacific even the present facilities.

It was also on November 19 that Tokyo cabled to various of its embassies the famous "winds code," [9] a special "weather" message to be used when "diplomatic relations" were "becoming dangerous," and then to be repeated five times at the beginning and at the end of broadcasts: viz.,

United States	Higashi nokaze ame	East wind, rain.
Russia	Kita nokaze kumori	North wind, cloudy.
England (including Thailand, Malaya, and the Netherlands East Indies)	Nishi nokaze hare	West wind, clear.

There were also further cable exchanges concerning the evacuation by ship of Japanese nationals. [10] More important were the cable exchanges between Tokyo and the Ambassadors concerning their proposed "truce," and whether or not "Proposal B" should be presented. [11] In the final upshot the "truce" was blended into "Proposal B" as a new and separate paragraph (2, as renumbered), but the date of November 25, by which agreement must be reached, remained "absolutely unalterable."

On November 20, 1941, although it was the official Thanksgiving Day, Mr. Hull met with the Japanese Ambassadors at noon for an hour and a half. [12] After some preliminary conversation, Mr. Kurusu presented "Proposal B" as modified. [13] This was the final Japanese proposition, and Mr. Hull knew that that was so. [14] The fifth item, that the United States would refrain from measures and actions prejudicial to endeavors to restore peace in China; *i.e.*, that it would discontinue military aid to Chiang Kai-shek, was the principal topic of discussion. Mr. Hull reiterated what he had previously said about the Tripartite Alliance, "that there was a partnership between Hitler and Japan aimed at enabling Hitler to take care of one-half of the world and Japan the other half," in consequence of which the United States was helping Great Britain on one hand and Chiang Kai-shek on the other. Until Japan made it clear that her policy was peaceful it would be impossible to cease aiding China: what was needed was that Japan should manifest a clear purpose for peace. After some further talk Ambassador Nomura said,

> * since the situation is so tense, if the tension between Japan and the United States can be relaxed, be it ever so little, particularly in the southwestern Pacific, and quickly clear the atmosphere, then I think we could go on and settle everything else.

Mr. Kurusu likewise urged the adoption of the *modus vivendi*, saying that

> * if we could go ahead with the present proposal the Japanese idea would be that we could go on working at fundamentals. *

Mr. Hull agreed upon the urgent importance of saving the situation at this juncture, but thought it would be hard to do so. He said that he wanted to think over the Japanese proposal fully and sympathetically, and he asked Ambassador Nomura if the Japanese statesmen could tone down the situation in Japan. Mr. Hull complimented the two Ambassadors on the recent "marked subsidence in warlike utterances" coming from Tokyo: he said that

> * if so much had been accomplished within the course of two days, much more could be accomplished in the course of a longer period.

The conference ended here, and Ambassador Nomura, following up Mr. Hull's request, at once cabled Tokyo to continue their efforts in keeping newspaper editorial comment calm. [15] In the light of a reply received two days later we may also confidently infer that at this time the Japanese Ambassadors insisted upon some extension of the "deadline" of November 25 because of what they believed were excellent prospects for the achievement of agreement on the *modus vivendi*. Hopes of such agreement were indeed so high in Japan that on Friday, November 21, 1941, Tokyo cabled the Ambassadors forms of notes [16] to be sent to Great Britain and to the Netherlands setting forth and explaining the agreement reached with America, and inviting those other countries to negotiate similar agreements.

On the other hand, if the testimony given four years later in the light of hindsight was accurate, Mr. Hull believed the situation was "critical and virtually hopeless"; the only solution he could think of was, at long last, "to present a reasonable counter-proposal." [17] Accordingly on the morning of Friday, November 21, 1941, Mr. Hull called in Admiral Stark and General Gerow, Chief of the War Plans Division and Acting Assistant Chief of Staff (General Marshall was out of town), and asked their opinion of the revised Morgenthau proposal. Admiral Stark had some relatively minor objections; General Gerow had none. Their views were submitted later in the day in written form, [18] General Gerow observing,

> * The adoption of its provisions would attain one of our present major objectives—the avoiding of war with Japan. Even a temporary peace in the Pacific, would permit us to complete defensive preparations in the Philippines and at the same time insure continuance of material assistance to the British—both of which are highly important.

Word had been received that day from the Dutch that a Japanese force had arrived near Palao, close to the heart of the Netherlands East Indies; extensive reinforcements of Japanese troops and equipment in Indo-China had been reported by our consuls there. [19] And although the Americans did not know it, November 21, 1941, was the day when the Japanese naval task force which later attacked Pearl Harbor had been ordered to assemble at Hitokappu Bay. [20]

In an endeavor to satisfy Mr. Hull's objections to the operation and existence of the Tripartite Pact, Mr. Kurusu called on Mr. Hull on November 21, 1941, [21] and gave him a draft letter [22] emphasizing that Japan was not Germany's puppet under that agreement:

> * Japan is in a position to interpret its obligation freely and independently and is not to be bound by the interpretation which the other high contracting parties may make of it. * my Government is not obligated by the aforementioned treaty or any other international engagement to become a collaborator or cooperator in any aggression whatever by any third Power or Powers.
>
> My Government would never project the people of Japan into war at the behest of any foreign Power; it will accept warfare only as the ultimate, inescapable necessity for the maintenance of its security and the preservation of national life against active injustice.
>
> I hope that the above statement will assist you in removing entirely the popular suspicion which Your Excellency has repeatedly referred to. *

Mr. Hull looked at the paper and then asked Mr. Kurusu whether he had anything more to offer on the whole subject of a peaceful settlement. He replied that he did not. Mr. Hull rather brusquely said, at this critical time,

> * I did not think this would be of any particular help and so dismissed it. *

It was at or about this time that Mr. Roosevelt momentarily took a personal hand in the attempts to prepare a *modus vivendi*. It was Mr. Roosevelt's idea that such an arrangement should be for "six months," as follows:

1. U. S. to resume economic relations—some oil and rice now—more later.
2. Japan to send no more troops to Indo-China or Manchurian border or any place South (Dutch, Brit. or Siam.)
3. Japan to agree not to invoke tripartite pact even if U. S. gets into European war.
4. U. S. to *introduce* Japs to Chinese to talk things over but U. S. to take no part in their conversations.

Later on Pacific agreements. (Emphasis in original.)

This memorandum was given to Mr. Hull, [23] and was no doubt much in the mind of the State Department as it redrafted the Morgenthau proposal for the second time, the new redraft being dated November 22, 1941. [24]

On Saturday, November 22, Mr. Hull called in the British and Chinese Ambassadors and the Netherlands and Australian Ministers for a conference which lasted about two and a half hours. [25] After Mr. Hull had recapitulated the high spots of the prior conversations with the Japanese, he gave them the Japanese proposal for a *modus vivendi* to read, with the exception of the Chinese Ambassador, who was late in arriving. All the other diplomats agreed that the November 22 draft, which Mr. Hull was "considering handing to the Japanese," was satisfactory. Dr. Hu Shih then came in; he

> * was somewhat disturbed, as he always is when any question concerning China arises not entirely to his way of thinking. *

Mr. Hull said that there was probably not one chance in three that the Japanese would accept this proposal. Each of the diplomats immediately reported to his respective Government. They were all to meet again on Monday the 24th.

Mr. Churchill's account of these manoeuverings and negotiations is scanty. He seems to have felt that Japan was America's problem, and he does not appear to have kept in close touch with the immediate progress of the conversations. Mr. Churchill's eyes were primarily fixed on Germany, not on Japan. He had sought and he would have welcomed an American declaration of war against Germany, but in early November he felt that he had gone as far as he could in that direction.[26] In the Pacific it seems plain that he would have preferred to maintain peace. He had sufficient warfare on his hands elsewhere. And so far as he could choose he preferred not to have the American strength and resources diluted or dissipated in a Pacific war.[27] Consequently Mr. Churchill wrote Mr. Eden, the British Foreign Secretary, on November 23 as to the general line to be taken in Washington by Lord Halifax on the following day.[28]

> Our major interest is: no further encroachments and no war, as we already have enough of this latter. * * The formal denunciation of the Axis Pact by Japan is not, in my opinion, necessary. Their stopping out of the war is in itself a great disappointment and injury to the Germans. *
>
> * it would be worth while to ease up upon Japan economically sufficiently for them to live from hand to mouth—even if we only got another three months. *
>
> I must say I should feel pleased if I read that an American-Japanese agreement had been made by which we were to be no worse off three months hence in the Far East than we are now.

Meanwhile, in apparent response to a cable from the Japanese Ambassadors, Tokyo extended the deadline to November 29, but warned them,[29]

> * This time we mean it, that the deadline absolutely cannot be changed. After that things are automatically going to happen. *

On the evening of November 22 Mr. Hull met with the Japanese Ambassadors again. [30] He told them of his conference with the other diplomats earlier in the day, and that he expected to be able to give the Japanese Ambassadors a reply on Monday, November 24. Mr. Hull then pushed rather hard and at length for some public peaceful statements to be made in Japan by Japanese statesmen. He referred to the damage which had been done to Japanese-American relations by the Japanese advance in Indo-China in July, and he warned the Ambassadors that "one move on Japan's part might kill dead [sic] our peace effort." There was then some discussion of the situation in Indo-China, from which Mr. Hull felt the Japanese troops should withdraw: this discussion broadened to include China. Ambassador Nomura then reverted to the desire of Japan for a quick settlement, and he again asked Mr. Hull to state what points in the Japanese proposal were acceptable, and what points required modification. The Japanese thought that Mr. Hull's ensuing reply "was a complete evasion." Mr. Hull said that if the Japanese could not wait until Monday, November 24, before having his answer there was nothing he could do about it: he would first have to talk to the other diplomats after they had consulted their governments. He hinted that a counterproposal would be made, involving the release of exports to Japan. Admiral Nomura responded that the Japanese would be quite ready to wait until Monday. There was some general talk of bilateral agreements to be negotiated in the future, and the conference closed.

At Tokyo, on November 23, 1941, Admiral Toyoda, the Foreign Minister, requested Mr. Grew to call and said [31]

> * that while it seems that England, Holland and Australia as well as America are not satisfied with merely the movement of the Japanese forces stationed in Southern French Indo-China to the northern part of that country, neither do we [Japan] consider it

sufficient merely to restore conditions as they were previous to the putting into effect of the freezing order, a thing which we with reluctance dared to propose and which we anticipate * it will be impossible to reach a settlement so long as no understanding with America is reached also with regard to the cessation of aid to Chiang Kai-shek and with regard to the securing of raw materials from the Dutch East Indies.

On November 24, 1941, Mr. Roosevelt announced that he had sent American troops to occupy Dutch Guiana "because disturbed conditions in the Pacific made it inadvisable for the Netherlands to strengthen the Dutch Guiana defense by drawing upon the defense forces now stationed in the Netherlands East Indies." [32] This led to immediate Japanese suspicions that, if the current negotiations were broken off, the United States and Great Britain would promptly occupy the Netherlands East Indies. [33]

It was also on November 24 that all of the top American naval and military commanders were telegraphed: [34]

> Chances of favorable outcome of negotiations with Japan very doubtful. This situation coupled with statements of Japanese Government and movements their naval and military forces indicate in our opinion that a surprise aggressive movement in any direction including attack on Philippines or Guam is a possibility. * Utmost secrecy necessary in order not to complicate an already tense situation or precipitate Japanese action. *

At Washington Mr. Hull met with the British and Chinese Ambassadors and the Netherlands and Australian Ministers [35] in the late afternoon. Mr. Hull had earlier conferred with General Marshall and Admiral Stark, [36] and had discussed with them a third redraft [37] of the Morgenthau proposal which the State

Department had worked up over the week end. Why the second redraft was abandoned, and what the sentiments of the various governments were towards it, does not appear. As previously was the case, the Chinese Ambassador made objections. Even though General Marshall had just expressed the opinion that to permit 25,000 Japanese troops to remain in Indo-China "would be no menace," Dr. Hu Shih objected to allowing more than 5000 Japanese troops to stay there. Mr. Hull explained that this was a mere "temporary agreement," desired primarily

> * because the heads of our Army and Navy often emphasize to me that time is the all-important question for them, and that it is necessary to be more fully prepared to deal effectively with the situation in the Pacific area in case of an outbreak by Japan. * there are real possibilities that such an outbreak may soon occur—any day after this week [which ended on Nov. 29]—unless a temporary arrangement is effected *.

Dr. Hu Shih stubbornly came back to the 5000 troops. Mr. Hull then suffered some disillusionment over the selfishness of America's prospective cobelligerents. He had been dwelling on the general advantages to all these countries of gaining a further three-months' respite by entering into the proposed *modus vivendi*, when it transpired that, except for the Netherlands, none of the diplomats had been given instructions by their respective Governments relative to this phase. Noting their self-centered attitudes, Mr. Hull soliloquized,

> *They seemed to be thinking of the advantages to be derived without any particular thought of what *we* should pay for them * . * (Emphasis supplied.)

Mr. Hull very justly remarked that

> * each of their Governments was more interested in the defense of that area of the world than this country, and at the same time they expected this country, in case of a Japanese military outbreak, to * take the lead in defending the entire area. * I made it clear that I was definitely disappointed at * the lack of interest and lack of a disposition to cooperate. They said nothing except the Netherlands Minister who then replied that * his Government * would support the *modus vivendi* proposal. I then indicated that I was not sure that I would present it to the Japanese Ambassador without knowing anything about the views and attitude of their Governments. The meeting broke up in this fashion.

However, in fairness to the other governments it should be pointed out that there was possibly another and equally valid point of view which they might have held. Mr. Roosevelt and Mr. Hull had been carrying on their dilatory conversations with Japan in secret; secret not only from the American people, but also largely secret from the governments of America's prospective cobelligerents. [38] Late in the eleventh hour Mr. Hull had suddenly given those governments, already becoming apprehensive because of the visible trend of international affairs, a peep behind the scenes. That peep revealed the imminence of a collision.

Foreign offices usually do not hurry, particularly in unexpected and novel situations. They were perhaps attempting to adjust themselves to the suddenly revealed circumstances, to estimate the courses and speeds of the Japanese and American ships of state, and to appraise the chances and risks of the collision. It is also conceivable that they distrusted the diplomatic seamanship of Mr. Roosevelt and of Mr. Hull, who had manoeuvered the diplomatic situation into a position where it was *in extremis*, without regard to the subsidiary question of whether the blundering course was negligently or deliberately chosen. Was it not reasonable for the other foreign offices to hesitate and to consider whether the newly proposed course was any safer than the old course?

Mr. Hull, so far as we know, made no mental allowance for any of these possibilities. By the time the meeting broke up he felt that he had been deserted by his allies; that they had let him down in a selfish and self-centered way.

Disillusioned, Mr. Hull then prepared a draft message for Mr. Roosevelt to send to Mr. Churchill, informing him of the pending *modus vivendi*. [39] Mr. Roosevelt personally added to its end [40] this comment:

> This seems to me a fair proposition for the Japanese but its acceptance or rejection is really a matter of internal Japanese politics. I am not very hopeful and we must all be prepared for real trouble, very soon.

The message was sent off that night.

At Tokyo, Ambassador Grew called on the Foreign Minister, Mr. Togo, on the afternoon of November 24. [41] Mr. Togo had received a report of Mr. Hull's remarks on the evening of November 22 concerning the withdrawal of the Japanese troops from both northern and southern Indo-China, and he wished to explain to Ambassador Grew that that was quite impossible at the moment. He dwelt somewhat on the Chinese situation, and expressed his inability to understand why the most recent Japanese proposal concerning that problem had not been accepted by the United States. He also referred to American aid to Chiang Kai-shek in such a way that Mr. Grew received the impression that the Japanese proposal on that point (#4) was "largely to save face," and Mr. Grew so reported to Washington.

The Japanese Ambassadors thus did not get their promised answer on Monday, November 24. Neither did they get it on Tuesday, November 25, 1941.

By 9:30 on the morning of November 25, 1941, the *modus vivendi* had been redrafted in the State Department for the fourth time and was now in "final" form. ⁴² At that hour Messrs. Stimson and Knox met at the State Department with Mr. Hull for their "usual Tuesday morning meeting." Mr. Hull showed them ⁴³

> * the proposal for a 3-months' truce, which he was going to lay before the Japanese today or tomorrow. It adequately safeguarded all our interests I [Secretary Stimson] thought as we read it *. *

But Mr. Stimson doubted that the Japanese would agree to all that they were asked to do by the *modus vivendi* proposal.

At noon that same day the War Council met at the White House for about an hour and a half. ⁴⁴ There were present Mr. Roosevelt, Mr. Hull, Mr. Stimson, Mr. Knox, General Marshall, and Admiral Stark. Mr. Stimson wrote in his diary:

> * There the President, instead of bringing up the Victory Parade [a nickname for the General Staff's European war plans], brought up entirely the relations with the Japanese. He brought up the event that we were likely to be attacked perhaps (as soon as) next Monday [December 1], for the Japanese are notorious for making an attack without warning, and the question was what should we do. *The question was how we should maneuver them into the position of firing the first shot without allowing too much danger to ourselves.* It was a difficult proposition. Hull laid out his general broad propositions on which the thing should be rested—the freedom of the seas and the fact that Japan was in alliance with Hitler and was carrying out his policy of world aggression. The others brought out the fact that any expedition to the South as the Japanese were likely to take would be an encirclement of our interests in the Philippines and cutting into our vital supplies of rubber from Malaysia [*sic*]. I pointed out to the President that he had already taken the first steps towards an ultimatum in notifying Japan way back last summer that if she crossed the border into Thailand she was violating our safety and that therefore he had only to point out (to Japan) that to follow any such expedition was a violation of a warning we had already given. So Hull is to go to work on preparing that. * (Emphasis supplied.)

It is all very bewildering. At 9:30 Mr. Stimson was in favor of the *modus vivendi:* by midday he and everyone else had apparently abandoned it, and without further discussion. Why? What had happened? In fact it seems doubtful that the *modus vivendi* was then and there abandoned. It is more likely that there was a discussion of the expediency of abandoning it, but that an absolutely final decision to abandon it was not made then and there. This view is supported by another contemporary record, a letter which Admiral Stark wrote to Admiral Kimmel that same afternoon, in which Admiral Stark makes it clear that he could not figure out what decision would be made by Mr. Roosevelt: [45]

> P.S. I held this up pending a meeting with the President and Mr. Hull today. I have been in constant touch with Mr. Hull and it was only after a long talk with him that I sent the message to you a day or two ago showing the gravity of the situation. He confirmed it all in today's meeting, as did the President. Neither would be surprised over a Japanese surprise attack. *
>
> I won't go into the pros and cons of what the United States may do. I will be damned if I know. I wish I did. The only thing I do know is that we may do most anything and that's the only thing I know to be prepared for; or we may do nothing—I think it is more likely to be "anything."

Mr. Hull, as will appear subsequently, put the final abandonment of the *modus vivendi* some hours later, and he ought to know. But later that day Admiral Stark took a war precaution and ordered all trans-Pacific shipping to be routed near Australia [46] and furnished with a naval escort. At 1:30 P.M. (Washington time) the Japanese fleet which later attacked Pearl Harbor had sailed from Hitokappu Bay. [47] By a curious coincidence it was almost the exact moment of termination of the White House War Council at which Mr. Roosevelt and his advisors had been trying to solve the problem of "how we should maneuver [the Japanese] into the position of firing the first shot without * too much danger to ourselves."

In the North Atlantic the American Navy, "spread extremely thin," was convoying British troop transports in high secrecy: in the South Atlantic it was likewise convoying 20,000 British troops "to Cape Town and possibly to Durban." [48]

In the afternoon of November 25, after the War Cabinet meeting, Mr. Hull returned to the State Department and Mr. Stimson to the War Department. The latter wrote in his diary: [49]

> * When I got back to the Department I found news from G-2 that an (a Japanese) expedition had started. Five divisions have come down from Shantung and Shansi to Shanghai and there they had embarked on ships—30, 40, or 50 ships—and have been sighted south of Formosa. I at once called up Hull [4:30 p.m] and told him about it and sent copies to him and to the President of the message from G-2.

In the meantime Mr. Hull was meeting with discouragement and even with opposition to his proposal for a three-months' truce. Only the Netherlands Government seemed to approve of a *modus vivendi*, [50] and they foresaw no difficulty in lifting the sanctions piecemeal and proportionately to the Japanese withdrawal. So far as discussions went, the Netherlands Minister of Foreign Affairs was willing to "fully entrust" them to Mr. Hull. Lord Halifax called in order to present various objections, [51] and left a somewhat critical British memorandum [52] which in part adopted the Chinese position.

The Chinese had once again pulled all the strings and pushed all the buttons, without regard either to diplomatic proprieties or to using official channels of communications.

Mr. T. V. Soong, the brother of Mrs. Chiang Kai-shek, immediately got in touch, not with Mr. Hull, but with Mr. Stimson and Mr. Knox, and gave them copies of a cable, dated November 25, 1941, from the Generalissimo: [53]

I presume Ambassador Hu Shih has given you a copy of my telegram yesterday. Please convey contents of the message to Secretaries Knox and Stimson immediately.

Please explain to them the gravity of the situation. If America should relax the economic blockade and freezing of Japanese assets, or even if reports that the United States is considering this should gain currency, the morale of our troops will be sorely shaken. During the past two months the Japanese propaganda have spread the belief that in November an appeasement will be successfully reached with the United States. They have even come to a silent but none the less definite understanding with the doubtful elements in our country. If, therefore, there is any relaxation of the embargo or freezing regulations, or if a belief of that gains ground, then the Chinese people would consider that China has been completely sacrificed by the United States. The morale of the entire people will collapse and every Asiatic nation will lose faith, and indeed suffer such a shock in their faith in democracy that a most tragic epoch in the world will be opened. The Chinese army will collapse, and the Japanese will be enabled to carry through their plans, so that even if in the future America would come to the rescue the situation would be already hopeless. Such a loss would not be to China alone.

We could therefore only request the United States Government to be uncompromising, and announce that if the withdrawal of Japanese armies from China is not settled, the question of relaxing of the embargo or freezing could not be considered. If, on the other hand, the American attitude remains nebulous Japanese propaganda will daily perform its fell purpose so that at no cost to them this propaganda will effect the breakdown of our resistance. Our more than four years of struggle with the loss of countless lives and sacrifices and devastation unparalleled in history would have been in vain. The certain collapse of our resistance will be an unparalleled catastrophe to the world, and I do not indeed know how history in future will record this episode.

The telegram to Dr. Hu Shih was from the Chinese Foreign Minister, Quo Tai-chi, and referred to the November 22 meeting of the diplomats with Mr. Hull: [54]

> After reading your telegram, the Generalissimo showed rather strong reaction. He got the impression that the United States Government has put aside the Chinese question in its conversation with Japan instead of seeking a solution, and is still inclined to appease Japan at the expense of China. * We are, however, firmly opposed to any measure which may have the effect of increasing China's difficulty in her war of resistance, or of strengthening Japan's power in her aggression against China.
>
> Please inform the Secretary of State.

Pressure was also brought by the Chinese to bear directly on Mr. Roosevelt. The Generalissimo's American advisor, Mr. Owen Lattimore, on November 25 cabled to one of Mr. Roosevelt's administrative assistants, Mr. Lauchlin Currie: [55]

> After discussing with the Generalissimo the Chinese Ambassador's conference with the Secretary of State, I feel you should urgently advise the President of the Generalissimo's very strong reaction. I have never seen him really agitated before. Loosening of economic pressure or unfreezing would dangerously increase Japan's military advantage in China. A relaxation of American pressure while Japan has its forces in China would dismay the Chinese. Any "Modus Vivendi" now arrived at with China would be disastrous to Chinese belief in America and analogous to the closing of the Burma Road, which permanently destroyed British prestige. Japan and Chinese defeatists would instantly exploit the resulting disillusionment and urge oriental solidarity against occidental treachery. It is doubtful whether either past assistance or increasing aid could compensate for the feeling of being deserted at this hour. The Generalissimo has deep confidence in the President's fidelity to his consistent policy but I must warn you that even the Generalissimo questions his

ability to hold the situation together if the Chinese national trust in America is undermined by reports of Japan's escaping military defeat by diplomatic victory.

In the evening of November 25 the Chinese Ambassador called on Dr. Hornbeck, Mr. Hull's political advisor, to repeat some of his objections: he was followed by the Netherlands Minister, who was now becoming lukewarm in his support of the plan to establish a three-months' truce.[56] Finally the Chinese Ambassador called on Mr. Hull that same evening[57] and presented the telegram already mentioned from Quo Tai-chi. Mr. Hull replied, with some natural indignation, that

> * in the first place the official heads of our Army and Navy for some weeks have been most earnestly urging that we not get into war with Japan until they have had an opportunity to increase further their plans and methods and means of defense in the Pacific area. In the second place, at the request of the more peaceful elements in Japan for conversations with this Government looking toward a broad peaceful settlement for the entire Pacific area, we have been carrying on conversations and making some progress thus far; and the Japanese are urging the continuance of these general conversations for the purpose of a broad Pacific area settlement. The situation, therefore, is that the proposed *modus vivendi* is really a part and parcel of the efforts to carry forward these general conversations *.

I said that very recently the Generalissimo and Madame Chiang Kai-shek almost flooded Washington with strong and lengthy cables telling us how extremely dangerous the Japanese threat is to attack the Burma Road through Indo-china and appealing loudly for aid, whereas practically the first thing this present proposal of mine and the President does is to require the Japanese troops to be taken out of Indochina and thereby to protect the Burma

Road from what Chiang Kai-shek said was an imminent danger. Now, I added, Chiang Kai-shek ignores that situation which we have taken care of for him and inveighs loudly about another matter relating to the release of certain commodities to Japan corresponding to the progress made with our conversations concerning a general peace agreement. He also overlooks the fact that our proposal would relieve the menace of Japan in Indochina to the whole South Pacific area, including Singapore, the Netherlands East Indies, Australia, and also the United States, with the Philippines and the rubber and tin trade routes. All of this relief from menace to each of the countries would continue for ninety days. One of our leading admirals stated to me recently that the limited amount of more or less inferior oil products that we might let Japan have during that period would not to any appreciable extent increase Japanese war and naval preparations. I said that, of course, we can cancel this proposal but it must be with the understanding that we are not to be charged with failure to send our fleet into the area near Indochina and into Japanese waters, if by any chance Japan makes a military drive southward.

So this interview terminated, and Mr. Hull was free to reflect upon the events of a long and busy day. He had ended the day with an excellent statement as to why it was expedient that there should be a three-months' truce, but later that evening of November 25 he seems to have experienced a complete revulsion of feeling and tentatively to have decided to abandon the proposed *modus vivendi*. In part he was no doubt motivated by the tentative decision for war reached at the War Council meeting at midday. In part he was motivated by pique—the "Chinese had exploded without knowing half the true facts or waiting to ascertain them."[58] But in part, the Chinese objections had prevailed and had influenced Mr. Hull to drop his plans to avoid an immediate conflict with Japan. As

Admiral Nomura had feared, China, in the event, had held the key to peace or war with Japan. Mr. Hull was also troubled and perplexed by the threatening political potentialities: he testified [59] *à propos* of this decision:

> It was manifest that there would be widespread opposition from American opinion to the *modus vivendi* aspect of the proposal especially to the supplying to Japan of even limited quantities of oil. The Chinese Government violently opposed the idea. The other interested governments were sympathetic to the Chinese view and fundamentally were unfavorable or lukewarm. Their cooperation was a part of the plan. It developed that the conclusion with Japan of such an arrangement would have been a major blow to Chinese morale. In view of these considerations it became clear that the slight prospects of Japan's agreeing to the *modus vivendi* did not warrant assuming the risks involved in proceeding with it, especially the serious risk of collapse of Chinese morale and resistance and even of disintegration of China. It therefore became perfectly evident that the *modus vivendi* aspect would not be feasible.

On November 26, 1941, American B-24s "fully equipped with gun ammunition" were ordered out to reconnoitre the Japanese naval bases at Truk and Jaluit. [60] Available also on November 26 to the American officials was an intercepted message from Japanese Foreign Office officials at Hanoi, Indo-China, to Tokyo, dated November 25, stating, [61]

> We are advised by the military that we are to have a reply from the United States on the 25th. If this is true, *no doubt the Cabinet will make a decision between peace and war within the next day or two.* *
> (Emphasis supplied.)

When the perplexed Mr. Hull arrived at his office early on the morning of Wednesday, November 26, 1941, further discouragement awaited him; a cabled reply had been sent the previous night from Mr. Churchill to Mr. Roosevelt: [62]

> Your message about Japan received tonight. Also full accounts from Lord Halifax of discussions and your counter project to Japan on which Foreign Secretary [Eden] has sent some comments. Of course, it is for you to handle this business and we certainly do not want an additional war. There is only one point that disquiets us. What about Chiang Kai-shek? Is he not having a very thin diet? Our anxiety is about China. If they collapse our joint dangers would enormously increase. We are sure that the regard of the United States for the Chinese cause will govern your action. We feel that the Japanese are most unsure of themselves.

At 9:20 A.M. [63] Mr. Stimson telephoned Mr. Hull, and thus recorded the conversation: [64]

> Hull told me over the telephone this morning that *he had about made up his mind* not to give (make) the proposition that Knox and I passed on the other day to the Japanese but *to kick the whole thing over*—to tell them that he has no other proposition at all. The Chinese have objected to that proposition—when he showed it to them; that is, to the proposition which he showed to Knox and me, because it involves giving to the Japanese the small modicum of oil for civilian use during the interval of the truce of the 3 months. Chiang Kai-shek had sent a special message to the effect that that would make a terrifically bad impression in China; that it would destroy all their courage and that they (it) would play into the hands of his, Chiang's, enemies and that the Japanese would use it. T. V. Soong had sent me this letter and asked to see me and I called Hull up this morning to tell him so and ask him what he wanted me to do about it. He replied as I have just said above—that *he had about made up his mind to give up the whole thing in respect to a truce* and to simply tell the Japanese that he had no further action to propose. (Emphasis supplied.)

CHINESE INTRIGUE TRIUMPHS | 491

A few minutes later Mr. Stimson telephoned Mr. Roosevelt to ask him whether he had received the previous day's report concerning the Japanese expeditionary force moving south from Shanghai. Mr. Stimson wrote that Mr. Roosevelt [65]

> * fairly blew up—jumped into the air, so to speak, and said he hadn't seen it and that *that changed the whole situation* because it was an evidence of bad faith on the part of the Japanese that while they were negotiating for an entire truce—an entire withdrawal (from China)—they should be sending this expedition down there to Indochina. I told him that it was a fact that had come to me through G-2 and through the Navy Secret Service and I at once got another copy of the paper I had sent last night and sent it over by special messenger. [66] (Emphasis supplied.)

At 9:50 A.M. Mr. Stimson again telephoned Mr. Hull [67] and we may conjecture that it was to report this conversation. Probably this last event finally made up Mr. Hull's mind, because that morning he dictated a memorandum to Mr. Roosevelt which, after reciting the alternatives, read, [68]

> In view of the opposition of the Chinese Government and either the half-hearted support or the actual opposition of the British, the Netherlands and the Australian Governments, and in view of the wide publicity of the opposition and of the additional opposition that will naturally follow through utter lack of an understanding of the vast importance and value otherwise of the *modus vivendi*, without in any way departing from my views about the wisdom and the benefit of this step to all of the countries opposed to the aggressor nations who are interested in the Pacific area, I desire very earnestly to recommend that at this time I call in the Japanese Ambassadors and hand them a copy of the comprehensive basic proposal for a general peaceful settlement, and at the same time withhold the *modus vivendi* proposal.

So far as the Japanese expedition from Shanghai was concerned it was not so sinister as appeared at first glance, and from the professional military point of view it did not warrant anyone in going off at halfcock. The military intelligence memorandum which Mr. Roosevelt received from Mr. Stimson contained this qualifying statement: [69]

> The officers concerned, in the Military Intelligence Division, feel that unless we receive other information, *this is more or less a normal movement* *. (Emphasis supplied.)

There was also a further qualification in the Military Intelligence statement about which Mr. Roosevelt was apparently not informed, which shed light on, and which importantly qualified, the meaning of this preliminary military movement, namely, that the Japanese plans were probably not to be put into effect until "after the armed services feel that the Kurusu mission is a definite failure." [70]

There was also on the morning of November 26 an Army-Navy Joint Board meeting at which the imminence of war was a principal topic of discussion. Admiral Ingersoll "presented at that meeting the arguments why we should not precipitate a war," [71] and once again it was decided that a cautious memorandum should be prepared for Mr. Roosevelt, which was done in draft form. Possibly General Marshall signed it on the night of the 26th: it represented his idea at the time. [72] In contrast to Mr. Stimson, General Marshall was [73]

> * hunting for time, so that whatever did happen we would be better prepared than we were at that time. *

> So it was a question of resolving his views as to the honor, we will say, of the United States * and mine, which * were * that we should get as much time as we could in order to make good the terrible deficiencies in our defensive arrangements.

Soon after midday Mr. Roosevelt sent off a secret message to Mr. Sayre, the High Commissioner for the Philippines, [74] asking him to consult President Quezon "in great confidence" in order to be sure that the Filipinos would support America in the impending war. Mr. Roosevelt, in that message, referred to the southward moves of the Japanese and said,

* I consider it possible that this next Japanese aggression might cause an outbreak of hostilities between the U. S. and Japan. *

Moreover, Mr. Roosevelt stated, the Japanese were reenforcing the mandated islands in order to prepare them

* as quickly as possible against a possible attack on them by U. S. Forces. *

At 2:30 that afternoon the Chinese Ambassador and Mr. T. V. Soong called on Mr. Roosevelt, but we do not know the substance of the conversation. [75] Later in the afternoon Mr. Hull conferred with Mr. Roosevelt [76] and he approved of Mr. Hull's calling in the Japanese Ambassadors and handing them the new and generalized proposals, usually called the Ten Point Proposal, while withholding the *modus vivendi* plan of a truce. Upon his return from the conference with Mr. Roosevelt, Mr. Hull conferred with his Far Eastern experts and then met the Japanese Ambassadors at the State Department at 5:00 P.M., [77] the appointment having been made for 4:45. [78] Mr. Hull began [79] by handing them the ten-point proposal [80] and also an explanatory "oral" statement. [81]

After the Japanese Ambassadors had read the papers, Mr. Kurusu asked incredulously if this was the American response to the Japanese proposal for a *modus vivendi*. Mr. Hull replied that the United States had to treat the Japanese proposal this way because "there was so much turmoil and confusion among the public both in the United States and in Japan." Mr. Kurusu objected to various of the American topics, and said that if this was the idea of the American Government no agreement was possible; it was not even worth reporting to Tokyo, for if this was done the Japanese Government would be likely to throw up its hands. Admiral Nomura pointed out that the prior negotiations had been addressed to the problem of reconciling the Japanese proposals of September 25 with the American proposals of June 21: these new proposals were "vastly different from either." The interview lasted for almost two hours and seems to have been rather heated. Towards its close Ambassador Nomura recollected that Mr. Roosevelt had said to them on November 17, quoting Mr. Bryan, "There is no last word between friends." [82] Ambassador Nomura therefore asked for an interview with Mr. Roosevelt. Ambassador Kurusu then observed that this American note was "tantamount to meaning the end," and he incredulously asked again if America was not really interested in a *modus vivendi*. Diplomatically Mr. Hull said, no. Mr. Kurusu asked if this was "because the other powers would not agree" with the American view. Diplomatically Mr. Hull declined to answer, and the interview was essentially over.

The Japanese Ambassadors were about at their wits' end, as they cabled Tokyo. [83] If the situation remained tense, the negotiations would "inevitably be ruptured, if indeed they may not already be called so." Such a rupture, they cabled, in their opinion,

* does not necessarily mean war between Japan and the United States, but after we break off, as we said, the military occupation of the Netherlands India is to be expected of England and the United States. Then we would attack them and a clash with them would be inevitable. *

Once again dispelling all notions that German and Japanese foreign policy was integrated or coordinated, they gloomily continued:

* Now, the question is whether or not Germany would feel duty bound by the third article of the treaty to help us. *We doubt if she would.* * (Emphasis supplied.)

Perhaps, they suggested, they could propose that Mr. Roosevelt

> *wire you that for the sake of posterity he hopes that Japan and the United States will cooperate for the maintenance of peace in the Pacific *, and that you in turn reply with a cordial message, thereby not only clearing the atmosphere, but also gaining a little time. *

This suggestion was perhaps the genesis of Mr. Roosevelt's subsequent idea of sending a message to the Emperor [84] at a time, late in the evening of December 6, 1941, when he knew it would be futile.

When Mr. Roosevelt approved Mr. Hull's idea "to kick the whole thing over," he understood that the probable consequence would be war. Indeed war was so clearly foreseen that Mr. Roosevelt's planning went a step in advance—"how we should maneuver them into the position of firing the first shot." This plan was coupled with a proviso, "without allowing too much danger to ourselves." In the ultimate event, the proviso backfired and the war began with a major disaster and for some months continued with only reverses and defeats. It is therefore quite understandable why the major participants in this ill-omened decision later sought to avoid responsibility for it, and sometimes to throw the blame for it on others.

In later years Mr. Hull was sensitive on the topic of his share in the responsibility for the outbreak of war with Japan. The report of the Army Pearl Harbor Board, adopting a phrase of Ambassador Grew's, [85] stated that Mr. Hull's note of November 26, 1941, [86]

> * was the document that touched the button that started the war *.

This irked Mr. Hull, [87] and if the existence of such a charge against him affected the emphasis which, four years later, he placed on certain events, it is not strange.

As the events of the next day, November 27, 1941, showed, Mr. Hull understood that the decision made by Mr. Roosevelt and himself on November 26 was a decision for probable war.

Nor were Mr. Roosevelt and Mr. Hull guessing in an uninformed way as to what might eventuate. It is as if they were playing poker in a game where there was a mirror hanging right behind their adversaries. They admittedly had "a wealth of intelligence concerning the purposes of the Japanese" [88] —"not only * what Japan and her ambassadors were *saying* but literally what they were *thinking*." [89] Therefore when Mr. Roosevelt and Mr. Hull deliberately discarded the prior endeavors to agree on a truce, it was because they equally deliberately elected to risk a Japanese attack upon the United States. And, it seems superfluous to add, this decision was cloaked in contemporaneous secrecy.

At 9:17 [90] on the morning of Thursday, November 27, 1941, Mr. Stimson, who had not been told of the decision, telephoned Mr. Hull [91]

> *to find out what his finale had been with the Japanese—whether he had handed them the new proposal which we passed on 2 or 3 days ago or whether, as he suggested yesterday he would, he broke the whole matter off. He told me now that he had broken the whole matter off. As he put it, "I have washed my hands of it and it is now in the hands of you and Knox—the Army and the Navy."

Evidently this reversal of policy took Mr. Stimson's breath away: he at once telephoned Mr. Roosevelt for confirmation and received it, but with a domestic political angle put upon it. Mr. Roosevelt [92]

> * said they had ended up, but they ended up with a magnificent statement prepared by Hull. *

That is, Mr. Roosevelt was now anticipatorily lining up his domestic publicity statements, to be issued after the actual war had begun. Mr. Stimson then suggested and Mr. Roosevelt approved sending a warning to General MacArthur "that he should be on the qui vive for any attack and telling him how the situation was."

In preparation for fixing the political responsibility for the anticipated war, Mr. Hull held a "special and lengthy" press conference on the morning of November 27, [93] commencing at 10 o'clock. Mr. Hull was trying to precondition the country by such publicity to the breakdown of the negotiations and to the possibility of war. He refused to be quoted, telling the correspondents that they could only use the information as their own, or as having come from "authoritative sources." Much of his statement was general historical background, but in due course he said that "a large [Japanese] military movement was taking place" and that the Japanese Navy might attack "around Siam, any time within a few days."

Putting his own interpretation on his own actions, some of the high spots of Mr. Hull's anticipatory claims were:

* we were straining Heaven and Earth to work out understandings that might mitigate the situation before it got out of hand *.

* * * * * *

We had exhausted all our efforts to work out phases of this matter with the Japanese. *

* * * * * *

* I had sought * always to omit consideration of any proposal that would contemplate the stoppage of the conversations and search for a general agreement for peace. (Emphasis supplied.)

While this long morning press conference was going on, Lord Halifax came in "urgently at his request." Mr. Hull being thus occupied in planting the seeds of domestic propaganda, the British Ambassador spoke to Mr. Welles, the Under Secretary, instead. Lord Halifax said [94]

* that Secretary Hull had called him on the telephone last night to inform him of the nature of the document which he had handed the Japanese envoys. The Ambassador said that he was not quite clear in his own mind as to the reasons which prompted this sudden change in presenting the Japanese Government with a document other than the *modus vivendi* document which had so recently been under discussion.

Mr. Welles tartly responded that

* Secretary Hull had requested me to say to the Ambassador in this regard that one of the reasons for the determination reached was the half-hearted support given by the British Government to the earlier proposal * and the raising of repeated questions * in regard thereto.

There was then a discussion of Mr. Churchill's message, which, Lord Halifax explained,

* had been intended merely to express the objections on the part of the Chinese Government. *

He, Lord Halifax, "had been surprised by the vigor of the Chinese objections," and had stated to Dr. Hu Shih that the proposed *modus vivendi* would ensure that the Burma Road would be kept open. The Chinese attitude, said Lord Halifax,

* was based partly on faulty information and partly on the almost hysterical reaction because of the fear that any kind of an agreement reached between Japan and the United States at this time would result in a complete breakdown of Chinese morale.

Mr. Welles concluded the conference by referring to recent reports of Japanese troop movements, perhaps against Thailand: "The gravity of the situation, I thought, could not be exaggerated."

A little later in the day the Australian Minister called on Mr. Hull [95] "to enquire whether the proposed *modus vivendi* had been abandoned permanently." Mr. Hull said that it had, and Mr. Casey "expressed great concern." Mr. Hull partly blamed Messrs. Churchill and Eden, and amplified his own reasons to show that he was frightened by possible Chinese publicity in the United States, and by the prospect of

> * a bitter fight that would be projected by Chiang Kai-shek and carried forward by all of the malcontents in the United States *.

Dr. Loudon, the Netherlands Minister, also called on Mr. Hull that day. To his sympathetic ears Mr. Hull unburdened himself, and to him he fixed the time and circumstances of his unhappy decision. Mr. Hull's contemporaneous memorandum reads: [96]

> The Minister wanted to make clear that he had supported me unequivocally in connection with the proposed *modus vivendi* arrangement which I abandoned on Tuesday evening, November twenty-fifth, or practically abandoned when the Chinese had exploded without knowing half the true facts or waiting to ascertain them. I said that I had determined early Wednesday morning, November twenty-sixth, to present to the Japanese later in the day the document containing a proposed draft of an agreement which set forth all of the basic principles for which this Government stands and has stood for, for many years, especially including the maintenance of the territorial integrity of China. I reminded the Minister that the central point in our plan was the continuance of the conversations with Japan looking toward the working out of a general agreement for a complete peaceful settlement in the Pacific area and that the so-called *modus vivendi* was really a part and parcel of these conversations and their objectives, intended to facilitate and keep them alive and that, of course, there was nothing that in any way could be construed as a departure from the basic principles which were intended to go into the general peace agreement. The Minister said he understood the situation.

Now since the *modus vivendi* "was * part and parcel * of the conversations with Japan looking toward * a complete peaceful settlement," it follows that to abandon the *modus vivendi* meant that the attempts to maintain peace had also been abandoned. And this was exactly the contemporaneous construction which Mr. Hull and everyone else who knew of that abandonment placed on it.

Mr. Grew, therefore, was warned by telegram [97] of the "probability" that the Japanese discussions would lapse, that in consequence the American Embassy and Consulates in Japan might be closed, and that he should consider making the necessary arrangements to pack up his official and personal effects.

Also on November 27 Mr. Hull sent off a long and resentful telegram [98] to the American Ambassador to China, "strictly confidential" and for his eyes "only," in which he narrated the unsatisfactory behavior of the parties involved, repeated some of his own irritated retorts to the Chinese Ambassador, and stated that it had been "decided that we should drop the draft *modus vivendi* *."

During the morning of November 27 there was a conference between Mr. Stimson, Mr. Knox, Admiral Stark, and General Gerow. [99] Admiral Stark and General Gerow were seeking "for more time," but Mr. Stimson "didn't want it at any cost of humility on the part of the United States or of reopening the thing which would show a weakness on our part."

Accordingly the draft was discussed of the proposed memorandum which the Army-Navy Joint Board, the previous day, had ordered to be submitted to Mr. Roosevelt. [100] Mr. Stimson

> * wanted to be sure that the memorandum would not be construed as a recommendation to the President that he request Japan to reopen the conversations. He was reassured on that point. It was agreed that the memorandum would be shown to both Secretaries before dispatch.

This was done later, and Mr. Stimson recommended some changes, which were made. Of even greater importance was the sending of war warnings, which went out that day. As sent to the Navy, the war warning commenced; [101]

> This despatch is to be considered a war warning. Negotiations with Japan looking toward stabilization of conditions in the Pacific have ceased and an aggressive move by Japan is expected within the next few days. The number and equipment of Japanese troops and the organization of naval task forces indicates an amphibious expedition against either the Philippines, Thai or Kra peninsula or possibly Borneo. *

But as sent to the Army, the warning was vastly more significant: [102]

> Negotiations with Japan appear to be terminated to all practical purposes with only the barest possibilities that the Japanese Government might come back and offer to continue. Japanese future action unpredictable but hostile action possible at any moment. If hostilities cannot, repeat cannot, be avoided *the United States desires that Japan commit the first overt act.* * (Emphasis supplied.)

The significance of this warning lies in two facts. *First*, that Mr. Stimson telephoned Mr. Hull, and in order that it should be strictly accurate [103]

> * got his exact statement as to the status of the negotiations, which was then incorporated in the first sentence of the messages.

Second, that the orders concerning the commission of "the first overt act" were inserted as "a direct instruction from the President," [104] probably to General Marshall. Its phraseology prevented the ordering of an all-out alert.

Admiral Thomas C. Hart, who commanded the weak Asiatic fleet from the Philippines, interpreted the warning message with accuracy. He testified: [105]

> The Asiatic fleet had to await attack. It could not attack. So, manifestly, the measure was to so dispose ourselves that when the attack came it would inflict as little damage as was possible; and under the circumstances that obtained out there, the only way to do that was following the principle of dispersal and concealment. That is what we did.

Accordingly, and about ten days before December 7, or, about November 27, 1941, Admiral Hart "had word conveyed over to Admiral Helfrich [who commanded in the Netherlands East Indies] informally what I was doing," [106] and Admiral Hart then sent the American warships to lie concealed in the ports of the Netherlands East Indies, "ostensibly to get fuel." Thus he preserved them from suffering a minor Pearl Harbor disaster at Manila. They never were brought back. [107]

At 2:20 on the afternoon of November 27 Mr. Hull went to the White House to see Mr. Roosevelt, [108] and at 2:30 the Japanese Ambassadors had an appointment with Mr. Roosevelt and Mr. Hull which lasted for about an hour. It was quite inconclusive. [109] Ambassador Nomura expressed disappointment over the failure to reach any agreement on a *modus vivendi*. Mr. Roosevelt referred to the general peaceful intentions of the United States. Difficulties had been caused by the Japanese occupation of Indo-China, and there were fears, according to recent reports, of more difficulties. He still had hopes of a peaceful settlement, involving a "substantial relaxation" of the American economic restrictions, provided that Japan would first give "some clear manifestation of peaceful intent." There was some desultory reference as to how a peace

CHINESE INTRIGUE TRIUMPHS | 503

conference with China would be initiated. Mr. Hull, as usual, lectured the Ambassadors and said that

> * unless the opposition to the peace element in control of the [Japanese] Government should make up its mind definitely to act and talk and move in a peaceful direction, no conversations could or would get anywhere *.

Saying that no instructions had been received from Japan concerning the most recent American note, Ambassador Nomura expressed the hope that Mr. Roosevelt would "find some way that will lead to a settlement." Mr. Roosevelt said in answer, and in closing the interview, that he had twice postponed his planned vacation; that he expected to leave for Warm Springs on the following afternoon, November 28, to be gone until December 3; that he would like to talk to the Ambassadors after that time, and that "it would be very gratifying if some means of a settlement could be discovered in the meantime."

At 3:45, immediately after this conference, Mr. Roosevelt had an appointment with Admiral King. [110]

To add a touch of humor to the close of an ill-omened day, some mention might be made of a memorandum which Dr. Hornbeck, the political advisor to Mr. Hull, wrote in the Department of State on November 27, estimating the probabilities of the Japanese situation. [111] He expressed the opinions that America was not now "on the immediate verge of 'war' in the Pacific"; that "the Japanese Government does not desire or intend or expect to have *forthwith* armed conflict with the United States," and, particularly, "Were it a matter of placing bets" he would give odds of 5 to 1 that the United States and Japan would *not* be at war on or before December 15, 1941; 3 to 1 against war on or before January 15, 1942, and even money against war by March 1, 1942.

Early in the morning of Friday, November 28, 1941, General Marshall returned from inspecting the Army manoeuvres in the South. The Army-Navy joint memorandum was brought to his attention, and he probably signed it then as "the first business of the day." [112] It was probably sent immediately to Mr. Roosevelt, although this cannot be established with precision. [113] The memorandum, as censored by Mr. Stimson, [114] was an attempt to estimate where Japan might make an attack "If the current negotiations end without agreement *." The most probable points were thought to be the Burma Road, Thailand, or the Philippines. Hawaii was nowhere mentioned. Then, even as censored, the memorandum stated,

> The most essential thing now, from the United States viewpoint is to gain time. *

The military and naval reasons why this was essential were set forth, and it was added,

> * Precipitance of military action on our part should be avoided so long as consistent with national policy. *

Was not the latter part of the quoted sentence Stimsonian? Reference was then made, by generality, to the most secret "American-Dutch-British Conversations" [115] held at Singapore in April 1941, in which the "military authorities * agreed that joint military counteraction" be taken against Japan if she attacked or directly threatened certain specified areas in the southwest Pacific. Therefore the memorandum recommended:

1. That until the Philippines were completely reenforced no military action be taken unless Japan attacked or directly threatened the defined areas. [116]

2. That if Japan advanced into Thailand a joint warning be issued by the United States, Britain, and the Netherlands, and that no military action be taken prior to such a warning.

3. That agreement be reached with the British and the Dutch to issue such a warning.

The American intelligence system in the Far East was by no means inefficient. Reports came in from our diplomatic and consular representatives [117] and, at the moment, the Japanese forces were being watched by our airplanes and trailed by our submarines. [118] Mr. Stimson had directed that Military Intelligence prepare him a summary of such information about the Japanese movements, and it was on his desk when he came in on the morning of November 28. Mr. Stimson's diary states that [119]

> * it amounted to such a formidable statement of dangerous possibilities that I decided to take it over to the President before he got up. *
> He branched into an analysis of the situation himself as he sat there on his bed, saying there were three alternatives and only three that he could see before us. I told him I could see two. His alternatives were—first, to do nothing; second, to make something in the nature of an ultimatum again, stating a point beyond which we would fight; third, to fight at once. I told him my only two were the last two, because I did not think anyone would do nothing in this situation, and he agreed with me. I said of the other two my choice was the latter one.

By implication Mr. Roosevelt did not agree with Mr. Stimson's choice to fight at once, and there the conference ended.

It was now apparent to Mr. Roosevelt that he had simply exchanged one dilemma for another, because, as will presently appear, the Japanese expedition seemed to be steering for territory which was not only not American territory but which was geographically exceedingly remote from the United States and from all American interests. Under such circumstances how could Mr. Roosevelt [120]

> * insure the support of the American people for a decision to fight Japan. *?

Stated more bluntly, Mr. Roosevelt's problem was, [121]

* would the American people be willing to fight for Singapore and Bandoeng?

These were the problems which Mr. Roosevelt must have debated in his mind prior to the meeting of the War Cabinet (Messrs. Hull, Stimson, and Knox and General Marshall and Admiral Stark) with him in the White House at noon that day. Mr. Stimson's diary continues with an account of the debate: [122]

> When we got back there at 12 o'clock [Mr. Roosevelt] had read the paper that I had left with him. The main point of the paper was a study of what the expeditionary force, which we know has left Shanghai and is headed south, is going to do. [Military Intelligence] pointed out that it might develop into an attack on the Philippines or a landing of further troops in Indochina, or an attack on the Dutch Netherlands [East Indies], or on Singapore. After the President had read these aloud, he pointed out that there was one more. It might, by attacking the Kra Isthmus, develop into an attack on Rangoon, which lies only a short distance beyond the Kra Isthmus and the taking of which by the Japanese would effectually stop the Burma Road at its beginning. This, I think, was a very good suggestion on his part and a very likely one. It was the consensus that the present move * completely changed the situation when we last discussed whether or not we could address an ultimatum to Japan about moving the troops which she already had on land in Indochina. It was now the opinion of everyone that if this expedition was allowed to get around the southern point of Indochina and to go off and land in the Gulf of Siam, either at Bangkok or further west, it would be a terrific blow at all of the three Powers, Britain at Singapore, the Netherlands, and ourselves in the Philippines. It was the consensus of everybody that this must not be allowed. Then we discussed how to prevent it. It

was agreed that if the Japanese got into the Isthmus of Kra, the British would fight. *It was also agreed that if the British fought, we would have to fight.* And it now seems clear that if this expedition was allowed to round the southern point of Indochina, this whole chain of disastrous events would be set on foot of going [*sic*].

It further became a consensus of views that rather than strike at the Force as it went by without any warning on the one hand, which we didn't think we could do: or sitting still and allowing it to go on, on the other, which we didn't think we could do—that the only thing for us to do was to address it a warning that if it reached a certain place, or a certain line, or a certain point, we should have to fight. The President's mind evidently was running towards a special telegram from himself to the Emperor of Japan. This he had done with good results at the time of the Panay incident, but for many reasons this did not seem to me to be the right thing now, and I pointed them out to the President. In the first place, a letter to the Emperor of Japan could not be couched in terms which contained an explicit warning. One does not warn an Emperor. In the second place it would not indicate to the people of the United States what the real nature of the danger was. Consequently I said there ought to be a message by the President to the people of the United States, and I thought that the best form of a message would be an address to Congress reporting the danger, reporting what we would have to do if the danger happened. The President accepted this idea of a message but he first thought of incorporating in it the terms of his letter to the Emperor. But again I pointed out that he could not publicize a letter to an Emperor in such a way; that he had better send his letter to the Emperor separate as one thing and a secret thing, and then make his speech to the Congress as a separate and a more understandable thing to the people of the United States. This was the final decision at that time, and the President asked Hull and Knox and myself to try to draft such papers. (Emphasis supplied.)

At this same War Cabinet meeting Mr. Hull testified that he had [123]

> * pointed out that there was practically no possibility of an agreement being achieved with Japan. I emphasized that in my opinion the Japanese were likely to break out at any time with new acts of conquest and that the matter of safeguarding our national security was in the hands of the Army and Navy. With due deference I expressed my judgment that any plans for our military defense should include an assumption that the Japanese might make the element of surprise a central point in their strategy and also might attack at various points simultaneously with a view to demoralizing efforts of defense and of coordination.

Shortly afterwards, at 2:30 P.M., Mr. Roosevelt left Washington for a vacation at Warm Springs, [124] telling reporters that the Japanese situation might require his return at any time. [125]

At some time on November 28 Mr. Hull telephoned Captain R. E. Schuirmann, the Navy's liaison officer with the State Department, and said, in effect, [126]

> I know you Navy fellows are always ahead of me but I want you to know that I don't seem to be able to do anything more with these Japanese and they are liable to run loose like a mad dog and bite anyone.

Captain Schuirmann assured Mr. Hull "that a war warning had been sent out." Navy orders were issued this same day to bomb unidentified submarines found near Hawaii or near our ships at sea. [127] American submarines were put on continuous war patrols from Midway and Wake Islands. [128] Also on November 28 the Army's "let Japan commit the first overt act" dispatch was telegraphed at full length to Admiral Kimmel at Hawaii with this additional order to him: [129]

> *Undertake no offensive action until Japan has committed an overt act.*

Admiral Halsey sailed that day with Task Force 8 from Hawaii to Wake Island to deliver some airplanes there. In popular language it was said that they sailed [130] "under absolute war orders. * the secrecy of our mission was to be protected at all costs. We were to shoot down anything we saw in the sky and bomb anything we saw on the sea." It is certain that the Admiral signalled, [131] "Current operations involve necessity readiness for instant action."

On the diplomatic front a telegram came in from Tokyo to the two Japanese Ambassadors, confirming the instructions over the telephone [132] the previous night from Mr. Yamamoto, the Chief of the American Division of the Japanese Foreign Office, to Ambassador Kurusu not to break off the negotiations. The telegram complimented the Ambassadors on their "superhuman efforts" and referred to the American ten-point note as a "humiliating proposal." [133] The telegram continued:

> * This was quite unexpected and extremely regrettable. The Imperial Government can by no means use it as a basis for negotiations. Therefore, with a report of the views of the Imperial Government on this American proposal which I will send you in two or three days, the negotiations will be de facto ruptured. This is inevitable. However, I do not wish you to give the impression that the negotiations are broken off. *

Instructions followed as to what they were to say, and, finally, they were informed that "Since things have come to this pass" the Japanese Minister of the Navy said that "under the present circumstances" their previous suggestion of November 26 of an exchange of peace messages "is entirely unsuitable." Tentatively and secretly Japan had now decided on war. [134] Another Japanese message of November 28 was intercepted, in which it was stated that the American note would be disregarded: [135]

* There is nothing to do but break off negotiations, and our relations with England and the United States within the next few days will assuredly take a critical turn. *

On November 28, 1941, the British Minister, Sir Ronald Campbell, called on Dr. Hornbeck, [136] stating that if negotiations had "broken down" it would become "necessary to issue certain instructions to the [British] armed forces": he enquired if that was so. Dr. Hornbeck frostily said that he "was not in a position to confirm or deny statements attributed to any American official agency that the negotiations have 'broken down.'" So far as Dr. Hornbeck was aware, neither Government "has declared or indicated that the negotiations are terminated.*"

Whether it was prior or subsequent to the Campbell-Hornbeck interview cannot be determined, but on the morning of November 28, 1941, Lord Halifax called on Mr. Welles. [137] Mr. Welles stated that Lord Halifax quoted the British Government as being "greatly excited." Mr. Welles continued his account of the interview by narrating that Lord Halifax

* read to me a telegram from his government which indicated that our naval officials in London had been informed by the Navy Department that the negotiations between Japan and the United States had been broken off and that an immediate movement by Japan was anticipated, and that consequently precautionary measures must at once be undertaken. The Ambassador inquired whether this was in fact the case. I replied that * I could not say technically that the negotiations had been broken off, although it was, of course, the assumption on the part of the Government of the United States that the Japanese Government would not accept the basis proposed by the Government of the United States. *

According to Mr. Stimson the rest of America's last complete week end at peace "was largely taken up with preparing a suggested draft of a message for the President to deliver to Congress *."[138] On Saturday, November 29, 1941, Mr. Stimson and Mr. Knox each sent proposed drafts [139] to Mr. Hull, who had been working on it with his associates in the State Department. Mr. Knox also sent a copy of his draft direct to Mr. Roosevelt, noting that Admirals Stark and Turner had helped him with it. [140] These draft suggestions were combined by Mr. Hull into a revised draft, [141] which was ready by noon, [142] together with a draft of a proposed message to the Emperor [143] and a memorandum to Mr. Roosevelt from Mr. Hull. [144] Subsequently there was prepared a second revised draft with additional material supplied by Mr. Knox and Admiral Turner. [145]

On November 29 Mr. Hull also found time for a lengthy conversation with the British Ambassador, Lord Halifax, who was not content to rest under the rebuff of Dr. Hornbeck to Sir Ronald Campbell the previous day. Mr. Hull was still resentful of the intrigues against any truce by Dr. Hu Shih and T. V. Soong. With noticeable irritation Mr. Hull first commented, "in a preliminary way," and as if the United States was already a cobelligerent, that [146] * the mechanics for the carrying on of diplomatic relations between the governments resisting aggressor nations are so complicated that it is nearly impossible to carry on such relations in a manner at all systematic and safe and sound. * [147]

In righteous grief Mr. Hull then elaborated upon his current troubles: [146]

> I referred to the fact that Chiang Kai-shek, for example, has sent numerous hysterical cable messages to different Cabinet officers and high officials in the Government other than the State Department, and sometimes even ignoring the President, intruding into a delicate and serious situation with no real idea of what the facts are. * Chiang Kai-shek has his brother-in-law, located here in Washington, disseminate damaging reports at times to the press and others, apparently with no particular purpose in mind;

that we have correspondents from London who interview different officials here, which is entirely their privilege to do, except that at times we all move too fast without fully understanding each other's views * . * this was well illustrated in the case of the recent outburst by Chiang Kai-shek. * it would have been better if, when Churchill received Chiang Kai-shek's loud protest about our negotiations here with Japan, instead of passing the protest on to us without objection on his part, thereby qualifying and virtually killing what we knew were the individual views of the British Government towards these negotiations, he had sent a strong cable back to Chiang Kai-shek telling him to brace up and fight with the same zeal as the Japanese and the Germans are displaying instead of weakening and telling the Chinese people that all of the friendly countries were now striving primarily to protect themselves and to force an agreement between China and Japan, every Chinese should understand from such a procedure that the best possible course was being pursued and that this calls for resolute fighting until the undertaking is consummated by peace negotiations which Japan in due course would be obliged to enter into with China.

Lord Halifax did not disagree with Mr. Hull, who then turned from the past to the present and the future:

I expressed the view that *the diplomatic part of our relations with Japan was virtually over and that the matter will now go to the officials of the Army and the Navy with whom I have talked and to whom I have given my views* for whatever they are worth. Speaking in great confidence, I said that *it would be a serious mistake* for our country and other countries interested in the Pacific situation *to make plans of resistance without including the possibility that Japan may move suddenly and with every possible element of surprise* and spread out over considerable areas and capture certain positions and posts before the peaceful countries interested in the Pacific would have time to confer and formulate plans to meet these new conditions; that this would be on the theory that the Japanese recognize that their course of unlimited conquest now renewed all along the line probably is a desperate gamble and requires the utmost boldness and risk. (Emphasis supplied.)

After a brief résumé of Japanese political potentialities, Mr. Hull concluded,

> * at least it would be a mistake not to consider this possibility as entirely real, rather than to assume that they would virtually halt and engage in some movements into Thailand and into the Burma Road while waiting the results on the Russian front. *

On this latter point Lord Halifax seemed to have had his reservations, and the discussion ended.

Throughout the British Empire there was apparent dismay at the American *volte-face*. Nowhere was the dismay more keen than in the Antipodes. Therefore on November 29, 1941, the Australian Minister, Mr. Richard G. Casey, called on Mr. Hull to propose that Australia should act as a mediator between the United States and Japan. According to his own account of the conversation, Mr. Hull was impatient and brusque to Mr. Casey: he wrote, [148]

> * *I really gave the matter no serious attention* except to tell him that *the diplomatic stage was over* and that nothing would come of a move of that kind. I interrupted to make this conclusive comment before the Minister could make a detailed statement of the matter *. (Emphasis supplied.)

It would appear to be evident that war with Japan was being invited. The diplomatic stage was over. Mediation was unacceptable. The matter had gone to the Army and the Navy. It is therefore not unjust to say that Mr. Hull had pushed the button that started the war. But one must add that the Chinese had joggled his elbow. Mr. Hull and Mr. Roosevelt had not differed on foreign policies once during the past eight years; they were as "two in one," and consequently Mr. Hull ought not to bear the sole onus. Rather the truth is that Mr. Roosevelt was pushing the buttons which might start a war.

The intrigues and manoeuvres and countermanoeuvres of power politics were now practically universal. Far away in Germany, where the Russian campaign was now known to the highest officials to be a failure, the hard-pressed Germans sniffed the ill-wind blowing from the Pacific and attempted to catch at straws of discord. The Japanese Ambassador to Germany was called in by von Ribbentrop for a coaxing on November 29, 1941. His intercepted message to Tokyo reported the ensuing interview as follows: [149]

> Ribbentrop opened our meeting by again inquiring whether I had received any reports regarding the Japanese-United States negotiations. I replied that I had received no official word.
>
> Ribbentrop: "It is essential that Japan effect the New Order in East Asia without losing this opportunity. There never has been and probably never will be a time when closer cooperation under the Tripartite Pact is so important. If Japan hesitates at this time, and Germany goes ahead and establishes her European New Order, all the military might of Britain and the United States will be concentrated against Japan.
>
> "As Fuehrer Hitler said today, there are fundamental differences in the very right to exist between Germany and Japan, and the United States. We have received advice to the effect that there is practically no hope of the Japanese-United States negotiations being concluded successfully because of the fact that the United States is putting up a stiff front.

"If this is indeed the fact of the case, and if Japan reaches a decision to fight Britain and the United States, I am confident that that will not only be to the interest of Germany and Japan jointly, but would bring about favorable results for Japan and herself."

Then the Japanese Ambassador replied:

"I can make no definite statement as I am not aware of any concrete intentions of Japan. Is Your Excellency indicating that a state of actual war is to be established between Germany and the United States?"

The German Foreign Minister evaded making any commitment:

Ribbentrop: "Roosevelt's a fanatic, so it is impossible to tell what he would do."

The Japanese Ambassador thereupon expressed this opinion to Tokyo:

Concerning this point, in view of the fact that Ribbentrop has said in the past that the United States would undoubtedly try to avoid [war] and from the tone of Hitler's recent speech, as well as that of Ribbentrop's, I feel that German attitude toward the United States is being considerably stiffened. There are indications at present that Germany would not refuse to fight the United States if necessary.

Part 3 of the Japanese message quotes von Ribbentrop as follows:

"In any event, Germany has absolutely no intention of entering into any peace with England. We are determined to remove all British influence from Europe. Therefore, at the end of this war, England will have no influence whatsoever in international affairs. The Island Empire of Britain may remain, but all of her other possessions throughout the world will probably be divided three ways by Germany, the United States, and Japan. In Africa, Germany will be satisfied with, roughly, those parts which were formerly German colonies. Italy will be given the greater share of the African colonies. Germany desires, above all else, to control European Russia."

In reply the Japanese Ambassador said:

"I am fully aware of the fact that Germany's war campaign is progressing according to schedule smoothly. However, suppose that Germany is faced with the situation of having not only Great Britain as an actual enemy, but also having all of those areas in which Britain has influence and those countries which have been aiding Britain as actual enemies as well. Under such circumstances, the war area will undergo considerable expansion, of course. What is your opinion of the outcome of the war under such an eventuality?"

Ribbentrop: "We would like to end this war during next year [1942]. However, under certain circumstances, it is possible that it will have to be continued on into the following year [1943].

"Should Japan become engaged in a war against the United States, Germany, of course, would join the war immediately. There is absolutely no possibility of Germany's entering into a separate peace with the United States under such circumstances. The Fuehrer is determined on that point."

This interview may or may not have put new ideas into the minds of the Japanese Cabinet; in any event it led to important consequences during the following week, and it was promptly followed up from Tokyo the following day.

Far away in Thailand the Japanese were plotting to bring that country into the war on their own side, and to manoeuvre the British into committing the first overt act. [150] An intercepted message to Tokyo from the Japanese Ambassador Tsubokami at Bangkok, dated November 29, 1941, read: [151]

CHINESE INTRIGUE TRIUMPHS | 517

Conferences now in progress in Bangkok considering plans aimed at forcing British to attack Thai at Padang Bessa near Singora as counter move to Japanese landing at Kota Bharu. Since Thai intends to consider first invader as her enemy, Japan believes this landing in Malay would force British to invade Thai at Padang Bessa. Thai would then declare war and request [Japanese] help. This plan appears to have approval of Thai Chief of Staff Bijitto. Thai Government circles have been sharply divided between pro-British and pro-[Japanese] until 25 November but now Wanitto and Shin who favor joint military action with [Japan] have silenced anti-[Japanese] group and intend to force Premier Pibul to make a decision. Early and favorable developments are possible.

On the evening of November 29, 1941, Mr. Roosevelt spoke at Warm Springs, prophesying [152] that by Thanksgiving of 1942 Americans might be "looking back on a peaceful past," and that our boys, who are now in training at the naval and military academies, "may actually be fighting in the defense of this country."

November 29 was the final deadline set in the intercepted Japanese messages, and consequently official Washington was on the alert for developments. Speaking in Japan on November 30, which was late in the day of November 29 by Washington time, Prime Minister Tojo was reported [153] to have made a speech before a rally in Tokyo, in the course of which he referred to "many countries who are indulging in actions hostile to us." He was reported to have continued,

> The fact that Chiang Kai-shek is dancing to the tune of Britain, America and communism at the expense of able-bodied and promising young men in his futile resistance against Japan is only due to the desire of Britain and the United States to fish in the troubled waters of East Asia by pitting the East Asiatic peoples against each other and to grasp the hegemony of East Asia. This is a stock in trade of Britain and the United States.
>
> For the honor and pride of mankind we must purge this sort of practice from East Asia with a vengeance. [154]

Mr. Hull was of the opinion that this speech "reflected the extreme acuteness of the situation": it prompted him to telephone Mr. Roosevelt at Warm Springs on the night of November 29, and to advise him to advance the date of his return to Washington. [155] The conversation was lengthy, and Mr. Roosevelt decided to leave Warm Springs on Sunday, November 30, arriving in Washington Monday, December 1, before noon. [156] There was another lengthy telephone conversation between Mr. Hull and Mr. Roosevelt on Sunday morning, November 30. [157]

At Washington on Sunday afternoon, November 30, 1941, a message from Mr. Churchill arrived for Mr. Roosevelt, which inferentially accorded with the decision already reached at the War Cabinet meeting on November 28. Mr. Churchill said: [158]

> It seems to me that one important method remains unused in averting war between Japan and our two countries, namely a plain declaration, secret or public as may be thought best, that any further act of aggression by Japan will lead immediately to the gravest consequences. I realize your constitutional difficulties but it would be tragic if Japan drifted into war by encroachment without having before her fairly and squarely the dire character of a further aggressive step. I beg you to consider whether, at the moment which you judge right which may be very near, you should not say that "any further Japanese aggression would compel you to place the gravest issues before Congress" or words to that effect. We would, of course, make a similar declaration or share in a joint declaration, and in any case arrangements are being made to synchronize our action with yours. Forgive me, my dear friend, for presuming to press such a course upon you, but I am convinced that it might make all the difference and prevent a melancholy extension of the war.

It was not only Mr. Churchill who was anxious to avoid rushing into war. Mr. Casey, the Australian Minister, called on Mr. Hull at his apartment and, referring to his notes, said that [159]

* the British Ambassador desired to urge along with him, the Australian Minister, that I do the best possible to continue our relations with Japan so as to avoid a military conflict at this time, the idea being that they needed more time for preparation to resist in the Pacific area. This view has been asserted constantly during recent weeks by the British Ambassador, the Australian Minister, and twice by the Netherlands Minister

The British Ambassador also called on Mr. Hull on November 30, partly to seek for more time, and partly to deal with the Japanese plans in Thailand: [160] he seemed to be quite unaware of the Japanese plot already mentioned. [161] Lord Halifax left with Mr. Hull a memorandum [162] outlining the British plans for occupying the Kra Isthmus (an additional memorandum was sent the next morning), [163] and he asked what the United States would do if the British took such action. Mr. Hull promised to lay this before Mr. Roosevelt at noon on Monday, December 1, and did so at that time.

From Tokyo on November 30, 1941, Foreign Minister Togo replied to the German bid in a message of the greatest importance. It was telegraphed in three parts, of which the second was never intercepted, nor subsequently found after the war in the Japanese files. [164] We can, however, confidently infer both from Count Ciano's diaries and from a later dispatch, that in the missing parts of the message the respective Japanese Ambassadors to Berlin and to Rome, "invoking the pertinent clause of the Tripartite Pact," were instructed to ask that Germany and "Italy declare war on the United States as soon as the conflict begins." [165] The intercepted parts of this momentous dispatch read: [168]

1. The conversations begun between Tokyo and Washington last April during the administration of the former cabinet, in spite of the sincere efforts of the Imperial Government, now stand

ruptured—broken. * In the face of this, our Empire faces a grave situation and must act with determination. Will Your Honor, therefore, immediately interview Chancellor Hitler and Foreign Minister Ribbentrop and confidentially communicate to them a summary of the developments. Say to them that lately England and the United States have taken a provocative attitude, both of them. Say that they are planning to move military forces into various places in East Asia and that we will inevitably have to counter by also moving troops. Say very secretly to them that there is extreme danger that war may suddenly break out between the Anglo-Saxon nations and Japan through some clash of arms and add that the time of the breaking out of this war may come quicker than anyone dreams.

* * * * * *

4 If, when you tell them this, the Germans and Italians question you about our attitude toward the Soviet, say that we have already clarified our attitude toward the Russians in our statement of last July. Say that by our present moves southward we do not mean to relax our pressure against the Soviet and that if Russia joins hands tighter with England and the United States and resists us with hostilities, we are ready to turn upon her with all our might; however, right now, it is to our advantage to stress the south and for the time being we would prefer to refrain from any direct moves in the north.

5. This message is important from a strategic point of view and must under all circumstances be held in the most absolute secrecy. This goes without saying. Therefore, will you please impress upon the Germans and Italians how important secrecy is.

6. As for Italy, after our Ambassador in Berlin has communicated this to the Germans, he will transmit a suitable translation to Premier Mussolini and Foreign Minister Ciano. As soon as a date is set for a conference with the Germans and Italians, please let me know.

Will you please send this message also to Rome, together with the separate message?

This message was translated and available in Washington on Monday, December 1, 1941: Mr. Roosevelt regarded it as being of such great importance that, contrary to the usual cautious practice in handling the intercepts, he retained a copy of it. [167] We may safely assume, however, that the message was not to be acted upon by the Japanese Ambassadors involved until further instructions were sent.

In Tokyo, on Monday, December 1, 1941, the Japanese Cabinet met at the official residence of Prime Minister Tojo. [168] For public consumption it was stated that the Cabinet had decided to continue negotiations with the United States, and Ambassador Grew telegraphed this report. [169] Actually it is now known that the final decision for war was made at this meeting. [170] Immediately thereafter, on instructions from the Imperial General Headquarters, an Imperial Naval Order was issued, declaring that [171]

> Japan, under the necessity of her self-preservation and self-defense, has reached a position [decision] to declare war on the United States of America *.

This was followed by another order, issued on December 2, under the same instructions: [171]

> The hostile actions against the United States of America * shall be commenced on December 8 [Japanese time, corresponding to December 7 at Hawaii].

Also on December 1, 1941, Tokyo sent messages to its diplomats at London, Hongkong, Singapore, and Manila to destroy their code machines immediately and report such destruction. [172]

And on this same day Malaya was placed in the second degree of readiness for war, and a proclamation of a state of emergency was issued. [173]

At Washington the Japanese Ambassadors called on Mr. Hull on Monday morning, December 1, 1941, [174] before Mr. Roosevelt had returned. In preliminary talk Mr. Hull dwelt upon the better news from Libya and from Russia. He also expressed at some length his resentment of the reported speech of Prime Minister Tojo. The Japanese Ambassadors, who had been much disturbed by the reported speech, as their intercepted communications with Tokyo show, [175] made mollifying remarks, doubting the accuracy of the reports, and they said that they would attempt to clear up the matter, as indeed they did the next day. [176] The Japanese Ambassadors had been instructed by Tokyo under date of November 29 to "make one more attempt" [177] towards peace. This message Mr. Kurusu delivered,

> * that the Japanese Government believed that the proposal * [of] November 20 was equitable *; that the Japanese Government finds it difficult to understand the position taken by the Government of the United States; and that the proposal which [the United States] had communicated to them seemed to fail to take cognizance of the actual conditions in the Far East. * his Government directed him to inquire what was the ultimate aim of the United States in the conversations and to request [the American] Government to make "deep reflection of this matter." * the Japanese offer to withdraw its troops from southern Indochina still stands; that Japan has shown its extreme desire to promote a peaceful settlement.

Mr. Hull went off on a tangent, and the discussion seems to have become more heated than illuminating. At one point he declaimed "that we will not allow ourselves to be kicked out of the Pacific," but his principal complaint appeared to be about the Japanese military moves, past and anticipated, into Indo-China. The conversation had been diverging into Hitler's purposes, off and on, and Mr. Kurusu disclaimed any similarity of purpose. Finally Ambassador Nomura said, almost pathetically, that

> * wars never settle anything and that war in the Pacific would be a tragedy, but he added that the Japanese people believe that the United States wants to keep Japan fighting with China and to keep Japan strangled. He said that the Japanese people feel that they are faced with the alternative of surrendering to the United States or of fighting. * that he was still trying to save the situation. *

Mr. Hull said that he had

> * practically exhausted himself here, that the American people are going to assume that there is real danger to this country in the situation, and that there is nothing he can do to prevent it.

The last feeble candle of hope that war might be averted flickered out as the interview ended on Mr. Hull's note of helplessness.

Yet it was the Japanese Ambassadors who alone refused to give up hope, and who cudgelled their wits for some new idea which might help to preserve peace. After this meeting was over, erroneously believing "that the United States desires to continue the negotiations," they cabled Tokyo a new expedient [178] suggesting that, in place of "a leaders' meeting," a second-rank conference be arranged "between persons in whom the leaders have complete confidence," such as Mr. Wallace or Mr. Hopkins for the United States, and the former Prime Minister, Prince Konoye, or Viscount Ishii for Japan, to be held at "some midway point, such as Honolulu," to "make one final effort to reach some agreement" and thus "facilitate the final decision as to war or peace."

 A MORAL PROBLEM IS SOLVED

SHORTLY BEFORE NOON on December 1, 1941, Mr. Roosevelt, who had just returned to Washington, conferred with Mr. Hull and with Admiral Stark.[1] In his prepared statement for the Congressional Committee Mr. Hull omitted all reference to this meeting,[2] and possibly because of this omission he was never examined on the point and did not volunteer any reference to it.[3] Likewise Admiral Stark was never directly examined on the point and did not volunteer any reference to it in his prepared statement.[4]

Mr. Hopkins was driven in from the Naval Hospital, "where he has been ill for weeks,"[5] to participate in a luncheon conference with Mr. Roosevelt. Clearly some highly important decision was about to be made. And clearly this important decision required such secrecy that Mr. Roosevelt dared not use the telephone to consult the "crafty"[6] Mr. Hopkins, as the adulatory Mr. Ludwig characterized him.

In the light of the swift developments it can almost surely be conjectured that the problem discussed at the White House that noon was how to get America to enter the war if only Thailand, or only Singapore, should be attacked by Japan. And it can further be conjectured that the method finally devised was to create an "incident" in which Japan would commit the first overt act by firing on the American flag and simultaneously sinking one or more American warships.

Thus was born at this conference the Case of the Cockleshell Warships.

So far as it is possible to ascertain, this was the only occasion on which Admiral Stark saw Mr. Roosevelt that day. Later that afternoon Admiral Stark sent out to Admiral Hart, commanding the United States Asiatic Fleet in the Far East, a message of extraordinary significance in the light of Mr. Roosevelt's purposes and problems.

The problem was, it must be repeated, how, in the absence of a direct attack on America, could the American people be persuaded to fight for Singapore or for Bandoeng? Or, how could the Japanese be manoeuvered into the position of firing the first shot without too much danger to the United States? Mr. Roosevelt, as has already been noted, liked to do a job the smart way, and he had personally instructed [7] Admiral Stark, presumably that same day, to send the following dispatch: [8]

> *President directs* that the following be done as soon as possible and within two days if possible after receipt this despatch. Charter 3 small vessels to form a "defensive information patrol." Minimum requirements to establish identity as U. S. men-of-war are command by a naval officer and to mount a small gun and 1 machine gun would suffice. Filipino crews may be employed with minimum number naval ratings to accomplish purpose which is to

observe and report by radio Japanese movements in west China Sea and Gulf of Siam. One vessel to be stationed between Hainan and Hue, one vessel off the Indo-China Coast between Camranh Bay and Cape St. Jacques and one vessel off Pointe de Camau. *Use of Isabel authorized by President* as one of the three but *not* other naval vessels. Report measures taken to carry out President's views. * (Emphasis supplied.)

On December 2 Admiral Hart responded that he was recalling the *Isabel* from her current mission.[9] This was perhaps not swift enough for the development of Mr. Roosevelt's plans, and Admiral Stark telegraphed back that the *Isabel* might be replaced by a chartered vessel at Admiral Hart's discretion.[10]

Fortunately for the men aboard her, the *Isabel* finally departed on this mission only a few hours before the attack on Pearl Harbor and came back at once: the other vessels never did start out.[11] No "incident" occurred, no Japanese overt act took place with respect to these three cockleshell warships in those particular waters.

What a "smart" plan it was! First, the beguiling and misleading name, adapted from the one first used in the Atlantic—"defensive information patrol." Next, the use of the American flag, and the attempt to convert these pitifully *"small"* chartered vessels into "U. S. men-of-war." Next, the provocation offered. These vessels were "to be stationed," that is, put in fixed positions (perhaps anchored), in what was believed to be the principal and direct path of the Japanese advance. There they were "to observe and report by radio," no mention being required of the use of code, the "Japanese movements." Next, the lack of need for sending out these little "men-of-war." The *Isabel*, the only vessel previously on the Navy list, was merely a converted yacht, used occasionally by the Commander in Chief of the Asiatic Fleet. Planes from Manila were conducting frequent reconnaissances, and getting from these searches what the Navy believed was "sufficient information." Indeed the Navy pointedly stated that it "did not initiate this movement," and "would not have done this unless" Mr. Roosevelt had specifically ordered it to be done. [12] Guardedly answering a question, Admiral Hart hinted [13] that in his opinion these small vessels were *not* being sent out for patrol purposes: "I wouldn't say that your analysis was quite correct." Finally, note the combination of frugality and of helplessness, presumably for emphasis in the ensuing indignant publicity—"a *small* gun and one machine gun would suffice." Such miserably small vessels would be at the utter mercy of any Japanese warship whatsoever in a hopelessly unequal and foredoomed encounter. And such vessels, with a frugal "minimum number [of] naval ratings" and "Filipino crews" would represent no substantial loss to the nation's naval strength. It is small wonder that, having personally directed the issuance of such an order, Mr. Roosevelt had a "terrible moral problem" [14] on his conscience for the rest of the week.

After this noon-day conference on December 1, 1941, Mr. Roosevelt called Mr. Welles to the White House; next, Mr. Welles "on orders" conferred with Lord Halifax, and then Mr. Welles returned to confer with Mr. Roosevelt for an hour and a half. [15] All that was said remains secret. Indicative of the trend of the official thinking of the moment was an interview which Mr. Hugh G. Grant, who had recently resigned as United States Minister to Thailand, gave to the press on December 1, 1941, in which he declared that [16]

> If the Japanese really want war, now is the time to let them have it.
>
> I believe we could smash them within a few months with our superior air and naval forces.

On the morning of Tuesday, December 2, 1941, Mr. Soong and Dr. Alfred Sze came in to see Mr. Stimson. [17] The latter felt that the suspicious Chinese merely wanted to have a witness to corroborate Mr. Stimson's statement that we intended to fortify the Philippines. Mr. Stimson said that there was no change in American policy, and he then threw out a broad but guarded hint: tell "the Generalissimo * to have just a little more patience and then I think all things will be well." Apparently that was all the Chinese callers wanted to know; they at once got up and thanked Mr. Stimson and went away.

At the State Department the same day the Chinese were attempting to mollify Mr. Hull. The Chinese Ambassador called in order to hand Mr. Hull, who was absent, due to a cold, a statement [18] from the Generalissimo and from Dr. Quo, the Foreign Minister. Yet at the same time this statement insisted on the Chinese viewpoint and referred to the "truly panicky feeling throughout China" at "the mere rumor of any possibility" of the relaxation of the Japanese embargo.

In Mr. Hull's absence Mr. Welles called in the Japanese Ambassadors on the morning of December 2 and, at Mr. Roosevelt's direct instructions, formally demanded the Japanese reasons for sending additional troops into Indo-China. [19] Some tendentious conversation followed, in the course of which Admiral Nomura repeated his remark that wars did not settle anything, and that "some agreement, even though it is not satisfactory, is better than no agreement at all." A little later in the conversation Ambassador Kurusu asked if the conversations could not be resumed on the old basis which existed prior to the American ten-point note of November 26. Mr. Welles said that he would refer this suggestion to Mr. Hull, and the interview ended.

It was on December 2, 1941, that Tokyo cabled the Japanese Embassy at Washington and at various other places [20] to destroy all copies of all codes, except one copy each of two specified codes, and to destroy all files and all other secret documents: this message was intercepted and available on December 3.

Soon after his meeting with the Japanese Ambassadors, [21] Mr. Welles went to the White House at noon to attend a meeting at which only Mr. Roosevelt, Mr. Stimson, Mr. Knox, and Mr. Welles were present. Mr. Stimson wrote in his diary: [22]

> * The President went step by step over the situation and I think has made up his mind to go ahead. He has asked the Japanese through Sumner Welles what they intend by this new occupation of southern Indochina—just what they are going to do—and has demanded a quick reply. The President is still deliberating the possibility of a message to the Emperor, although all the rest of us are rather against it, but in addition to that he is quite settled, I think, that he will send a message to the Congress and will perhaps back that up with a speech to the country. He said that he was going to take the matters right up when he left us.

The meaning of this guarded statement is clear: Mr. Roosevelt had already "made up his mind to go ahead" to war. Not only is this confirmed by the *Isabel* order: it is also confirmed by the "quite settled" decision to "send a message to the Congress," and by the fact that Mr. Hull in his memorandum to Mr. Roosevelt accompanying the draft message wrote: [23]

> * I think *we agree* that you will not send message [*sic*] to Congress *until* the *last* stage of our relations, *relating to actual hostilities, has been reached*. (Emphasis supplied.)

Mr. Roosevelt held a press conference on the afternoon of December 2, 1941. The State Department's official copy of what Mr. Roosevelt said is as follows: [24]

The President was asked if the Japanese marched into Thailand what would the United States Government do? *The President evaded the question.* Another correspondent asked if the President could give any indication of the nature of the information requested from the Japanese Representatives this morning. The President said let us put it this way, and this answers again many questions at the same time. Since last April we have been discussing with the Japanese some method to arrive at an objective that is permanent peace in the whole area in the Pacific and at times it seemed that progress was being made. During the whole period up to the end of June we assumed that as both nations were negotiating toward that objective—there would be no act contrary to the desired end of peace. We were therefore somewhat surprised when the Japanese Government sent troops to a specific over-all total into Indo-China after very brief negotiations with the Vichy Government at the conclusion of which the Vichy Government let it be understood clearly that they had agreed to this number of troops principally because they were powerless to do anything else.

Sometime later conversations were resumed with the United States and again we made it perfectly clear that the objective we were seeking meant the taking of no additional territory by anyone in the Pacific area. We received word the other day that there were large additional bodies of Japanese forces of various kinds, including troops, planes, war vessels, etc., in Indo-China and that other forces were on the way. Before these forces had arrived the number of forces already there had greatly exceeded the original amount agreed to by the French and the number on the way were much greater, and the question asked this morning, very politely, at my request, was as to what the purpose and intention of the Japanese Government was as to the future, eliminating the necessity of policing Indo-China which is a very peaceful spot and we hope to receive a reply in the near future.

In reply to a question as to whether any time for a reply had been set, the President said that there had naturally been no time limit set.

As reported by the New York *Times*, [25] Mr. Roosevelt is reported also to have said that Japan was "a friendly power with which the United States was at peace."

It was probably on December 2, 1941, that the Japanese Ambassadors in Berlin and Rome were ordered to take action, because on Wednesday morning, December 3, at 11:00 the Japanese Ambassador called on Mussolini and Count Ciano and asked Italy to declare war on the United States as soon as the conflict began. [26] The Italians were quite unprepared for this request, which Count Ciano characterized in his diary as "A stunning move by the Japanese." [27] Mussolini, whose mental and physical powers were failing, was "happy about it," [27] and proudly boasted of his foresight. [28] The intelligent Count Ciano felt quite otherwise and glumly set forth in his diary: [27]

> * that Roosevelt has succeeded in his maneuvre, not being able to enter the war directly, he has succeeded by an indirect route—forcing the Japanese to attack him. *

As reported to Count Ciano, the German reaction, on second thought, was not enthusiastic: [27]

> Berlin reaction to the Japanese step is extremely cautious. * the idea of provoking American intervention is less and less liked by the Germans. *

Halfway across the world, what was described as a "New British Fleet" steamed into Singapore upon December 2, 1941. [29] Its principal elements were the ill-fated *Prince of Wales* and *Repulse:* its equally ill-fated Admiral, Sir Tom S. V. Phillips, had arrived there a week ahead of the fleet. [30]

Von Ribbentrop, when interviewed by the Japanese Ambassador on December 3, was highly cautious. He declined to make any official reply to the Japanese request for participation in an American war until he had been in touch with, and had secured the approval of, Hitler, who "was at a distant place," and he insisted on seeing Hitler personally, refusing to telephone him. Von Ribbentrop thought that he might have word for the Japanese by December 4 or 5. [31]

On December 3, 1941, Tokyo cabled a noncommittal reply to Mr. Roosevelt's inquiry. [32] The Japanese Ambassadors doubted the expediency of delivering this reply, and that same day asked for a reconsideration of it by Tokyo, observing, [33]

> * it is being rumored among the journalists that this reply is to be the key deciding whether there will be war or peace between Japan and the United States. There is no saying but what the United States Government will take a bold step depending upon how our reply is made. If it is really the intention of our government to arrive at a settlement, the explanation you give, I am afraid, would neither satisfy them nor prevent them taking the bold step referred to—even if your reply is made for the mere purpose of keeping the negotiations going. *

And, in addition, that same day they sent this further warning to Tokyo: [34]

> Judging from all indications, we feel that some joint military action between Great Britain and the United States, with or without a declaration of war, is a definite certainty in the event of an occupation of Thailand.

Likewise on December 3, 1941, Tokyo cabled the Ambassadors and with reference to their recent proposal for a second-rank conference stated [35] "that it would be inappropriate for us to propose such a meeting again at this time."

There were further Japanese messages concerning code destruction on December 3, 1941, and it was on this day that General Miles, with General Marshall's knowledge and approval, cabled the American Embassy at Tokyo to destroy our code machine there.[36]

At Washington, on December 3, 1941, Mr. Hull held a press conference at which he reviewed the matters which he had already covered at the November 27 press conference.[37] He made his position plain that at no time had the Japanese Government shown any disposition to modify its basic policies, which he described as being at complete variance with those of the United States.[38]

These mid-week days were the lull before the final storm. On the morning of Thursday, December 4, 1941, six majority and minority leaders of the Senate and of the House of Representatives met with Mr. Roosevelt for two hours [39] in what he no doubt intended to be a preliminary seminar "in connection with the defense of our own territories and vital interests in the Far East." They were said to have left the White House "with the impression that the situation is critical, but will not necessarily come to a show-down *." That afternoon the Senate adjourned until December 8, and the next day the House also adjourned until December 8. At 3:30 that afternoon of December 4, Mr. Hull conferred with Mr. Roosevelt,[40] but we do not know anything about the discussion. That evening unidentified individuals,[41] "Cabinet members having close relations with the President and * individuals equally influential," dined with Mr. Roosevelt and

> * advised him against a Japanese-American war and urged him to do the "introducing" at once between Japan and China. However, the President did not make known what he had in mind. According to these men, this attitude of the President is his usual attitude. *

On December 4 Tokyo cabled the Japanese Ambassadors and declined to give more explanations: they were instructed to deliver the reply to Mr. Roosevelt's questions as originally sent. [42] There was also another message concerning the destruction of codes. [43] The Japanese Embassy in Berlin cabled Tokyo as to the evacuation of the Embassy in London, [44] and Tokyo cabled various points in China as to a possible war with the Netherlands. [45] Likewise the Navy received the controverted "winds" code message, "War with England, War with America, Peace with Russia." [46]

At the State Department, on the afternoon of December 4, the First Secretary of the British Embassy, Mr. Hayter, called on Mr. Hamilton of the Far Eastern Division [47] to discuss a possible arrangement with Japan for the evacuation of officials and nationals "in the event of British-Japanese hostilities." Mr. Hamilton felt the American Government should attempt to make a similar arrangement, but, he concluded,

> As the making of such an approach would be interpreted by the American public as a definite indication that this Government expects war between Japan and the United States *—

Mr. Hull might wish to consult Mr. Roosevelt first before expressing any opinion.

Mr. Stimson went up to New York to see his dentist [48] because, as he told his press conference on December 5, the following day, he was assured that "the conversations with Japan were still in progress." [49] This assertion was made, the minority of the Pearl Harbor Committee states, "notwithstanding [his] intimate knowledge of the imminence of war." [50] At this same press conference Mr. Stimson also complained in bitter language of the action of the Chicago *Tribune* in revealing the secret plan of the Administration to conscript an army of ten million men, half of whom were to form a new expeditionary force to be sent in Europe in 1943. [51]

In Australia, on December 5, active steps were being taken in preparation for war—active, but pessimistic, because the existence in the near future of a state of blockade was foreseen. [52]

On the morning of Friday, December 5, 1941, Mr. Hull conferred with Mr. Roosevelt for a short time before meeting the Japanese Ambassadors. [53] The Japanese Ambassadors presented their reply, [54] as ordered, which stated that the Japanese troops in Indo-China had been reinforced because the Chinese troops along the frontier had "recently shown frequent signs of movements *." In the ensuing discussion [55] Mr. Hull said sarcastically, "so Japan has assumed the defensive against China." There was some further talk about the situation in Indo-China and then Admiral Nomura said to Mr. Hull:

> You keep bringing up the subject of our occupation of French Indo-China. Basically this is merely a phase of "power politics." Your country herself, has stated that the "best defense is an offense." Your military men in particular have taken this adage literally, and as proof thereof, have been making every effort to strengthen the army and the fleet of the ABCD [American-British-Chinese-Dutch]. With this situation being flaunted before their eyes, our army and navy cannot remain unconcerned.

Mr. Hull asked whether these observations applied to the American measures being taken against Hitler. Admiral Nomura backed away from that, and went back to the Japanese proposal of November 20. Mr. Hull returned to his own favorite topic—"the matter of the aid Japan is giving to Hitler." Mr. Kurusu asked, how? Mr. Hull said "by keeping large forces *of this country* and other countries immobilized in the Pacific *." *Sotto voce* Admiral Nomura said, in Japanese, "this isn't getting us anywhere!" So the conversation went round and round, and ended with some criticism of the press of each country. Following this conference Mr. Hull lunched at the White House with Mr. Roosevelt.

A MORAL PROBLEM IS SOLVED | 537

That morning Mr. Roosevelt had dictated a letter to Mr. Willkie, in connection with a proposed visit to Australia, in which the latter was warned: [56]

> * There is always the Japanese matter to consider. The situation is definitely serious and there might be an armed clash at any moment if the Japanese continued their forward progress against the Philippines, Dutch Indies or Malaya or Burma. Perhaps the next four or five days will decide the matter.

At 2:00 o'clock there was a general cabinet meeting, [57] but what happened at it remains unknown. Perhaps it had to do with a cable which was sent that day to Ambassador Winant in London to be read to Mr. Eden personally. [58] Mr. Eden was about to leave to confer with the Russians, and the Russians were already commencing to make territorial demands. Mr. Roosevelt, who initialled the cable message, now viewed the United States as being to all intents and purposes wholly in the war, so much so that the post-war arrangements were already being discussed. The more significant portions of this cable read: [58]

> It is our conviction that the test of our good faith with regard to the Soviet Union is the measure to which we fulfill the commitments our representatives made in Moscow. *
>
> In so far as our post war policies are concerned, it is our belief that these have been delineated in the Atlantic Charter which today represents the attitude not only of the United States but also of Great Britain and of the Soviet Union.
>
> In view of this fact in our considered opinion it would be unfortunate were any of the three governments * to express any willingness to enter into commitments regarding specific terms of the post war settlement. * Upon the conclusion of hostilities those nations contributing to the defeat of the Hitler forces will join in an effort to restore peace and order. The participation at that

time of the Soviet Government will be no less than that of Great Britain and our own. In order not to jeopardize * an enduring peace it is evident that *no commitments as to individual countries should be entered into at this time. * Above all there must be no secret accords.* (Emphasis supplied.)

It is a pity that a little more than three years later, at Yalta, Mr. Roosevelt reversed himself on this principle.

Later in the day of December 5, 1941—probably in the evening—Lord Halifax called at Mr. Hull's apartment. Mr. Hull's report of the conversation was guarded and extremely brief. [59] The British Ambassador

* said he had a message from Eden, head of the British Foreign Office, setting forth the British view that the time has now come for immediate cooperation with the Dutch East Indies by mutual understanding. This of course relates to the matter of defense against Japan.

At 10:00 o'clock that evening Mr. Hull sent a telegram to the American Embassy at Tokyo, [60] to apply to "all offices in Japan, Japanese occupied areas in China, Hong Kong, Indo China and Thailand," giving them authority to destroy

* all confidential files, seals, codes, ciphers, true readings, protectograph dies, et cetera *.

It was also on December 5, 1941, that the Japanese Embassy at Washington reported to Tokyo the destruction of codes, but asked authority to keep one machine, [61] which, on December 6, Tokyo authorized "for the time being." [62] Then, on December 7, it ordered the destruction of the remaining machine, codes, and secret documents. [63] Likewise on December 5 the Japanese ministry at Panama reported [64] to Tokyo the destruction of its code books, while

Peking reported to Tokyo its own proposed similar arrangements, [65] "Concurrent with opening war on Britain and America * [and] In case war breaks out with Holland *." War was obviously just around the corner, and everybody in the topmost official positions knew it. In fact the final order to attack Pearl Harbor had that day been sent to the Japanese fleet, then 800 miles north of Hawaii. [66]

The significant events of Saturday, December 6, 1941, began early in the day. Between 7:15 and 7:20 A.M. a Navy monitoring station intercepted a message [67] from Tokyo to the Japanese Ambassadors which has subsequently been called the "pilot message." The pilot message read: [68]

1. The Government has deliberated deeply on the American proposal of the 26th of November and as a result we have drawn up a memorandum for the United States contained in my separate message No. 902 in English.

2. This separate message is a very long one. I will send it in fourteen parts and I imagine you will receive it tomorrow. However, I am not sure. The situation is extremely delicate, and when you receive it I want you to please keep it secret for the time being.

3. Concerning the time of presenting this memorandum to the United States, I will wire you in a separate message. However, I want you in the meantime to put it in nicely drafted form and make every preparation to present it to the Americans just as soon as you receive instructions.

The pilot message was delivered by the Navy to the Army for decoding and translation by 12:05 P.M., [69] while shortly before that time the first five or six parts of the fourteen parts of the following longer message were also received by the Navy for decoding. [70] This took less time than ordinarily, because, already being in English, the longer message did not have to be translated. [71]

Later on in the morning Admiral Stark received a message from Admiral Hart at Manila [72] stating that two Japanese convoys were "sailing slowly westwards toward Kra 14 hours distant in time." This was sent to Mr. Hull about 1:50 P.M. [73] Meanwhile, at 10:40 A.M. the State Department had received the same information, via Ambassador Winant, marked "Personal and secret to the Secretary and the President," both of whom received it. [74]

Mr. Roosevelt's appointments that morning were negligible. [75] Presumably it was after his receipt of the message concerning the two Japanese convoys that he found time to peruse two special memoranda, which he had asked to be prepared on December 5, concerning the total number of Japanese troops in Indo-China, [76] and the Japanese naval forces in that vicinity. [77] At or about the same time Admiral Hart, in the Far East, was considering this and other problems, such as the American objections to the ABD plan, in secret conference [78] concerning "the war which then was coming, within a day or two" with the British Admiral Sir Tom S. V. Phillips, the British Far Eastern naval commander, who, as has been mentioned, had arrived at Singapore a little ahead of the *Prince of Wales* and *Repulse*. [79] Admiral Hart's joint report of his war plans made with Admiral Phillips was received at Washington late on December 6, 1941. [80] Earlier in the day Admiral Hart had received, and had then enquired of Washington [81] about, a dispatch from the United States Naval Attaché at Singapore, which referred to British Air Marshal Sir Robert Brooke-Popham, who simultaneously commanded the Royal Air Force in Malaya and the British Army there. [82] The dispatch read: [83]

> Brooke Popham received Saturday from War Department London:—
>
> "We have now received assurance of American armed support in cases as follows:
>
> "A. We are obliged execute our plans to stall Japs landing Isthmus of Kra or take action in reply to Nips invasion any other part of Siam;

"B. If Dutch Indies are attacked and we go to their defense;

"C. If Japs attack us, the British.

"Therefore without reference to London, put plan in action if

"First; you have good info [information] Jap expedition advancing with the apparent intention of landing in Kra,

"Second; if the Nips violate any part of Thailand.

"If N[etherlands] E[ast] I[ndies] are attacked put into operation plans agreed upon between British and Dutch."

From Budapest there came this astonishing report to Tokyo as of December 6: [84]

On the 6th the American Minister presented to the Government of this country a British Government communique to the effect that a state of war would break out on the 7th.

This was thought to be of such importance that it was relayed to Berlin.

Also during December 6 a Japanese message was received which was a complete tip-off on the declaration of war. [85] It was, unfortunately, not decoded until December 8, perhaps because it seemed to be garbled. It read (bracketing the garbled or variant words) as follows:

$$\text{The} \begin{Bmatrix} \text{proclamation} \\ \text{or} \\ \text{declaration} \end{Bmatrix} \text{day (X day) decided by the} \begin{Bmatrix} \text{ambassadorial} \\ \text{or} \\ \text{China} \end{Bmatrix}$$

$$\text{liaison conference on} \begin{Bmatrix} \text{November} \\ \text{or} \\ \text{the sixth} \end{Bmatrix} \text{is the 8th and the day on which}$$

the notice is to be given is the 7th (Sunday). As soon as you have received this message, please reply to that effect.

Japan in fact declared war—"X-day"—at 6:00 A.M. on December 8, [86] Japanese time, and "the day on which the notice [was] given" at Washington was December 7, Washington time! Among all the tragic blunders which accompanied the American entry into the war the failure to observe promptly the importance of this message was not the least.

Joint action against Japan was not only being planned on December 6; probably it had already been tentatively agreed upon. On December 7 Mr. Churchill submitted for Mr. Roosevelt's comments a long and formal draft of a proposed declaration to Japan in the name of Great Britain and of the various dominions. The Netherlands Government had already seen the draft, and by inference approved of it: the Dominion Governments were being "consulted urgently" to approve it. [87] That this joint action had been tentatively agreed upon on December 6 is proved by a message from the Australian Minister in Washington, sent to Australia on December 6, which was quoted and contained in the telegraphed consent which Australia sent to London: [88]

> Subject to conditions that President gives prior approval to text of warning as drafted and also gives signal for actual delivery of warning, we concur in draft as a joint communication from all His Majesty's Governments. I point out that message from Australian Minister at Washington just received notes that,
>
> 1. President has decided to send message to Emperor.
> 2. President's subsequent procedure is that if no answer is received by him from the Emperor by Monday evening [Dec. 8],
>   a. he will issue his warning on Tuesday afternoon or evening [Dec. 9],
>   b. warning or equivalent by British or others will not follow until Wednesday morning [Dec. 10], i.e., after his own warning has been delivered repeatedly to Tokyo and Washington.

The information regarding the procedure to be followed by Mr. Roosevelt came orally from him to the Australian Minister late in the afternoon of December 6. [89]

The draft of the proposed British warning [90] recited that the various British Governments had "followed closely in consultation with the United States" the Japanese negotiations. Mr. Roosevelt's inquiry of December 2 was mentioned, and the Japanese reply was characterized as "extremely disquieting." The note then referred to the Japanese troops in Indo-China, and expressed an

> * assumption that the Japanese Government are preparing for some further aggressive move directed against the Netherlands East Indies, Malaya or Thailand.

With reference to the first territory, the note stated,

> Relations between the Governments of the British Commonwealth and the Netherlands Government are too well known for the Japanese Government to be under any illusion as to their reaction to an attack on territories of the Netherlands. *

As to an attack upon Thailand,

> * They [H. M. Governments] feel bound therefore to warn the Japanese Government in the most solemn manner that if Japan attempts to establish her influence in Thailand by force or threat of force she will do so at her own peril and His Majesty's Governments will at once take all appropriate measures. Should hostilities unfortunately result the responsibility will rest with Japan.

The reader will have noted that no guarantee was offered by Britain to the United States if the Philippines alone were attacked by Japan.

In mid-afternoon a second message came in from Ambassador Winant in London, referring in part to the destination of the

Japanese convoys, but also confirming the pending arrangement with Britain: [91]

> British feel pressed for time in relation to guaranteeing support Thailand fearing Japan might force them to invite invasion on pretext protection before British have opportunity to guarantee support but wanting to carry out President's wishes in message transmitted by Welles to Halifax.

Mr. Hull had now prepared and had sent to Mr. Roosevelt, at his request, a redraft of a proposed message [92] to the Japanese Emperor which was genuinely peaceable in tone and which embodied a "stand-still arrangement." It proposed a ninety-day armistice between China and Japan, an approach by Mr. Roosevelt to China to negotiate peace, a reduction of forces in Indo-China, and a resumption of the conversations between Japan and America "looking to a peaceful settlement in the entire Pacific area." For unknown reasons this peaceable approach was promptly abandoned. A further redraft was made and submitted. [93] Except for the additional redrafting of one page, referring to the most recent concentration of Japanese troops in Indo-China, it thereafter remained in this form, in which it was finally sent.

Part of this Saturday afternoon activity, unusual in Washington, may be presumed to have been due to the knowledge that a long and important message from Japan was coming in. The "pilot message" was decoded, translated, and available to Mr. Hull, Mr Stimson, and various military personalities by 3:00 P.M. [94] The Army's head of the Far Eastern Section had had it by 2:00 P.M. [95] And the balance of the longer message—except for the final, fourteenth part—was received in the Navy Department at Washington at 2:51 P.M. [96] Captain Safford, in charge of the Navy's Communications Intelligence Unit, [97] promptly realized the great importance of the longer message: it was unusual because, for the first time, the Japanese "became very abusive in their language," and he concluded [98]

> That they were breaking off diplomatic relations with the presentation of that note, and this was particularly in view of the instructions which they had given in the pilot message about its presentation and holding its presentation until they were told to do it.

Whether, in addition to knowledge from the pilot message that this important communication from Japan was arriving, Mr. Roosevelt knew by preliminary telephone calls of its nature cannot now be determined. Whatever the facts may be, Mr. Roosevelt rushed over to Mr. Hull at the end of the day, for his approval, the final draft of his message to the Emperor with these instructions: [99]

> O.K.—send the amended p. 3 to the British Ambassador *.
>
> F.D.R.

and [100]

> Shoot this to Grew. I think [it] can go in gray code—saves time—I don't mind if it gets picked up.
>
> F.D.R.

Accordingly, at 8:00 P.M. a preliminary cable was sent to Ambassador Grew [101] to expect "an important telegram" to be communicated "at earliest possible moment * to the Emperor." At 9:00 P.M. the full message was sent out to Mr. Grew. [102] Simultaneously a copy was sent to Ambassador Gauss at Chungking, to be communicated "in person if feasible, at the earliest possible moment to Chiang Kai-shek." The telegram to Mr. Gauss concluded: [103]

> In communicating copy of this message to Chiang Kai-shek, please state orally as from the President that the quoted message has already been sent by the President to the Emperor; that this message, as the situation now stands, would seem to represent very nearly the last diplomatic move that this Government can make toward causing Japan to desist from its present course; that if the slender chance of acceptance by Japan should materialize, a very effective measure would have been taken toward safeguarding the Burma Road; and that it is very much hoped that Chiang Kai-shek will not make or allow to be spread in Chinese Government circles adverse comment.

It seems obvious that this final paragraph was intended to prevent another outburst of Chinese hysterics, publicity, and propaganda.

After Mr. Hull, Mr. Stimson, and Mr. Knox had received [104] the first thirteen parts of the Japanese fourteen-part message on the evening of December 6, they arranged over the telephone for a conference on Sunday morning, December 7, 1941, at 10:00. [105] The records show a spate of telephone calls among them from 8:30 to 8:50 on the evening of December 6, viz.: [106]

Secretary Knox called Secretary Stimson.
Secretary Knox called Secretary Hull.
Secretary Hull called Secretary Knox.
Secretary Knox called Secretary Stimson.
Secretary Knox called Operations, War Department.

No later calls are recorded. It is evident that the decoded message was delivered to them before 8:30 P.M. or else that by that time they had word of its substance.

General Marshall disclaimed knowledge of the message that evening. [107] He was probably staying home with his sick wife, but he was not quite certain, [108] until later. [109] General Marshall's subordinates "all caught hell" if Admiral Stark ever got an intercept before General Marshall did. [110] Afterwards General Marshall made no investigation of this alleged failure to send the intercept to him. [111] It is odd.

Mr. Roosevelt, who had been giving a large dinner at 8:00 o'clock [112] received the intercept about 9:30. [113] He was in his study with Mr. Hopkins, and the naval officer noted that Mr. Roosevelt "was expecting" the papers. He read them, which took about ten minutes, and gave them to Mr. Hopkins to read. Then Mr. Roosevelt said, in substance, that this meant war. For perhaps five minutes Mr. Roosevelt and Mr. Hopkins discussed where the Japanese troops were, and then,

> Mr. Hopkins * expressed a view that since war was undoubtedly going to come at the convenience of the Japanese, it was too bad that we could not strike the first blow and prevent any sort of surprise.

Mr. Roosevelt nodded, but he replied,

> * "No, we can't do that. We are a democracy and a peaceful people." Then he raised his voice, and this much I remember definitely. He said, "But we have a good record."

The last remark in the louder voice appears to have been for the benefit of the naval officer. Mr. Roosevelt then attempted to telephone Admiral Stark, who was at the National Theatre seeing "The Student Prince." Mr. Roosevelt said "that he would reach the Admiral later, that he did not want to cause public alarm by having the Admiral paged *." The naval officer left about 10:00. After Admiral Stark got home he telephoned Mr. Roosevelt and, after doing so, said to his guests "that the situation with Japan was very serious." [114] This must have been at least fourteen hours before the attack began at Pearl Harbor.

Nobody did anything.

No warnings were sent out.

All of the top American personalities went promptly to bed, slept soundly, and awoke late on Sunday morning, December 7, 1941.

Everybody seemed to be ostentatiously casual that fatal Sunday morning, almost as if they were preparing alibis. General Marshall had breakfast, looked at the Sunday papers, went for a horseback ride in Virginia, and was having a shower after his ride when he was finally summoned to the War Department. [115] Admiral Stark "was lazy on Sunday mornings": he took a walk around his grounds and greenhouse and "didn't hurry about getting down" to his office, which he reached about 10:30 or 11:00. [116]

Mr. Roosevelt, knowing that war was imminent, had decided to take the day off so as to catch up with his neglected stamp collection: Mr. Hopkins was still lounging around the White House in pajamas and dressing gown at 1:00 P.M. [117]

Ordinary American citizens, if that day they were reading the *Herald Tribune* in or near New York, no doubt noticed and were reassured by Mr. Knox's annual report as Secretary of the Navy. It was prominently displayed in Section I on page 1, column 1, and the so-soon-to-be-bitterly-mocking headline read:

KNOX ASSERTS NAVY IS NOW EQUAL OF ANY

The body of the article continued:

> Mr. Knox pointed out the international situation was such that the United States naval defenses must be prepared for an attack by any possible combination of powers.

* * * * * *

---

* He pointed out that the degree of effectiveness of a warship is determined by the efficiency of its crew.

One of Mr. Knox's policies was

> To make effectiveness in war the objective of all developments and training.

In the New York *Times* the body of the article on the same topic was about the same in substance, but the headline was superlative: [118]

Navy Is Superior to Any, Says Knox

The earliest risers in Washington seem to have been the elderly Messrs. Hull and Stimson, who were to outlive the younger Mr. Knox, but even their planned 10:00 o'clock conference at the State Department did not start until 10:30. [119]

Meanwhile the last and fourteenth part of the Japanese note had been intercepted about 3:00 A.M. The "one o'clock" message had been intercepted at 4:37 A.M.: [120] it was available at the Navy Department at 5:00 A.M., [121] but did not come to the attention of Admiral Stark until at least 10:30 A.M. [122] The fourteenth part of the long message was available shortly after 8:00 o'clock on Sunday morning: it was delivered to Admiral Stark's office about 9:30 and to the White House and the Department of State by 9:40 to 9:45 A.M. [122]

At about 10:00 A.M. these papers were taken in to Mr. Roosevelt in his bedroom. After reading them he said, in substance, [123]

> It looks like the Japanese are going to break off negotiations.

One of the most curious things is that no one would admit either having telephoned Mr. Roosevelt, or having been called by him, the whole morning long. By the middle of the morning, or sooner, there was also available [124] a later message [125] instructing the Japanese Embassy, after deciphering part 14 of the long message, to destroy the remaining cipher machine, all codes, and secret documents.

The previous evening Mr. Stimson had asked the Navy Department to furnish him with a compilation of the British, American, Japanese, Dutch and Russian men-of-war in the Far East, and also with a compilation of the American warships in the Pacific Fleet together with their locations. This was available at the morning conference, and it showed that almost all of the ships of the Pacific Fleet were in Pearl Harbor. [126] The morning meeting of the three secretaries is thus narrated in Mr. Stimson's diary: [127]

> Today is the day that the Japanese are going to bring their answer to Hull, and everything in MAGIC [the intercepted messages] indicated that they had been keeping the time back until now in order to accomplish something hanging in the air. Knox and I arranged a conference with Hull at 10:30 and we talked the whole matter over. Hull is very certain that the Japs are planning some deviltry and *we are all wondering where the blow will strike*. We three stayed together in conference until lunch time, *going over the plans for what should be said* or done. The main thing is to hold the main people who are interested in the Far East together—the British, ourselves, the Dutch, the Australians, the Chinese. Hull expressed his views, giving the broad picture of it, and I made him dictate it to a stenographer *. Knox also had his views as to the importance of showing immediately how these different nations must stand together and I got him to dictate that *. Hull was to see the Japanese envoys at 1 o'clock but they were delayed in keeping the appointment and did not come until later—as it turned out, till 2 o'clock or after. I returned to Woodley to lunch *. * (Emphasis supplied.)

There is other evidence that the conference terminated at about 11:30. [128] The interesting thing about both Mr. Hull's and Mr. Knox's statements [129] is that each one assumes that America would not be directly attacked, and each one sets forth for American consumption why the United States ought to lead the rescue party for the other nations.

Colonel Bratton, head of the Army's Far Eastern Section in Military Intelligence, having read the various Japanese intercepts, had been trying to locate General Marshall since about 9:00 that morning.[130] Finally General Marshall telephoned him, near 10:30, and Colonel Bratton managed to see him at 11:25.[131] At about 11:30 General Marshall called Admiral Stark on the telephone.[132] The Admiral thought a warning message "might confuse" the various commanders.[133] Nevertheless the General wrote out a longhand message, at 11:40 the General and the Admiral again spoke over the telephone.[132] The Admiral was willing to have added to the Army message, "Show this to your Naval officers," which was done.[133] For what seems like a labored reason, General Marshall testified that he was unwilling to use his special "scrambler" telephone.[134] There was some delay while the War Department debated how the message should be sent:[135] as is well known, it arrived at Pearl Harbor long after the damage had been done.[136] Except for consenting to the inclusion of Naval officers in this Army message, Admiral Stark sent no warning whatever.

About noon the Japanese Embassy telephoned Mr. Hull and asked for an appointment at 1:00 P.M. Somewhat later the Embassy telephoned again and moved the appointment on to 1:45, because Ambassador Nomura was not ready.[137] Mr. Hull had been waiting in the State Department, mentally composing his anticipated oral reply to the Japanese Ambassadors.

By this time war was inevitable, but disaster was not yet inevitable; one barrier still remained. Mr. Stimson had been working earnestly to get radar to Hawaii, and he had succeeded.[138] At the northernmost point of the island of Oahu, atop a mountain called Opana, the best site on the island, was such a station. It was in normal operation only until 7:00 A.M.,[139] Hawaii time (12:30 P.M., Washington time). Third-class specialist Joseph L. Lockard[140] was in charge, with Private George E. Elliott[141] assisting him. The truck to take them back to their barracks was late and had not arrived at 7:00 o'clock that morning, so that the radar set continued in operation in order to instruct Private Elliott.[142] It had been a rather dull morning, with not much activity.[143] At 7:02,[144] 137 miles out,[145] Private Elliott located a large flight of planes approaching from the northwest. Specialist Lockard checked it: it was larger than any he had ever seen before; "something completely out of the ordinary"; "probably more than 50"; the biggest flight that he had ever picked up.[146] After some discussion, Lockard arguing that their time on duty was over, Elliott prevailed and telephoned the Information Center on the direct line, the tactical line, in order to report the news. No one answered.[147] Elliott persisted. He had a second line, the administrative line, and on it he finally reached the switchboard operator, who said that there was nobody around; but on Elliott's insistence the operator agreed to try to find "somebody that would know what to do and pass on the information, and have him take care of it."[148]

Lieutenant Kermit A. Tyler was still at the Information Center, which was located at Fort Shafter. This was his second tour of duty, and he had had no previous instruction.[149] He was the only officer there, because at 7:00 o'clock all except the telephone operator and himself "folded up their equipment and left."[150] Lieutenant Tyler had no particular duty assigned to him; he didn't know why he was there at all, and there was nothing for him to do but twiddle his thumbs (as General Grunert later put it)[151] which, as the same General conservatively stated, "seems all cock-eyed."[152]

The telephone operator found Lieutenant Tyler, who called back. Specialist Lockard answered, and stated the facts.[153] Lieutenant Tyler told him to forget it, not to worry about it.[154] Lockard argued back—as long as he thought it was reasonably safe to do so—[155] and then rang off. He had received an order from an officer; his duty was done, and he dared not go over the officer's head to some higher officer to try to do anything more.[156]

The last barrier to disaster crashed down. [157]

Private Elliott on his radar set piloted the big airfleet in—120 miles, 112 miles, 101 miles, 96, 88, 84, 79, 74, 67, 60, 55, 50, 45, 40, 35, 30 [158]—and lost it behind the distant mountains, 20 miles away, at 7:39. [159] They shut off the radar set at 7:45 and walked down their own mountain to find their truck. [160]

At Pearl Harbor, Japan committed the first overt act and the war began at 7:50 A.M. [161] (1:20 P.M., Washington time.) But the decoy was not the pitiful little *Isabel*. The sitting ducks were some of the finest battleships in the American Navy—the *Arizona*, [162] *California*, [163] *West Virginia*, [164] *Oklahoma*, [165] *Nevada*, [166] *Maryland*, [167] *Pennsylvania*, [168] and *Tennessee*. [169] Half of the total roster of our battleships was at Pearl Harbor, although on a numerical basis 60 per cent of the Navy was in the Atlantic. [170] Two thousand three hundred and twenty-six died in the Services and one thousand one hundred and nine were wounded. [171] It was "the greatest military and naval disaster in our Nation's history." [172]

Back in Washington, word of the attack was received by the Navy at 1:50 P.M. [173] Mr. Knox was talking with Admirals Stark and Turner when the message came in. Highly evidentiary of the direction in which the eyes of the top American officials were turned was his involuntary ejaculation: [174] "My God, this can't be true! this must mean the Philippines."

Yet, except for the unexpected locality and the circumstances involved, the outbreak of the war was hardly news to the top insiders. Mrs. Roosevelt later wrote: [175]

> December 7th was just like any of the later D-Days to us. We clustered at the radio and waited for more details *but it was far from the shock it proved to the country in general. We had expected something of the sort for a long time.* (Emphasis supplied.)

Mr. Stimson was still sitting at lunch, at just about 2:00 o'clock, when Mr. Roosevelt telephoned him [176] and "in a rather excited voice" asked him, "Have you heard the news?" Mr. Stimson's first reaction was geographically erroneous, just like Mr. Knox's, but he selected another locality and referred to the Gulf of Siam. Mr. Roosevelt said, "Oh, no. I don't mean that. They have attacked Hawaii. They are now bombing Hawaii." Well, thought Mr. Stimson, that was an excitement indeed. He then reflected on the plans of the three secretaries that morning and on

> * our efforts this morning in drawing our papers * to see whether or not we should all act together. The British will have to fight if they [the Japanese] attack the Kra Peninsula. We three all thought that we must fight if the British fought. *

It might have been very difficult to persuade the American people about that, Mr. Stimson thought, and mentally he felt a great relief:

> But now *the Japs have solved the whole thing* by attacking us *directly* in Hawaii. (Emphasis supplied.)

This desired conclusion continued to buoy him up through the rest of what would otherwise have been a somber day, as Mr. Stimson set down in his diary:

> When the news first came that Japan had attacked us, my first feeling was of relief that the indecision was over and that a crisis had come in a way which would unite all our people. This continued to be my dominant feeling in spite of the news of catastrophes which quickly developed. *

Before the Japanese Ambassadors finally arrived at 2:05 P.M., Mr. Hull had heard a report of the attack, and he asked for confirmation of it. [177] Perhaps this is why he kept the Ambassadors waiting for a quarter of an hour. [178] Ambassador Nomura handed

Mr. Hull the fourteen-part note [179] and Mr. Hull glanced over it perfunctorily. It was not news to him. Mr. Hull then addressed Admiral Nomura, beginning defensively, and working himself up to end on a note of defiance. He said [180] of himself,

> I must say that in all my conversations with you during the last nine months I have never uttered one word of untruth. This is borne out absolutely by the record. In all my fifty years of public service I have never seen a document that was more crowded with infamous falsehoods and distortions—infamous distortions and falsehoods on a scale so huge that I never imagined until today that any Government on this planet was capable of uttering them.

Mr. Hull's lecturing was likewise not new to Admiral Nomura, but at least this one was the last. He endured it patiently. Without making any comment the Japanese Ambassadors then left. Later in the day Mr. Hull issued a seven-sentence press release, [181] which twice accused Japan of treachery and which said that the recent Japanese professions "of desire for peace" had been "infamously false and fraudulent." Moreover,

> At the very moment when representatives of the Japanese Government were discussing * principles and courses of peace, the armed forces of Japan were preparing * to launch new attacks * upon nations * with which Japan was professedly at peace including the United States.

This was less candor than propaganda.

The outsiders of the Cabinet were widely scattered that Sunday, and by long-distance telephone were summoned back to Washington for a cabinet meeting that evening at 8:30.

As with Mr. Stimson, war had brought peace to Mr. Roosevelt. He was more "serene" than he had been for a long time, [182] because he had accomplished his purpose, as it had finally turned out, without the aid of visible manoeuvres or the use of smart devices. Technically he had even kept the promise of the plank in the 1940 Democratic Platform—not to go to war unless attacked.

What lay beneath the surface nobody knew, but Miss Perkins had a shrewd intuitive feeling. Of the Cabinet meeting held on the evening of Sunday, December 7, 1941, she wrote [183] —and note the sequence of the important psychological considerations—

> * in spite of the terrible blow to his pride, to his faith in the Navy and its ships, and to his confidence in the American Intelligence Service. * [Mr. Roosevelt] had, nevertheless, a much calmer air. His terrible moral problem had been resolved by the event.

As with Mr. Stimson again, Mr. Roosevelt's relief persisted through the rest of the day, in spite of the cumulating news of catastrophe and defeat. It was illustrated by a remark which he made to a selected group of Senators and Congressmen later that evening: [184]

> * Well, we were attacked. *There is no question about that.* (Emphasis supplied.)

This relief was so obvious that it impressed a news commentator who saw Mr. Roosevelt soon after midnight—"he was completely relaxed."

Far away in England that night, Mr. Churchill also understood very well how the Japanese attack upon an American possession had vastly simplified the problems of Mr. Roosevelt and of himself. Mr. Churchill was more than serene; he was full of "the greatest joy." [186] For now the second British coalition had officially secured its most important member, and with the power of America joined to that of Britain "we could subdue everybody else in the world." [187]

On Thursday in the following week, December 11, 1941, Germany and Italy [188] declared war upon the United States. The Nation was then completely at war; back door and front door; Pacific and Atlantic; Asia and Europe.

As it eventuated, Japan was the first enemy to fire upon us and the last enemy to surrender to us. Yet always a malign miasma seemed to haunt that air. It was against Japan that the atom bombs were released and thus revealed to the world—needlessly, as it transpired. And needlessly, as it also transpired, secret deals and agreements were made with Russia at Yalta in order to persuade that country to aid us with its might—for four days—and to help us conquer the supposed tremendous forces of Japan.

Thus Russia came into North Korea. The end of that story is a tale yet to unfold, a tale yet to be told. Perhaps future historians will some day trace here the origins of the Third World War.

Designs, least of all designs for war, do not always eventuate as their planners intended. The design for the war which began at Pearl Harbor was a zigzag pattern of secret power politics and of secret diplomacy, conducted by a very few men, and at times conducted in the United States by only one man.

The American people were steadily kept uninformed, as were their representatives and also many high officials, including generals and admirals. There were even times when the prospective allies in the future coalition were left to guess in the dark. Almost all of the developments were treated as if they were the private concerns of a small coterie.

The American people were informed only that the secret war policy was really a peace policy, or a defense policy. The Senate did not advise, and in fact it was not consulted. There was not then, and there still is not today, any equivalent of the King's Council or of the more modern British Cabinet to consider, debate, and advise on the great questions of policy which one man so often decided alone. As Congressman Frank B. Keefe wrote, [189]

> In the future the people and their Congress must know how close American diplomacy is moving to war so they may check its advance if imprudent and support its position if sound. A diplomacy which relies on the enemy's first overt act to insure effective popular support for the nation's final war decision is both outmoded and dangerous in the atomic age. To prevent any future Pearl Harbor more tragic and damaging than that of December 7, 1941, there must be constant close coordination between American public opinion and American diplomacy.

A contemplated war may or may not be useful and necessary. On such a question an adequately informed nation should be the ultimate judge. The people are entitled to ask—and to have sufficient knowledge to decide the problem—what advantage will a prospective war be to this nation? And in order to judge wisely, the people should be fully informed, and not kept in ignorance nor misinformed by those whom they have elected to high office.

It has always been true that eternal vigilance is the price of liberty. It is more than ever true in the atomic era.

BIBLIOGRAPHY

Armstrong, Hamilton Fish, *Chronology of Failure*, New York, 1941.
Beard, Charles A., *American Foreign Policy in the Making*, New Haven, 1946; *President Roosevelt and the Coming of the War, 1941*, New Haven, 1948.
Bullitt, William C., *The Great Globe Itself*, New York, 1946.
Busch, Noel F., *What Manner of Man*, New York, 1946.
Butcher, Harry C., *My Three Years With Eisenhower*, New York, 1946.
Byrnes, James F., *Speaking Frankly*, New York, 1947.
Carmichael, Donald Scott, *F.D.R., Columnist*, New York, 1947.
Churchill, Winston S., *The Gathering Storm*, Boston, 1948; *Their Finest Hour*, Boston, 1949; *The Grand Alliance*, Boston, 1950.
Ciano Diaries, The, Garden City, 1946.
Ciechanowski, Jan, *Defeat in Victory*, Garden City, 1947.
Clapper, Olive Ewing, *Washington Tapestry*, New York, 1946.
Creel, George, *Rebel at Large*, New York, 1947.
Davis, Forrest, and Ernest K. Lindley, *How War Came*, New York, 1942.
Eisenhower, Dwight D., *Crusade in Europe*, New York, 1948.
Farley, James A., *Behind the Ballots*, New York, 1938; *Jim Farley's Story: The Roosevelt Years*, New York, 1948.
Flynn, Edward J., *You're the Boss*, New York, 1947.
Flynn, John T., *Country Squire in the White House*, New York, 1940; *The Roosevelt Myth*, New York, 1948.
Foreign Relations of the United States, Japan: 1931-1941, Vol. II, Department of State, Washington, 1943.
Fuehrer Conferences on Matters Dealing With the German Navy, 1939, and 1940, Office of Naval Intelligence, Navy Department, Washington, D.C., 1947.
Goebbels Diaries, The, ed. by Louis P. Lochner, Washington and Garden City, 1948.

Grew, Joseph C., *Ten Years in Japan*, New York, 1944.
Hayes, Carlton J. H., *Wartime Mission in Spain*, New York, 1945.
Hitler, Adolf, *My New Order*, ed. by Raoul de Roussy de Sales, New York, 1941.
Hull, Cordell, *The Memoirs of*, 2 vols., New York, 1948.
International Transactions of the United States During the War, 1940-1945, U. S. Department of Commerce, Washington, D.C., 1948.
Kournakoff, Sergei N., *Russia's Fighting Forces*, New York, 1942.
Kravchenko, Victor, *I Chose Freedom*, New York, 1946.
Krivitsky, W. G., *In Stalin's Secret Service*, New York, 1939.
Lane, Arthur Bliss, *I Saw Poland Betrayed*, New York, 1948.
Langer, William L., *Our Vichy Gamble*, New York, 1947.
Leahy, William D., *I Was There*, New York, 1950.
Lindley, Ernest K., *Franklin D. Roosevelt*, New York, 1934.
Ludwig, Emil, *Roosevelt, a Study in Fortune and Power*, New York, 1938.
McIntire, Ross T., *White House Physician*, New York, 1946.
Millis, Walter, *This Is Pearl*, New York, 1947.
Moley, Raymond, *After Seven Years*, New York, 1939.
Morgenstern, George, *Pearl Harbor*, New York, 1947.
Nazi Conspiracy and Aggression, 8 vols., U. S. Government Printing Office, Washington, D.C., 1946.
Nazi-Soviet Relations, 1939-1941, Department of State, Washington, D.C., 1948.
Peace and War, United States Foreign Policy, 1931-1941, U. S. Government Printing Office, Washington, D.C., 1942.
Pearl Harbor Attack, Hearings Before the Joint Committee on the Investigation of the, 39 Parts, U. S. Government Printing Office, Washington, D.C., 1946.
Pearl Harbor Committee Report, 79th Congress, 2d Session, Senate Document No. 244, U. S. Government Printing Office, Washington, D.C., 1946.

Perkins, Frances, *The Roosevelt I Knew*, New York, 1946.
Roosevelt, Eleanor, *This I Remember*, New York, 1949.
Roosevelt, Elliott, *As He Saw It*, New York, 1946.
Roosevelt, Franklin D., *The Public Papers and Addresses of*, New York. 5 volumes for 1928-1936 pub'd in 1938; 4 volumes for 1937-1940 pub'd in 1941; 4 volumes for 1941-1945 pub'd in 1950.
Sevareid, Eric, *Not So Wild a Dream*, New York, 1946.
Sherwood, Robert E., *Roosevelt and Hopkins*, New York, 1948.
Shirer, William L., *Berlin Diary*, New York, 1941.
Smith, Walter Bedell, *My Three Years in Moscow*, Philadelphia and New York, 1950.
Stettinius, Edward R., Jr., *Lend-Lease, Weapon for Victory*, New York, 1944.
Stimson, Henry L., and Bundy, McGeorge, *On Active Service in Peace and War*, New York, 1948.
Taylor, Myron C., *Wartime Correspondence Between President Roosevelt and Pope Pius XII*, New York, 1947.
United States and Italy, 1936-1946, Documentary Record, U. S. Government Printing Office, Washington, D.C., 1946.
United States at War, The, Historical Reports on War Administration, Bureau of the Budget, No. 1, Washington, D.C., 1946.
United States Relations With China, Department of State, Washington, D.C., 1949.
Von Hassell Diaries, The, Garden City, 1947.
Welles, Sumner, *The Time for Decision*, New York, 1944.

NOTES

CHAPTER I

[1] *The United States at War*, p. 506.
[2] Welles, *The Time for Decision*, p. 288.

CHAPTER II

[1] *The Public Papers, etc., of F.D.R.*, Vol. 5, p. 288.
[2] *Ibid.*, Vol. 2, p. 9.
[3] *Ibid.*, Vol. 5, p. 8; Vol. 2, p. 14.
[4] *Ibid.*, Vol. 2, p. 98.
[5] *Ibid.*, Vol. 2, pp. 186–187.
[6] *Ibid.*, Vol. 2, p. 264.
[7] *Ibid.*, Vol. 2, p. 394.
[8] *Ibid.*, Vol. 2, p. 472.
[9] *Ibid.*, Vol. 2, pp. 472–475.
[10] *Ibid.*, Vol. 2, p. 545. This was not an addition to, but a reversal of, President Wilson's policies; e.g. towards Huerta in Mexico in 1914; towards the Dominican Republic in 1914; towards Haiti in 1915, and, some might assert, the First World War. See also *ibid.*, Vol. 3, p. 270.
[11] *Ibid.*, Vol 2, p. 547.
[12] *Ibid.*, Vol. 3, p. 12.
[13] *Ibid.*, Vol. 3, p. 172.
[14] *Ibid.*, Vol. 3, pp. 164–165.
[15] *Ibid.*, Vol. 3, p. 173.
[16] *Ibid.*, Vol. 4, p. 24.
[17] *Ibid.*, Vol. 4, p. 251.
[18] *Ibid.*, Vol. 4, pp. 345–346.
[19] *Ibid.*, Vol. 4, p. 410.
[20] *Ibid.*, Vol. 4, p. 450.
[21] *Ibid.*, Vol. 4, p. 416.
[22] *Ibid.*, Vol. 4, p. 423.
[23] *Ibid.*, Vol. 4, p. 425.
[24] *Ibid.*, Vol. 4, p. 440.
[25] *Ibid.*, Vol. 4, pp. 442–443.
[26] *Ibid.*, Vol. 4, pp. 452–453.
[27] *Ibid.*, Vol. 4, p. 482.
[28] *Ibid.*, Vol. 4, p. 493.
[29] *Ibid.*, Vol. 5, p. 12.
[30] *Ibid.*, Vol. 5, p. 217.
[31] *Ibid.*, Vol. 5, p. 225.
[32] *Ibid.*, 1937 Vol., p. 191.
[33] *Ibid.*, Vol. 5, p. 622.
[34] *Ibid.*, Vol. 5, p. 623.
[35] *Ibid.*, Vol. 5, p. 634. A stop-gap resolution was passed on Jan. 8, 1937; ibid., 1937 Vol., p. 191.
[36] *Ibid.*, Vol. 5, p. 285.
[37] *Ibid.*, Vol. 5, pp. 288–292.
[38] Over three years later the extreme "interventionists" numbered only 2½%; Sherwood, *Roosevelt and Hopkins*, pp. 127–128.
[39] *The Public Papers, etc., of F.D.R.*, Vol. 5, p. 417.
[40] *Ibid.*, Vol. 5. p. 421.
[41] *Ibid.*, Vol. 5, pp. 440, 463, 474–475, 491.
[42] *Ibid.*, Vol. 5, p. 567.
[43] *Ibid.*, Vol. 5, pp. 598–600, 604–608.
[44] *Ibid.*, Vol. 5, p. 640.
[45] *Ibid.*, Vol. 5, p. 659.
[46] *Our Navy at War:* Report of Admiral King to the Secretary of the Navy, dated March 27, 1944. Their names do not appear in action until the latter part of 1942; p. 34.

CHAPTER III

[1] *The Morgenthau Diaries, Collier's,* Oct. 4, 1947; Vol. 120, No. 14, p. 20.

[2] *The Public Papers, etc., of F.D.R.,* 1938 Vol., p. 84.

[3] *The Morgenthau Diaries, Collier's,* Oct. 25, 1947, Vol. 120, No. 17, p. 85.

[4] Mr. Roosevelt's later recommendation to the Congress on February 11, 1939, for a Federal Planning Agency, *The Public Papers, etc., of F.D.R.,* 1939 vol., pp. 134–135, was not welcomed. After the outbreak of the Second World War, and after the declaration of a "limited national emergency on September 8, 1939, he finally created such a board by executive order; *ibid.,* 1939 vol., p. 493.

[5] *The 168 Days,* by Alsop and Catledge, pp. 306, 307, 309.

[6] *The Morgenthau Diaries, Collier's,* Oct. 11, 1947, Vol. 120, No. 15, p. 77.

[7] *The Public Papers, etc., of F.D.R.,* 1937 Vol., p. 152.

[8] *Ibid.,* 1937 vol., p. 284.

[9] *Ibid.,* 1937 vol., p. 185.

[10] *Ibid.,* 1937 vol., p. 191.

[11] Sherwood, *Roosevelt and Hopkins,* p. 405.

[12] *The Public Papers, etc., of F.D.R.,* 1937 vol., p. 354: *Peace and War,* pp. 47–48.

[13] *The Public Papers, etc., of F.D.R.,* 1937 vol., p. 355.

[14] *Peace and War,* p. 47.

[15] *The Public Papers, etc., of F.D.R.,* 1937 vol., p. 192.

[16] *Ibid.,* 1937 vol., pp. 352–354; Press Conference of Sept. 14, 1937.

[17] *The 168 Days,* by Alsop and Catledge, p. 312.

[18] *The Public Papers, etc., of F.D.R.,* 1937 vol., pp. 414–415.

[19] *Ibid.,* 1937 vol., pp. 406–411.

[20] *Ibid.,* 1937 vol., pp. 414, 423–425.

[21] Cf. McIntire, *White House Physician,* p. 109.

[22] Flynn, *Country Squire in the White House,* p. 103; cf. Leahy, *I Was There,* p. 64; *The Memoirs of Cordell Hull,* Vol. II, p. 1111.

[23] Churchill, *The Second World War: The Gathering Storm,* p. 247.

[24] Byrnes, *Speaking Frankly,* p. 6.

[25] *The Public Papers, etc., of F.D.R.,* 1939 vol., p. 121: "secret records [which] should not be disclosed * even to a Senatorial Committee."

[26] *Ibid.,* 1938 vol., p. 548.

[27] *Peace and War,* p. 50.

[28] Grew, *Ten Years in Japan,* p. 221.

[29] *The Public Papers, etc., of F.D.R.,* 1937 vol., p. 463: Mr. Roosevelt's phraseology in his annotation at this point.

[30] Grew, *Ten Years in Japan,* pp. 226–227.

[31] *The Public Papers, etc., of F.D.R.,* 1937 vol., p. 521. At his press conference on November 23, 1937.

[32] The *Panay,* an American gunboat, was anchored in the Yangtze River. She was bombed and sunk by Japanese airplanes.

[33] *The Public Papers, etc., of F.D.R.,* 1937 vol., p. 541.

[34] *Ibid.,* 1937 vol., p. 542.

[35] McIntire, *White House Physician,* p. 110.

[36] *The Public Papers, etc., of F.D.R.*, 1937 vol., p. 554.

[37] See Mr. Churchill's secret speech of April 23, 1942: *Life* magazine, Vol. 20 (Jan. 28, 1946), at p. 46.

Bataan had fallen, the Philippines had been overrun, Singapore had fallen, the Allied naval forces had been utterly destroyed in the Java Sea action; the Netherlands East Indies, Borneo, New Guinea, New Britain, and the Solomon Islands had been occupied by the Japanese, and Australia was threatened. But Mr. Roosevelt wrote Mr. Churchill, "I am frank to say that I feel better about the war than at any time in the past two years"; *ibid.*, p. 46. Obviously Mr. Roosevelt's thoughts must have been fixed on Europe, since the Pacific war was about at its nadir. Also see General Marshall's Report, N.Y. *Times*, Oct. 10, 1945, p. 2S, col. 1. Also *Pearl Harbor Attack*, Part 9, pp. 4288–4289.

[38] Moley, *After Seven Years*, p. 379. See *The Memoirs of Cordell Hull*, Vol. I, p. 684, which acknowledges the truth of the fact.

[39] Churchill, *The Gathering Storm*, pp. 251–254, 346.

[40] Emil Ludwig, *Roosevelt*, p. 272.

[41] *Pearl Harbor Attack*, Part 9, pp. 4272–4276.

[42] *Ibid.*, Part 14, p. 924.

[43] *Ibid.*, Part 1, p. 309: cf. Part 14, p. 924.

[44] Ludwig, *Roosevelt*, p. 269.

[45] *American Journal of International Law*, Vol. 32, p. 581.

[46] *Ibid.*, Vol. 32, p. 817.

[47] *Ibid.*, Vol. 33, p. 572: for a general study see *ibid.*, Vol. 33, p. 521.

[48] N.Y. *Times*, Oct. 24, 1947, p. 1, cols. 2–3.

[49] Ludwig, *Roosevelt*, pp. 274-275.

[50] *The Public Papers, etc., of F.D.R.*, 1937 vol., p. 373.

[51] *Ibid.*, 1937 vol., pp. 436, 490, 520: the last in response to a taunt from Senator Vandenberg on Nov. 22, 1937. See also Mr. Roosevelt's excuses in the introduction to his 1938 vol., pp. xxii-xxiii.

[52] Moley, *After Seven Years*, pp. 374–375.

[53] Byrnes, *Speaking Frankly*, p. 6.

[54] *The Public Papers, etc., of F.D.R.*, 1938 vol., p. 67.

[55] *Peace and War*, p. 52.

[56] Farley, *Behind the Ballots*, p. 362.

[57] *The Public Papers, etc., of F.D.R.*, 1938 vol., p. 67.

[58] Mr. Roosevelt said more at this point on this topic, but it has been omitted from the printed volume.

[59] *Ibid.*, 1938 vol., pp. 68–71.

[60] Byrnes, *Speaking Frankly*, p. 6.

[61] *Peace and War*, pp. 54–55: cf. Moley, *After Seven Years*, p. 380.

[62] *The Public Papers, etc., of F.D.R.*, 1938 vol., pp. 249–258.

[63] *Ibid.*, 1938 vol., pp. 286–287.

[64] *Ibid.*, 1938 vol., p. 221.

[65] *Ibid.*, 1938 vol., p. 305.

[66] *Ibid.*, 1938 vol., p. 366.

[67] *Ibid.*, 1938 vol., p. 378.

[68] *Ibid.*, 1938 vol., p. 413.

[69] *Ibid.*, 1938 vol., p. 456.

[70] *Ibid.,* 1938 vol., p.406, and cf. his defensive apologetics in 1939 vol., p. 293. For Hitler's recent boasts see Reichstag speech of Feb. 20, 1938; *My New Order,* p. 435.

[71] See the testimony of Mr. Louis A. Johnson, N. Y. *Sun,* Oct. 23, 1947, p.1, cols. 5–6: N. Y. *Times,* Oct. 24, 1947, p. 1, cols. 2–3.

[72] *Peace and War,* p. 86; *U. S. Relations With China,* pp. 24–25.

[73] N. Y. *Times,* Nov. 18, 1938, pp. 1, 12, 13.

[74] *Ibid.,* Nov. 18, 1938, p. 1, col. 7.

[75] *Ibid.,* Nov. 18, 1938, p. 1, col 8, continued on p. 12, cols. 3–4.

[76] *The Public Papers, etc., of F.D.R.,* 1938 vol., p. 504.

[77] *Ibid.,* 1938 vol., pp. 510–511.

[78] *Ibid.,* 1938 vol., pp. 521, 548.

[79] *Ibid.,* 1939 vol., pp. 544–546.

[80] Sherwood, *Roosevelt and Hopkins,* p. 100.

[81] *Ibid.,* pp. 76, 100–101

[82] Moley, *After Seven Years,* p. 380.

[83] *Peace and War,* p. 86.

[84] *Ibid.,* p. 87; *U. S. Relations With China,* p. 24.

[85] Churchill, *The Gathering Storm,* p. 293.

[86] *The Public Papers, etc., of F.D.R.,* 1938 vol., p. 531.

[87] *Ibid.,* 1938 vol., pp. 535–536, 537.

[88] Churchill, *The Gathering Storm,* p. 223.

[89] *The Public Papers, etc., of F.D.R.,* 1938 vol., p. 542.

[90] *Ibid.,* 1938 vol., pp. 546–548.

[91] *Ibid.,* 1938 vol., pp. 564, 566.

[92] *Ibid.,* 1938 vol., p. 574.

[93] *Ibid.,* 1938 vol., p. 597. Although our State Department now says that it was: *Peace and War,* p. 58.

[94] *Ibid.,* 1938 vol., p. 602.

[95] *Ibid.,* 1938 vol., p. 623.

[96] Moley, *After Seven Years,* pp. 379–380.

[97] *The United States at War,* p. 12.

[98] *The Public Papers, etc., of F.D.R.,* 1938 vol., p. 615.

[99] *Ibid.,* 1938 vol., pp. 624–627.

[100] *Ibid.,* 1938 vol., p. 651.

[101] *The Ciano Diaries,* p. 3.

[102] *Ibid.,* p. 5.

[103] *Ibid.,* p. 7; cf. pp. 38–39.

[104] *Ibid.,* pp. 58, 72, 73, 77, 82, 91, 126, 293, 296.

[105] *Ibid.,* p. 145.

[106] *The Public Papers, etc., of F.D.R.,* 1939 vol., pp. xxxviii– xxxix.

[107] *Ibid.,* 1939 vol., pp. 1–12.

[108] *Ibid.,* 1939 vol., p. 523.

[109] *Ibid.,* 1939 vol., pp. 70–74.

CHAPTER IV

[1] See Mr. Roosevelt's opinions, as declared to Vice Admiral McIntire, soon after the commencement of the Second World War; *White House Physician,* p. 115.

[2] *The Ciano Diaries,* p. 10.

[3] *The Morgenthau Diaries, Collier's,* Oct. 18, 1947, Vol. 120, No. 16, p. 17.

[4] *The Public Papers, etc., of F.D.R.,* 1939 vol., p. 110.

[5] *Ibid.,* 1940 vol., pp. 323–324.

[6] *The Morgenthau Diaries, Collier's,* Oct. 18, 1947, vol. 120, No. 16, p. 17.

[7] *The Public Papers, etc., of F.D.R.*, 1939 vol., pp. 199-201.
[8] *Ibid.*, 1939 vol., p. 69.
[9] *Ibid.*, 1939 vol., pp. 115, 126–133.
[10] *Ibid.*, 1939 vol., pp. 115, 227–228.
[11] *Ibid.*, 1939 vol., pp. 155–157.
[12] *Ibid.*, 1939 vol., p. 155.
[13] *Ibid.*, 1939 vol., p. xxxii.
[14] *Ibid.*, 1939 vol., p. 387.
[15] *Ibid.*, 1939 vol., pp. 381-387.
[16] *Ibid.*, 1939 vol., p. 380.
[17] *The Ciano Diaries*, pp. 42–44.
[18] *The Public Papers, etc., of F.D.R.*, 1939 vol., pp. 165-166.
[19] *The Ciano Diaries*, p. 45.
[20] Ludwig, *Roosevelt*, p. 332.
[21] Note Professor Moley's observations, *After Seven Years*, p. 388.
[22] Ernest K. Lindley, *Franklin D. Roosevelt*, pp. 50, 68.
[23] Moley, *After Seven Years*, pp. 378–379. See Baron Hiranuma's penetrating observations: *Pearl Harbor Attack*, Part 20, pp. 4158–4161.
[24] Butcher, *My Three Years With Eisenhower*, p. 386.
[25] Butcher, *op. cit.*, p. 518. General Fuller wrote that unconditional surrender thenceforth hung "like a putrefying albatross around the necks of America and Britain." *Army Ordnance*, March–April 1947, p. 416. See also *The Goebbels Diaries*, pp. 30, 145.
[26] "Human Events," Vol. III, No. 9, Feb. 27, 1946, p. 5: N.Y. *Times*, March 18, 1946, p. 8, col. 4.
[27] *The Ciano Diaries*, pp. 49, 87, 127, 211, 216, 227–228, 237, 241, 298, 333, 392, 402, 437, 492:—and anti-Fascist, p. 352.
[28] *Ibid.*, pp. 47–48, 50, 120–125, 128, 131, 173, 186, 208, 210, 215, 216, 245, 438, 442–443, 445, 456.
[29] *Ibid.*, pp. 136, 255: cf. Welles, *The Time for Decision*, pp. 143, 146.
[30] *The Public Papers, etc., of F.D.R.*, 1938 vol., p. 400.
[31] General Fuller believes that, with proper support, the German revolt would have taken place, successfully, a year before its actual date (July 20, 1944): *Army Ordnance*, March–April 1947, p. 416. *The Von Hassell Diaries* also mention earlier conspiratorial attempts, e.g., Oct. 19, 1939, pp. 81–84, etc.
[32] At p. 49.
[33] *The Public Papers, etc., of F.D.R.*, 1939 vol., pp. 185–186.
[34] *United States and Italy*, pp. 3–4.
[35] *The Public Papers, etc., of F.D.R.*, 1939 vol., pp. 189–191.
[36] *Ibid.*, 1939 vol., p. 192.
[37] *Ibid.*, 1939 vol., pp. 195-199.
[38] *My New Order*, pp. 615–628.
[39] *The Public Papers, etc., of F.D.R.*, 1939 vol., pp. 201–205.
[40] Mr. Roosevelt said, next day: "Nobody was advised [that this action was being taken]. * And in the same way, our embassies and legations in Europe were advised of it by cable last night. * Great Britain, France or any other nation in the world was not consulted in any way and did not know anything about it." 1939 vol., p. 217.

[41] Moley, *op. cit.*, pp. 394–395.
[42] *The Public Papers, etc., of F.D.R.*, 1939 vol., pp. 209–217.
[43] *Ibid.*, 1939 vol., p. 205.
[44] *The Ciano Diaries*, p. 66.
[45] *Ibid.*, p. 68.
[46] *The Public Papers, etc., of F.D.R.*, 1939 vol., p. 151.
[47] *My New Order*, pp. 630–677.
[48] *The Ciano Diaries*, p. 74.
[49] *The Memoirs of Cordell Hull*, Vol. I, p. 630.
[50] *The Ciano Diaries*, p. 83.
[51] *Nazi Conspiracy and Aggression*, Vol. VI, p. 890.
[52] *The Ciano Diaries*, p. 69.
[53] *Ibid.*, p. 84. Cf. *Nazi-Soviet Relations*, p. 79.
[54] *The Ciano Diaries*, p. 113.
[55] *Ibid.*, p. 110.
[56] *Ibid.*, pp. 111–114.
[57] Krivitsky, *In Stalin's Secret Service*, pp. 3–4, 7–15, 21–25.
[58] *Nazi-Soviet Relations*, pp. 1–2.
[59] *Ibid.*, pp. 2–3.
[60] *Ibid.*, pp. 8–9.
[61] *Ibid.*, pp. 28–30, 32–36.
[62] *Ibid.*, pp. 41–42.
[63] *Ibid.*, pp. 42, 47.
[64] *Ibid.*, pp. 38, 41, 45–49.
[65] *Ibid.*, pp. 50–52.
[66] *Ibid.*, pp. 53, 58, 63–65, 67–68.
[67] *Ibid.*, p. 62.
[68] *Ibid.*, pp. 52–56.
[69] *Ibid.*, pp. 58, 62–63, 69.
[70] *Ibid.*, p. 70. Cf. p. 47.
[71] *Ibid.*, pp. 71–76.
[72] *Ibid.*, pp. 76–77.
[73] *Ibid.*, p. 78.
[74] *Ibid.*, p. 54. The episode is not referred to in *The Ciano Diaries*.
[75] *The Ciano Diaries*, pp. 118–120.
[76] *Nazi Conspiracy and Aggression*, Vol. IV, pp. 514–515.
[77] *The Public Papers, etc., of F.D.R.*, 1939 vol., p. 122.
[78] *Ibid.*, 1939 vol., pp. 160–161.
[79] *Ibid.*, 1939 vol., at pp. 350–351.
[80] Moley, *After Seven Years*, at pp. 382 and 385.
[81] Ludwig, *Roosevelt*, p. 279.
[82] *The Public Papers, etc., of F.D.R.*, 1939 vol., p. 344.
[83] Ludwig, *Roosevelt*, p. x.
[84] Farley, *Behind the Ballots*, p. 353.
[85] Flynn, *You're the Boss*, pp. 154–155; Sherwood, *Roosevelt and Hopkins*, p. 117.
[86] Grew, *Ten Years in Japan*, P. 281. See Baron von Weizsäcker's reproaches to the Japanese Ambassador on Aug. 22, 1939: *Nazi-Soviet Relations*, pp. 70–71.
[87] Grew, *op. cit.*, p. 283.
[88] *Pearl Harbor Attack*, Part 20, pp. 4145–4147.
[89] *Ibid.*, Part 20, pp. 4148–4150: cf. pp. 4165–4167.
[90] *Ibid.*, Part 20, pp. 4135–4138.
[91] *Ibid.*, Part 20, p. 4134.
[92] *Ibid.*, Part 20, p. 4139.
[93] *Ibid.*, Part 20, pp. 4140–4143.
[94] *Ibid.*, pp. 4144–4164.
[95] *Ibid.*, Part 20, p. 4168. Nine years later Mr. Hull claimed that he was "more than skeptical": *The Memoirs of Cordell Hull*, Vol. I, p. 631. No suggestion of skepticism appears in the 1939 memorandum.

[96] *Pearl Harbor Attack*, Part 20, p. 4168.
[97] *Ibid.*, Part 20, p. 4169.
[98] *Ibid.*, Part 20, p. 4175.
[99] *Ibid.*, Part 20, pp. 4177–4190.
[100] *Ibid.*, Part 20, p. 4176.
[101] *Ibid.*, Part 20, pp. 4171–4174.
[102] *Ibid.*, Part 20, p. 4170.
[103] *Ibid.*, Part 20, pp. 4191-4192.
[104] *Ibid.*, Part 20, pp. 4193–4194.
[105] *Ibid.*, Part 20, pp. 4196–4199.
[106] *Ibid.*, Part 20, pp. 4200–4202.
[107] *Ibid.*, Part 20, pp. 4203–4204.
[108] *Ibid.*, Part 20, pp. 4205–4206.
[109] *Ibid.*, Part 20, pp. 4207–4208.
[110] *Nazi-Soviet Relations*, p. 47.
[111] *The Ciano Diaries*, p. 126.
[112] *Nazi-Soviet Relations*, pp. 70–71, 80.
[113] *Ibid.*, p. 82.
[114] *Peace and War*, p. 88.
[115] *Ibid.*, p. 89.

CHAPTER V

[1] *The Public Papers, etc., of F.D.R.*, 1939 vol., pp. 390–397.
[2] *Ibid.*, 1939 vol., p. 429.
[3] McIntire, *White House Physician*, p. 112.
[4] *Peace and War*, p. 61; *International Transactions of the U. S., etc.*, p. 27; *The Memoirs of Cordell Hull*, Vol. I, p. 625.
[5] *The Public Papers, etc., of F.D.R.*, 1939 vol., p. 568.
[6] *Ibid.*, 1939 vol., p. 438.
[7] *The United States at War*, p. 16.
[8] *The Public Papers, etc., of F.D.R.*, 1939 vol., pp. 586–587.
[9] *Ibid.*, 1939 vol., pp. 444–448.
[10] *Ibid.*, 1939 vol., p. 452.
[11] *Ibid.*, 1939 vol., pp. 449–450.
[12] *Ibid.*, 1939 vol., pp. 448–449.
[13] McIntire, *White House Physician*, pp. 112–113.
[14] *The Von Hassell Diaries*, p. 63.
[15] *The Ciano Diaries*, p. 130.
[16] *United States and Italy*, p. 6.
[17] *The Ciano Diaries*, pp. 129–130.
[18] *Ibid.*, p. 132.
[19] *Ibid.*, p. 134.
[20] *Ibid.*, p. 136: *The Von Hassell Diaries*, p. 73.
[21] *The Public Papers, etc., of F.D.R.*, 1939 vol., p. 457.
[22] *Ibid.*, 1939 vol., pp. 460–464.
[23] *N.Y. Times*, Sept. 18, 1947, p. 52, col. 8.
[24] Churchill, *The Gathering Storm*, p. 440.
[25] *Ibid.*, p. 441.
[26] Churchill, *The Second World War: Their Finest Hour*, p. 23.
[27] *Ibid.*, p. 23.
[28] *The Public Papers, etc., of F.D.R.*, 1939 vol., pp. 464–473.
[29] *Ibid.*, 1939 vol., pp. 473–478.
[30] *Ibid.*, 1939 vol., pp. 479–487.

[31] *Ibid.*, 1939 vol., pp. 478–479.
[32] The previous press conference is omitted from Mr. Roosevelt's published papers.
[33] *The Public Papers, etc., of F.D.R.*, 1939 vol., pp. 487–488.
[34] *Ibid.*, pp. 525–527.
[35] *Fuehrer Conferences*, 1940, Vol. II, p. 48.
[36] Our Navy at War, by Admiral Ernest J. King, p. 5.
[37] *The Public Papers, etc., of F.D.R.*, 1939 vol., pp. 552–554.
[38] Churchill, *The Gathering Storm*, pp. 513–514.
[39] *The Public Papers, etc., of F.D.R.*, 1939 vol., pp. 507, 509: "* the Department of Agriculture announced on Sept. 7 that reserves of sugar * were adequate for any requirements of customers,*" and on Sept. 11 all marketing quotas and restrictions on sugar were removed. But in 1947 sugar was the only article still being rationed!
[40] *The United States at War*, p. 464.
[41] *The Public Papers, etc., of F.D.R.*, 1939 vol., pp. 491, 493, 502-503.
[42] *The United States at War*, p. 21.
[43] *The Public Papers, etc., of F.D.R.*, 1939 vol., p. 510.
[44] *Nazi-Soviet Relations*, pp. 89–96.
[45] N. Y. *Sun*, Oct. 23, 1946, p. 9 col. 1: cf. *The Von Hassell Diaries*, pp. 80–81.
[46] Sherwood, *Roosevelt and Hopkins*, p. 126.
[47] *The Public Papers, etc., of F.D.R.*, 1939 vol., pp. 512–522.
[48] Mr. Hull wrote, "Nowhere in his message did the President mention the thought that had been in the minds of all of us, that lifting the arms embargo would assist Britain and France." *The Memoirs of Cordell Hull*, Vol. I, p. 683. See also *ibid.*, p. 684.
[49] *The Public Papers, etc., of F.D.R.*, 1939 vol., p. 528.
[50] *Ibid.*, 1939 vol., p. 528.
[51] *The Ciano Diaries*, p. 146.
[52] *My New Order*, pp. 722–756.
[53] *The Ciano Diaries*, p. 156.
[54] *Ibid.*, p. 157.
[55] 187 pages for the first quarter, 192 pages for the second quarter, 152 pages for the third quarter, but only 81 pages for the last quarter.
[56] Churchill, *The Second World War: The Gathering Storm*, p. 551.
[57] *The Public Papers, etc., of F.D.R.*, 1939 vol., pp. 554–557,
[58] *The Public Papers, etc., of F.D.R.*, 1939 vol., p. 524.
[59] *Ibid.*, 1939 vol., p. 559.
[60] *Ibid.*, 1939 vol., p. 524.
[61] *Ibid.*, 1939 vol., pp. 559–564.
[62] *Ibid.*, 1939 vol., 568–569.
[63] *The Morgenthau Diaries, Collier's*, Oct. 18, 1947, vol. 120, No. 16, p. 72.
[64] *Nazi-Soviet Relations*, pp. 105-108.
[65] *Fuehrer Conferences on Matters Dealing With the German Navy, 1939*, Office of Naval Intelligence, Navy Dept., 1947, pp. 12, 21. This base was abandoned about a year later in favor of Norwegian bases: *Nazi-Soviet Relations*, p. 185.
[66] *The Public Papers, etc., of F.D.R.*, 1939 vol., pp. 538–539.
[67] *Ibid.*, 1939 vol., p. 539.

[68] *Ibid.*, 1939 vol., pp. 587–588.
[69] *Ibid.*, 1939 vol., p. 589.
[70] *The Ciano Diaries*, pp. 174–175, 177, 191, 196.
[71] *Ibid.*, pp. 177, 180, 191.
[72] *Ibid.*, pp. 200–203.
[73] *The Public Papers, etc., of F.D.R.*, 1939 vol., p. 592.
[74] *Ibid.*, 1939 vol., pp. 606–608.
[75] *Ibid.*, 1939 vol., p. 609.
[76] *The Public Papers, etc., of F.D.R.*, 1940 vol., pp. 101–102.
[77] *Ibid.*, 1940 vol., p. 51.
[78] *The United States at War*, p. 48.
[79] *The Public Papers, etc., of F.D.R.*, 1939 vol., pp. 582, 604–605; 1940 vol., p. 70.
[80] Ernest K. Lindley, *Franklin D. Roosevelt*, p. 343.
[81] *Ibid.*, p. 100.
[82] Perkins, *The Roosevelt I Knew*, p. 128.
[83] *The Public Papers, etc., of F.D.R.*, 1940 vol., p. xxv. But Vice Admiral McIntire says that our unpreparedness was "pitiful": *White House Physician*, p. 115.
[84] *The Public Papers, etc., of F.D.R.*, 1940 vol., pp. 2–3.
[85] *Ibid.*, 1940 vol., p. 9.
[86] *Ibid.*, 1940 vol., pp. 49–50.
[87] *Pearl Harbor Attack*, Part 14, pp. 924–927.
[88] From 1937 to 1938: *Pearl Harbor Attack*, Part 1, p. 254.
[89] *Ibid.*, Part 14, p. 1007.
[90] "Orange" was the Navy code word for "Japan" or "Japanese": *Pearl Harbor Attack*, Part 1, pp. 258, 330: Part 3, p. 1002.
[91] *The Public Papers, etc., of F.D.R.*, 1940 vol., p. 77.
[92] *Ibid.*, 1940 vol., pp. 78–80.
[93] *Ibid.*, 1940 vol., pp. 111–112.
[94] Cf. the statements in Welles, *The Time for Decision*, pp. 73–77, and his preface to *The Ciano Diaries*, p. xxv. Also *The Von Hassell Diaries*, pp. 113, 120–121.
[95] *The Public Papers, etc., of F.D.R.*, 1940 vol., pp. 81–82.
[96] Taylor, *Wartime Correspondence Between President Roosevelt and Pope Pius XII*, p. 5.
[97] *Ibid.*, p. 27.
[98] *The Von Hassell Diaries*, pp. 125, 131.
[99] *Ibid.*, pp. 115–118, 133–134.
[100] Shirer, *Berlin Diary*, p. 296.
[101] *The Von Hassell Diaries*, p. 111.
[102] *Ibid.*, p. 120.
[103] *The Ciano Diaries*, p. 222: cf. Welles, *The Time for Decision*, p. 135.
[104] *The Ciano Diaries*, p. 222: cf. Welles, *The Time for Decision*, p. 139.
[105] *The Von Hassell Diaries*, p. 121.
[106] *The Ciano Diaries*, p. 224.
[107] *Ibid.*, p. 225.
[108] *Ibid.*, p. 229.
[109] *The Von Hassell Diaries*, p. 76.
[110] *Ibid.*, pp. 106–107.
[111] *The Ciano Diaries*, pp. 167–168, 183, 191, 193, 197.
[112] Shirer, *Berlin Diary*, pp. 291-292: cf. p. 307.
[113] *The Von Hassell Diaries*, pp. 123–125, 130–132.

[114] Churchill, *The Gathering Storm*, pp. 543–547; 573–574. He was confident that if Britain sent troops to occupy Norway the United States would handle the matter in the way most calculated to help Britain: *ibid.*, at p. 547.
[115] *The Public Papers, etc., of F.D.R.*, 1940 vol., p. 51.
[116] Churchill, *Their Finest Hour*, p. 228.
[117] *The Public Papers, etc., of F.D.R.*, 1940 vol., pp. 104–108.
[118] *Ibid.*, 1940 vol., p. 133.
[119] N. Y. *Times*, May 8, 1946, p. 4, col. 7.
[120] *The Public Papers, etc., of F.D.R.*, 1940 vol., p. 157.
[121] *Ibid.*, 1940 vol., pp. 158–162.
[122] *Ibid.*, 1940 vol., pp. 166-170.
[123] *The Ciano Diaries*, p. 237.
[124] Taylor, *Wartime Correspondence, etc.*, p. 28: *The Von Hassell Diaries*, p. 135.
125 *The Ciano Diaries*, p. 241.
[126] Taylor, *Wartime Correspondence, etc.*, p. 27.
[127] *The Ciano Diaries*, p. 241: cf. *Peace and War*, pp. 70–71.
[128] *The Von Hassell Diaries*, p. 135.
[129] *The Ciano Diaries*, pp. 241–242: cf. *Peace and War*, p. 71.
[130] *United States and Italy*, p. 10.
[131] *The Ciano Diaries*, p. 250: cf. Armstrong, *Chronology of Failure*, p. 29
[132] *United States and Italy*, p. 10.
[133] *The Public Papers, etc., of F.D.R.*, 1940 vol., p. 195.
[134] Churchill, *Their Finest Hour*, pp. 121–122.
[135] *Ibid.*, p. 122.
[136] *Ibid.*, p. 123.
[137] *United States and Italy*, pp. 10–11: cf. *Peace and War*, p. 72.
[138] *The Ciano Diaries*, p. 255.
[139] *Ibid.*, p. 255.
[140] *United States and Italy*, p. 11: cf. *Peace and War*, p. 72.
[141] *The Ciano Diaries*, pp. 257–258.
[142] *United States and Italy*, pp. 12–13.
[143] *Ibid.*, pp. 13–14: *The Ciano Diaries*, p. 258.
[144] *Newsweek*, Jan. 13, 1947, vol. 29, No. 2, p. 36.
[145] *The Public Papers, etc., of F.D.R.*, 1940 vol., pp. 184–187.
[146] *Ibid.*, 1940 vol., p. 189.
[147] *Ibid.*, 1940 vol., pp. 190–196.
[148] *Ibid.*, 1940 vol., p. 203.
[149] *Ibid.*, 1940 vol., p. 600.
[150] Churchill, *Their Finest Hour*, p. 24–25.
[151] *The Public Papers, etc., of F.D.R.*, 1940 vol., pp. 198–205.
[152] *Ibid.*, 1940 vol., p. 203.
[153] *Ibid.*, 1940 vol., p. 198.
[154] *Ibid.*, 1940 vol., pp. 199–200.
[155] Churchill, *Their Finest Hour*, pp. 576–577: *The Grand Alliance*, pp. 379, 465.
[156] Eisenhower, *Crusade in Europe*, pp. 206–252.
[157] *The Public Papers, etc., of F.D.R.*, 1940 vol., p. 192.
[158] *Ibid.*, 1940 vol., p. 213.
[159] Churchill, *Their Finest Hour*, p. 25: Hull, *op. cit.*, Vol. I, p. 831.
[160] *Pearl Harbor Attack*, Part 1, pp. 255–256.

161 *Ibid.*, Part 14, pp. 933-934.
162 *Ibid.*, Part 14, pp. 935–937.
163 *Ibid.*, Part 14, pp. 938–939.
164 Churchill, *Their Finest Hour*, p. 56.
165 *Ibid.*, pp. 56–57.
166 Churchill, *The Grand Alliance*, p. 388.
167 *The Memoirs of Cordell Hull*, Vol. I., p. 772.
168 N. Y. *Times*, May 25, 1940, p. 1, col. 2.
169 *Hearings Before the Special Senate Committee Investigating Petroleum Resources: 79th Congress, 1st Session*; Vol. of Nov. 15–17, 1945, p. 47.
170 Sherwood, *Roosevelt and Hopkins*, p. 161.
171 Sherwood, *Roosevelt and Hopkins*, p. 136: cf. *The Memoirs of Cordell Hull*, Vol. I, p. 208.
172 N. Y. *Sun*, Oct. 23, 1947, p. 1., cols. 5–6; N. Y. *Times*, Oct. 24, 1947, p. 1., cols. 2–3.
173 This was Mr. Churchill's expectation: *Their Finest Hour*, p. 147.
174 *The Public Papers, etc., of F.D.R.*, 1940 vol., pp. 230–240.
175 *Ibid.*, 1940 vol., p. 216.
176 At a later date he asked Mr. Hull to refer to him, even within the cabinet, as Commander in Chief and not as President. *The Memoirs of Cordell Hull*, Vol. II, p. 1111.
177 *The Public Papers, etc., of F.D.R.*, 1940 vol., p. 200.
178 *Ibid.*, 1940 vol., p. 215: May 17, 1940.
179 *Ibid.*, 1940 vol., p. 217.
180 *The United States at War*, p. 173.
181 *Ibid.*, p. 29.
182 *Ibid.*, p. 41.
183 Churchill, *The Grand Alliance*, p. 641.
184 *Pearl Harbor Attack*, Part 14, pp. 943–945.
185 *The Public Papers, etc., of F.D.R.*, 1940 vol., pp. 241–250.
186 *Ibid.*, 1940 vol., p. 205.
187 *Ibid.*, 1940 vol., pp. 249–250.
188 *Ibid.*, 1940 vol., pp. 250–252: *Peace and War*, pp. 77–78.
189 Stettinius, *Lend-Lease, Weapon for Victory*, pp. 24–25. The weapons were sold to the United States Steel Export Company, which forthwith resold them to Britain. "The subterfuge was obvious *'" admitted Mr. Stimson: *On Active Service in Peace and War*, p. 356.
190 Churchill, *Their Finest Hour*, p. 557
191 *Ibid.*, p. 118.
192 *The Public Papers, etc., of F.D.R.*, 1940 vol., *Introduction*, dated July 17, 1941, pp. xxiv–xxv, xxix.
193 From the historical point of view, and in the light of events prior to 1812, and prior to 1917, a strangely inaccurate remark.
194 Vice Admiral McIntire wrote that "Mr. Churchill begged for help": *White House Physician*, p. 117.
195 Churchill, *Their Finest Hour*, pp. 145-146.
196 *Ibid.*, pp. 400–401.
197 Armstrong, *Chronology of Failure*, p. 70. Note that it was later

believed that Mr. Roosevelt's telephone calls, at least to Ambassador Bullitt, were intercepted by the Germans. *Pearl Harbor Attack*, Part 3, p. 1213.

[198] Stettinius, *Lend-Lease, Weapon for Victory*, p. 29.

[199] *The Public Papers, etc., of F.D.R.*, 1940 vol., pp. 253–254.

[200] *Ibid.*, 1940 vol., pp. 673–674.

[201] *The Morgenthau Diaries, Collier's*, Oct. 18, 1947, Vol. 120, No. 16, p. 72.

[202] *The Public Papers, etc., of F.D.R.*, 1940 vol., pp. 259–264.

[203] Armstrong, *Chronology of Failure*, p. 81.

[204] *The Public Papers, etc., of F.D.R.*, 1940 vol., pp. 265–266.

[205] Churchill, *Their Finest Hour*, p. 152.

[206] *Ibid.*, pp. 132–133.

[207] *Ibid.*, p. 178.

[208] *Pearl Harbor Attack*, Part 15, pp. 1916–1917.

[209] *Ibid.*, Part 15, p. 1908.

[210] Churchill, *Their Finest Hour*, pp. 178–183.

[211] *Peace and War*, pp. 74–75: Churchill, *Their Finest Hour*, pp. 183–184. Sherwood, *Roosevelt and Hopkins*, p. 145, has a slightly different version—perhaps not paraphrased?

[212] Churchill, *Their Finest Hour*, p. 184.

[213] *Ibid.*, p. 185–186.

[214] *Ibid.*, pp. 184–185.

[215] *Peace and War*, p. 75.

[216] *The Public Papers, etc., of F.D.R.*, 1940 vol., 266–267.

[217] Churchill, *Their Finest Hour*, p. 187.

[218] *Ibid.*, p. 187.

[219] *Ibid.*, pp. 188–189.

[220] Armstrong, *Chronology of Failure*, p. 100.

[221] Churchill, *Their Finest Hour*, pp. 194–196.

[222] Armstrong, *Chronology of Failure*, pp. 103–104: text in N. Y. *Times*, June 18, 1940, p. 9, cols. 2–4, and in Churchill, *Their Finest Hour*, p. 208–209. Those who are interested in the genesis of this imaginative idea should read *If, Or History Rewritten*, p. 279, an analogous fictional proposal written in 1931 by Mr. Churchill.

[223] Churchill, *Their Finest Hour*, p. 200.

[224] Armstrong, *Chronology of Failure*, p. 105.

[225] *Peace and War*, p. 76.

[226] *Ibid.*, p. 76.

[227] Armstrong, *Chronology of Failure*, p. 110.

[228] *Pearl Harbor Attack*, Part 1, p. 271; Part 14, p. 949; Part 15, pp. 1594, 1597.

[229] *Ibid.*, Part 14, p. 947; Part 15, p. 1595.

[230] *Ibid.*, Part 15, pp. 1929–1931; 1908–1910.

[231] Leahy, *I Was There*, p. 444; *Peace and War*, pp. 76, 103.

[232] *The Ciano Diaries*, p. 265.

[233] *United States and Italy*, p. 18.

[234] *The Public Papers, etc., of F.D.R.*, 1940 vol., pp. 271–272.

[235] *Life* magazine, Vol. 9, No. 1, p. 7: July 1, 1940.

[236] *Life* magazine, Vol. 9, No. 11, p. 26: Sept, 9, 1940.
[237] *Life* magazine, Vol. 9, No. 1, pp. 7–8: July 1, 1940.
[238] N.Y. *Times*, June 16, 1940, Section 4, p. E-8, col. 2.
[239] See *34 American Journal of International Law*, pp. 569–572.
[240] *The Public Papers, etc., of F.D.R.*, 1940 vol., pp. 273–274.
[241] Churchill, *Their Finest Hour*, p. 227.
[242] Sherwood, *Roosevelt and Hopkins*, p. 147.
[243] Churchill, *Their Finest Hour*, p. 227.
[244] *Ibid.*, pp. 228–229.
[245] Stettinius, *Lend-Lease, Weapon for Victory*, pp. 27–28.
[246] *The United States at War*, p. 27.
[247] *Peace and War*, p. 91: cf. Churchill, *The Grand Alliance*, pp. 423, 426—eleven months later.
[248] Sherwood, *Roosevelt and Hopkins*, p. 407.
[249] *The Public Papers, etc., of F.D.R.*, 1940 vol., pp. 274–275.
[250] McIntire, *White House Physician*, p. 117.
[251] Churchill, *Their Finest Hour*, p. 171; cf. *The Von Hassell Diaries*, p. 145.
[252] *The Public Papers, etc., of F.D.R.*, 1940 vol., p. 281.
[253] On this topic compare Churchill, *The Grand Alliance*, p. 137, with Sherwood, *Roosevelt and Hopkins*, p. 271.
[254] Churchill, *The Grand Alliance*, p. 424.
[255] *The United States at War*, p. 31.
[256] Leahy, *I Was There*, p. 444.
[257] Sherwood, *Roosevelt and Hopkins*, p. 149.
[258] Armstrong, *Chronology of Failure*, p. 166: Churchill, *Their Finest Hour*, p. 235.
[259] Armstrong, *Chronology of Failure*, pp. 166–167.
[260] *The Public Papers, etc., of F.D.R.*, 1940 vol., p. 276.
[261] *Ibid.*, 1940 vol., pp. 277–280.
[262] *Ibid.*, 1940 vol., p. 281.
[263] *The Ciano Diaries*, p. 272.
[264] *The Public Papers, etc., of F.D.R.*, 1940 vol., p. 672.
[265] *Ibid.*, 1940 vol., pp. 284–285.
[266] *Ibid.*, 1940 vol., pp. 286–291: *The United States at War*, p. 21.

CHAPTER VI

[1] *The Public Papers, etc., of F.D.R.*, 1940 vol., p. 292.
[2] *Ibid.*, 1940 vol., pp. 293–303.
[3] *Ibid.*, 1940 vol., pp. 415, 495: see also Commager, *Documents of American History*, p. 622.
[4] Commager, *Documents of American History*, p. 617.
[5] Byrnes, *Speaking Frankly*, pp. 10–11: N.Y. *Times*, Oct. 29, 1941, p. 4, cols. 3–4.
[6] Sherwood, *Roosevelt and Hopkins*, pp. 176–177.
[7] Flynn, *You're the Boss*, pp. 156–159.

⁸ *Newsweek,* Vol. 28, No. 22, Nov. 25, 1946; p. 24, col. 3.
⁹ *The Ciano Diaries,* p. 293: cf. p. 218, where it did not come off so well.
¹⁰ *The Public Papers, etc., of F.D.R.,* 1940 vol., pp. 293–303.
¹¹ *The Wilson Era, Years of Peace, 1910–1917,* by Josephus Daniels, pp. 472–473.
¹² Ludwig, *Roosevelt,* p. 117; cf. pp. 99, 330, 339–340.
¹³ *Ibid.,* p. 63.
¹⁴ *The Public Papers, etc., of F.D.R.,* 1940 vol., pp. 306–311.
¹⁵ *Ibid.,* 1940 vol., pp. 312–313, where the places and dates are itemized. He also made "short talks" which are not printed: *ibid.,* p. 467.
¹⁶ *Ibid.,* 1940 vol., pp. 407–416.
¹⁷ *Ibid.,* 1940 vol., 435–442.
¹⁸ *Ibid.,* 1940 vol., pp. 446–449.
¹⁹ *Life* magazine, Vol. 9, No. 10, p. 30: Sept. 2, 1940.
²⁰ *Pink Pepper,* by Wesley Price, *Saturday Evening Post,* Aug. 31, 1946, p. 118.
²¹ *The Public Papers, etc., of F.D.R.,* 1940 vol., p. 450.
²² *Ibid.,* 1940 vol., pp. 460–467.
²³ *Ibid.,* 1940 vol., pp. 480–481.
²⁴ *Ibid.,* 1940 vol., p. 481.
²⁵ *Ibid.,* 1940 vol., pp. 483–485, 539–543.
²⁶ *Ibid.,* 1940 vol., pp. 485, 510, 524, 553, 558.
²⁷ *Ibid.,* 1940 vol., pp. 483–485.
²⁸ *Ibid.,* 1940 vol., pp. 485–495.
²⁹ *Ibid.,* 1940 vol., pp. 499–510.
³⁰ The characterization is Mr. Sherwood's: *Roosevelt and Hopkins,* p. 189.
³¹ *The Public Papers, etc., of F.D.R.,* 1940 vol., pp. 514–524.
³² Sherwood, *Roosevelt and Hopkins,* pp. 192–201.
³³ *The Public Papers, etc., of F.D.R.,* 1940 vol., p. 570.
³⁴ *Ibid.,* 1940 vol., pp. 530–539.
³⁵ *Ibid.,* 1940 vol., pp. 539–541.
³⁶ *Ibid.,* 1940 vol., pp. 541–543.
³⁷ *Ibid.,* 1940 vol., p. 499.
³⁸ *Ibid.,* 1940 vol., pp. 544–553.
³⁹ But after the election he "weaseled" away from it: 1940 vol., p. 560.
⁴⁰ *The Public Papers, etc., of F.D.R.,* 1940 vol., pp. 554–558.
⁴¹ *Ibid.,* Vol. 5, p. 582, and 1940 vol., p. 558.
⁴² See Mr. Sherwood's unhappy reflections about the election—the "false faces," and the "smear" left on Mr. Roosevelt's record: *Roosevelt and Hopkins,* pp. 200–201.
⁴³ *The Public Papers, etc., of F.D.R.,* 1940 Vol., p. 554.
⁴⁴ *Ibid.,* 1940 vol., p. 651.

CHAPTER VII

¹ "The Lost Peace," by Major General J. F. C. Fuller, *Army Ordnance,* March–April 1947, pp. 415–416.
² N. Y. *Herald Tribune,* June 22, 1947, p. 1, col. 5.
³ *The Public Papers, etc., of F.D.R.,* 1940 vol., p. 674.
⁴ *Ibid.,* 1940 vol., pp. 563–564, 612.

⁵ *Life* magazine, Vol. 9, No. 11, p. 26: Sept. 9, 1940.

⁶ *We Saw It Happen*, Ch. 6, "Britain—A Story of Old Age," by Ferdinand Kuhn, p. 186.

⁷ Armstrong, *Chronology of Failure*, pp. 128, 158–160.

⁸ Butcher, *My Three Years With Eisenhower*, p. 257; cf. p. 622 as to "Britain's ebbing manpower in July 1944.

⁹ *Life* magazine, Vol. 21, No. 6, p. 46: Aug. 5, 1946.

¹⁰ Churchill, *Their Finest Hour*, pp. 226–227; cf. pp. 222–223.

¹¹ *Note:* this opinion contradicts his many statements to Mr. Roosevelt that the British fleet would have to be surrendered as a part of the price of obtaining peace.

¹² Sherwood, *Roosevelt and Hopkins*, p. 364.

¹³ *My New Order*, pp. 809–838; especially pp. 836–838.

¹⁴ Shirer, *Berlin Diary*, pp. 453, 457, 459, 550–552: *The Ciano Diaries*, p. 277.

¹⁵ Shirer, *Berlin Diary*, pp. 458, 561.

¹⁶ *Ibid.*, p. 461: The *Ciano Diaries*, pp. 281, 288: *The Von Hassell Diaries*, p. 145.

¹⁷ *The Ciano Diaries*, p. 286.

¹⁸ Churchill, *Their Finest Hour*, p. 260.

¹⁹ *The United States at War*, pp. 507–508.

²⁰ *Nazi Conspiracy and Aggression*, Vol. III, pp. 399–400.

²¹ *The Ciano Diaries*, p. 296.

²² *Nazi Conspiracy and Aggression*, Vol. III, pp. 406–407: see also *Fuehrer Conferences on Matters Dealing with the German Navy*, Vol. II, pp. 22–23.

²³ *The Von Hassell Diaries*, pp. 146, 156, 197–198.

²⁴ *The Ciano Diaries*, p. 182.

²⁵ *Ibid.*, p. 269; cf: p: 272.

²⁶ Shirer, *Berlin Diary*, p. 550.

²⁷ *Ibid.*, p. 450.

²⁸ *Nazi Conspiracy and Aggression*, Vol. V, p. 741.

²⁹ *Ibid.*, Vol. V, pp. 734, 740.

³⁰ *The Ciano Diaries*, p. 293.

³¹ Nazi Conspiracy and Aggression, Vol. VI, p. 889.

³² *The Ciano Diaries*, pp. 298–299.

³³ *Nazi-Soviet Relations*, p. 215.

³⁴ *Ibid.*, pp. 207–213.

³⁵ *Nazi-Soviet Relations*, pp. 217–225.

³⁶ *Ibid.*, pp. 226–234.

³⁷ *Ibid.*, pp. 234–247.

³⁸ Churchill, *Their Finest Hour*, pp. 584, 586.

³⁹ *Nazi-Soviet Relations*, pp. 247–254.

⁴⁰ *Ibid.*, pp. 258–259.

⁴¹ *Ibid.*, pp. 270–271.

⁴² *Ibid.*, pp. 271–273.

⁴³ *Nazi Conspiracy and Aggression*, Vol. III, pp. 406–407.

⁴⁴ Ibid., Vol. III, pp. 407–408; Vol. V, p. 740: *Nazi-Soviet Relations*, pp, 260–264.

⁴⁵ *Saturday Evening Post*, May 13, 1950: "How Russia Almost Lost the War," by General Alexei Markoff; p. 175, col. 1.

⁴⁶ Sherwood, *Roosevelt and Hopkins*, p. 175.
⁴⁷ Churchill, *Their Finest Hour*, p. 401.
⁴⁸ *Life* magazine, Vol. 9, No. 3, pp. 24–25: July 15, 1940.
⁴⁹ *Peace and War*, p. 79.
⁵⁰ *The United States at War*, p. 33.
⁵¹ Churchill, *Their Finest Hour*, pp. 401–402.
⁵² *Ibid.*, pp. 402–403.
⁵³ *Ibid.*, pp. 404–405.
⁵⁴ *Ibid.*, pp. 405–406.
⁵⁵ *The Public Papers, etc., of F.D.R.*, 1940 vol., p. 322.
⁵⁶ *Ibid.*, 1940 vol., pp. 333–334. Mr. Stimson states, *On Active Service, etc.*, p. 356, that on August 13 Mr. Roosevelt had drafted the essential principles of the agreement which was later reached.
⁵⁷ Churchill, *Their Finest Hour*, pp. 406–407.
⁵⁸ *Ibid.*, pp. 409–410.
⁵⁹ *The Public Papers, etc., of F.D.R.*, 1940 vol., p. 394: see also *The Memoirs of Cordell Hull*, Vol. I, pp. 831–842.
⁶⁰ Churchill, *Their Finest Hour*, pp. 410–412.
⁶¹ *Ibid.*, pp. 412–413.
⁶² *Ibid.*, pp. 413–414.
⁶³ Churchill, *Their Finest Hour*, p. 414.
⁶⁴ *The Public Papers, etc., of F.D.R.*, 1940 vol., pp. 376–385.
⁶⁵ *Ibid.*, 1940 vol., p. 391–394.
⁶⁶ *American Journal of International Law*, Vol. 34, pp. 569, 690.

⁶⁷ *The Public Papers, etc., of F.D.R.*, 1940 vol., pp. 394–405.
⁶⁸ Churchill, *Their Finest Hour*, p. 404, where he expresses the opinion that it would have justified a German declaration of war against America, for which he felt his hope was in vain.
⁶⁹ N. Y. *Times*, Sept. 4, 1940, p. 1, col. 3.
⁷⁰ *Ibid.*, Sept. 7, 1940, p. 8, col. 1. Compare a similar statement in the N. Y. *Times*, Sept. 6, 1940, p. 16, col. 5. It has been asserted that before the destroyer deal was consummated Mr. Roosevelt approached Mr. Willkie through a secret emissary and obtained his promise that the deal would not be made a campaign issue: *The Aspirin Age*, "Wendell Willkie: a Study in Courage," at p. 453. Mr. Sherwood, *Roosevelt and Hopkins*, pp. 175–176, states that the emissary was Mr. William Allen White. In the light of Mr. Willkie's statements it is difficult to believe that he gave such a promise.
⁷¹ *The Public Papers, etc., of F.D.R.*, 1940 vol., pp. 377–379, 382.
⁷² "there already"? Mr. Roosevelt obviously checked himself from what he thought would be an imprudent expression. In late August well-informed observers thought that the destroyers were already in Canadian waters. We are told that the British crews were already there. Churchill, *Their Finest Hour*, pp. 407, 415.
⁷³ *The Public Papers, etc., of F.D.R.*, 1940 vol., p. 331.
⁷⁴ *Life* magazine, Vol. 9, No. 10, p. 22: Sept. 2, 1940.

[75] *Fuehrer Conferences on Matters Dealing with the German Navy*, 1940, Vol. II, pp. 19–20, 24–25, 28, 31, 33–34, 40–41, 53–55.

[76] *The Memoirs of Cordell Hull*, Vol. I, p. 834.

[77] *Ibid.*, pp. 796–797.

[78] *Ibid.*, p. 790. See note 197 to Ch. V.

[79] Leahy, *I Was There*, pp. 15–16.

[80] *The Public Papers, etc., of F.D.R.*, 1940 vol., pp. 313–314.

[81] *Ibid.*, 1940 vol., p. 315.

[82] *Ibid.*, 1940 vol., pp. 357–359.

[83] *Ibid.*, 1940 vol., p. 321.

[84] *Ibid.*, 1940 vol., p. 322.

[85] *Ibid.*, 1940 vol., pp. 323–327.

[86] *Peace and War*, pp. 79–80.

[87] *The Public Papers, etc., of F.D.R.*, 1940 vol., pp. 337–341.

[88] *Ibid.*, 1940 vol., p. 353. See also the same vol., p. 434, for a similar argument on September 16, 1940.

[89] Churchill, *Their Finest Hour*, p. 277.

[90] *Ibid.*, p. 672.

[91] *Ibid.*, pp. 487–488. Mr. Stimson, *On Active Service, etc.*, p. 359, states that these rifles, thirty million rounds of ammunition, and five bombers, formed part of the destroyer deal, and were omitted from the final document through mere inadvertence.

[92] *The Public Papers, etc., of F.D.R.*, 1940 vol., pp. 370–375.

[93] *Peace and War*, p. 81.

[94] *Ibid.*, pp. 81–82.

[95] *Ibid.*, p. 86.

[96] *The Public Papers, etc., of F.D.R.*, 1940 vol., p. 428.

[97] *Ibid.*, 1940 vol., pp. 429, 432, 473–475.

[98] *Ibid.*, 1940 vol., pp. 422–444.

[99] *Ibid.*, 1940 vol., pp. 510–514.

[100] *Ibid.*, 1940 vol., pp. 321, 432.

[101] *Ibid.*, 1940 vol., pp. 433–434.

[102] *Ibid.*, 1940 vol., p. 443.

[103] *Ibid.*, 1940 vol, pp. 474, 511, 512, 516.

[104] *Ibid.*, 1940 vol., pp. 444, 512, 513, 517.

[105] *Ibid.*, 1940 vol., p. 434: "* intelligently led, comfortably clothed, well fed and adequately armed and equipped * . * physically hardened, mentally disciplined and properly trained in fundamentals *." Cf. *ibid.*, p. 513.

[106] *Ibid.*, 1940 vol., pp. 434, 473–474, 475, 513–514.

[107] *The Memoirs of Cordell Hull*, Vol. I, p. 870:—"We were working closely with the British Government in diplomatic matters in many parts of the world *." Cf. Welles, *The Time for Decision*, pp. 155–156.

[108] Churchill, *Their Finest Hour*, pp. 487–488.

[109] Leahy, *I Was There*, p. 9.

[110] Churchill, *Their Finest Hour*, p. 513.

[111] *Ibid.*, pp. 513–514.

[112] *Ibid.*, p. 514: cf. Welles, *The Time for Decision*. pp. 155–156.

[113] *Peace and War*, pp. 82–83.

[114] *Pearl Harbor Attack*, Part 14, p. 964.

[115] *Ibid.*, Part 11, p. 5239.
[116] Stettinius, *Lend-Lease, Weapon for Victory*, p. 57.
[117] Churchill, *Their Finest Hour*, pp. 516–517.
[118] *Ibid.*, pp. 517–518; Leahy, *I Was There*, p. 445.
[119] Churchill, *Their Finest Hour*, pp. 529–530.
[120] Sherwood, *Roosevelt and Hopkins*, p. 221.
[121] Churchill, *Their Finest Hour*, p. 558.

CHAPTER VIII

[1] *Pearl Harbor Attack*, Part 14, page 972; Part 16, pp. 2448–2450.
[2] *Ibid.*, Part 20, pp. 4072–4074.
[3] *The Public Papers, etc., of F.D.R.*, 1940 vol., p. 562: see N. Y. *Times*, Nov. 14, 1940, p. 18, col. 1.
[4] *The Public Papers, etc., of F.D.R.*, 1940 vol., p. 564.
[5] Olive E. Clapper, *Washington Tapestry*, pp. 260–262.
[6] Churchill, *Their Finest Hour*, p. 558.
[7] Sherwood, *Roosevelt and Hopkins*, p. 223.
[8] Churchill, *Their Finest Hour*, pp. 558–567; *The Morgenthau Diaries*, *Collier's*, Oct. 18, 1947, Vol. 120, No. 16, p. 72.
[9] On Dec. 13, 1940, Mr. Churchill (*Their Finest Hour*, pp. 606–607) threatened to cut off all British shipping from Eire, intending to force the grant of bases. He asked for Mr. Roosevelt's "reactions" to this. Mr. Roosevelt's initial reactions seem to have been favorable. For some days he was thinking what action to take, and how to negotiate with Eire, and who should be sent as his representative; perhaps Joseph P. Kennedy, perhaps General Donovan: Sherwood, *Roosevelt and Hopkins*, p. 230.
[10] Churchill, *Their Finest Hour*, p. 409.
[11] *Pearl Harbor Attack*, Part 14, p. 984; Part 20, pp. 4075–4076.
[12] *Ibid.*, Part 4, pp. 1929–1930; Part 5, p. 2102.
[13] *The Public Papers, etc., of F.D.R.*, 1940 vol., pp. 604–615.
[14] *Ibid.*, 1940 vol., p. 674. Messrs. Davis and Lindley state that "The bottom of the barrel was constructively in sight" by Sept. 1940: *op. cit.*, p. 108. This was in substance the phrase which Secretary Morgenthau used when testifying to a House subcommittee on December 17, 1940; Davis and Lindley, *op. cit.*, p. 119. Nevertheless "On December 18 the British Purchasing Commission was advised to place new orders for $3,000,000,000 in war materials without delay, and the orders, for which no British cash was available, were so placed." Davis and Lindley, *op. cit.*, p. 120.
[15] *The Public Papers, etc., of F.D.R.*, 1940 vol., pp. 645, 647, 649.
[16] Sherwood, *Roosevelt and Hopkins*, pp. 234–260; Davis and Lindley, *How War Came*, pp. 173, 182.
[17] *The Public Papers, etc., of F.D.R.*, 1940 vol., pp. 622–631; see also *ibid.*, pp. 679–702.

[18] *Ibid.*, 1940 vol., pp. 633–644.
[19] *Peace and War*, p. 81.
[20] *The Morgenthau Diaries, Collier's*, Oct. 18, 1947; vol. 120, No. 16, p. 74.
[21] Churchill, *Their Finest Hour*, pp. 573–575.
[22] Delbert Clark, *Washington Dateline*, p. 301.
[23] *The Public Papers, etc., of F.D.R.*, 1940 vol., p. 645; see also pp. 715–716.
[24] *Ibid.*, 1940 vol., pp. 651–662.
[25] *Ibid.*, 1940 vol., pp. 663–672.
[26] *Ibid.*, 1940 vol., p. 689.
[27] N. Y. *Times*, Jan. 8, 1941, p. 1, cols. 4–5.
[28] *Ibid.*, Jan. 9, 1941, p. 19, col. 5.
[29] N. Y. *Times*, Jan. 9, 1941, p. 1, col. 5.
[30] *Our Navy at War*, Official Report by Admiral Ernest J. King, p. 20.
[31] *Pearl Harbor Attack*, Part 16, p. 2144.
[32] Admiral King's own words, *op. cit.*, p. 25. Admiral Stark steadily opposed "sending more combatant ships to the Far East." *Pearl Harbor Attack*, Part 16, pp. 2147–2148, 2151.
[33] Admiral King, *op. cit.*, p. 25.
[34] N. Y. *Times*, Jan. 7, 1941, p. 7, col. 1.
[35] *Ibid.*, Jan. 10, 1941, p. 18, col. 5.
[36] *Ibid.*, Jan. 10, 1941, p. 6, cols. 3–6.
[37] *Ibid.*, Jan. 25, 1941, p. 1, col. 8.
[38] *Ibid.*, Jan, 25, 1941, p. 3, cols. 3–4.
[39] *Ibid.*, Jan. 11, 1941, p. 3, col. 1.
[40] *Nazi Conspiracy and Aggression*, Vol. VII, p. 753.
[41] *Ibid.*, Vol. VII, pp. 800–814.
[42] *Ibid.*, Vol. VI, pp. 893–905.
[43] *Ibid.*, Vol. VII, p. 588.
[44] *Nazi Conspiracy and Aggression*, Vol. VI, pp. 276–278; also printed in *Nazi-Soviet Relations*, pp. 199–201, in a slightly different form of translation.
[45] *Nazi Conspiracy and Aggression*, Vol. III, p. 407.
[46] *Ibid.*, Vol. III, pp. 403–407.
[47] *Ibid.*, Vol. VII, p. 928: cf. *Fuehrer Conferences*, 1940, Vol. II, pp. 33, 51, 69.
[48] *The Von Hassell Diaries*, pp. 166, 197–198. At a later date Admiral Leahy, *I Was There*, p. 24, thought that the invasion of England was "impossible."
[49] Taylor, *Wartime Correspondence, etc.*, p. 49; Kravchenko, *I Chose Freedom*, pp. 352, 363. Vice Admiral Ross T. McIntire, *White House Physician*, p. 134, says that Mr. Roosevelt had predicted from the first that the Russo-German alliance would not last, and that "Under his instructions * Welles had been conducting conversations with Constantine Oumansky. * trying to drive a wedge between the two mismated partners.*"
[50] Taylor, *Wartime Correspondence, etc.*, p. 49: *Peace and War*, p. 105: *The Memoirs of Cordell Hull*, Vol. II, pp. 967–969: Welles, *The Time for Decision*, pp. 170–171.
[51] Stettinius, *Lend-Lease*, p. 120.
[52] N. Y. *Times*, Jan. 22, 1941, p. 1, col. 5.
[53] *Ibid.*, Jan. 22, 1941, p. 9, col. 1.
[54] Kravchenko, *I Chose Freedom*, pp. 335, 362–365, 466–467.

[55] N. Y. *Times*, Jan. 25, 1941, p. 14, col. 5.

[56] *Nazi Conspiracy and Aggression*, Vol. V, p. 740.

[57] *The Morgenthau Diaries*, *Collier's*, Oct. 18, 1947, Vol. 120, No. 16, p. 74: cf. Sherwood, *op. cit.*, p. 228.

[58] N. Y. *Times*, Jan. 10, 1941, p. 1, col. 8.

[59] *Ibid.*, Jan. 11, 1941, p. 1, col. 7.

[60] N. Y. *Times*, Jan. 9, 1941, p. 1, cols. 6–7.

[61] *Ibid.*, Jan. 9, 1941, p. 14 (entire page).

[62] *Ibid.*, Jan. 15, 1941, p. 1, cols. 6–7.

[63] *Ibid.*, Jan. 13, 1941, p. 4, cols. 2–4. Mr. Stimson, *On Active Service, etc.*, p. 357, says that here again Mr. Willkie was persuaded through the activities of an intermediary.

[64] N. Y. *Times*, Jan. 13, 1941, p. 1, col. 8.

[65] *Ibid.*, Jan. 15, 1941, p. 22, col. 5.

[66] *Ibid.*, Jan. 13, 1941, p. 14, col. 5.

[67] *Ibid.*, Jan. 16, 1941, p. 1, col. 8: *Peace and War*, pp. 96, 113.

[68] *The Morgenthau Diaries*, *Collier's*, Oct. 18, 1947; Vol. 120, No. 16, p. 75. Mr. Stimson, *On Active Service, etc.*, p. 360, says that all of these lend-lease statements were planned in advance in a unified way.

[69] N. Y. *Times*, Jan. 16, 1941, p. 8, cols. 1–5.

[70] Six weeks earlier, Count Ciano had found Mussolini "discouraged as never before." He said: "There is nothing else to do. This is grotesque and absurd, but it is a fact. We have to ask for a truce through Hitler." *The Ciano Diaries*, p. 318: Dec. 4, 1940.

[71] N. Y. *Times*, Jan. 16, 1941, p. 10, cols. 2–6.

[72] N. Y. Times, Jan. 16, 1941, p. 1, col. 8.

[73] *Ibid.*, Jan. 16, 1941, p. 23, col. 2. The reader will perhaps have noticed that this news, while not suppressed, was hardly featured.

[74] *Ibid.*, Jan. 17, 1941, p. 1, col. 8.

[75] *Ibid.*, Jan. 17, 1941, p. 6, cols. 3–6.

[76] *Ibid.*, Jan. 18, 1941, p. 1, col. 5. Mr. Stimson, *On Active Service, etc.*, pp. 365–366, and Mr. Knox had become convinced that war was inevitable. They could not tell the American people that it was necessary to fight because they would at once lose their audience. They never allowed themselves to say that the final result of Mr. Roosevelt's policies was war, because their loyalty to him bound them to be silent.

[77] *Pearl Harbor Attack*, Part 20, p. 4275.

[78] *Ibid.*, Part 20, pp. 4276–4280.

[79] N. Y. *Times*, Jan. 18, 1941, p. 1, col. 4.

[80] *Ibid.*, Jan. 18, 1941, p. 1, col. 8: cf. Sherwood, *op. cit.*, at p. 247.

[81] It has been stated that at this time there were many trans-Atlantic telephone conversations between Mr. Churchill and Mr. Hopkins in Britain, and Mr. Roosevelt: Davis and Lindley, *How War Came*, pp. 181–182.

[82] N. Y. *Times*, Jan. 19, 1941, p. 1, cols. 6–7; text at p. 35, cols. 1–7.

[83] The interested student of Butcher, *My Three Years with Eisenhower*, will have observed the many months of planning which preceded the channel crossing, and will have noted the vast quantities of material and equipment which were prerequisite; e.g., pp. 500, 502, 524, 527, 530, etc.

[83a] *The Ciano Diaries*, p. 338.

[84] N. Y. *Times*, Jan. 21, 1941, p. 2, cols. 3–4.

[85] *Ibid.*, Jan. 22, 1941, p. 1, col. 2.

[86] *Ibid.*, Jan. 21, 1941, p. 20, col. 5.

[87] *Ibid.*, Jan. 20, 1941, p. 16, col. 5.

[88] *Ibid.*, Jan. 25, 1941, p. 4, cols. 4–5.

[89] *Ibid.*, Jan. 29, 1941, p. 1, col. 5.

[90] *Ibid.*, Jan. 30, 1941, p. 1, col. 1.

[91] *Ibid.*, Jan. 26, 1941, p. 1, col. 6: p. 5, col. 1.

[92] *Ibid.*, Jan. 21, 1941, p. 1, cols. 5–6.

[93] *Ibid.*, Jan. 29, 1941, p. 1, col. 8.

[94] *Ibid.*, Jan. 30, 1941, p. 1, col. 8.

[95] *Ibid*, Feb. 1, 1941, p. 5, cols. 2–4.

[96] *Pearl Harbor Attack*, Part 14, p. 1422.

[97] N. Y. *Times*, Feb. 1, 1941, p. 1, col. 8.

[98] *Ibid.*, Jan. 21, p. 1, col. 4.

[99] *Ibid.*, Feb. 11, 1941, p. 11, col. 2. They left together by clipper on Feb. 27; N. Y. *Times*, Feb. 28, 1941, col. 6.

[100] *Ibid.*, Feb. 7, 1941, p. 18, col. 5; Feb. 16, 1941, Sec. 4, p. 3, col. 1.

[101] McIntire, *White House Physician*, p. 156; Elliott Roosevelt, *As He Saw It*, pp. 36–38.

[102] Elliott Roosevelt, *op. cit.*, pp. 74–77, 86, 114–116, 121–122, 165.

[103] McIntire, *op. cit.*, p. 152: Elliott Roosevelt, *op. cit.*, pp. 110–112.

[104] Elliott Roosevelt, *op. cit.*, pp. 223–224.

[105] McIntire, *op. cit.*, pp. 230–231; Elliott Roosevelt, *op. cit.*, p. 245.

[106] *Pearl Harbor Attack*, Part 11, p. 5240.

[107] *Ibid.*, Part 4, pp. 1931–1933; Part 15, pp. 1485–1584.

[108] *Ibid.*, Part 14, p. 993.

[109] *Ibid.*, Part 2, p. 726; Part 5, p. 2372.

[110] Text in *Pearl Harbor Attack*, Part 15, pp. 1485–1550.

[111] Text in *Pearl Harbor Attack*, Part 15, pp. 1551–1584.

[112] *Pearl Harbor Attack*, Part 3, pp. 994–997.

[113] *Ibid.*, Part 5, p. 2391.

[114] *Our Navy at War*, p. 3.

[115] *Pearl Harbor Attack*, Part 15, p. 1564.

[116] *Pearl Harbor Committee Report*, p. 508.

[117] *Pearl Harbor Attack*, Part 7, p. 3199; Part 9, pp. 4317—4320, 4564—4565.

[118] N. Y. *Times*, April 3, 1941, p. 1, col. 3.

[119] *Ibid.*, April 4, 1941, p. 1, col. 5.

[120] *Ibid.*, April 8, 1941, p. 9, col. 1.

[121] *Pearl Harbor Attack*, Part 12, pp. 3, 9, 27, 57, 88, 98, 110, 120, 121, 128, 149, 152, 161, 165, 172, 175, 182, 206, 227.

[122] *Ibid.*, Part 19, pp. 3442–3444.

[123] *Ibid.*, Part 19, pp. 3447–3449.

[124] *Ibid.*, Part 19, pp. 3450–3451.
[125] *Ibid.*, Part 19, pp. 3445–3446.
[126] *Ibid.*, Part 21, pp. 4720–4721.
[127] *Ibid.*, Part 19, pp. 3452–3453.
[128] See *Foreign Relations, Japan; 1931–1941*, Vol. II, p. 388, line 5.
[129] *Pearl Harbor Attack*, Part 19, p. 3454.
[130] N. Y. *Times*, Feb, 6, 1941, p. 1, cols. 2–3.
[131] *Pearl Harbor Attack*, Part 15, p. 1602: cf. Churchill, *The Grand Alliance*, pp. 142–145.
[132] N. Y. *Times*, Feb. 9, 1941, p. 35, cols. 4–5.
[133] *Ibid.*, Feb. 10, 1941, p. 8, cols. 2–6.
[134] Sherwood, *Roosevelt and Hopkins*, pp. 260–261.
[135] *The United States at War*, p. 46.
[136] Churchill, *The Grand Alliance*, p. 128.
[137] N. Y. *Times*, Feb. 11, 1941, p. 6, col. 6.
[138] *Ibid.*, Feb. 10, 1941, p. 1, cols. 2–3.
[139] *Ibid.*, Feb. 10, 1941, p. 16, col. 5.
[140] *Ibid.*, Feb. 10, 1941, p. 1, col. 1.
[141] *Ibid.*, Feb. 12, 1941, p. 1, col. 8.
[142] *Ibid.*, Feb. 12, 1941, p. 4, col. 1, to p. 5, col. 8.
[143] Minority report in N. Y. *Times*, Feb. 19, 1941, p. 4, cols. 2–7.
[144] *Ibid.*, Feb. 17, 1941, p. 1, col. 5.
[145] *Ibid.*, Feb. 18, 1941, p. 1, col. 1.
[146] *Ibid.*, Feb. 19, 1941, p. 5, col. 5.
[147] *Ibid.*, Feb. 28, 1941, p. 9, col. 2.
[148] *Ibid.*, Feb. 18, 1941, p. 1, cols. 2–3.
[149] *Ibid.*, Feb. 21, 1941, p. 1, col. 6; p. 4, col. 6.
[150] *Ibid.*, Feb. 18, 1941, p. 22, col. 5.
[151] *Pearl Harbor Attack*, Part 11, p. 5239.
[152] N. Y. *Times*, Feb. 21, 1941, p. 1, col. 8.
[153] *Pearl Harbor Attack*, Part 3, pp. 1229–1230, 1383.
[154] N. Y. *Times*, Feb, 22, 1941, p. 1, cols. 2–3.
[155] *Ibid.*, Feb. 22, 1941, p. 7, col. 6.
[156] *Ibid.*, Feb. 22, 1941, p. 6, col. 2.
[157] *Ibid.*, Feb. 25, 1941, p. 1, col. 1.
[158] *Ibid.*, Feb. 25, 1941, p. 10, col. 1.
[159] *Ibid.*, Feb. 26, 1941, p. 1, col. 8.
[160] *Ibid.*, Feb. 27, 1941, p. 1, col. 8.
[161] *Ibid.*, Feb. 27, 1941, p. 18, col. 5.
[162] *Ibid.*, Feb. 28, 1941, p. 1, col. 2.
[163] *Ibid.*, March 7, 1941, p. 1, col. 4.
[164] *Ibid.*, March 6, 1941, p. 10, col. 5.
[165] *Ibid.*, March 5, 1941, p. 11, col. 1.
[166] *Pearl Harbor Attack*, Part 15, p. 1489. On March 25 Mr. Stimson had already met with the senior British officials in Washington in order to discuss with them the need for American

aid in convoying: *On Active Service, etc.*, p. 368.

[167] *Pearl Harbor Attack*, Part 17, pp. 2462–2463.

[168] *International Transactions of the U. S., etc.*, p. 35.

[169] Sherwood, *Roosevelt and Hopkins*, p. 270.

[170] Churchill, *The Grand Alliance*, p. 138: Stettinius, *Lend-Lease*, p. 141.

[171] Churchill, *The Grand Alliance*, pp. 127, 732, 741.

[172] *The United States at War*, p. 145.

[173] *Pearl Harbor Attack*, Part 19, pp. 3456–3457.

[174] *Ibid.*, Part 19, pp. 3460–3461.

[175] Sevareid, *Not So Wild a Dream*, pp. 193–194.

[176] *Ibid.*, p. 199.

[177] *Saturday Evening Post*, Oct. 11, 1941, p. 28.

[178] "Capital Parade," by Joseph Alsop and Robert Kintner; *The Washington Post*, June 4, 1941, p. 9, col. 6.

[179] N. Y. *Times*, March 30, 1941, p. 42, cols. 2–5.

[180] Beard, *Basic History of the U. S.*, pp. 482–483.

CHAPTER IX

[1] Langer, *Our Vichy Gamble*, p. 126; see N. Y. *Times*, March 5, 1946, pp. 12–13.

[2] N. Y. *Times*, Feb. 13, 1941, p. 1, col. 1.

[3] *Ibid.*, Feb. 1, 1941, p. 1, col. 4.

[4] *The Ciano Diaries*, p. 339.

[5] *Nazi Conspiracy and Aggression*, Vol. VII, pp. 928, 975.

[6] *Ibid.*, Vol. VII, p. 928: Leahy, *I Was There*, p. 19; cf. Hayes, *Wartime Mission in Spain*, pp. 61–66.

[7] *The Ciano Diaries*, pp. 321, 331–333, 339.

[8] *Ibid.*, pp. 318, 324–325, 336–337.

[9] *Ibid.*, p. 339.

[10] *Nazi Conspiracy and Aggression*, Vol. V, p. 740.

[11] N. Y. *Times*, March 2, 1941, p. 1, cols. 5 and 8: see *The Ciano Diaries*, pp. 331, 335; and *Nazi-Soviet Relations*, pp. 276–279.

[12] N. Y. *Times*, March 3, 1941, p. 1, col. 8.

[13] *Ibid.*, Feb. 25, 1941, p. 1, cols. 4–5; see also *Our Frontier on the Danube, Saturday Evening Post*, May 24, 1941, p. 118: Churchill, *The Grand Alliance*, pp. 110, 158: Leahy, *I Was There*, p. 21.

[14] N. Y. *Times*, April 12, 1941, p. 3, col. 6.

[15] *Our Frontier on the Danube, Saturday Evening Post*, May 24, 1941, pp. 9, 118: cf. *Peace and War*, pp. 98–99; *The Von Hassell Diaries*, p. 179.

[16] *Nazi Conspiracy and Aggression*, Vol. VI, p. 996, item 141.

[17] N. Y. *Times*, April 12, 1941, p. 3, col. 6; cf. *United States and Italy*, p. 25.

[18] *Our Frontier on the Danube, Saturday Evening Post*, May 24, 1941, p. 118.

[19] N. Y. *Times*, Sept. 17, 1947, p. 12, cols. 3–4.

[20] *Ibid.*, April 1, 1941, p. 1, cols. 3–4.

[21] *Ibid.*, April 7, 1941, p. 1, col. 6; see *Fuehrer Conferences*, 1940, Vol. II, p. 68, under date of Dec. 27, 1940.

[22] For a succinct review of these unfortunate campaigns, see Hitler's speech of May 4, 1941, *My New Order*, pp. 957–962.

[23] N. Y. *Times*, May 21, 1941, p. 1, col. 8.

[24] *Ibid.*, June 2, 1941, p. 1, col. 8.

[25] *Pearl Harbor Attack*, Part 9, pp. 4299–4300.

[26] *Newsweek*, July 14, 1941, p. 23.

[27] *Our Frontier on the Danube*, *Saturday Evening Post*, May 24, 1941, p. 120.

[28] Text in Taylor, *op. cit.*, pp. 51–52.

[29] Text in Taylor, *op. cit.*, pp. 53–54.

[30] Churchill, *The Grand Alliance*, pp. 131–134.

[31] *Ibid.*, pp. 235–236.

[32] *Ibid.*, pp. 254, 754.

[33] *Ibid.*, pp. 793–794, 797, 351.

[34] *Ibid.*, pp. 139–140.

[35] *Ibid.*, p. 764.

[36] N. Y. *Times*, Dec. 4, 1941, p. 1, col. 2.

[37] N. Y. *Times*, June 6, 1941, p. 1, col. 8; text, p. 6, cols. 4–6.

[38] Elliott Roosevelt, *As He Saw It*, pp. 14–15.

[39] *Pearl Harbor Attack*, Part 16, pp. 2162–2163. It was on April 10 that Mr. Roosevelt conferred with Mr. Stimson, *On Active Service, etc.*, p. 368, at the White House. Mr. Roosevelt feared that the Congress would refuse if he asked for the power to convoy. Mr. Roosevelt was therefore "trying to see how far over in the direction of Great Britain we could get and how would be the best way to do it.*"

[40] *Pearl Harbor Attack*, Part 16, pp. 2160–2161.

[41] Admiral King, *Our Navy at War*, p. 6; cf. *Peace and War*, pp. 99–100.

[42] *Pearl Harbor Attack*, Part 5, p. 2170; Part 17, p. 2483.

[43] *The United States at War*, p. 44.

[44] *Ibid.*, pp. 48–49.

[45] *Ibid.*, pp. 56–57.

[46] *Ibid.*, p. 63.

[47] *The United States at War*, p. 61.

[48] *Ibid.*, p. 60.

[49] Blair Bolles, *Foreign Policy Reports*, Aug. 1, 1945, p. 145. "Meanwhile, the ocean policy led to an undeclared naval war between the United States and Germany.*"

[50] N. Y. *Times*, May 17, 1941, p. 1, col. 8, continued on p. 4, col. 2.

[51] *The United States at War*, p. 59.

[52] *Ibid.*, p. 24.

[53] *The United States at War*, p. 207.

[54] N. Y. *Times*, May 28, 1941, p. 2, cols. 2–8; *The United States at War*, p. 66; cf. Sherwood, *Roosevelt and Hopkins*, pp. 292–293, 296–298.

[55] *The Ciano Diaries*, p. 359.

[56] *Pearl Harbor Attack*, Part 5, p. 2113; Part 16, pp. 2168–2170.

[57] *Ibid.*, Part 11, p. 5503; Part 9, p. 4290.

[58] *Ibid.*, Part 5, pp. 2107, 2113; Part 6, p. 2505; Part 16, pp. 2163–2165.

[59] *Ibid.*, Part 1, p. 125.

[60] *Nazi Conspiracy and Aggression,* Vol. I, p. 801.
[61] *Pearl Harbor Attack,* Part 18, p. 2877.
[62] *Ibid.,* Part 18, pp. 2877, 2882, 2908–2909, 2914.
[63] *Ibid.,* Part 18, p. 2882.
[64] *Ibid.,* Part 18, p. 2911.
[65] *Ibid.,* Part 18, pp. 2885–2886, 2915.
[66] *Ibid.,* Part 18, pp. 2887, 2897, 2918.
[67] *Ibid.,* Part 18, pp. 2917, 2897, 2918.
[68] *Ibid.,* Part 18, p. 2916.
[69] *Ibid.,* Part 18, p. 2910.
[70] *Ency. Brit.,* 11th Ed., Vol. 22, pp. 142, 149.
[71] *Pearl Harbor Committee Report,* p. 168.
[72] *Our Navy at War,* p. 48; cf. Sherwood, *Roosevelt and Hopkins,* p. 290.
[73] *Pearl Harbor Committee Report,* p. 168.
[74] *The Washington Post,* June 1, 1941, Section II, p. 5, cols. 5–6; article, "The Strategy of the War—as the President Sees It," by Joseph Alsop and Robert Kintner. See also *Pearl Harbor Attack,* Part 20, p. 3992.
[75] Leahy, *I Was There,* p. 7.
[76] *The Washington Post,* June 4, 1941, p. 9, cols. 6–8; "Capital Parade," by Joseph Alsop and Robert Kintner.
[77] *Pearl Harbor Attack,* Part 16, p. 2238. Note, that as of the end of April 1941 a Gallup poll showed that 80% of the American people were opposed to immediate entry into the war; Stimson, *On Active Service, etc.,* p. 374.
[78] Judgment of the International Military Tribunal at Nuremberg, Nov. 1, 1946; *American Journal of International Law,* Vol. 41, p. 214.
[79] *Pearl Harbor Attack,* Part 5, p. 2293: Churchill, *The Grand Alliance,* pp. 140–141, 144–145, 244. On May 5, 1941, Mr. Stimson made a speech, the text of which was approved by Mr. Roosevelt, in which he called for direct naval aid to Britain. The elderly gentleman also called upon all young Americans to be prepared to sacrifice and to die. Mr. Knox also made a similar speech. Stimson, *On Active Service, etc.,* pp. 370–371.
[80] *Pearl Harbor Attack,* Part 15, p. 1902.
[81] Churchill, *The Grand Alliance,* p. 144.
[82] Frances Perkins, *The Roosevelt I Knew,* p. 380.
[83] *Ibid.,* pp. 3 and 4.
[84] *Ibid.,* p. 66.
[85] *Ibid.,* p. 163.
[86] *The Ciano Diaries,* p. 131, Mussolini thinks Hitler is jealous of his prestige; p. 155, Mussolini "is somewhat bitter about Hitler's sudden rise to fame. He would be greatly pleased if Hitler were slowed down *": p. 167, in Mussolini's opinion, "no Italian feels any great joy over the fact that Hitler had escaped death *." For other instances see *The Ciano Diaries,* pp. 197, 234, 262, 351, 358, 370, 390, 424.
[87] Thus, Hitler said: "The [Japanese] Emperor is * Weak, cowardly,

irresolute * . * Let us think of ourselves as masters and consider these people at best as lacquered half-monkeys, who need to feel the knout." *Nazi Conspiracy and Aggression*, Vol. VII, p. 754. Cf. *The Ciano Diaries*, pp. 172, 178, 213, 263, 279, 364, 389, 391, 393–394, 403.

[88] *The Ciano Diaries*, pp. 346, 357, 359, 363, 364–365, 372, 374, 402.

[89] *Ibid.*, pp 150, 161, 191, 204, 240, 277, 294, 339, 343–344, 351, 359–360, 366, 421.

[90] *Ibid.*, pp. 119, 121, 131, 147, 176–177, 180, 182, 272, 309.

[91] *Ibid.*, p. 356: "Bismarck gave Filippo to understand that the Germans are in possession of our secret codes and read our telegrams. This is good to know; in the future they will also read what I *want* them to read." Also Germany and Russia were reading the Japanese code messages; *Pearl Harbor Attack*, Vol. 4, p. 1851; cf. Part 5, p. 2070: Krivitsky, *In Stalin's Secret Service*, p. 17; see also *The Von Hassell Diaries*, p. 214.

[92] "The Japanese must not be given any intimation of the Barbarossa operation." *Nazi Conspiracy and Aggression*, Vol. VI, p. 908. They were kept in ignorance of the pending World War until Aug. 23, 1939: *The Ciano Diaries*, p. 126. For other episodes see *The Ciano Diaries*, pp. 130, 151, 181, 221, 233, 234, 280, 283, 300, 317, 365, 370, 582–583.

[93] Thus, Russia reproved Bulgaria for joining the Axis: N. Y. *Times*, March 3, 1941, p. 1, col. 8. *The Ciano Diaries*, p. 125: "* if * the Axis * should * collapse * I would not be the one to weep over it." For other episodes see *The Ciano Diaries*, pp. 170, 172, 175, 183, 186, 191, 229, 269, 272, 309, 379–380, 403, 409. Germany was secretly intriguing against Japan in Thailand: *Pearl Harbor Attack*, Part 14, p. 1346.

[94] "Japan will definitely act according to her own interests. *" *Nazi Conspiracy and Aggression*, Vol. VII, p. 804. "I have a suspicion that the Germans are preparing to put one over on us": *The Ciano Diaries*, p. 143: for other instances see *ibid.*, pp. 215, 231, 254, 279, 291–293, 304, 342, 368, 371–372, 377, 383, 390, 392, 397, 400.

[95] Thus, in late 1939 Germany was torpedoing Japanese merchant ships wherever "it can be made to appear that ships are striking mines," *Fuehrer Conferences, etc.*, 1939; p. 69.

[96] Note Mussolini's expectations of war between Italy and Germany: *The Ciano Diaries*, pp. 374, 379–380, 383. Note the Japanese secret judgment of the relationship: *Pearl Harbor Attack*, Part 12, p. 13. See *The United States at War*, pp. 507–508, 510.

[97] See *Pearl Harbor Attack*, Part 14, p. 1354.

[98] See Ambassador Grew's opinions: *Pearl Harbor Attack*, Part 14, p. 1047.

[99] Grew, *Ten Years in Japan*, p. 288.

[100] *Ibid.*, p. 198.

[101] Krivitsky, *In Stalin's Secret Service*, pp. 15–20.

[102] Kournakoff, *Russia's Fighting Forces*, pp. 111–119; *Pearl Harbor Attack*, Part 14, p. 1335; Grew, *Ten Years in Japan*, p. 251.
[103] *Pearl Harbor Attack*, Part 2, p. 412.
[104] *Ibid.*, Part 2, p. 409.
[105] Grew, *Ten Years in Japan*, p. 301.
[106] *The Public Papers, etc., of F.D.R.*, 1940 vol., pp. 593–594.
[107] *Ibid.*, 1940 vol., pp. 587, 594, 595.
[108] *U. S. Relations With China*, pp. 23–24.
[109] Grew, *Ten Years in Japan*, p. 314.
[110] *Ibid.*, p. 318.
[111] *Foreign Relations, Japan; 1931–1941*, Vol. II, pp. 281–282. The text of the Japanese declaration appears at p. 281.
[112] Churchill, *Their Finest Hour*, p. 256.
[113] *Peace and War*, p. 91.
[114] *Ibid.*, p. 93.
[115] *The Public Papers, etc., of F.D.R.*, 1940 vol., p. 594; *Peace and War*, p. 94.
[116] *The Ciano Diaries*, p. 293.
[117] Shirer, *Berlin Diary*, p. 535.
[118] *Ibid.*, p. 535: *The Ciano Diaries*, p. 293; *Nazi-Soviet Relations*, pp. 232–233: *The Von Hassell Diaries*, p. 152.
[119] *Foreign Relations, Japan; 1931–1941*, Vol. II, p. 169.
[120] *Peace and War*, p. 93.
[121] *The Public Papers, etc., of F.D.R.*, 1940 vol., p. 594: *United States and Italy*, pp. 19–20.
[122] *Peace and War*, p. 93.
[123] *Pearl Harbor Attack*, Part 1, p. 259; Part 14, p. 932.
[124] *Ibid.*, Part 1, p. 260; Part 14, pp. 933–934.
[125] *Ibid.*, Part 14, pp. 936, 940, 956–957.
[126] *Ibid.*, Part 1, pp. 265–266: Part 20, p. 4411; Part 14, p. 962.
[127] Sherwood, *Roosevelt and Hopkins*, pp. 258–259.
[128] *Pearl Harbor Attack*, Part 1, pp: 305–306, 318–319; Part 14, p. 1006.
[129] *Ibid.*, Part 1, pp. 323–324.
[130] *Ibid.*, Part 14, p. 964. Cf. Stimson, *On Active Service, etc.*, pp. 384–385.
[131] Churchill, *Their Finest Hour*, pp. 435–437.
[132] *Ibid.*, pp. 497–498.
[133] Davis and Lindley, *How War Came*, p. 160.
[134] *Pearl Harbor Attack*, Part 14, p. 1064.
[135] *N. Y. Times*, Feb. 2, 1941, p. 2, col. 1.
[136] Grew, *Ten Years in Japan*, pp. 339, 347, 354, 357.
[137] *Ibid.*, pp. 354–355.
[138] *Pearl Harbor Attack*, Part 20, pp. 3986, 4297–4299; Part 17, p. 2463.
[139] *Ibid.*, Part 15, p. 1860.
[140] "The Trial of Yamashita," by Col. J. Gordon Feldhaus, *South Dakota Bar Journal*, Vol. XV, p. 182; Oct. 1946.
[141] The secret American process for decoding Japanese messages was given to England as early as January 1941: *Pearl Harbor Attack*, Part 2, pp. 946–947. The United States had been using it during all of 1940: *Pearl*

Harbor Attack, Part 3, p. 1353; Part 18. p. 3335.

[142] N. Y. *Times,* Jan. 15, 1941, p. 1, cols. 4–5.

[143] N. Y. *Sun,* Feb. 7, 1946, p. 6.

[144] Grew, *Ten Years in Japan,* p. 350.

[145] *Pearl Harbor Attack,* Part 20, p. 3985.

[146] *Ibid.,* Part 20, pp. 4285–4286.

[147] *Ibid.,* Part 20, p. 4284.

[148] *Ibid.,* Part 20, pp. 4287–4288.

[149] *Ibid.,* Part 20, p. 4289.

[150] *Ibid.,* Part 20, p. 4292.

[151] N. Y. *Times,* Jan. 23, 1941, p. 4, col. 2.

[152] *Pearl Harbor Committee Report,* p. 293, paraphrasing *Foreign Relations, Japan;* Vol. II, pp. 328–329.

[153] *Pearl Harbor Attack,* Part 2, p. 417. He expressed no such extreme skepticism in his contemporary "Confidential Memorandum" to Mr. Roosevelt concerning the Walsh proposals, *ibid.,* Part 20, pp. 4289–4291.

[154] Grew, *Ten Years in Japan,* pp. 362–363.

[155] *Ibid.,* p. 365.

[156] *Fuehrer Conferences,* 1940, Vol. II, p. 69.

[157] *Pearl Harbor Attack,* Part 19, pp. 3644–3647: also printed in *Nazi Conspiracy and Aggression,* Vol. IV, p. 471.

[158] *Nazi Conspiracy and Aggression,* Vol. I, pp. 843–846; Vol. IV, pp. 469–475.

[159] *Nazi Conspiracy and Aggression,* Vol. I, pp. 844–845; Vol. IV, p. 472.

[160] *Pearl Harbor Attack,* Part 19, p. 3453; cf. Churchill, *The Grand Alliance,* pp. 178–179, where the paraphrase is differently expressed: "inspire the Japanese with * fear."

[161] *Pearl Harbor Attack,* Part 16, 2150.

[162] *Ibid.,* Part 2, pp. 726–727.

[163] N. Y. *Times,* Feb. 13, 1941, p. 5, col. 1.

[164] *Ibid.,* Feb. 15, 1941, p. 1, col. 4.

[165] *Foreign Relations, Japan;* Vol. II, p. 331.

[166] N. Y. *Times,* Feb. 16, 1941, Section I, p. 1, col. 5.

[167] *Ibid.,* Feb. 17, 1941, p. 1, col. 7.

[168] *Ibid.,* Feb. 18, 1941, p. 1, col. 8; cf. Grew, *Ten Years in Japan,* p. 372.

[169] *Ibid.,* Feb. 19, 1941, p. 1, cols. 6–7.

[170] *Ibid.,* Feb. 20, 1941, p. 1, col. 5.

[171] *Ibid.,* Feb. 25, 1941, p. 1, col. 6. Yet it is likely that there was some substance to it: see *The Von Hassell Diaries,* pp. 170, 194.

[172] See Sherwood, *Roosevelt and Hopkins,* pp. 258–259.

[173] N. Y. *Times,* Feb. 21, 1941, p. 4, col. 5.

[174] *Ibid.,* Feb. 21, 1941, p. 4, col. 6.

[175] *Ibid.,* Feb. 23, 1941, Section 4, p. 4, cols. 1–2.

[176] *Ibid.,* March 5, 1941, p. 8, col. 2:cf. Churchill, *The Grand Alliance,* pp. 179–181.

[177] N. Y. *Times,* March 6, 1941, p. 6, col. 3.

[178] *Nazi Conspiracy and aggression,* Vol. I, pp. 847–849; Vol. VI, pp. 906–908. See *The Von Hassell Diaries,* p. 173.

179 *Nazi Conspiracy and Aggression,* Vol. I, p. 849; Vol. VI, p. 996.
180 N. Y. *Times,* March 13, 1941, p. 7, col. 2.
181 *Nazi Conspiracy and Aggression,* Vol. 1, pp. 850–853, 863–866; Vol. IV, pp. 520–526: *Nazi-Soviet Relations,* pp. 281–316: *Pearl Harbor Attack,* Part 15, pp. 1754–1756. Matsuoka left Berlin for Rome on March 30, 1941; N. Y. *Times,* March 31, 1941, p. 4, col. 5.
182 *The Ciano Diaries,* p. 229.
183 *Ibid.,* p. 371.
184 *Pearl Harbor Attack,* Part 15, p. 1559: cf. Grew, *op. cit.,* pp. 250–251.
185 For an estimate of Matsuoka's purposes while at Berlin, and for a declaration by Matsuoka himself while at Moscow, before the Russian reversal, see *Foreign Policy, Japan;* Vol. II, pp. 182–185.
186 *Nazi Conspiracy and Aggression,* Vol. I, p. 850.
187 N. Y. *Times,* April 8, 1941, p. 9, col. 1.
188 *Ibid.,* April 9, 1941, p. 11, col. 1.
189 *Ibid.,* April 13, 1941, Section I, p. 25, cols. 3–4.
190 *Ibid.,* April 14, 1941, p. 1, col. 8; *Nazi-Soviet Relations,* pp. 321–324.
191 N. Y. *Times,* April 14, 1941, p. 8, col. 6.
192 *Foreign Relations, Japan;* 1931–1941, Vol. II, p. 331.
193 *Ibid.,* Vol. II, pp. 389–396.
194 *Pearl Harbor Attack,* Part 2, p. 418; cf. *Foreign Relations, Japan;* Vol. II, pp. 396-398, in which report there appear to be omissions, presumably significant; see also *Nazi-Soviet Relations,* p. 321, and Grew, *op. cit.,* pp. 381–384.
195 *Foreign Relations, Japan;* Vol. II, pp. 398–402.
196 *Ibid.,* Vol. II, pp. 402–406.
197 *Ibid.,* Vol. II, pp. 406–410.
198 The ensuing account follows Prince Konoye's Memoirs, *Pearl Harbor Attack,* Part 20, pp. 3985-3990.
199 *Foreign Relations, Japan;* Vol. II, pp. 411–415.
200 *Ibid.,* Vol. II, pp. 418–425.
201 *Ibid.,* Vol. II, p. 421.
202 *Pearl Harbor Attack,* Part 20, p. 3990.
203 *The Ciano Diaries,* p. 350.
204 *Nazi Conspiracy and Aggression,* Vol. IV, pp. 499–508; at p. 506.
205 *The Ciano Diaries,* p. 351; N. Y. *Sun,* Feb. 7, 1946, p. 1.
206 *The Ciano Diaries,* p. 351.
207 *Foreign Relations, Japan;* Vol. II, pp. 145–148.
208 *Ibid.,* Vol, II, pp. 427–434.
209 *Pearl Harbor Attack,* Part 2, p. 420.
210 *Foreign Relations, Japan;* Vol. II, pp. 432–433.
211 *Pearl Harbor Attack,* Part 20, p. 3991.
212 *Ibid.,* Part 20, pp. 3990–3991.
213 *Ibid.,* Part 3, pp. 1077, 1436–1437.
214 *Ibid.,* Part 15, p. 1631.
215 Sherwood, *Roosevelt and Hopkins,* p. 295.
216 Churchill, *The Grand Alliance,* p. 426.

[217] *Ibid.*, p. 423.
[218] Sherwood, *Roosevelt and Hopkins*, pp. 390-391.
[219] *Nazi Conspiracy and Aggression*, Vol. IV, p. 100.
[220] *Foreign Relations, Japan;* Vol. II, pp. 440–443.
[221] *Pearl Harbor Attack*, Part 20, p. 3992.
[222] *Foreign Relations, Japan;* Vol. II, pp. 446–454.
[223] *Ibid.*, Vol. II, pp. 454–455.
[224] *Pearl Harbor Attack*, Part 2, p. 420.
[225] *Foreign Relations, Japan;* Vol. II, pp. 455–483.
[226] N. Y. *Times*, June 6, 1941, p. 1, col. 8; text, p. 6, cols. 4–6: cf. Langer, *Our Vichy Gamble*, pp. 158–161, 173.
[227] N. Y. *Times*, May 17, 1941, p. 1, col. 8; Churchill, *The Grand Alliance*, p. 282.
[228] N. Y. *Times*, June 21, 1941, p. 1, col. 8; text, p. 6, cols. 2–4: *Peace and War*, p. 105.
[229] *International Transactions of the United States*, p. 223; *United States and Italy*, pp. 27–28.
[230] N. Y. *Times*, June 17, 1941, p. 1, col. 8; see *United States and Italy*, p. 29.
[231] N. Y. *Times*, June 20, 1941, p. 1. col. 8.
[232] *The Ciano Diaries*, p. 367.
[233] *Nazi Conspiracy and Aggression*, Vol. VI, p. 997; *Nazi-Soviet Relations*, p. 330.
[234] *The Ciano Diaries*, pp. 364, 367, 368.
[235] *Foreign Relations, Japan;* Vol. II, pp. 483–492.

[236] Mr. Roosevelt never did know, within the meaning of the American Neutrality Act, that there was anything but peace in China.
[237] *Foreign Relations, Japan;* Vol. II, p. 485.
[238] Prince Konoye's phrase; *Pearl Harbor Attack*, Part 20, p. 3993; see also Part 14, pp. 1345–1346: cf. Grew, *op. cit.*, pp. 395–396, 401–402.
[239] *Pearl Harbor Attack*, Part 14, p. 1049.
[240] *The Ciano Diaries*, p. 371.
[241] *Pearl Harbor Attack*, Part 20, p. 3993.
[242] *Ibid.*, Part 16, p. 2175.
[243] *Ibid.*, Part 14, p. 1397.
[244] See Ambassador Grew's cable of Sept. 12, 1940; *Pearl Harbor Attack*, Part 14, especially pp. 1305–1306.

CHAPTER X

[1] *Newsweek*, July 14, 1941, p. 26.
[2] *Pearl Harbor Attack*, Part 12, pp. 1–2; cf. Part 20, p. 3993.
[3] *Ibid.*, Part 20, pp. 4018–4019.
[4] *Foreign Relations, Japan;* Vol. II, p. 496; cf. Stimson, *On Active Service, etc.*, p. 387.
[5] *Pearl Harbor Attack*, Part 2, p. 412.
[6] *Ibid.*, Part 14, pp. 1397–1398.
[7] *Ibid.*, Part 14, p. 1398.
[8] Langer, *Our Vichy Gamble*, p. 178.
[9] Sumner Welles, *Where Are We Heading?*, p. 3.
[10] N. Y. *Times*, July 1, 1941, p. 1, col. 4.
[11] *Ibid.*, July 3, 1941, p. 8, col. 1.

[12] *Newsweek,* July 14, 1941, p. 24.
[13] *Our Navy at War,* p. 6.
[14] *Ibid.,* p. 6.
[15] *Newsweek,* July 7, 1941, pp. 7, 13.
[16] N.Y. *Times,* July 2, 1941, p. 1, col. 4,
[17] Churchill, *The Grand Alliance,* p. 753.
[18] *Ibid.,* p. 776.
[19] Sherwood, *Roosevelt and Hopkins,* pp. 308, 310.
[20] Churchill, *The Grand Alliance,* pp. 799, 802.
[21] N.Y. *Times,* July 4, 1941, p. 1, col. 6. See Stimson, *On Active Service, etc.,* p. 372, which confirms this.
[22] *Saturday Evening Post,* Aug. 16, 1941, p. 26.
[23] N.Y. *Times,* July 4, 1941, p. 1, cols. 6–8.
[24] *Pearl Harbor Attack,* Part 14, p. 1396.
[25] Text in N.Y. *Times,* July 5, 1941, p. 6, cols. 2–3.
[26] *Pearl Harbor Attack,* Part 20, p. 3993: Grew, *op. cit.,* pp. 396–400.
[27] N.Y. *Times,* July 5, 1941, p. 1, col. 3.
[28] *Ibid.,* July 8, 1941, p. 8, col. 2.
[29] *Ibid.,* July 5, 1941, p. 24, col. 2; cf. *Pearl Harbor Attack,* Part 15, p. 1637.
[30] *Pearl Harbor Attack,* Part 5, p. 2113.
[31] Text in N.Y. *Times,* July 8, 1941, p. 3, cols. 2–6: *Peace and War,* p. 106. Mr. Stimson, *On Active Service, etc.,* p. 373, states that Mr. Roosevelt deliberately omitted any suggestion that war was imminent because he believed that the "defense" story was more palatable to the American people.
[32] Mr. Churchill omits all reference to this, except for the brief statement that it was Mr. Roosevelt who had made the decision in June. *The Grand Alliance,* p. 150.
[33] *Newsweek,* July 21, 1941, p. 11.
[34] N.Y. *Times,* July 9, 1941, p. 12, cols. 5–6.
[35] *Pearl Harbor Attack,* Part 20, p. 3993.
[36] N.Y. *Times,* July 9, 1941, p. 1, col. 4.
[37] *Ibid.,* July 10, 1941, p. 1, col. 4.
[38] *Ibid.,* July 10, 1941, p. 1, col. 3.
[39] *Ibid.,* July 11, 1941, p. 1, cols. 6–7.
[40] *Pearl Harbor Attack,* Part 16, p. 2175.
[41] *Saturday Evening Post,* Sept. 20, 1941, p. 26, col. 3.
[42] N.Y. *Times,* July 11, 1941, p. 1, col. 8.
[43] *Pearl Harbor Attack,* Part 15, pp. 1636–1639: Part 3, pp. 1094–1095.
[44] *Nazi Conspiracy and Aggression,* Vol. V, pp. 564–565; I, 854–855.
[45] *Ibid.* Vol. I p. 856.
[46] *Foreign Relations, Japan;* Vol. II, p. 339.
[47] *Pearl Harbor Attack,* Part 14, p. 1399.
[48] *Ibid.,* Part 14, p. 1398.
[49] Wm. L. Langer, *Our Vichy Gamble,* p. 177.
[50] *Pearl Harbor Attack,* Part 20, p. 3993.
[51] *Newsweek,* July 28, 1941, p. 20; *Pearl Harbor Attack,* Part 14, p. 1343; Part 15, p. 1849.

[52] *Newsweek*, July 21, 1941, pp. 22–23.
[53] *Pearl Harbor Attack*, Part 20, pp. 3994–3997.
[54] *Ibid.*, Part 12, p. 3.
[55] *Ibid.*, Part 20, p. 3994.
[56] For their text, see *Pearl Harbor Attack*, Part 14, p. 1398.
[57] Langer, *Our Vichy Gamble*, p. 177.
[58] *Newsweek*, July 21, 1941, p. 13.
[59] *Nazi Conspiracy and Aggression*, Vol. VI, p. 916.
[60] N. Y. *Times*, May 9, 1946, p. 12, cols. 2–3.
[61] *Pearl Harbor Attack*, Part 16, p. 2164.
[62] *Ibid.*, Part 16, p. 2177.
[63] *Ibid.*, Part 16, p. 2225.
[64] *The Fuehrer Conferences, etc.*, 1940, Vol. II, p. 18.
[65] Davis and Lindley, *How War Came*, p. 47; cf. Sherwood, *op. cit.*, p. 269.
[66] Grew, *Ten Years in Japan*, p. 417: cf. p. 415.
[67] Leahy, *I Was There*, p. 71; cf. Sherwood, Roosevelt and Hopkins, p. 386.
[68] *The Ciano Diaries*, pp. 380–386.
[69] *Ibid.*, p. 386.
[70] *The United States at War*, p. 72.
[71] Sumner Welles, *Where Are We Heading?*, p. 5. The same opinion was held in French military circles; Leahy, *I Was There*, p. 40.
[72] *Newsweek*, July 7, 1941, p. 12; *Pearl Harbor Attack*, Part 14, p. 1344.
[73] *Newsweek*, Aug. 4, 1941, p. 14.
[74] *Ibid.*, July 28, 1941, p. 13; *The United States at War*, p. 72.
[75] *Newsweek*, Aug. 18, 1941, pp. 15–16.
[76] *The United States at War*, p. 72.
[77] *Newsweek*, Aug. 25, 1941, pp. 16–17.
[78] *The United States at War*, pp. 72–73.
[79] *Newsweek*, Aug. 4, 1941, p. 11; Aug. 11, 1941, p. 15: Stimson, *op. cit.*, pp. 358, 415.
[80] *Pearl Harbor Attack*, Part 14, p. 1064.
[81] *Ibid.*, Part 14, p. 1398.
[82] *Foreign Relations, Japan;* Vol. II, pp. 516–518.
[83] *Pearl Harbor Attack*, Part 5, pp. 2382–2384.
[84] These were the exact reasons which were also assigned by Admiral Yamamoto, prior to the attack; *Pearl Harbor Attack*, Part 1, p. 179. See Ambassador Grew's frequent misgivings, *Ten Years in Japan*, pp. 272, 295, 304, 314, 345, 410–411.
[85] *Foreign Relations, Japan;* Vol. II, pp. 340–341, 522–526.
[86] *Ibid.*, Vol. II, p. 315–317.
[87] *Ibid.*, Vol. II, pp. 527–530.
[88] Sherwood, *Roosevelt and Hopkins*, pp. 318–319.
[89] *Pearl Harbor Attack*, Part 20, p. 4373.
[90] *Foreign Relations, Japan;* Vol. II, pp. 266–267.
[91] *Newsweek*, Aug. 4, 1941, pp. 11–12.
[92] Sherwood, *op. cit.*, pp. 317–318.
[93] Hayes, *Wartime Mission in Spain*, p. 80.

[94] *Pearl Harbor Attack*, Part 12, p. 9.
[95] It is to be found in *Pearl Harbor Aftack*, Part 12. p. 9.
[96] *Newsweek*, Sept. 10, 1945, p. 48.
[97] *Pearl Harbor Attack*, Part 20, pp. 3999–4000.
[98] *Ibid.*, Part 20, p. 4000.
[99] *Ibid.*, Part 12, p. 12.
[100] *Foreign Relations, Japan;* Vol. II, pp. 550–551: *Peace and War,* p. 122.
[101] Hayes, *Wartime Mission in Spain,* p. 11; cf. *Newsweek,* March 5, 1945, p. 60.
[102] *Pearl Harbor Attack,* Part 2, p. 490. For further references to the Thailand situation see *ibid.*, Part 15, pp. 1721–1725; Part 19, pp. 3696–3798.
[103] *Ibid.,* Part 2, p. 490: *Peace and War,* p. 123.
[104] *Pearl Harbor Attack,* Part 2, p. 487.
[105] Sherwood, *Roosevelt and Hopkins,* p. 308; Churchill, *The Grand Alliance,* p. 424.
[106] *Newsweek,* July 28, 1941, pp. 7, 13.
[107] *Ibid.*, Aug. 11, 1941, p. 17; *Pearl Harbor Attack,* Part 20, p. 4373.
[108] *Pearl Harbor Attack,* Part 20, p. 4384.
[109] *Ibid.,* Part 16, p. 2177.
[110] *Ibid.,* Part 16, p. 2182.
[111] *N. Y. Times,* July 31, 1941, p. 1, col. 2.
[112] Bullitt, *The Great Globe Itself,* p. 11.
[113] *Newsweek,* Aug. 4, 1941, p. 7; cf. *Pearl Harbor Attack,* Part 16, p. 2175; cf. Part 20, pp. 4352, 4357.
[114] *Pearl Harbor Attack,* Part 16, p. 2175.
[115] *Ibid.,* Part 16, p. 2182.
[116] *Ibid.,* Part 16, p. 2450.
[117] *Newsweek,* Aug. 11, 1941, p. 17. Within several months it *was* put under lend-lease, Stettinius, *op. cit.,* pp. 126, 130.
[118] The ultimate total was approximately ten billion dollars: *International Transactions of the United States,* p. 148.
[119] *Pearl Harbor Attack,* Part 16, p. 2174.
[120] *Ibid.,* Part 16, p. 2242.
[121] *Ibid.,* Part 26, p. 265.
[122] Churchill, *Their Finest Hour,* pp. 252–253.
[123] Churchill, *The Grand Alliance,* pp. 806–807.
[124] *N. Y. Times,* July 30, 1941, p. 1, col. 5; text on p. 6, cols. 3–6.
[125] Cf. *N. Y. Times,* Aug. 1, 1941, p. 34, cols. 3–8.
[126] *N. Y. Times,* Aug. 2, 1941, p. 1, col. 5.
[127] *Newsweek,* Aug. 11, 1941, p. 43: *N. Y. Times,* Aug. 1, 1941; p. 1, col. 8.
[128] *Newsweek,* Aug. 18, 1941, p. 14.
[129] *Ibid.,* Aug. 18, 1941, pp. 13–14.
[130] McIntire, *White House Physician,* p. 130.
[131] *Pearl Harbor Attack,* Part 12, p. 14.
[132] Elliott Roosevelt, *As He Saw It,* p. 22.
[133] *Ibid.,* p. 33.
[134] McIntire, *op. cit.,* p. 133.
[135] Elliott Roosevelt, *op. cit.,* pp. 27–30, 41.
[136] *Ibid.,* pp. 22–23.

[137] Churchill, *The Grand Alliance*, p. 593.
[138] Elliott Roosevelt, *op. cit.*, p. 39.
[139] Sumner Welles, *Where Are We Heading?*, p. 6: Churchill, *The Grand Alliance*, p. 434.
[140] *Ibid.*, pp. 6–17: See *Pearl Harbor Attack*, Part 14, pp. 1269–1299.
[141] *Pearl Harbor Committee Report*, pp. 508–509.
[142] *Pearl Harbor Attack*, Part 14, pp. 1275–1278: Churchill, *The Grand Alliance*, pp. 437–438.
[143] Churchill, *The Grand Alliance*, p. 441.
[144] *Ibid.*, pp. 440–441.
[145] *Pearl Harbor Attack*, Part 14, pp. 1254–1274.
[146] *Ibid.*, Part 16, pp. 2182–2183.
[147] *Foreign Relations, Japan*; Vol. II, p. 345.
[148] *Pearl Harbor Attack*, Part 14, p. 1283.
[149] Churchill, *The Grand Alliance*, pp. 439–441, 855, 859.
[150] *Pearl Harbor Attack*, Part 14, pp. 1280–1281.
[151] Elliott Roosevelt, *op. cit.*, p. 11; cf. *Foreign Relations, Japan*; Vol. II, pp. 264–265.
[152] *Pearl Harbor Attack*, Part 2, pp. 483–484.
[153] *Newsweek*, Aug. 25, 1941, p. 11.
[154] Note Mr. Roosevelt's labored efforts to show that by inference "freedom of religion was included": also "freedom of information." N. Y. *Times*, Aug. 22, 1941, p. 4, cols. 1 and 3. "Freedom of information" was to be a Russian substitute for freedom of speech.
[155] *Prefaces to Peace; a Symposium*, pp. 3–4: *Department of State Bulletin*, Aug. 16, 1941, p. 125; etc.
[156] But see the N. Y. *Times*, Aug. 17, 1941, Section 4, p. 1, col. 1.
[157] Jan Ciechanowski, *Defeat in Victory*, pp. 50–51.
[158] *Newsweek*, Aug. 25, 1941, p. 11.
[159] *Ibid.*, Aug. 25, 1941, pp. 14, 24.
[160] Cf. Ciechanowski, *op. cit.*, p 42: *Newsweek*, Aug. 25, 1941, p. 14.
[161] In his broadcast of Aug. 24, 1941, Mr. Churchill said clearly that both he and Mr. Roosevelt were opposed to the vindictive and impractical idea which was the seed of the Morgenthau plan:

"The second difference is this: that instead of trying to ruin German trade by all kinds of additional trade barriers and hindrances, as was the mood of 1917, we have definitely adopted the view that it is not in the interests of the world and of our two countries that any large nation should be unprosperous or shut out from the means of making a decent living for itself and its people by its industry and enterprise."

N. Y. *Times*, Aug. 25, 1941, p. 4, col. 4.
[162] *Prefaces to Peace; a Symposium*, p. 422.
[163] *Newsweek*, Aug. 25, 1941, p. 33.
[164] *Ibid.*, Aug. 25, 1941, p 31.
[165] See Churchill, *The Grand Alliance*, p. 447.
[166] *Newsweek*, Aug. 25, 1941, p. 31.

[167] *Peace and War*, p. 108.
[168] *Foreign Relations, Japan*; Vol. II, pp. 553–554.
[169] *Pearl Harbor Attack*, Part 12, p. 17.

CHAPTER XI

[1] A memorandum by Mr. Hull of the conversation appears in *Foreign Relations, Japan*; Vol. II, pp. 554–555: cf. *Pearl Harbor Attack*, Part 15, p. 1682; Part 17, pp. 2749–2756.
[2] Text of the statement in *Foreign Relations, Japan*; Vol. II, pp. 556–557; *Pearl Harbor Attack*, Part 15, pp. 1683–1684.
[3] *Pearl Harbor Attack*, Part 14, pp. 1255–1268.
[4] *Foreign Relations, Japan*; Vol. II, p. 345.
[5] *Ibid.*, Vol. II, pp. 554–557.
[6] *Pearl Harbor Attack*, Part 3, p. 1253.
[7] *Foreign Relations, Japan*; Vol. II, p. 555.
[8] *Ibid.*, Vol. II, pp. 557–559; *Pearl Harbor Attack*, Part 15, pp. 1685–1688.
[9] *Foreign Relations, Japan*; Vol. II, p. 568.
[10] *Pearl Harbor Attack*, Part 17, pp. 2749–2756.
[11] *Ibid.*, Part 15, pp. 1717–1718.
[12] *Ibid.*, Part 2, pp. 486, 515; Part 4, p. 1695; Part 11, pp. 5388–5389.
[13] *Ibid.*, Part 19, pp. 3717–3719.
[14] *Foreign Relations, Japan*; Vol. II, pp. 1–2.
[15] Memorandum of the interview in *Foreign Relations, Japan*; Vol. II, pp. 559–560.
[16] Memorandum of the interview in *Foreign Relations, Japan*; Vol. II, pp. 560–564; *Pearl Harbor Attack*, Part 17, p. 2770; See Grew, *Ten Years in Japan*, pp. 416–421.
[17] *Pearl Harbor Committee Report*, p. 314; cf. *Foreign Relations, Japan*; Vol. II, pp. 559–560.
[18] *Foreign Relations, Japan*; Vol. II, p. 565.
[19] *Ibid.*, Vol. II, p. 560; cf. Grew, *op. cit.*, p. 415.
[20] *Nazi Conspiracy and Aggression*, Vol. VI, p. 545; *Pearl Harbor Attack*, Part 18, p. 2948.
[21] N. Y. *Times*, Aug. 22, 1941, p. 4, cols. 2–3.
[22] *Foreign Relations, Japan*; Vol. II, pp. 565–567.
[23] *Pearl Harbor Attack*, Part 17, p. 2772.
[24] *Foreign Relations, Japan*; Vol. II, p. 568; *Pearl Harbor Attack*, Part 17, p. 2773.
[25] N. Y. *Times*, Aug. 25, 1941, p. 1, col. 8; text on p. 4, cols. 2–8: also *Pearl Harbor Attack*, Part 2, pp. 524–528.
[26] See *Pearl Harbor Attack*, Part 4, pp. 1695–1696.
[27] Ciechanowski, *Defeat in Victory*, pp. I, 5–6.
[28] *Pearl Harbor Attack*, Part 14, pp. 1400–1401; Part 5, pp. 2294–2296.
[29] *Ibid.*, Part 12, p. 21.
[30] *Ibid.*, *Department of State Bulletin*, Aug. 30, 1941; *Foreign Relations, Japan*; Vol. II, p. 580; N. Y. *Times*, Aug. 27, 1941, p. 1, col. 7.
[31] *Pearl Harbor Attack*, Part 16, p. 2177.
[32] *Ibid.*, Part 16, p. 2450.

[33] *U. S. Relations with China*, p. 25: Stettinius, *Lend-Lease*, pp. 116–118; Churchill, *The Grand Alliance*, p. 832; *Pearl Harbor Attack*, Part 3, pp. 1229–1230, 1383; Part 14, p. 1081.

[34] *Foreign Relations, Japan;* Vol. II, pp. 568–569.

[35] *Ibid.*, Vol. II, pp. 569–570.

[36] *Ibid.*, Vol. II. Memorandum of the conversation, pp. 571–572; message, pp. 572–573; statement of views, pp. 573–575. See also pp. 346–347; also pp. 346–347; also *Pearl Harbor Attack*, Part 17, pp. 2776–2796.

[37] *Foreign Relations, Japan;* Vol, II, pp. 576–579; *Peace and War,* p, 125.

[38] *Pearl Harbor Attack*, Part 14, p. 1401; Part 6, p. 2667.

[39] *Foreign Relations, Japan;* Vol. II, pp. 582–583: *Pearl Harbor Attack*, Part 17, p. 2796.

[40] *Foreign Relations, Japan;* Vol. II, pp. 579–587, 592: *Pearl Harbor Attack*, Part 17, pp. 2797–2799.

[41] *Pearl Harbor Committee Report*, p. 309.

[42] *Nazi Conspiracy and Aggression*, Vol. VI, pp. 547–551: *Pearl Harbor Attack*, Part 18, pp. 2948–2951.

[43] *The United States at War*, pp. 68–69, 80.

[44] Text in N. Y. *Times*, Sept. 2, 1941, p. 10, cols. 2-5.

[45] *Pearl Harbor Attack*, Part 15, pp. 1509, 1524, 1540; Part 18, p. 2918.

[46] Churchill, *The Grand Alliance*, p. 491.

[47] *Ibid.*, p. 492.

[48] *Ibid.*, p. 493. Cf. Admiral Stark's regrets: *Pearl Harbor Attack*, Part 16, p. 2221.

[49] Churchill, *The Grand Alliance*, p. 668.

[50] *Ibid.*, p. 493.

[51] *Ibid.*, p. 517.

[52] *Foreign Relations, Japan;* Vol. II, pp. 583–585.

[53] *Pearl Harbor Attack*, Part 12, p. 25.

[54] *Foreign Relations, Japan;* Vol. II, pp. 586–587.

[55] Text in *Foreign Relations, Japan;* Vol. II, pp. 589–592.

[56] *Ibid.*, pp. 588–589.

[57] *Pearl Harbor Committee Report* (majority), p. 25.

[58] Churchill, *The Grand Alliance*, pp. 455, 589.

[59] *Pearl Harbor Attack*, Part 2, 425–426: see also *Peace and War,* pp. 126–127.

[60] As Mr. Hull suggested: *Foreign Relations, Japan;* Vol. II, p. 595.

[61] Germany claimed that this was "an unprovoked aggressive act by the United States," and the Japanese feared that Germany "may claim that it falls within the purview of article 3 of the Tripartite Pact." *Foreign Relations, Japan;* Vol. II, p. 609. Note that Admiral Stark testified, "we attacked German submarines under this order." *Pearl Harbor Attack*, Part 5, p. 2296.

[62] In *Newsweek*, Nov. 10, 1941, p. 21, Mr. Lindley stated that the *Greer* had been following the submarine, and then a British plane came up and dropped depth charges "before the Nazi commander struck." Admiral King, *Our Navy at War*, p. 6, says that one torpedo was fired, that then the *Greer* dropped the depth charges,

and then the second torpedo was fired. He omits any reference to the British plane.

⁶³ Stettinius, *Lend-Lease*, p. 141.

⁶⁴ *Pearl Harbor Attack*, Part 16, p. 2210.

⁶⁵ N. Y. *Times*, Sept. 5, 1941, p. 1, cols. 6–7; texts on p. 4, cols. 2–6.

⁶⁶ *Pearl Harbor Attack*, Part 20, pp. 4413–4416: *Foreign Relations, Japan;* Vol. II, pp. 593–595.

⁶⁷ *Foreign Relations, Japan;* Vol. II, pp. 608–609.

⁶⁸ *Ibid.*, Vol. II, pp. 595–596.

⁶⁹ *Ibid.*, Vol. II, pp. 597–600.

⁷⁰ *Ibid.*, Vol II, pp. 487–490.

⁷¹ *Ibid.*, Vol. II, p. 595.

⁷² *Ibid.*, Vol. II, p. 351. It was also on Sept. 4 that the Chinese Ambassador called on Mr. Hull to enquire "* about the reported conversations *." Mr. Hull said "* that exploratory conversations * were taking place but that no common basis for negotiations had as yet been revealed. *"

Mr. Hull then promised that "* before considering negotiations with Japan affecting * China" he "would * discuss the entire subject with" China and "with the British, the Dutch and the Australian Governments as well." *Foreign Relations, Japan;* Vol. II, pp. 347–348.

⁷³ *Foreign Relations, Japan;* Vol. II, p. 621.

⁷⁴ *Pearl Harbor Attack*, Part 20, pp. 4085–4087; cf. Part 16, p. 2214.

⁷⁵ *Ibid.*, Part 20, pp. 4004–4005, 4022–4023.

⁷⁶ *Foreign Relations, Japan;* Vol. II, pp. 601–603.

⁷⁷ *Ibid.*, pp. 603–604.

⁷⁸ *Foreign Relations, Japan;* Vol. II, pp. 604–606; 349–350: Grew, *Ten Years in Japan*, pp. 425–428.

⁷⁹ *Foreign Relations, Japan;* Vol. II, p. 606.

⁸⁰ *Ibid.*, Vol. II, pp. 608–609.

⁸¹ *Ibid.*, Vol. II, p. 608, footnote 5.

⁸² *Ibid.*, Vol. II, p. 607.

⁸³ *Ibid.*, Vol. II, p. 610.

⁸⁴ *Ibid.*, Vol. II, pp. 610–613.

⁸⁵ *Ibid.*, Vol. II, pp. 613–614.

⁸⁶ *Foreign Relations, Japan;* Vol. II, pp. 614–619.

⁸⁷ N. Y. *Times*, March 19, 1937, p. 1, col. 3; official abstract on p. 10, cols. 3–6.

⁸⁸ Taylor, *Wartime Correspondence*, etc., pp. 61–62.

⁸⁹ *Ibid.*, p. 58.

⁹⁰ In late June 1941 Mr. Roosevelt wrote, "* I do not think we need worry about any possibility of Russian domination. *" Leahy, *I Was There*, p. 460.

⁹¹ Taylor, *Wartime Correspondence*, etc., pp. 63–64.

⁹² *Ibid.*, p. 67.

CHAPTER XII

¹ *The United States at War*, p. 80: *Pearl Harbor Attack*, Part 16, pp: 2209–2210.

² N. Y. *Times*, Sept. 12, 1941, p. 1, cols. 6–7; p. 4, cols. 2–5: *Peace and War*, pp. 109–110.

³ *Pearl Harbor Attack*, Part 16, p. 2248.

⁴ *Ibid.*, Part 5, p. 2295.

⁵ *Ibid.*, Part 3, p. 1389.

6 N.Y. *Times,* Sept. 18, 1941, p. 1, col. 8.
7 *Pearl Harbor Attack,* Part 5, p. 2117: see also pp. 2296, 2310.
8 *Foreign Relations, Japan;* Vol. II, pp. 620–622.
9 *Ibid.,* pp. 623–624.
10 *Pearl Harbor Attack,* Part 12, p. 27.
11 *Ibid.,* Part 12, p. 28.
12 Postmaster General Walker?
13 *Foreign Relations, Japan;* Vol. II, pp. 624–625.
14 *Ibid.,* Vol. II, pp. 626–629.
15 *Foreign Relations, Japan;* Vol. II, pp. 631–633.
16 *Ibid.,* Vol. II, pp. 489–490.
17 *Pearl Harbor Attack,* Part 14, pp. 1357–1358.
18 *Ibid.,* Part 20, p. 4214.
19 *Ibid.,* Part 11, pp. 5257–5258.
20 *Ibid.,* Part 12, pp. 29–31.
21 *Foreign Relations, Japan;* Vol. II, pp. 634–636.
22 *Pearl Harbor Attack,* Part 16, pp. 2212–2214.
23 *Foreign Relations, Japan;* Vol. II, pp. 637–641.
24 Cf. *ibid.,* Vol. II, p. 673.
25 Since "ratification" is not used in Mr. Hull's draft, it is obvious that he did not envisage that this "understanding" would rise to the formal level of a treaty.
26 *Foreign Relations, Japan;* Vol. II, pp. 325–386.
27 *Ibid.,* Vol. II, p. 354.
28 *Ibid.,* Vol. II, p. 353.
29 *Ibid.,* Vol. II, p. 352.
30 *Pearl Harbor Attack,* Part 20, pp. 4424–4427.
31 *Foreign Relations, Japan;* Vol. II, pp. 641–645.
32 *Pearl Harbor Attack,* Part 20, p. 4423.
33 *Foreign Relations, Japan;* Vol. II, pp. 645–650.
34 *Pearl Harbor Committee Report,* p. 315.
35 *Foreign Relations, Japan;* Vol. II, pp. 651–652.
36 *Ibid.,* Vol. II, pp. 652–654.
37 *Pearl Harbor Attack,* Part 12, pp. 44–45.
38 *Ibid.,* Part 12, pp. 48–49.
39 Stettinius, *Lend-Lease,* p. 125: cf. Churchill, *The Grand Alliance,* pp. 468–470.
40 Bullitt, *The Great Globe Itself,* p. 14. As late as Dec. 1, 1941, the British Military Mission to Russia was given nothing more than the official communiqués: *Pearl Harbor Attack,* Part 5, p. 2078; cf. Part 16, p. 2452.
41 *Pearl Harbor Attack,* Part 12, p. 52.
42 Bullitt, *The Great Globe Itself,* p. 16.
43 Stettinius, *Lend-Lease,* p. 126: cf. Sherwood, *Roosevelt and Hopkins,* pp. 396–398.
44 Ciechanowski, *Defeat in Victory,* pp. 54–55: cf. Bullitt, *The Great Globe Itself,* p. 15.
45 N.Y. *Times,* Oct. 13, 1941, p. 1, col. 5.
46 *Ibid.,* Oct. 14, 1941, p. 1, col. 8.
47 *Newsweek,* Oct. 20, 1941, p. 25.
48 Stettinius, *Lend-Lease,* p. 127.

49 *Pearl Harbor Attack,* Part 16, p. 2452.
50 *The Ciano Diaries,* p. 447.
51 See, for example, Stettinius, *Lend-Lease,* p. 123.
52 *The United States at War,* p. 152.
53 *Ibid.,* p. 80.
54 *Ibid.,* p. 82.
55 *Ibid.,* p. 79; cf. p. 82.
56 Note the guarded statements in an article captioned "McNair Finds Army Unready to Fight Nazis," N. Y. *Herald Tribune,* Dec. 7, 1941, Section I, p. 52, cols. 1–6: "Anti-tank guns are being taken away from the forces in training to be sent elsewhere * . * Guns still are simulated, many units lack their full quotas of transportation and communication facilities * . *" And by the first four months of 1942, it was said, live ammunition would be available.
57 *Foreign Relations, Japan;* Vol. II, pp. 656–661.
58 *Ibid.,* Vol. II, pp. 654–656.
59 *Pearl Harbor Attack,* Part 14, pp. 1357–1359, 1385–1388.
60 *Ibid.,* Part 14, p. 1388. See similar sentiments in Stimson, *On Active Service, etc.,* pp. 388–389.
61 *Pearl Harbor Attack,* Part 12, pp. 50–51.
62 *Ibid.,* Part 12, pp. 51–53.
63 *Pearl Harbor Committee Report,* p. 322.
64 *Pearl Harbor Attack,* Part 20, p. 4008.
65 *Foreign Relations, Japan;* Vol. II, pp. 662–663.
66 *Ibid.,* Vol. II, pp. 663–665.

67 *Pearl Harbor Attack,* Part 20, p. 4008.
68 *Ibid.,* Part 20, pp. 4008–4009.
69 *Foreign Relations, Japan;* Vol. II, pp. 666–667.
70 *The United States at War,* p. 82.
71 Bullitt, *The Great Globe Itself,* pp. 145–146; *Pearl Harbor Attack,* Part 5, pp. 2296, 2389, 2436; Part 6, pp. 2666–2670.
72 *Pearl Harbor Attack,* Part 5, p. 2360.
73 N. Y. *Times,* Oct. 10, 1941, p. 1, col. 8; text on p. 4, cols. 2–6; *Pearl Harbor Committee Report,* p. 13; *The United States at War,* pp. 88–89.
74 *Pearl Harbor Attack,* Part 5, pp. 2292, 2296.
75 *Foreign Relations, Japan;* Vol. II, pp. 667–669.
76 *Pearl Harbor Attack,* Part 12, p. 61.
77 *Foreign Relations, Japan;* Vol. II, pp. 670–672.
78 *Ibid.,* Vol. II, pp. 672–677; cf. *Pearl Harbor Attack,* Part 12, pp. 61–62.
79 *Newsweek,* Sept. 10, 1945, p. 48; cf. Grew, *Ten Years in Japan,* p. 453.
80 *Pearl Harbor Attack,* Part 12, pp. 62–63.
81 *Foreign Relations, Japan;* Vol. II, pp. 677–679.
82 Grew, *Ten Years in Japan,* p. 455.
83 *Pearl Harbor Attack,* Part 20, p. 4009.
84 *Ibid.,* Part 20, p. 4009.
85 *Foreign Relations, Japan;* Vol. II, pp. 680–686.
86 *Ibid.,* Vol. II, p. 686.

[87] *Pearl Harbor Attack,* Part 20, pp. 4009–4010.
[88] *Ibid.,* Part 20, p. 4010.
[89] *Ibid.,* Part 20, pp. 4010–4011.
[90] *Foreign Affairs, Japan;* Vol. II, p. 697.
[91] *Pearl Harbor Attack,* Part 19, pp. 3463–3466.
[92] *Pearl Harbor Attack,* Part 19, p. 3462.
[93] *Ibid.,* Part 20, pp. 4059–4071.
[94] *Ibid.,* Part 14, pp. 1327, 1402. By official instruction this dispatch was passed on to General Short by Admiral Kimmel: *ibid.,* Part 27, p. 154. Cf. *ibid.,* Part 16, p. 2214.
[95] *Ibid.,* Part 16, p. 2150; cf. Part 12, p. 88.
[96] *Ibid.,* Part 12, p. 71.
[97] *Foreign Relations, Japan;* Vol. II, p. 686.
[98] *Pearl Harbor Attack,* Part 12, p. 117.
[99] *Foreign Relations, Japan;* Vol. I, pp. 690–692, 697–699; *Pearl Harbor Attack,* Part 12, pp. 76, 81.
[100] *Pearl Harbor Attack,* Part 12, pp. 79–81.
[101] *Ibid.,* Part 12, p. 82.
[102] *Ibid.,* Part 12, p. 81.
[103] *Ibid.,* Part 14, p. 1327.
[104] Churchill, *The Grand Alliance,* p. 547.
[105] N. Y. *Times,* Oct. 25, 1941, p. 1, col. 8.
[106] *Ibid.,* Oct. 29, 1941, p. 1, col. 3.
[107] *Ibid.,* Oct. 24, 1941, p. 3, cols. 2–3.
[108] *Foreign Relations, Japan;* Vol. II, pp. 692–697.
[109] *Ibid.,* Vol. II, pp. 698–699; *Peace and War,* p. 112.
[110] N. Y. *Times,* Oct. 28, 1941, p. 1, col. 1; text on p. 4, cols. 2–6.
[111] *Newsweek,* Nov. 10, 1941, p. 21.
[112] *Ibid.,* Nov. 10, 1941, p. 21.
[113] N. Y. *Times,* Oct. 29, 1941, p. 4, cols. 3–4.
[114] *Newsweek,* Nov. 3, 1941, p. 9.
[115] *Pearl Harbor Attack,* Part 16, p. 2214; cf. Part 5, p. 2296; also cf. N. Y. *Times,* Oct. 29, 1941, p. 3, col. 1.
[116] N. Y. *Times,* Oct. 29, 1941, p. 1, cols. 2–3.
[117] *The Ciano Diaries,* p. 398.
[118] Churchill, *The Grand Alliance,* p. 545.
[119] *Ibid.,* p. 552.
[120] *Pearl Harbor Attack,* Part 14, pp. 1061, 1077–1080; Part 15, pp. 1476–1481.
[121] *Foreign Relations, Japan;* Vol. II, pp. 699–700.
[122] Admiral King, *Our Navy at War,* p. 6.
[123] *Newsweek,* Nov. 10, 1941, p. 19.
[124] *Pearl Harbor Attack,* Part 16, p. 2456.
[125] *Ibid.,* Part 16, pp. 2220, 2224.
[126] *Newsweek,* Nov. 10, 1941, p. 35.
[127] Churchill, *The Grand Alliance,* p. 586.
[128] Sherwood, *Roosevelt and Hopkins,* p. 397.
[129] *Ibid.,* p. 383; cf. p. 420; also Churchill, *The Grand Alliance,* p. 539.
[130] Sherwood, *Roosevelt and Hopkins,* p. 420.

CHAPTER XIII

[1] *Pearl Harbor Attack*, Part 6, pp. 2910–2911.
[2] *Ibid.*, Part 11, p. 5292; cf. Churchill, *The Grand Alliance*, p. 528.
[3] *Pearl Harbor Attack*, Part 14, pp. 1063, 1066.
[4] *Foreign Relations, Japan;* Vol. II, pp. 700–701.
[5] *Ibid.*, Vol. II, pp. 701–704.
[6] *Pearl Harbor Attack*, Part 14, pp. 1066–1067.
[7] *Ibid.*, Part 14, pp. 1062–1065; Part 5, pp. 2085–2086.
[8] *Ibid.*, Part 3, pp. 1167–1168, 1244–1247, 1252.
[9] *Foreign Relations, Japan;* Vol. II, p. 355.
[10] *Pearl Harbor Attack*, Part 14, p. 1065.
[11] *Ibid.*, Part 15, pp. 1476.
[12] *Ibid.*, Part 15, pp. 1476–1478.
[13] *Ibid.*, Part 19, pp. 3469–3476.
[14] *Ibid.*, Part 2, pp. 443–444.
[15] *Ibid.*, Part 2, p. 428.
[16] *Ibid.*, Part 12, pp. 92–94.
[17] *Ibid.*, Part 12, pp. 94–97.
[18] *Ibid.*, Part 12, p. 99.
[19] *Foreign Relations, Japan;* Vol. II, p. 679.
[20] *Ibid.*, Vol. II, p. 704.
[21] *Pearl Harbor Attack*, Part 12, pp. 97, 101.
[22] *Ibid.*, Part 12, p. 98.
[23] *Ibid.*, Part 12, p. 98.
[24] *Ibid.*, Part 12, p. 100.
[25] *Ibid.*, Part 12, p. 100.
[26] *Ibid.*, Part 19, pp. 3467–3468.
[27] *Ibid.*, Part 13, p. 415.
[28] *Ibid.*, Part 13, p. 415.
[29] *Ibid.*, Part 14, pp. 1061–1062; Part 16, pp. 2222–2223.
[30] *Ibid.*, Part 11, pp. 5420, 5431.
[31] *Ibid.*, Part 3, pp. 1394–1395.
[32] *Ibid.*, Part 2, p. 429; Part 20, pp. 4111–4112; cf. *Peace and War*, p. 130.
[33] *Pearl Harbor Attack*, Part 11, p. 5432; cf. p. 5420.
[34] *Ibid.*, Part 20, p. 4112.
[35] *Ibid.*, Part 5, pp. 2121, 2292, 2310.
[36] Bullitt, *The Great Globe Itself*, p. 5.
[37] Stettinius, *Lend-Lease*, pp. 131, 205.
[38] *Pearl Harbor Attack*, Part 14, pp. 1081–1082.
[39] *Ibid.*, Part 20, p. 4457.
[40] *Foreign Relations, Japan;* Vol. II, pp. 706–709.
[41] *Ibid.*, Vol. II, pp. 709–710.
[42] *Pearl Harbor Attack*, Part 12, p. 106.
[43] *Ibid.*, Part 12, p. 106.
[44] *N. Y. Times*, Nov. 11, 1941, p. 1, col. 1; text on p. 4, cols. 2–6.
[45] *Ibid.*, Nov. 12, 1941, p. 1, col. 5; text on p. 3, cols. 3–6.
[46] *Ibid.*, Nov. 12, 1941, p. 2, col. 2; *Pearl Harbor Attack*, Part 20, p. 4112.
[47] *N. Y. Times*, Nov. 12, 1941, p. 3, col. 1; p. 1, col. 5; *Pearl Harbor Attack*, Part 20, p. 4112.
[48] *Foreign Relations, Japan;* Vol. II, pp. 710–714; *Pearl Harbor Attack*, Part 12, pp. 109–111.
[49] *Foreign Relations, Japan;* Vol. II, pp. 715–719; *Pearl Harbor Attack*, Part 12, pp. 112–116.

[50] *Foreign Relations, Japan;* Vol. II, p. 719.
[51] *Pearl Harbor Attack,* Part 12, p. 111.
[52] Postmaster General Walker?
[53] *Pearl Harbor Attack,* Part 12, pp. 111–112.
[54] *Ibid.,* Part 12, pp. 116–117.
[55] *Ibid.,* Part 12, p. 119.
[56] *Ibid.,* Part 19, pp. 3479–3481.
[57] *Ibid.,* Part 12, pp. 117–119.
[58] *Foreign Relations, Japan;* Vol. II, pp. 719–722.
[59] *Ibid.,* Vol. II, pp. 722–726; *Pearl Harbor Attack,* Part 12, pp. 119–122.
[60] *Foreign Relations, Japan;* Vol. II, pp. 726–727.
[61] *Ibid.,* Vol. II, pp. 727–729.
[62] *Ibid.,* Vol. II, pp. 729–731; *Pearl Harbor Attack,* Part 12, pp. 123–125.
[63] *Pearl Harbor Attack,* Part 14, p. 1070.
[64] *Ibid.,* Part 14, p. 1069.
[65] *Ibid.,* Part 20, p. 4242.
[66] *Ibid.,* Part 14, pp. 1072–1076.
[67] *Ibid.,* Part 16, pp. 2221–2224.
[68] *Ibid.,* Part 12, pp. 125–126.
[69] *Ibid.,* Part 12, pp. 127–129.
[70] *Ibid.,* Part 12, pp. 137–138.
[71] *Foreign Relations, Japan;* Vol. II, pp. 731–734; *Pearl Harbor Attack,* Part 12, pp. 131–132, 134–137.
[72] *Foreign Relations, Japan;* Vol. II, pp. 734–736.
[73] *Ibid.,* Vol. II, pp. 736–737.
[74] *Pearl Harbor Attack,* Part 12, pp. 133–134.
[75] *Ibid.,* Part 12, p. 137.
[76] *Foreign Relations, Japan;* Vol. II, pp. 738–739.
[77] *Ibid.,* Vol. II, pp. 739–740: *Pearl Harbor Attack,* Part 12, p. 138.
[78] *Foreign Relations, Japan;* Vol. II, p. 740; *Pearl Harbor Attack,* Part 12, p. 144.
[79] *Pearl Harbor Attack,* Part 12, pp. 139-140.
[80] *Foreign Relations, Japan;* Vol. II, pp. 740–743; *Pearl Harbor Attack,* Part 12, pp. 139, 141–143.
[81] *Foreign Relations, Japan;* Vol. II, pp. 743–744.
[82] *The United States at War,* p. 88.
[83] Postmaster General Walker? See *Pearl Harbor Committee Report,* p. 356; *Pearl Harbor Attack,* Part 11, p. 5192; Part 20, pp. 4284–4285.
[84] *Pearl Harbor Attack,* Part 12, p. 154.
[85] Messrs. Stimson and Knox?
[86] *Foreign Relations, Japan;* Vol. II, pp. 744–750; *Pearl Harbor Attack,* Part 12, pp. 146–153.
[87] *Pearl Harbor Attack,* Part 19, pp. 3683–3685.
[88] This was the first information which the Netherlands had received from Mr. Hull in three months, and that Government had finally persuaded Ambassador Winant to cable Mr. Hull for some definite word: *Pearl Harbor Attack,* Part 20, pp. 4082–4084. A Netherlands attempt to obtain a little information two months earlier was suavely brushed off by Mr. Hull's subordinates: *Pearl Harbor Attack,* Part 20, pp. 4080–4081.
[89] *Pearl Harbor Attack,* Part 19, pp. 3686–3687.
[90] *Foreign Relations, Japan;* Vol. II, pp. 751–753.

CHAPTER XIV

1. *Pearl Harbor Attack*, Part 6, pp. 2912–2913.
2. *Ibid.*, Part 10, p. 5147.
3. *Ibid.*, Part 19, pp. 3668–3682.
4. *Ibid.*, Part 19, p. 3667.
5. *Ibid.*, Part 14, pp. 1098–1102.
6. *Ibid.*, Part 14, p. 1097.
7. Cf. *ibid.*, Part 14, p. 1104–1107.
8. *Ibid.*, Part 4, pp. 1704–1705.
9. *Ibid.*, Part 12, pp. 154–155.
10. *Ibid.*, Part 12, pp. 153–159.
11. *Ibid.*, Part 12, pp. 155–159.
12. *Foreign Relations, Japan;* Vol. II, pp. 753–755: *Pearl Harbor Attack*, Part 12, pp. 161–162; Part 18, p. 2952.
13. *Foreign Relations, Japan;* Vol. II, pp. 755–756.
14. *Pearl Harbor Attack*, Part 2, p. 431.
15. *Ibid.*, Part 12, pp. 162–163.
16. *Ibid.*, Part 12, pp. 163–164.
17. *Ibid.*, Part 2, p. 432.
18. *Ibid.*, Part 14, pp. 1104–1107.
19. *Ibid.*, Part 2, p. 431.
20. *Ibid.*, Part 1, p. 179.
21. *Foreign Relations, Japan;* Vol. II, p. 756.
22. *Ibid.*, Vol. II, pp. 756–757.
23. *Pearl Harbor Attack*, Part 14, pp. 1108–1109.
24. *Ibid.*, Part 14, pp. 1110–1121.
25. *Ibid.*, Part 14, pp. 1122–1123: Part 18, p. 2953.
26. Churchill, *The Grand Alliance*, pp. 593–594.
27. Cf. *ibid.*, pp. 622–624, 641–643.
28. *Ibid.*, p. 595.
29. *Pearl Harbor Attack*, Part 12, p. 165.
30. *Foreign Relations, Japan;* Vol. II, pp. 757–762; *Pearl Harbor Attack*, Part 12, pp. 167–171; Part 18, p. 2953.
31. *Pearl Harbor Attack*, Part 18, p. 2953.
32. *Ibid.*, Part 6, p. 2862: N.Y. *Times*, Nov. 25, 1941, p. 1, col. 8.
33. *Pearl Harbor Attack*, Part 12, pp. 180–181, 192.
34. *Ibid.*, Part 14, pp. 1328, 1405.
35. *Ibid.*, Part 14, pp. 1143–1146.
36. *Ibid.*, Part 2, p. 442.
37. *Ibid.*, Part 14, pp. 1124–1137.
38. *Ibid.*, Part 12, p. 117; Part 19, p. 3480; Part 20, pp. 4080–4084.
39. *Ibid.*, Part 14, pp. 1138–1141.
40. *Ibid.*, Part 14, p. 1142.
41. *Foreign Relations, Japan;* Vol. II, pp. 762–764; *Pearl Harbor Attack*, Part 12, pp. 172–173.
42. *Pearl Harbor Attack*, Part 14, pp. 1147–1159.
43. *Ibid.*, Part 11, p. 5433.
44. *Ibid.*, Part 11, p. 5433; Part 20, pp. 4113–4114.
45. *Ibid.*, Part 16, pp. 2224–2225.
46. *Ibid.*, Part 1, p. 82; Part 12, p. 317.
47. *Ibid.*, Part 1, pp. 184, 192, 220. Instructions had been issued for their return if the negotiations were successful: Part 13, pp. 395, 417.
48. *Ibid.*, Part 16, p. 2224.
49. *Ibid.*, Part 11, pp. 5433–5434.
50. *Ibid.*, Part 4, pp. 1692–1693.
51. *Ibid.*, Part 14, pp. 1162–1163.
52. *Ibid.*, Part 14, pp. 1164–1166.
53. *Ibid.*, Part 14, p. 1161.
54. *Ibid.*, Part 14, p. 1170.

[55] *Ibid.*, Part 14, p. 1160; Part 20, p. 4473.
[56] *Ibid.*, Part 14, pp. 1171–1174.
[57] *Ibid.*, Part 14, pp. 1167–1169.
[58] *Ibid.*, Part 4, p. 1694.
[59] *Ibid.*, Part 2, pp. 434–435, 742–743. Mr. Hull closely paraphrased this testimony in his later *Memoirs*, Vol. II, p. 1081.
[60] *Pearl Harbor Attack*, Part 14, p. 1328.
[61] *Ibid.*, Part 12, p. 174.
[62] *Ibid.* Part 14, p. 1300: Cf. Churchill, *The Grand Alliance*, pp. 595–596.
[63] *Pearl Harbor Attack*, Part 2, p. 442.
[64] *Ibid.*, Part 11, p. 5434.
[65] *Ibid.*, Part 11, p. 5434.
[66] *Ibid.*, Part 20, p. 4476.
[67] *Ibid.*, Part 2, p. 442; Part 5, p. 2093.
[68] *Ibid.*, Part 14, pp. 1176–1177.
[69] *Ibid.*, Part 16, p. 2014; Part 20, p. 4476.
[70] *Ibid.*, Part 3, p. 1336.
[71] *Ibid.*, Part 9, p. 4259.
[72] *Ibid.*, Part 11, p. 5192.
[73] *Ibid.*, Part 11, p. 5197.
[74] *Ibid.*, Part 11, p. 5214.
[75] *Ibid.*, Part 20, p. 4438.
[76] *Ibid.*, Part 2, p. 435.
[77] *Ibid.*, Part 5, p. 2323.
[78] *Ibid.*, Part 12, p. 179.
[79] *Foreign Relations, Japan*; Vol. II, pp. 764–766; *Pearl Harbor Attack*, Part 12, pp. 179–185; Part 15, pp. 1751–1753.
[80] *Foreign Relations, Japan*; Vol. II, pp. 768–770; *Pearl Harbor Attack*, Part 15, pp. 1746–1750; Part 19, pp. 3656–3660.
[81] *Foreign Relations, Japan*; Vol. II, pp. 776–767; *Pearl Harbor Attack*, Part 15, pp. 1745–1746; Part 19, pp. 3652–3655.
[82] *Pearl Harbor Attack*, Part 12, p. 141.
[83] *Ibid.*, Part 12, pp. 180–181.
[84] *Ibid.*, Part 11, p. 5374.
[85] *Ibid.*, Part 39, p. 83.
[86] *Ibid.*, Part 39, p. 137.
[87] *Ibid.*, Part 11, p. 5309.
[88] *Pearl Harbor Committee Report*, p. 179.
[89] *Ibid.*, p. 47; emphasis contained in the Majority Report.
[90] *Pearl Harbor Attack*, Part 5, p. 2094.
[91] *Ibid.*, Part 11, p. 5434.
[92] *Ibid.*, Part 11, p. 5435; Part 15, p. 1471.
[93] *Ibid.*, Part 2, pp. 438–440.
[94] *Ibid.*, Part 14, pp. 1179–1181.
[95] *Ibid.*, Part 14, pp. 1182–1183.
[96] *Ibid.*, Part 4, pp. 1693–1694.
[97] *Ibid.*, Part 14, pp. 1184–1185.
[98] *Ibid.*, Part 14, pp. 1188–1193.
[99] *Ibid.*, Part 11, p. 5435; cf. p. 5423.
[100] *Ibid.*, Part 15, p. 1471.
[101] *Ibid.*, Part 14, p. 1406.
[102] *Ibid*, Part 14, pp. 1328–1329; Part 18, p. 3173.
[103] *Ibid.*, Part 11, p. 5423.
[104] *Ibid.*, Part 3, pp. 1310, 1501; cf. pp. 1173, 1289.
[105] *Ibid.*, Part 10, p. 4812.
[106] *Ibid.*, Part 10, p. 4827.
[107] *Ibid.*, Part 10, p. 4828.
[108] *Ibid.*, Part 20, p. 4439.

[109] *Foreign Relations, Japan;* Vol. II, pp. 770–772; *Pearl Harbor Attack,* Part 12, pp. 188–195; Part 20, pp. 4477–4478.
[110] *Pearl Harbor Attack,* Part 15, p. 1632.
[111] *Ibid.,* Part 5, pp. 2089–2090; Part 16, pp. 2437–2443.
[112] *Ibid.,* Part 3, pp. 1263, 1264, 1292, 1294–1295, 1403, 1407.
[113] *Ibid.,* Part 3, pp. 1295, 1405.
[114] *Ibid.,* Part 14, p. 1083.
[115] *Ibid.,* Part 15, pp. 1551–1584.
[116] This memorandum adopted the exact territorial definitions contained in the "A.—D.—B. Conversations": see *Pearl Harbor Attack,* Part 15, at p. 1564, paragraph no. 26. It protected Burma, the Indian Ocean, Malaya, and the Netherlands East Indies.
[117] *Pearl Harbor Attack,* Part 14, p. 1253; note Part 18, pp. 3486–3440.
[118] *Ibid.,* Part 8, p. 3388.
[119] *Ibid.,* Part 11, p. 5435.
[120] Stimson, *On Active Service, etc.,* p. 390; cf. Sherwood, *Roosevelt and Hopkins,* pp. 428–430.
[121] Davis and Lindley, *How War Came,* p. 156.
[122] *Pearl Harbor Attack,* Part 11, pp. 5435–5436.
[123] *Ibid.,* Part 2, p. 440; Part 20, pp. 4113–4114.
[124] *Ibid.,* Part 20, p. 4440.
[125] *Pearl Harbor Committee Report,* p. 395.
[126] *Pearl Harbor Attack,* Part 26, p. 451.
[127] *Ibid.,* Part 17, p. 2496; Part 32, p. 232.
[128] *Ibid.,* Part 6, p. 2532; cf. *Pearl Harbor Committee Report,* p. 109.
[129] *Pearl Harbor Attack,* Part 14, p. 1407.
[130] *Ibid.,* Part 5, pp. 2471–2472.
[131] *Ibid.,* Part 11, p. 5477.
[132] *Ibid.,* Part 12, pp. 188–191.
[133] *Ibid.,* Part 12, p. 195.
[134] N.Y. *Sun,* Aug. 19, 1947, p. 12, col. 1.
[135] *Pearl Harbor Attack,* Part 12, p. 196.
[136] *Ibid.,* Part 14, pp. 1186–1187.
[137] *Ibid.,* Part 2, p. 495.
[138] *Ibid.,* Part 11, p. 5427.
[139] *Ibid.,* Part 19, pp. 3509–3515.
[140] *Ibid.,* Part 19, p. 3508.
[141] *Ibid.,* Part 14, pp. 1204–1223.
[142] *Ibid.,* Part 19, pp. 3520–3521.
[143] *Ibid.,* Part 14, pp. 1224–1225.
[144] *Ibid.,* Part 14, pp. 1202–1203.
[145] *Ibid.,* Part 19, pp. 3523–3533.
[146] *Ibid.,* Part 14, pp. 1194–1197.
[147] This phrase is repeated in Mr. Hull's dispatch of Dec. 1, 1941, to Chungking; see *Pearl Harbor Attack,* Part 19, p. 3692, at pp. 3694–3695.
[148] *Pearl Harbor Attack,* Part 19, p. 3689.

[149] *Nazi Conspiracy and Aggression,* Vol. II, pp. 505–506; also *Pearl Harbor Attack,* Part 12, pp. 200–202.

[150] For earlier material on Thailand, see *Pearl Harbor Attack,* Part 15, pp. 1721–1725; Part 19, pp. 3696–3788: Grew, *Ten Years in Japan,* p. 464.

[151] *Pearl Harbor Attack,* Part 17, p. 2484.

[152] Merriman Smith, *"Thank You, Mr. President,"* p. 109.

[153] The Japanese denied that *any* speech had been delivered; they said that a privately prepared manuscript for a proposed speech was given to the press before it had been officially examined or approved: they also questioned the translation: *Foreign Relations, Japan;* Vol. II, p. 778; *Pearl Harbor Attack,* Part 12, p. 223.

[154] *Foreign Relations, Japan;* Vol. II, pp. 148–149: cf. Grew, *op. cit.,* pp. 483–484, 486.

[155] *Pearl Harbor Attack,* Part 11, pp. 5401–5402.

[156] *Ibid.,* Part 11, p. 5400.

[157] N. Y. *Times,* Dec. 1, 1941, p. 1, col. 8.

[158] *Pearl Harbor Attack,* Part 14, 1300.

[159] *Ibid.,* Part 19, pp. 3690–3691.

[160] *Ibid.,* Part 2, p. 491; Part 14, pp. 1249–1250.

[161] For further developments in this intrigue, see *Pearl Harbor Attack,* Part 12, pp. 202–203.

[162] *Pearl Harbor Attack,* Part 14, p. 1251.

[163] *Ibid.,* Part 19, pp. 3484–3485.

[164] *Pearl Harbor Committee Report,* p. 409.

[165] *The Ciano Diaries,* p. 414; see also *Pearl Harbor Attack,* Part 12, pp. 228–229, for explicit references to the contents of paragraphs 2 and 3.

[166] *Pearl Harbor Attack,* Part 12, pp. 204–205.

[167] *Ibid.,* Part 9, p. 4072.

[168] *Pearl Harbor Committee Report,* p. 414.

[169] *Pearl Harbor Attack,* Part 14, pp. 1301–1302.

[170] *Ibid.,* Part 18, p. 2945.

[171] *Ibid.,* Part 1, p. 180; cf. p. 178; Part 13, p. 393.

[172] *Ibid.,* Part 12, p. 209.

[173] *Ibid.,* Part 5, p. 2072.

[174] *Foreign Relations, Japan;* Vol. II, pp. 772–777; *Pearl Harbor Attack,* Part 12, pp. 210–212.

[175] *Pearl Harbor Attack,* Part 12, pp. 206–207; 212–215.

[176] *Foreign Relations, Japan;* Vol. II, pp. 777–778.

[177] *Pearl Harbor Attack,* Part 12, p. 199.

[178] *Ibid.,* Part 12, pp. 213–214.

CHAPTER XV

[1] *Pearl Harbor Attack*, Part 15, p. 1632.
[2] See *Pearl Harbor Attack*, Part 2, p. 441.
[3] See *ibid.*, Part 11, p. 5405.
[4] *Ibid.*, Part 5, pp. 2097–2135.
[5] N. Y. *Times*, Dec. 2, 1941, p. 1, col. 8.
[6] Ludwig, *Roosevelt*, p. 318.
[7] *Pearl Harbor Attack*, Part 5, p. 2190.
[8] *Ibid.*, Part 14, p. 1407.
[9] *Ibid.*, Part 5, p. 2416; Part 6, pp. 2670–2671.
[10] *Ibid.*, Part 5, p. 2417; Part 6, p. 2671.
[11] *Ibid.*, Part 5, p. 2190; Part 10, p. 4807.
[12] *Ibid.*, Part 9, pp. 4252–4253.
[13] *Ibid.*, Part 10, pp. 4807–4808.
[14] Frances Perkins, *The Roosevelt I Knew*, p. 380.
[15] *Pearl Harbor Committee Report*, pp. 413–414.
[16] N. Y. *Times*, Dec. 2, 1941, p. 4, col. 5.
[17] *Pearl Harbor Attack*, Part 11, p. 5437.
[18] *Ibid.*, Part 14, pp. 1198–1200.
[19] *Foreign Relations, Japan*; Vol. II, pp. 778–781; *Pearl Harbor Attack*, Part 12, 221–223.
[20] *Pearl Harbor Attack*, Part 12, pp. 215–216; Part 15, p. 1866.
[21] *Pearl Harbor Committee Report*, p. 416.
[22] *Pearl Harbor Attack*, Part 11, p. 5437.
[23] *Ibid.*, Part 14, p. 1203; cf. Mr. Stimson's answer to Question 3, *ibid.*, Part 11, p. 5457; that Mr. Roosevelt "was undoubtedly considering such a decision."
[24] *Pearl Harbor Attack*, Part 19, pp. 3664–3665.
[25] N. Y. *Times*, Dec. 3, 1941, p. 1, col. 8.
[26] *The Ciano Diaries*, p. 414. It was on Dec. 2 that a Japanese Imperial Naval Order was issued, setting the date for the commencement of hostilities: *Pearl Harbor Attack*, Part 13, p. 393.
[27] *The Ciano Diaries*, p. 414.
[28] *Pearl Harbor Attack*, Part 12, pp. 228–229; cf. *Nazi Conspiracy and Aggression*, Vol. VI, p. 310.
[29] N. Y. *Times*, Dec. 3, 1941, p. 1, cols. 6–7.
[30] *Ibid.*, Dec. 3, 1941, p. 4, col. 2.
[31] *Pearl Harbor Attack*, Part 9, p. 4200.
[32] *Ibid.*, Part 12, p. 224.
[33] *Ibid.*, Part 12, pp. 227–228.
[34] *Ibid.*, Part 12, p. 227.
[35] *Ibid.*, Part 12, p. 224.
[36] *Ibid.*, Part 3, pp. 1317–1318; Part 14, p. 1409.
[37] *Ibid.*, Part 2, p. 441.
[38] *Pearl Harbor Committee Report*, p. 418.
[39] *Ibid.*, p. 419.
[40] *Pearl Harbor Attack*, Part 15, p. 1632; cf. Part 2, p. 441.
[41] *Ibid.*, Part 12, p. 247.
[42] *Ibid.*, Part 12, p. 232.
[43] *Ibid.*, Part 12, p. 231.
[44] *Ibid.*, Part 12, p. 234.
[45] *Ibid.*, Part 12, p. 233.

[46] *Ibid.*, Part 3, pp. 1445–1447; Part 6, p. 2702; Part 8, pp. 3586–3590; Part 12, pp. 154–155.
[47] *Ibid.*, Part 15, pp. 1741–1743.
[48] *Ibid.*, Part 11, p. 5461.
[49] N. Y. *Times*, Dec. 6, 1941, p. 3, col. 1.
[50] *Pearl Harbor Committee Report*, p. 571.
[51] N. Y. *Times*, Dec. 6, 1941, p. 3, col. 1.
[52] N. Y. *Times*, Dec. 6, 1941, p. 1, col. 7.
[53] *Pearl Harbor Committee Report*, p. 421, footnote 1.
[54] *Foreign Relations, Japan;* Vol. II, p. 784: *Pearl Harbor Attack*, Part 12, p. 224.
[55] *Foreign Relations, Japan;* Vol. II, pp. 781–783: *Pearl Harbor Attack*, Part 12, pp. 235–236.
[56] *Pearl Harbor Attack*, Part 17, p. 2457.
[57] *Ibid.*, Part 15, p. 1632.
[58] *Ibid.*, Part 19, pp. 3648–3651.
[59] *Ibid.*, Part 11, p. 5472.
[60] *Ibid.*, Part 2, pp. 744–745.
[61] *Ibid.*, Part 12, p. 236.
[62] *Ibid.*, Part 12, p. 237.
[63] *Ibid.*, Part 12. p. 249.
[64] *Ibid.*, Part 12. p. 237.
[65] *Ibid.*, Part 12, p. 236.
[66] *Ibid.*, Part 1, pp. 185, 190.
[67] *Ibid.*, Part 14. p. 1413.
[68] *Ibid.*, Part 12, pp. 238–239.
[69] *Ibid.*, Part 8, p. 3557.
[70] *Ibid.*, Part 8, p. 3558; Part 14, pp. 1413–1415.
[71] *Ibid.*, Part 8, pp. 3560–3561.
[72] *Ibid.*, Part 15, p. 1680.
[73] *Ibid.*, Part 15, p. 1681; Part 2, pp. 441–443.
[74] *Ibid.*, Part 14, p. 1246.
[75] *Ibid.*, Part 15, p. 1634.
[76] *Ibid.*, Part 20, pp. 4117–4120.
[77] *Ibid.*, Part 20, pp. 4115–4116.
[78] *Ibid.*, Part 10, p. 4803; Part 4, p. 1932; Part 5, p. 2369.
[79] *Ibid.*, Part 10, p. 5083.
[80] *Ibid.*, Part 4, pp. 1933–1935; Part 19, pp. 3547–3553, 3555.
[81] *Ibid.*, Part 14, p. 1412.
[82] *Ibid.*, Part 10, p. 5083; Part 5, p. 2072.
[83] *Ibid.*, Part 10, pp. 5082–5083.
[84] *Ibid.*, Part 12, p. 252; see Part 10, p. 5148.
[85] *Ibid.*, Part 12, p. 247.
[86] *Foreign Relations, Japan;* Vol. II, p. 786, footnote 72.
[87] *Pearl Harbor Attack*, Part 11, p. 5165.
[88] *Ibid.*, Part 11, p. 5166.
[89] *Ibid.*, Part 11, p. 5509.
[90] *Ibid.*, Part 11, pp. 5165–5166.
[91] Ibid., Part 14, p. 1247.
[92] *Ibid.*, Part 14, pp. 1231–1235.
[93] *Ibid.*, Part 14, pp. 1240–1245.
[94] *Ibid.*, Part 9, p. 4513.
[95] *Ibid.*, Part 9, p. 4512.
[96] *Ibid.*, Part 14, pp. 1414–1415.
[97] *Ibid.*, Part 8, p. 3556.
[98] *Ibid.*, Part 8, pp. 3573–3574.
[99] *Ibid.*, Part 14, p. 1239.
[100] *Ibid.*, Part 14, p. 1238.
[101] *Ibid.*, Part 14, p. 1236.
[102] *Foreign Relations, Japan;* Vol. II, pp. 784–786; cf. *Pearl Harbor Attack*, Part 14, pp. 1240–1245.

[103] *Pearl Harbor Attack,* Part 11, p. 5473.
[104] *Ibid.*, Part 8, p. 3568.
[105] *Ibid.*, Part 9, p. 3990; Part 11, p. 5393.
[106] *Ibid.*, Part 2, p. 443; Part 15, p. 1633.
[107] *Ibid.*, Part 3, pp. 1108, 1319, 1321.
[108] *Ibid.*, Part 3, pp. 1110, 1328, 1430.
[109] *Ibid.*, Part 11, p. 5194.
[110] *Ibid.*, Part 3, p. 1325.
[111] *Ibid.*, Part 3, p. 1327.
[112] *Ibid.*, Part 15, pp. 1633–1634.
[113] *Ibid.*, Part 10, pp. 4660–4664.
[114] *Ibid.*, Part 11, p. 5544.
[115] *Ibid.*, Part 3, p. 1108.
[116] *Ibid.*, Part 5, p. 2183.
[117] Davis and Lindley, *How War Came,* p. 4.
[118] N. Y. *Times,* Dec. 7, 1941, Section 1, p. 1, col. 4.
[119] *Pearl Harbor Attack,* Part 11, p. 5437.
[120] *Ibid.*, Part 14, pp. 1415–1416; Part 12, p. 248.
[121] *Ibid.*, Part 9, p. 3997.
[122] *Ibid.*, Part 9, pp. 4006–4007; 4523–4524.
[123] *Ibid.*, Part 11, pp. 5282–5283.
[124] *Ibid.*, Part 9, p. 3998.
[125] *Ibid.*, Part 12, p. 249.
[126] *Ibid.*, Part 20, pp. 4121–4131, especially 4123.
[127] *Ibid.*, Part 11, pp. 5437–5438.
[128] *Ibid.*, Part 8, p. 3828.
[129] *Ibid.*, Part 11, pp. 5439–5440.
[130] *Ibid.*, Part 9, p. 4524.
[131] *Ibid.*, Part 9, p. 4525.
[132] *Ibid.*, Part 3, p. 1111.
[133] *Ibid.*, Part 3, p. 1109; Part 5, pp. 2132–2133.
[134] *Ibid.*, Part 3, pp. 1288–1289.
[135] *Ibid.*, Part 3, pp. 1109–1110.
[136] *Ibid.*, Part 7, p. 3116; Part 14, pp. 1409–1410.
[137] *Foreign Relations, Japan;* Vol. II, pp. 379–380, 786.
[138] *Pearl Harbor Attack,* Part 11, p. 5458.
[139] *Ibid.*, Part 10, p. 5029.
[140] Testified; *Pearl Harbor Attack,* Part 10, pp. 5076–5080; Part 27, pp. 526–536; Part 32, pp. 475–485.
[141] Testified, *Pearl Harbor Attack,* Part 10, pp. 5027–5076; Part 27, pp. 517–526; Part 32, pp. 485–496.
[142] *Pearl Harbor Attack,* Part 32, pp. 478, 482–483; Part 27, p. 531; Part 10, p. 5036.
[143] *Ibid.*, Part 27, p. 531.
[144] *Ibid.*, Part 10, pp. 5028; Part 27, p. 520.
[145] *Ibid.*, Part 10, p. 5037; Part 27, p. 522.
[146] *Ibid.*, Part 27, pp. 520, 532, 570; Part 32, pp. 348, 478, 488; Part 10, pp. 5041, 5045–5047, 5068, 5078.
[147] *Ibid.*, Part 10, pp. 5029–5031; Part 32, p. 489; Part 27, p. 520.
[148] *Ibid.*, Part 10, p. 5031; Part 32, p. 478; Part 27, p. 532.
[149] *Ibid.*, Part 27, p. 567; see Part 18, pp. 3014–3015.
[150] *Ibid.*, Part 27, pp. 568, 570–571.
[151] *Ibid.*, Part 27, pp. 570–571; Part 32, pp. 347–348.

152 *Ibid.*, Part 27, p. 572.
153 *Ibid.*, Part 10, p. 5078.
154 *Ibid.*, Part 32, p. 349; Part 27, pp. 521, 568–570; Part 10, pp. 5031–5032, 5045.
155 *Ibid.*, Part 27, p. 533.
156 *Ibid.*, Part 10, p. 5079; Part 32, p. 494.
157 *Ibid.*, Part 5, p. 2340.
158 See chart, facing p. 5058, Part 10, *Pearl Harbor Attack;* cf. Part 32, p. 489.
159 *Pearl Harbor Attack*, Part 32, p. 479; Part 27, pp. 521, 533; Part 10, pp. 5037, 5046.
160 *Ibid.*, Part 32, p. 490; Part 10, p. 5033.
161 *Ibid.*, Part 11, p. 5308; cf. Part 1, p. 43; Part 6, p. 2675.
162 Sunk; *ibid.*, Part 1, p. 46; Part 6, p. 2674; Part 12, p. 354; Part 5, p. 2210.
163 Sunk; *ibid.*, Part 1, p. 46; Part 6, p. 2674; Part 12, p. 354; Part 5, p. 2210.
164 Sunk; *ibid.*, Part 1, p. 46; Part 5, p. 2210; Part 6, p. 2674.
165 Capsized; *ibid.*, Part 1, p. 47; Part 6, p. 2674; Part 12, p. 354.
166 Heavily damaged; *ibid,* Part 1, p. 48; Part 6, p. 2674; Part 12, p. 355.
167 Damaged; *ibid.*, Part 5, p. 2210; Part 6, p. 2674; Part 12, p. 355.
168 Damaged; *ibid.*, Part 6, p. 2674; Part 12, p. 355.
169 Seriously damaged; Part 1, p. 46; Part 6, p. 2674; Part 12, p. 355; Part 20, p. 4522.
170 *Pearl Harbor Attack,* Part 1, pp. 29, 62.
171 *Ibid.*, Part 1, pp. 58–59.
172 *Pearl Harbor Committee Report*, p. 65.
173 *Pearl Harbor Attack,* Part 11, p. 5351; Part 19, p. 3556.
174 *Ibid.*, Part 8, p. 3829.
175 *Ibid.*, Part 6, p. 2837.
176 *Ibid.*, Part 11, p. 5438.
177 *Ibid.*, Part 2, p. 607.
178 *Foreign Relations, Japan;* Vol. II, p. 786.
179 *Ibid.*, Vol. II, pp. 787–792: *Pearl Harbor Attack*, Part 12, pp. 239–245.
180 *Foreign Relations, Japan;* Vol. II, p. 787.
181 *Ibid.*, Vol. II, p. 793.
182 Mrs. Eleanor Roosevelt, *This I Remember*, p. 233.
183 Perkins, *The Roosevelt I Knew*, pp. 379–380.
184 *Pearl Harbor Attack,* Part 19, p. 3505.
185 *The Aspirin Age,* "Pearl Harbor Sunday: The End of an Era," by Jonathan Daniels, p. 485.
186 Churchill, *The Grand Alliance*, p. 606.
187 *Ibid.*, p. 607.
188 *Peace and War*, p. 143.
189 *Pearl Harbor Committee Report*, p. 266–W.

INDEX

A

Abyssinia, conquest of, 34
Agar, Herbert, 257
Alaska, danger to, 329
Albania,
    Italian occupation of, 63
    Russian occupation of, 63
Alien Registration Act, 149
Allied Purchasing commission, 135,
Alsop, Joseph W., 257
Amau, Eiji, 357-358, 367-368, 379, 426
Amile, Thomas R., 59
American Society of Newspaper Editors, 40
Andrews, General Frank M., 143
Argentia, Newfoundland, 341, 342, 343, 352, 358
Arita, 75, 76, 278
Arizona (battleship), 553
Arkansas (battleship), 20
Army-Navy Joint Board (U. S.), 439, 492, 500
Arnold, General Henry H., Jr., 56, 343
Atlantic Charter, 342, 343, 358, 360, 361, 383, 406, 537
Atlantic Conference, 325, 336, 359, 370, 373, 383
Attolico, Bernardo, 68
Auchinleck, Sir Claude, 318, 321, 339
Augusta (cruiser), 341, 346
Australia, 35, 245, 255, 283, 336, 436, 467, 483, 513, 536
Austria, invaded by Germany, 38
Azores, 192, 233, 246, 252, 256, 266, 268, 321, 343

B

Baldwin, Hanson, 319
Ballantine, Joseph W., 382, 416, 456, 458-460, 462
Bardia, 259
Barkley, Senator Alben, W., 155
Baruch, Bernard M., 46
Basra, 262
Baudouin, Paul, 143, 151
Beaverbrook, Lord, 138, 340, 406, 407
Belgium, invaded by Germany, 115, 131, 221
Bengazi, 259
Bess, Demaree, 261
Bessarabia, 70, 137
Bevin, Ernest, 239
Bibliography, 559-561
Biddle, Francis J., 143
Bismarck (battleship), 304
Bismarck Archipelago, 264
Black, Hugo, 21. 22, 25
Bolshevism, 82, 223
Bratton, Colonel Rufus S., 540
Britain, see England Brooke-Popham, Sir Robert, 240, 241, 540
Brown, Senator Prentiss M., 253
Bryan, William Jennings, 494
Buchanan, President James, 275
Bulgaria, 63, 183, 260
Bullitt, William C., 46, 48, 51, 56, 67, 150, 193, 237, 328, 338, 427
Burma Road, 279, 281-282, 431, 440, 486, 487, 498, 504, 506, 513, 546
Butler, Richard Austen, 289
Butler, W.M., 241
Byas, Hugh, 288, 290
Byrd, Harry F., 196
Byrnes, James F., 156

INDEX | 613

C

Cadogan, Sir Alexander, 343
California (battleship), 553
Campbell, Sir Ronald, 467, 510
Canada, 41, 122, 191, 203, 266
Canary Islands, 192, 223, 335
Canton Island, 35, 264, 324
Cape Verde Islands, 43, 119, 223, 266, 269, 321, 344
Case of the Cockleshell Worships, 526, 527
Casey, Richard G., 499, 513, 518
Cayuga (Coast Guard cutter), 264
Chamberlain, Neville, 23, 34, 44, 45, 56, 63, 92, 99, 115
Chiang Kai-shek,
    attitude towards U.S. negotiations with Japan, 481, 487, 488, 490, 499, 511, 517, 545, 546
    Japan's request for cessation of U. S. aid to, 471, 478, 481
    Japan's secret peace offer to, 283
    Message to Morgenthau, 431
    plea for British aid, 445
    plea for United States aid, 487-488, 499
    Roosevelt's policy toward, 335
    Russian aid to, 336
    Truce terms offered to Japan, 285
    United States aid to, 496, 549-553
Chiang Kai-shek, Madame, 487
China
    Lend-lease aid to, 451
    Roosevelt's policy towards, 24, 39, 296, 489
    Sino-Japanese war, 24, 33, 60, 182
    United States loan to, 48
    Christian Science Monitor, 23
    Christmas Island, 264
    Churchill, Winston, agreement on defending Canada, 191-192

Atlantic Charter, 360, 361
Atlantic Conference, 325, 336, 359, 370, 373, 383
Becomes Prime Minister, 115
Burma Road, 282
Chinese policy, 452
Egypt reinforced by, 224
General control over British fighting forces, 115
Japan and, 287-288, 305, 332, 334
Landing on Norway planned, 110
Led Opposition in Parliament, 45
Message to Mussolini, 113
Opposition to peace in 1940, 178
"parallel action" between Roosevelt and, 352, 354, 358, 359
Request for U.S. aid, 133-134, 137, 139, 141, 144, 162, 186, 198, 201, 203, 204, 212, 216, 218, 231, 232, 234, 237, 238, 248, 251, 255, 262, 266, 270, 336, 368, 440
Roosevelt's quarantine speech prompted by, 33
Sealed communication sent personally to Roosevelt, 92
U. S. aid to France requested by, 139-144
U. S. "neutral zone," 95
"we will never surrender" speech 133, 224
Ciano, Count Galeazzo, 56, 60, 62, 66, 70, 90, 108, 110, 112, 151, 181
Ciechanowski, Jan, 407
Citrine, Sir Walter, 251
Civilian Conservation Corps, 123
Clapper, Mrs. Olive E., 207
Cohen, Benjamin V., 238
Columbus (German merchant vessel), 90
Compton, Lewis, 146
Cooke, Captain Charles M., Jr., 320, 362
Cooper, Rt. Hon. Alfred Duff, 45, 394

Corcoran, Thomas J., 72
Council of National Defense,
    Advisory Commission to, 131
Craig, May, 131
Craigie, Sir Robert L., 338, 411, 457
Crete, 261
Currie, Lauchlin, 486
Czechoslovakia, 44, 64, 346

D

Dakar, 192, 201, 266, 270
Daladier, Edouard, 99
Darlan, Jean Francois, 150, 263, 326, 328
Davies, Joseph E., 67
Davis, Norman, 14
Davis, William, R., 97
Declaration of Lima, 58
Declaration of Panama, 94
Defense Plant Corporation, 148
Defense Supplies Corporation, 148
DeGaulle, General Charles, 339
Democratic Party, anti-war plank, 155, 156, 165, 267, 429, 430, 556
Denmark,
    Export-Import Bank loan to, 110
    Invaded by Germany, 111
Dill, Sir John, 260, 343
Division of State and Local Cooperation, 265
Doenitz, Admiral Karl, 111, 327
Donovan, Col. William J., 260, 407
Dooman, Counselor Eugene H., 73, 76, 77, 78, 79, 81, 83, 84, 288, 354, 363, 392, 413, 415
Draft,
    Act signed by Roosevelt, 154,
    Amendment to Act, 319, 320, 321, 328, 329
    Plans for, 96
    Roosevelt quoted on, 58, 137, 165, 195

Drought, Father, 284
Dunkirk, 131, 133, 176
Dutch Guiana, 478

E

Early, Stephen T., 146
Eden, Anthony, 30, 45, 49, 187, 243, 260, 336, 411, 476, 490, 499, 537
Edison, Charles, Secretary of the Navy, 144
Egypt, 224, 261, 262
Eisenhower, General Dwight D., 115
Elizabeth, Queen, 67
Elliott, George E., 551-552
Emmons, General Delos C., 149
Enderbury Island, 35
England,
    destroyer deal with, 146, 280
    Finland aided by, 102
    Lend-lease aid to, 204, 205, 209, 212, 215, 216, 217, 341
    Navy code broken by Germany, 328
    trade agreement (1938), 41
    was declared on Germany, 90
Estonia, 63, 102, 137
Ethiopia, 12-15
Export-Import Bank,
    Capital increased, 110
    Loans,
        to Denmark, 110
        to Finland, 102, 105, 110
        to Iceland, 110
        to Sweden, 110

F

Fair Labor Standards Act (1938), 37
Farley, James A., 37, 72
Federal Bureau of Investigation, 93
Federal Power Commission 135
Fiji Islands, 264
Finland, 102, 103, 105, 110

INDEX | 615

Flynn, Edward J., 157
Four Freedoms, 217, 218, 262, 346
France,
    air mission to United States, 56
    declaration of war against Germany, 90
    fall of, 149-150
    fleet of, 143, 150
    Italy's declaration of war against, 136
    sit-down strikes, 15
Franco, Francisco, 61, 223, 259, 335, 336
Freeman, Vice Chief Air Wilfred, 343
Fujii, Sadamubu, 85
Fuller, General J. F. C., 175

G

Garner, Vice-President John N., 225
Gauss, Ambassador Clarence E., 431, 440, 545
George, David Lloyd, 99
George II, King, 261
George V (H.M.S.), 214
George VI, King, 67
Germany,
    Ambassador to Washington called home, 47
    Attack on Russia planned, 181
    Austria invaded by, 38
    Belgium invaded by, 115, 131, 221
    Bulgaria invaded by, 260
    Czechoslovakia occupied by, 63
    Denmark invaded by, 111
    England's declaration of war against, 90
    English Navy code broken by, 328
    Finland aided by, 103
    France occupied by, 135
    France's declaration of war against, 90
    Greece attacked by, 261
    Luxembourg invaded by, 115
    Netherlands invaded by, 115, 118
    Norway invaded by, 111
    Poland invaded by, 90, 118, 221
    Rhineland reoccupied by, 15
    Russia attacked by, 308, 309,
    Saar reunion with, 11
    Sudetenland occupied by, 44
    United States diplomatic code broken by, 328
    Universal military service, 11
    War declared on United States, 557
    Yugoslavia invaded by, 260
Gerow, General Leonard T., 438, 473, 500
Ghormley, Admiral Robert L., 150, 205
Gibraltar, 223, 224, 259
Gilbert Islands, 264
Goering, Marshal Hermann, 97, 108, 221
Good Neighbor policy, 8
Grant, Hugh, G., 528
Great Britain, *see* England Greece, 238, 261, 262
Greer (destroyer), 374, 385, 386, 430
Greenland, 218, 264
Grew, Joseph C.,
    Attempts to improve U. S.-Japanese relations, 73-74, 391, 402, 428, 465, 521
    Conference of Nine-Power Washington Treaty signatories, 32
    Conference with Shigemitsu, 391
    Conference with Konoye, 318, 379-380
    Conference with Matsuoka, 288, 318
    Conference with Terasaki, 379, 414
    Conference with Togo, 454-455, 481
    Conference with Toyoda, 336, 354-355, 357, 375, 381-382, 401, 402, 414, 477
    Confidence in Dooman, 354
    Message to Hull, 372, 402, 437
    Opinion of Konoye, 404
    Opinion of Nomura, 286

616 | DESIGN FOR WAR

Quoted on China campaign, 278
Quoted on German policy concerning U.S.-Japanese relations, 286
Roosevelt's message to Hirohito sent to, 537
Russo-Japanese partition of China reported by, 137
Terasaki's message to, 363
Warned of probability of lapse of Japanese discussion, 500
Grunert, General George, 552
Guam, 53, 478

H

Hague, Frank, 157
Halifax, Lord,
Ambassador to U. S., 220, 244,
Arrival in U. S., 236
Cable to London intercepted by Japanese Navy, 306
Conference to review clauses in Versailles Treaty, 90
Conference with Nomura, 421-423
Conference with Reynaud, 138
Conference with Hull, 484, 512-514, 519, 538
Conference with Welles, 498-499, 510, 528
Conversation with Ciano, 56
Requests for U. S. aid, 67, 336
Speech (August 22, 1940) 179
Halsey, Admiral William F., 509
Hamilton, Maxwell M., 241, 382, 470, 535
Harkness, Richard L., 152
Harriman, W. Averell, 406
Hart, Admiral Thomas C., 205, 339, 362, 432, 502, 526, 527, 540
Hassell, Ulrich von, 108
Hawaii, 53
Hayes, Carlton J. H., 335, 336

Hayter, Mr., 535
Helfrich, Admiral C. E. L., 502
Helsinki, Finland, bombing of, 102
Henderson, Leon, 408
Henderson, Sir Nevile, 89
Henri-Haye, Gaston, 191
Herron, General Charles D., 198
Hess, Rudolf, 302
Hiranuma, Baron Kiichiro, 76, 77, 78, 83, 84, 326
Hirohito, Emperor,
attitude, toward proposed Konoye-Roosevelt meeting, 334
conference with chiefs of Japanese high command, 413, 442
desire for peace, 377, 422, 437
Roosevelt's message to, 495, 511, 530, 542, 544, 545
Hirota, Koki, 32
Hitler, Adolf,
Conference with Matsuoka, 290-293
Conference with Molotov, 182
Czechoslovakia occupied by, 63
Desire for peace, 99, 178, 222, 472
Hatred of Bolshevism, 223
Invasion of England planned by, 179, 222, 235
Message to Roosevelt, 66
Opposition to war with U. S., 272, 291, 300, 327
Plan to break through Maginot Line, 109
Planned Japanese attack on British possessions in the Far East, 287, 291
Roosevelt's message to, 495
Russian invasion, 176, 180, 308
Speeches (1937), 28
Triparite Treaty and, 279
Underground movement and, 62
Hitokappu Bay, 474, 483
Hopkins, Harry,
Advisor to Roosevelt on lend-lease, 264

INDEX | 617

Appointed to Production Planning Board, 250
Illness, 525
Ludwig quoted on, 525
On cruises with Roosevelt, 209, 257
On Supply Priorities and Allocations Board, 408
Roosevelt's personal envoy to England, 212, 220, 232, 248, 251, 264, 289, 333, 337-338
Russia visited by, 338
Survey of national capacity to build military airplanes, 43
Third-term movement, 72, 155
Views on war with Japan, 547
Horinouchi, Kensuke, 82
Hornbeck, Dr. Stanley K., 439, 448, 487, 503, 510, 511
Hu Shih, Dr., 475, 479, 485, 486, 498, 511
Hull, Cordell,
    Aid to Britain promised by, 201, 286
    Chinese policy, 277, 431, 441, 514, 536
    Conference of Nine-Power Washington Treaty Signatories, 32
    Conference with Minister from Thailand, 354
    Conference with Kurusu, 463, 466, 468, 471-472, 474, 492-494, 529, 536
    Conference with Nomura, 298, 299, 300, 302-303, 306, 307, 309, 331, 335, 348, 349, 354, 358, 359, 362, 363, 365, 366, 371, 372, 375, 376, 380, 381, 382, 390, 395, 396, 404, 409, 410, 412, 415, 416, 417, 421, 424, 445, 451, 452, 456, 457, 458, 459, 462, 463, 466, 467, 468, 472, 489, 494, 503, 523, 529, 536, 551, 554, 555
France and, 263
Havana conference, 195

Japanese situation and, 25, 77, 78, 82, 83, 84, 85, 149, 198, 213, 242, 243, 253, 279, 280, 283, 285, 286, 288, 298, 299, 301, 303, 305, 306, 332, 345, 346, 349, 358, 359, 363, 365-366, 371, 373, 377, 395, 398, 400-402, 410, 454, 460, 474, 478, 480-82, 511-515, 537, 539-552
Joint United States-Japanese declaration on economic policy proposed by, 462
Lend-lease and, 225, 228, 253
National Defense, 202
Neutrality Act modified by, 131
Opinion of Tojo's speech, 518
Panay incident, 32
Peace Act, 59, 60
Permanent Joint Board on Defense, 192
responsibility for outbreak of war with Japan, 495
Roosevelt's proposed message to Emperor drafted by, 511, 544
Russo-German war, 308
Speech (3/17/38), 39
Ten point Proposal, 493
Tripartite Treaty, 213
War Council, 482, -484, 488, 511-514
Hungary, 63
Hutchins, Robert, M., 256
Hyperion (British destroyer), 95

I

Iceland, 252, 264, 266, 269, 319-320
    Export-Import Bank loan to, 110
Ickes, Harold L., 72, 123, 157, 161, 186, 250, 340
Ikawa, Tadao, 284
Indo-China, 279-280, 310-311, 314-315, 318, 322-323, 326, 331-333, 336, 380, 398, 399, 431, 443, 444, 458, 465, 467, 474, 475, 477, 479, 481, 487, 489, 502, 523, 527, 529, 536, 540, 543-544

618 | DESIGN FOR WAR

Industrial Mobilization Plan, 36, 88
Ingersoll, Admiral Royal E., 35, 106, 424, 441, 492
Inglis, Admiral T. B., 268
Institute of Public Affairs, 23
Interstate Commerce Commission, 59
Iraq, 263
Isabel (U.S.S.), 527, 530, 553,
Ishii, Viscount, 523
Italo-Ethiopian war, 12, 14, 15
Italy,
    Albania occupied by, 60, 63
    Finland aided by, 102
    Italo-Ethiopian war, 12, 14, 15
    United States diplomatic code broken by, 328, 357
    Was declared against France, 136
    War declared on United States, 557
Iwakuro, Colonel Hideo, 284

J

Jackson, Robert, H., 134, 146, 157, 189
Jaluit, 489
Japan
    German pressure on, 425
    Hull's antipathy against, 25
    Imperial conference, 313, 379, 443, 444,
    "moral embargo" against, 41
    Oil agreement with Netherlands East Indies, 432
    Panay incident, 32
    Relations with United States prior to Pearl Harbor, 32-33, 73-85, 104-105, 149, 250-253, 273-296, 300-385, 390-401, 419-433, 435-558
    Resignation of Knoyo's cabinet, 422, 424, 426
    Sino-Japanese war, 24, 33, 58, 72, 73, 78, 182, 278-282
    United States warning to, 352
    War declared against United States, 521, 542-543
    "winds code", 471, 535
Jodl, General Alfred, 181, 291
Johnsin, Louis, A., 56, 123, 151
Jones, Jesse, H., 250

K

Kalinin, President Mikhail I., 102
Kearny (U.S.S.), 428, 430
Keefe, Frank B., 558
Keitel, General Wilhelm, 181, 290, 291
Kelly, Edward J., 151
Kennedy, Joseph, 48, 51, 67, 167, 206, 233-234, 235, 237, 247
Kido, Marquis, 419
Kimmel, Admiral Husband E., 219, 263, 264, 318, 327, 331, 338, 339, 396, 424, 483, 508
King, Admiral Ernest J., 95, 125, 268, 269, 316, 317, 343, 503
King, Mackenzie, 134, 191, 375
Knox, Frank,
    "American blood" speech, 316, 318
    American Legion address, 389
    annual report (1941), 548
    appointed Secretary of the Navy
    censorship, 216
    Chinese policy, 441
    Draft of Roosevelt's message to Congress, 511
    Foreign military purchases and, 103
    Japanese situation, 427-428, 500, 506, 546, 549
    Lend-lease favored by, 230-234, 238
    Opinion on intervention, 151, 317, 320
    Pearl Harbor attack, 553
    Providence speech, 453
    Quoted on escort of convoys, 389
    War Council meeting, 488
Knudsen, William S., 213, 265

INDEX | 619

Konoye, Prince Fumimaro, conferences with Tojo, 413, 420-421
    Grew's opinion, 404
    Imperial Conference, 377
    Japan's counter-policy proposed by, 278
    Meeting with Grew, 379
    Proposed meeting with Roosevelt, 334-336, 348, 353, 355-356, 363, 364, 367, 372, 379, 390, 397, 399, 404, 409
    Proposed second-rank conference with, 523
    Resignation, 421
    Tripartite Treaty, 314
    Views on United States-Japanese relations, 301-304, 316-318, 353
Korean war, 4, 557
Kra Isthmus, 506, 519, 541, 554
Krock, Arthur, 221, 236, 238, 239, 252
Ku Klux Klan, 21
Kunming, 431, 438, 441
Kurusu, Saburo,
    Appointed ambassador, 445
    Conference with Welles, 529, 530
    Conferences with Hull, 463, 468, 471, 472, 474, 493, 494, 522, 523, 536, 554

L

LaGuardia, Fiorello H., 226
Land, Admiral Emory Scott, 88
Landon, Alfred M., 227
Lattimore, Owen, 486
Latvia, Russian occupation of, 63, 102, 137
Le Brun, President Albert, 150
League of Nations,
    Russia expelled from, 102
    United States and, 8, 9, 14, 16
Leahy, Admiral William D., 193, 201, 325, 328
Lehman, Governor Herbert H., 226
Lend-Lease,
    Aid to China, 451
    Aid to England, 198, 203, 204, 212, 216, 263, 337
    Aid to Greece, 261
    Aid to Russia, 337, 338, 339, 407, 408
    Ellender amendment, 252, 253
    Escort for convoys, 269, 316
    Hopkins and, 212, 264
    Origin of, 204
    Roosevelt and, 212, 216, 337, 341
    Second appropriation bill, 407
    Shortages in Hawaii due to, 408
    Synthetic crisis at birth of, 205-258
Leopold III, King, 88, 116, 131
Liberia, 201
Libya, 224, 226, 228, 261, 522
Lindley, Ernest K., 29, 428
Lindsay, Sir Ronald, 33
Lithuania, 63, 70, 102, 137
Litvinov, Maxim, 68
Lockard, Joseph L., 551-551
    Conference with Hull, 149, 197, 198, 206
    Conference with Roosevelt, 121, 134
    Deceased, 214
    Defense of Canada, 191
    Destroyer gift, 118, 185
    Request for U. S. aid, 198
Loudon, Dr. Alexander, 499
Ludlow, Louis, 31, 36, 37, 59
Ludwig, Emil, 34, 35, 36, 72, 525
Luxembourg, 115
Luzon, 438

M

McCormick, Ann O'Hare, 225, 236
McIntire, Vice Admiral Ross T., 560
MacArthur, General Douglas, 33, 119, 496

Maginot Line, 109
Magruder, General John A., 362, 431
Malaya, 331, 522, 537
Malaya (H.M.S.), 177, 216
Manila, 305
Marshall, General George C., aid to Britain, 132, 238
    Army-Navy Joint Board, 439, 492, 500, 504
    Atlantic Conference, 343
    Chinese policy, 438
    Combat planes for China, 251
    Conference of Generals in office of, 142
    Danger to Alaska, 329
    Draft amendment, 318, 320, 321, 329
    Expeditionary Force, 322
    Far Eastern situation, 446, 448, 551
    Joint U.S.-British war plan approved by, 251
    Mission to Britain, 149
    Monies for military expansion, 43
    Morgenthau proposal, 478
    Occupation of Azores considered by, 246
    "surplus" military material, 135
    Views on proposed seizure of Martinique, 304
    War Cabinet meeting, 506
    War Council, 482
Martin, Representative Joseph W., Jr., 1
Martinique, 304, 321
Maryland (battleship), 553
Mason, Representative, 218
Matsudaira, Koto, 382
Matsuoka, Foreign Minister Yosuke, 246, 288-306, 310, 311, 313, 315, 318, 322, 324, 326, 368, 403
Mencken, H. L., 177
Merekalov, Alexei, 68
Metals Reserve Company, 148

Miles, General Sherman, 244, 534
Moley, Raymond, 33, 61, 71
Molotov, Vyacheslav M., 68, 69, 70, 85, 181, 182, 183, 184, 298
Monroe Doctrine, 144
Moore, John Bassett, 232
Morgenthau, Henry,
    Aid to Britain, 134
    Armaments, 27,
    Champion of China, 431
    foreign military purchases, 103
    French air mission visits, 56
    lend-lease, 216, 225, 229, 238
    proposal for eliminating tension with Japan and insuring defeat of Germany, 469, 474, 476
    Roosevelt's third term, 155
Morocco, 431
Moscicki, Ignace, 89
Mount Vernon (U.S.S.), 370
Muller, Dr. Joseph, 115
Munich agreement, 44
Massolini, Benito,
    Albania seized by, 60
    Attempt to conciliate Japan, 85
    Conference with Franco, 259
    Conference with Hitler, 235
    Conference with Japanese ambassador, 532
    Conference with von Ribbentrop, 302
    Desire for peace, 68
    Ethiopia invaded by, 12
    Meeting with Roosevelt proposed, 109
    Opposed to alliance with Hitler, 62
    Roosevelt's messages to, 64, 112-114, 136
    Versailles Treaty, 90
    War considered inevitable by, 49

N

Nash, Patrick, 157
National Defense Advisory Commission, 213
National Defense Research Committee, 148
National Guard, 142, 193, 194
National Resources Planning Board, 96
Naval Appropriations Act, 146, 189
Naval Conference (1935), 10, 14
Netherlands, 115, 118, 239
Netherlands East Indies, 278, 310, 331, 336, 380, 398, 444, 471, 488, 502, 543
Neutrality Act (1935),
    Amendment (1937), 16, 27, 29
    Amendment (1939), 36, 48, 93, 94, 97, 98, 100, 101, 102,
    Amendment (1941), 415, 465
    Embargo and arms and munitions under,
    Hull and,
    Roosevelt and, 11, 29, 50, 51, 88, 94-95, 98, 100, 101, 166
    Nevada (battleship), 553
New Caledonia, 264
New Deal,
    Collapse of, 21
    Objectives of, 8
    Production and, 127
New Guinea, 469
New Hebrides, 264
New York (battleship), 20
New Zealand, 245, 256, 283, 336, 436
Newfoundland, 229
Nine-Power Washington Treaty, 32
Nomura, Admiral Kichisaburo,
    Appointed Ambassador, 284
    Atlantic Conference reported by, 341
    Conference with Lord Halifax, 421-424
    Conference with Welles, 331-332
    Conference with Hull, 298, 299, 302, 303, 306, 307, 309, 348, 358, 393, 404, 423-424, 445, 451-455, 458, 459-460, 462-463, 464, 466-469, 477, 503, 529, 536, 551, 555
    Conference with Roosevelt, 243, 246, 288, 298, 332, 353, 372, 457, 503, 529, 536, 551
    Desire for peaceful relations with U. S., 286, 353, 419
    Desire to resign, 426
    Germany's attitude towards, 283, 284, 289
    Grew's opinion of, 284
    Instructions to, 443, 463-500
North Carolina (battleship), 20
Norway, 107, 110, 111
Nye, Senator Gerald P., 249
Obata, Shigeyoshi, 382
Office of Civilian Defense, 265
Office of Price Administration and Civilian Supply, 264
Office of Production Management, 206, 265
Ohashi, Chuichi, 288
Oklahoma, (battleship), 553
Oldham, Bishop, 14
Oshima, General Hiroshi, 287, 303, 311
Ott, General Eugene, 303, 322-324, 357, 358, 367-369, 322
Oumansky, Constantine, 224, 229, 338, 339
Outer Mongolia, 138, 183

P

Panama, 53
Panama Canal, 42, 188, 318
Panama Conference (1939), 95
Panay (U.S.S.), 32, 507, 563
Paris, France, fall of, 149, 150
Patterson, Robert, P., 135

622 | DESIGN FOR WAR

Paul, Prince, 254
Peace Act, 59-60
Pearl Harbor, 176, 219, 280, 370, 404, 412, 413, 474, 483, 527, 539, 547, 553
Pearl Harbor Committee, 307, 334, 404, 412, 535, 560
Pennsylvania, (battleship), 553
Pepper, Senator Claude E., 161, 427
Perkins, Frances, 123, 157, 273, 556
Permanent Joint Board, 192
Perry, Commodore Oliver Hazard, 275
Pétain, Marshal Henri Philippe, 141, 150, 151, 201, 203, 259, 263
Philippine Air Force, 438
Philippine Islands, 399, 411, 448, 478, 482, 501, 504, 537, 543, 553
Phillips, Sir Frederick, 216
Phillips, Sir Tom S. V., 532, 540
Phillips, William, 48, 112, 113, 151, 302
Piedmont, Prince of, 62
Pittman, Senator Key, 59
Pius XII, Pope, 103, 108, 112, 149, 179, 262, 383, 384
Poland,
 Collapse of Army, 90
 Invaded by Germany, 90, 118, 221
 Partition of, 70
 Russian occupation of, 63, 118
Portugal, 266
Potomac (U.S.S.), 257, 341
Pound, Admiral Sir Dudley, 203, 343
Pratt, Admiral William V., 316
President, checks and balances, 3
Prince of Wales (H.M.S.), 341, 436, 532, 540
Production Planning Board, 250
Purvis, Arthur B., 215

Q

Quadripartite Pact, 184
Quezon, Manuel Luis, 493
Quo Tai-chi, 486, 487, 529

R

Raeder, Admiral Erich, 181, 291
Reconstruction Finance Corporation, 58, 148
Republican Party, anti-war plank, 156
Repulse (H.M.S.), 532, 540
Reuben James, 432
Reynaud, Paul, 113, 135, 136, 137, 138, 139, 140, 141, 142
Rhineland, 15
Ribbentrop, Joachim von, attitude toward Nomura, 284, 302
 Conference with Molotov, 182-184
 Conference with Mussolini, 302
 Conference with Oshima, 287
 Conference with Stalin, 70
 Conference with Ciano, 70, 144, 181, 302
 Conference with Matsuoka, 293-298
 Desire for peace, 144
 Japanese relations, 315, 322-324, 514-516, 533
 Note to Matsuoka, 310
 Richardson, Admiral James O., 35, 106, 121, 129, 202, 219, 280, 281, 282
Roberts, Floyd, 59
Robin Moor, (vessel), 308, 386
Roosevelt, Mrs. Eleanor, 218, 561
Roosevelt, Elliott, 263, 341
Roosevelt, Franklin Delano,
 A. F. of L. Teamsters Union address, 159
 Alien Registration Act approved by, 149
 American Retail Federation address, 71
 Annual Message to the Congress (1934), 10
 Annual Message to the Congress (1935), 11
 Annual Message to the Congress

INDEX | 623

(1936), 15
Annual Message to the Congress (1937), 20
Annual Message to the Congress (1939), 50
Annual Message to the Congress (1940), 104
Annual Message to the Congress (1941), 217
armament program, 33, 48, 108, 136
Armistice Day address (1935), 13
Armistice Day address (1941), 445
Arms embargo repealed, 94
"Arsenal of democracy" speech, 213-215
Atlantic Conference, 325, 336, 359, 370, 373, 383
Battleship construction approved by, 20
Boston campaign speech (1940), 167
Brooklyn campaign speech (1940), 168
Buffalo campaign speech (1940), 169
Case of the Cockleshell Warships, 526-527
Chautauqua speech, 8, 16-18
Chicago speech, 14
Chinese policy, 24, 40, 296
Cleveland campaign speech (1940), 171-172
conduct of foreign affairs, 3, 4, 5, 6
Conference of Nine-Power Washington Treaty signatories, 32
Conferences with cabinet, 534
cooperation with Great Britain, 33, 34, 42-43
court-packing plans, 21, 37
Dallas speech, 15
Depression (1937-1989) 21, 37, 40, 41, 47, 71
Destroyer deal, 10, 120, 127, 142, 146, 173, 186-191

Executive Department reorganization plans, 21
Food shortages, 95
four freedoms, 108, 217, 218, 262, 346,
fourth term, 171
Good Neighbor policy, 8
government spending, 50
Great Smoky Mountains National Park speech, 197-199
"hemisphere defense," 161
Herald Tribune Forum address, 46
inaugural address first, 8
inaugural address third, 235
inauguration, first, 7
intervention in Europe, 116
isolationist, 7-20
Italo-Ethiopian war and, 12-14, 24
Japanese policy, 40, 277, 287, 288, 345, 411, 482, 494, 495
Labor Day speech (1941), 369
League of Nations, 8, 9, 116
Madison Square Garden speech (1936), 19
Madison Square Garden speech (1940), 166-167
Meeting with Konoye proposed, 334, 336, 345, 348, 353, 355, 356, 357, 363, 372, 379, 390, 397, 409
Message to Hirohito, 495, 511, 530, 540
Message to Sayre, 493
Morgenthau plan, 62
Moscow Protocol approved by, 415
National defense program, 31, 43, 45, 47, 117, 118, 120, 124, 131, 135, 148, 160, 194, 213, 235, 250, 321
Navy Day speech (1941), 428-430
Neutrality Act (1935), 11, 23, 50, 51, 59, 87, 93, 97, 98, 100, 101, 102, 166, 415, 465
Neutrality and, 12, 15, 17, 18, 24,

26, 29, 39, 49, 51, 59, 77, 81, 91, 93, 94, 95, 97, 101, 118
Nomura's conference with, 246, 288, 298, 302, 332, 348, 349, 455
North Carolina Univ. address, 48
"on hand or on order" speech, 124-126
one hundred days, 7
Pan American Scientific Congress address, 111-115
Pan American Union address (1939), 64
Pan American Union address (1940), 111
Pan American Union address (1941), 265
Panay incident, 32
"parallel action" between Churchill and, 352, 354, 359, 358
Peace Act, 59
Philadelphia speech, 163-164
Political purges, 37, 258
Proclamation of Limited Emergency, 93
Proclamation of unlimited Emergency, 265
Quarantine speech, 24-30, 33, 137
Reaction to Pearl Harbor attack, 558
Rochester campaign speech, (1940), 169
San Diego Exposition, 11
Sino-Japanese war, 24, 33
South American trip, 20
Spanish Civil War, 16, 23, 24, 40,
special message on defense, 51
third term, 72, 96, 103, 155-174
unconditional surrender, 62
University of Virginia speech, 136
War Council, 482-484
"we-are-planning-it-that-way" speech 12, 131
West Point address, 11
World Court, 8, 9

world disarmament favored by, 23
World Economic Conference ended by, 8
Yalta Conference, 538
Young Democratic Clubs of America address, 111
Roosevelt, Theodore, 170, 197
Rubber Reserve Company, 148
Rumania, 259
Bessarabia ceded to Rumania, 137
Russian occupation of, 63
Russia,
Aid in war against Japan, 557
Albania occupied by, 63-64
Attack on Germany planned by, 181
Attacked by Germany, 308
Bessarabia, ceded to, 137
Bulgaria occupied by, 63
Czechoslovakia occupied by, 63-64
diplomatic relations with United States, 9
Estonia occupied by, 63, 102, 137
expelled from the League of Nations, 102
Finland invaded by, 102
Hungary occupied by, 63
Latvia occupied by, 63, 183
Lend-lease aid to, 337, 407, 450
Lithuania occupied by, 63, 102, 137
Poland occupied by, 63
Rumania occupied by, 63
undeclared wars with Japan, 276
United States aid to, 387, 406, 407
Russo-German treaty, 88

S

Saar, 11
Safford, Captain Laurence F., 544
Samoa, 438
Sayre, Francis B., 493

INDEX | 625

Schmidt, Max W., 382
Schnurre, Dr. Karl, 222
Schuirmann, Captain R. E., 508
Schulenburg, Ambassador F. W., 181
Selassie, Haile, 15
Sevareid, 256
Sherwood, Robert E., 168, 255
Shaw, George Bernard, 99
Shigemitsu, Mamoru, 290, 391, 392
Short, General Walter C., 427
Siam, *see* Thailand
Siberia, 329
Sierra Leone, 201
"American-Dutch-British Conversations" held at, 504
American warships visit, 35
British permission for U. S. to use, 118, 198, 242, 244, 245
Chinese request for use of British air force at, 441
Mount Vernon diverted to, 370
"New British Fleet" at, 532
Possible Japanese attack, 289-291, 295, 305, 336, 380, 526
Sinkiang, 183
Sino-Japanese war, 24, 33, 60, 73, 74, 78, 182, 280, 286
Sofia, Bulgaria, 260
Solomon Islands, 264
Soong, T. V., 149, 431, 484, 490, 493, 511, 529
Spain, 203, 223, 259, 266, 333
Civil war in, 16, 23, 24
Stalin, Joseph,
　Atlantic Charter, 342
　Attitude toward Ribbentrop, 181
　Chinese policy, 296
　Conference with Hopkins, 337
　Conference with Matsuoka, 296-298
　Conference with Ribbentrop, 70
　Desire for stalemate in the war between Germany and England, 225
　German policy, 68
　Request for War materials, 406
　Roosevelt's opinion of 429
　Views about Japan, 305
Stark, Admiral Harold R., aid to Britain, 238
　Conference with Roosevelt, 268, 310, 331, 506, 511, 525, 526, 527
　Draft of Roosevelt's message to Congress, 511
　Isabel, 530
　Kearny incident, 430
　Letter to Hull, 415
　Letters to Cooke, 320, 362
　Letters to Hart, 205-206, 339, 362, 432, 450
　Letters to Kimmel, 263, 338, 339, 396, 432, 460, 483
　Letters to Richardson, 121, 129-130
　Magruder mission, 362
　mission to Britain, 149
　Morgenthau proposal, 470, 473, 475, 478
　Naval collaboration between U. S. and Britain, 202, 203, 255, 261
　Secret memorandum to Roosevelt, 446, 450
　Trans-Pacific shipping order, 483
　Views on war situation, 121, 129, 202-203, 206, 218, 219, 238, 240, 261, 263, 310, 318, 319, 320, 325, 327, 331, 338, 343, 362, 388, 389, 396, 415, 424, 432, 448, 460, 470, 478, 482, 500, 546, 549, 551, 553
　War Council, 482
Stimson, Henry L.,
　Appointed Secretary of War, 144
　Army-Navy Joint memorandum, 500
　Conference about Martinique, 304
　Draft and, 144, 195, 196, 348, 535, 544, 546
　Draft of Roosevelt's message to

Congress, 512
Foreign military purchases committee, lend-lease and, 228, 237, 238
Peace-time conscription advocated by, 144
Radar in Hawaii, 551
Views on intervention, 151
Views on war situation, 410-411, 448-449, 482-483, 484-485, 490-491, 500-501, 504-506, 529-530, 544, 546, 549-551, 554-556
Warning to MacArthur, 496
Strong, General George V., 143, 197
Sudetenland, 43
Suñer, Ramon Serrano, 223, 259
Supply Priorities and Allocations Board, 203, 408
Sweden, 110
Syria, 66, 263
Sze, Dr. Alfred, 529

T

Taft, Senator Robert A., 248
Taxes,
  excess profits, 151
  war-time, 96
Taylor, Myron, C., 103, 108, 383, 384
Tennessee (battleship), 553
Terasaki, Hindenari, 299, 354, 363, 379, 414, 415
Texas, (battleship), 20
Thailand, Japanese threat to, 314, 336, 354, 398, 399, 458, 498, 504, 513, 516, 519, 526, 528, 531, 538, 543
Thomas, Senator Elmer, 456
Tinkham, Representative George H., 228, 231
Tobruk, 259
Togo, Shigenori, 431, 437, 443, 454-455, 457, 458, 461, 481, 519

Tojo, General Hideki, 334, 413, 414, 418, 420, 421, 426, 463, 517, 521, 522
Toyoda, Admiral Teijiro, becomes Foreign Minister, 326
  Conference with Craigie, 328
  Conference with Ott, 367
  Conference with Grew, 336, 354-355, 356, 372, 375, 378, 389-390, 391, 414, 477
  Desire for peaceful relations terms with United States, 333-334
  Proposed Japanese peace terms with China,
  Quoted on Japan relations with United States, 333-336
  Views on proposed meeting between Roosevelt and Konoye, 372
Treaty of Versailles, 11, 90
Tripartite Treaty, 181, 183, 213, 279, 280, 372, 426, 462, 463, 466, 472, 519
Truk, 489
Truman, Harry S.,
  Korean war and, 4
  Morgenthau plan abandoned by, 62
Truman Investigation Committee, 251, 347
Tsubokami, Ambassador, 516
Turkey, 183, 263
Turner, Rear Admiral Richmond K., 331, 333, 340, 511, 553
Tuscaloosa (cruiser), 95, 207, 209
Tyler, Lt. Kermit A., 552

U

United States,
  Aid to Russia, 383, 407, 415, 450
  diplomatic code broken, 328, 357
  diplomatic relations with Russia, 9
  Finland aided by, 103, 105, 110
  French air mission, 56
  German declaration of war against, 557

INDEX | 627

isolationism, 8-20, 25, 26
Italian declaration of war against, 557
Japanese declaration of war on, 521, 542
League of Nations and, 8, 9, 14, 16
Loan to China, 48
Neutrality, 11, 12, 15, 16, 17, 18, 23, 24, 26, 29
Relations with Japan prior to Pearl Harbor, 32-33, 73-85, 106, 149, 243-244, 245, 246, 250, 251, 252, 253, 273-290, 298-384, 398-406, 408-428, 431-558
Warning to Japan, 352
United States Air Corps, expansion of, 123
United States Army, 195, 449
  War warning to, 501, 508
United States Maritime Commission, 88
United States Navy,
  War warning to, 501, 508
Ushiba, Tomohiko, 392, 413

V

Victor, Emmanuel III, King, 62, 89
Vinson Navy Bill, 10

W

W. P. A., 71
Wakasugi, Kaname, 419, 420, 426, 427, 428, 455, 456, 58, 459, 460, 462, 463
Wake Islands, 508
Walker, Frank C., 284-285
Wallace, Henry A., 95, 157, 161, 408, 523
Walsh, Senator David I., 146
Walsh, Bishop James E., 284
Wang Ching-wei, 278, 295, 296, 309
War Plans Division, 436, 438
War Resources Board, 88
war-risk insurance, 96, 144
Washington, (battleship), 20
Washington, George, 4, 25

Wavell, Sir Archibald P., 318, 321, 339
Welles, Summer,
  Atlantic Conference, 343, 346
  Conferences with Japanese ambassadors, 332-334, 529
  Conferences with Lord Halifax, 458, 497, 510, 528
  European mission, 107-110
  Japanese policy, 289
  "parallel action" between Roosevelt and Churchill, 352
  Quoted, 316, 346, 347, 454
  Request that American military observers visit Russian combat zones, 338
  Russia warned of German attack b, 224
  Statement scolding Germany, 60
  Views on foreign policy, 6
  Warning to Japan, 346, 352
West Virginia, (battleship), 553
Wheeler, Senator Burton K., 317
wichita (vessel), 24
Willkie, Wendell, 158-162, 167, 173, 189, 227, 248, 249, 537
Wilson, Ambassador Hugh R., 46, 48
Wilson, Woodrow, 9, 61, 158, 163
Winant, Ambassador John G., 92, 207, 233, 238, 424, 537, 540, 543
Woodring, Harry H., 56, 123, 144, 151
World Court, 8, 9
World Economic Conference,

Y

Yalta Conference, 538, 557
Yamamoto, Kumaicho, 509
Yamashita, General Tomoyuki, 283
Yugoslavia, 260
Yunnan, 440, 446

Z

Zeeland, Paul van, 47